Praise for *Baltimore Book of Prayers*

"The *Baltimore Book of Prayers* is a source of nourishment and devotion for Catholics in this country and beyond."

—Archbishop Timothy P. Broglio,
Military Services, USA

"As a successor of those bishops who first compiled the *Baltimore Book of Prayers*, I find it a pleasure to see this book back in print today."

— Bishop James Wall,
Diocese of Gallup, New Mexico

"In this time of Eucharistic Revival, there is a need for faithful Catholics to get 'back to basics' by embracing the enduring classics of the Faith. This book is at the heart of nourishing a life of meaningful prayer and devotion."

— Archbishop Salvatore Cordileone,
Archdiocese of San Francisco

"I wholeheartedly welcome this new edition of the *Baltimore Book of Prayers* as an outstanding instrument for attaining to the deep roots of Catholic spirituality. The prayers and devotions herein have withstood the test of time because they have been, and remain, an efficacious means for the contemplation of the Holy Face of Jesus, who is, in His own words to us, "the way, and the truth, and the life" (John 14:6). Thanks to the present publication, may they continue to be so for many years to come."

— Raymond Leo Cardinal Burke

"I pray that this beautiful new version of the *Baltimore Book of Prayers* has the effect of renewing and nourishing the devotional lives of Catholics in this country and beyond."

— Bishop Joseph Strickland

"I thank the Lord for this new edition of the *Baltimore Prayer Book*, a gift from God in this time of Eucharistic Revival for the pilgrim Church in the United States of America. Be assured of my prayers for the Lord's abundant blessings on this undertaking and for American Catholics who, even in the midst of many trials, offer a luminous testimony to the world in their defense of the Faith, life, marriage, and the family."

— ARCHBISHOP EMERITUS HÉCTOR AGUER,
Archdiocese of La Plata, Argentina

Baltimore Book of Prayers

BALTIMORE
Book of Prayers

Prepared and Published
By Order of the
Third Plenary Council of Baltimore

SOPHIA INSTITUTE PRESS
Manchester, New Hampshire

Sophia Institute Press
Box 5284, Manchester, NH 03108
1-800-888-9344
www.SophiaInstitute.com

Sophia Institute Press is a registered trademark of Sophia Institute.

ISBN 978-1-64413-892-2

eBook ISBN 978-1-64413-893-9

Library of Congress Control Number: 2024934184

First printing

CONTENTS

(For full alphabetical index, see end of book.)

Contents

Contents

PUBLISHER'S

PREFACE

Given the relative youth of the Catholic Church in America, no occasions have been more significant in its history than the three Plenary Councils of Baltimore, held in 1852, 1866, and 1884. Representing the first official gatherings of North American bishops apart from Canada, these councils would enduringly shape American Catholics' instruction in the truths of Faith and their life of prayer—chiefly by means of the major books emanating from Baltimore III.

The decrees of Baltimore III prompted the publication of two texts that would become its lasting legacy: *A Catechism of Christian Doctrine* (1885), best known around the world as the "Baltimore Catechism," and *A Manual of Prayers for the Use of the Catholic Laity* (1889), or the "Baltimore Prayer Book," which served generations of Catholics as their definitive collection of approved prayers and devotions.

At once authoritative and comprehensive, this prayer book first appeared as a magnificent, nearly eight-hundred page compendium: serving clergy, laymen, and families as a primary devotional reference. Running into several editions (of varying quality) in later years, the present *Baltimore Book of Prayers* has painstakingly remastered the original Baltimore text approved in 1889, while carefully incorporating relevant content from later editions and making precise editorial adjustments, to produce a more intuitive and readable layout overall.

While the original 1889 text has been retained here, several changes are worth special mention. Subsequent editions added over thirty new feasts, many of which became most beloved to the faithful (e.g., feasts of the Sacred Heart, St. Joseph, St. Thérèse of Lisieux); these have been included with other, later ritual texts as indicated by a double-dagger symbol (‡). The copious use of the in-text asterisk (*) in the original has here been modified to simply indicate a Psalmody breathing mark, or to point out an intratext page reference. The clutter of notes pertinent to indulgences under past legislation has been removed, while a new table of moveable feasts and an equation for finding the future date of Easter in any year have been added. Where the original left certain devotions, Mass texts, or rubrical notes incomplete or in more basic form (trusting to the customary knowledge of American Catholics in the 1800s), these have been filled out wherever it seemed advisable.

The hoped-for result has been to produce an edition of the *Baltimore Prayer Book* that is at once faithful to the 1889 text, and still readily usable for Catholics today: a manual worthy to succeed the time-honored original, sharing the riches of classical Catholic prayer and devotion with the faithful of today and tomorrow.

Baltimore Book of Prayers

The Calendar

OF FEASTS CELEBRATED IN THE
UNITED STATES OF AMERICA

(Holy days of obligation are marked with a ✠)

ABBREVIATIONS EXPLAINED:
Ap. signifies Apostle or Apostles; *M.*, Martyr or Martyrs; *P.*, Pope; *Abp.*, Archbishop; *B.*, Bishop; *C.*, Confessor; *D.*, Doctor; *Abb.*, Abbot; *V.*, Virgin; *W.*, Widow; *K.*, King; *Q.*, Queen; *Pr.*, Priest; *H.*, Hermit.

OTHER MOVABLE FEASTS NOT INCLUDED IN THE FOLLOWING CALENDAR

‡Sunday during the Octave of the Epiphany—*The Holy Family.*
Second Sunday after Epiphany—*Holy Name of Jesus.*
Friday after Quinquagesima—*Passion of Our Lord.*
Friday after First Sunday in Lent—*Holy Crown of Thorns.*
Friday after Second Sunday in Lent—*Spear and Nails.*
Friday after Third Sunday in Lent—*Five Wounds.*
Friday after Fourth Sunday in Lent—*Most Precious Blood.*
Friday after Passion Sunday—*Seven Sorrows of the Blessed Virgin Mary (B. V. M.)*
Third Sunday after Easter—*Patronage of St. Joseph.*
Thursday after Trinity Sunday—*Corpus Christi.*
Friday after Octave of Corpus Christi—*Sacred Heart of Jesus.*
First Sunday of July—*Most Precious Blood.*
Sunday within the Octave of the Assumption—*St. Joachim, Father of the B. V. M.*
Sunday within the Octave of Nativity of B. V. M.—*Holy Name of Mary.*
Third Sunday of September—*Seven Sorrows of the B. V. M.*
First Sunday of October—*Rosary Sunday.*
Second Sunday of October—*Maternity of the B. V. M.*
‡Last Sunday of October—*Christ Our King.*
Second Sunday of November—*Patronage of the B. V. M.*

The Calendar

JANUARY. Hath thirty-one days.

1. ✠ CIRCUMCISION OF OUR LORD.
2. Octave of St. Stephen, *First Martyr.*
3. Octave of St. John, *Ap. and Evangelist.*
4. Octave of the Holy Innocents, *M.*
5. Vigil.
6. EPIPHANY OF OUR LORD.
7. Of the Octave.
8. Of the Octave.
9. Of the Octave.
10. Of the Octave.
11. Of the Octave. ‡Conv. of St. Hyginus, *P.M.*
12. Of the Octave.
13. Octave of the *Epiphany.*
14. St. Hilary, *B.C.D.* ‡Conv. of St. Felix, *Pr.M.*
15. St. Paul, First *H.*
16. St. Marcellus, *P.M.*
17. St. Anthony, *Abb.*
18. St. Peter's Chair at Rome.
19. St. Canute of Denmark, *K.M.* ‡Sts. Marius and his companions, *M.*
20. Sts. Fabian and Sebastian, *M.*
21. St. Agnes, *V.M.*
22. Sts. Vincent and Anastasius, *M.*
23. *Espousals of the B.V.M.*
24. St. Timothy, *B.M.*
25. *Conversion of St. Paul, Ap.*
26. St. Polycarp, *B.M.*
27. St. John Chrysostom, *Patriarch, C.D.*
28. St. Agnes, *the second time.*
29. St. Francis de Sales, *B.C.D.*
30. St. Martina, *V.M.*
31. St. Peter Nolasco, *C.* ‡St. John Bosco, *C.*

The Calendar

FEBRUARY. Hath twenty-eight or twenty-nine days.

1. St. Ignatius, *B. M.*
2. PURIFICATION OF THE B. V. M.
3. St. Blase, *B. M.*
4. St. Andrew Corsini, *B. C.*
5. St. Philip of Jesus, *M.*
6. St. Titus, *Abp. C.*
7. St. Romuald, *Abb.*
8. St. John of Matha, *C.*
9. St. Cyril of Alexandria, *B. C. D.*
10. St. Scholastica, *V.*
11. St. Raymond of Pennafort, *C.* ‡Apparition of the B. V. M. at Lourdes.
12. St. Agatha, *V. M.* ‡The Seven Holy Founders of the Servites, *C.*
13. Of the Season.
14. St. Valentine, *Pr. M.*
15. Sts. Faustinus and Jovita, *M.*
16. Of the Season.
17. Of the Season.
18. St. Simeon, *B. M.*
19. Of the Season.
20. Of the Season.
21. Of the Season.
22. St. Peter's Chair at Antioch.
23. St. Peter Damian, *B. C. D.* Vigil.
24. *St. Matthias, Ap.*[1]
25. Of the Season.
26. Of the Season.
27. Of the Season. ‡St. Gabriel of The Seven Dolors, *C.*
28. Of the Season.

[1]   In Leap Year, on the 25th.

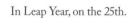

The Calendar

MARCH. Hath thirty-one days.

1. Of the Season.
2. Of the Season.
3. Of the Season.
4. St. Casimir, *C.*
5. Of the Season.
6. Of the Season. ‡Sts. Perpetua and Felicitas, *M.*
7. St. Thomas Aquinas, *C.D.*
8. St. John of God, *C.*
9. St. Frances of Rome, *W.*
10. The Forty Martyrs.
11. Of the Season.
12. St. Gregory the Great, *P.C.D.*
13. Of the Season.
14. Of the Season.
15. Of the Season. ‡St. Louise de Marillac, *W.*
16. Of the Season.
17. St. Patrick, *Abp. C., Apostle of Ireland.*
18. *St. Gabriel, Archangel.*
19. ST. JOSEPH, *Patron of the Universal Church.*
20. St. Cyril of Jerusalem, *B.C.D.*
21. St. Benedict, *Abb.*
22. Of the Season.
23. Of the Season.
24. Of the Season.
25. ANNUNCIATION OF THE B. V. M.
26. Of the Season.
27. Of the Season. ‡St. John of Damascus, *C.D.*
28. Of the Season. ‡St. John Capistran, *Pr. C.*
29. Of the Season.
30. Of the Season.
31. Of the Season.

The Calendar

APRIL. Hath thirty days.

1. Of the Season.
2. St. Francis of Paula, *C.*
3. Of the Season.
4. St. Isidore, *Abp. C. D.*
5. St. Vincent Ferrer, *C.*
6. Of the Season.
7. Of the Season.
8. Of the Season. ‡Bl. Julie Billiart, V.
9. Of the Season.
10. Of the Season.
11. St. Leo the Great, *P. C. D.*
12. Of the Season.
13. St. Hermenegild of Spain, *K. M.*
14. St. Justin, *M.*
15. Of the Season.
16. Of the Season.
17. St. Anicetus, *P. M.*
18. Of the Season.
19. Of the Season.
20. Of the Season.
21. St. Anselm, *Abp. C. D.*
22. Sts. Soter and Caius, *P. M.*
23. St. George, *M.*
24. St. Fidelis of Sigmaringen, *M.*
25. *St. Mark, Evangelist.*
26. Sts. Cletus and Marcellinus, *P. M.*
27. St. Turibius, *B. C.* ‡Peter Canisius, *C. D.*
28. St. Paul of the Cross, *C.*
29. St. Peter, *M.*
30. St. Catherine of Siena, V.

The Calendar

MAY. Hath thirty-one days.

1. *Sts. Philip and James, Ap.*
2. St. Athanasius, *B. C. D.*
3. *Finding of the Holy Cross.*
4. St. Monica, *W.*
5. St. Pius V, *P. C.*
6. St. John before the Latin Gate.
7. St. Stanislaus, *B. M.*
8. *Apparition of St. Michael, Archangel.*
9. St. Gregory Nazianzen, *Patriarch C. D.*
10. St. Antoninus, *Abp. C.*
11. Of the Season. ‡St. Lucia Filippini, *V.*
12. Sts. Nereus, Achilleus, and Comp., *M.*
13. Of the Season. ‡St. Robert Bellarmine, *B. C. D.*
14. St. Boniface, *M.*
15. Of the Season. ‡St. John Baptist de la Salle, *C.*
16. St. Ubald, *B. C.*
17. St. Paschal Baylon, *C.*
18. St. Venantius, *M.*
19. St. Peter Celestin, *P. C.*
20. St. Bernardine of Siena, *C.*
21. Of the Season.
22. St. John Nepomucene, *M.*
23. Of the Season.
24. *Our Blessed Lady, Help of Christians.*
25. St. Gregory VII, *P. C.*
26. St. Philip Neri, *C.*
27. St. Mary Magdalen de' Pazzi, V. ‡St. Bede the Venerable, *C. D.*
28. St. Augustine of Canterbury, *B. C.*
29. Of the Season.
30. St. Felix, *P. M.*
31. St. Angela Merici, *V.*

The Calendar

JUNE. Hath thirty days.

1. Of the Season.
2. Sts. Marcellinus and Peter, *M.*
3. Of the Season.
4. St. Francis Caracciolo, *C.*
5. St. Boniface, *Abp. M.*
6. St. Norbert, *Abp. C.*
7. Of the Season.
8. Of the Season.
9. Sts. Primus and Felician, *M.*
10. St. Margaret of Scotland, *Q. W.*
11. *St. Barnabas, Ap.*
12. St. John of San Fagondez, *C.*
13. St. Anthony of Padua, *C.*
14. St. Basil the Great, *Abp. C. D.*
15. Sts. Vitus and Modestus, *M.*
16. St. John Francis Regis, *C.*
17. Of the Season.
18. Sts. Mark and Marcellian, *M.* ‡St. Ephrem, *C. D.*
19. St. Juliana de' Falconieri, V.
20. St. Silverius, *P. M.*
21. St. Aloysius Gonzaga, *C.*
22. St. Paulinus, *B. C.*
23. Vigil.
24. *Nativity of St. John the Baptist.*
25. St. William, *Abb.*
26. Sts. John and Paul, *M.*
27. Of the Octave.
28. St. Irenæus, *B. M.* Vigil.
29. STS. PETER AND PAUL, *Ap.* (Solemnity transferred to following Sunday.)
30. *Commemoration of St. Paul, Ap.*

The Calendar

JULY. Hath thirty-one days.

1. Octave of St. John the Baptist.
2. *Visitation of the B. V. M.*
3. St. Leo II, *P. C.*
4. Of the Octave.
5. Sts. Cyril and Methodius, *B. C.* ‡St. Anthony Mary Zaccaria, *C.*
6. Octave of Sts. Peter and Paul, *Ap.*
7. Of the Season.
8. St. Elizabeth of Portugal, *Q. W.*
9. Of the Season.
10. Seven Brothers, *M.*
11. St. Pius I, *P. M.*
12. St. John Gualberto, *Abb.*
13. St. Anacletus, *P. M.*
14. St. Bonaventure, *B. C. D.*
15. St. Henry, *K. C.*
16. *Our Lady of Mount Carmel.*
17. St. Alexius, *C.*
18. St. Camillus de' Lelli, *C.*
19. St. Vincent of Paul, *C.*
20. St. Jerome Miani, *C.*
21. St. Praxedes, *V.*
22. St. Mary Magdalen, *Penitent.*
23. St. Apollinaris, *B. M.*
24. St. Francis Solano, *C.* Vigil. ‡St. Christina *V. M.*
25. *St. James, Ap.*
26. *St. Ann, Mother of the B. V. M.*
27. St. Pantaleon, *M.*
28. Sts. Nazarius and others, *M.*
29. St. Martha, *V.*
30. Sts. Abdon and Sennen, *M.*
31. St. Ignatius of Loyola, *C.*

The Calendar

AUGUST. Hath thirty-one days.

1. St. Peter's Chains.
2. St. Alphonsus de' Liguori, *B. C. D.*
3. Finding of St. Stephen, *First Martyr.*
4. St. Dominic, *C.*
5. *Our Lady of the Snows.*
6. TRANSFIGURATION OF OUR LORD.
7. St. Cajetan, *C.*
8. Sts. Cyriacus and others, *M.*
9. Vigil. ‡St. John Vianney, *C.*
10. *St. Lawrence, M.*
11. Of the Octave. ‡Sts. Tibertius and Susanna, *M.*
12. St. Clare, V.
13. Of the Octave. ‡Sts. Hippolytus and Cassian, *M.*
14. *Vigil. Fast.*
15. ✠ ASSUMPTION OF THE B. V. M.
16. St. Hyacinth, C.
17. Octave of St. Lawrence.
18. Of the Octave.
19. Of the Octave. ‡St. John Eudes, *C.*
20. St. Bernard, *Abb. D.*
21. St. Jane Frances de Chantal, *W.*
22. Octave of the Assumption. ‡Immaculate Heart of Mary.
23. St. Philip Benizzi. Vigil.
24. *St. Bartholomew, Ap.*
25. St. Louis of France, *K. C.*
26. St. Zephyrinus, *P. M.*
27. St. Joseph Casalanz, *C.*
28. St. Augustine, *B. C. D.*
29. Beheading of St. John the Baptist.
30. St. Rose of Lima, V.
31. St. Raymond Nonnatus, *C.*

The Calendar

SEPTEMBER. Hath thirty days.

1. St. Giles, *Abb.*
2. St. Stephen, *K. C.*
3. Of the Season.
4. Of the Season.
5. St. Lawrence de' Giustiniani, *Patriarch C.*
6. Of the Season.
7. Of the Season.
8. *Nativity of the B. V. M.*
9. Of the Octave. ‡St. Peter Claver, *C.*
10. St. Nicholas of Tolentino, *C.*
11. Of the Octave. ‡Sts. Protus and Hyacinth, *M.*
12. Of the Octave.
13. Of the Season.
14. *Exaltation of the Holy Cross.*
15. Octave of the Nativity of the B. V. M.
16. Sts. Cornelius, *P.M.*, and Cyprian, *B.M.*
17. The Stigmata of St. Francis, *C.*
18. St. Joseph of Cupertino, *C.*
19. Sts. Januarius and Companions, *M.*
20. Sts. Eustace and Companions, *M.* Vigil.
21. *St. Matthew, Ap. and Evangelist.*
22. St. Thomas of Villanova, *Abp. C.*
23. St. Linus, *P.M.*
24. *Our Lady of Ransom.*
25. Of the Season.
26. Sts. Cyprian and Justina, M. ‡Jesuit Saints of North America, M.
27. Sts. Cosmas and Damian, *M.*
28. St. Wenceslaus of Bohemia, *K. M.*
29. *Dedication of St. Michael, Archangel.*
30. St. Jerome, *Pr. C. D.*

The Calendar

OCTOBER. Hath thirty-one days.

1. St. Remy, *B. C.*
2. *Holy Guardian Angels.*
3. Of the Season. ‡St. Thérèse of the Child Jesus, V.
4. St. Francis of Assisi, *C.*
5. St. Placid and Companions, *M.*
6. St. Bruno, *C.*
7. St. Mark, *P. C.*
8. St. Bridget of Sweden, *W.*
9. Sts. Denys and Companions, *M.*
10. St. Francis Borgia, *C.*
11. Of the Season.
12. Of the Season.
13. St. Edward, *K. C.*
14. St. Callistus, *P. M.*
15. St. Teresa, *V.*
16. St. Hedwiges, *W.*
17. St. Margaret Mary Alacoque, *V.*
18. *St. Luke, Evangelist.*
19. St. Peter of Alcantara, *C.*
20. St. John of Kenty, *C.*
21. St. Hilarion, *Abb.*
22. Of the Season.
23. Of the Season. ‡Bl. Mary Clotilde Angela, *V. M.*
24. *St. Raphael, Archangel.*
25. Sts. Chrysanthus and Darias, *M.*
26. St. Evaristus, *P. M.*
27. Vigil.
28. *Sts. Simon and Jude, Ap.*
29. Of the Season.
30. Of the Season.
31. *Vigil. Fast.*

The Calendar

NOVEMBER. Hath thirty days.

1. ✠ ALL SAINTS' DAY.
2. *All Souls' Day.*
3. Of the Octave.
4. St. Charles Borromeo, *Abp. C.*
5. Of the Octave.
6. Of the Octave.
7. Of the Octave.
8. Octave of ALL SAINTS.
9. Dedication of St. John Lateran Basilica.
10. St. Andrew Avellino, *C.*
11. St. Martin of Tours, *B. C.*
12. St. Martin, *P.M.*
13. St. Diego, *C.*
14. St. Stanislaus Kostka, *C.*
15. St. Gertrude, *V.* ‡St. Albert the Great, *B. C. D.*
16. St. Josaphat, *B. M.*
17. St. Gregory the Wonder-Worker, *B. C.*
18. Dedication of Sts. Peter and Paul's Basilica.
19. St. Elizabeth of Hungary, *W.*
20. St. Felix of Valois, *C.*
21. *Presentation of the B. V. M.*
22. St. Cecilia, *V. M.*
23. St. Clement, *P.M.*
24. St. John of the Cross, *C.* ‡*D.*
25. St. Catherine, *V. M.*
26. St. Peter of Alexandria, *B. M.* ‡St. Sylvester, *Abb.*
27. Of the Season. ‡Our Lady of Miraculous Medal.
28. Of the Season. ‡St. Catherine Labouré, *V.*
29. Vigil.
30. *St. Andrew, Ap.*

The Calendar

DECEMBER. Hath thirty-one days.

1. Of the Season.
2. St. Bibiana, *V. M.*
3. St. Francis Xavier, *C.*
4. St. Peter Chrysologus, *Abp. C. D.*
5. St. Saba, *Abb.*
6. St. Nicholas, *Abp. C.*
7. St. Ambrose, *B. C. D.* Vigil.
8. ✠ IMMACULATE CONCEPTION OF THE B. V. M. PATRONAL FEAST OF THE UNITED STATES.
9. Of the Octave.
10. Of the Octave.
11. St. Damasus, *P. C.*
12. Of the Octave.
13. St. Lucy, *V. M.*
14. Of the Octave.
15. Octave of the IMMACULATE CONCEPTION.
16. St. Eusebius, *B. M.*
17. Of the Season.
18. *Expectation of the B. V. M.*
19. Of the Season.
20. Vigil.
21. *St. Thomas, Ap.*
22. Of the Season. ‡St. Frances Xavier Cabrini.
23. Of the Season.
24. *Vigil. Fast.*
25. ✠ NATIVITY OF OUR LORD.
26. *St. Stephen, First Martyr.*
27. *St. John, Ap. and Evangelist.*
28. *The Holy Innocents, M.*
29. St. Thomas of Canterbury, *Abp. M.*
30. Of the Octaves.
31. St. Sylvester, *P. C.*

TABLE OF MOVABLE FEASTS

Year of Our Lord	Ash Wednesday	Easter Sunday	Ascension Day	Whitsunday	Corpus Christi	First Sunday of Advent
2024	Feb. 14	Mar. 31	May 9	May 19	May 30	Dec. 1
2025	Mar. 5	Apr. 20	May 29	June 8	June 29	Nov. 30
2026	Feb. 18	Apr. 5	May 14	May 24	June 4	Nov. 29
2027	Feb. 10	Mar. 28	May 6	May 16	May 27	Nov. 28
2028	Mar. 1	Apr. 16	May 25	June 4	June 15	Dec. 3
2029	Feb. 14	Apr. 1	May 10	May 20	May 31	Dec. 2
2030	Mar. 6	Apr. 21	May 30	June 9	June 20	Dec. 1
2031	Feb. 26	Apr. 13	May 22	June 1	June 12	Nov. 30
2032	Feb. 11	Mar. 28	May 6	May 16	May 27	Nov. 28
2033	Mar. 2	Apr. 17	May 26	June 5	June 16	Nov. 27
2034	Feb. 22	Apr. 9	May 18	May 28	June 8	Dec. 3
2035	Feb. 7	Mar. 25	May 3	May 13	May 24	Dec. 2
2036	Feb. 27	Apr. 13	May 22	June 1	June 12	Nov. 30
2037	Feb. 18	Apr. 5	May 14	May 24	June 4	Nov. 29
2038	Mar. 10	Apr. 25	June 3	June 13	June 24	Nov. 28
2039	Feb. 23	Apr. 10	May 19	May 29	June 9	Nov. 27
2040	Feb. 15	Apr. 1	May 10	May 19	May 30	Dec. 2
2041	Mar. 6	Apr. 21	May 30	June 9	June 20	Dec. 1
2042	Feb. 19	Apr. 6	May 15	May 25	June 5	Nov. 30
2043	Feb. 11	Mar. 29	May 7	May 17	May 28	Nov. 29
2044	Mar. 2	Apr. 17	May 26	June 5	June 16	Nov. 27
2045	Feb. 22	Apr. 9	May 18	May 28	June 8	Dec. 3
2046	Feb. 7	Mar. 25	May 3	May 13	May 24	Dec. 2
2047	Feb. 27	Apr. 14	May 23	June 2	June 13	Dec. 1
2048	Feb. 19	Apr. 5	May 14	May 24	June 4	Nov. 29
2049	Mar. 3	Apr. 18	May 27	June 6	June 17	Nov. 28
2050	Feb. 23	Apr. 10	May 19	May 29	June 9	Nov. 27

Year of Our Lord	Ash Wednesday	Easter Sunday	Ascension Day	Whitsunday	Corpus Christi	First Sunday of Advent
2051	Feb. 15	Apr. 2	May 11	May 21	June 1	Dec. 3
2052	Mar. 6	Apr. 21	May 30	June 9	June 20	Dec. 1
2053	Feb. 19	Apr. 6	May 15	May 25	June 5	Nov. 30
2054	Feb. 11	Mar. 29	May 7	May 17	May 28	Nov. 29
2055	Mar. 3	Apr. 18	May 27	June 6	June 17	Nov. 28
2056	Feb. 16	Apr. 2	May 11	May 21	June 1	Dec. 3
2057	Mar. 7	Apr. 22	May 31	June 10	June 21	Dec. 2
2058	Feb. 27	Apr. 14	May 23	June 2	June 13	Dec. 1
2059	Feb. 12	Mar. 30	May 8	May 18	May 29	Nov. 30
2060	Mar. 3	Apr. 18	May 27	June 6	June 17	Nov. 28
2061	Feb. 23	Apr. 10	May 19	May 29	June 9	Nov. 27
2062	Feb. 8	Mar. 26	May 4	May 14	May 25	Dec. 3
2063	Feb. 28	Apr. 15	May 24	June 3	June 14	Dec. 2
2064	Feb. 20	Apr. 6	May 15	May 25	June 5	Nov. 30
2065	Feb. 11	Mar. 29	May 7	May 17	May 28	Nov. 29
2066	Feb. 24	Apr. 11	May 20	May 30	June 10	Nov. 28
2067	Feb. 16	Apr. 3	May 12	May 22	June 2	Nov. 27
2068	Mar. 7	Apr. 22	May 31	June 10	June 21	Dec. 2
2069	Feb. 27	Apr. 14	May 23	June 2	June 13	Dec. 1
2070	Feb. 12	Mar. 30	May 8	May 18	May 29	Nov. 30
2071	Mar. 4	Apr. 19	May 28	June 7	June 18	Nov. 29
2072	Feb. 24	Apr. 10	May 19	May 29	June 9	Nov. 27
2073	Feb. 8	Mar. 26	May 4	May 14	May 25	Dec. 3
2074	Feb. 28	Apr. 15	May 24	June 3	June 14	Dec. 2

Note. — Easter Day (on which all the other movable feasts depend) is always the first Sunday after the full moon which happens upon or next after the twenty-first day of March; and if the full moon happens upon a Sunday, Easter Day is the Sunday after.

Advent Sunday is always the nearest Sunday to the feast of St. Andrew, whether before or after.

Septuagesima (*Sexagesima, Quinquagesima, Quadragesima*) Sunday is nine (eight, seven, six) weeks before *Easter* (respectively).

Rogation Sunday (*Ascension Day, Whitsunday, Trinity Sunday*) is five weeks (forty days, seven weeks, eight weeks) after *Easter* (respectively).

The calendar as at present used was reformed, in the year of Our Lord 1582, by Pope Gregory XIII, who ordered the *historical* or civil year to be thenceforward reckoned from the first day of January. It was not adopted by English-speaking people until January 1, 1753. The *ecclesiastical* year still begins on the First Sunday in Advent.

A Rule

FOR FINDING EASTER OF ANY YEAR IN THIS CENTURY OR THE NEXT

1st. Divide the date of the year by 19, and call the remainder a;
2nd. Divide the date of the year by 4, and call the remainder b;
3rd. Divide the date of the year by 7, and call the remainder c;
4th. Divide the date of the year by 100 (disregarding any remainder), and call the quotient k;
5th. Divide $(13 + 8k)$ by 25 (disregarding any remainder), and call the quotient p;
6th. Divide k by 4 (disregarding any remainder), and call the quotient q;
7th. Divide $(15 - p + k - q)$ by 30, and call the remainder M;
8th. Divide $(4 + k - q)$ by 7, and call the remainder N;
9th. Divide $(19a + M)$ by 30, and call the remainder d;
10th. Divide $(2b + 4c + 6d + N)$ by 7, and call the remainder e;
Then Easter Sunday will be the $(d + e + 22)$ of March; or the $(d + e - 9)$ of April.

Exceptions.
If $d = 29$ and $e = 6$, then Easter Sunday is April 19th.
If $d = 28$ and $e = 6$ and $a > 10$, then Easter Sunday is April 18th.

A Table

OF ALL THE FEASTS THAT ARE OBSERVED BY THE CATHOLICS OF THE UNITED STATES, WITH OBLIGATION OF HEARING MASS AND ABSTAINING FROM SERVILE WORK.

All the Sundays of the year.
January 1—The Circumcision of Our Lord, or New Year's Day.
August 15—The Assumption of the Blessed Virgin Mary.
November 1—All Saints' Day.
December 8—The Immaculate Conception of the Blessed Virgin Mary.
December 25—The Nativity of Our Lord, or Christmas Day.
Also Ascension Day, or the Thursday forty days after Easter.

On Fasting and Abstinence

Our holy mother, the Catholic Church, does not leave her children without guidance, and to their own devices, in this important matter; she tells them not only *when* but *how* to fast and abstain, and the rules she has established are those inspired by her heavenly wisdom, and shaped and fashioned by centuries of practical experience. Every Catholic is bound to keep these mild and gentle rules *first of all* before any other form of bodily mortification can be worthily undertaken. If these are willfully neglected, no amount of self-imposed austerity can ever make up the loss, or atone for the disobedience.

The law of **abstinence** affects only the *kind* of food, and has no reference to its *quantity*. On abstinence days, the faithful are obliged to abstain from flesh-meat only; the number of meals and the amount of food may be the same as on other days.

The law of **fasting** includes that of abstinence, and adds special requirements of its own; it affects both the *kind* and the *quantity* of food. On fasting days, besides the obligation of abstaining from flesh-meat, the number and quantity of meals are restricted. Only *one full meal* is allowed, to be taken about noon or later. Besides this full meal, a collation of eight ounces is allowed. If the full meal is taken about the middle of the day, the collation will naturally be taken in the evening; if the full meal is taken late in the day, the collation may be taken about noon. Besides the full meal and collation, general custom has made it lawful to take about two ounces of bread (without butter) and a cup of some warm liquid—as coffee or tea—in the morning. This is important to observe, for by means of this many persons are enabled—and therefore *obliged*—to keep the fast who could not otherwise do so.

It should be borne in mind that these practices of fasting and abstinence are not merely penitential works of *counsel*, recommended to our observance, but acts of mortification of *precept*, enjoined by laws binding strictly on the conscience; and therefore not to be evaded or omitted without mortal sin. Various reasons, however, may exist for excuse or dispensation from these laws (especially from the law of *fasting*), which are commonly noted in the published "Regulations for Lent" in every diocese. But as to *abstinence*, legitimate excuses are very few; and generally no one can proceed safely in excusing himself from abstinence before consulting his confessor.

ABSTINENCE DAYS

All the Fridays of the year.

Note.—When a Friday happens to be *Christmas Day*, it is not a day of abstinence.

FASTING DAYS

1. The Fridays of Advent.[2]
2. Every day in Lent; except *Sundays*.
3. The four Quarter Tenses, or Ember Days, viz.: the *Wednesday*, *Friday*, and *Saturday* following—1) the First Sunday in Lent; 2) Whitsunday; 3) the fourteenth day of September; and, 4) the Third Sunday of Advent.
4. The Vigils of *Whitsunday*, of the *Assumption*, of *All Saints*, and of *Christmas*.

Note.—When a fasting day falls upon a Sunday, it is kept on the *Saturday* previous.

THE TIMES

Wherein Marriages are not solemnized.

From *Advent Sunday* until the *Epiphany*, and from *Ash Wednesday* until *Low Sunday*.

---

[2]   In some dioceses (as in the Province of New Orleans) the Fridays of Advent are not fasting days.

Brief Statement of Christian Doctrine

The Ten Commandments of God — Ex 20

1. I AM the Lord thy God, Who brought thee out of the land of Egypt, out of the house of bondage. Thou shalt not have strange gods before Me. Thou shalt not make to thyself a graven thing, nor the likeness of anything that is in heaven above, or in the earth beneath, nor of those things that are in the waters under the earth. Thou shalt not adore them, nor serve them.
2. Thou shalt not take the name of the Lord thy God in vain.
3. Remember thou keep holy the Sabbath day.
4. Honor thy father and thy mother.
5. Thou shalt not kill.
6. Thou shalt not commit adultery.
7. Thou shalt not steal.
8. Thou shalt not bear false witness against thy neighbor.
9. Thou shalt not covet thy neighbor's wife.
10. Thou shalt not covet thy neighbor's goods.

The Six Commandments of the Church

1. To hear Mass on Sundays, and holy days of obligation.
2. To fast and abstain on the days appointed.
3. To confess at least once a year.
4. To receive the Holy Eucharist during the Easter time.
5. To contribute to the support of our pastors.
6. Not to marry persons who are not Catholics, or who are related to us within the fourth degree of kindred, nor privately without witnesses, nor to solemnize marriage at forbidden times.

The Seven Sacraments

Baptism (Mt 28:19). Extreme Unction (Jas 5:14).
Confirmation (Acts 8:17). Holy Orders (Lk 22:19).
Holy Eucharist (Mt 26:26). Matrimony (Mt 19:6).
Penance (Jn 20:23).

The Three Theological Virtues

Faith. Hope. Charity.

The Four Cardinal Virtues

Prudence.	Fortitude.
Justice.	Temperance.

The Seven Gifts of the Holy Ghost — Is 11:2–3

Wisdom.	Knowledge.
Understanding.	Piety.
Counsel.	The fear of the Lord.
Fortitude.	

The Twelve Fruits of the Holy Ghost

Charity.	Long-suffering.
Joy.	Mildness.
Peace.	Faith.
Patience.	Modesty.
Benignity.	Continency.
Goodness.	Chastity.

The Spiritual Works of Mercy

To admonish the sinner.	To bear wrongs patiently.
To instruct the ignorant.	To forgive all injuries.
To counsel the doubtful.	To pray for the living and the dead.
To comfort the sorrowful.	

The Corporal Works of Mercy

To feed the hungry.	To harbor the harborless.
To give drink to the thirsty.	To visit the sick.
To clothe the naked.	To bury the dead.
To ransom the captive.	

The Eight Beatitudes — Mt 5

1. Blessed are the poor in spirit; for theirs is the Kingdom of heaven.
2. Blessed are the meek; for they shall possess the land.
3. Blessed are they that mourn; for they shall be comforted.
4. Blessed are they that hunger and thirst after justice; for they shall be filled.
5. Blessed are the merciful; for they shall obtain mercy.
6. Blessed are the clean of heart; for they shall see God.
7. Blessed are the peacemakers; for they shall be called the children of God.
8. Blessed are they that suffer persecution for justice' sake; for theirs is the Kingdom of heaven.

The Seven Deadly Sins, and the Opposite Virtues

Seven Deadly Sins		Seven Contrary Virtues
Pride		Humility
Covetousness		Liberality
Lust		Chastity
Anger	VS.	Meekness
Gluttony		Temperance
Envy		Brotherly love
Sloth		Diligence

The Sins against the Holy Ghost

Presumption of God's mercy.
Despair.
Impugning the known truth.

Envy at another's spiritual good.
Obstinacy in sin.
Final impenitence.

The Sins Crying to Heaven for Vengeance

Willful murder.
The sin of Sodom.

Oppression of the poor.
Defrauding laborers of their wages.

The Nine Ways of Being Accessory to Another's Sin

By counsel.
By command.
By consent.
By provocation.
By praise or flattery.

By concealment.
By partaking.
By silence.
By defense of the ill done.

The Three Eminent Good Works

Prayer.   Fasting.   Almsgiving.

The Evangelical Counsels

Poverty.   Chastity.   Obedience.

The Four Last Things to Be Remembered

Death.   Judgment.   Hell.   Heaven.

Subjects for Daily Meditation

Remember, Christian soul, that thou hast this day and every day of thy life:

God to glorify,	Eternity to prepare for,
Jesus to imitate,	Time to profit by,
The angels and saints to invoke,	Neighbors to edify,
A soul to save,	The world to despise,
A body to mortify,	Devils to combat,
Sins to expiate,	Passions to subdue,
Virtues to acquire,	Death perhaps to suffer,
Hell to avoid,	And judgment to undergo.
Heaven to gain,	

Lay Baptism

Provided an infant is in danger of dying before a priest can be procured, any other person, whether man, woman, or child, may baptize it in the following manner:

While pouring common water on the head or face of the infant, pronounce the words:

"I baptize thee in the name of the Father, and of the Son, and of the Holy Ghost."

A Summary of Christian Faith and Practice

WHAT EVERY CHRISTIAN MUST BELIEVE

1. Every Christian must believe that there is one God, and no more than one God: that God is a pure Spirit, the Lord and Maker of heaven and earth, Who has neither beginning nor end, but is always the same; Who is everywhere present; knows and sees all things; can do all things whatsoever He pleases; and is infinite in all perfections.

2. Every Christian is bound to believe that in one God there are three distinct Persons, perfectly equal, of the same substance, and having the same nature: the Father, Who proceeds from no one; the Son, Who is born of the Father before all ages; and the Holy Ghost, Who proceeds eternally from the Father and the Son as from one principle; and that the three Persons are all equally eternal, equal in wisdom and power, and are all three one and the same Lord, one and the same God.

3. We must believe that God created the angels to be with Him forever, and that one part of them fell from God by sin, and became devils; that God also created Adam and Eve, the first parents of all mankind, and placed them in the earthly paradise, from whence they were justly banished for the sin they committed in eating of the fruit of the forbidden tree; and that, by this transgression of Adam, we are all conceived and born in sin, and must have been lost forever, if God had not sent us a Savior.

4. We are bound to believe in the Savior of all mankind, Jesus Christ, the Son of God, true God and true man; perfect God from all eternity, equal to His Father in all things; and perfect man, from the time of His coming down from heaven for us, having a body and soul like ours.

5. We must believe that Jesus Christ, our Savior, Who had been long foretold by the prophets, was, at God's appointed time, by the power of the Holy Ghost, without having any man for His father, conceived in the womb of the Virgin Mary; whom God had prepared for this wonderful maternity in a wonderful manner: in that by a singular grace and privilege, in view of the merits of Jesus Christ, she was in the first instant of her conception preserved free from every taint of Original Sin. Of her, who is blessed among women forevermore, was born Our Lord—she still remaining a pure Virgin. During the time of His mortal life, Jesus Christ founded the Christian religion; and then offered Himself a sacrifice for the sins of the whole world, by dying upon a Cross, to obtain mercy, grace, and salvation for us; and that neither mercy, nor grace, nor salvation can, or ever could, since Adam's Fall, be obtained except through the mediation of the Son of God.

6. We must believe that Jesus Christ, after He died and was buried, arose on the third day from death to life, never to die again; and that, for the space of forty days, He was pleased, at different times, to manifest Himself to His disciples, and then ascended into heaven in their sight; where, as God-Man, He continually intercedes for us. Thence He sent down the Holy Ghost upon His disciples, to abide with them forever, as He had promised, and to guide them and their successors into all truth.

7. We must believe the Catholic or universal Church of Christ, of which He is the perpetual Head, and His Spirit the perpetual Guide; which is founded upon a rock, and is ever victorious over all the powers of earth and hell. The Church is always one, in all its members professing one Faith, in one communion, under one chief pastor, called the pope, succeeding St. Peter, to whom Christ committed His whole flock. The Church is always holy, in teaching a holy doctrine, in inviting all to a holy life, and in the eminent holiness of many of its children. It is catholic, or universal, for it subsists in all ages, and teaches all nations, and maintains all truth. It is apostolic, for it derives its doctrine, its communion, its orders, and its mission, by an uninterrupted succession, from the apostles of Christ.

8. With the Catholic Church the Scriptures, both of the Old and New Testaments, were deposited by the apostles. It is the guardian and interpreter of them, and the judge of all controversies relating to them. The Scriptures, thus interpreted, together with the traditions of the apostles, are to be received and admitted by all Christians for the rule of their faith and practice.

9. We must believe that, when the pope speaks *ex cathedra*—that is, when, in discharge of his office of pastor and teacher of all Christians, he defines, in virtue of his supreme apostolic authority, a doctrine of faith or morals to be held by the universal Church—he is endowed, by the divine assistance promised to him in blessed Peter, with that infallibility with which the divine Redeemer willed that His Church should be furnished, in defining doctrine of faith or morals. And therefore such definitions of the pope are irreformable *of themselves*, and not in virtue of the consent of the Church.

10. We must believe that Jesus Christ has instituted in His Church seven Sacraments, or mysterious signs and instrumental causes of divine grace in our souls: **Baptism**, by way of a new birth, by which we are made children of God, and cleansed from sin; **Confirmation**, by which we receive the Holy Ghost, by the imposition of the hands of the successors of the apostles; the Blessed **Eucharist**, which feeds and nourishes our souls with the Body and Blood of Christ, really present under the forms of bread and wine, or under either of them; **Penance**, by which penitent sinners are absolved from their sins, by virtue of the commission given by Christ to His ministers; **Extreme Unction**, which wipes away the remains of sin, and arms the soul with the grace of God in the time of sickness; **Holy Orders**, by which the ministers of God are consecrated; and **Matrimony**, which, as a sacred sign of the indissoluble union of Christ and His Church, unites the married couple in a holy bond, and imparts to them a grace suitable to that state.

11. We must believe that Jesus Christ has also instituted the great Eucharistic sacrifice of His Body and Blood in remembrance of His Passion and death. In this sacrifice, called the Mass, He is mystically immolated every day upon our altars, being Himself both Priest and Victim. This sacrifice is the principal worship of the New Law, in which, and by which, we unite ourselves to Jesus Christ; and, with Him and through Him, we adore God in spirit and truth; give Him thanks for all His blessings; obtain His grace for ourselves and the whole world, and pardon for all our sins; and pray for the living and the dead.

12. We must believe that there is, in the Catholic or universal Church of God, a communion of saints, by means of which we communicate with all holy persons and in all holy things. We communicate with the saints in heaven, as our fellow members under the same Head, Christ Jesus; we give thanks to God for His gifts to them, and we beg a share in their prayers. We communicate with all the saints upon earth in the same Sacraments and sacrifice, and in a holy union of faith and charity. And we also communicate with the faithful who have departed this life in a more imperfect state—and who, by the law of God's justice, are for a while in a state of suffering—by offering prayers and alms and sacrifice to God for them.

13. We must believe that, by the full concession of Christ, there ever resides in the Church the active power of forgiving sin, and of granting indulgences for the remission of the temporal punishments of sin; which may be applied to the souls both of the living and of the dead who have died friends of God and in the peace of Christ.

14. We must believe also the necessity of divine grace, without which we cannot make so much as one step toward heaven; and that all our good and all our merits are the gift of God; that Christ died for all men, and that His grace does not take away or oppress our free will.

15. We must believe that Jesus Christ will come from heaven at the Last Day to judge all men; that all the dead, both good and bad, shall arise from their graves, and shall be judged by Him according to their works; that the good shall go to heaven with Him, body and soul, to be happy for all eternity in the enjoyment of the sovereign Good; and that the wicked shall be condemned, both body and soul, to the torments of hell.

WHAT EVERY CHRISTIAN MUST DO

1. Every Christian, in order to attain life everlasting, must worship God as his first beginning and last end. This worship is to be rendered, first, by **faith**: which makes both the understanding and the will humbly adore and embrace all those truths which God has taught, however obscure and incomprehensible they may be to our weakness. Secondly, by **hope**: which honors the infinite power, goodness, and mercy of God, and the truth of His promises; and, upon these grounds, raises the soul to an assured expectation of mercy, grace, and salvation, through the merits of Jesus

Christ. Thirdly, by **charity**: which teaches us to love God with our whole hearts, for His own sake, and our neighbor as ourselves, for God's sake. Fourthly, by the virtue of **religion**: the chief acts of which are *adoration, praise, thanksgiving, oblation of ourselves to God, sacrifice,* and *prayer*; which ought to be the daily employments of a Christian soul. We must flee all idolatry and all false religions; also superstition, under which name are comprehended all manner of divinations, all fortune-telling, all witchcraft, charms, spells, observations of omens, dreams, and the like. All these things are heathenish, and contrary to the worship of the true and living God, and to that entire dependence which a Christian soul ought to have on Him. But we must devoutly honor the ever Blessed Virgin Mary, Mother of God, the holy angels, and the saints reigning in glory; whose intercessions we shall always most profitably invoke. We should likewise duly reverence all sacred emblems and pious memorials of Our Lord and His saints, and honor the relics of God's servants whom holy Church has canonized.

2. We must reverence the name of God and His truth by a religious observance of all lawful oaths and vows, and by carefully avoiding all false, rash, or unjust oaths, and blasphemies.

3. We must dedicate some notable part of our time to His divine service; and, more especially, consecrate to Him those days which are ordered by His Church to be sanctified or kept holy.

4. Under God, we must love, reverence, and obey our parents, and other lawful superiors, spiritual and temporal; and observe the laws of the Church and state: as also we must have a due care of our children, and of others that are under our charge, both as to their souls and their bodies.

5. We must abstain from all injuries to our neighbor's person, by murder or any other violence; and from all hatred, envy, and desire of revenge; as also from *spiritual* murder, which is committed by drawing him into sin, by words, actions, or bad example.

6. We must abstain from all uncleanness in thoughts, words, or actions.

7. We must not steal, cheat, or any other way do wrong to our neighbor in his goods and possessions; we must give every one his own, pay our debts, and make restitution for all damages which we have caused through our fault.

8. We must not wrong our neighbor in his *character* or good name, by calumny, detraction, or rash judgment; or in his *honor* by reproaches or affronts; or rob him of his *peace of mind*, by scoffs or contempt; or of his *friends*, by carrying stories backward and forward. In all such cases, whosoever wrongs his neighbor is obliged to make reparation or satisfaction.

9, 10. As we are commanded to abstain from all deeds of lust and injustice, so are we also strictly obliged to restrain all *desires* of these kinds, and to resist the irregular motions of concupiscence. So far the Ten Commandments of God; which are a short abridgment of the whole eternal and natural law, which admits of no dispensation.

Every Christian is, moreover, bound to keep the commandments of God's Church.

1. We must sanctify Sundays and holy days of obligation by devout attendance at Holy Mass, and by resting from servile work.

2. We must strictly observe those days of fasting and abstinence appointed by ecclesiastical authority.

3. We must humbly confess our sins at least once a year to a priest having competent jurisdiction — that is approved by the bishop of the diocese.

4. We must be careful to make our *Easter duty*, by receiving Holy Communion at some time during the interval between the First Sunday in Lent and Trinity Sunday.

5. According to our means, we must contribute to the support of those who minister to us in spiritual things.

6. We must not marry non-Catholics, or anyone related to us within the fourth degree of kindred; we must not marry clandestinely, or solemnize marriage within the prohibited times.

PRAYERS WHICH EVERY CHRISTIAN SHOULD KNOW BY HEART

The Invocation

In nomine Patris, ✠ et Filii, et Spiritus Sancti. *Amen.*

In the name of the Father, ✠ and of the Son, and of the Holy Ghost. *Amen.*

The Lord's Prayer

Pater noster, qui es in cœlis, sanctificetur nomen tuum: adveniat regnum tuum: fiat voluntas tua, sicut in cœlo, et in terra. Panem nostrum quotidianum da nobis hodie: et dimitte nobis debita nostra, sicut et nos dimittimus debitoribus nostris. Et ne nos inducas in tentationem: sed libera nos a malo. *Amen.*

Our Father, Who art in heaven, hallowed be Thy name: Thy Kingdom come: Thy will be done on earth as it is in heaven. Give us this day our daily bread: and forgive us our trespasses as we forgive those who trespass against us. And lead us not into temptation; but deliver us from evil. *Amen.*

The Hail Mary

Ave, Maria, gratia plena; Dominus tecum: benedicta tu in mulieribus, et benedictus fructus ventris tui Jesus. Sancta Maria, Mater Dei, ora pro nobis peccatoribus, nunc et in hora mortis nostræ. *Amen.*

Hail, Mary, full of grace; the Lord is with thee: blessed art thou among women, and blessed is the fruit of thy womb, Jesus. Holy Mary, Mother of God, pray for us sinners, now and at the hour of our death. *Amen.*

The Creed

Credo in Deum, Patrem omnipotentem, Creatorem cœli et terræ; et in Jesum Christum, Filium ejus unicum, Dominum nostrum: qui conceptus est de Spiritu Sancto, natus ex Maria Virgine, passus sub Pontio Pilato, crucifixus; mortuus, et sepultus. Descendit ad inferos; tertia die resurrexit a mortuis; ascendit ad cœlos, sedet ad dexteram Dei Patris omnipotentis: inde venturus est judicare vivos et mortuos. Credo in Spiritum Sanctum, Sanctam Ecclesiam Catholicam, Sanctorum communionem, remissionem peccatorum, carnis resurrectionem, vitam æternam. *Amen.*

I believe in God, the Father Almighty, Creator of heaven and earth; and in Jesus Christ, His only Son, Our Lord: Who was conceived by the Holy Ghost, born of the Virgin Mary, suffered under Pontius Pilate, was crucified; died, and was buried. He descended into hell; the third day He arose again from the dead; He ascended into heaven, sitteth at the right hand of God the Father Almighty; from thence He shall come to judge the living and the dead. I believe in the Holy Ghost, the holy Catholic Church, the communion of saints, the forgiveness of sins, the resurrection of the body, and the life everlasting. *Amen.*

The Confiteor

Confiteor Deo omnipotenti, beatæ Mariæ semper Virgini, beato Michaeli Archangelo, beato Joanni Baptistæ, sanctis Apostolis Petro et Paulo, omnibus Sanctis, (et tibi, Pater,) quia peccavi nimis cogitatione, verbo, et opere: mea culpa, mea culpa, mea maxima culpa. Ideo precor beatam Mariam semper Virginem, beatum Michaelem Archangelum, beatum Joannem Baptistam, sanctos Apostolos Petrum et Paulum, omnes Sanctos, (et te, Pater,) orare pro me ad Dominum Deum nostrum.

I confess to Almighty God, to Blessed Mary ever Virgin, to blessed Michael the archangel, to blessed John the Baptist, to the holy apostles Peter and Paul, and to all the saints, (and to you, Father,) that I have sinned exceedingly in thought, word, and deed, through my fault, through my fault, through my most grievous fault. Therefore I beseech Blessed Mary ever Virgin, blessed Michael the archangel, blessed John the Baptist, the holy apostles Peter and Paul, and all the saints, (and you, Father,) to pray to the Lord our God for me.

Misereatur nostri omnipotens Deus, et dimissis peccatis nostris, perducat nos ad vitam æternam. *Amen.*

May Almighty God have mercy upon us, and forgive us our sins, and bring us unto life everlasting. *Amen.*

Indulgentiam, ✠ absolutionem, et remissionem peccatorum nostrorum, tribuat nobis omnipotens et misericors Dominus. *Amen.*

May the Almighty and merciful Lord grant us pardon, ✠ absolution, and remission of our sins. *Amen.*

The Gloria Patri, or Lesser Doxology

Gloria Patri, et Filio, et Spiritui Sancto. Sicut erat in principio, et nunc, et semper, et in sæcula sæculorum. *Amen.*

Glory be to the Father, and to the Son, and to the Holy Ghost. As it was in the beginning, is now, and ever shall be, world without end. *Amen.*

Morning Prayers

THE OFFICE OF PRIME

Before Prime are said inaudibly the Our Father, *the* Hail Mary, *and the* Creed.

Then is said aloud:
Come unto my help, O God.
℟. O Lord, make haste to help me.
Glory be to the Father, etc.
Alleluia (*or, in Lent,* Praise to Thee, O Lord, King of eternal glory).

Then is said the following Hymn:[3]
The star of morn to night succeeds;
We therefore meekly pray,
May God, in all our words and deeds,
Keep us from harm this day.

May He in love restrain us still
From tones of strife and words of ill,
And wrap around and close our eyes
To earth's absorbing vanities.

May wrath and thoughts that gender shame
Ne'er in our breasts abide,
And painful abstinences tame
Of wanton flesh the pride;

So when the weary day is o'er,
And night and stillness come once more,
Blameless and clean from spot of earth
We may repeat with reverent mirth—

To God the Father glory be,
And to His only Son,
And to the Spirit, one and three,
While endless ages run. Amen.

Then follow the Psalms which are said under one Antiphon:
Ant. for Sundays. Alleluia.

---

[3]   Translation by Cardinal Newman.

Ant. for weekdays. Blessed are they that walk.

Psalm 53

Save me, O God, by Thy name: and judge me in Thy strength.

Hear my prayer, O God: give ear unto the words of my mouth.

For strangers have risen up against me, and the mighty have sought after my soul: and they have not set God before their eyes.

For behold, God is my helper: and the Lord is the protector of my soul.

Turn back evil upon mine enemies: and destroy Thou them in Thy truth.

I will freely sacrifice unto Thee, and will praise Thy name, O Lord: for it is good:

For Thou hast delivered me out of all my trouble: and mine eye hath looked down upon mine enemies.

Glory be to the Father, etc.

Psalm 118

Blessed are the undefiled in the way: who walk in the law of the Lord.

Blessed are they that search His testimonies: that seek Him with their whole heart.

For they that work iniquity: have not walked in His ways.

Thou hast commanded that Thy commandments be kept most diligently.

O that my ways may be so directed: that I may keep Thine ordinances.

Then shall I not be confounded: when I shall have regard to all Thy commandments.

I will praise Thee with uprightness of heart: when I shall have learned the judgments of Thy justice.

I will keep Thine ordinances: O forsake me not utterly.

By what doth a young man correct his way? even by keeping Thy words.

With my whole heart have I sought after Thee: let me not stray from Thy commandments.

Thy words have I hidden within my heart: that I may not sin against Thee.

Blessed art Thou, O Lord: O teach me Thine ordinances.

With my lips have I declared: all the judgments of Thy mouth.

I have had delight in the way of Thy testimonies: even as in all riches.

I will meditate on Thy commandments: and I will consider Thy ways.

I will think upon Thine ordinances: I will not forget Thy words.

Glory be to the Father, etc.

Deal bountifully with Thy servant: quicken Thou me, and I shall keep Thy words.

Open Thou mine eyes: and I shall see the wondrous things of Thy law.

I am a sojourner upon earth: O hide not Thy commandments from me.

My soul hath longed greatly: to desire Thine ordinances at all times.

Thou hast rebuked the proud: cursed are they that do err from Thy commandments.

O take from me shame and contempt: for I have sought after Thy testimonies.

Princes also did sit and speak against me: but Thy servant was occupied in Thy statutes.

For Thy testimonies are my meditation: and Thine ordinances are my counsel.

My soul hath cleaved to the earth: O quicken Thou me according to Thy word.

I have declared my ways, and Thou heardest me: teach me Thy statutes.

Make me to understand the way of Thine ordinances: and I will meditate on Thy wondrous works.

My soul hath slumbered through weariness: strengthen Thou me in Thy words.

Remove from me the way of iniquity: and have mercy on me in Thy law.

I have chosen the way of truth: I have not forgotten Thy judgments.

I have cleaved unto Thy testimonies, O Lord: put me not to shame.

I have run in the way of Thy commandments: when Thou didst enlarge my heart.

Glory be to the Father, etc.

[*The following Creed is said only on* Sundays, *when the* Sunday Office *is recited:*

The Creed of St. Athanasius

Quicumque vult salvus esse, *
    ante omnia opus est, ut teneat
    Catholicam fidem.

Whosoever desires to be saved, before
    all things it is necessary that he hold
    the Catholic Faith.

Quam nisi quisque integram inviolat-
    amque servaverit, * absque dubio
    in æternum peribit

Which Faith, except every one do keep
    entire and inviolate, without doubt
    he shall perish everlastingly.

Fides autem Catholica hæc est, *
    ut unum Deum in Trinitate, et
    Trinitatem in unitate veneremur.

Now the Catholic Faith is this: that we
    worship one God in Trinity, and
    Trinity in Unity.

Neque confundentes personas, * neque
    substantiam separantes.

Neither confounding the Persons nor
    dividing the substance.

Alia est enim persona Patris, alia Filii,
    * alia Spiritus Sancti.

For there is one Person of the Father,
    another of the Son, another of the
    Holy Ghost.

Sed Patris, et Filii, et Spiritus Sancti
    una est divinitas, * æqualis gloria,
    cœterna majestas.

But the Godhead of the Father, and of
    the Son, and of the Holy Ghost is
    one; the glory equal, the majesty
    coeternal.

Qualis Pater, talis Filius, * talis Spiritus
Sanctus.

As the Father is, such is the Son, such
    the Holy Ghost.

Increatus Pater, increatus Filius, * increatus Spiritus Sanctus.

The Father uncreate, the Son uncreate, the Holy Ghost uncreate.

Immensus Pater, immensus Filius, * immensus Spiritus Sanctus.

The Father infinite, the Son infinite, the Holy Ghost infinite.

Æternus Pater, æternus Filius, * æternus Spiritus Sanctus.

The Father eternal, the Son eternal, the Holy Ghost eternal.

Et tamen non tres æterni, * sed unus æternus.

And yet they are not three eternals, but one Eternal.

Sicut non tres increati, nec tres immensi, * sed unus increatus, et unus immensus.

As also they are not three uncreates, nor three infinites; but one Uncreate, and one Infinite.

Similiter omnipotens Pater, omnipotens Filius, * omnipotens Spiritus Sanctus.

In like manner the Father is Almighty, the Son Almighty, and the Holy Ghost Almighty.

Et tamen non tres omnipotentes, * sed unus omnipotens.

And yet they are not three almighties, but one Almighty.

Ita Deus Pater, Deus Filius, * Deus Spiritus Sanctus.

So the Father is God, the Son God, and the Holy Ghost God.

Et tamen non tres Dii, * sed unus est Deus.

And yet they are not three gods, but one God.

Ita Dominus Pater, Dominus Filius, * Dominus Spiritus Sanctus.

So the Father is Lord, the Son is Lord, and the Holy Ghost is Lord.

Et tamen non tres Domini, * sed unus est Dominus.

And yet they are not three lords, but one Lord.

Quia sicut singillatim unamquamque personam Deum ac Dominum confiteri Christiana veritate compellimur: * ita tres Deos aut Dominos dicere Catholica religione prohibemur.

For as we are obliged by the Christian truth to acknowledge every Person singly to be God and Lord: so we are forbidden by the Catholic religion to say there are three gods or three lords.

Pater a nullo est factus, * nec creatus, nec genitus.

The Father was made by no one, neither created, nor begotten.

Filius a Patre solo est: * non factus, nec creatus, sed genitus.

Spiritus Sanctus a Patre et Filio: * non factus, nec creatus, nec genitus, sed procedens.

Unus ergo Pater, non tres Patres: unus Filius, non tres Filii: * unus Spiritus Sanctus, non tres Spiritus Sancti.

Et in hac Trinitate nihil prius aut posterius, nihil majus aut minus: * sed totæ tres personæ coæternæ sibi sunt, et coæquales.

Ita ut per omnia, sicut jam supra dictum est, * et unitas in Trinitate, et Trinitas in unitate veneranda sit.

Qui vult ergo salvus esse, * ita de Trinitate sentiat.

Sed necessarium est ad æternam salutem, * ut incarnationem quoque Domini nostri Jesu Christi fideliter credat.

Est ergo fides recta, ut credamus et confiteamur, * quia Dominus noster Jesus Christus Dei Filius, Deus et homo est.

Deus est ex substantia Patris ante sæcula genitus: * et homo est ex substantia matris in sæculo natus.

Perfectus Deus, perfectus homo: * ex anima rationali, et humana carne subsistens.

The Son is by the Father alone, not made, nor created, but begotten.

The Holy Ghost is from the Father and the Son, not made, nor created, nor begotten, but proceeding.

So there is one Father, not three fathers: one Son, not three sons: one Holy Ghost, not three holy ghosts.

And in this Trinity there is nothing before or after, nothing greater or less; but the whole three Persons are coeternal together and coequal.

So that in all things, as is aforesaid, the Unity is to be worshipped in Trinity, and the Trinity in Unity.

He, therefore, that desires to be saved, must thus believe of the Trinity.

Furthermore, it is necessary to everlasting salvation that he also believe faithfully the Incarnation of Our Lord Jesus Christ.

Now the right faith is that we believe and confess that Our Lord Jesus Christ, the Son of God, is both God and man.

He is God of the substance of His Father, begotten before the world; and He is man of the substance of His Mother, born in the world:

Perfect God and perfect man; of rational soul and human flesh subsisting.

Æqualis Patri secundum divini-
tatem: * minor Patre secundum
humanitatem.

Qui, licet Deus sit et homo, * non duo
tamen, sed unus est Christus.

Unus autem, non conversione divinitatis in carnem, * sed assumptione
humanitatis in Deum.

Unus omnino, non confusione substantiæ, * sed unitate personæ.

Nam, sicut anima rationalis et caro
unus est homo, * ita Deus et homo
unus est Christus:

Qui passus est pro salute nostra,
descendit ad inferos, * tertia die
resurrexit a mortuis:

Ascendit ad cœlos, sedet ad dexteram
Dei Patris omnipotentis: * inde
venturus est judicare vivos et
mortuos:

Ad cujus adventum omnes homines
resurgere habent cum corporibus
suis, * et reddituri sunt de factis
propriis rationem.

Et qui bona egerunt, ibunt in vitam
æternam: * qui vero mala, in ignem æternum.

Hæc est fides Catholica: * quam nisi
quisque fideliter firmiterque cred-
iderit, salvus esse non poterit.

Gloria Patri, etc.

Equal to the Father according to His
divinity; and less than the Father
according to His humanity.

Who, although He be both God and
man, yet He is not two, but one
Christ:

One, not by the conversion of the
Godhead into flesh, but by the as-
suming of human nature unto God:

One altogether, not by confusion of substance, but by unity of Person.

For as the rational soul and the body
constitutes one man, so God and
man is one Christ:

Who suffered for our salvation, descended into hell, arose again the
third day from the dead:

He ascended into heaven; He sitteth at
the right hand of God the Father
Almighty; thence He shall come to
judge the living and the dead:

At Whose coming all men must arise
again with their bodies, and must
give an account of their own works.

And they that have done good shall go
into life everlasting; and they that
have done evil, into everlasting fire.

This is the Catholic Faith, which except
a man believe faithfully and steadfastly he cannot be saved.

Glory be to the Father, etc.

Antiphon for Sundays. Alleluia, alleluia, alleluia.
At Easter a fourth Alleluia.

Antiphon for weekdays. Blessed are they that walk in Thy law, O Lord.

Then is said the Chapter:
Sundays:
Unto the King of ages, the Immortal, Invisible, only God, be honor and glory
forever and ever.
℞. Thanks be to God.

Weekdays:
Love peace and truth, saith the Lord Almighty.
℞. Thanks be to God.

Then follows the Short Responsory:
Christ, Thou Son of the living God, have mercy on us.
℞. Christ, Thou Son of the living God, have mercy on us.
℣. Thou that sittest at the right hand of the Father,
℞. Have mercy on us.
℣. Glory be to the Father, and to the Son, and to the Holy Ghost.
℞. Christ, Thou Son of the living God, have mercy on us.
℣. Arise, O Christ, and help us.
℞. And deliver us for Thy name's sake.

After the Short Responsory follow these prayers, called the Preces, *except on* double feasts
and within octaves, *when they are omitted down to the mark* (*):
Lord, have mercy.
Christ, have mercy.
Lord, have mercy.
Our Father (*inaudibly*).
℣. And lead us not into temptation.
℞. But deliver us from evil.
I believe in God (*inaudibly*).
℣. The resurrection of the body.
℞. And the life everlasting. Amen.
℣. But I, O Lord, have cried unto Thee.
℞. And in the morning my prayer shall come early before Thee.
℣. Let my mouth be filled with praise.
℞. That I may sing of Thy glory; and of Thy greatness all the day long.
℣. O Lord, turn away Thy face from my sins.
℞. And blot out all my iniquities.

℣. Create in me a clean heart, O God.

℟. And renew a right spirit within me.

℣. Cast me not away from Thy face.

℟. And take not Thy Holy Spirit from me.

℣. Restore unto me the joy of Thy salvation.

℟. And strengthen me with a perfect spirit.

[*These prayers within the brackets are said only on weekdays:*

Deliver me, O Lord, from the evil man.

℟. And rescue me from the unjust man.

℣. Deliver me from mine enemies, O my God.

℟. And defend me from them that rise up against me.

℣. Deliver me from them that work iniquity.

℟. And save me from the men of blood.

℣. So will I sing a psalm unto Thy name forever and ever.

℟. That I may pay my vows from day to day.

℣. Hear us, O God our Savior.

℟. Who art the hope of all the ends of the earth, and in the sea afar off.

℣. Come unto my help, O God.

℟. O Lord, make haste to help me.

℣. Holy God, Holy and Mighty, Holy and Immortal,

℟. Have mercy on us.

℣. Bless the Lord, O my soul.

℟. And let all that is within me bless His holy name.

℣. Bless the Lord, O my soul.

℟. And forget not all His benefits.

℣. Who forgiveth thee all thine iniquities.

℟. Who healeth all thine infirmities.

℣. Who redeemeth thy life from destruction.

℟. Who crowneth thee with mercy and compassion.

℣. Who satisfieth thy desire with good things.

℟. Thy youth shall be renewed like the eagle's.]

℣. Our help is in the name of the Lord.

℟. Who hath made heaven and earth.

The Confiteor (*p. 32*).

Then the Office continues as follows:

Vouchsafe, O Lord, this day

℟. To keep us without sin.

℣. Have mercy on us, O Lord.

℟. Have mercy on us.

℣. Let Thy mercy, O Lord, be upon us.

℟. As we have hoped in Thee.

Here the Office is resumed, when the Preces *have been omitted:*

℣. O Lord, hear my prayer.

℟. And let my cry come unto Thee.

Let us pray.

O Lord, God Almighty, Who hast brought us to the beginning of this day: let Thy power so defend us therein, that this day we fall into no sin, but that all our thoughts, words, and works may always tend to what is just in Thy sight. Through Our Lord Jesus Christ, Thy Son, Who liveth and reigneth with Thee in the unity of the Holy Ghost, one God, world without end. ℟. Amen.

℣. O Lord, hear my prayer.

℟. And let my cry come unto Thee.

℣. Let us bless the Lord.

℟. Thanks be to God.

Here is read the Martyrology, *if read at all; after which the Office proceeds thus:*

℣. Precious in the sight of Lord

℟. Is the death of His saints.

May the Blessed Virgin Mary and all the saints plead for us with the Lord, that we may deserve to be helped and delivered by Him Who liveth and reigneth, world without end. ℟. Amen.

℣. Come unto my help, O God.

℟. O Lord, make haste to help me. (*This versicle and response is said thrice.*)

℣. Glory be to the Father, etc.

℟. As it was in the beginning, etc.

Lord, have mercy.

Christ, have mercy.

Lord, have mercy.

Our Father (*inaudibly*).

℣. And lead us not into temptation.

℟. But deliver us from evil.

℣. Look upon Thy servants, O Lord, and upon Thy works, and direct their children.

℟. And let the brightness of the Lord our God be upon us, and direct Thou the works of our hands over us: yea, the work of our hands do Thou direct.

℣. Glory be to the Father, etc.

℟. As it was in the beginning, etc.

Let us pray.

O Lord God, King of heaven and earth, vouchsafe this day to direct and to sanctify, to rule and to govern, our souls and bodies, our senses, words, and actions, in Thy law, and in the works of Thy commandments; that both now and forever we may deserve to be saved and delivered through Thy protection, O Savior of the world, Who livest and reignest, world without end. ℟. Amen.

℣. O Lord, grant Thy blessing.

THE BLESSING

May the Lord Almighty order our days and deeds in His peace. ℟. Amen.

Then is read the Short Lesson:

And may the Lord direct our hearts in the love of God, and the patience of Christ. And do Thou, O Lord, have mercy on us.

℟. Thanks be to God.

℣. Our help is in the name of the Lord.

℟. Who hath made heaven and earth.

℣. Bless ye.

℟. God.

THE BLESSING

The Lord bless us, and keep us from all evil, and bring us unto life everlasting: and may the souls of the faithful departed, through the mercy of God, rest in peace. ℟. Amen.

ANOTHER FORM OF MORNING PRAYERS

As soon as you are awake, make the sign of the cross, and say:

Holy, holy, holy, Lord God of hosts: the earth is full of Thy glory. Glory be to the Father, glory be to the Son, glory be to the Holy Ghost. *Amen.*

When you are dressed, calling to mind the greatness of God, and your own nothingness, place yourself in His presence, and kneel down and say:

In the name of the Father, ✠ and of the Son, and of the Holy Ghost. *Amen.*

Come, Holy Ghost, fill the hearts of Thy faithful, and kindle in them the fire of Thy love.

Most Holy and adorable Trinity, one God in three Persons, I believe that Thou art here present; I adore Thee with the deepest humility, and render to Thee, with my whole heart, the homage which is due to Thy sovereign Majesty.

O my God, I most humbly thank Thee for all the favors Thou hast bestowed upon me up to the present moment. I give Thee thanks from the bottom of my heart that Thou hast created me after Thine own image and likeness, that Thou hast redeemed me by the Precious Blood of Thy dear Son, and that Thou hast preserved me and brought me safe to the beginning of another day. I offer to Thee, O Lord, my whole being, and, in particular, all my thoughts, words, actions, and sufferings of this day. I consecrate them all to the glory of Thy name, beseeching Thee that through the infinite merits of Jesus Christ my Savior they may all find acceptance in Thy sight. May Thy divine love animate them, and may they all tend to Thy greater glory.

Adorable Jesus, my Savior and Master, Model of all perfection, I resolve and will endeavor this day to imitate Thy example, to be, like Thee, mild, humble, chaste, zealous, charitable, and resigned. I will redouble my efforts that I may not fall this day into any of those sins which I have heretofore committed (*here you may name any besetting sin*), and which I sincerely desire to forsake.

O my God, Thou knowest my poverty and weakness, and that I am unable to do anything good without Thee; deny me not, O God, the help of Thy grace; proportion it to my necessities; give me strength to avoid everything evil which Thou forbiddest, and to practice the good which Thou hast commanded; and enable me to bear patiently all the trials which it may please Thee to send me.

Our Father. Hail Mary. Creed. Confiteor.

[*Here the* Litany of the Holy Name, *p. 47, may be said.*]

AN ACT OF FAITH

O my God! I firmly believe that Thou art one God in three divine Persons, the Father, the Son, and the Holy Ghost; I believe that Thy divine Son became man, and died for our sins, and that He will come to judge the living and the dead. I believe these and all the truths which the holy Catholic Church teaches, because Thou hast revealed them, Who canst neither deceive nor be deceived.

AN ACT OF HOPE

O my God! relying on Thy infinite goodness and promises, I hope to obtain pardon of my sins, the help of Thy grace, and life everlasting, through the merits of Jesus Christ, my Lord and Redeemer.

AN ACT OF CHARITY

O my God! I love Thee above all things, with my whole heart and soul, because Thou art all-good and worthy of all love. I love my neighbor as myself for the love of Thee. I forgive all who have injured me, and ask pardon of all whom I have injured.

AN ACT OF CONTRITION

O my God! I am heartily sorry for having offended Thee, and I detest all my sins, because I dread the loss of heaven and the pains of hell, but most of all because they offend Thee, my God, Who art all-good and deserving of all my love. I firmly resolve, with the help of Thy grace, to confess my sins, to do penance, and to amend my life. *Amen.*

O holy Virgin, Mother of God, my Mother and patroness, I place myself under thy protection, I throw myself with confidence into the arms of thy compassion. Be to me, O Mother of mercy, my refuge in distress, my consolation under suffering, my advocate with thy adorable Son, now and at the hour of my death. *Amen.*

O faithful guardian and father of virgins, blessed Joseph, to whom was confided the care of Jesus, and of Mary the Queen of virgins, I most humbly supplicate thee, by the love thou dost bear Jesus and Mary, to obtain for me that, being preserved from every stain during my whole life, I may be ever able to serve them with unspotted purity of mind and body. *Amen.*

Angel of God, my guardian dear,
To whom His love commits me here,
Ever this day be at my side,
To light and guard, to rule and guide. *Amen.*

O great saint, whose name I bear, protect me, pray for me, that, like thee, I may serve God faithfully on earth, and glorify Him eternally with thee in heaven. *Amen.*

May the power of the Father govern and protect me! May the wisdom of the Son teach and enlighten me! May the influence of the Holy Ghost renew and quicken me! May the blessing of the All-Holy Trinity, the Father, ✠ the Son, and the Holy Ghost, be with me, now and forevermore. *Amen.*

THE ANGELUS

To be said morning, noon, and night; kneeling, except on Saturday evening and throughout Sunday.

Angelus Domini nuntiavit Mariæ.
℟. Et concepit de Spiritu Sancto.
Ave, Maria, etc.
℣. Ecce ancilla Domini.
℟. Fiat mihi secundum verbum tuum.

The angel of the Lord declared unto Mary.
℟. And she conceived by the Holy Ghost.
Hail, Mary, etc.
℣. Behold the handmaid of the Lord.
℟. Be it done unto me according to Thy word.

Ave, Maria, etc.

Hail, Mary, etc.

℣. ET VERBUM CARO FACTUM EST.
℟. Et habitavit in nobis.
Ave, Maria, etc.

℣. AND THE WORD WAS MADE FLESH.
℟. And dwelt among us.
Hail, Mary, etc.

‡℣. Ora pro nobis, Sancta Dei Genitrix.
℟. Ut digni efficiamur promissionibus Christi.

[‡℣. Pray for us, O holy Mother of God.
℟. That we may be made worthy of the promises of Christ.]

Oremus.

Gratiam tuam, quæsumus, Domine, mentibus nostris infunde, ut qui, Angelo nuntiante, Christi Filii tui incarnationem cognovimus, per passionem ejus et crucem ad resurrectionis gloriam perducamur; per eundem Christum Dominum nostrum. *Amen.*

Let us pray.

Pour forth, we beseech Thee, O Lord, Thy grace into our hearts; that as we have known the Incarnation of Christ Thy Son by the message of an angel, so, by His Passion and Cross, we may be brought to the glory of His Resurrection; through the same Christ Our Lord. *Amen.*

In Eastertide, *instead of the* Angelus, *the* Regina cœli *(p. 59) is said standing.*

A PRAYER FOR THE CHURCH, THE CIVIL AUTHORITIES, ETC.[4]

We pray Thee, O Almighty and eternal God, Who through Jesus Christ hast revealed Thy glory to all nations, to preserve the works of Thy mercy; that Thy Church, being spread through the whole world, may continue, with unchanging faith, in the confession of Thy name.

We pray Thee, Who alone art good and holy, to endow with heavenly knowledge, sincere zeal, and sanctity of life our chief bishop, N., the Vicar of Our Lord Jesus Christ in the government of His Church; our own bishop, (*or* archbishop,)

---

[4]   Composed by Archbishop Carroll, A.D. 1800.

N., (*if he is not consecrated,* our bishop-elect); all other bishops, prelates, and pastors of the Church; and especially those who are appointed to exercise among us the functions of the holy ministry, and conduct Thy people into the ways of salvation.

We pray Thee, O God of might, wisdom, and justice, through Whom authority is rightly administered, laws are enacted, and judgment decreed, assist, with Thy Holy Spirit of counsel and fortitude, the president of these United States, that his administration may be conducted in righteousness, and be eminently useful to Thy people, over whom he presides, by encouraging due respect for virtue and religion; by a faithful execution of the laws in justice and mercy; and by restraining vice and immorality. Let the light of Thy divine wisdom direct the deliberations of Congress, and shine forth in all the proceedings and laws framed for our rule and government; so that they may tend to the preservation of peace, the promotion of national happiness, the increase of industry, sobriety, and useful knowledge, and may perpetuate to us the blessings of equal liberty.

We pray for his Excellency the governor of this state, for the members of the assembly, for all judges, magistrates, and other officers who are appointed to guard our political welfare; that they may be enabled, by Thy powerful protection, to discharge the duties of their respective stations with honesty and ability.

We recommend likewise to Thy unbounded mercy all our brethren and fellow citizens, throughout the United States, that they may be blessed in the knowledge, and sanctified in the observance of Thy most holy law; that they may be preserved in union, and in that peace which the world cannot give; and, after enjoying the blessings of this life, be admitted to those which are eternal.

Finally, we pray Thee O Lord of mercy, to remember the souls of Thy servants departed who are gone before us with the sign of faith, and repose in the sleep of peace: the souls of our parents, relations, and friends; of those who, when living, were members of this congregation; and particularly of such as are lately deceased; of all benefactors who, by their donations or legacies to this Church, witnessed their seal for the decency of divine worship, and proved their claim to our grateful and charitable remembrance. To these O Lord, and to all that rest in Christ, grant, we beseech Thee, a place of refreshment, light, and everlasting peace, through the same Jesus Christ, Our Lord and Savior. *Amen.*

GRACE BEFORE MEALS

Bless us, O Lord, and these Thy gifts, which we are about to receive from Thy bounty. Through Christ Our Lord. ℟. Amen.

GRACE AFTER MEALS

We give Thee thanks, O Almighty God, for all Thy mercies. Who livest and reignest world without end. ℟. Amen.

Vouchsafe, O Lord, to reward with eternal life all those who do us good for Thy name's sake. ℟. Amen.

℣. Let us bless the Lord.

℟. Thanks be to God.

May the souls of the faithful departed, through the mercy of God, rest in peace.

℟. Amen.

Litany of the Most Holy Name of Jesus

Kyrie, eleison.	Lord, have mercy on us.
Christe, eleison.	*Christ, have mercy on us.*
Kyrie, eleison.	Lord, have mercy on us.
Jesu, audi nos.	Jesus, hear us.
Jesu, exaudi nos.	*Jesus, graciously hear us.*
Pater de cœlis Deus,	God the Father of heaven,
Fili Redemptor mundi Deus,	God the Son, Redeemer of the world,
Spiritus Sancte Deus,	God the Holy Ghost,
Sancta Trinitas, unus Deus,	Holy Trinity, one God,
Jesu, Fili Dei vivi,	Jesus, Son of the living God,
Jesu, splendor Patris,	Jesus, Splendor of the Father,
Jesu, candor lucis æternæ,	Jesus, Brightness of eternal light,
Jesu, rex gloriæ,	Jesus, King of glory,
Jesu, sol justitiæ,	Jesus, Sun of justice,
Jesu, Fili Mariæ Virginis,	Jesus, Son of the Virgin Mary,
Jesu amabilis,	Jesus, most amiable,
Jesu admirabilis,	Jesus, most admirable,
Jesu, Deus fortis,	Jesus, mighty God,
Jesu, pater futuri sæculi,	Jesus, Father of the world to come,
Jesu, magni consilii Angele,	Jesus, Angel of the great counsel,
Jesu potentissime,	Jesus, most powerful,
Jesu patientissime,	Jesus, most patient,
Jesu obedientissime,	Jesus, most obedient,
Jesu mitis et humilis corde,	Jesus, meek and humble of heart,
Jesu, amator castitatis,	Jesus, Lover of chastity,
Jesu, amator noster,	Jesus, Lover of us,
Jesu, Deus pacis,	Jesus, God of peace,

Jesu, auctor vitæ,	Jesus, Author of life,
Jesu, exemplar virtutum,	Jesus, Model of virtues,
Jesu, zelator animarum,	Jesus, zealous for souls,
Jesu, Deus noster,	Jesus, our God,
Jesu, refugium nostrum,	Jesus, our Refuge,
Jesu, pater pauperum,	Jesus, Father of the poor,
Jesu, thesaure fidelium,	Jesus, Treasure of the faithful,
Jesu, bone pastor,	Jesus, Good Shepherd,
Jesu, lux vera,	Jesus, true Light,
Jesu, sapientia æterna,	Jesus, eternal Wisdom,
Jesu, bonitas infinita,	Jesus, infinite Goodness,
Jesu, via et vita nostra,	Jesus, our Way and our Life,
Jesu, gaudium Angelorum,	Jesus, Joy of angels,
Jesu, rex Patriarcharum,	Jesus, King of patriarchs,
Jesu, magister Apostolorum,	Jesus, Master of apostles,
Jesu, doctor Evangelistarum,	Jesus, Teacher of evangelists,
Jesu, fortitudo Martyrum,	Jesus, Strength of martyrs,
Jesu, lumen Confessorum,	Jesus, Light of confessors,
Jesu, puritas Virginum,	Jesus, Purity of virgins,
Jesu, corona Sanctorum omnium.	Jesus, Crown of all saints,

Propitius esto, *parce nobis, Jesu.* — Be merciful, *spare us, O Jesus.*
Propitius esto, *exaudi nos, Jesu.* — Be merciful, *graciously hear us, O Jesus.*

Ab omni malo,	From all evil,
Ab omni peccato,	From all sin,
Ab ira tua,	From Thy wrath,
Ab insidiis diaboli,	From the snares of the devil,
A spiritu fornicationis,	From the spirit of fornication,
A morte perpetua,	From everlasting death,
A neglectu inspirationum tuarum,	From neglect of Thy inspirations,
Per mysterium sanctæ incarnationis tuæ,	Through the mystery of Thy holy Incarnation,
Per nativitatem tuam,	Through Thy nativity,
Per infantiam tuam,	Through Thine infancy,
Per divinissimam vitam tuam,	Through Thy most divine life,
Per labores tuos,	Through Thy labors,
Per agoniam et passionem tuam,	Through Thine agony and Passion,
Per crucem et derelictionem tuam,	Through Thy Cross and abandonment,

Per languores tuos,

Per mortem et sepulturam tuam,

Per resurrectionem tuam,

Per ascensionem tuam,

‡Per sanctissimæ Eucharistiæ institutionem tuam,

Per gaudia tua,

Per gloriam tuam,

Agnus Dei, qui tollis peccata mundi, *parce nobis, Jesu.*

Agnus Dei, qui tollis peccata mundi, *exaudi nos, Jesu.*

Agnus Dei, qui tollis peccata mundi, *miserere nobis, Jesu.*

Jesu, audi nos.

Jesu, exaudi nos.

Oremus.

Domine Jesu Christe, qui dixisti: Petite, et accipietis; quærite, et invenietis; pulsate, et aperietur vobis: quæsumus, da nobis petentibus divinissimi tui amoris affectum, ut te toto corde, ore et opere diligamus, et a tua nunquam laude cessemus.

Sancti Nominis tui, Domine, timorem pariter et amorem fac nos habere perpetuum, quia nunquam tua gubernatione destituis quos in soliditate tuæ dilectionis instituis. Qui vivis et regnas, etc. *Amen.*

Through Thy sufferings,

Through Thy death and burial,

Through Thy Resurrection,

Through Thine Ascension,

‡Through Thy institution of the most Holy Eucharist,

Through Thy joys,

Through Thy glory,

Lamb of God, Who takest away the sins of the world, *spare us, O Jesus.*

Lamb of God, Who takest away the sins of the world, *graciously hear us, O Jesus.*

Lamb of God, Who takest away the sins of the world, *have mercy on us, O Jesus.*

Jesus, hear us.

Jesus, graciously hear us.

Let us pray.

O Lord Jesus Christ, Who hast said, "Ask, and ye shall receive; seek, and ye shall find; knock, and it shall be opened unto you": grant, we beseech Thee, unto us who ask, the gift of Thy most divine love, that we may ever love Thee with our whole hearts, and in all our words and actions, and never cease from showing forth Thy praise.

Make us O Lord, to have a perpetual fear and love of Thy holy name; for Thou never failest to govern those whom Thou dost solidly establish in Thy love. Who livest and reignest, etc. *Amen.*

Litany of the Blessed Virgin,

COMMONLY CALLED
THE LITANY OF LORETO

Sub tuum præsidium confugimus, Sancta Dei Genitrix. Nostras deprecationes ne despicias in necessitatibus nostris; sed a periculis cunctis libera nos semper, Virgo gloriosa et benedicta.

We fly to thy patronage, O holy Mother of God. Despise not our petitions in our necessities; but deliver us from all dangers, O ever glorious and Blessed Virgin.

Kyrie, eleison.
Christe, eleison.
Kyrie, eleison.
Christe, audi nos.
Christe, exaudi nos.

Lord, have mercy on us.
Christ, have mercy on us.
Lord, have mercy on us.
Christ, hear us.
Christ, graciously hear us.

Pater de cœlis Deus, *miserere nobis.*
Fili Redemptor mundi Deus, *miserere nobis.*
Spiritus Sancte Deus, *miserere nobis.*
Sancta Trinitas, unus Deus, *miserere nobis.*

God the Father of heaven, *have mercy on us.*
God the Son, Redeemer of the world, *have mercy on us.*
God the Holy Ghost, *have mercy on us.*
Holy Trinity, one God, *have mercy on us.*

Sancta Maria,
Sancta Dei Genitrix,
Sancta Virgo virginum,
Mater Christi,
Mater divinæ gratiæ,
Mater purissima,

Holy Mary,
Holy Mother of God,
Holy Virgin of virgins,
Mother of Christ,
Mother of divine grace,
Mother most pure,

Mater castissima,
Mater inviolata,
Mater intemerata,
Mater amabilis,
Mater admirabilis,
‡Mater boni consilii,

Mother most chaste,
Mother inviolate,
Mother undefiled,
Mother most amiable,
Mother most admirable,
‡Mother of good counsel,

Mater Creatoris,	Mother of our Creator,
Mater Salvatoris,	Mother of our Savior,
Virgo prudentissima,	Virgin most prudent,
Virgo veneranda,	Virgin most venerable,
Virgo prædicanda,	Virgin most renowned,
Virgo potens,	Virgin most powerful,
Virgo clemens,	Virgin most merciful,
Virgo fidelis,	Virgin most faithful,
Speculum justitiæ,	Mirror of justice,
Sedes sapientiæ,	Seat of wisdom,
Causa nostræ lætitiæ,	Cause of our joy,
Vas spirituale,	Spiritual vessel,
Vas honorabile,	Vessel of honor,
Vas insigne devotionis,	Singular vessel of devotion,
Rosa mystica,	Mystical rose,
Turris Davidica,	Tower of David,
Turris eburnea,	Tower of ivory,
Domus aurea,	House of gold,
Fœderis arca,	Ark of the covenant,
Janua cœli,	Gate of heaven,
Stella matutina,	Morning star,
Salus infirmorum,	Health of the sick,
Refugium peccatorum,	Refuge of sinners,
Consolatrix afflictorum,	Comforter of the afflicted,
Auxilium Christianorum,	Help of Christians,
Regina Angelorum,	Queen of angels,
Regina Patriarcharum,	Queen of patriarchs,
Regina Prophetarum,	Queen of prophets,
Regina Apostolorum,	Queen of apostles,
Regina Martyrum,	Queen of martyrs,
Regina Confessorum,	Queen of confessors,
Regina Virginum,	Queen of virgins,
Regina Sanctorum omnium,	Queen of all saints,
Regina sine labe originali concepta,	Queen conceived without Original Sin,
Regina sacratissimi Rosarii,	Queen of the most holy Rosary,
‡Regina pacis,	‡Queen of peace,

Agnus Dei, qui tollis peccata mundi,
parce nobis, Domine.
Agnus Dei, qui tollis peccata mundi,
exaudi nos, Domine.
Agnus Dei, qui tollis peccata mundi,
miserere nobis.
℣. Ora pro nobis, Sancta Dei Genitrix.
℟. Ut digni efficiamur promissionibus
Christi.

Oremus.
Gratiam tuam, quæsumus, Domine,
mentibus nostris infunde, ut qui,
Angelo nuntiante, Christi filii tui
incarnationem cognovimus, per
passionem ejus et crucem ad resurrectionis gloriam perducamur;
per eundem Christum Dominum
nostrum. *Amen.*

℣. Divinum auxilium maneat semper
nobiscum.
℟. Amen.

Sub tuum præsidium confugimus,
Sancta Dei Genitrix. Nostras deprecationes ne despicias in necessitatibus nostris; sed a periculis cunctis
libera nos semper, Virgo gloriosa et
benedicta.

Lamb of God, Who takest away the sins
of the world, *spare us, O Lord.*
Lamb of God, Who takest away the
sins of the world, *graciously hear us,
O Lord.*
Lamb of God, Who takest away the sins
of the world, *have mercy on us.*
℣. Pray for us, O holy Mother of God.
℟. That we may be made worthy of the
promises of Christ.

Let us pray.
Pour forth, we beseech Thee, O Lord,
Thy grace into our hearts; that as
we have known the Incarnation of
Christ Thy Son by the message of an
angel, so, by His Passion and Cross,
we may be brought to the glory of
His Resurrection; through the same
Christ Our Lord. Amen.

℣. May the divine assistance remain always with us.
℟. Amen.

We fly to thy patronage, O holy Mother
of God. Despise not our petitions in
our necessities; but deliver us from
all dangers, O ever glorious and
Blessed Virgin.

Evening Prayers

THE OFFICE OF COMPLINE

Lord, grant Thy blessing.

THE BLESSING

May the Lord Almighty grant us a quiet night, and a perfect end. ℟. Amen.

SHORT LESSON

Bretheren, be sober, and vigilant, for your adversary the devil as a roaring lion goeth about, seeking whom he may devour; whom resist strong in faith. And do Thou, O Lord, have mercy on us.

℟. Thanks be to God.

℣. Our help is in the name of the Lord.

℟. Who hath made heaven and earth.

Our Father (*inaudibly*).

Then follows the Confiteor (*p. 32*).

Then is said:

Convert us, O God our Savior.

℟. And turn away Thine anger from us.

℣. Come unto my help, O God.

℟. O Lord, make haste to help me.

Glory be to the Father, and to the Son, and to the Holy Ghost.

As it was in the beginning, is now, and ever shall be, world without end. Amen.

Alleluia (*or, in Lent*, Praise to Thee, O Lord, King of eternal glory).

Ant. Have mercy.

In Paschal time, Ant. Alleluia.

PSALM 4

When I called upon Him, the God of my justice heard me: when I was in straits, Thou didst set me at liberty.

Have mercy on me: and hear my prayer.

O ye sons of men, how long will ye be dull of heart? Why do ye love vanity, and seek after lying?

Know ye also that the Lord hath exalted His holy one: the Lord will hear me when I cry unto Him.

Be ye angry, and sin not: the things ye say in your hearts, be sorry for upon your beds.

Offer up the sacrifice of justice, and trust in the Lord: many say, Who showeth us good things?

The light of Thy countenance, O Lord, is signed upon us: Thou hast given gladness in my heart.

By the fruit of their corn, and wine, and oil: are they multiplied.

In peace in the selfsame: I will sleep and I will rest.

For Thou, O Lord, alone: hast established me in hope.

Glory be to the Father, etc.

PSALM 30

In Thee, O Lord, have I hoped, let me never be confounded: deliver me in Thy justice.

Bow down Thine ear unto me: make haste to deliver me.

Be Thou unto me a God, a protector: and a house of refuge to save me.

For Thou art my strength and my refuge: and for Thy name's sake Thou wilt lead me, and nourish me.

Thou wilt bring me out of this snare, which they have hidden for me: for Thou art my protector.

Into Thy hands I commend my spirit: Thou hast redeemed me, O Lord, God of truth.

Glory be to the Father, etc.

PSALM 90

He that dwelleth in the help of the Most High: shall abide under the protection of the God of heaven.

He shall say unto the Lord: Thou art my upholder, and my refuge: my God, in Him will I hope.

For He hath delivered me from the snare of the hunters; and from the sharp word.

He shall overshadow thee with His shoulders: and under His wings shalt thou trust.

His truth shall compass thee with a shield: thou shalt not be afraid for the terror of the night;

For the arrow that flieth in the day; for the plague that walketh in the darkness; for the assault of the evil one in the noonday.

A thousand shall fall at thy side, and ten thousand at thy right hand: but it shall not come nigh thee.

But with thine eyes shalt thou behold: and shalt see the reward of the wicked.

For Thou, O Lord, art my hope: thou hast made the most High thy refuge.

There shall no evil approach unto thee: neither shall the scourge come nigh thy dwelling.

For He hath given His angels charge over thee: to keep thee in all thy ways.

In their hands they shall bear thee up: lest haply thou dash thy foot against a stone.

Thou shalt walk upon the asp and the basilisk: the lion and the dragon shalt thou trample underfoot.

Because he hath hoped in Me, I will deliver him: I will protect him because he hath known My name.

He shall cry unto Me, and I will hear him: I am with him in trouble, I will deliver him, and I will glorify him.

I will fill him with length of days: and will show him My salvation.

Glory be to the Father, etc.

PSALM 133

Behold, now bless ye the Lord: all ye servants of the Lord.

Ye that stand in the house of the Lord: in the courts of the house of our God.

Lift up your hands by night to the holy places: and bless ye the Lord.

May the Lord bless thee out of Sion: Who hath made heaven and earth.

Glory be to the Father, etc.

Ant. Have mercy on me, O Lord, and hear my prayer.

‡*In Paschal time, Ant.* Alleluia, Alleluia, Alleluia.

THE HYMN[5]

Now that the daylight dies away.
By all Thy grace and love,
Thee, Maker of the world, we pray
To watch our bed above.

Let dreams depart and phantoms fly,
The offspring of the night;
Keep us, like shrines, beneath Thine eye,
Pure in our foes' despite.

This grace on Thy redeemed confer,
Father, coequal Son,
And Holy Ghost, the Comforter,
Eternal Three in One. *Amen.*

THE LITTLE CHAPTER

Thou, O Lord, art among us, and Thy holy name is called upon us: forsake us not, O Lord our God.

---

[5]   Translation by Cardinal Newman.

℟. Thanks be to God.

Short Responsory

Into Thy hands, O Lord, I commend my spirit.

℟. Into Thy hands, O Lord, I commend my spirit.

℣. Thou hast redeemed us, O Lord, God of truth.

℟. I commend my spirit.

℣. Glory be to the Father, and to the Son, and to the Holy Ghost.

℟. Into Thy hands, O Lord, I commend my spirit.

℣. Keep us, O Lord, as the apple of Thine eye.

℟. Protect us under the shadow of Thy wings.

THE CANTICLE OF SIMEON

Ant. Save us.

Now, O Lord, lettest Thou Thy servant depart in peace: according to Thy word.

For mine eyes have seen: Thy salvation.

Which Thou hast prepared: in sight of all nations.

Light to enlighten the Gentiles: and glory of Thy people Israel.

Glory be to the Father, etc.

Ant. Save us, O Lord, watching, guard us sleeping: that we may watch with Christ, and may rest in peace. (*At Eastertide*, Alleluia.)

Lord, have mercy.

Christ, have mercy.

Lord, have mercy.

Our Father (*inaudibly*).

℣. And lead us not into temptation.

℟. But deliver us from evil.

I believe in God (*inaudibly*).

℣. The resurrection of the body.

℟. And the life everlasting. Amen.

℣. Blessed art Thou, O Lord, the God of our fathers.

℟. And worthy to be praised and glorified forever.

℣. Let us bless the Father and the Son with the Holy Ghost.

℟. Let us praise and exalt Him above all forever.

℣. Blessed art Thou, O Lord, in the firmament of heaven.

℟. And worthy to be praised, and glorified, and exalted above all forever.

℣. May the Almighty and merciful Lord bless and protect us.

℟. Amen.

℣. Vouchsafe, O Lord, this night

℟. To keep us without sin.

℣. Have mercy on us, O Lord.
℟. Have mercy on us.
℣. Let Thy mercy, O Lord, be upon us.
℟. As we have hoped in Thee.

℣. O Lord, hear my prayer.
℟. And let my cry come unto Thee.

Let us pray.
Visit, we beseech Thee, O Lord, this habitation, and drive far from it all snares of
the enemy: let Thy holy angels dwell therein to keep us in peace: and may Thy
blessing be upon us always. Through Our Lord, etc. ℟. Amen.
℣. O Lord, hear my prayer.
℟. And let my cry come unto Thee.
℣. Let us bless the Lord.
℟. Thanks be to God.

THE BLESSING

May the Almighty and merciful Lord bless and protect us; the Father, ✠ the Son,
and the Holy Ghost. ℟. Amen.

Then is said one of the Antiphons of the Blessed Virgin, *according to the season. The*
Antiphon *is to be said kneeling, except in Eastertide, when it is to be said standing.*

I.
From Vespers of Saturday before the First Sunday in Advent *to the* Purification,
inclusive.

Alma Redemptoris Mater, quæ per-
via cœli
Porta manes, et Stella maris, succurre
cadenti,
Surgere qui curat, populo: tu quæ
genuisti,
Natura mirante, tuum sanctum
Genitorem:
Virgo prius ac posterius, Gabrielis
ab ore
Sumens illud Ave, peccatorum
miserere.

Mother of Christ! Hear thou thy people's
cry,
Star of the deep, and portal of the sky!
Mother of Him Who thee from nothing
made,
Sinking we strive, and call to thee for aid:
Oh, by that joy which Gabriel brought to
thee,
Thou Virgin first and last, let us thy mercy
see.

In Advent.

Angelus Domini nuntiavit Mariæ.	The angel of the Lord declared unto Mary.
℟. Et concepit de Spiritu Sancto.	℟. And she conceived by the Holy Ghost.

Oremus.

Let us pray.

Gratiam tuam, quæsumus, Domine, mentibus nostris infunde, ut qui, Angelo nuntiante, Christi Filii tui incarnationem cognovimus, per passionem ejus et crucem ad resurrectionis gloriam perducamur; per eundem Christum Dominum nostrum. ℟. Amen.

Pour forth, we beseech Thee, O Lord, Thy grace into our hearts; that as we have known the Incarnation of Christ Thy Son by the message of an angel, so, by His Passion and Cross, we may be brought to the glory of His Resurrection; through the same Christ Our Lord. ℟. Amen.

From Christmas Day *to the* Purification.

Post partum virgo inviolata permansisti.	After childbirth, thou didst remain a pure Virgin.
℟. Dei Genitrix, intercede pro nobis.	℟. O Mother of God, intercede for us.

Oremus.

Let us pray.

Deus, qui salutis æternæ, beatæ Mariæ virginitate fœcunda, humano generi præmia præstitisti: tribue, quæsumus; ut ipsam pro nobis intercedere sentiamus, per quam meruimus auctorem vitæ suscipere, Dominum nostrum Jesum Christum Filium tuum. ℟. Amen.

O God, Who, by the fruitful virginity of Blessed Mary, hast given unto mankind the rewards of eternal salvation; grant, we beseech Thee, that we may feel that she intercedes for us, through whom we have been made worthy to receive the Author of life, Our Lord Jesus Christ, Thy Son. ℟. Amen.

II.

From the feast of the Purification *to* Maundy Thursday, *exclusively.*

Ave, Regina cœlorum!
Ave, Domina angelorum!
Salve, radix, salve, porta,
Ex qua mundo Lux est orta:
Gaude, Virgo gloriosa,
Super omnes speciosa,
Vale, o valde decora!
Et pro nobis Christum exora.
℣. Dignare me laudare te, Virgo sacrata.
℟. Da mihi virtutem contra hostes tuos.

Oremus.
Concede, misericors Deus, fragilitati nostræ præsidium; ut qui sanctæ Dei Genitricis memoriam agimus; intercessionis ejus auxilio a nostris iniquitatibus resurgamus. Per eundem Christum Dominum nostrum. ℟. Amen.

Hail! O Queen of heav'n enthron'd!
Hail! by angels mistress own'd!
Root of Jesse, Gate of morn,
Whence the world's true Light was born.
Glorious Virgin! joy to thee,
Loveliest whom in heaven they see.
Fairest thou where all are fair!
Plead with Christ our sins to spare.
℣. Vouchsafe that I may praise thee, O sacred Virgin.
℟. Give me strength against thine enemies.

Let us pray.
Grant, O merciful God, defense to our weakness; that we who now celebrate the memory of the holy Mother of God may, by the aid of her intercession, rise again from our sins. Through the same Christ Our Lord ℟ Amen.

III.

From Holy Saturday *till* Trinity Eve.

Regina Cœli, lætare! alleluia.
Quia quem meruisti portare, alleluia,
Resurrexit, sicut dixit, alleluia.
Ora pro nobis Deum, alleluia.
℣. Gaude et lætare, Virgo Maria, alleluia.
℟. Quia surrexit Dominus vere, alleluia.

O Queen of heaven, rejoice! alleluia.
For He Whom thou didst merit to bear, alleluia,
Hath arisen, as He said, alleluia.
Pray for us to God, alleluia.
℣. Rejoice and be glad, O Virgin Mary, alleluia.
℟. For the Lord hath risen indeed, alleluia.

Oremus.

Deus, qui per resurrectionem Filii tui Domini nostri Jesu Christi mundum lætificare dignatus es; præsta, quæsumus, ut, per ejus Genitricem Virginem Mariam perpetuæ capiamus gaudia vitæ. Per eundem Christum Dominum nostrum. ℟. Amen.

Let us pray.

O God, Who, through the Resurrection of Thy Son Our Lord Jesus Christ, didst vouchsafe to fill the world with joy; grant, we beseech Thee, that, through His Virgin Mother, Mary, we may lay hold on the joys of everlasting life. Through the same Christ Our Lord. ℟. Amen.

IV.

From Vespers of Trinity Sunday to Advent.

Salve, Regina, mater misericordiæ; vita, dulcedo, et spes nostra, salve. Ad te clamamus exules filii Hevæ; ad te suspiramus, gementes et flentes in hac lacrymarum valle. Eia ergo, Advocata nostra, illos tuos misericordes oculos ad nos converte; et Jesum, benedictum fructum ventris tui, nobis post hoc exilium ostende, O clemens, o pia, o dulcis Virgo Maria.

℣. Ora pro nobis, sancta Dei Genitrix.
℟. Ut digni efficiamur promissionibus Christi.

Hail, holy Queen, Mother of mercy; our life, our sweetness, and our hope. To thee do we cry, poor banished children of Eve; to thee do we send up our sighs, mourning and weeping in this valley of tears. Turn, then, most gracious Advocate, thine eyes of mercy toward us; and after this our exile, show unto us the blessed fruit of thy womb, Jesus; O clement, O pious, O sweet Virgin Mary.

℣. Pray for us, O holy Mother of God.
℟. That we may be made worthy of the promises of Christ.

Oremus.

Omnipotens sempiterne Deus, qui gloriosæ Virginis Matris Mariæ corpus et animam, ut dignum Filii tui habitaculum effici mereretur, Spiritu Sancto cooperante, præparasti; da ut cujus commemoratione lætamur; ejus pia intercessione ab instantibus malis et a morte perpetua liberemur. Per eundem Christum Dominum nostrum. ℟. Amen.

Let us pray.

Almighty, everlasting God, Who, by the cooperation of the Holy Ghost, didst prepare the body and soul of the glorious Virgin Mother, Mary, to become the fit habitation of Thy Son; grant that we who now rejoice in her commemoration may, by her gracious intercession, be delivered from all the evils that threaten us, and from everlasting death. Through the same Christ Our Lord. ℟. Amen.

℣. Divinum auxilium maneat semper nobiscum.

℟. Amen.

Pater noster, Ave Maria, Credo (*secreto*).

℣. May the divine assistance remain always with us.

℟. Amen.

Our Father. Hail Mary. Creed (*inaudibly*).

ANOTHER FORM OF EVENING PRAYERS

In the name of the Father, ✠ and of the Son, and of the Holy Ghost. *Amen.*

Come, Holy Ghost, fill the hearts of Thy faithful, and kindle in them the fire of Thy love.

O my God, I present myself before Thee at the end of another day, to offer Thee anew the homage of my heart. I humbly adore Thee, my Creator, my Redeemer, and my Judge! I believe in Thee, because Thou art Truth itself; I hope in Thee, because Thou art faithful to Thy promises; I love Thee with my whole heart, because Thou art infinitely worthy of being loved; and for Thy sake I love my neighbor as myself.

Enable me, O my God, to return Thee thanks as I ought for all Thine inestimable blessings and favors. Thou hast thought of me, and loved me from all eternity; Thou hast formed me out of nothing; Thou hast delivered up Thy beloved Son to the ignominious death of the Cross for my redemption; Thou hast made me a member of Thy holy Church; Thou hast preserved me from falling into the abyss of eternal misery, when my sins had provoked Thee to punish me; and Thou hast graciously continued to spare me, even though I have not ceased to offend Thee. What return, O my God, can I make for Thine innumerable blessings, and particularly for the favors of this day? O all ye angels and saints, unite with me in praising the God of mercies, Who is so bountiful to so unworthy a creature.

Our Father. Hail Mary. Creed.

Ask of God light to discover the sins committed this day.

O my God, sovereign Judge of men, Who desirest not the death of a sinner, but that he should be converted and saved, enlighten my mind, that I may know the sins which I have this day committed in thought, word, or deed, and give me the grace of true contrition.

Here examine your conscience; then say:

O my God, I heartily repent, and am grieved that I have offended Thee, because Thou art infinitely good, and sin is infinitely displeasing to Thee. I humbly ask of Thee mercy and pardon, through the infinite merits of Jesus Christ. I resolve, by the assistance of Thy grace, to do penance for my sins, and I will endeavor nevermore to offend Thee.

Confiteor.

[*Here may be said the* Litany of Loreto, *p. 50.*]

O God, hear my prayers on behalf of our Holy Father Pope N., our bishop N., our clergy, and for all that are in authority over us. Bless, I beseech Thee, the whole Catholic Church, and convert all heretics and unbelievers. Pour down Thy blessings, O Lord, upon all my friends, relations, and acquaintances, and upon my enemies, if I have any. Help the poor and sick, and those who are in their last agony. O God of mercy and goodness, have compassion on the souls of the faithful in purgatory; put an end to their sufferings, and grant to them eternal light, rest, and happiness. *Amen.*

O Almighty and eternal God, Who savest all, and willest not that any should perish, look, we beseech Thee, upon the souls that are led astray by the deceits of the devil; that, rejecting all errors, the hearts of those who err may be converted, and return to the unity of Thy truth. Through Christ Our Lord. *Amen.*

Bless, O Lord, the repose I am about to take, that, my bodily strength being renewed, I may be the better enabled to serve Thee. *Amen.*

O Blessed Virgin Mary, Mother of mercy, pray for me, that I may be preserved this night from all evil, whether of body or soul. Blessed St. Joseph, and all ye saints and angels of paradise, especially my guardian angel and my chosen patron, watch over me. I commend myself to your protection now and always. *Amen.*

Holy, holy, holy, Lord God of hosts: the earth is full of Thy glory. Glory be to the Father, glory be to the Son, glory be to the Holy Ghost. *Amen.*

𝕴𝖓𝖘𝖙𝖗𝖚𝖈𝖙𝖎𝖔𝖓𝖘 𝖋𝖔𝖗 𝕳𝖊𝖆𝖗𝖎𝖓𝖌 𝕸𝖆𝖘𝖘

WHAT THE MASS IS, AND FOR WHAT END IT IS TO BE OFFERED

From the beginning of the world, the servants of God were always accustomed to offer sacrifice to Him, by way of acknowledging His sovereignty and paying their homage to Him; and in all ancient religions, true or false, this worship of sacrifice was always regarded as a most solemn act of religion, due to the Deity worshipped.

In the law of nature, and in the Law of Moses, there was a great variety of sacrifices: some bloody, in which the victim was slain; others unbloody. Some were called holocausts, or whole burnt offerings, in which the whole host or victim was consumed in fire upon God's altar, for His honor and glory; others were called sin offerings, which were offered for sins; others were offerings of thanksgivings; others were pacific or peace offerings, which were offered for obtaining favors of God—the word *peace* in the Scripture style signifying all manner of good and prosperity.

All these sacrifices of the law of nature, and of the Law of Moses, were of themselves but "weak and needy elements" (Gal 4:9), and only figures of a sacrifice to come, namely that of Jesus Christ; in consideration of which sacrifice only, and of the faith of the offerers, by which they believed in the Redeemer to come, those ancient sacrifices were then accepted by the divine Majesty, when they were accompanied with the inward sacrifice of the heart; but not for any intrinsic worth or dignity of the things offered, for no other blood but the blood of Christ could wash away sins. Hence, St. Paul says, quoting from the thirty-ninth Psalm: "Sacrifice and oblation Thou wouldst not have: but Thou hast fitted to Me a body" (Heb 10:5). This gives us to understand that, by reason of the insufficiency of the sacrifices of the Old Law, Christ Himself would come to be our Sacrifice, and would offer up His own body and blood for us.

Accordingly, our Savior Jesus Christ, at the time appointed by His Father, having taken flesh for us, was pleased to offer Himself a Sacrifice for us, dying upon the Cross for the sins of the whole world. By this one offering we were completely redeemed, inasmuch as our ransom was paid, and all mercy, grace, and salvation were purchased for us. Neither can there now be any need of His dying anymore, or purchasing any other graces for us than those for which He has already paid the price of His blood.

Nevertheless, for the daily application of this one eternal Redemption to our souls, and that the mercy, grace, and salvation which He has purchased for us may be actually communicated to us, He not only continually appears in our behalf in the sanctuary of heaven, there representing and offering to His Father His Passion and death for us, but He has also instituted the Blessed Eucharist, the night before His

Passion, in which He bequeathed us His Body and Blood, under the sacramental veils, not only to be received by us as a Sacrament, for the food and nourishment of our souls, but also (mystically delivered) to be offered and presented by His ministers to His Father as a Sacrifice: not by way of a new death, but by way of a standing memorial of His death; a daily celebrating and representing of His death to God, and an applying to our souls of the fruits thereof.

This Eucharistic sacrifice of the Body and Blood of Christ, daily offered under the forms of bread and wine, in remembrance of His Passion, is what we call the Mass. This is the solemn liturgy of the Catholic Church. This is that pure offering which is made to God in every place among the Gentiles, according to the prophecy of Malachi (see 1:10–11). By this, Christ is a Priest forever according to the order of Melchisedech (see Ps 109), whose sacrifice was bread and wine (see Gn 14:18).

This Sacrifice of the Mass is the same in substance with that which Christ offered for us upon the Cross; because both the Victim offered, and the Priest or principal Offerer, is the same Jesus Christ. The difference is only in the *manner* of the offering: upon the Cross, our Savior offered Himself in such a manner as really to shed His blood and die for us; whereas now, He does not really shed His blood, or die. And therefore, this is called an unbloody sacrifice; and that of the Cross a bloody sacrifice.

By virtue of this essential sameness, the Sacrifice of the Mass completely answers all the different ends of sacrifice, and that in a way infinitely more effective than any of the ancient sacrifices. Christ is here both Priest and Victim, representing in Person and offering up His Passion and death to His Father.

This Sacrifice of the Mass is offered up to God, in the Catholic Church, first as a daily remembrance of the Passion of Christ: "This do for the commemoration of Me" (1 Cor 11:24); secondly, as a most solemn worship of the divine Majesty; thirdly, as a most acceptable thanksgiving to God, from whence it has the name of Eucharist; fourthly, as a most powerful means to move God to show mercy to us in the forgiveness of our sins, for which reason we call it propitiatory; and, lastly, as a most effectual way to obtain of God all that we need, coming to Him, as we here do, with Christ and through Christ.

For these ends both priest and people ought to offer up the Sacrifice of the Mass—the priest, as Christ's minister and in His Person; and the people, by the hands of the priest; and both the one and the other by the hands of the great High Priest Jesus Christ. And with this offering of Christ, both the one and the other should make a total offering of themselves also by His hands and in union with Him.

OF THE CEREMONIES OF MASS

Although the homage which man owes to His Creator so essentially consists in the interior dispositions of the soul that without these all outward worship is unprofitable and vain, yet the constitution of our nature is such as to require external signs and ceremonies which may operate through the medium of the bodily senses upon our souls, and elevate them to God. To this end are directed all the ceremonies of the Church, and it is the Christian's duty to learn how to use them accordingly. Hence—

1. The custom of placing a vessel containing *blessed* or **holy water** at the entrance of the Church has been handed down to us from the apostolic age. Into this vessel the faithful dip the fingers of the right hand, and make upon themselves the sign of the cross, repeating at the same time the invocation of the ever Blessed Trinity. As water denotes purity and innocence, by using it on entering a place of worship, we are admonished with what purity of heart and mind we should appear in the presence of our Maker.

2. The **sign of the cross**, which we make upon ourselves in taking holy water, as well as on many other occasions, is a sign or ceremony in which, with St. Paul (see Gal 6:14), we should place our greatest happiness and glory, as being a striking memorial of the sufferings and death of our Redeemer—that mystery whence are derived all our hopes for mercy, grace, and salvation. By the words that accompany this ceremony we are no less forcibly reminded that God Whom we serve, although *one* in nature, exists in *three Persons* really distinct from each other.

3. The first object that arrests the Christian's notice on entering a church is the **altar**, with its **tabernacle** and **crucifix**. The *altar* is the place of sacrifice—another Calvary, as it were—whereon is celebrated, as Christ ordained, the memorial of His Passion and death by the pure and unbloody sacrifice of His Body and Blood. Upon the altar we always see a *crucifix*, or image of our Savior upon the Cross; that, as the Mass is said in remembrance of Christ's Passion and death, both priest and people may have before their eyes during this sacrifice the image which puts them in mind of those mysteries. The *tabernacle* contains the Blessed Sacrament. It is to Jesus Christ, therefore, truly present within the tabernacle, that we bend the knee in homage and adoration when we enter or depart from the church.

4. As the Mass represents the Passion of Christ, and the priest officiates in His Person, so the **vestments** in which he officiates represent those in which Christ was ignominiously clothed at the time of His Passion. Thus, the *amice* represents the cloth with which the Jews muffled our Savior's face when at every blow they bade Him prophesy who it was that struck Him. The *alb* represents the white garment with which He was vested by Herod. The *girdle*, *maniple*, and *stole* represent the cords and bands with which He was bound in the different stages of His Passion. The *chasuble*, or outward vestment, represents the purple garment with which He was clothed as a mock King; upon this is embroidered a cross, to represent that which Christ bore upon His sacred shoulders. Lastly, the priest's *tonsure*, which is worn in all Catholic countries, is to represent the crown of thorns which our Savior wore.

Moreover, as in the Old Law, the priests who were wont to officiate in the sacred functions had, by the appointment of God, *vestments* assigned for that purpose—as well for the greater decency and solemnity of the divine worship as to signify the virtues which God required of His ministers—so it was proper that, in the Church of the New Testament, Christ's ministers should in their sacred functions be distinguished in like manner from the laity by their sacred vestments; which might also represent the virtues which God requires in them. Thus, the *amice* represents divine *hope*, which St. Paul calls the helmet of salvation (see 1 Thes 5:8); the *alb*, *innocence of life*; the *girdle*, *purity* and *chastity*; the *maniple*, *patience* in enduring the labors of this mortal life; the *stole*, the sweet *yoke of Christ*, to be borne in this life in order to attain a happy immortality; the *chasuble*, which covers all the rest, the virtue of *charity*, which, as St. Peter tells us, "covereth a multitude of sins" (1 Pt 4:8).

In these vestments, the Church uses five colors, namely: *white*, on the feasts of Our Lord, of the Blessed Virgin, of the angels, and of the saints who were not martyrs, and on the Sundays in Eastertide; *red*, on the feasts of Pentecost, of the Finding and Exaltation of the Cross, and of the apostles and martyrs; *violet*, in the penitential seasons of Advent and Lent, and upon vigils and Ember days; *green*, on most other Sundays and ordinary days throughout the year; and *black*, on Good Friday, and in Masses for the Dead.

5. There are always **lighted candles** upon the altar during Mass, as well to honor the victory and triumph of our great King by these lights, which are tokens of our joy and of His glory, as to denote the *light of faith*, without which it is impossible to please Him.

6. A small **bell** is occasionally rung. This is done to give notice of certain more solemn parts of the sacrifice; to recall the wandering mind from distraction; and to excite all to greater fervor and devotion.

7. **Incense** is used at Solemn Mass. It is symbolical of prayer, according to the saying of the psalmist: "Let my prayer, O Lord, be directed as incense in Thy sight" (Ps 140:2).

ON THE MANNER OF HEARING MASS

There are various methods of profitably hearing Mass. One method is to follow the priest in the Ordinary of the Mass as contained in the Missal; joining with him, as far as the laity may, in the very words of the service, and uniting our intention with him in what he does as priest for the people. To enable all persons, even those who do not understand Latin, to follow the service, translations of the Ordinary and Canon of the Mass have been made into almost all languages, and circulated by authority. Another method is to accompany the priest through the different parts of the service with appropriate devotions, similar to those he is using and directed to the same general ends, uniting our intention with his, but not using or not confining ourselves to the words of the Ordinary. A third method is to apply the service to the purpose of meditation on the life or Passion of Our Lord, or on any other appropriate subject. Whatever be the method followed, our first care should be to recollect ourselves, by calling home our wandering thoughts, and taking them off from all other concerns. We should humble ourselves profoundly in the presence of God, in Whose temple we are; and represent to ourselves, by a lively faith, the dread majesty of God, and humbly beg His mercy and grace, that we may participate in this Holy Sacrifice in a worthy and becoming manner.

PRAYERS BEFORE MASS

Come, Holy Ghost, fill the hearts of Thy faithful, and kindle in them the fire of Thy love.

℣. Send forth Thy Spirit, and they shall be created.

℟. And Thou shalt renew the face of the earth.

Let us pray.

O God, Who by the light of Thy Holy Spirit didst teach the hearts of Thy faithful, grant us by the same Spirit to have a right judgment in all things, and evermore to rejoice in His holy comfort. Through Christ, Our Lord. *Amen.*

Look down, O Lord, from Thy sanctuary, and from heaven, Thy dwelling place, and behold this holy Victim which our great High Priest, Thy holy Child, the Lord Jesus, offers up to Thee for the sins of His brethren; and let not Thy wrath be kindled because of the multitude of our transgressions. Behold, the voice of the blood of Jesus our Brother calls to Thee from the Cross. Give ear, O Lord; be appeased, O Lord; hearken, and tarry not, for Thine own sake, O my God; because Thy name is called upon in behalf of this city, and of Thy people; but deal with us according to Thy great mercy. *Amen.*

That Thou vouchsafe to defend, pacify, keep, preserve, and bless this city: we beseech Thee to hear us.

𝔇𝔢𝔳𝔬𝔱𝔦𝔬𝔫𝔰 𝔣𝔬𝔯 𝔐𝔞𝔰𝔰

PART I

THE PREPARATION, BY ACTS OF HUMILITY, PRAISE, FAITH, ETC.

Prayer at the beginning of Mass, while the priest says the Judica me, Deus, *etc.*
O Almighty Lord of heaven and earth, behold I, a wretched sinner, presume to appear before Thee this day, to offer up unto Thee, by the hands of our High Priest, Jesus Christ, Thy Son, the sacrifice of His Body and Blood, in union with that sacrifice which He offered to Thee upon the Cross: first, for Thine own honor, praise, adoration, and glory; secondly, in remembrance of His Passion and death; thirdly, in thanksgiving for all Thy blessings bestowed upon Thy whole Church, whether

triumphant in heaven or militant on earth, and especially for those bestowed upon me, the most unworthy of all; fourthly, for obtaining pardon and remission of all my sins, and of those of all others, whether living or dead, for whom I ought to pray (*here mention their names*); and, lastly, for obtaining all graces and blessings both for myself and for Thy whole Church (*here mention your particular requests*). Oh, be Thou pleased to assist me by Thy grace, that I may behave myself this day as I ought to do in Thy divine presence, and that I may so commemorate the Passion and death of Thy Son as to partake most plentifully of the fruits thereof. Through the same Jesus Christ, Our Lord. *Amen.*

At the Confiteor.
O Blessed Trinity, one God, Father, Son, and Holy Ghost, prostrate in spirit before Thee, I here confess, in the sight of the whole court of heaven and of all Thy faithful, my innumerable treasons against Thy divine Majesty. I have sinned, O Lord, I have sinned; I have grievously offended Thee through the whole course of my life, in thought, word, and deed; and therefore am unworthy to lift mine eyes to heaven, or so much as to utter Thy sacred name. How much more am I unworthy to appear here in Thy sanctuary, and to mingle among Thine angels at these heavenly mysteries, which require so much purity, because Jesus Christ Himself is here in Person, both Priest and Victim! But, O my God, Thy mercies are above all Thy works, and Thou wilt not despise a contrite and humble heart: and therefore I here venture to come into Thy temple, and with the poor publican, and, as I hope, with the same penitential spirit, I strike my breast and say: "God be merciful to me, a sinner." And I humbly hope to find this mercy which I crave, through that Passion and death which are here celebrated. O Fountain of mercy, grant this mercy to me and to all poor sinners. *Amen.*

When the priest ascends the steps of the altar.
Take away from us our iniquities, we beseech Thee, O Lord; that we may be worthy to enter with pure minds into the Holy of Holies. Through Christ, Our Lord. Amen.

At the Introit.
Grant, O Lord, that we may be truly prepared for offering this great sacrifice unto Thee this day; and because our sins alone can render us displeasing to Thee, therefore we cry aloud to Thee for mercy.

At the Kyrie, eleison.
Either repeat with the priest, or say:
Have mercy on me, O Lord, and forgive me all my sins.
Have mercy on me, O Lord, have mercy on me.

The Gloria in excelsis, *or* Greater Doxology. *Repeat this with the priest.*
Glory be to God on high, and on earth peace to men of good will. We praise Thee; we bless Thee; we worship Thee; we glorify Thee. We give Thee thanks for Thy great glory, O Lord God, heavenly King, God the Father Almighty. O Lord, the only begotten Son, Jesus Christ; O Lord God, Lamb of God, Son of the Father, Who takest away the sins of the world, have mercy on us: Thou Who takest away the sins of the world, receive our prayer; Thou Who sittest at the right hand of the Father, have mercy on us. For Thou only art holy: Thou only art the Lord: Thou only, O Jesus Christ, with the Holy Ghost, art most High in the glory of God the Father. *Amen.*

At the Collects.
O Almighty and eternal God, we humbly beseech Thee mercifully to hear the prayers here offered unto Thee by Thy servant in the name of Thy whole Church, and in behalf of us Thy people. Accept them, to the honor of Thy name, and the good of our souls; and grant us all mercy, grace, and salvation. Through Our Lord Jesus Christ. Amen.

(*Or, on a saint's day.*)
Grant, we beseech Thee, Almighty God, that the examples of Thy saints may effectually move us to reform our lives; that while we celebrate their festivals, we may also imitate their actions. Through Our Lord Jesus Christ. Amen.

At the Epistle.
Thou hast vouchsafed, O Lord, to teach us Thy sacred truths by the prophets and apostles: oh, grant that we may so improve by their doctrine and examples in the love of Thy holy name, and of Thy holy law, that we may show forth by our lives Whose disciples we are; that we may no longer follow the corrupt inclinations of flesh and blood, but master all our passions; that we may be ever directed by Thy light, and strengthened by Thy grace, to walk in the way of Thy commandments, and to serve Thee with clean hearts. Through Our Lord Jesus Christ. Amen.

At the Gradual.
How admirable, O Lord, is Thy name, in the whole earth! I will bless Thee, O Lord, at all times; Thy praise shall be always in my mouth. Be Thou my God and Protector forever: I will put my whole trust in Thee; oh, let me never be confounded.

At the Gospel.
Mayest Thou be ever adored and praised, O Lord, Who, not content to instruct and inform us by Thy prophets and apostles, hast even vouchsafed to speak to us by Thine only Son our Savior Jesus Christ; commanding us by a voice from heaven to hear Him: grant us, O merciful God, the grace to profit by His divine and heavenly doctrine. All that is written of Thee, O Jesus, in Thy Gospel, is Truth itself: nothing

but wisdom in Thine actions, power and goodness in Thy miracles, light and instruction in Thy words. With Thee, sacred Redeemer, are the words of eternal life: to whom shall we go but to Thee, eternal Fountain of truth? Give me, O God, grace to practice what Thou commandest, and command what Thou pleasest.

At the Credo. *Say this with the priest.*
I believe in one God the Father Almighty, Maker of heaven and earth, and of all things visible and invisible. And in one Lord Jesus Christ, the only begotten Son of God, born of the Father before all ages. God of God; Light of Light; very God of very God; begotten, not made; being of one substance with the Father, by Whom all things were made. Who for us men, and for our salvation, came down from heaven *and was incarnate by the Holy Ghost of the Virgin Mary:* AND WAS MADE MAN. [*Here all kneel down.*] He was crucified also for us, suffered under Pontius Pilate, and was buried. The third day He rose again according to the Scriptures; and ascended into heaven, and sitteth at the right hand of the Father: and He shall come again with glory to judge both the living and the dead: of Whose kingdom there shall be no end.

And I believe in the Holy Ghost, the Lord and Giver of life, Who proceedeth from the Father and the Son: Who together with the Father and the Son is worshipped and glorified; Who spoke by the prophets. And one, holy, catholic, and apostolic Church. I confess one Baptism for the remission of sins. And I look for the resurrection of the dead, and the life of the world to come. *Amen.*

PART II

THE OBLATION AND SANCTIFICATION OF THE BREAD AND WINE FOR THE SACRIFICE

At the Offertory *of the bread and wine.*
Accept, O eternal Father, this offering which is here made to Thee by Thy priest, in the name of us here present, and of Thy whole Church. It is as yet only bread and wine: but, by a miracle of Thy power, will shortly become the Body and Blood of Thy beloved Son. He is our High Priest and our Victim. With Him and through Him we desire to approach Thee this day, and by His hands to offer Thee this sacrifice, for Thine own honor, praise, and glory; in thanksgiving for all Thy benefits; in satisfaction for all our sins; and for obtaining conversion for all unbelievers, and mercy, grace, and salvation for all Thy faithful. And with this offering of Thine only begotten Son, we offer Thee ourselves, our souls and bodies, begging that by virtue of this sacrifice we may be happily united to Thee, and that nothing in life or death may ever separate us from Thee. Through Jesus Christ, Our Lord. *Amen.*

In a humble spirit, and a contrite heart, may we be accepted by Thee, O Lord: and let our sacrifice be so made in Thy sight this day that it may be pleasing unto

Thee, O Lord God. Come, O Sanctifier, Almighty, eternal God, and bless this sacrifice set forth to Thy holy name.

At the Washing of the Fingers.
Oh, what cleanliness and purity of heart ought we to bring with us to this great sacrifice! But, alas! I am a poor unclean sinner. Oh, wash me, dear Lord, from all the stains of sin in the blood of the Lamb, that I may be worthy to be present at these heavenly mysteries.

After the Lavabo, *when the priest bows down at the middle of the altar.*
O most Holy and adorable Trinity, vouchsafe to receive this our sacrifice in remembrance of our Savior's Passion, Resurrection, and glorious Ascension: and grant that we may die with Him to our sins, rise with Him to newness of life, and ascend with Him to Thee. Let those saints whose memory we celebrate on earth remember us before Thy throne in heaven, and obtain mercy for us. Through the same Jesus Christ, Our Lord. *Amen.*

At the Orate, fratres.
May the Lord receive the sacrifice from thy hands, to the praise and glory of His name, to our benefit, and to that of all His holy Church.

At the Secreta.
Mercifully hear our prayers, O Lord, and graciously accept this oblation which we Thy servants make unto Thee; and as we offer it to the honor of Thy name, so may it be to us a means of obtaining Thy grace here and life everlasting hereafter. Through Jesus Christ, Our Lord. *Amen.*

(Or, on a saint's day.)
Sanctify, O Lord, we beseech Thee, these gifts which we offer Thee in this solemnity of Thy holy servant N., and so strengthen us by Thy grace that, both in prosperity and adversity, our ways may be ever directed to Thine honor. Through Jesus Christ, Our Lord. *Amen.*

At the Sursum corda.
℣. Lift up your hearts.
℟. We lift them up unto the Lord.
℣. Let us give thanks unto the Lord our God.
℟. It is worthy and just.

The Preface.
It is truly worthy and just, right and profitable unto salvation, that we should at all times, and in all places, give thanks unto Thee, O holy Lord, Father Almighty,

eternal God. Who, with Thine only begotten Son and the Holy Ghost, art one God, one Lord: not in the singleness of one only person, but in the Trinity of one substance. For what we believe of Thy glory, as Thou hast revealed it, that we believe of Thy Son, and that of the Holy Ghost, without any difference or inequality. That, in the confession of the true and eternal Godhead, distinction in Persons, unity in essence, and equality in majesty may be adored. Whom the angels and archangels, the cherubim also and seraphim, do praise; who cease not daily to cry out, with one voice saying:

(*Here the bell is rung.*)
Holy, holy, holy, Lord God of hosts. Heaven and earth are full of Thy glory. Hosanna in the highest. Blessed is He Who cometh in the name of the Lord. Hosanna in the highest.

PART III

THE CANON OF THE MASS, OR MAIN ACTION OF THE SACRIFICE

At the beginning of the Canon.
O eternal and most merciful Father, behold we come to offer Thee our homage this day. We desire to adore, praise, and glorify Thee, joining our hearts and voices with all Thy blessed in heaven, and with Thy whole Church upon earth. But acknowledging our great unworthiness and innumerable sins, for which we are heartily sorry and humbly crave Thy pardon, we dare not venture to approach Thee, save through Thy Son, our Advocate and Mediator, Jesus Christ, Whom Thou hast given us to be both our High Priest and Sacrifice. With Him, therefore, and through Him, we venture to offer Thee this sacrifice: to His most sacred intentions we desire to unite ours: and with this offering which He makes of Himself we wish to make an offering of our whole being unto Thee. With Him, and through Him, we beseech Thee to exalt Thy holy Catholic Church throughout the world; to maintain her in peace, unity, holiness, and truth; to have mercy on Thy servant, N. our pope, N. our bishop, N. our pastor, [our parents, children, friends, benefactors, etc.,] on all whom we have in any way scandalized, injured, or offended, or for whom we ought to pray; on all who are dying; on all who are under temptation, or in other necessity of either body or soul; on all our enemies; and on us all poor sinners; that we may all be converted to Thee, and find mercy through Jesus Christ, Thy Son; through Whom we hope one day to be admitted into the company of all Thy saints and elect, whose memory we here celebrate, whose prayers we desire, and with whom we communicate in these holy mysteries.

When the priest spreads his hands over the oblation.
(*Here the bell is again rung.*)

Give ear, we beseech Thee, to the prayers of Thy servant, who is here appointed to make this oblation in our behalf; and grant it may be effectual for the obtaining of all those blessings which he asks for us.

Behold, O Lord, we all here present unto Thee in this bread and wine the symbols of our perfect union. Grant, O Lord, that they may be made for us the true Body and Blood of Thy dear Son; that, being consecrated to Thee by this holy Victim, we may live in Thy service, and depart this life in Thy grace.

At the Consecration.
Bow down in solemn adoration; make an act of faith in the Real Presence of your Savior's Body and Blood, Soul and Divinity, under the sacramental veils. Offer your whole self to Him, and through Him to His Father: beg that your heart and soul may be happily united to Him.

At the Elevation *of the Host.*
(*Here the bell is rung again.*)
Most adorable Body, I adore Thee with all the powers of my soul. Lord, Who hast given Thyself entire to us, grant we may become entirely Thine. I believe, O Lord; help mine unbelief.

Most merciful Savior, be Thou my Protector; strengthen and defend me by Thy heavenly grace, now, and especially at the hour of my death, good Jesus. *Amen.*

At the Elevation *of the chalice.*
(*Here also the bell is rung.*)
Most adorable Blood, that washest away all our sins, I adore Thee: happy we, could we return our life and blood for Thine, O blessed Victim.

O Jesus, do Thou cleanse, sanctify, and preserve our souls to eternal life. Live, Jesus, in us, and may we live in Thee. *Amen.*

After the Elevation.
And now, O Lord, with grateful hearts, we call to mind the sacred mysteries of Thy Passion and death, of Thy Resurrection and Ascension. Here is Thy Body that was delivered; here is Thy Blood that was shed for us; of which these exterior signs are but the figures and yet in reality contain the substance. Now we truly offer Thee, O Lord, that pure and holy Victim which Thou hast been pleased to give us; of which all the other sacrifices were but so many types and figures.

At the Memento *for the dead.*
I offer Thee, O Almighty Father, this Holy Sacrifice of the Body and Blood of Thine only Son, in behalf of the faithful departed, and in particular for the souls of N. [*here name whom you chiefly propose to pray for*]. Likewise of such as I have in any way injured, or of whose sins I have by any means been the cause or occasion; of

such as have injured me, and been my enemies; of such as die in war, or have none to pray for them. To these, O Lord, and to all that rest in Christ, grant, we beseech Thee, a place of refreshment, of light, and of peace. Through the same Christ, Our Lord. *Amen.*

At the Nobis quoque peccatoribus, *when the priest strikes his breast.*
Vouchsafe to grant the same to us also, poor and miserable sinners; judge us not according to our demerits, but through the infinite multitude of Thy tender mercies, in which we put all our trust, graciously extend to us Thy grace and pardon.

We ask it of Thee, in the name of Thy dear Son, Who liveth and reigneth eternally with Thee; and in that form of prayer which He Himself hath taught us.

PART IV

THE COMMUNION, OR SACRAMENTAL PART OF THE CANON

At the Pater noster.
Our Father, etc.
Deliver us, O Lord, from those evils which we labor under at present; from past evils, which are our manifold sins; and from all evils to come, which will be the just chastisement of our offenses, if our prayers, and those more powerful ones of Thy saints, who intercede for us, intercept not Thy justice or excite not Thy bounty.

At the Pax Domini.
Thy body was delivered and Thy blood was shed for us; grant that the commemoration of this holy mystery may obtain for us peace, and that those who receive it may find everlasting rest.

At the Agnus Dei.
Say with the priest:
Lamb of God, Who takest away the sins of the world, have mercy on us.
Lamb of God, Who takest away the sins of the world, have mercy on us.
Lamb of God, Who takest away the sins of the world, grant us Thy peace.

After the Agnus Dei.
In saying to Thine apostles, "Peace I leave you. My peace I give you," Thou hast promised, O Lord, to all Thy Church, that peace which the world cannot give — peace with Thee, and peace with ourselves. Let nothing, O Lord, ever interrupt this holy peace; let nothing separate us from Thee, to Whom we heartily desire to be united, through this Blessed Sacrament of peace and reconciliation. Let this Food of angels strengthen us in every Christian duty, so as nevermore to yield under temptations or fall into our common weaknesses.

At the Domine, non sum dignus.
Say with the priest three times, striking your breast:
(*Here the bell is rung.*)
Lord, I am not worthy that Thou shouldst enter under my roof; but only say the word, and my soul shall be healed.

Such as do not intend to communicate sacramentally may communicate spiritually, as follows:
Most loving Jesus, I adore Thee with a lively faith, Who art present in this Sacrament by virtue of Thine infinite power, wisdom, and goodness. All my hope is in Thee. I love Thee, O Lord, with all my heart, Who hast so loved me; and therefore I desire to receive Thee now spiritually. Come, therefore, O Lord, to me in spirit, and heal my sinful soul. Feed me, for I am hungry; strengthen me, for I am weak; enliven and sanctify me with Thy sacred Body and Blood; deliver me from all sin, and make me always obedient to Thy commandments; and let me never be separated from Thee, my Savior, Who, with the Father and the Holy Ghost, livest and reignest one God, world without end. *Amen.*

A FAVORITE PRAYER OF ST. IGNATIUS LOYOLA
Anima Christi
Soul of Christ, sanctify me!
Body of Christ, save me!
Blood of Christ, inebriate me!
Water from the side of Christ, wash me!
Passion of Christ, strengthen me!
O good Jesus, hear me!
Within Thy wounds, hide me!
Suffer me not to be separated from Thee!
From the malicious enemy, defend me!
In the hour of my death, call me,
And bid me come to Thee;
That with Thy saints I may praise Thee
Forever and ever. Amen.

At the Communion.
Let it be now, O Lord, the effect of Thy mercy, that we who have been present at this holy mystery may find the benefit of it in our souls.

PART V

THE PUBLIC THANKSGIVING AFTER COMMUNION

At the Postcommunion.
We give Thee thanks, O God, for Thy mercy in admitting us to have a part in offering this sacrifice to Thy holy name: accept it now to Thy glory, and be ever mindful of our weakness. Most gracious God, Father of mercy, grant, I beseech Thee, that this adorable sacrifice of the blessed Body and Blood of Thy Son, Our Lord Jesus Christ, may obtain for us at Thy hands mercy and the remission of all our sins. *Amen.*

Concluding Prayer
I return Thee now most hearty thanks, O my God, through Jesus Christ Thy Son, that Thou hast been pleased to deliver Him up to death for us, and to give us His Body and Blood, both as a Sacrament and a sacrifice, in these holy mysteries, at which Thou hast permitted me, a most unworthy sinner, to be present this day. May all heaven and earth bless and praise Thee ever for all Thy mercies. Pardon me, O Lord, all the distractions and the manifold negligences of which I have been guilty this day in Thy sight; and let me not depart without Thy blessing. Behold, I desire from this moment to give up myself, and all that belongs to me, into Thy hands; and I beg that all my undertakings, all my thoughts, words, and actions, may henceforward tend to Thy glory. Through the same Jesus Christ, Our Lord. *Amen.*

The Gospel of St. John[6]
In the beginning was the Word, and the Word was with God, and the Word was God. This was in the beginning with God. All things were made through Him, and without Him was made nothing that was made: in Him was life, and the life was the light of men: and the light shineth in darkness, and the darkness did not comprehend it.

There was a man sent from God, whose name was John. This one came for a witness, to testify concerning the light, that all might believe through him. He was not the light, but he was to testify concerning the light. The true Light, which enlighteneth every man, cometh into this world.

He was in the world, and the world was made through Him, and the world knew Him not. He came to His own possessions, and His own people received Him not. But to as many as received Him He gave power to become children of God, to those who believe in His name, who are born not of blood, nor of the will of the flesh, nor of the will of man, but of God. AND THE WORD WAS MADE FLESH [*Here all kneel*], and dwelt among us; and we saw His glory, the glory as of the only begotten of the Father, full of grace and truth.

---

[6]   When a feast of greater rank falls on a Sunday, the Sunday Gospel is substituted for that of St. John.

A PRAYER AFTER MASS

Almighty, everlasting God, we humbly beseech Thee graciously to look down from Thy high and holy place upon this congregation, and mercifully hear and accept the prayers of Thy Church. Of Thine infinite mercy be pleased to grant us pardon of all our sins, soundness of mind, health of body, and all the necessaries of life: grant also peace in our days, freedom from tempests, and fruitful seasons. Grant also to our prayers the unity of the Catholic Faith, the extirpation of heresies, the destruction of wicked counsels, the increase of true religion, fervor of love and piety, sincere devotion, patience and long-suffering in affliction, and joy in hope. Finally, grant us all things needful for the welfare of our souls and bodies, but, above all, whatever may promote the increase of Thy glory. Through Jesus Christ, Our Lord. *Amen.*

‡AN ACT OF REPARATION FOR BLASPHEMY.

Blessed be God.
Blessed be His holy name.
Blessed be Jesus Christ, true God and true man.
Blessed be the name of Jesus.
Blessed be His most Sacred Heart.
Blessed be His most Precious Blood.
Blessed be Jesus in the most Holy Sacrament of the Altar.
Blessed be the Holy Ghost, the Paraclete.
Blessed be the great Mother of God, Mary most holy.
Blessed be her holy and Immaculate Conception.
Blessed be her glorious Assumption.
Blessed be the name of Mary, Virgin and Mother.
Blessed be St. Joseph, her most chaste spouse.
Blessed be God in His angels and in His saints.

[‡Hail, Mary (*three times*).

Hail, holy Queen, Mother of mercy; our life, our sweetness, and our hope. To thee do we cry, poor banished children of Eve; to thee do we send up our sighs, mourning and weeping, in this valley of tears! Turn, then, most gracious Advocate, thine eyes of mercy toward us; and after this our exile, show unto us the blessed fruit of thy womb, Jesus: O clement, O loving, O sweet Virgin Mary.
℣. Pray for us, O holy Mother of God.
℞. That we may be made worthy of the promises of Christ.

Let us pray.
    O God, our refuge and our strength, graciously look upon Thy people who cry to Thee; and through the intercession of the glorious and Immaculate Virgin Mary,

Mother of God, of blessed Joseph, her spouse, and Thy holy apostles Peter and Paul, and all the saints, in Thy mercy and kindness hear the prayers which we pour forth for the conversion of sinners, for the freedom and exaltation of holy Mother the Church. Through the same Christ Our Lord. Amen.

St. Michael, the archangel, defend us in the battle; be our protection against the wickedness and snares of the devil.—Rebuke him, O God, we suppliantly beseech Thee: and do thou, O prince of the heavenly host, by the divine power, drive into hell Satan and the other evil spirits, who wander through the world seeking the ruin of souls. Amen.

Most Sacred Heart of Jesus, have mercy on us (*three times*).]

The Manner of Serving a Priest at Mass

The priest begins, and the server, kneeling at his left hand, answers him as follows:

‡In nomine Patris, et Filii, et Spiritus Sancti. Amen.

P. Introibo ad altare Dei.

S. Ad Deum, qui lætificat juventutem meam.

P. Judica me, Deus, et discerne causam meam de gente non sancta: ab homine iniquo, et doloso erue me.

S. Quia tu es, Deus, fortitudo mea: quare me repulisti, et quare tristis incedo, dum affligit me inimicus?

P. Emitte lucem tuam, et veritatem tuam: ipsa me deduxerunt, et adduxerunt in montem sanctum tuum, et in tabernacula tua.

S. Et introibo ad altare Dei: ad Deum, qui lætificat juventutem meam.

P. Confitebor tibi in cithara, Deus, Deus meus: quare tristis es, anima mea, et quare conturbas me?

S. Spera in Deo, quoniam adhuc confitebor illi: salutare vultus mei, et Deus meus.

P. Gloria Patri, et Filio, et Spiritui Sancto.

S. Sicut erat in principio, et nunc, et semper: et in sæcula sæculorum. Amen.

P. Introibo ad altare Dei.

S. Ad Deum, qui lætificat juventutem meam.

P. Adjutorium nostrum in nomine Domini.

S. Qui fecit cœlum et terram.

P. Confiteor Deo, etc.

S. Misereatur tui omnipotens Deus, et, dimissis peccatis tuis, perducat te ad vitam æternam.

P. Amen.

S. Confiteor Deo omnipotenti, beatæ Mariæ semper Virgini, beato Michaeli Archangelo, beato Joanni Baptistæ, sanctis Apostolis Petro et Paulo, omnibus Sanctis, et tibi, pater, quia peccavi nimis cogitatione, verbo, et opere: [*Strike your breast thrice, and say,*] mea culpa, mea culpa, mea maxima culpa. Ideo precor beatam Mariam semper Virginem, beatum Michaelem Archangelum, beatum Joannem Baptistam, sanctos Apostolos Petrum et Paulum, omnes Sanctos, et te, pater, orare pro me ad Dominum Deum nostrum.

P. Misereatur vestri, etc.

S. Amen.

P. Indulgentiam, absolutionem, etc.

S. Amen.

[*At a bishop's Mass, here give him the maniple.*]

P. Deus, tu conversus vivificabis nos.

S. Et plebs tua lætabitur in te.

P. Ostende nobis, Domine, misericordiam tuam.
S. Et salutare tuum da nobis.
P. Domine, exaudi orationem meam.
S. Et clamor meus ad te veniat.
P. Dominus vobiscum.
S. Et cum spiritu tuo.

When the priest goes from the book to the middle of the altar:
P. Kyrie, eleison.
S. Kyrie, eleison.
P. Kyrie, eleison.
S. Christe, eleison.
P. Christe, eleison.
S. Christe, eleison.
P. Kyrie, eleison.
S. Kyrie, eleison.
P. Kyrie, eleison.
P. Dominus vobiscum.
S. Et cum spiritu tuo.
[*At a bishop's Mass:*
B. Pax vobis.
S. Et cum spiritu tuo.]
When the priest says, Flectamus genua, *as is the case a few times in the year, answer,*
Levate.
P. Per omnia sæcula sæculorum.
S. Amen.

At the end of the Epistle say, Deo gratias; *then remove the book to the other side of the altar, and always kneel or stand on the side opposite to that on which the book has been placed.*

P. Dominus vobiscum.
S. Et cum spiritu tuo.
P. Sequentia sancti evangelii secundum N.
Making the sign of the cross on your forehead, mouth, and breast, say:
S. Gloria tibi. Domine.

Stand during the Gospel, and at the end say:
S. Laus tibi, Christe.
P. Dominus vobiscum.
S. Et cum spiritu tuo.

Here give the wine and water, and prepare the basin, water, and towel for the priest. When the priest has washed his fingers, kneel in your former place, and answer:

P. Orate, fratres, etc.
S. Suscipiat Dominus sacrificium de manibus tuis ad laudem, et gloriam nominis sui, ad utilitatem quoque nostram, totiusque Ecclesiæ suæ sanctæ.
P. Per omnia sæcula sæculorum.
S. Amen.
P. Dominus vobiscum.
S. Et cum spiritu tuo.
P. Sursum corda.
S. Habemus ad Dominum.
P. Gratias agamus Domino Deo nostro.
S. Dignum et justum est.

At Sanctus, Sanctus, Sanctus, *ring the bell.*

When you see the priest spread his hands over the chalice, give warning, by the bell, of the Consecration which is about to be made. Then, holding up the vestment with your left hand, and having the bell in your right, ring during the Elevation of the Host and of the chalice. As often as you pass by the Blessed Sacrament, make a genuflection.

P. Per omnia sæcula sæculorum.
S. Amen.
P. Et ne nos inducas in tentationem
S. Sed libera nos a malo.
P. Per omnia sæcula sæculorum.
S. Amen.
P. Pax Domini sit semper vobiscum.
S. Et cum spiritu tuo.

When the priest says, Domine, non sum dignus, *ring the bell; and after his Communion, if there are communicants, prepare the cloth and say the* Confiteor. *After they have received, serve the priest with wine and water, for the ablutions. Then remove the book to the other side of the altar, take away the cloth from the communicants, and return to your place.*

P. Dominus vobiscum.
S. Et cum spiritu tuo.
P. Per omnia sæcula sæculorum.
S. Amen.
P. Dominus vobiscum.
S. Et cum spiritu tuo.

P. Ite, missa est *or*, Benedicamus Domino.
S. Deo gratias.
[In Masses for the Dead:
P. Requiescant in pace.
S. Amen.]
[At a bishop's Mass:
B. Sit nomen Domini benedictum.
S. Ex hoc nunc, et usque in sæculum.
B. Adjutorium nostrum in nomine Domini.
S. Qui fecit cœlum, et terram.
B. Benedicat vos omnipotens Deus, Pater ✠, et Filius ✠, et Spiritus ✠ Sanctus.
S. Amen.]

Remove the book to the Gospel side, if it be left open; kneel as you pass, to receive the priest's blessing, answering, Amen.
P. Dominus vobiscum.
S. Et cum spiritu tuo.
P. Initium (*or*, Sequentia) sancti evangelii, etc.
S. Gloria tibi, Domine.
At the end say, Deo gratias.

THE ORDER OF BLESSING WATER

On Sundays, and whenever need arises, the salt and clean water being prepared, in the church or in the sacristy, the priest, vested in surplice and violet stole, first says:
Our help is in the name of the Lord.
℟. Who hath made heaven and earth.

THE EXORCISM OF THE SALT

I exorcise thee, O creature of salt, by the living God, ✠ by the true God, ✠ by the holy God, ✠ by the God Who commanded thee to be cast into the water by Eliseus the prophet, that the barrenness of the same might be healed; that thou become salt for the preservation of them that believe, and be to all who take thee salvation of soul and body; and from the place wherein thou shalt be sprinkled, let every delusion and wickedness of the devil, and all unclean spirits, fly and depart when adjured by Him Who shall come to judge the living and the dead, and the world by fire. ℟. Amen.

Let us pray.
　　We humbly implore Thy boundless clemency, Almighty and everlasting God, that of Thy bounty Thou wouldst deign to bless ✠ and sanctify ✠ this creature of salt, which Thou hast given for the use of mankind; let it be unto all who take it health of mind and body; that whatsoever shall be touched or sprinkled with it be

freed from all manner of uncleanness, and from all assaults of spiritual wickedness. Through Our Lord Jesus Christ, etc. ℟. Amen.

THE EXORCISM OF THE WATER

I exorcise thee, O creature of water, in the name of God ✠ the Father Almighty; and in the name of Jesus Christ, ✠ His Son, Our Lord; and in the power of the Holy ✠ Ghost; that thou mayest become water exorcised for the chasing away of all the power of the enemy; that thou mayest have strength to uproot and cast out the enemy himself and his apostate angels, by the power of the same Our Lord Jesus Christ, Who shall come to judge the living and the dead, and the world by fire. ℟. Amen.

Let us pray.

O God, Who for the salvation of mankind hast founded one of Thy greatest Sacraments in the element of water, graciously give ear when we call upon Thee, and pour upon this element, prepared for divers purifications, the power of Thy ✠ blessing; let Thy creature serving in Thy mysteries, by divine grace be effectual for casting out devils and for driving away diseases, that on whatsoever in the houses or places of the faithful this water shall be sprinkled, it may be freed from all uncleanness, and delivered from hurt. Let not the blast of pestilence nor disease remain there; let every enemy that lieth in wait depart; and if there be aught which hath ill-will to the safety and quietness of the inhabitants, let it flee away at the sprinkling of this water, that they, being healed by the invocation of Thy holy name, may be defended from all that rise up against them. Through Our Lord Jesus Christ, etc. ℟. Amen.

The priest thrice mingles salt with water in the form of a cross, saying once:
Let this become a mixture of salt and water, in the name of the Father, ✠ and of the Son, ✠ and of the Holy ✠ Ghost. ℟. Amen.
℣. The Lord be with you.
℟. And with thy spirit.

Let us pray.

O God, Author of invincible might, King of unconquerable dominion, and ever a Conqueror Who doest wonders, Who puttest down the strength of all that rise up against Thee; Who overcomest the rage of the adversary; Who by Thy power dost cast down his wickedness; we, O Lord, with fear and trembling, humbly entreat and implore Thee mercifully to look upon this creature of salt and water, to graciously illumine and sanctify it with the dew of Thy favor; that, wheresoever it shall be sprinkled, by the invocation of Thy holy name all troubling of unclean spirits may be cast out, and the dread of the poisonous serpent be chased far away; and let the presence of the Holy Ghost vouchsafe to be with us, who ask Thy mercy in every place. Through Our Lord Jesus Christ, etc. ℟. Amen.

THE ASPERGES

The Asperges, *or* sprinkling with Holy Water, *is performed every Sunday, immediately before High Mass, except when the bishop celebrates pontifically.*

The priest who is about to celebrate High Mass first blesses the holy water according to the preceding form, and then enters the sanctuary vested in alb and stole (and sometimes in a cope also), accompanied by an acolyte bearing the vessel of holy water (at Solemn Mass he is accompanied also by the deacon and subdeacon). Arriving at the foot of the altar, the priest, while intoning the following Anthem, *sprinkles the altar three times; then himself, and afterward his assistants. Then, going down into the church, he sprinkles the congregation.*

Asperges me, Domine, hyssopo, et mundabor: lavabis me, et super nivem dealbabor.
Ps. Miserere mei, Deus, secundum magnam misericordiam tuam.
℣. Gloria Patri, etc.
Ant. Asperges me, etc.

Thou shalt sprinkle me, O Lord, with hyssop, and I shall be cleansed: Thou shalt wash me, and I shall be made whiter than snow.
Ps. Have mercy on me, O God, according to Thy great mercy.
℣. Glory be to the Father, etc.
Ant. Thou shalt sprinkle me, etc.

The priest, being returned to the foot of the altar, says:

Ostende nobis, Domine, misericordiam tuam.
℟. Et salutare tuum da nobis.
℣. Domine, exaudi orationem meam.
℟. Et clamor meus ad te veniat.
℣. Dominus vobiscum.
℟. Et cum spiritu tuo.

Show us Thy mercy, O Lord.
℟. And grant us Thy salvation.
℣. O Lord, hear my prayer.
℟. And let my cry come unto Thee.
℣. The Lord be with you.
℟. And with thy spirit.

Oremus.
Exaudi nos, Domine sancte, Pater omnipotens, æterne Deus: et mittere digneris sanctum Angelum tuum de cœlis, qui custodiat, foveat, protegat, visitet, atque defendat omnes habitantes in hoc habitaculo. Per Christum Dominum nostrum. ℟. Amen.

Let us pray.
Hear us, O holy Lord, Father Almighty, everlasting God; and vouchsafe to send Thy holy angel from heaven, to guard, cherish, protect, visit, and defend all those that are assembled together in this house. Through Christ Our Lord. ℟. Amen.

From Easter to Whitsunday inclusively, instead of the foregoing Anthem, *the following is sung, and* Alleluia *is added to the* ℣. Ostende nobis, *and also to its* ℟. Et salutare.

Vidi aquam egredientem de templo, a latere dextro, alleluia: et omnes, ad quos pervenit aqua ista, salvi facti sunt, et dicent, Alleluia, alleluia.

I saw water flowing from the right side of the temple, alleluia; and all unto whom that water came were saved, and they shall say, Alleluia, alleluia.

Confitemini, Domino, quoniam bonus: quoniam in sæculum misericordia ejus. Gloria Patri, etc.

O praise the Lord, for He is good; for His mercy endureth forever. Glory be to the Father, etc.

The Antiphon Vidi aquam *is repeated.*

The Ordinary of the Holy Mass

[N.B.—At Low Mass the parts within brackets are to be passed over.]

The priest, standing at the foot of the altar, and making the usual reverence, signs himself with the sign of the cross from the forehead to the breast, and says in an audible voice:[7]

In nomine Patris, ✠ et Filii, et Spiritus Sancti. *Amen.*

In the name of the Father, ✠ and of the Son, and of the Holy Ghost. *Amen.*

Then, joining his hands before his breast, he begins the Antiphon:

℣. Introibo ad altare Dei.

℣. I will go in unto the altar of God.

℟. Ad Deum, qui lætificat juventutem meam.

℟. Unto God, Who giveth joy to my youth.

[In Masses for the Dead, and in those of the Season from Passion Sunday till Holy Saturday exclusively, the following Psalm is omitted:]

PSALM 42

Judica me, Deus, et discerne causam meam de gente non sancta: ab homine iniquo, et doloso erue me.

Judge me, O God, and distinguish my cause from the nation that is not holy: deliver me from the unjust and deceitful man.

M. Quia tu es, Deus, fortitudo mea, quare me repulisti? et quare tristis incedo, dum affligit me inimicus?

℟. For Thou, O God, art my strength: Why hast Thou cast me off? And why go I sorrowful whilst the enemy afflicteth me?

S. Emitte lucem tuam, et veritatem tuam: ipsa me deduxerunt, et adduxerunt in montem sanctum tuum, et in tabernacula tua.

P. Send forth Thy light and Thy truth: they have led me and brought me unto Thy holy hill, and into Thy tabernacles.

---

[7] At the beginning of High Mass, when the priest commences at the foot of the altar, the choir sings the *Kyrie eleison,* etc. (sometimes the *Introit* is sung first), which usually lasts until the *Gloria in excelsis.* Those parts of the service that are sung by the choir are also said in a low voice by the priest.

M. Et introibo ad altare Dei: ad Deum qui lætificat juventutem meam.

℟. And I will go in unto the altar of God: unto God, Who giveth joy to my youth.

S. Confitebor tibi in cithara, Deus, Deus meus: quare tristis es, anima mea, et quare conturbas me?

P. I will praise Thee upon the harp, O God, my God: Why art thou sad, O my soul? And why dost thou disquiet me?

M. Spera in Deo, quoniam adhuc confitebor illi: salutare vultus mei, et Deus meus.

℟. Hope thou in God, for I will yet praise Him: Who is the salvation of my countenance, and my God.

S. Gloria Patri, et Filio, et Spiritui Sancto.

P. Glory be to the Father, and to the Son, and to the Holy Ghost.

M. Sicut erat in principio, et nunc, et semper, et in sæcula sæculorum. Amen.

℟. As it was in the beginning, is now, and ever shall be, world without end. Amen.

℣. Introibo ad altare Dei.

℣. I will go in unto the altar of God.

℟. Ad Deum, qui lætificat juventutem meam.

℟. Unto God, Who giveth joy to my youth.

℣. Adjutorium nostrum in nomine Domini.

℣. Our help is in the name of the Lord.

℟. Qui fecit cœlum et terram.

℟. Who hath made heaven and earth.

Then, joining his hands and humbly bowing down, he says the Confiteor, *as on p. 32:*

S. Confiteor Deo omnipotenti, etc.

P. I confess to Almighty God, etc.

M. Misereatur tui omnipotens Deus, et, dimissis peccatis tuis, perducat te ad vitam æternam.

℟. May Almighty God have mercy upon thee, and forgive thee thy sins, and bring thee unto life everlasting.

S. Amen.

P. Amen.

The server recite the Confiteor.
Then the priest, with his hands joined, gives the absolution, saying:

Misereatur vestri omnipotens Deus, et, dimissis peccatis vestris, perducat vos ad vitam æternam.

May Almighty God have mercy upon you, and forgive you your sins, and bring you unto life everlasting.

M. Amen.

℟. Amen.

Signing himself with the sign of the cross, he says:

Indulgentiam, ✠ absolutionem, et re-missionem peccatorum nostrorum tribuat nobis omnipotens et miseri-cors Dominus.	May the Almighty and merciful Lord grant us pardon, ✠ absolution, and remission of our sins.
M. Amen.	℟. Amen.

Then, bowing down, he proceeds:

℣. Deus, tu conversus vivificabis nos.	℣. Thou shalt turn again, O God, and quicken us.
℟. Et plebs tua lætabitur in te.	℟. And Thy people shall rejoice in Thee.
℣. Ostende nobis, Domine, misericor-diam tuam.	℣. Show us Thy mercy, O Lord.
℟. Et salutare tuum da nobis.	℟. And grant us Thy salvation.
℣. Domine, exaudi orationem meam.	℣. O Lord, hear my prayer.
℟. Et clamor meus ad te veniat.	℟. And let my cry come unto Thee.
℣. Dominus vobiscum.	℣. The Lord be with you.
℟. Et cum spiritu tuo.	℟. And with thy spirit.

The priest then, extending and afterward joining his hands, says:

Oremus.	Let us pray.

Then, going up to the altar, he says inaudibly:

Aufer a nobis, quæsumus, Domine, iniquitates nostras: ut ad Sancta Sanctorum puris mereamur mentibus introire. Per Christum Dominum nostrum. *Amen.*	Take away from us our iniquities, we beseech Thee, O Lord: that we may be worthy to enter with pure minds into the Holy of Holies. Through Christ Our Lord. *Amen.*

Bowing down over the altar, he kisses it and says:

Oramus te, Domine, per merita Sanctorum tuorum quorum reliquiæ hic sunt, et omnium Sanctorum, ut indulgere digneris omnia peccata mea. *Amen.*	We beseech Thee, O Lord, by the mer-its of Thy saints whose relics are here, and of all the saints, that Thou wouldst vouchsafe to forgive me all my sins. *Amen.*

[*At Solemn Mass the altar is here incensed.*]
Then the priest, signing himself with the sign of the cross, reads

THE INTROIT,

during which one of the following may be read:
Blessed be the Holy Trinity and undivided Unity: we will give praise to Him, because He hath shown His mercy unto us.
O Lord, Our Lord, how admirable is Thy name in the whole earth!
Glory be to the Father, Who hath created us.
Glory be to the Son, Who hath redeemed us.
Glory be to the Holy Ghost, Who hath sanctified us.
Glory be to the Holy and undivided Trinity, one God, world without end. *Amen.*

Or on a saint's day:
The just shall flourish like the palm tree; he shall grow up like a cedar of Libanus: they that are planted in the house of the Lord shall flourish in the courts of the house of our God.

It is good to give praise unto the Lord; and to sing unto Thy name, O Thou most High.

The Kyrie, eleison *is then said:*

Kyrie, eleison.	Lord, have mercy.
M. Kyrie, eleison.	℟. Lord, have mercy.
S. Kyrie, eleison.	P. Lord, have mercy.
M. Christe, eleison.	℟. Christ, have mercy.
S. Christe, eleison.	P. Christ, have mercy.
M. Christe, eleison.	℟. Christ, have mercy
S. Kyrie, eleison.	P. Lord, have mercy.
M. Kyrie, eleison.	℟. Lord, have mercy.
S. Kyrie, eleison.	P. Lord, have mercy.

Afterward, standing at the middle of the altar, extending and then joining his hands, and slightly bowing, he says (when it is to be said[8]*) the* Gloria in excelsis.

[*At High Mass the choir sings the* Gloria, *and the officiating clergy wait until its conclusion.*]

---

[8]   The *Gloria* is omitted in Masses of the Season during Lent and Advent, and in Masses for the Dead.

Gloria in excelsis Deo; et in terra pax hominibus bonæ voluntatis. Laudamus te; benedicimus te; adoramus te; glorificamus te. Gratias agimus tibi propter magnam gloriam tuam. Domine Deus, Rex cœlestis, Deus Pater omnipotens. Domine Fili unigenite, Jesu Christe: Domine Deus, Agnus Dei, Filius Patris, qui tollis peccata mundi, miserere nobis: qui tollis peccata mundi, suscipe deprecationem nostram: qui sedes ad dexteram Patris, miserere nobis: quoniam tu solus sanctus: tu solus Dominus: tu solus altissimus, Jesu Christe, cum Sancto Spiritu, in gloria Dei Patris. *Amen.*

Glory be to God on high, and on earth peace to men of good will. We praise Thee; we bless Thee; we worship Thee; we glorify Thee. We give Thee thanks for Thy great glory, O Lord God, heavenly King, God the Father Almighty. O Lord, the only begotten Son, Jesus Christ; O Lord God, Lamb of God, Son of the Father, Who takest away the sins of the world, have mercy on us: Thou Who takest away the sins of the world, receive our prayer; Thou Who sittest at the right hand of the Father, have mercy on us. For Thou only art holy: Thou only art the Lord: Thou only, O Jesus Christ, with the Holy Ghost, art most High in the glory of God the Father. *Amen.*

The priest kisses the altar, and turning to the people, says:

℣. Dominus vobiscum.

℣. The Lord be with you.

℟. Et cum spiritu tuo.

℟. And with thy spirit.

Then follow the Collect *and other prayers, if prescribed; at the end of the first and last of which the acolyte answers,* Amen.

The Collects *vary with the season.*[9] *They may be found in their proper place (p. 506). Any of the following may be used instead:*

O God, the Protector of all that hope in Thee, without Whom nothing is strong, nothing is holy, multiply upon us Thy mercy; that, Thou being our Ruler and Guide, we may so pass through temporal blessings that we finally lose not those which are eternal. Through Our Lord Jesus Christ, etc. Amen.

Defend us, O Lord, we beseech Thee, from all dangers both of soul and body; and, by the intercession of the glorious and Blessed Mary ever Virgin, Mother of God, of blessed Joseph, of Thy holy apostles Peter and Paul, of blessed N. [*here insert the name of your patron saint*], and of all Thy saints, grant us, in Thy mercy, health and

---

[9] The same remark applies to the Introit, Epistle, Gradual, Gospel, Offertory, Communion, and Postcommunion.

peace; that all adversities and errors being done away, Thy Church may serve Thee with a pure and undisturbed devotion.

Almighty and everlasting God, by Whose Spirit the whole body of the Church is sanctified and governed: receive our humble supplications which we offer before Thee for all degrees and orders of men in Thy holy Church, that, by the assistance of Thy grace, they may faithfully serve Thee.

O God, the Pastor and Ruler of all the faithful, look down, in Thy mercy, upon Thy servant N. [*here mention the pope's name*], whom Thou hast appointed to preside over Thy Church; and grant, we beseech Thee, that both by word and example he may edify all those who are under his charge; so that, with the flock entrusted to him, he may arrive at length unto life everlasting. Through Our Lord Jesus Christ, etc. *Amen.*

Then the Epistle *for the day is read, which may be found in its proper place (p. 506); or the following may be used instead:*
(Phil 4:4–9)
Rejoice in the Lord always: again I say, rejoice. Let your moderation be known to all men. The Lord is nigh. Be anxious about nothing: but in everything, by prayer and supplication, with thanksgiving, let your petitions be made known to God. And may the peace of God, which surpasseth all understanding, guard your hearts and minds in Christ Jesus. As to the rest, brethren, whatever things are true, whatever modest, whatever just, whatever holy, whatever amiable, whatever of good report, if there be any virtue, if any praise of discipline, think on these things. The things which ye have both learned and received, and heard and seen in me, these do ye, and the God of peace shall be with you.

After the Epistle *is said:*

℟. Deo gratias.   ℟. Thanks be to God.

Then the Gradual, Tract, Alleluia, *or* Sequence, *according to the time.*

FOR THE GRADUAL.[10]

Be Thou unto me a God, a Protector, and a House of refuge to save me. In Thee, O God, have I hoped; O Lord, let me never be confounded.

Deal not with us, O Lord, according to our sins which we have committed, nor punish us according to our iniquities.

℣. Help us, O God our Savior; and for the glory of Thy name, O Lord, deliver us, and forgive us our sins for Thy name's sake.

---

[10]   The choir sings the *Gradual* while the book is moved to the Gospel side, and the priest says the prayer *Munda cor meum,* "Cleanse my heart," etc.

Come, ye children, hearken unto me: I will teach you the fear of the Lord. Come ye to Him, and be enlightened; and your faces shall not be confounded. Alleluia, alleluia. O clap your hands, all ye nations; shout unto God with the voice of joy. Alleluia.

Before the Gospel the priest bows down before the middle of the altar, and says:

Munda cor meum, ac labia mea, om-nipotens Deus, qui labia Isaiæ Prophetæ calculo mundasti ignito: ita me tua grata miseratione dignare mundare, ut sanctum Evangelium tuum digne valeam nuntiare. Per Christum Dominum nostrum. Amen.

Jube, Domine, benedicere.

Cleanse my heart and my lips, O Almighty God, Who didst cleanse the lips of the prophet Isaias with a burning coal; and vouchsafe, through Thy gracious mercy, so to purify me that I may worthily proclaim Thy holy Gospel. Through Christ Our Lord. *Amen.*

Lord, grant Thy blessing.

Dominus sit in corde meo et in labiis meis: ut digne et competenter an-nuntiem Evangelium suum. *Amen.*

The Lord be in my heart and on my lips, that I may worthily and fittingly proclaim His holy Gospel. *Amen.*

Then, going to the Gospel side, he says:

℣. Dominus vobiscum.
℟. Et cum spiritu tuo.
℣. Sequentia sancti Evangelii secundum N.
℟. Gloria tibi, Domine.

℣. The Lord be with you.
℟. And with thy spirit.
℣. The continuation of the holy Gospel according to N.
℟. Glory be to Thee, O Lord.

Then is read

THE GOSPEL (p. 506).

For the Gospel *may be read:*
(Lk 12:35–40)
Let your loins be girded round, and lamps burning in your hands. And be ye like men waiting for their lord, when he shall return from the wedding; that when he cometh, and knocketh, they may open to him immediately. Happy are those servants whom the Lord, when He cometh, shall find watching. Truly I say to you, that He will gird Himself, and make them recline at table, and will come and serve them. And if He shall come in the second watch, or shall come in the third watch, and so find, happy are those servants. But know this, that if the master of the house did know at what hour the thief would come, he would surely watch, and would not suffer his house to be broken open. Be ye then also ready; for at what hour ye think not, the Son of Man will come.

After the Gospel *is said:*

℟. Laus tibi, Christe.   ℟. Praise be to Thee, O Christ.

The priest says inaudibly:

Per Evangelica dicta deleantur nostra   By the words of the Gospel may our sins
   delicta.   be blotted out.

[*At Solemn Mass, after the* Epistle *is sung, the deacon places the Gospel-book on the table of the altar, and the celebrant blesses the incense. The deacon then, kneeling before the altar with his hands joined, says the* Munda cor meum, *as above. He then takes the book from the altar, and kneeling, asks the celebrant's blessing, saying:*

Jube, Domne, benedicere.   Pray, sir, a blessing.

To which the celebrant replies in the words of the prayer Dominus sit in corde, *etc., above, only using the second person instead of the first, and blessing with the sign of the cross.*

The deacon then proceeds, with attendants bearing incense and lights, to the Gospel side of the sanctuary, and, standing with hands joined, sings:

Dominus vobiscum, etc.   The Lord be with you, etc.

When he sings Sequentia, *etc., he makes the sign of the cross upon the book and upon himself; and thereupon incenses the book thrice.*

After the Gospel, *the subdeacon takes the book to the celebrant, who kisses it, and is then incensed by the deacon.*]

[*Here the sermon is usually preached.*[11]]

Then, at the middle of the altar, extending, elevating, and joining his hands, the priest says the Nicene Creed (when it is to be said), keeping his hands joined. At the words, and was incarnate, *he kneels down, and continues kneeling to the words,* WAS MADE MAN.

---

[11]   *Prayer before the sermon.*
    I will hear what the Lord will say unto me. O Jesus, Light of the world, enlighten my understanding, that I may understand Thy word; and cleanse my heart, that it may bring forth the fruits of Thy holy teaching.

    After the sermon.
    I give Thee thanks, O Lord God, that Thou hast been pleased to refresh my soul by Thy word. Direct my steps according to Thy commandments.

Credo in unum Deum, Patrem omnipotentem, Factorem cœli et terræ, visibilium omnium et invisibilium. Et in unum Dominum Jesum Christum, Filium Dei unigenitum, et ex Patre natum ante omnia sæcula. Deum de Deo; Lumen de Lumine; Deum verum de Deo vero; genitum, non factum; consubstantialem Patri, per quem omnia facta sunt. Qui propter nos homines, et propter nostram salutem, descendit de cœlis, *et incarnatus est de Spiritu Sancto, ex Maria Virgine:* ET HOMO FACTUS EST. [*Hic genuflectitur.*] Crucifixus etiam pro nobis: sub Pontio Pilato passus et sepultus est. Et resurrexit tertia die secundum Scripturas; et ascendit in cœlum, sedet ad dexteram Patris: et iterum venturus est cum gloria judicare vivos et mortuos: cujus regni non erit finis.

I believe in one God the Father Almighty, Maker of heaven and earth, and of all things visible and invisible. And in one Lord Jesus Christ, the only begotten Son of God, born of the Father before all ages. God of God; Light of Light; very God of very God; begotten, not made; being of one substance with the Father, by Whom all things were made. Who for us men, and for our salvation, came down from heaven *and was incarnate by the Holy Ghost of the Virgin Mary:* AND WAS MADE MAN. [*Here all kneel down.*] He was crucified also for us, suffered under Pontius Pilate, and was buried. The third day He rose again according to the Scriptures; and ascended into heaven, and sitteth at the right hand of the Father: and He shall come again with glory to judge both the living and the dead: of Whose kingdom there shall be no end.

Et in Spiritum Sanctum, Dominum et vivificantem, qui ex Patre, Filioque procedit: qui cum Patre et Filio simul adoratur et conglorificatur; qui locutus est per prophetas. Et unam sanctam Catholicam et Apostolicam Ecclesiam. Confiteor unum baptisma in remissionem peccatorum. Et expecto resurrectionem mortuorum, et vitam venturi sæculi. *Amen.*

And I believe in the Holy Ghost, the Lord and Giver of life, Who proceedeth from the Father and the Son: Who together with the Father and the Son is worshipped and glorified; Who spoke by the prophets. And one, holy, catholic, and apostolic Church. I confess one Baptism for the remission of sins. And I look for the resurrection of the dead, and the life of the world to come. *Amen.*

[*At High Mass the choir sings the* Credo, *and the clergy sit down until its conclusion.*]

Then the celebrant kisses the altar, and, turning to the people, says:

℣. Dominus vobiscum.

℟. Et cum spiritu tuo.

℣. The Lord be with you.

℟. And with thy spirit.

He then reads

THE OFFERTORY.[12]

The following may be read:

The angel of the Lord shall encamp round about them that fear Him, and shall deliver them; O taste and see that the Lord is sweet.

Bless the Lord, O my soul, and forget not all His benefits: and thy youth shall be renewed like the eagle's.

I will extol Thee, O Lord, for Thou hast lifted me up: and hast not made my foes to rejoice over me: O Lord, my God, I have cried unto Thee: and Thou hast healed me.

This being finished, the priest takes the paten with the host [if it is Solemn Mass, the deacon hands the priest the paten with the host], and, offering it up, says:

Suscipe, sancte Pater, omnipotens æterne Deus, hanc immaculatam Hostiam, quam ego indignus famulus tuus offero tibi Deo meo vivo, et vero, pro innumerabilibus peccatis, et offensionibus, et negligentiis meis, et pro omnibus circumstantibus, sed et pro omnibus fidelibus Christianis, vivis atque defunctis: ut mihi et illis proficiat ad salutem in vitam æternam. *Amen.*

Accept, O holy Father, Almighty, everlasting God, this stainless host, which I, Thine unworthy servant, offer unto Thee, my God, living and true, for mine innumerable sins, offences, and negligences, and for all here present; as also for all faithful Christians, both living and dead, that it may be profitable for my own and for their salvation unto life eternal. *Amen.*

---

[12]   The choir sings the *Offertory*, or some suitable Anthem or Hymn.

Then, making the sign of the cross with the paten, he places the host upon the corporal. The priest pours wine and water into the chalice, blessing the water before it is mixed, saying:

Deus, ✠ qui humanæ substantiæ dignitatem mirabiliter condidisti, et mirabilius reformasti: da nobis per hujus aquæ et vini mysterium, ejus divinitatis esse consortes, qui humanitatis nostræ fieri dignatus est particeps, Jesus Christus Filius tuus Dominus noster: qui tecum vivit et regnat in unitate Spiritus Sancti Deus, per omnia sæcula sæculorum. *Amen.*

O God, ✠ Who hast wonderfully framed man's exalted nature, and still more wonderfully restored it: grant us, by the mystic signification of this commingling of water and wine, to become partakers of His Godhead Who vouchsafed to become partaker of our manhood, Jesus Christ, Thy Son, Our Lord; Who liveth and reigneth with Thee in the unity of, etc. *Amen.*

[If it is a Solemn Mass, the deacon ministers the wine, the subdeacon the water.]

Offering up the chalice, he says:

Offerimus tibi, Domine, calicem salutaris, tuam deprecantes clementiam: ut in conspectu divinæ Majestatis tuæ, pro nostra et totius mundi salute cum odore suavitatis ascendat. *Amen.*

We offer unto Thee, O Lord, the chalice of salvation, beseeching Thy clemency that, in the sight of Thy divine Majesty, it may ascend with the odor of sweetness, for our salvation, and for that of the whole world. *Amen.*

Then making the sign of the cross with the chalice, and placing it on the corporal, he covers it with the pall.

[At Solemn Mass the subdeacon here receives the paten, and, wrapping it up in the veil with which his shoulders are covered, he goes and stands behind the celebrant until toward the end of the Pater noster.*]*

Bowing down, the priest says:

In spiritu humilitatis, et in animo contrito, suscipiamur a te, Domine: et sic fiat sacrificium nostrum in conspectu tuo hodie, ut placeat tibi, Domine Deus.

In a humble spirit and a contrite heart may we be received by Thee, O Lord; and let our sacrifice be so made in Thy sight this day that it may please Thee, O Lord God.

Raising his eyes and stretching out his hands he says:

Veni, sanctificator, omnipotens, æterne Deus, et bene ✠ dic hoc sacrificium, tuo sancto nomini præparatum.

Come, O Sanctifier, Almighty, eternal God, and bless ✠ this sacrifice set forth to Thy holy name.

[At Solemn Mass the celebrant blesses the incense:

Per intercessionem beati Michaelis Archangeli, stantis a dextris altaris incensi, et omnium electorum suorum, incensum istud digne-tur Dominus bene ✠ dicere, et in odorem suavitatis accipere. Per Christum Dominum nostrum. *Amen.*

By the intercession of blessed Michael the archangel, standing at the right hand of the altar of incense, and of all His elect, may the Lord vouchsafe to bless ✠ this incense, and receive it as an odor of sweetness. Through Our Lord, etc. *Amen.*

He incenses the bread and wine, saying:

Incensum istud a te benedictum, as-cendat ad te, Domine: et descendat super nos misericordia tua.

May this incense which Thou hast blessed, O Lord, ascend to Thee, and may Thy mercy descend upon us.

Then he incenses the altar, saying:

Dirigatur, Domine, oratio mea, sicut incensum, in conspectu tuo: eleva-tio manuum mearum sacrificium vespertinum.
Pone, Domine, custodiam ori meo, et ostium circumstantiæ labiis meis:
Ut non declinet cor meum in verba malitiæ, ad excusandas excusationes in peccatis.

Let my prayer, O Lord, be directed as incense in Thy sight: and the lift-ing up of my hands as the evening sacrifice.
Set a watch, O Lord, before my mouth, and a door round about my lips.
That my heart may not incline to evil words, to make excuses in sins.

Giving the censer to the deacon, he says:

Accendat in nobis Dominus ignem sui amoris, et flammam æternæ carita-tis. *Amen.*

May the Lord enkindle in us the fire of His love, and the flame of everlasting charity. *Amen.*

Here the celebrant is incensed by the deacon, who next incenses the clergy present in the choir and the other ministers at the altar.]

The priest, with his hands joined, goes to the Epistle side of the altar, where he washes his fingers while he recites the following Ps 25:

Lavabo inter innocentes manus meas: et circumdabo altare tuum, Domine:	I will wash my hands among the innocent: and I will compass Thine altar, O Lord.
Ut audiam vocem laudis, et enarrem universa mirabilia tua.	That I may hear the voice of praise, and tell of all Thy wondrous works.
Domine, dilexi decorem domus tuæ, et locum habitationis gloriæ tuæ.	O Lord, I have loved the beauty of Thy house, and the place where Thy glory dwelleth.
Ne perdas cum impiis, Deus, animan meam, et cum viris sanguinum vitam meam:	Take not away my soul, O God, with the wicked, nor my life with men of blood.
In quorum manibus iniquitates sunt: dextera eorum repleta est muneribus.	In whose hands are iniquities: their right hand is filled with gifts.
Ego autem in innocentia mea ingressus sum: redime me, et miserere mei.	But as for me, I have walked in my innocence: redeem me, and be merciful unto me.
Pes meus stetit in directo: in ecclesiis benedicam te, Domine.	My foot hath stood in the right way: in the churches I will bless Thee, O Lord.
Gloria Patri, etc.	Glory be to the Father, etc.[13]

Returning, and bowing before the middle of the altar, with joined hands, he says:

[13] In Masses for the Dead, and in Passion time, the *Gloria* is omitted.

Suscipe, sancta Trinitas, hanc oblationem, quam tibi offerimus ob memoriam Passionis, Resurrectionis,
et Ascensionis Jesu Christi Domini
nostri: et in honorem beatæ
Mariæ semper Virginis, et beati
Joannis Baptistæ, et sanctorum
Apostolorum Petri et Pauli, et isto-
rum, et omnium Sanctorum: ut illis
proficiat ad honorem, nobis autem
ad salutem: et illi pro nobis intercedere dignentur in cœlis, quorum
memoriam agimus in terris. Per
eundem Christum Dominum nostrum. *Amen.*

Receive, O Holy Trinity, this oblation,
which we offer unto Thee, in memory of the Passion, Resurrection, and
Ascension of Our Lord Jesus Christ,
and in honor of Blessed Mary ever
Virgin, of blessed John the Baptist,
of the holy apostles Peter and Paul,
of these and of all Thy saints: that
it may be to their honor and to our
salvation: and may they vouchsafe
to intercede for us in heaven, whose
memory we celebrate on earth.
Through the same Christ Our Lord.
Amen.

Then he kisses the altar, and having turned himself toward the people, extending and joining his hands, he raises his voice a little, and says:

Orate, fratres: ut meum ac vestrum sacrificium acceptabile fiat apud Deum
Patrem omnipotentem.

Pray, my brethren, that my sacrifice and
yours may be acceptable to God the
Father Almighty.

The server then answers:

Suscipiat Dominus sacrificium de manibus tuis, ad laudem et gloriam nominis sui, ad utilitatem quoque nostram,
totiusque Ecclesiæ suæ sanctæ.

May the Lord receive the sacrifice from
thy hands, to the praise and glory of
His name, to our benefit, and to that
of all His holy Church.

The priest answers in a low voice, Amen.

Then, with outstretched hands, he recites the Secret Prayers.

AT THE SECRETA.

Mercifully hear our prayers, O Lord, and graciously accept this oblation which we
Thy servants make unto Thee; and as we offer it to the honor of Thy name, so may it
be to us a means of obtaining Thy grace here, and life everlasting hereafter. Through
Our Lord Jesus Christ, etc. *Amen.*

On a saint's day.
Sanctify, O Lord, we beseech Thee, these gifts which we offer Thee in this solemnity
of Thy holy servant N., and so strengthen us by Thy grace that both in prosperity

and adversity our ways may be ever directed to Thine honor. Through Our Lord Jesus Christ, etc.

Which being finished, he says in an audible voice:

Per omnia sæcula sæculorum.

℞. Amen.

℣. Dominus vobiscum.

℞. Et cum spiritu tuo.

World without end.

℞. Amen.

℣. The Lord be with you.

℞. And with thy spirit.

Here he uplifts his hands:

℣. Sursum corda.

℞. Habemus ad Dominum.

℣. Lift up your hearts.

℞. We lift them up unto the Lord.

He joins his hands before his breast and bows his head while he says:

℣. Gratias agamus Domino Deo nostro.

℟. Dignum et justum est.

℣. Let us give thanks unto the Lord our God.

℟. It is worthy and just.

He then disjoins his hands, and keeps them in this posture until the end of the Preface, *after which he again joins them, and, bowing, says,* Sanctus, *etc.*[14] *When he says* Bencdictus, *etc., he signs himself with the cross.*

The following Preface *is said on every Sunday in the year that has no special Preface of its own.*

Vere dignum et justum est, æquum et salutare, nos tibi semper et ubique gratias agere, Domine sancte, Pater omnipotens, æterne Deus. Qui cum unigenito Filio tuo, et Spiritu Sancto, unus es Deus, unus es Dominus: non in unius singularitate Personæ, sed in unius Trinitate substantiæ. Quod enim de tua gloria, revelante te, credimus, hoc de Filio tuo, hoc de Spiritu Sancto, sine differentia discretionis sentimus. Ut in confessione veræ sempiternæque Deitatis, et in Personis proprietas, et in essentia unitas, et in Majestate adoretur æqualitas. Quam laudant angeli atque archangeli, cherubim quoque ac seraphim, qui non cessant clamare quotidie, una voce dicentes:

It is truly worthy and just, right and profitable unto salvation, that we should at all times and in all places give thanks unto Thee, O holy Lord, Father Almighty, eternal God. Who, with Thine only begotten Son and the Holy Ghost, art one God, one Lord: not in the singleness of one only person, but in the Trinity of one substance. For what we believe of Thy glory, as Thou hast revealed it, that we believe of Thy Son, and that of the Holy Ghost, without any difference of inequality. That in the confession of the true and eternal Godhead, distinction in Persons, unity in essence, and equality in majesty may be adored. Whom the angels and archangels, the cherubim also and seraphim, do praise; who cease not daily to cry out, with one voice saying:

(*Here the bell is rung thrice.*)

---

[14] At High Mass the choir sings the *Sanctus* (while the priest is proceeding with the Canon) as far as the first *Hosanna in excelsis* before the Elevation; and after the Elevation, *Benedictus qui venit*, etc.

Sanctus, sanctus, sanctus, Dominus Deus Sabaoth. Pleni sunt cœli et terra gloria tua. Hosanna in excelsis. Benedictus qui venit in nomine Domini. Hosanna in excelsis.

Holy, holy, holy, Lord God of hosts. Heaven and earth are full of Thy glory. Hosanna in the highest. Blessed is He Who cometh in the name of the Lord. Hosanna in the highest.

THE CANON OF THE MASS.

The priest, first extending, then elevating and joining his hands, raising his eyes toward heaven, says in a low voice:

Te igitur, clementissime Pater, per Jesum Christum Filium tuum Dominum nostrum, supplices rog-amus ac petimus,

We, therefore, humbly pray and beseech Thee, most merciful Father, through Jesus Christ Thy Son, Our Lord,

He kisses the altar.

Uti accepta habeas et benedicas hæc ✠ dona, hæc ✠ munera, hæc ✠ sancta sacrificia illibata, in primis, quæ tibi offerimus pro Ecclesia tua sancta Catholica: quam pacificare, custo-dire, adunare, et regere digneris toto orbe terrarum, una cum famulo tuo Papa nostro N., et Antistite nostro N., et omnibus orthodoxis, atque Catholicæ et Apostolicæ Fidei cultoribus.

That Thou wouldst accept and bless these ✠ gifts, these ✠ presents, these ✠ holy unspotted sacrifices, which, in the first place, we offer Thee for Thy holy Catholic Church: which vouchsafe to pacify, guard, unite, and govern throughout the whole world, together with Thy servant N. our pope; N. our bishop; as also all orthodox believers and professors of the Catholic and apostolic Faith.

THE COMMEMORATION OF THE LIVING.

Memento, Domine, famulorum famu-larumque tuarum, N. et N.,

Remember, O Lord, Thy servants and handmaids, N. and N.,

He pauses, and, joining his hands, prays silently for those he wishes to pray for in partic-ular; and proceeds:

Et omnium circumstantium, quorum tibi fides cognita est, et nota devotio, pro quibus tibi offerimus, vel qui tibi offerunt hoc sacrificium laudis, pro se, suisque omnibus, pro redemptione animarum suarum, pro spe salutis et incolumitatis suæ: tibique reddunt vota sua æterno Deo, vivo et vero.

And all here present, whose faith and devotion are known to Thee; for whom we offer, or who offer up to Thee this sacrifice of praise for themselves and all pertaining to them, for the redemption of their souls, for the hope of their salvation and well-being, and who pay their vows unto Thee, the eternal God, living and true.

Communicantes, et memoriam venerantes, in primis gloriosæ semper Virginis Mariæ, Genitricis Dei et Domini nostri Jesu Christi: sed et beatorum Apostolorum ac Martyrum tuorum, Petri et Pauli, Andreæ, Jacobi, Joannis, Thomæ, Jacobi, Philippi, Bartholomæi, Matthæi, Simonis et Thaddæi, Lini, Cleti, Clementis, Xysti, Cornelii, Cypriani, Laurentii, Chrysogoni, Joannis et Pauli, Cosmæ et Damiani, et omnium Sanctorum tuorum; quorum meritis precibusque concedas, ut in omnibus protectionis tuæ muniamur auxilio. Per eundem Christum Dominum nostrum. *Amen.*

In communion with, and honoring the memory, especially of the glorious ever Virgin Mary, Mother of our God and Lord Jesus Christ; as also of Thy blessed apostles and martyrs, Peter and Paul, Andrew, James, John, Thomas, James, Philip, Bartholomew, Matthew, Simon and Thaddeus; Linus, Cletus, Clement, Xystus, Cornelius, Cyprian, Lawrence, Chrysogonus, John and Paul, Cosmas and Damian, and all Thy saints; by whose merits and prayers grant that we may in all things be defended by the aid of Thy protection. Through the same Christ Our Lord. *Amen.*

Spreading his hands over the oblation, he says:
(*Here the bell is rung once.*)

Hanc igitur oblationem servitutis nostræ, sed et cunctæ familiæ tuæ, quæsumus, Domine, ut placatus accipias; diesque nostros in tua pace disponas, atque ab æterna damnatione nos eripi, et in electorum tuorum jubeas grege numerari. Per Christum Dominum nostrum. *Amen.*

This oblation, therefore, of our service, and that of Thy whole family, we beseech Thee, O Lord, graciously to accept; and to dispose our days in Thy peace, and to command us to be delivered from eternal damnation, and to be numbered in the flock of Thine elect. Through Christ Our Lord. *Amen.*

Quam oblationem tu Deus, in omnibus, quæsumus, bene ✠ dictam, adscrip ✠ tam, ra ✠ tam, rationabilem, acceptabilemque facere digneris: ut nobis cor ✠ pus et san ✠ guis fiat dilectissimi Filii tui Domini nostri Jesu Christi.

Which oblation do Thou, O God, we beseech Thee, vouchsafe to make in all things blessed, ✠ approved, ✠ ratified, ✠ reasonable, and acceptable: that it may become for us the Body ✠ and Blood ✠ of Thy dearly beloved Son, Our Lord Jesus Christ.

Qui pridie quam pateretur, accepit panem in sanctas ac venerabiles manus suas, et elevatis oculis in cœlum, ad te Deum patrem suum omnipotentem: tibi gratias agens, bene ✠ dixit, fregit, deditque discipulis suis, dicens: Accipite, et manducate ex hoc omnes.

Who, the day before He suffered, took bread into His holy and venerable hands, and with eyes lifted up toward heaven, unto Thee, O God, His Almighty Father, giving thanks to Thee, did bless, ✠ break, and give unto His disciples, saying: Take, and eat ye all of this.

Holding the host with both hands, the priest pronounces the words of Consecration, secretly, distinctly, and attentively:

HOC EST ENIM CORPUS MEUM.

FOR THIS IS MY BODY.

After pronouncing the words of Consecration, the priest, kneeling upon one knee, adores the Sacred Host; then, rising, he elevates it, and replaces it upon the corporal, kneeling once again.

(At the Elevation of the Host the bell is rung three times.)

Simili modo postquam cœnatum est, accipiens et hunc præclarum calicem in sanctas ac venerabiles manus suas: item tibi gratias agens, bene ✠ dixit, deditque discipulis suis, dicens: Accipite, et bibite ex eo omnes.

In like manner, after supper, taking also this excellent chalice into His holy and venerable hands: and giving thanks to Thee, He blessed, ✠ and gave to His disciples, saying: Take, and drink ye all of it.

The priest then pronounces the words of Consecration over the chalice, holding it slightly elevated, saying:

HIC EST ENIM CALIX SANGUINIS MEI NOVI ET ÆTERNI TESTAMENTI: MYSTERIUM FIDEI; QUI PRO VOBIS ET PRO MULTIS EFFUNDETUR IN REMISSIONEM PECCATORUM.

FOR THIS IS THE CHALICE OF MY BLOOD OF THE NEW AND ETERNAL TESTAMENT: THE MYSTERY OF FAITH; WHICH SHALL BE SHED FOR YOU, AND FOR MANY, FOR THE REMISSION OF SINS.

He then replaces the chalice on the corporal, and says:

Hæc quotiescumque feceritis, in mei memoriam facietis.

As often as ye do these things, ye shall do them in remembrance of Me.

Making a genuflection, he adores; then, rising, he elevates the chalice, and, replacing it upon the corporal, makes another genuflection.

(At the Elevation of the chalice the bell is rung three times.)

He then proceeds:

Unde et memores, Domine, nos servi tui, sed et plebs tua sancta, ejusdem Christi Filii tui Domini nostri tam beatæ passionis, necnon et ab inferis resurrectionis, sed et in cœlos gloriosæ ascensionis: offerimus præclaræ Majestati tuæ, de tuis donis ac datis, Hostiam ✠ puram, Hostiam ✠ sanctam, Hostiam ✠ immaculatam, panem ✠ sanctum vitæ æternæ, et calicem ✠ salutis perpetuæ.

Wherefore, O Lord, we Thy servants, and likewise Thy holy people, calling to mind the blessed Passion of the same Christ Thy Son, Our Lord, together with His Resurrection from the grave, and also His glorious Ascension into heaven, offer unto Thy excellent Majesty, of Thy gifts and presents, a pure ✠ Victim, a holy ✠ Victim, an immaculate ✠ Victim, the holy ✠ Bread of eternal life, and the chalice ✠ of everlasting salvation.

Extending his hands, he proceeds:

Supra quæ propitio ac sereno vultu respicere digneris, et accepta habere, sicuti accepta habere dignatus es munera pueri tui justi Abel, et sacrificium Patriarchæ nostri Abrahæ; et quod tibi obtulit summus sacerdos tuus Melchisedech, sanctum sacrificium, immaculatam hostiam.

Upon which do Thou vouchsafe to look with favorable and gracious countenance, and accept them, as Thou didst vouchsafe to accept the gifts of Thy just servant Abel, and the sacrifice of our patriarch Abraham, and that which Thy high priest Melchisedech offered unto Thee, a holy Sacrifice, an unspotted Victim.

Bowing profoundly, with hands joined and placed upon the altar, he says:

Supplices te rogamus, omnipotens Deus, jube hæc perferri per manus sancti angeli tui in sublime altare tuum, in conspectu divinæ Majestatis tuæ, ut quotquot ex hac altaris participatione, sacrosanctum Filii tui cor ✠ pus et San ✠ guinem sumpserimus, omni benedictione cœlesti et gratia repleamur. Per eundem Christum Dominum nostrum. *Amen.*

We humbly beseech Thee, Almighty God, command these to be carried by the hands of Thy holy angel to Thine altar on high, in the presence of Thy divine Majesty, that as many of us as shall, by partaking at this altar, receive the most sacred Body ✠ and Blood ✠ of Thy Son, may be filled with all heavenly blessing and grace. Through the same Christ Our Lord. *Amen.*

COMMEMORATION OF THE DEAD.

Memento etiam, Domine, famulorum famularumque tuarum N. et N., qui nos præcesserunt cum signo fidei, et dormiunt in somno pacis.

Remember also, O Lord, Thy servants and handmaids, N. and N., who have gone before us with the sign of faith, and sleep the sleep of peace.

Here the priest, with hands joined, prays for such of the dead as he wishes to pray for in particular. Then, extending his hands, he continues:

Ipsis, Domine, et omnibus in Christo quiescentibus, locum refrigerii, lucis et pacis, ut indulgeas, deprecamur. Per eundem Christum Dominum nostrum. *Amen.*

To these, O Lord, and to all who rest in Christ, grant, we pray Thee, a place of refreshment, of light, and of peace. Through the same Christ Our Lord. *Amen.*

Here, striking his breast and slightly raising his voice, he says:

Nobis quoque peccatoribus famulis tuis, de multitudine miserationum tuarum sperantibus partem aliquam et societatem donare digneris, cum tuis sanctis Apostolis et Martyribus; cum Joanne, Stephano, Matthia, Barnaba, Ignatio, Alexandro, Marcellino, Petro, Felicitate, Perpetua, Agatha, Lucia, Agnete, Cæcilia, Anastasia, et omnibus Sanctis tuis: intra quorum nos consortium, non æstimator meriti, sed veniæ, quæsumus, largitor admitte. Per Christum Dominum nostrum.

To us also, Thy sinful servants, who hope in the multitude of Thy mercies, vouchsafe to grant some part and fellowship with Thy holy apostles and martyrs: with John, Stephen, Matthias, Barnabas, Ignatius, Alexander, Marcellinus, Peter, Felicitas, Perpetua, Agatha, Lucy, Agnes, Cecilia, Anastasia, and all Thy saints: into whose company, not weighing our merits, but pardoning our offenses, we beseech Thee to admit us. Through Christ Our Lord.

Per quem hæc omnia, Domine, semper bona creas, sancti ✠ ficas, vivi ✠ ficas, bene ✠ dicis, et præstas nobis.

By Whom, O Lord, Thou dost always create, sanctify, ✠ quicken, ✠ bless, ✠ and bestow upon us all these good things.

He uncovers the chalice, and makes a genuflection; then taking the Host in his right hand, and holding the chalice in his left, he makes thrice the sign of the cross over the chalice, saying:

Per ip✠sum, et cum ip✠so, et in ip✠so, est tibi Deo Patri ✠ omnipotenti, in unitate Spiritus ✠ Sancti, omnis honor et gloria.

Through Him, ✠ and with Him, ✠ and in Him, ✠ is unto Thee, God the Father ✠ Almighty, in the unity of the Holy ✠ Ghost, all honor and glory.

He here replaces the Sacred Host upon the corporal, covers the chalice, and makes a genuflection; and rising again, he says aloud:

℣. Per omnia sæcula sæculorum.
℟. Amen.

℣. World without end.
℟. Amen.

Oremus.
Præceptis salutaribus moniti, et divina institutione formati, audemus dicere:

Let us pray.
Admonished by Thy saving precepts, and following Thy divine institution, we make bold to say:

Pater noster, qui es in cœlis, sanctificetur nomen tuum: adveniat regnum tuum: fiat voluntas tua sicut in cœlo, et in terra. Panem nostrum quotidianum da nobis hodie: et dimitte nobis debita nostra, sicut et nos dimittimus debitoribus nostris. Et ne nos inducas in tentationem.
M. Sed libera nos a malo.
S. Amen.

Our Father, Who art in heaven, hallowed be Thy name: Thy kingdom come: Thy will be done on earth as it is in heaven. Give us this day our daily bread: and forgive us our trespasses as we forgive those who trespass against us. And lead us not into temptation.
℟. But deliver us from evil.
P. Amen.

[At Solemn Mass, the deacon, toward the conclusion of the Pater noster, *goes to the right hand of the priest, where he awaits the approach of the subdeacon, from whom he receives the paten, which he puts into the hands of the priest.]*

He takes the paten between his first and second finger, and says:

Libera nos, quæsumus, Domine, ab omnibus malis, præteritis, præsentibus, et futuris: et intercedente beata et gloriosa semper Virgine Dei Genitrice Maria, cum beatis Apostolis tuis Petro et Paulo, atque Andrea, et omnibus Sanctis,

Deliver us, we beseech Thee, O Lord, from all evils, past, present, and to come: and by the intercession of blessed and glorious Mary ever Virgin, Mother of God, together with Thy blessed apostles Peter and Paul, and Andrew, and all the saints,

Making the sign of the cross on himself with the paten, he kisses it, and says:

Da propitius pacem in diebus nostris: ut ope misericordiæ tuæ adjuti, et a peccato simus semper liberi, et ab omni perturbatione securi.

Graciously give peace in our days: that, aided by the help of Thy mercy, we may be always free from sin, and secure from all disturbance.

He then uncovers the chalice, makes a genuflection, and, rising again, takes the Sacred Host and breaks it in the middle, over the chalice, saying:

Per eundem Dominum nostrum Jesum Christum Filium tuum,

Through the same Our Lord Jesus Christ, Thy Son,

He then places the part of the Host which he has in his right hand on the paten. Then, breaking off a particle of that which remains in his left hand, he says:

Qui tecum vivit et regnat in unitate Spiritus Sancti Deus,

Who liveth and reigneth with Thee in the unity of the Holy Ghost, God,

Then placing on the paten what remains in his left hand of the Sacred Host, and holding in his right hand, over the chalice, the particle which he had broken off, he says aloud:

℣. Per omnia sæcula sæculorum.
℟. Amen.

℣. World without end.
℟. Amen.

He then with the same particle of the Sacred Host makes the sign of the cross over the chalice, saying:

℣. Pax ✠ Domini sit ✠ semper vobis ✠ cum.
℟. Et cum spiritu tuo.

℣. May the peace ✠ of the Lord be ✠ always with ✠ you.
℟. And with thy spirit.

He then puts the particle in the chalice, saying in a low voice:

Hæc commixtio et consecratio corporis et sanguinis Domini nostri Jesu Christi fiat accipientibus nobis in vitam æternam. *Amen.*

May this mingling and consecration of the Body and Blood of Our Lord Jesus Christ be unto us that receive it effectual unto life everlasting. *Amen.*

He covers the chalice, makes a genuflection, and, bowing down and striking his breast three times, says:[15]

---

[15]   The choir sings the *Agnus Dei*, which generally continues during the priest's Communion and the ablutions.

Agnus Dei, qui tollis peccata mundi, miserere nobis.

Lamb of God, Who takest away the sins of the world, have mercy on us.

Agnus Dei, qui tollis peccata mundi, miserere nobis.

Lamb of God, Who takest away the sins of the world, have mercy on us.

Agnus Dei, qui tollis peccata mundi, dona nobis pacem.

Lamb of God, Who takest away the sins of the world, grant us Thy peace.

[*In Masses for the Dead he says twice,* Grant them rest; *and lastly,* Grant them eternal rest.]

Then inclining toward the altar, with hands joined upon it, the priest says the following prayers:

Domine Jesu Christe, qui dixisti Apostolis tuis, Pacem relinquo vobis, pacem meam do vobis: ne respicias peccata mea, sed fidem Ecclesiæ tuæ; eamque secundum voluntatem tuam pacificare et coadunare digneris: qui vivis et regnas Deus, per omnia sæcula sæculorum. *Amen.*

O Lord Jesus Christ, Who saidst to Thine apostles, Peace I leave you, My peace I give you: look not upon my sins, but upon the faith of Thy Church; and vouchsafe to it that peace and unity which is agreeable to Thy will: Who livest and reignest God world without end. *Amen.*

(*The preceding prayer is omitted in Masses for the Dead.*)

[*At Solemn Mass the deacon kisses the altar at the same time with the celebrating priest, by whom he is saluted with the* kiss of peace *with these words:*

℣. Pax tecum.

℣. Peace be with thee.

To which the deacon answers:

℟. Et cum spiritu tuo.

℟. And with thy spirit.

And then salutes in like manner the subdeacon, who in turn salutes the clergy who may be present.]

Domine Jesu Christe, Fili Dei vivi, qui ex voluntate Patris, cooperante Spiritu Sancto, per mortem tuam mundum vivificasti: libera me per hoc sacrosanctum corpus et sanguinem tuum ab omnibus iniquitatibus meis, et universis malis: et fac me tuis semper inhærere mandatis, et a te nunquam separari permittas. Qui cum eodem Deo Patre et Spiritu Sancto vivis et regnas Deus in sæcula sæculorum. *Amen.*

O Lord Jesus Christ, Son of the living God, Who, by the will of the Father and the cooperation of the Holy Ghost, hast by Thy death given life to the world: deliver me by this Thy most sacred Body and Blood from all my iniquities and from all evils; and make me always adhere to Thy commandments, and suffer me never to be separated from Thee. Who with the same God the Father and the Holy Ghost livest and reignest God world without end. *Amen.*

Perceptio corporis tui, Domine Jesu Christe, quod ego indignus sumere præsumo, non mihi proveniat in judicium et condemnationem; sed pro tua pietate prosit mihi ad tutamentum mentis et corporis, et ad medelam percipiendam. Qui vivis et regnas cum Deo Patre, in unitate Spiritus Sancti, Deus per omnia sæcula sæculorum. *Amen.*

Let not the partaking of Thy Body, O Lord Jesus Christ, which I, though unworthy, presume to receive, turn to my judgment and condemnation; but by Thy mercy be it profitable to the safety and health both of soul and body. Who with God the Father, in the unity of the Holy Ghost, livest and reignest God world without end. *Amen.*

Making a genuflection, and taking the Host in his hands, the priest says:

Panem cœlestem accipiam, et nomen Domini invocabo.

I will take the Bread of heaven, and will call upon the name of the Lord.

The priest then, slightly inclining, takes both parts of the Sacred Host, and, striking his breast and raising his voice a little, he says three times, humbly and with devotion: (Here the bell is rung thrice.)

Domine, non sum dignus ut intres sub tectum meum; sed tantum dic verbo, et sanabitur anima mea.

Lord, I am not worthy that Thou shouldst enter under my roof; but only say the word, and my soul shall be healed.

He then makes the sign of the cross on himself with the Sacred Host, holding it in his right hand over the paten, saying:

Corpus Domini nostri Jesu Christi custodiat animam meam in vitam æternam. *Amen.*

The Body of Our Lord Jesus Christ preserve my soul unto life everlasting. *Amen.*

He then reverently takes both parts of the Host, joins his hands, and remains a short time in meditation on the most Holy Sacrament. Then he uncovers the chalice, makes a genuflection, collects whatever fragments may remain, and wipes the paten over the chalice, saying meanwhile:

Quid retribuam Domino pro omnibus quæ retribuit mihi? Calicem salutaris accipiam, et nomen Domini invocabo. Laudans invocabo Dominum, et ab inimicis meis salvus ero.

What shall I render unto the Lord for all the things that He hath rendered unto me? I will take the chalice of salvation, and call upon the name of the Lord. I will call upon the Lord and give praise: and I shall be saved from mine enemies.

He takes the chalice in his right hand, and, making the sign of the cross with it on himself, he says:

Sanguis Domini nostri Jesu Christi custodiat animam meam in vitam æternam. *Amen.*

The Blood of Our Lord Jesus Christ preserve my soul unto life everlasting. *Amen.*

He then reverently takes the Precious Blood. After which he gives Communion to all who are to communicate.

Those who are to communicate go up to the sanctuary at the Domine, non sum dignus, *when the bell rings. The acolyte spreads a cloth before them, and says the* Confiteor.

During the Confiteor *the priest removes from the tabernacle of the altar the ciborium, or vessel containing the Blessed Sacrament; and placing it upon the corporal, he makes a genuflection, and, turning to the communicants, pronounces the Absolution:*

Misereatur vestri omnipotens Deus, et dimissis peccatis vestris, perducat vos ad vitam æternam.
℞. Amen.

May Almighty God have mercy upon you, and forgive you your sins, and bring you unto life everlasting.
℞. Amen.

Signing them with the sign of the cross, he continues:

Indulgentiam, ✠ absolutionem, et remissionem peccatorum vestrorum
tribuat vobis omnipotens et misericors Dominus.

℞. Amen.

May the Almighty and merciful Lord
grant you pardon, ✠ absolution,
and remission of your sins.

℞. Amen.

Elevating a particle of the Blessed Sacrament, and turning toward the people, he says:

Ecce Agnus Dei, ecce qui tollit peccata
mundi.

Behold the Lamb of God, behold Him
Who taketh away the sins of the
world.

And then says three times:

Domine, non sum dignus ut intres
sub tectum meum; sed tantum dic
verbo, et sanabitur anima mea.

Lord, I am not worthy that Thou
shouldst enter under my roof; but
only say the word, and my soul
shall be healed.

Descending the steps of the altar to the communicants, he administers the Holy Communion, saying to each:

Corpus Domini nostri Jesu Christi
custodiat animam tuam in vitam
æternam. *Amen.*

The Body of Our Lord Jesus Christ
preserve thy soul unto life everlasting. *Amen.*

The priest then, returning to the altar, replaces the ciborium in the tabernacle, makes a genuflection, and closes the door. Then the acolyte pours a little wine into the chalice and the priest takes the first ablution, saying:

Quod ore sumpsimus, Domine, pura
mente capiamus; et de munere
temporali fiat nobis remedium
sempiternum.

What we have taken with our mouth,
O Lord, may we receive with a
pure heart; and of a temporal gift
may it become to us an everlasting
healing.

Here the acolyte, at the Epistle corner, pours wine and water over the priest's fingers, and the priest, returning to the middle of the altar, wipes his fingers and takes the second ablution, saying:

Corpus tuum, Domine, quod sumpsi, et sanguis quem potavi, adhæreat visceribus meis: et præsta; ut in me non remaneat scelerum macula, quem pura et sancta refecerunt sacramenta. Qui vivis et regnas in sæcula sæculorum. *Amen.*

May Thy Body, O Lord, which I have received, and Thy Blood which I have drunk, cleave unto my inmost parts; and grant that no stain of sin may remain in me, who have been refreshed with pure and holy mysteries. Who livest and reignest, etc. *Amen.*

Then he wipes his lips and the chalice, which he covers, and, having folded the corporal, places on the altar, as at first; he goes to the book, and reads the Communion.

[*At Solemn Mass the choir sings the* Communion. *The subdeacon removes the chalice to the credence table.*]

FOR THE COMMUNION.

One thing I have asked of the Lord, this will I seek after: that I may dwell in the house of the Lord all the days of my life.

O taste and see that the Lord is sweet: blessed is the man that hopeth in Him.

(*On a saint's day.*)
Happy are those servants whom the Lord when He cometh shall find watching.

If any man will come after Me, let him deny himself, and take up his cross, and follow Me.

Then, going to the middle of the altar, he turns to the people, and says:

℣. Dominus vobiscum.

℞. Et cum spiritu tuo.

℣. The Lord be with you.

℞. And with thy spirit.

Then, returning to the missal, he reads the Postcommunions; *at the end of the first and last of which the acolyte answers,* Amen.

FOR THE POSTCOMMUNIONS.

Pour forth upon us, O Lord, the spirit of Thy love, that, by Thy mercy, Thou mayst make those of one mind whom Thou hast fed with one celestial Food. Through Our Lord Jesus Christ, etc. *Amen.*

Graciously hear the prayers of Thy family, O Almighty God; and grant that these sacred mysteries which we have received from Thee may by Thy grace be preserved incorrupt within us.

(*On a saint's day.*)

We have received the heavenly mysteries, O Lord, in the commemoration of the Blessed Mary ever Virgin, of blessed Joseph, of blessed N. [*here insert the name of your patron saint*], and of all Thy saints; grant, we beseech Thee, that what we celebrate in time we may obtain in the joys of eternity. Through Our Lord, etc. *Amen.*

Afterward he turns again toward the people, and says:

℣. Dominus vobiscum.
℟. Et cum spiritu tuo.
℣. Ite, missa est;
℟. Deo gratias.

℣. The Lord be with you.
℟. And with thy spirit.
℣. Go, the Mass is ended;
℟. Thanks be to God.

Or, when the Gloria in excelsis *has been omitted, he turns to the altar and says:*

℣. Benedicamus Domino.
℟. Deo gratias.

℣. Let us bless the Lord.
℟. Thanks be to God.

In Masses for the Dead:

℣. Requiescant in pace.
℟. Amen.

℣. May they rest in peace.
℟. Amen.

[*At Solemn Mass,* Ite, missa est, *or* Benedicamus Domino *is chanted by the deacon.*]

Bowing before the altar, the priest says:

Placeat tibi, sancta Trinitas, obsequium servitutis meæ; et præsta, ut sacrificium quod oculis tuæ Majestatis indignus obtuli, tibi sit acceptabile, mihique, et omnibus pro quibus illud obtuli, sit, te miserante, propitiabile. Per Christum Dominum nostrum. *Amen.*

May the performance of my homage be pleasing to Thee, O Holy Trinity; and grant that the sacrifice which I, though unworthy, have offered up in the sight of Thy Majesty, may be acceptable unto Thee, and may, through Thy mercy, be a propitiation for myself, and all those for whom I have offered it. Through Christ Our Lord. *Amen.*

Then he kisses the altar, and raising his eyes, and extending, raising, and joining his hands, he bows his head, and says:

Benedicat vos omnipotens Deus, Pater, et Filius, ✚ et Spiritus Sanctus.
℟. Amen.

May Almighty God bless you; the Father, and the Son, ✚ and the Holy Ghost.
℟. Amen.

At the word Deus *he turns toward the people, and makes the sign of the cross over them.* [*The* Benediction *is omitted in Masses for the Dead.*] *Then, turning to the Gospel side of the altar, he says:*

℣. Dominus vobiscum.

℟. Et cum spiritu tuo.

℣. The Lord be with you.

℟. And with thy spirit.

He then makes the sign of the cross, first upon the altar, then upon his forehead, lips, and breast, begins the Gospel according to St. John, saying:

Initium sancti Evangelii secundum Joannem.

M. Gloria tibi, Domine.

The beginning of the holy Gospel according to John.

℟. Glory be to Thee, O Lord.

In principio erat Verbum, et Verbum erat apud Deum; et Deus erat Verbum: hoc erat in principio apud Deum. Omnia per ipsum facta sunt, et sine ipso factum est nihil quod factum est: in ipso vita erat, et vita erat lux hominum; et lux in tenebris lucet, et tenebræ eam non comprehenderunt.

In the beginning was the Word, and the Word was with God, and the Word was God. This was in the beginning with God. All things were made through Him, and without Him was made nothing that was made: in Him was life, and the life was the light of men: and the light shineth in darkness, and the darkness did not comprehend it.

Fuit homo missus a Deo, cui nomen erat Joannes. Hic venit in testimonium, ut testimonium perhiberet de lumine, ut omnes crederent per illum. Non erat ille lux: sed ut testimonium perhiberet de lumine. Erat lux vera quæ illuminat omnem hominem venientem in hunc mundum.

There was a man sent from God, whose name was John. This one came for a witness, to testify concerning the light, that all might believe through him. He was not the light, but he was to testify concerning the light. The true Light, which enlighteneth every man, cometh into this world.

In mundo erat, et mundus per ipsum factus est, et mundus eum non cognovit. In propria venit, et sui eum non receperunt. Quotquot autem receperunt eum, dedit eis potestatem filios Dei fieri: his qui credunt in nomine ejus, qui non ex sanguinibus, neque ex voluntate carnis, neque ex voluntate viri, sed ex Deo nati sunt. ET VERBUM CARO FACTUM EST [*Hic genuflectitur*], et habitavit in nobis; et vidimus gloriam ejus, gloriam quasi Unigeniti a Patre, plenum gratiæ et veritatis.

M. Deo gratias.

He was in the world, and the world was made through Him, and the world knew Him not. He came to His own possessions, and His own people received Him not. But to as many as received Him He gave power to become children of God, to those who believe in His name, who are born not of blood, nor of the will of the flesh, nor of the will of man, but of God. AND THE WORD WAS MADE FLESH [*Here all kneel*], and dwelt among us; and we saw His glory, the glory as of the only begotten of the Father, full of grace and truth.

℞. Thanks be to God.

When a feast falls on a Sunday, or other day which has a proper Gospel of its own, the Gospel of the day is read instead of the Gospel of St. John.

‡*Proper Prefaces,* Communicantes, *and* Hanc Igitur

1. *From Christmas Day till the Epiphany (except in the Octave of St. John), on the Purification, Corpus Christi and its octave, the Transfiguration, the Holy Name of Jesus, and in Masses of the Blessed Sacrament.*

Vere dignum et justum est, æquum et salutare, nos tibi semper et ubique gratias agere Domine sancte, Pater omnipotens, æterne Deus. Quia per incarnati Verbi mysterium, nova mentis nostræ oculis lux tuæ claritatis infulsit: ut dum visibiliter Deum cognoscimus, per hunc in invisibilium amorem rapiamur. Et ideo cum angelis et archangelis, cum thronis et dominationibus, cumque omni militia cœlestis exercitus, hymnum gloriæ tuæ canimus, sine fine dicentes: Sanctus, etc. (*p. 102*).

It is truly worthy and just, right and profitable unto salvation, that we should at all times and in all places give thanks unto Thee, O holy Lord, Father Almighty, eternal God. Because, by the mystery of the Word made flesh, a new ray of Thy glory has shone upon the eyes of our minds: that while we know our God visibly, we may by Him be drawn to the love of things invisible. And therefore, with angels and archangels, with thrones and dominations, and with the whole army of heavenly hosts, we sing a hymn to Thy glory, saying unceasingly: Holy, etc. (*p. 102*).

Besides, on Christmas Day and during its octave, the following Communicantes *is said (at Midnight Mass alone is said instead,* noctem sacratissimam celebrantes, qua *[celebrating the most sacred night on which]):*

Communicantes, et (noctem sacratissimam celebrantes, qua, *vel*) diem sacratissimum celebrantes, quo beatæ Mariæ intemerata virginitas huic mundo edidit Salvatorem: sed et memoriam venerantes, in primis ejusdem gloriosæ semper Virginis Mariæ, Genitricis ejusdem Dei, et Domini nostri Jesu Christi: sed et beatorum Apostolorum ac Martyrum tuorum, Petri et Pauli, Andreæ, Jacobi, Joannis, Thomæ, Jacobi, Philippi, Bartholomæi,

In communion with, and (celebrating the most sacred night on which, *or*) celebrating that most sacred day in which the undefiled virginity of Blessed Mary brought forth the Savior into this world; and honoring the memory especially of the same glorious ever Virgin Mary, Mother of the same our God and Lord Jesus Christ; as also of Thy blessed apostles and martyrs, Peter and Paul, Andrew, James, John, Thomas, James, Philip, Bartholomew,

Matthæi, Simonis et Thaddæi, Lini, Cleti, Clementis, Xysti, Cornelii, Cypriani, Laurentii, Chrysogoni, Joannis et Pauli, Cosmæ et Damiani, et omnium Sanctorum tuorum; quorum meritis precibusque concedas, ut in omnibus protectionis tuæ muniamur auxilio. Per eundem Christum Dominum nostrum. *Amen. (p. 103)*.

Matthew, Simon and Thaddeus; Linus, Cletus, Clement, Xystus, Cornelius, Cyprian, Lawrence, Chrysogonus, John and Paul, Cosmas and Damian, and all Thy saints; by whose merits and prayers grant that we may in all things be defended by the aid of Thy protection. Through the same Christ Our Lord. *Amen.*etc., *(p. 103)*.

2. *On the Epiphany and during its octave.*

Vere dignum et justum est, æquum et salutare, nos tibi semper et ubique gratias agere Domine sancte, Pater omnipotens, æterne Deus. Quia, cum Unigenitus tuus in substantia nostræ mortalitatis apparuit, nova nos immortalitatis suæ luce reparavit. Et ideo cum angelis et archangelis, cum thronis et dominationibus, cumque omni militia cœlestis exercitus, hymnum gloriæ tuæ canimus, sine fine dicentes: Sanctus, etc. *(p. 102)*.

It is truly worthy and just, right and profitable unto salvation, that we should at all times and in all places give thanks unto Thee, O holy Lord, Father Almighty, eternal God. Because when Thy only begotten Son appeared in the substance of our mortality, He reestablished us by the new light of His immortality. And therefore, with angels and archangels, with thrones and dominations, and with the whole army of heavenly hosts, we sing a hymn to Thy glory, saying unceasingly: Holy, etc. *(p. 102)*.

Communicantes, et diem sacratissimum celebrantes, quo Unigenitus tuus in tua tecum gloria coæternus, in veritate carnis nostræ visibiliter corporalis apparuit: sed et memoriam venerantes, in primis gloriosæ semper Virginis Mariæ, Genitrices ejusdem Dei et Domini nostri Jesu Christi: sed et beatorum Apostolorum ac Martyrum tuorum, Petri et Pauli, Andreæ, Jacobi, Joannis, Thomæ, Jacobi, Philippi, Bartholomæi,

In communion with, and celebrating that most sacred day on which Thy only begotten Son, coeternal with Thee in Thy glory, appeared visibly as man in the reality of our own flesh; and honoring the memory, in the first place of the glorious Mary ever Virgin, Mother of the same our God and Lord Jesus Christ; as also of Thy blessed apostles and martyrs, Peter and Paul, Andrew, James, John, Thomas, James, Philip, Bartholomew,

Matthæi, Simonis et Thaddæi, Lini, Cleti, Clementis, Xysti, Cornelii, Cypriani, Laurentii, Chrysogoni, Joannis et Pauli, Cosmæ et Damiani, et omnium Sanctorum tuorum; quorum meritis precibusque concedas, ut in omnibus protectionis tuæ muniamur auxilio. Per eundem Christum Dominum nostrum. *Amen.*

Matthew, Simon and Thaddeus; Linus, Cletus, Clement, Xystus, Cornelius, Cyprian, Lawrence, Chrysogonus, John and Paul, Cosmas and Damian, and all Thy saints; by whose merits and prayers grant that we may in all things be defended by the aid of Thy protection. Through the same Christ Our Lord. *Amen.*

3. *From Ash Wednesday to Passion Sunday exclusively, except in feasts which have a proper preface.*

Vere dignum et justum est, æquum et salutare, nos tibi semper et ubique gratias agere Domine sancte, Pater omnipotens, æterne Deus. Qui corporali jejunio vitia comprimis, mentem elevas, virtutem largiris et præmia: per Christum Dominum nostrum. Per quem Majestatem tuam laudant angeli, adorant dominationes, tremunt potestates. Cœli cœlorumque virtutes, ac beata seraphim, socia exultatione concelebrant. Cum quibus et nostras voces, ut admitti jubeas, deprecamur, supplici confessione dicentes: Sanctus, etc. (*p. 102*).

It is truly worthy and just, right and profitable unto salvation, that we should at all times and in all places give thanks unto Thee, O holy Lord, Father Almighty, eternal God. Who, by a bodily fast restraineth vices, upliftest our minds, and grantest strength and rewards: through Christ Our Lord. Through Whom the angels praise, the dominations adore, and the powers fear Thy Majesty: the heavens also and the heavenly forces, and the blessed seraphim glorify it in common exultation. With whom, we beseech Thee, bid that our voices also be admitted in suppliant praise, saying, Holy, etc. (*p. 102*).

4. *From Passion Sunday to Maundy Thursday; at all the Masses of the Holy Cross, the Passion of Our Lord, and His most Precious Blood.*

Vere dignum et justum est, æquum et salutare, nos tibi semper et ubique gratias agere Domine sancte, Pater omnipotens, æterne Deus. Qui salutem humani generis in ligno Crucis constituisti: ut unde mors oriebatur, inde vita resurgeret: et qui in ligno vincebat, in ligno quoque vinceretur: per Christum Dominum nostrum. Per quem Majestatem tuam laudant angeli, adorant dominationes, tremunt potestates. Cœli cœlorumque virtutes, ac beata seraphim, socia exultatione concelebrant. Cum quibus et nostras voces, ut admitti jubeas, deprecamur, supplici confessione dicentes: Sanctus, etc. (*p. 102*).

It is truly worthy and just, right and profitable unto salvation, that we should at all times and in all places give thanks unto Thee, O holy Lord, Father Almighty, eternal God. Who didst establish the salvation of mankind in the wood of the Cross: that life should thence arise whence death had come: and that he who had overcome in the tree, should in the tree also be overcome, by Christ Our Lord. Through Whom the angels praise, the dominations adore, and the powers fear Thy Majesty: the heavens also and the heavenly forces, and the blessed seraphim glorify it in common exultation. With whom, we beseech Thee, bid that our voices also be admitted in suppliant praise, saying, Holy, etc. (*p. 102*).

5. *From Holy Saturday till Ascension Day, and on festivals occurring in this time, unless they have proper prefaces of their own. In the Mass of Holy Saturday is said,* in hac potissimum nocte *(more especially on this night); on Easter Day, until the Saturday following,* in hac potissimum die *(more especially on this day); after that,* in hoc potissimum *(more especially now).*

Vere dignum et justum est, æquum et salutare: Te quidem, Domine, omni tempore, sed (in hac potissimum nocte *vel* die, *vel*) in hoc potissimum gloriosius prædicare, cum Pascha nostrum immolatus est Christus. Ipse enim verus est Agnus, qui abstulit peccata mundi. Qui mortem nostram moriendo destruxit, et vitam resurgendo reparavit.

It is truly worthy and just, right and profitable unto salvation, at all times indeed to glorify Thee, O Lord, but more especially (on this night, *or* on this day, *or*) now, when Christ our Passover is sacrificed. For He is the true Lamb that took away the sins of the world. Who dying destroyed our death, and rising again restored us unto life.

Et ideo cum angelis et archangelis, cum thronis et dominationibus, cumque omni militia cœlestis exercitus, hymnum gloriæ tuæ canimus, sine fine dicentes: Sanctus, etc. (*p. 102*).

And therefore, with angels and archangels, with thrones and dominations, and with the whole army of heavenly hosts, we sing a hymn to Thy glory, saying unceasingly: Holy, etc. (*p. 102*).

Besides, from Holy Saturday to the following Saturday, inclusive, the following Communicantes *and* Hanc igitur *are said (but in the Mass of Holy Saturday is said* noctem sacratissimam [the most sacred night]).

Communicantes et (noctem sacratissimam, *vel*) diem sacratissimum celebrantes Resurrectionis Domini nostri Jesu Christi secundum carnem: sed et memoriam venerantes, in primis gloriosæ semper Virginis Mariæ, Genitrices ejusdem Dei et Domini nostri Jesu Christi: sed et beatorum Apostolorum ac Martyrum tuorum, Petri et Pauli, Andreæ, Jacobi, Joannis, Thomæ, Jacobi, Philippi, Bartholomæi, Matthæi, Simonis et Thaddæi, Lini, Cleti, Clementis, Xysti, Cornelii, Cypriani, Laurentii, Chrysogoni, Joannis et Pauli, Cosmæ et Damiani, et omnium Sanctorum tuorum; quorum meritis precibusque concedas, ut in omnibus protectionis tuæ muniamur auxilio. Per eundem Christum Dominum nostrum. *Amen.*

In communion with, and celebrating the most sacred (night, *or*) day of the Resurrection of Our Lord Jesus Christ according to the flesh: and honoring the memory, in the first place of the glorious Mary ever Virgin, Mother of the same our God and Lord Jesus Christ; as also of Thy blessed apostles and martyrs, Peter and Paul, Andrew, James, John, Thomas, James, Philip, Bartholomew, Matthew, Simon and Thaddeus; Linus, Cletus, Clement, Xystus, Cornelius, Cyprian, Lawrence, Chrysogonus, John and Paul, Cosmas and Damian, and all Thy saints; by whose merits and prayers grant that we may in all things be defended by the aid of Thy protection. Through the same Christ Our Lord. *Amen.*

Hanc igitur oblationem servitutis nostræ, sed et cunctæ familiæ tuæ, quam tibi offerimus pro his quoque, quos regenerare dignatus es ex aqua et Spiritu Sancto, tribuens eis remissionem omnium peccatorum, quæsumus, Domine, ut placatus accipias; diesque nostros in tua pace disponas, atque ab æterna damnatione nos eripi, et in electorum tuorum jubeas grege numerari. Per Christum Dominum nostrum. *Amen.*

This oblation, therefore, of our service, and that of Thy whole family, which we offer unto Thee for these also, whom Thou hast vouchsafed to regenerate by water, and the Holy Ghost, granting them the remission of all their sins, we beseech Thee, O Lord, graciously to accept; and to dispose our days in Thy peace, and to command us to be delivered from eternal damnation, and to be numbered in the flock of Thine elect. Through Christ Our Lord. *Amen.*

6. *From Ascension Day to Whitsunday Eve, exclusively, except on feasts which have their proper prefaces.*

Vere dignum et justum est, æquum et salutare, nos tibi semper et ubique gratias agere Domine sancte, Pater omnipotens, æterne Deus. Per Christum Dominum nostrum. Qui post resurrectionem suam omnibus discipulis suis manifestus apparuit, et ipsis cernentibus est elevatus in cælum, ut nos divinitatis suæ tribueret esse participes. Et ideo cum angelis et archangelis, cum thronis et dominationibus, cumque omni militia cœlestis exercitus, hymnum gloriæ tuæ canimus, sine fine dicentes: Sanctus, etc. (*p. 102*).

It is truly worthy and just, right and profitable unto salvation, that we should at all times and in all places give thanks unto Thee, O holy Lord, Father Almighty, eternal God. Through Christ Our Lord: Who after His Resurrection appeared openly to all His disciples, and whilst they looked on, was taken up into heaven, that He might grant us the fellowship of His Godhead. And therefore, with angels and archangels, with thrones and dominations, and with the whole army of heavenly hosts, we sing a hymn to Thy glory, saying unceasingly: Holy, etc. (*p. 102*).

Communicantes, et diem sacratissimum celebrantes, quo Dominus
noster, unigenitus Filius tuus, uni-
tam sibi fragilitatis nostræ substan-
tiam, in gloriæ tuæ dextera collo-
cavit: sed et memoriam venerantes,
in primis gloriosæ semper Virginis
Mariæ, Genitrices ejusdem Dei et
Domini nostri Jesu Christi:

In communion with, and celebrating
that most sacred day on which Our
Lord, Thy only begotten Son, did
place on the right hand of Thy glory,
that substance of our frailty which
He had united to Himself, and honoring the memory, in the first place
of the glorious Mary ever Virgin,
Mother of the same our God and
Lord Jesus Christ;

sed et beatorum Apostolorum ac
Martyrum tuorum, Petri et Pauli,
Andreæ, Jacobi, Joannis, Thomæ,
Jacobi, Philippi, Bartholomæi,
Matthæi, Simonis et Thaddæi, Lini,
Cleti, Clementis, Xysti, Cornelii,
Cypriani, Laurentii, Chrysogoni,
Joannis et Pauli, Cosmæ et
Damiani, et omnium Sanctorum
tuorum; quorum meritis preci-
busque concedas, ut in omnibus
protectionis tuæ muniamur auxilio.
Per eundem Christum Dominum
nostrum. *Amen.*

as also of Thy blessed apostles and
martyrs, Peter and Paul, Andrew,
James, John, Thomas, James, Philip,
Bartholomew, Matthew, Simon and
Thaddeus; Linus, Cletus, Clement,
Xystus, Cornelius, Cyprian,
Lawrence, Chrysogonus, John and
Paul, Cosmas and Damian, and all
Thy saints; by whose merits and
prayers grant that we may in all
things be defended by the aid of Thy
protection. Through the same Christ
Our Lord. *Amen.*

7. *From Whitsunday Eve to the following Saturday; and in Masses of the Holy Ghost, omitting the words,* hodierna die (this day).

Vere dignum et justum est, æquum et salutare, nos tibi semper et ubique gratias agere Domine sancte, Pater omnipotens, æterne Deus. Per Christum Dominum nostrum. Qui ascendens super omnes cœlos, sed-ensque ad dexteram tuam, promis-sum Spiritum Sanctum (hodierna die) in filios adoptionis effudit. Quapropter profusis gaudiis, totus in orbe terrarum mundus exultat. Sed et supernæ virtutes, atque angelicæ potestates, hymnum riæ tuæ concinunt, sine fine dicentes: Sanctus, etc., (*p. 102*).

It is truly worthy and just, right and profitable unto salvation, that we should at all times and in all places give thanks unto Thee, O holy Lord, Father Almighty, eternal God. Through Christ Our Lord: Who, ascending above all the heavens and sitting at Thy right hand, (this day) poured forth the promised Holy Ghost upon the children of adop-tion. Wherefore the whole world exults with exceeding joy. But the heavenly forces also, and the angelic powers, sound forth the hymn of Thy glory: saying without end: Holy, etc., (*p. 102*).

Besides, from Whitsunday Eve to the following Saturday, inclusive, the following Communicantes *and* Hanc igitur *are said.*

Communicantes, et diem sacratissimum Pentecostes celebrantes, quo Spiritus Sanctus Apostolis innumeris linguis apparuit: sed et memoriam venerantes, in primis gloriosæ semper Virginis Mariæ, Genitrices ejusdem Dei et Domini nostri Jesu Christi: sed et beatorum Apostolorum ac Martyrum tuorum, Petri et Pauli, Andreæ, Jacobi, Joannis, Thomæ, Jacobi, Philippi, Bartholomæi, Matthæi, Simonis et Thaddæi, Lini, Cleti, Clementis, Xysti, Cornelii, Cypriani, Laurentii, Chrysogoni, Joannis et Pauli, Cosmæ et Damiani, et omnium Sanctorum tuorum; quorum meritis precibusque concedas, ut in omnibus protectionis tuæ muniamur auxilio. Per eundem Christum Dominum nostrum. *Amen.*

In communion with, and celebrating that most sacred day of Pentecost, on which the Holy Ghost appeared to the apostles in numberless tongues; and honoring the memory, in the first place of the glorious Mary ever Virgin, Mother of the same our God and Lord Jesus Christ; as also of Thy blessed apostles and martyrs, Peter and Paul, Andrew, James, John, Thomas, James, Philip, Bartholomew, Matthew, Simon and Thaddeus; Linus, Cletus, Clement, Xystus, Cornelius, Cyprian, Lawrence, Chrysogonus, John and Paul, Cosmas and Damian, and all Thy saints; by whose merits and prayers grant that we may in all things be defended by the aid of Thy protection. Through the same Christ Our Lord. *Amen.*

Hanc igitur oblationem servitutis nostræ, sed et cunctæ familiæ tuæ, quam tibi offerimus pro his quoque, quos regenerare dignatus es ex aqua, et Spiritu Sancto, tribuens eis remissionem omnium peccatorum, quæsumus, Domine, ut placatus accipias; diesque nostros in tua pace disponas, atque ab æterna damnatione nos eripi, et in electorum tuorum jubeas grege numerari. Per Christum Dominum nostrum. *Amen.*

This oblation, therefore, of our service and of Thy whole family, which we offer unto Thee for these also, whom Thou hast vouchsafed to regenerate by water, and the Holy Ghost, granting them remission of all their sins, we beseech Thee, O Lord, graciously to accept; and to dispose our days in Thy peace, and to command us to be delivered from eternal damnation, and to be numbered in the flock of Thine elect. Through Christ Our Lord. *Amen.*

8. *At the Masses of Our Lord Jesus Christ, King.*

Vere dignum et justum est, æquum et salutare, nos tibi semper et ubique gratias agere Domine sancte, Pater omnipotens, æterne Deus. Qui unigenitum Filium tuum Dominum nostrum Jesum Christum. Sacerdotem æternum et universorum Regem, oleo exultationis unxisti: ut seipsum in ara crucis, hostiam immaculatam et pacificam offerens, redemptionis humanæ sacramenta perageret: et suo subjectis imperio omnibus creaturis, æternum et universale regnum, immensæ tuæ traderet Majestati: regnum veritatis et vitæ; regnum sanctitatis et gratiæ; regnum justitiæ, amoris, et pacis. Et ideo cum angelis et archangelis, cum thronis et dominationibus, cumque omni militia cœlestis exercitus, hymnum gloriæ tuæ canimus, sine fine dicentes: Sanctus, etc. (*p. 102*).

It is truly worthy and just, right and profitable unto salvation, that we should at all times and in all places give thanks unto Thee, O holy Lord, Father Almighty, eternal God. Who didst anoint with the oil of gladness Thine only begotten Son, Our Lord Jesus Christ, the eternal Priest and universal King, that He might accomplish the mystery of man's Redemption by immolating Himself an unspotted sacrifice and peace offering, on the altar of the Cross; and having subjected all creatures to His dominion, might deliver up to Thine infinite Majesty, an eternal and universal kingdom: a kingdom of truth and life; a kingdom of sanctification and grace; a kingdom of justice, love, and peace. And therefore, with angels and archangels, with thrones and dominations, and with the whole army of heavenly hosts, we sing a hymn to Thy glory, saying unceasingly: Holy, etc. (*p. 102*).

9. *On festivals of the Blessed Virgin Mary (B. V. M.) (except the Purification, on which is said the Preface of Christmas), and within their octaves, and on Votive Masses of the B. V. M., the words,* Annunciation, Visitation, Assumption, Nativity, Presentation, Conception, Espousal, *are inserted after,* and extol Thee on this. *On the Dedication of the B. V. M. ad Nives, as also on the feast of her Holy Name; and on the feast of the B. V. M. of Mercy, are inserted,* the festival. *On the feast of the Seven Dolors is inserted,* transfixion. *On the feast of Mount Carmel,* commemoration; *and on that of the most Holy Rosary,* solemnity. *In Votive Masses and on Saturday,* veneration.

Vere dignum et justum est, æquum et salutare, nos tibi semper et ubique gratias agere Domine sancte, Pater omnipotens, æterne Deus. Et te in N. beatæ Mariæ semper Virginis collaudare, benedicere, et prædicare. Quæ et Unigenitum tuum Sancti Spiritus obumbratione concepit: et virginitatis gloria permanente, lumen æternum mundo effudit, Jesum Christum Dominum nostrum. Per quem Majestatem tuam laudant angeli, adorant dominationes, tremunt potestates. Cœli cœlorumque virtutes, ac beata seraphim, socia exultatione concelebrant. Cum quibus et nostras voces, ut admitti jubeas, deprecamur, supplici confessione dicentes: Sanctus, etc. (*p. 102*).

It is truly worthy and just, right and profitable unto salvation, that we should at all times and in all places give thanks unto Thee, O holy Lord, Father Almighty, eternal God. And that we should praise, bless, and extol Thee on this festival of Blessed Mary ever Virgin: who both conceived Thy only begotten Son by the overshadowing of the Holy Ghost, and, the glory of her virginity still enduring, brought forth to the world the everlasting Light, Jesus Christ Our Lord. Through Whom the angels praise, the dominations adore, and the powers fear Thy Majesty: the heavens also and the heavenly forces, and the blessed seraphim glorify it in common exultation. With whom, we beseech Thee, bid that our voices also be admitted in suppliant praise, saying, Holy, etc. (*p. 102*).

10. *At the Masses of St. Joseph.*

‡Vere dignum et justum est, æquum et salutare, nos tibi semper et ubique gratias agere Domine sancte, Pater omnipotens, æterne Deus. Et te in Festivitate beati Joseph debitis magnificare præconiis, benedicere et prædicare. Qui et vir justus, a te Deiparæ Virgini Sponsus est datus: et fidelis servus ac prudens, super Familiam tuam est constitutus: ut Unigenitum tuum, Sancti Spiritus obumbratione conceptum, paterna vice custodiret, Jesum Christum Dominum nostrum. Per quem Majestatem tuam laudant angeli, adorant dominationes, tremunt potestates. Cœli cœlorumque virtutes, ac beata seraphim, socia exultatione concelebrant. Cum quibus et nostras voces, ut admitti jubeas, deprecamur, supplici confessione dicentes: Sanctus, etc. (*p. 102*).

It is truly worthy and just, right and profitable unto salvation, that we should at all times and in all places give thanks unto Thee, O holy Lord, Father Almighty, eternal God. And that we should bless and proclaim Thee, and magnify Thee with fitting praise on the feast of blessed Joseph. Who, being a just man, was given by Thee to the Virgin Mother of God as a spouse, and who also, as a faithful and prudent servant, was set over Thy family, in order that he might watch over, as a father, Thy only begotten Son, conceived by the overshadowing of the Holy Spirit, Jesus Christ, Our Lord. Through Whom the angels praise, the dominations adore, and the powers fear Thy Majesty: the heavens also and the heavenly forces, and the blessed seraphim glorify it in common exultation. With whom, we beseech Thee, bid that our voices also be admitted in suppliant praise, saying, Holy, etc. (*p. 102*).

11. *On feasts of apostles and evangelists* (*December 27 excepted*), *and their octaves, except in feasts which have proper prefaces of their own.*

Vere dignum et justum est, æquum et salutare: Te, Domine, suppliciter exorare, ut gregem tuum, pastor æterne, non deseras: sed per beatos Apostolos tuos continua protectione custodias: Ut iisdem rectoribus gubernetur, quos operis tui vicarios eidem contulisti præesse pastores. Et ideo cum angelis et archangelis, cum thronis et dominationibus,

It is truly worthy and just, right and profitable unto salvation, suppliantly to beseech Thee, Lord, the everlasting Shepherd, not to forsake Thy flock, but through Thy blessed apostles to keep it under Thy continued protection. That it may be governed by those rulers whom, as the vicars of Thy work, Thou hast given to preside over it as pastors. And therefore, with angels and archangels, with thrones and dominations,

cumque omni militia cœlestis exercitus, hymnum gloriæ tuæ canimus,
sine fine dicentes: Sanctus, etc.
(*p. 102*).

and with the whole army of heavenly
hosts, we sing a hymn to Thy glory,
saying unceasingly: Holy, etc.
(*p. 102*).

12. *On all festivals and weekdays which have none proper.*

Vere dignum et justum est, æquum et
salutare, nos tibi semper et ubique
gratias agere Domine sancte, Pater
omnipotens, æterne Deus. Per
Christum Dominum nostrum. Per
quem Majestatem tuam laudant
angeli, adorant dominationes,
tremunt potestates. Cœli cœlorumque virtutes, ac beata seraphim, socia exultatione concelebrant. Cum
quibus et nostras voces, ut admitti
jubeas, deprecamur, supplici confessione dicentes: Sanctus, etc. (*p. 102*).

It is truly worthy and just, right and
profitable unto salvation, that we
should at all times and in all places
give thanks unto Thee, O holy Lord,
Father Almighty, eternal God.
Through Christ Our Lord. Through
Whom the angels praise, the dominations adore, and the powers fear
Thy Majesty: the heavens also and
the heavenly forces, and the blessed
seraphim glorify it in common exultation. With whom, we beseech
Thee, bid that our voices also be
admitted in suppliant praise, saying,
Holy, etc., (*p. 102*).

13. *In Masses for the Dead.*

Vere dignum et justum est, æquum et salutare, nos tibi semper et ubique gratias agere Domine sancte, Pater omnipotens, æterne Deus. Per Christum Dominum nostrum. In quo nobis spes beatæ resurrectionis effulsit, ut quos contristat certa moriendi condito, eosdem consoletur futuræ immortalitatis promissio. Tuis enim fidelibus, Domine, vita mutatur, non tollitur, et, dissoluta terrestris hujus incolatus domo, æterna in cælis habitatio comparatur. Et ideo cum angelis et archangelis, cum thronis et dominationibus, cumque omni militia cœlestis exercitus, hymnum gloriæ tuæ canimus, sine fine dicentes: Sanctus, etc., (*p. 102*).

It is truly worthy and just, right and profitable unto salvation, that we should at all times and in all places give thanks unto Thee, O holy Lord, Father Almighty, eternal God. Through Christ Our Lord. In Whom the hope of a blessed resurrection has shone forth to us, so that the promise of future immortality may console those who are saddened by the certain lot of dying. For to Thy faithful, O Lord, life is changed, not taken away, and while the earthly house of this habitation is dissolved, an eternal dwelling place in the heavens is being prepared. And therefore, with angels and archangels, with thrones and dominations, and with the whole army of heavenly hosts, we sing a hymn to Thy glory, saying unceasingly: Holy, etc. (*p. 102*).

14. *On the feast of the Sacred Heart.*

‡Vere dignum et justum est, æquum et salutare, nos tibi semper et ubique gratias agere Domine sancte, Pater omnipotens, æterne Deus. Qui Unigenitum tuum in cruce penden-tem lancea militis transfigi voluisti, ut apertum cor, divinæ largitatis sacrarium, torrentes nobis funderet miserationis et gratiæ, et quod amore nostri flagrare numquam destitit, piis esset requies et pœni-tentibus pateret salutis refugium. Et ideo cum angelis et archangelis, cum thronis et dominationibus, cumque omni militia cœlestis exer-citus, hymnum gloriæ tuæ canimus, sine fine dicentes: Sanctus, etc. (*p. 102*).

It is truly worthy and just, right and profitable unto salvation, that we should at all times and in all places give thanks unto Thee, O holy Lord, Father Almighty, eternal God. Who didst will that Thy only begotten Son should be pierced by the soldier's lance as He hung on the Cross, so that from His open Heart as from a treasury of divine bounty, He might pour out on us torrents of mercy and grace, and in that Heart, always burning with love of us, the devout might find rest and the pen-itent a saving refuge. And therefore, with angels and archangels, with thrones and dominations, and with the whole army of heavenly hosts, we sing a hymn to Thy glory, saying unceasingly: Holy, etc. (*p. 102*).

Special Prayers

The Te Deum laudamus

Te Deum laudamus: * te Dominum confitemur.	We praise Thee, O God: we acknowledge Thee to be the Lord.
Te æternum Patrem * omnis terra veneratur.	All the earth doth worship Thee: the Father everlasting.
Tibi omnes angeli, * tibi cœli, et universæ potestates:	To Thee all angels: to Thee the heavens and all the powers therein:
Tibi cherubim et seraphim * incessabili voce proclamant:	To Thee the cherubim and seraphim: cry with unceasing voice:
Sanctus, sanctus, sanctus * Dominus Deus Sabaoth.	Holy, holy, holy: Lord God of hosts.
Pleni sunt cœli et terra * majestatis gloriæ tuæ.	The heavens and the earth are full: of the majesty of Thy glory.
Te gloriosus * Apostolorum chorus,	Thee the glorious choir: of the apostles,
Te Prophetarum * laudabilis numerus,	Thee the admirable company: of the prophets,
Te Martyrum candidatus * laudat exercitus.	Thee the white-robed army of martyrs: praise.
Te per orbem terrarum * sancta confitetur Ecclesia,	Thee the holy Church throughout all the world: doth acknowledge.
Patrem * immensæ majestatis;	The Father: of infinite majesty.
Venerandum tuum verum * et unicum Filium;	Thine adorable, true: and only Son.
Sanctum quoque * Paraclitum Spiritum.	Also the Holy Ghost: the Paraclete.
Tu Rex gloriæ, * Christe.	Thou art the King of glory: O Christ.
Tu Patris * sempiternus es Filius.	Thou art the everlasting Son: of the Father.

Tu ad liberandum suscepturus hominem, * non horruisti Virginis uterum.

Thou having taken upon Thee to deliver man: didst not abhor the Virgin's womb.

Tu devicto mortis aculeo, * aperuisti credentibus regna cœlorum.

Thou having overcome the sting of death: didst open to believers the kingdom of heaven.

Tu ad dexteram Dei sedes, * in gloria Patris.

Thou sittest at the right hand of God: in the glory of the Father.

Judex crederis * esse venturus.

We believe that Thou shalt come: to be our Judge.

Te ergo quæsumus, tuis famulis subveni, * quos pretioso sanguine redemisti.

[16]We beseech Thee, therefore, help Thy servants: whom Thou hast redeemed with Thy Precious Blood.

Æterna fac cum Sanctis tuis * in gloria numerari.

Make them to be numbered with Thy saints: in glory everlasting.

Salvum fac populum tuum, Domine, * et benedic hæreditati tuæ.

O Lord, save Thy people: and bless Thine inheritance.

Et rege eos, * et extolle illos usque in æternum.

Govern them: and lift them up forever.

Per singulos dies * benedicimus te;

Day by day: we bless Thee.

Et laudamus nomen tuum in sæculum, * et in sæculum sæculi.

And we praise Thy name forever: and world without end.

Dignare, Domine, die isto * sine peccato nos custodire.

Vouchsafe, O Lord, this day: to keep us without sin.

Miserere nostri, Domine, * miserere nostri.

Have mercy on us, O Lord: have mercy on us.

Fiat misericordia tua, Domine, super nos * quemadmodum speravimus in te.

Let Thy mercy, O Lord, be upon us: as we have hoped in Thee.

In te, Domine, speravi: * non confundar in æternum.

O Lord, in Thee have I hoped: let me never be confounded.

---

[16]   During this petition it is usual to kneel.

On occasions of solemn public thanksgiving the following prayers are added:

Benedictus es, Domine, Deus patrum nostrorum.

Blessed art Thou O Lord, the God of our fathers.

℞. Et laudabilis, et gloriosus in sæcula.

℞. And worthy to be praised, and glorified forever.

℣. Benedicamus Patrem et Filium, cum Sancto Spiritu.

℣. Let us bless the Father and the Son, with the Holy Ghost.

℞. Laudemus et superexaltemus eum in sæcula.

℞. Let us praise and exalt Him above all forever.

℣. Benedictus es, Domine, in firmamento cœli.

℣. Blessed art Thou, O Lord, in the firmament of heaven.

℞. Et laudabilis, et gloriosus, et superexaltatus in sæcula.

℞. And worthy to be praised, and glorified, and exalted above all forever.

℣. Benedic, anima mea, Domino.

℣. Bless the Lord, O my soul.

℞. Et noli oblivisci omnes retributiones ejus.

℞. And forget not all His benefits.

℣. Domine, exaudi orationem meam.

℣. O Lord, hear my prayer.

℞. Et clamor meus ad te veniat.

℞. And let my cry come unto Thee.

℣. Dominus vobiscum.

℣. The Lord be with you.

℞. Et cum spiritu tuo.

℞. And with thy spirit.

Oremus.

Let us pray.

Deus, cujus misericordiæ non est numerus, et bonitatis infinitus est thesaurus; piissimæ majestati tuæ pro collatis donis gratias agimus, tuam semper clementiam exorantes, ut qui petentibus postulata concedis, eosdem non deserens, ad præmia futura disponas.

O God, Whose mercies are without number, and the treasure of Whose goodness is infinite; we render thanks to Thy most gracious Majesty for the gifts Thou hast bestowed upon us, evermore beseeching Thy clemency that as Thou dost grant the petitions of them that ask Thee, so, never forsaking them, Thou wilt prepare them for the rewards to come.

Deus, qui corda fidelium Sancti Spiritus illustratione docuisti: da nobis in eodem Spiritu recta sapere, et de ejus semper consolatione gaudere.

O God, Who didst teach the hearts of Thy faithful by the light of Thy Holy Spirit: grant us, by the same Spirit, to have a right judgment in all things, and evermore to rejoice in His holy comfort.

Deus, qui neminem in te sperantem nimium affligi permittis, sed pium precibus præstas auditum: pro postulationibus nostris, votisque susceptis gratias agimus, te piissime deprecantes, ut a cunctis semper muniamur adversis. Per Dominum nostrum Jesum Christum Filium tuum, qui tecum vivit et regnat, in unitate Spiritus Sancti Deus, per omnia sæcula sæculorum. ℟. Amen.

O God, Who sufferest none that hope in Thee to be afflicted overmuch, but dost turn a gracious ear unto their prayers: we render Thee thanks for having heard our supplications and vows; most humbly beseeching Thee that we may evermore be protected from all adversities. Through Our Lord Jesus Christ, etc. ℟. Amen.

Occasional Prayers

For the Whole Church

Defend us, O Lord, we beseech Thee, from all dangers both of soul and body; and, by the intercession of the glorious and Blessed Mary ever Virgin, Mother of God, of blessed Joseph, of Thy holy apostles Peter and Paul, of blessed N. [*here insert the name of your patron saint*], and of all Thy saints, grant us, in Thy mercy, health and peace; that all adversities and errors being done away, Thy Church may serve Thee with a pure and undisturbed devotion.

For All Orders of Ecclesiastics

Almighty and everlasting God, by Whose Spirit the whole body of the Church is sanctified and governed: receive our humble supplications which we offer before Thee for all degrees and orders of men in Thy holy Church, that, by the assistance of Thy grace, they may faithfully serve Thee.

For the Pope

O God, the Pastor and Ruler of all the faithful, look down, in Thy mercy, upon Thy servant N. [*here mention the pope's name*], whom Thou hast appointed to preside over Thy Church; and grant, we beseech Thee, that both by word and example he may edify all those who are under his charge; so that, with the flock entrusted to him, he may arrive at length unto life everlasting. Through Our Lord Jesus Christ, etc. *Amen.*

For Bishops, and the People Committed to Them

Almighty and everlasting God, Who alone doest great wonders, send down upon Thy servants, and the congregations committed unto them, the spirit of Thy saving grace; and that they may truly please Thee, pour forth upon them the continual dew of Thy blessing.

For the Bishop of the Diocese

Grant, we beseech Thee, O Lord, to Thy servant our bishop, that, by preaching and doing such things as are right, he may by the example of good works edify the minds of those under his authority, and receive of Thee, most tender Shepherd, an everlasting recompense and reward.

For a Congregation or Family

Defend, we beseech Thee, O Lord, through the intercession of Blessed Mary, ever Virgin, this Thy family from all adversity; and, as in all humility they prostrate themselves before Thee, do Thou graciously protect them against all the snares of their enemies. Through Christ Our Lord. *Amen.*

For the Preservation of Concord in a Congregation

O God, the Giver of peace and Lover of charity, grant to Thy servants true concord and union with Thy holy will, that we may be delivered from all temptations which assault us.

Against the Persecutors of the Church

Mercifully hear, O Lord, we beseech Thee, the prayers of Thy Church: that, all adversities and errors being done away, we may serve Thee with a pure and undisturbed devotion.

In Any Necessity

O God, our refuge and strength, Who art the Author of all goodness: hear, we beseech Thee, the devout prayers of Thy Church; and grant that what we faithfully ask we may effectually obtain. Through Our Lord Jesus Christ, etc. *Amen.*

In Any Tribulation

O Almighty God, despise not Thy people who cry unto Thee in their affliction; but, for the glory of Thy name, turn away Thine anger, and help us in our tribulations.

In Time of Famine or Pestilence

Grant, we beseech Thee, O Lord, an answer to our hearty supplications; and, Thy wrath being appeased, turn away from us this famine (or pestilence), that the hearts of men may know that these scourges proceed from Thine anger, and cease by Thy mercy.

For Rain

O God, in Whom we live, and move, and are, grant us seasonable rain; that we, enjoying a sufficiency of support in this life, may with more confidence strive after the things which are eternal.

For Fair Weather

Hear us, O Lord, Who cry unto Thee, and grant fair weather to us, Thy suppliant servants; that we, who are justly afflicted for our sins, may by Thy preventing pity find mercy.

For the Gift of Tears

Almighty and most merciful God, Who didst cause a fount of living water to spring out of a rock, for Thy people in their thirst: draw forth tears of compunction from our stony hearts; that we may weep over our sins, and by Thy mercy deserve to obtain pardon for the same.

For Forgiveness of Sins

O God, Who rejectest none that come unto Thee, but in loving kindness art appeased even with the greatest sinners who repent: mercifully regard our prayers in our humiliation, and enlighten our hearts that we may be able to fulfill Thy commandments.

For the Tempted and Afflicted

O God, Who justifiest the ungodly, and willest not the death of a sinner: we humbly entreat Thy Majesty to protect Thy servants, who trust in Thy mercy, with Thy heavenly assistance, and preserve them by Thy continual protection; that they may constantly serve Thee, and by no temptation be separated from Thee.

Against Evil Thoughts

Almighty and most merciful God, graciously hearken unto our prayers: and free our hearts from the temptations of evil thoughts; that we may worthily become a fit habitation for Thy Holy Spirit.

For the Gift of Continence

Inflame, O Lord, our reins and our hearts with the fire of the Holy Ghost; that we may serve Thee with a chaste body, and please Thee with a pure mind.

For the Gift of Humility

O God, Who resistest the proud, and givest grace to the humble: grant us the virtue of true humility, whereof Thine only begotten showed in Himself a pattern for Thy faithful; that we may never by our pride provoke Thine anger, but rather by our meekness receive the riches of Thy grace.

For the Gift of Patience

O God, Who didst crush the pride of the enemy by the long-suffering of Thine only begotten Son: grant, we beseech Thee, that we may worthily recall those things which in His tender love He bore for us; and thus following His example may patiently endure all our adversities.

For the Gift of Charity

O God, Who makest all things to work together for good unto those who love Thee; give to our hearts the lasting affection of Thy love; that such desires as are inspired by Thee may never be changed by any temptation.

For Those at Sea

O God, Who didst bring our fathers through the Red Sea, and bear them through the great waters singing praises unto Thy name: we humbly beseech Thee to vouchsafe to turn away all adversities from Thy servants at sea, and to bring them with a calm voyage unto the haven where they would be.

For Heretics and Schismatics

O Almighty and everlasting God, Who hast compassion on all, and wouldst not that any should perish: favorably look down upon all those who are seduced by the deceit of Satan; that, all heretical impiety being removed, the hearts of such as err may repent and return to the unity of Thy truth.

For Jews

O Almighty and everlasting God, Who repellest not from Thy mercy even the perfidious Jews: hear the prayer which we offer for the blindness of that people; that the Light of Thy truth, Christ Our Lord, being known to them, they may be delivered from their darkness.

For Pagans

O Almighty and everlasting God, Who desirest not the death but the life of sinners: mercifully accept our prayers, and, delivering pagans from the worship of idols, unite them to Thy Church, to the praise and honor of Thy glorious name.

For Our Friends

O God, Who, by the grace of the Holy Spirit, hast poured into the hearts of Thy faithful the gifts of charity: grant to Thy servants and handmaids, for whom we implore Thy mercy, health both of body and soul; that they may love Thee with all their strength, and cheerfully perform those things which are pleasing unto Thee.

For Enemies

O God, the Lover and Preserver of peace and charity: grant unto all our enemies peace and true charity; give them remission of all their sins, and by Thy power deliver us from their snares.

A Short Recommendation to God

Into the hands of Thy unspeakable mercy, O Lord, I commend my soul and body; my senses, my words, my thoughts, and all my actions, with all the necessities of my body and soul; my going forth and my coming in; my faith and conversation; the course and end of my life; the day and hour of my death; my rest and resurrection with the saints and elect.

For the Sick

Almighty and eternal God, the everlasting Health of them that believe: hear us for Thy sick *servant*, N., for whom we implore the aid of Thy pitying mercy, that, with *his* bodily health restored, *he* may give thanks to Thee in Thy church. Through Christ Our Lord. *Amen.*

For a Sick Person near Death

Almighty and everlasting God, Preserver of souls, Who dost correct those whom Thou dost love, and for their amendment dost tenderly chastise those whom Thou dost receive, we call upon Thee, O Lord, to bestow Thy healing, that the soul of Thy servant, at the hour of its departure from the body, may by the hands of Thy holy angels be presented without spot unto Thee.

For the Dead

Almighty, everlasting God, Who hast dominion over the living and the dead, and showest mercy unto all whom Thou foreknowest will be Thine by faith and works: we humbly beseech Thee that they for whom we have resolved to pour forth our prayers, whether this present world still detain them in the flesh, or the world to come hath already received them stripped of their bodies, may, by the grace of Thy fatherly love, and through the intercession of all the saints, obtain the remission of all their sins. Through Our Lord Jesus Christ, etc. *Amen.*

A Prayer before Study or Instructions

Incomprehensible Creator, the true Fountain of light and only Author of all knowledge: vouchsafe, we beseech Thee, to enlighten our understandings, and to remove from us all darkness of sin and ignorance. [Thou, Who makest eloquent the tongues of those that want utterance, direct our tongues, and pour on our lips the grace of Thy blessing.] Give us a diligent and obedient spirit, quickness of apprehension, capacity of retaining, and the powerful assistance of Thy holy grace; that what we hear or learn we may apply to Thy honor and the eternal salvation of our own souls.

A Husband's Prayer

O gracious Father, Maker and Preserver of heaven and earth, Who in the beginning didst institute Matrimony, thereby foreshadowing the mystical union of the Church with our Savior Christ, Who, in the time of His ministry upon earth, did honor marriage with His first miracle: enable me, I pray Thee, by Thy grace to live in holiness and purity with the wife whom Thou hast given me. Mortify in me all violence of earthly passion, all selfishness and inconsiderateness (*here name any besetting sin which may be a hindrance to you*), that I may love her as Christ loved His Church, cherish and comfort her as my own body, and have as great care for her happiness as for my own. Grant that we may live in peace, without contention; in unity, without discord. [Give us, O Lord, discreet hearts and understanding minds, to bring up our children in Thy faith and fear, that they may be obedient to Thee and to Thy commandments, and to all that Thou requirest of them in duty toward their parents.] And give us, O Lord, a competency of estate, to maintain ourselves and our family according to that rank and calling wherein Thou hast placed us, without excess or vainglory, in singleness and pureness of heart. Grant this for Jesus Christ's sake, to Whom with Thee and the Holy Ghost, be all honor and glory, now and forever. *Amen.*

A Wife's Prayer

O merciful Lord God, Who in the beginning didst take Eve out of the side of Adam and didst give her to him as a helpmate: give me grace to live worthy of the honorable estate of Matrimony to which Thou hast called me, that I may love my husband with a pure and chaste love, acknowledging him as my head, and truly reverencing and obeying him in all good things; that thereby I may please him, and live with him in all Christian quietness. Keep me from all worldliness and vanity. Help me, O Lord, that I may, under him, prudently and discreetly guide and govern his household. Let no fault of mine aggravate any sins by which he may be especially tempted; enable me to soothe him in perplexity, to cheer him in difficulty, to refresh him in weariness, and, as far as may be, to advise him in doubt. [Give me understanding so to fulfill my part in the education of our children, that they may be our joy in this world and our glory in the next.] Grant that our perfect union here may be the beginning of the still more perfect and blissful union hereafter in Thy kingdom; and this I pray through Jesus Christ Our Lord. *Amen.*

A Prayer to Be Said by Husband or Wife

O merciful God, we humbly beseech Thee to send Thy blessing continually upon us, and to make us thankful for all that Thou hast already vouchsafed unto us; and as Thou hast made us one in the mystical grace of Matrimony, grant that we may be also inwardly of one heart and of one mind, paying due honor one to another, united in love to Thee and to each other in Thee; living together in peace and holiness, as faithful members of Thy Church, denying ourselves, and being a mutual help, comfort, and support to each other, all the days of our life. [Give us grace to train our children in Thy faith and fear.] Bless us with health and strength, if it be Thy will, and with whatever else Thy good providence shall see to be best for our souls and bodies. Fit and prepare us day by day for our departure hence, that we may together inherit eternal life in Thy heavenly kingdom. Through the merits of Jesus Christ, Our Lord and Savior. *Amen.*

Prayers of Parents, for Themselves and for Their Children

Almighty God, the Father and Maker of us all, Who of Thy blessing and goodness hast vouchsafed to make me a father [*or* mother] of children: be pleased to accept my hearty thanksgiving and devout praise for the same; grant me Thy heavenly grace and assistance so to train up my children in Thy faith, fear, and love that as they advance in years they may grow in grace and may hereafter be found in the number of Thine elect. Through Jesus Christ Our Lord. *Amen.*

O Father of mankind, Who hast given unto me these my children, and committed them to my charge to bring them up for Thee, and to prepare them for everlasting life: assist me with Thy heavenly grace, that I may be able to fulfill this most sacred duty and stewardship. Teach me both what to give and what to withhold; when to reprove and when to forbear; make me to be gentle, yet firm; considerate and watchful; and deliver me equally from the weakness of indulgence, and the excess of severity; and grant that, both by word and example, I may be careful to lead them in the ways of wisdom and true piety, so that at last I may, with them, be admitted to the unspeakable joys of our true home in heaven, in the company of the blessed angels and saints.

O heavenly Father, I commend my children unto Thee. Be Thou their God and Father; and mercifully supply whatever is wanting in me through frailty or negligence. Strengthen them to overcome the corruptions of the world, to resist all solicitations to evil, whether from within or without; and deliver them from the secret snares of the enemy. Pour Thy grace into their hearts, and confirm and multiply in them the gifts of Thy Holy Spirit, that they may daily grow in grace and in the knowledge of Our Lord Jesus Christ; and so, faithfully serving Thee here, may come to rejoice in Thy presence hereafter.

A Child's Prayer

O Almighty God, Who hast given unto me my father and mother, and made them to be an image of Thine authority, and love, and tender watchfulness; and hast commanded me to love, and honor, and obey them in all things: give me grace cheerfully and with my whole heart to keep this Thy law. Help me to love them fervently, to honor them truly, to yield a ready obedience to their commands, to comply with their wishes, to study their happiness in everything, and to bear their rebukes with patience and humility. Deliver me, O God, from pride, rebellion, and willfulness, from passion and stubbornness, from sloth and carelessness. Make me diligent in all my duties and studies, and patient in all my trials; that so living, I may deserve to be Thy child, Who art our Father in heaven.

A Prayer for Choosing a State of Life

O Lord, I beseech Thee to grant me Thy divine light, that I may know the designs of Thy providence concerning me, and that, filled with a sincere desire for my soul's salvation, I may say, with the young man in the Gospel: "What must I do to be saved?" All states of life are before me; but, still undecided what to do, I await Thy commands, I offer myself to Thee without restriction, without reserve, with a most perfect submission.

Far be it from me, O Lord, to oppose the order of Thy wisdom, and, unfaithful to the inspiration of Thy grace, to strive to subject the will of the Creator to the caprice of the creature. It is not for the servant to choose the way in which he will serve his master: do Thou lay upon me what commands Thou pleasest. My lot is in Thy hands. I make no exception, lest perchance what I except be that which Thou willest, and because I am too shortsighted to discover in the future the different obstacles I shall meet with, if, without Thy guidance, I make myself the arbiter of my own conduct. Speak, Lord, to my soul; speak to me as Thou didst to the youthful Samuel: Speak, Lord; for Thy servant heareth. I cast myself at Thy feet, and I am ready, if it be Thy will, to sacrifice myself as a victim to Thee for the remainder of my days, in such wise as Thou shalt deem most worthy of Thy greatness.

O my God, inspire the affections of my parents, and guide their projects according to the counsels of Thy wisdom. Lord, I sincerely desire to consult Thee Who art the eternal Truth; grant that my parents also may submit themselves to its decrees, faithfully and without reserve.

A Prayer in Times of Threatened Calamity

O Jesus Christ, we call upon Thee, holy, immortal God. Have mercy upon us and upon all men. Purify us by Thy holy blood, forgive us by Thy holy blood, save us by Thy holy blood, now and forever. Amen.

For Civil Authorities

We pray Thee, O Almighty and eternal God (*p. 45*).

A UNIVERSAL PRAYER[17]

For All Things Necessary to Salvation

O my God, I believe in Thee: do Thou strengthen my faith. All my hopes are in Thee; do Thou secure them. I love Thee; teach me to love Thee daily more and more. I am sorry that I have offended Thee; do Thou increase my sorrow.

I adore Thee as my first beginning; I aspire after Thee as my last end. I give Thee thanks as my constant benefactor; I call upon Thee as my sovereign protector.

Vouchsafe, O my God, to conduct me by Thy wisdom, to restrain me by Thy justice, to comfort me by Thy mercy, to defend me by Thy power.

To Thee I desire to consecrate all my thoughts, words, actions, and sufferings; that henceforward I may think of Thee, speak of Thee, refer all my actions to Thy greater glory, and suffer willingly whatever Thou shalt appoint.

Lord, I desire that in all things Thy will may be done, because it is Thy will, and in the manner that Thou willest.

I beg of Thee to enlighten my understanding, to inflame my will, to purify my body, and to sanctify my soul.

Give me strength, O my God, to expiate my offenses, to overcome my temptations, to subdue my passions, and to acquire the virtues proper for my state.

Fill my heart with tender affection for Thy goodness, hatred of my faults, love of my neighbor, and contempt of the world.

Let me always remember to be submissive to my superiors, courteous to my inferiors, faithful to my friends, and charitable to my enemies.

Assist me to overcome sensuality by mortification, avarice by almsdeeds, anger by meekness, and tepidity by devotion.

O my God, make me prudent in my undertakings, courageous in dangers, patient in affliction, and humble in prosperity.

Grant that I may be ever attentive at my prayers, temperate at my meals, diligent in my employments, and constant in my resolutions.

Let my conscience be ever upright and pure, my exterior modest, my conversation edifying, and my deportment regular.

---

[17] Composed by Pope Clement XI, A.D. 1721.

Assist me, that I may continually labor to overcome nature, to correspond with Thy grace, to keep Thy commandments, and to work out my salvation.

Discover to me, O my God, the nothingness of this world, the greatness of heaven, the shortness of time, and the length of eternity.

Grant that I may prepare for death; that I may fear Thy judgments, escape hell, and in the end obtain heaven; through Jesus Christ Our Lord. *Amen.*

Vespers

The public prayers of the Church, other than those in the great Sacrifice of the Mass, are contained in the Breviary. The whole Office for each day consists of Matins and Lauds; Prime, Tierce, Sext, and None (the prayers for the *first, third, sixth*, and *ninth* hours, the old Roman division of the day); Vespers and Compline. This Office was originally chanted daily by the faithful, and is still chanted by some religious orders, the preservers of primitive tradition and fervor. It is daily recited by the clergy; and, on Sundays and holy days, the Vespers are publicly chanted as part of the solemn worship of the day, to enable the faithful to join in so holy and venerable a form of prayer.

All the parts of the Office consist of psalms and canticles from the Holy Scripture, with lessons also from Scripture, or the holy Fathers, and appropriate to the day.

The psalms in the Vespers for Sunday are the 109th and the following, including the 113th, although very frequently the 116th is substituted for the last of these. This series of psalms is most suitable to the ordinary wants of the Church on her weekly festivals. The first is a kind of commemoration of all the great mysteries of our Redemption; the second alludes to the praise of God *in the congregation*; the third commemorates the graces and privileges of the just; the fourth is a psalm of praise, as is also that substituted occasionally for the fifth; the fifth celebrates the deliverance of the Israelites from Egyptian bondage. All are prophecies of Our Lord and of His Immaculate Mother, as well as of the Church. In them we sing the praises of Christ, Our Lord, as Priest forever, offering sacrifice, like Melchisedech, in the form of bread and wine; as Lord of Lords, and King of Kings; as true to His promises of ever abiding by His Church, investing her with miraculous powers; and ever spreading the mystic banquet: in them we praise Him as our Redeemer and our God, Whom we adore; in them we praise that Immaculate Virgin—the *joyful Mother of children*—and with her raise our hearts and voices to glorify God.

It is not, then, an unmeaning service, but one most appropriate and consoling. Hence, though it is not of obligation to attend Vespers, as it is to hear Mass, all the saints and spiritual writers of the Church urge the faithful to be present at this Office with piety and devotion. For there is always more benefit and comfort to be derived from the public Offices of the Church than from private devotions, God having ordained that *communion of prayers* should always have the preference.

VESPERS FOR SUNDAY

The priest, with his attendants, enters the sanctuary, and, kneeling before the altar, recites the following prayer:

Aperi, Domine, os meum ad benedicendum nomen sanctum tuum: munda quoque cor meum ab omnibus vanis, perversis, et alienis cogitationibus: intellectum illumina, affectum inflamma, ut digne, attente, ac devote hoc Officium recitare valeam, et exaudiri merear ante conspectum divinæ Majestatis tuæ. Per Christum Dominum nostrum. ℞. Amen.

Domine, in unione illius divinæ intentionis, qua ipse in terris laudes Deo persolvisti, has tibi Horas persolvo.

O Lord, open Thou my mouth that I may bless Thy holy name; cleanse my heart from all vain, evil, and wandering thoughts; enlighten my understanding; kindle my affections, that I may worthily, attentively, and devoutly recite this Office, and may deserve to be heard before the presence of Thy divine Majesty. Through Christ Our Lord. ℞. Amen.

Lord, in union with that divine intention wherewith Thou didst Thyself praise God while on earth, I offer these Hours unto Thee.

The celebrant and his attendants then proceed to the bench, on the Epistle side of the sanctuary; and after saying in silence the Our Father *and the* Hail Mary, *the celebrant intones:*

Deus ✠, in adjutorium meum intende.
℞. Domine, ad adjuvandum me festina.
℣. Gloria Patri, et Filio, et Spiritui Sancto.
℞. Sicut erat in principio, et nunc, et semper, et in sæcula sæculorum. Amen. Alleluia.

Come ✠ unto my help, O God.
℞. O Lord, make haste to help me.
℣. Glory be to the Father, and to the Son, and to the Holy Ghost.
℞. As it was in the beginning, is now, and ever shall be, world without end. Amen. Alleluia.

[*From* Septuagesima *to* Palm Sunday, *inclusively, is said:*

Laus tibi, Domine, Rex æternæ gloriæ.

Praise to Thee, O Lord, King of eternal glory.]

Ant. Dixit Dominus.

Ant. The Lord said.

In Eastertide the psalms are all said under this one Antiphon: Alleluia.

[18]A PSALM 109

Dixit Dominus Domino meo: * Sede a dextris meis:	The Lord said unto my Lord: Sit Thou at My right hand:
Donec ponam inimicos tuos, * scabellum pedum tuorum.	Until I make Thine enemies: Thy footstool.
Virgam virtutis tuæ emittet Dominus ex Sion: * dominare in medio inimicorum tuorum.	The Lord will send forth the scepter of Thy power out of Sion: rule Thou in the midst of Thine enemies.
Tecum principium in die virtutis tuæ in splendoribus Sanctorum: * ex utero ante luciferum genui te.	Thine shall be dominion in the day of Thy power, amid the brightness of the saints: from the womb before the daystar have I begotten Thee.
Juravit Dominus, et non pœnitebit eum: * Tu es sacerdos in æternum secundum ordinem Melchisedech.	The Lord hath sworn, and He will not repent: Thou art a priest forever after the order of Melchisedech.
Dominus a dextris tuis * confregit in die iræ suæ reges.	The Lord upon Thy right hand: hath overthrown kings in the day of His wrath.
Judicabit in nationibus, implebit ruinas: * conquassabit capita in terra multorum.	He shall judge among the nations; He shall fill them with ruins: He shall smite in sunder the heads in the land of many.
De torrente in via bibet: * propterea exaltabit caput.	He shall drink of the brook in the way: therefore shall He lift up His head.
Gloria Patri, etc.	Glory be to the Father, etc.
Ant. Dixit Dominus Domino meo: Sede a dextris meis.	*Ant.* The Lord said unto my Lord: Sit Thou at My right hand.
Ant. Fidelia.	*Ant.* Faithful.

---

[18] The letters prefixed to the Vesper psalms are for convenience in selecting them for different feasts. See the Directory (p. 172).

B PSALM 110

Confitebor tibi, Domine, in toto corde meo: * in consilio justorum, et congregatione.	I will praise Thee, O Lord, with my whole heart: in the assembly of the just, and in the congregation.
Magna opera Domini: * exquisita in omnes voluntates ejus.	Great are the works of the Lord: sought out are they according unto all His pleasure.
Confessio et magnificentia opus ejus, * et justitia ejus manet in sæculum sæculi.	His work is His praise and His honor: and His justice endureth forever and ever.
Memoriam fecit mirabilium suorum misericors et miserator Dominus: * escam dedit timentibus se.	A memorial hath the merciful and gracious Lord made of His marvelous works: He hath given meat unto them that fear Him.
Memor erit in sæculum testamenti sui: * virtutem operum suorum annuntiabit populo suo:	He shall ever be mindful of His covenant: He shall show forth to His people the power of His works:
Ut det illis hæreditatem gentium: * opera manuum ejus veritas et judicium.	That He may give them the heritage of the Gentiles: the works of His hands are truth and judgment.
Fidelia omnia mandata ejus, confirmata in sæculum sæculi, * facta in veritate et æquitate.	All His commandments are faithful: they stand fast forever and ever, they are done in truth and equity.
Redemptionem misit populo suo: * mandavit in æternum testamentum suum.	He hath sent redemption unto His people: He hath commanded His covenant forever.
Sanctum et terribile nomen ejus: * initium sapientiæ timor Domini.	Holy and terrible is His name: the fear of the Lord is the beginning of wisdom.
Intellectus bonus omnibus facientibus eum: * laudatio ejus manet in sæculum sæculi.	A good understanding have all they that do thereafter: His praise endureth forever and ever.
Gloria Patri, etc.	Glory be to the Father, etc.

Ant. Fidelia omnia mandata ejus, confirmata in sæculum sæculi.

Ant. Faithful are all His commandments; they stand fast forever and ever.

Ant. In mandatis.

Ant. In His commandments.

C PSALM 111

Beatus vir, qui timet Dominum: * in mandatis ejus volet nimis.

Blessed is the man that feareth the Lord: he shall delight exceedingly in His commandments.

Potens in terra erit semen ejus: * generatio rectorum benedicetur.

His seed shall be mighty upon earth: the generation of the upright shall be blessed.

Gloria et divitiæ in domo ejus, * et justitia ejus manet in sæculum sæculi.

Glory and riches shall be in his house: and his justice endureth forever and ever.

Exortum est in tenebris lumen rectis: * misericors, et miserator, et justus.

Unto the upright there hath risen up light in the darkness: he is merciful, and compassionate, and just.

Jucundus homo, qui miseretur et commodat, disponet sermones suos in judicio: * quia in æternum non commovebitur.

Acceptable is the man who is merciful and lendeth: he shall order his words with judgment, for he shall not be moved forever.

In memoria æterna erit justus: ab auditione mala non timebit.

The just man shall be in everlasting remembrance: he shall not be afraid for evil tidings.

Paratum cor ejus sperare in Domino, confirmatum est cor ejus: * non commovebitur donec despiciat inimicos suos.

His heart is ready to hope in the Lord: his heart is strengthened, he shall not be moved until he look down upon his enemies.

Dispersit, dedit pauperibus: justitia ejus manet in sæculum sæculi: * cornu ejus exaltabitur in gloria.

He hath dispersed abroad, he hath given to the poor; his justice endureth forever and ever: his horn shall be exalted in glory.

Peccator videbit, et irascetur; dentibus suis fremet et tabescet: * desiderium peccatorum peribit.

The wicked shall see it and shall be wroth; he shall gnash with his teeth, and pine away: the desire of the wicked shall perish.

Gloria Patri, etc.

Glory be to the Father, etc.

Ant. In mandatis ejus cupit nimis.

Ant. In His commandments He hath exceeding great delight.

Ant. Sit nomen Domini.

Ant. Blessed be the name.

D PSALM 112

Laudate, pueri, Dominum: * laudate nomen Domini.

Praise the Lord, ye children: praise ye the name of the Lord.

Sit nomen Domini benedictum: * ex hoc nunc, et usque in sæculum.

Blessed be the name of the Lord: from this time forth forevermore.

A solis ortu usque ad occasum, * laudabile nomen Domini.

From the rising up of the sun unto the going down of the same: the name of the Lord is worthy to be praised.

Excelsus super omnes gentes Dominus: * et super cœlos gloria ejus.

The Lord is high above all nations: and His glory above the heavens.

Quis sicut Dominus Deus noster, qui in altis habitat * et humilia respicit in cœlo et in terra?

Who is like unto the Lord our God, Who dwelleth on high: and regardeth the things that are lowly in heaven and on earth?

Suscitans a terra inopem: * et de stercore erigens pauperem:

Who raiseth up the needy from the earth: and lifteth the poor out of the dunghill;

Ut collocet eum cum principibus: * cum principibus populi sui.

That He may set him with the princes: even with the princes of His people.

Qui habitare facit sterilem in domo: * matrem filiorum lætantem.

Who maketh the barren woman to dwell in her house: the joyful mother of children.

Gloria Patri, etc.

Glory be to the Father, etc.

Ant. Sit nomen Domini benedictum in sæcula.

Ant. Blessed be the name of the Lord forevermore.

Ant. Nos qui vivimus.

Ant. We that live.

E PSALM 113

In exitu Israel de Ægypto: * domus Jacob de populo barbaro,

When Israel came out of Egypt: the house of Jacob from among a strange people,

Facta est Judæa sanctificatio ejus: * Israel potestas ejus.

Judea was made His sanctuary: and Israel His dominion.

Mare vidit, et fugit: * Jordanis conversus est retrorsum.

The sea saw it, and fled: Jordan was turned back.

Montes exultaverunt ut arietes: * et colles sicut agni ovium.

The mountains skipped like rams: and the little hills like the lambs of the flock.

Quid est tibi, mare, quod fugisti: * et tu, Jordanis, quia conversus es retrorsum?

What aileth thee, O thou sea, that thou fleddest: and thou, Jordan, that thou wast turned back?

Montes, exultastis sicut arietes: * et colles, sicut agni ovium?

Ye mountains, that ye skipped like rams: and ye little hills, like the lambs of the flock?

A facie Domini mota est terra: * a facie Dei Jacob.

At the presence of the Lord the earth was moved: at the presence of the God of Jacob.

Qui convertit petram in stagna aquarum: * et rupem in fontes aquarum.

Who turned the rock into a standing water: and the stony hill into a flowing stream.

Non nobis, Domine, non nobis: * sed nomini tuo da gloriam.

Not unto us, O Lord, not unto us: but unto Thy name give the glory.

Super misericordia tua, et veritate tua: * nequando dicant gentes, Ubi est Deus eorum?

For Thy mercy, and for Thy truth's sake: lest the Gentiles should say, Where is their God?

Deus autem noster in cœlo: * omnia quæcumque voluit fecit.

But our God is in heaven: He hath done all things whatsoever He would.

Simulacra gentium argentum et aurum: * opera manuum hominum.

The idols of the Gentiles are silver and gold: the work of the hands of men.

Os habent, et non loquentur: * oculos habent, et non videbunt.

They have mouths, and speak not: eyes have they, and see not.

Aures habent, et non audient: * nares habent, et non odorabunt.

They have ears, and hear not: noses have they, and smell not.

Manus habent, et non palpabunt; pedes habent, et non ambulabunt: * non clamabunt in gutture suo.

They have hands, and feel not: they have feet, and walk not; neither shall they speak through their throat.

Similes illis fiant, qui faciunt ea: et omnes qui confidunt in eis.

Let them that make them become like unto them: and all such as put their trust in them.

Domus Israel speravit in Domino: * adjutor eorum et protector eorum est.

The house of Israel hath hoped in the Lord: He is their helper and protector.

Domus Aaron speravit in Domino: * adjutor eorum et protector eorum est.

The house of Aaron hath hoped in the Lord: He is their helper and protector.

Qui timent Dominum, speraverunt in Domino: * adjutor eorum et protector eorum est.

They that fear the Lord have hoped in the Lord: He is their helper and protector.

Dominus memor fuit nostri, * et benedixit nobis.

The Lord hath been mindful of us: and hath blessed us.

Benedixit domui Israel: * benedixit domui Aaron.

He hath blessed the house of Israel: He hath blessed the house of Aaron.

Benedixit omnibus, qui timent Dominum: * pusillis cum majoribus.

He hath blessed all that fear the Lord: both small and great.

Adjiciat Dominus super vos: * super vos, et super filios vestros.

May the Lord add blessings upon you: upon you, and upon your children.

Benedicti vos a Domino: * qui fecit cœlum et terram.	Blessed be ye of the Lord: Who hath made heaven and earth.
Cœlum cœli Domino, * terram autem dedit filiis hominum.	The heaven of heavens is the Lord's: but the earth hath He given to the children of men.
Non mortui laudabunt te, Domine: * neque omnes, qui descendunt in infernum.	The dead shall not praise Thee, O Lord: neither all they that go down into hell.
Sed nos qui vivimus, benedicimus Domino: * ex hoc nunc, et usque in sæculum.	But we that live bless the Lord: from this time forth forevermore.
Gloria Patri, etc.	Glory be to the Father, etc.
Ant. Nos qui vivimus, benedicimus Domino.	*Ant.* We that live bless the Lord.

In Eastertide: Ant. Alleluia, alleluia, alleluia.

When the choir has ended the chanting of the psalms, the priest rises and chants the Little Chapter—generally the first sentence of the Epistle of the day (p. 506–593); but from the Third Sunday after Epiphany *till* Septuagesima, *and from the* Third Sunday after Pentecost *till* Advent, *the following:*

THE LITTLE CHAPTER

Benedictus Deus, et Pater Domini nostri Jesu Christi, Pater misericordiarum, et Deus totius consolationis, qui consolatur nos in omni tribulatione nostra.	Blessed be God, even the Father of Our Lord Jesus Christ, the Father of mercies, and God of all consolation, Who comforteth us in all our tribulation.
℟. Deo gratias.	℟. Thanks be to God.

The choir then sings the Hymn of the day, which varies according to season and solemnity (p. 172–175). The Hymn which corresponds to the Little Chapter, Benedictus, *is as follows:*

Lucis Creator optime,
Lucem dierum proferens,
Primordiis lucis novæ
Mundi parans originem:

[19]Father of lights, by Whom each day
Is kindled out of night,
Who, when the heavens were made, didst lay
Their rudiments in light;

Qui mane junctum vesperi
Diem vocari præcipis:
Illabitur tetrum chaos,
Audi preces cum fletibus.

Thou, Who didst bind and blend in one
The glistening morn and evening pale,
Hear Thou our plaint, when light is gone,
And lawlessness and strife prevail.

Ne mens gravata crimine,
Vitæ sit exul munere,
Dum nil perenne cogitat,
Seseque culpis illigat.

Hear, lest the whelming weight of crime
Wreck us with life in view;
Lest thoughts and schemes of sense and time
Earn us a sinner's due.

Cœleste pulset ostium:
Vitale tollat præmium:
Vitemus omne noxium:
Purgemus omne pessimum.

So may we knock at heaven's door,
And strive the immortal prize to win,
Continually and evermore
Guarded without and pure within.

Præsta, Pater piissime,
Patrique compar unice,
Cum Spiritu Paraclito
Regnans per omne sæculum. Amen.

Grant this, O Father, only Son,
And Spirit, God of grace,
To Whom all worship shall be done
In every time and place. Amen.

℣. Dirigatur, Domine, oratio mea.
℟. Sicut incensum in conspectu tuo.

℣. Let my prayer, O Lord, be directed
℟. As incense in Thy sight.

---

[19]   Translation by Cardinal Newman.

Then the choir chants the Magnificat, *or* Canticle of the Blessed Virgin—*preceded and followed by its proper* Antiphon—*during which the priest puts on the cope, if he has not worn it from the beginning, and, proceeding to the altar, blesses incense and puts it into the censer. He then incenses the altar in the same manner as at Solemn Mass.*

THE MAGNIFICAT, OR CANTICLE OF THE BLESSED VIRGIN

Magnificat * anima mea Dominum:

My soul doth magnify the Lord.

Et exultavit spiritus meus * in Deo, salutari meo.

And my spirit rejoiceth: in God my Savior.

Quia respexit humilitatem ancillæ suæ * ecce enim ex hoc beatam me dicent omnes generationes.

Because He hath looked down on the lowliness of His handmaid: for behold henceforth all generations will call me blessed.

Quia fecit mihi magna qui potens est: * et sanctum nomen ejus.

Because the Mighty One hath done great things for me: and holy is His name.

Et misericordia ejus a progenie in progenies * timentibus eum.

And His mercy is from generation to generation: on those who fear Him.

Fecit potentiam in brachio suo: * dispersit superbos mente cordis sui.

He showeth might in His arm: He scattereth the proud in the conceit of their heart.

Deposuit potentes de sede, * et exaltavit humiles.

He casteth down the mighty from their throne: and exalteth the lowly.

Esurientes implevit bonis: * et divites dimisit inanes.

He filleth the hungry with good things: and the rich He sendeth away empty.

Suscepit Israel, puerum suum, * recordatus misericordiæ suæ.

He hath received His servant Israel: being mindful of His mercy.

Sicut locutus est ad patres nostros, * Abraham, et semini ejus in sæcula.

As He spake to our fathers: to Abraham and to his seed forever.

Gloria Patri, etc.

Glory be to the Father, etc.

Here follow the proper Collect (*p. 506–593*) *and the* Commemorations, *if any.*

THE USUAL COMMEMORATIONS

These are said at the end of Vespers, from the Third Sunday after Epiphany *to the* Fourth Sunday of Lent; *and from the* Third *to the* Last Sunday after Pentecost *inclusively, except on doubles and within octaves.*

OF THE BLESSED VIRGIN MARY

Sancta Maria, succurre miseris, juva pusillanimes, refove flebiles, ora pro populo, interveni pro clero, intercede pro devoto fœmineo sexu: sentiant omnes tuum juvamen, quicumque celebrant tuam sanctam commemorationem.

℣. Ora pro nobis, sancta Dei Genitrix.

℟. Ut digni efficiamur promissionibus Christi.

Oremus.

Concede nos famulos tuos, quæsumus Domine Deus, perpetua mentis et corporis sanitate gaudere: et gloriosa beatæ Mariæ semper virginis intercessione, a præsenti liberari tristitia, et æterna perfrui lætitia.

Holy Mary, be thou a help to the helpless, a strength to the fearful, a comfort to the sorrowful; pray for the people, plead for the clergy, make intercession for all women vowed to God; may all feel thine assistance who keep thy holy remembrance.

℣. Pray for us, O holy Mother of God.

℟. That we may be made worthy of the promises of Christ.

Let us pray.

Grant, O Lord God, we beseech Thee, that we Thy servants may rejoice in continual health of mind and body; and through the glorious intercession of Blessed Mary ever Virgin, be freed from present sorrow and enjoy eternal gladness.

From the Third Sunday after Epiphany *to the* Purification, *the following* ℣., ℟., *and Prayer are said instead of the above:*

℣. Post partum virgo inviolata permansisti.

℟. Dei Genitrix, intercede pro nobis.

℣. After childbirth thou didst remain a pure Virgin.

℟. O Mother of God, intercede for us.

Oremus.

Deus, qui salutis æternæ, beatæ Mariæ virginitate fœcunda, humano generi præmia præstitisti: tribue, quæsumus, ut ipsam pro nobis intercedere sentiamus, per quam meruimus auctorem vitæ suscipere, Dominum nostrum Jesum Christum Filium tuum.

Let us pray.

O God, Who by the fruitful virginity of Blessed Mary hast given unto mankind the rewards of eternal salvation: grant, we beseech Thee, that we may feel that she intercedes for us, through whom we have been made worthy to receive the Author of life, Our Lord Jesus Christ, Thy Son.

OF ST. JOSEPH

Ecce fidelis servus et prudens, quem constituit Dominus super familiam suam.

℣. Gloria et divitiæ in domo ejus.

℞. Et justitia ejus manet in sæculum sæculi.

Behold a faithful and wise servant, whom the Lord hath set over His household.

℣. Glory and riches shall be in his house.

℞. And his justice endureth forever and ever.

Oremus.

Deus, qui ineffabili providentia beatum Joseph sanctissimæ Genitricis tuæ sponsum eligere dignatus es: præsta quæsumus, ut quem protectorem veneramur in terris, intercessorem habere mereamur in cœlis.

Let us pray.

O God, Who by Thine unspeakable providence didst vouchsafe to choose blessed Joseph to be the spouse of Thy most holy Mother: mercifully grant that, as we venerate him for our protector on earth, we may be found worthy to be aided by his intercession in heaven.

OF THE APOSTLES

Petrus Apostolus, et Paulus doctor Gentium, ipsi nos docuerunt legem tuam, Domine.

℣. Constitues eos principes super omnem terram.

℞. Memores erunt nominis tui, Domine.

Peter the apostle, and Paul the Doctor of the Gentiles, they have taught us Thy law, O Lord.

℣. Thou shalt make them princes over all the earth.

℞. They shall be mindful of Thy name, O Lord.

Oremus.

Deus, cujus dextera beatum Petrum ambulantem in fluctibus, ne mergeretur, erexit; et coapostolum ejus Paulum tertio naufragantem de profundo pelagi liberavit: exaudi nos propitius, et concede, ut amborum meritis æternitatis gloriam consequamur.

Let us pray.

O God, Whose right hand raised up blessed Peter when he walked amid the waves, and suffered him not to sink; and delivered his fellow apostle Paul, in his third shipwreck, from the depths of the sea: graciously hear us, and grant that by the merits of both we may attain unto everlasting glory.

[A Commemoration is made of the patron or titular of the church either before or after the above, according to dignity.]

FOR PEACE

Da pacem, Domine, in diebus nostris, quia non est alius qui pugnet pro nobis, nisi tu Deus noster.

℣. Fiat pax in virtute tua.

℟. Et abundantia in turribus tuis.

Grant peace in our days, O Lord, for there is none other that fighteth for us, but only Thou, our God.

℣. Let peace be in thy strength.

℟. And plenteousness in thy towers.

Oremus.

Deus, a quo sancta desideria, recta consilia, et justa sunt opera: da servis tuis illam, quam mundus dare non potest pacem; ut et corda nostra mandatis tuis dedita, et hostium sublata formidine, tempora sint tua protectione tranquilla.

Let us pray.

O God, from Whom are holy desires, right counsels, and just works: give unto Thy servants that peace which the world cannot give; that our hearts being given to the keeping of Thy commandments, and the fear of enemies being removed, our days, by Thy protection, may be peaceful.

From the Second Sunday after Easter *till the* Ascension, *the foregoing Commemorations are omitted, and the following is the only Commemoration made:*

OF THE CROSS

Crucem sanctam subiit, qui infernum confregit, accinctus est potentia, surrexit die tertia, alleluia.

℣. Dicite in nationibus, alleluia.

℟. Quia Dominus regnavit a ligno, alleluia.

He bore the holy Cross, Who broke the power of hell; He was girded with power, He arose again the third day, alleluia.

℣. Tell ye among the nations, alleluia.

℟. That the Lord hath reigned from the Tree, alleluia.

Oremus.

Deus, qui pro nobis Filium tuum
crucis patibulum subire voluisti, ut
inimici a nobis expelleres potestatem: concede nobis famulis tuis;
ut resurrectionis gratiam consequamur. Per eundem Dominum, etc. ℟.
Amen.

℣. Dominus vobiscum.
℟. Et cum spiritu tuo.
℣. Benedicamus Domino.
℟. Deo gratias.
℣. Fidelium animæ per misericordiam
Dei requiescant in pace.

℟. Amen.
Pater noster (*secreto*).
℣. Dominus det nobis suam pacem.
℟. Et vitam æternam. Amen.

Let us pray.

O God, Who didst will that Thy Son
should undergo for us the ignominy
of the Cross, that Thou mightest
drive away from us the power of the
enemy: grant unto us Thy servants
to be made partakers of the grace of
the Resurrection. Through the same
Christ Our Lord, etc. ℟. Amen.

℣. The Lord be with you.
℟. And with thy spirit.
℣. Let us bless the Lord.
℟. Thanks be to God.
℣. May the souls of the faithful departed,
through the mercy of God, rest in
peace.

℟. Amen.
Our Father (*inaudibly*).
℣. May the Lord grant us His peace.
℟. And life everlasting. Amen.

*Here follows the Antiphon of the Blessed Virgin proper for the season. See end of Compline
(p. 57).*

Last of all is said, kneeling and in silence:

Sacrosanctæ et individuæ Trinitati,
crucifixi Domini nostri Jesu Christi
humanitati, beatissimæ et glorio-
sissimæ semperque Virginis Mariæ
fœcundæ integritati, et omnium
Sanctorum universitati sit sempiterna laus, honor, virtus, et gloria ab
omni creatura, nobisque remissio
omnium peccatorum, per infinita
sæcula sæculorum. ℟. Amen.

℣. Beata viscera Mariæ Virginis, quæ
portaverunt æterni Patris Filium.

℟. Et beata ubera, quæ lactaverunt
Christum Dominum.

To the most Holy and undivided Trinity,
to the humanity of Our Lord Jesus
Christ Crucified, to the fruitful virginity of the most blessed and most
glorious Mary, ever Virgin, and to
the whole company of the saints, be
everlasting praise, honor, power, and
glory, by all creatures; and to us remission of all our sins, world without
end. ℟. Amen.

℣. Blessed be the womb of the Virgin
Mary, which bore the Son of the
eternal Father.

℟. And blessed be the breast which
nourished Christ the Lord.

Then are said the Our Father *and the* Hail Mary.

THE OTHER PSALMS SUNG ON FESTIVALS AND SUNDAYS DURING THE YEAR

A complete Directory for their use will be found at the end (p. 172). The reference is made by letters of the alphabet.

F PSALM 116

Laudate Dominum, omnes gentes: * laudate eum, omnes populi:

O praise the Lord, all ye nations: praise Him, all ye people.

Quoniam confirmata est super nos misericordia ejus: * et veritas Domini manet in æternum.

For His mercy is confirmed upon us: and the truth of the Lord endureth forever.

Gloria Patri, etc.

Glory be to the Father, etc.

G PSALM 115

Credidi, propter quod locutus sum: * ego autcm humiliatus sum nimis.

I believed, and therefore did I speak: but I was humbled exceedingly.

Ego dixi in excessu meo: * Omnis homo mendax.

I said in mine excess: All men are liars.

Quid retribuam Domino, * pro omnibus, quæ retribuit mihi?

What shall I render unto the Lord: for all the things that He hath rendered unto me?

Calicem salutaris accipiam: * et nomen Domini invocabo.

I will take the chalice of salvation: and call upon the name of the Lord.

Vota mea Domino reddam coram omni populo ejus: * pretiosa in conspectu Domini mors sanctorum ejus:

I will pay my vows unto the Lord, in the presence of all His people: precious in the sight of the Lord is the death of His saints.

O Domine, quia ego servus tuus: * ego servus tuus, et filius ancillæ tuæ.

O Lord, I am Thy servant: I am Thy servant, and the son of Thine handmaid.

Dirupisti vincula mea: * tibi sacrificabo hostiam laudis, et nomen Domini invocabo.

Thou hast broken my bonds in sunder: I will offer unto Thee the sacrifice of praise, and will call upon the name of the Lord.

Vota mea Domino reddam in conspectu omnis populi ejus: * in atriis domus Domini, in medio tui, Jerusalem.

I will pay my vows unto the Lord in the sight of all His people: in the courts of the house of the Lord, in the midst of thee, O Jerusalem.

Gloria Patri, etc.

Glory be to the Father, etc.

H PSALM 121

Lætatus sum in his, quæ dicta sunt mihi: * In domum Domini ibimus.

I was glad at the things that were said unto me: We will go into the house of the Lord.

Stantes erant pedes nostri, * in atriis tuis, Jerusalem.

Our feet were standing in thy courts: O Jerusalem.

Jerusalem, quæ ædificatur ut civitas: * cujus participatio ejus in idipsum.

Jerusalem, which is built as a city: that is in unity with itself.

Illuc enim ascenderunt tribus, tribus Domini: * testimonium Israel ad confitendum nomini Domini.

For thither did the tribes go up, even the tribes of the Lord: the testimony of Israel, to praise the name of the Lord.

Quia illic sederunt sedes in judicio, * sedes super domum David.

For there are set the seats of judgment: the seats over the house of David.

Rogate quæ ad pacem sunt Jerusalem: * et abundantia diligentibus te.

Pray ye for the things that are for the peace of Jerusalem: and plenteousness be to them that love thee.

Fiat pax in virtute tua: * et abundantia in turribus tuis.

Let peace be in thy strength: and plenteousness in thy towers.

Propter fratres meos, et proximos meos, * loquebar pacem de te:

For my brethren and companions' sake: I spake peace concerning thee.

Propter domum Domini Dei nostri, * quæsivi bona tibi.

Because of the house of the Lord our God: I have sought good things for thee.

Gloria Patri, etc.

Glory be to the Father, etc.

I PSALM 126

Nisi Dominus ædificaverit domum, * in vanum laboraverunt qui ædificant eam.

Unless the Lord build the house: they labor in vain that build it.

Nisi Dominus custodierit civitatem, * frustra vigilat qui custodit eam.

Unless the Lord keep the city: he watcheth in vain that keepeth it.

Vanum est vobis ante lucem surgere: * surgite postquam sederitis, qui manducatis panem doloris.

In vain do ye rise before the light: rise not till ye have rested, O ye that eat the bread of sorrow.

Cum dederit dilectis suis somnum: * ecce hæreditas Domini filii: merces, fructus ventris.

When He hath given sleep to His beloved: lo, children are a heritage from the Lord; and the fruit of the womb a reward.

Sicut sagittæ in manu potentis: * ita filii excussorum.

Like as arrows in the hand of the mighty one: so are the children of those that have been cast out.

Beatus vir qui implevit desiderium suum ex ipsis: * non confundetur cum loquetur inimicis suis in porta.

Blessed is the man whose desire is satisfied with them: he shall not be confounded when he speaketh with his enemies in the gate.

Gloria Patri, etc.

Glory be to the Father, etc.

J PSALM 147

Lauda, Jerusalem, Dominum: * lauda Deum tuum, Sion.

Praise the Lord, O Jerusalem: praise thy God, O Sion.

Quoniam confortavit seras portarum tuarum: * benedixit filiis tuis in te.

For He hath strengthened the bars of thy gates: He hath blessed thy children within thee.

Qui posuit fines tuos pacem: * et adipe frumenti satiat te.

Who hath made peace in thy borders: and filleth thee with the fat of corn.

Qui emittit eloquium suum terræ: *
velociter currit sermo ejus.

Who sendeth forth His speech upon the
earth: His word runneth very swiftly.

Qui dat nivem sicut lanam: * nebulam
sicut cinerem spargit.

Who giveth snow like wool: He scattereth mists like ashes.

Mittit crystallum suam sicut buccel-
las: * ante faciem frigoris ejus quis
sustinebit?

He sendeth His crystal like morsels:
Who shall stand before the face of
His cold?

Emittet verbum suum, et liquefaciet ea:
* flabit spiritus ejus, et fluent aquæ.

He shall send out His word, and shall
melt them: His wind shall blow, and
the waters shall run.

Qui annuntiat verbum suum Jacob: *
justitias et judicia sua Israel.

Who declareth His word unto Jacob:
His justice and judgments unto
Israel.

Non fecit taliter omni nationi: * et judicia sua non manifestavit eis.

He hath not done in like manner to
every nation: and His judgments He
hath not made manifest to them.

Gloria Patri, etc.

Glory be to the Father, etc.

K PSALM 125

In convertendo Dominus captivitatem
Sion: * facti sumus sicut consolati.

When the Lord turned again the captivity of Sion: we became like men
consoled.

Tunc repletum est gaudio os nostrum: *
et lingua nostra exultatione.

Then was our mouth filled with gladness: and our tongue with joy.

Tunc dicent inter Gentes: *
Magnificavit Dominus facere cum
eis.

Then shall they say among the Gentiles;
The Lord hath done great things for
them.

Magnificavit Dominus facere nobiscum: * facti sumus lætantes.

The Lord hath done great things for us:
we are become joyful.

Converte, Domine, captivitatem nostram: * sicut torrens in austro.

Turn again our captivity, O Lord: as a
river in the south.

Qui seminant in lacrimis, * in exultatione metent.

They that sow in tears: shall reap in joy.

Euntes ibant et flebant, * mittentes semina sua.

They went forth on their way and wept: scattering their seed.

Venientes autem venient cum exultatione * portantes manipulos suos.

But returning, they shall come with joy: carrying their sheaves with them.

Gloria Patri, etc.

Glory be to the Father, etc.

L PSALM 138

Domine, probasti me, et cognovisti me: * tu cognovisti sessionem meam, et resurrectionem meam.

Lord, Thou hast proved me, and known me: Thou hast known my sitting down, and my rising up.

Intellexisti cogitationes meas de longe: * semitam meam, et funiculum meum investigasti.

Thou hast understood my thoughts afar off: my path and my line hast Thou searched out.

Et omnes vias meas prævidisti: * quia non est sermo in lingua mea.

Thou hast foreseen also all my ways: for there is no speech in my tongue.

Ecce, Domine, tu cognovisti omnia novissima et antiqua: * tu formasti me, et posuisti super me manum tuam.

Behold, O Lord, Thou hast known all things, the newest and those of old: Thou hast formed me, and laid Thine hand upon me.

Mirabilis facta est scientia tua ex me * confortata est, et non potero ad eam.

Thy knowledge is become wonderful unto me: it is high, and I cannot reach unto it.

Quo ibo a spiritu tuo? * et quo a facie tua fugiam?

Whither shall I go from Thy spirit? Or whither shall I flee from Thy face?

Si ascendero in cœlum, tu illic es: * si descendero in infernum, ades.

If I ascend into heaven, Thou art there: if I descend into hell, Thou art present.

Si sumpsero pennas meas diluculo, * et habitavero in extremis maris:

If I take my wings early in the morning: and dwell in the uttermost parts of the sea,

Etenim illuc manus tua deducet me: * et tenebit me dextera tua.

Even there also shall Thy hand lead me: and Thy right hand shall hold me.

Et dixi: Forsitan tenebræ conculcabunt me: * et nox illuminatio mea in deliciis meis.

And I said, Perhaps darkness shall cover me: and night shall be my light in my pleasures.

Quia tenebræ non obscurabuntur a te, et nox sicut dies illuminabitur: * sicut tenebræ ejus, ita et lumen ejus.

But darkness shall not be dark to Thee; and night shall be as light as the day: the darkness and the light thereof shall be alike to Thee.

Quia tu possedisti renes meos: * suscepisti me de utero matris meæ.

For Thou hast possessed my reins: Thou hast upholden me from my mother's womb.

Confitebor tibi quia terribiliter magnificatus es: * mirabilia opera tua, at anima mea cognoscit nimis.

I will praise Thee, for Thou art fearfully magnified: wonderful are Thy works, and my soul knoweth them right well.

Non est occultatum os meum a te, quod fecisti in occulto: * et substantia mea in inferioribus terræ.

My bone is not hidden from Thee, which Thou hast made in secret: and my substance in the lower parts of the earth.

Imperfectum meum viderunt oculi tui, et in libro tuo omnes scribentur: * dies formabuntur, et nemo in eis.

Thine eyes did see my imperfect being, and in Thy book all shall be written: the days shall be formed, and no one in them.

Mihi autem nimis honorificati sunt amici tui, Deus: * nimis confortatus est principatus eorum.

But to me Thy friends, O God, are made exceedingly honorable: their principality is exceedingly strengthened.

Dinumerabo eos, et super arenam multiplicabuntur: * exurrexi, et adhuc sum tecum.

I will number them, and they shall be multiplied above the sand: I rose up, and am still with Thee.

Si occideris, Deus, peccatores: * viri sanguinum, declinate a me:

If Thou wilt slay the wicked, O God: ye men of blood, depart from me:

Quia dicitis in cogitatione: * Accipient in vanitate civitates tuas.

Because ye say in thought: They shall receive Thy cities in vain.

Nonne qui oderunt te, Domine, oderam: * et super inimicos tuos tabescebam?

Have I not hated them, O Lord, that hated Thee: and pined away because of Thine enemies?

Perfecto odio oderam illos: * et inimici facti sunt mihi.	I have hated them with a perfect hatred: and they became as enemies unto me.
Proba me, Deus, et scito cor meum: * interrogfa me, et cognosce semitas meas.	Prove me, O God, and know my heart: examine me, and know my paths.
Et vide, si via iniquitatis in me est: * et deduc me in via æterna.	And see if there be in me the way of iniquity: and lead me in the eternal way.
Gloria Patri, etc.	Glory be to the Father, etc.

M PSALM 131

Memento, Domine, David, * et omnis mansuetudinis ejus:	O Lord, remember David: and all his meekness.
Sicut juravit Domino, * votum vovit Deo Jacob:	How he swore unto the Lord: and vowed a vow to the God of Jacob:
Si introiero in tabernaculum domus meæ, * si ascendero in lectum strati mei:	If I shall enter into the tabernacle of my house; if I shall go up into my bed:
Si dedero somnum oculis meis, * et palpebris meis dormitationem.	If I shall give sleep to mine eyes: or slumber to mine eyelids,
Et requiem temporibus meis: donec inveniam locum Domino, * tabernaculum Deo Jacob.	Or rest unto the temples of my head: until I find a place for the Lord, a tabernacle for the God of Jacob.
Ecce audivimus eam in Ephrata: * invenimus eam in campis silvæ.	Lo, we heard of it in Ephrata: we found it in the fields of the wood.
Introibimus in tabernaculum ejus: * adorabimus in loco, ubi steterunt pedes ejus.	We will go into His tabernacle: we will worship in the place where His feet have stood.
Surge, Domine, in requiem tuam, * tu et arca sanctificationis tuæ.	Arise, O Lord, into Thy resting place: Thou and the ark of Thy holiness.
Sacerdotes tui induantur justitiam: * et sancti tui exultent.	Let Thy priests be clothed with justice: and let Thy saints rejoice.

Propter David servum tuum, * non avertas faciem Christi tui.

For Thy servant David's sake: turn not away the face of Thine anointed.

Juravit Dominus David veritatem, et non frustrabitur eam: * de fructu ventris tui ponam super sedem tuam.

The Lord hath sworn the truth unto David, and He will not make it void: Of the fruit of thy body I will set upon thy throne.

Si custodierint filii tui testamentum meum, * et testimonia mea hæc, quæ docebo eos:

If thy children will keep My covenant: and these My testimonies which I shall teach them.

Et filii eorum usque in sæculum, * sedebunt super sedem tuam.

Their children also shall sit upon thy throne: forevermore.

Quoniam elegit Dominus Sion: * elegit eam in habitationem sibi.

For the Lord hath chosen Sion: He hath chosen her for His dwelling.

Hæc requies mea in sæculum sæculi: * hic habitabo quoniam elegi eam.

This is My rest forever and ever: here will I dwell, for I have chosen her.

Viduam ejus benedicens benedicam: * pauperes ejus saturabo panibus.

With blessing I will bless her widows: I will satisfy her poor with bread.

Sacerdotes ejus induam salutari: * et sancti ejus exultatione exultabunt.

I will clothe her priests with salvation; and her saints shall rejoice with exceeding joy.

Illuc producam cornu David, * paravi lucernam Christo meo.

There will I bring forth a horn unto David: I have prepared a lamp for Mine anointed.

Inimicos ejus induam confusione: * super ipsum autem efflorebit sanctificatio mea.

His enemies I will clothe with confusion: but upon Him shall My sanctification flourish.

Gloria Patri, etc.

Glory be to the Father, etc.

N PSALM 127

Beati omnes, qui timent Dominum, * qui ambulant in viis ejus.

Blessed are all they that fear the Lord: that walk in His ways.

Labores manuum tuarum quia mandu- | For thou shalt eat the labors of thy
cabis: * beatus es, et bene tibi erit. | hands: blessed art thou, and it shall
be well with thee.

Uxor tua sicut vitis abundans, * in lat- | Thy wife shall be as a fruitful vine: on
eribus domus tuæ. | the walls of thy house.

Filii tui sicut novellæ olivarum, * in cir- | Thy children as olive plants: round about
cuitu mensæ tuæ. | thy table.

Ecce sic benedicetur homo, * qui timet | Behold, thus shall the man be blessed:
Dominum. | that feareth the Lord,

Benedicat tibi Dominus ex Sion: * et | May the Lord bless thee out of Sion:
videas bona Jerusalem omnibus die- | and mayest thou see the good things
bus vitæ tuæ. | of Jerusalem all the days of thy life.

Et videas filios filiorum tuorum, * pa- | Mayest thou see thy children's children:
cem super Israel. | and peace upon Israel.

Gloria Patri, etc. | Glory be to the Father, etc.

O PSALM 129

De profundis clamavi ad te, Domine: * | Out of the depths have I cried unto
Domine, exaudi vocem meam. | Thee, O Lord: Lord, hear my voice.

Fiant aures tuæ intendentes, * in vocem | O let Thine ears consider well: the voice
deprecationis meæ. | of my supplication.

Si iniquitates observaveris, Domine: * | If Thou, O Lord, wilt mark iniquities:
Domine, quis sustinebit? | Lord, who shall abide it?

Quia apud te propitiatio est: * et prop- | For with Thee there is merciful forgive-
ter legem tuam sustinui te, Domine. | ness: and because of Thy law I have
waited for Thee, O Lord.

Sustinuit anima mea in verbo ejus: * | My soul hath waited on His word: my
speravit anima mea in Domino. | soul hath hoped in the Lord.

A custodia matutina usque ad noctem: | From the morning watch even until
* speret Israel in Domino. | night: let Israel hope in the Lord.

Quia apud Dominum misericordia: * et | For with the Lord there is mercy: and
copiosa apud eum redemptio. | with Him is plenteous redemption.

Et ipse redimet Israel, * ex omnibus iniquitatibus ejus.

And He shall redeem Israel: from all his iniquities.

Gloria Patri, etc.

Glory be to the Father, etc.

ℙ PSALM 137

Confitebor tibi, Domine, in toto corde meo: * quoniam audisti verba oris mei.

I will praise Thee, O Lord, with my whole heart: for Thou hast heard the words of my mouth.

In conspectu Angelorum psallam tibi: * adorabo ad templum sanctum tuum, et confitebor nomini tuo:

I will sing praise unto Thee in the sight of the angels: I will worship toward Thy holy temple, and give glory unto Thy name.

Super misericordia tua, et veritate tua: * quoniam magnificasti super omne, nomen sanctum tuum.

For Thy mercy, and for Thy truth: for Thou hast magnified Thy holy name above all.

In quacumque die invocavero te, exaudi me: * multiplicabis in anima mea virtutem.

In what day soever I shall call upon Thee, hear Thou me: Thou shalt multiply strength in my soul.

Confiteantur tibi, Domine, omnes reges terræ: * quia audierunt omnia verba oris tui.

Let all the kings of the earth give glory unto Thee, O Lord: for they have heard all the words of Thy mouth.

Et cantent in viis Domini: * quoniam magna est gloria Domini.

And let them sing in the ways of the Lord: for great is the glory of the Lord.

Quoniam excelsus Dominus, et humilia respicit: * et alta a longe cognoscit.

For the Lord is high, and looketh on the lowly: and the lofty He knoweth afar off.

Si ambulavero in medio tribulationis, vivificabis me: * et super iram inimicorum meorum extendisti manum tuam, et salvum me fecit dextera tua.

If I shall walk in the midst of tribulation, Thou wilt quicken me: and Thou hast stretched forth Thy hand against the wrath of mine enemies, and Thy right hand hath saved me.

Dominus retribuet pro me: * Domine, misericordia tua in sæculum: opera manuum tuarum ne despicias.

Gloria Patri, etc.

The Lord will repay for me; Thy mercy, O Lord, endureth forever: O despise not the works of Thy hands.

Glory be to the Father, etc.

𝔇𝔦𝔯𝔢𝔠𝔱𝔬𝔯𝔶

For finding the Psalms and Hymns appointed to be sung on the Sundays and principal festivals of the Christian year.

I.
SUNDAYS AND FEASTS OF THE SEASON

THE SUNDAYS OF ADVENT: . . . . A, B, C, D, E
    HYMN, "CREATOR ALME," NO. 7, P. 448.

CHRISTMAS— . . . . FIRST VESPERS: A, B, C, D, F
    SECOND VESPERS: . . . . A, B, C, O, M
    HYMN, "JESU, REDEMPTOR," NO. 11, P. 453.

THE HOLY INNOCENTS—VESPERS AS FOR THE SECOND VESPERS OF CHRISTMAS
    HYMN, "SALVETE, FLORES MARTYRUM," NO. 13, P. 455.

THE CIRCUMCISION: . . . . A, D, H, I, J
    HYMN, "JESU, REDEMPTOR" AS ABOVE.

THE EPIPHANY—FIRST VESPERS: . . . . A, B, C, D, F
    SECOND VESPERS: . . . . A, B, C, D, E
    HYMN, "CRUDELIS HERODES," NO. 14, P. 455.

‡THE HOLY FAMILY: . . . . A, D, H, I, J
    HYMN, "O LUX BEATA," P. 456.

THE SUNDAYS FROM EPIPHANY TILL LENT: . . . . A, B, C, D, E
    HYMN, "LUCIS CREATOR," NO. 5, P. 447.

THE SUNDAYS OF LENT: . . . . A, B, C, D, E
    HYMN, "AUDI, BENIGNE CONDITOR," NO. 16, P. 458.

PASSION AND PALM SUNDAYS: . . . . A, B, C, D, E
    HYMN, "VEXILLA REGIS," NO. 18, P. 459.

EASTER SUNDAY: . . . . A, B, C, D, E
    NO HYMN, BUT INSTEAD THE ANTIPHON, "HÆC DIES," NO. 23, P. 467.

FROM LOW SUNDAY TILL THE ASCENSION: . . . . A, B, C, D, E
    HYMN, "AD REGIAS AGNI DAPES," NO. 24, P. 468.

ASCENSION DAY AND THE SUNDAY FOLLOWING: . . . . A, B, C, D, F
    HYMN, "SALUTIS HUMANÆ SATOR," NO. 25, P. 469.

WHITSUNDAY: . . . . A, B, C, D, E
    HYMN, "VENI, CREATOR," NO. 26, P. 469.

TRINITY SUNDAY: .... A, B, C, D, E
    HYMN, "JAM SOL RECEDIT IGNEUS," NO. 28, P. 471.

CORPUS CHRISTI AND THE SUNDAY FOLLOWING: .... A, B, G, N, J
    HYMN, "PANGE, LINGUA," NO. 29, P. 472.

THE SUNDAYS AFTER PENTECOST: .... A, B, C, D, E
    HYMN, "LUCIS CREATOR," NO. 5, P. 447.

‡LAST SUNDAY OF OCTOBER, THE KINGSHIP OF OUR LORD: ..... A, B, C, D, F
    HYMN, "TE SÆCULORUM PRINCIPEM," P. 478.

II.
PROPER FEASTS OF SAINTS, ETC.

THE CONVERSION OF ST. PAUL (JAN. 25)—FIRST VESPERS: ...... A, B, C, D, F
    SECOND VESPERS: .... A, D, G, K, L
    HYMN, "EGREGIE DOCTOR," NO. 15, P. 457.

THE HOLY NAME OF JESUS (SECOND SUNDAY AFTER EPIPHANY): . A, B, C, D, G
    HYMN, "JESU, DULCIS MEMORIA," NO. 33, P. 479.

[‡THE FEAST OF ST. JOSEPH (MARCH 19) AND] THE PATRONAGE OF ST. JOSEPH
    (THIRD SUNDAY AFTER EASTER): .... A, B, C, D, F
    HYMN, "TE, JOSEPH, CELEBRENT," NO. 34, P. 480.

THE NATIVITY OF ST. JOHN THE BAPTIST (JUNE 24): .... A, B, C, D, F
    HYMN, "UT QUEANT LAXIS," NO. 35, P. 481.

STS. PETER AND PAUL (JUNE 29): .... A, B, C, D, F
    HYMN, "DECORA LUX," NO. 36, P. 482.

THE MOST PRECIOUS BLOOD (FIRST SUNDAY OF JULY): .... A, B, C, D, J
    HYMN, "FESTIVIS RESONENT," NO. 37, P. 483.

THE TRANSFIGURATION OF OUR LORD (AUGUST 6): .... A, B, C, D, F
    HYMN, "QUICUMQUE CHRISTUM QUÆRITIS," NO. 38, P. 484.

ST. JOACHIM (SUNDAY WITHIN OCTAVE OF ASSUMPTION): .... A, B, C, D, F
    HYMN, "ISTE CONFESSOR," NO. 50, P. 496.

THE SEVEN SORROWS OF THE B. V. M.: .... A, D, H, I, J
    HYMN, "O QUOT UNDIS," NO. 39, P. 485.
    ‡HYMN, "JAM TOTO," P. 486.

ST. MICHAEL (SEPT. 29)—FIRST VESPERS: .... A, B, C, D, F
    SECOND VESPERS: .... A, B, C, D, P
    HYMN, "TE, SPLENDOR," NO. 40, P. 487.

THE ANGEL GUARDIAN (OCT. 2): SAME PSALMS AS ABOVE.
HYMN, "CUSTODES HOMINUM," NO. 41, P. 488.

‡THE MOST HOLY ROSARY OF THE BLESSED VIRGIN (OCT. 7): ..... A, D, H, I, J
HYMN, "TE GESTIENTEM," P. 489.

ST. RAPHAEL (OCT. 24): SAME PSALMS AS ABOVE.
HYMN, "TIBI CHRISTE SPLENDOR," NO. 42, P. 490.

ALL SAINTS (NOV. 1)—FIRST VESPERS: .... A, B, C, D, F
SECOND VESPERS: .... A, B, C, D, G
HYMN, "PLACARE, CHRISTE," NO. 44, P. 491.

III.
COMMON OFFICES OF SAINTS, ETC.

COMMON OF APOSTLES—FIRST VESPERS: .... A, B, C, D, F
SECOND VESPERS: .... A, D, G, K, L
HYMN, "EXULTET ORBIS," NO. 45, P. 492.
HYMN AT EASTERTIDE, "TRISTES ERANT," NO. 46, P. 493.

COMMON OF ONE MARTYR AND OF MANY MARTYRS—FIRST VESPERS: A, B, C, D, F
SECOND VESPERS: .... A, B, C, D, G
HYMN FOR ONE MARTYR, "DEUS TUORUM," NO. 47, P. 494.
HYMN FOR MANY MARTYRS, "SANCTORUM MERITIS," NO. 48, P. 494.
HYMN FOR MANY MARTYRS AT EASTERTIDE, "REX GLORIOSE," NO. 49, P. 496.

COMMON OF A CONFESSOR BISHOP—FIRST VESPERS: .... A, B, C, D, F
SECOND VESPERS: .... A, B, C, D, M
HYMN, "ISTE CONFESSOR," NO. 50, P. 496.

COMMON OF A CONFESSOR NOT A BISHOP: .... A, B, C, D, F
HYMN THE SAME AS ABOVE.

COMMON OF VIRGINS AND HOLY WOMEN: .... A, D, H, I, J
HYMN FOR VIRGINS, "JESU CORONA VIRGINUM," NO. 51, P. 497.
HYMN FOR HOLY WOMEN, "FORTEM VIRILI PECTORE," NO. 52, P. 498.

COMMON OF THE DEDICATION OF A CHURCH: .... A, B, C, D, J
HYMN, "CŒLESTIS URBS," NO. 53, P. 499.

COMMON FOR ALL FEASTS OF THE B. V. M.: .... A, D, H, I, J
HYMN, "AVE MARIS STELLA," NO. 54, P. 500.

TABLE OF PSALMS IN THIS BOOK SUITABLE FOR VARIOUS OCCASIONS

(The pages in which the psalms occur will be found in the index.)

DURING SICKNESS.—Pss. 6, 15, 19, 85, 90.

SORROW FOR SIN.—Pss. 6, 31, 37, 50, 101, 129, 142.

CONFIDENCE IN GOD.—Pss. 26, 90, 126, 127, 138.

BEWAILING OUR MISERIES.—Ps. 41.

PRAYER FOR DELIVERANCE.—Pss. 7, 24, 85.

PRAISE.—Pss. 118, 133, 148, 149, 150.

SONGS OF JOY.—Pss. 62, 83, 121.

THANKSGIVING.—Pss. 112, 113, 116, 125, 148.

IN TROUBLE.—Pss. 4, 5, 30, 142.

FOR SUPERIORS.—Ps. 19.

IN DISQUIETUDE OF MIND.—Ps. 6.

SHORTNESS OF THIS LIFE.—Pss. 101, 102.

THE GOOD AND THE WICKED.—Pss. 5, 7, 23, 24, 31, 83, 90, 118, 126, 127.

EXCELLENCE OF GOD'S LAW.—Ps. 118.

HISTORICAL.—Ps. 113.

SEEKING AFTER GOD.—Pss. 41, 62, 66, 83.

FOR HOLY COMMUNION.   Pss. 19, 24, 41, 53, 84, 117, 137, 148.

PSALMS SUITABLE FOR THE VARIOUS SEASONS

ADVENT.—Ps. 84.

CHRISTMAS.—Pss. 83, 102.

LENT.—Pss. 4, 30, 39, 110, 115, AND THE *SEVEN PENITENTIAL PSALMS*.

EASTER.—Pss. 15, 109, 117.

ASCENSION.—Pss. 23, 102, 131.

PENTECOST.—Pss. 133, 150.

THE BLESSED VIRGIN.—Pss. 23, 109, 112, 121, 126, 147.

THE HOLY ANGELS.—Pss. 90, 102, 148.

THE CHURCH.—Pss. 121, 131, 147, 149.

FOR THE DEAD.—Pss. 5, 6, 7, 22, 24, 26, 39, 40, 41, 50, 62, 64, 129, 131, 137.

Benediction of the Blessed Sacrament

The Benediction of the Blessed Sacrament is a rite in which Jesus, in the Sacrament of His love, is not only exposed to the adoration of the faithful, but in which He, present in that Sacrament, is implored to bless the faithful present before the altar. It is not so much the priest who blesses the people by this rite, as it is Jesus Christ Himself, in the Blessed Sacrament, Who bestows His benediction upon them.

In this country, Benediction usually follows Vespers. After the final Antiphon of the Blessed Virgin is said, the priest, vested in surplice, stole, and cope, goes up to the altar, while the choir sings the *O salutaris Hostia*; and opening the tabernacle, he makes a genuflection, and taking out a consecrated Host enclosed in a kind of locket, called a *luna*, places this in the center of the *monstrance* or *ostensorium*—a stand of gold or silver, with rays like the sun. He then descends to the foot of the altar, and puts incense in the censer; kneeling again, he receives the censer from the hand of the acolyte, and incenses the adorable Host. When the choir sings the second line of the *Tantum ergo*, all bow humbly down, and then, or during the *Genitori*, the priest again incenses the Blessed Sacrament.

As soon as the choir has ended the hymn, the priest chants the versicle; and after the response, he chants the Prayer of the Blessed Sacrament, and sometimes another prayer. He then kneels again, and a veil is placed around his shoulders, after which he ascends again to the altar, and, making a genuflection, takes the monstrance, and, turning to the people, gives the Benediction in silence, making the sign of the cross over the kneeling congregation.

Replacing the Host in the tabernacle, he descends, and, preceded by his assistants, retires, while the choir chants the 116th Psalm, *Laudate Dominum, omnes Gentes*, or some other psalm or canticle permitted by the usage of the place.

During this holy rite, the devout worshipper may either join in the chant of the choir, or pour out his soul in aspirations of love, adoration, gratitude, petition, or contrition to the Sacred Heart of Jesus, thus humbled for our love.

When the priest has exposed the Blessed Sacrament, the choir sings:

O salutaris Hostia,	O saving Victim! opening wide
Quæ cœli pandis ostium,	The gate of heaven to man below!
Bella premunt hostilia,	Our foes press on from every side;
Da robur, fer auxilium.	Thine aid supply, Thy strength bestow.
Uni trinoque Domino	To Thy great name be endless praise,
Sit sempiterna gloria:	Immortal Godhead! One in Three!
Qui vitam sine termino	O grant us endless length of days
Nobis donet in patria.	In our true native land with Thee!

Here is frequently sung the Litany of Loreto *(p. 50), or some hymn in honor of the Blessed Sacrament (pp. 472–477, 483–484, 501–503).*

Lastly is sung the Tantum ergo; *during which incense is again offered to the Blessed Sacrament, and all prostrate themselves at the second line.*

Tantum ergo Sacramentum	Down in adoration falling,
Veneremur cernui:	Lo! the Sacred Host we hail!
Et antiquum documentum	Lo! o'er ancient forms departing,
Novo cedat ritui:	Newer rites of grace prevail;
Præstet fides supplementum	Faith for all defects supplying
Sensuum defectui.	Where the feeble senses fail.
Genitori, Genitoque	To the everlasting Father,
Laus et jubilatio:	And the Son Who reigns on high,
Salus, honor, virtus quoque	With the Holy Ghost proceeding
Sit et benedictio:	Forth from each eternally,
Procedenti ab utroque	Be salvation, honor, blessing.
Compar sit laudatio. *Amen.*	Might, and endless majesty. *Amen.*

Still kneeling, the priest sings:

℣. Panem de cœlo præstitisti eis.

℟. Omne delectamentum in se habentem.

℣. Thou gavest them bread from heaven.

℟. Having in it the sweetness of every taste.

[*In Eastertide, and during the* Octave of Corpus Christi, Alleluia *is added to* ℣. *and* ℟.]

Rising, he sings the following prayer:

Oremus.

Deus, qui nobis sub sacramento mirabili passionis tuæ memoriam reliquisti: tribue, quæsumus, ita nos corporis et sanguinis tui sacra mysteria venerari; ut redemptionis tuæ fructum in nobis jugiter sentiamus. Qui vivis et regnas in sæcula sæculorum. ℟. Amen.

Let us pray.

O God, Who, under a wonderful Sacrament, hast left us a memorial of Thy Passion: grant us, we beseech Thee, so to venerate the sacred mysteries of Thy Body and Blood that we may ever feel within ourselves the fruit of Thy Redemption. Who livest and reignest, world without end. ℟. Amen.

The Benediction veil is now placed upon the shoulders of the priest. He ascends the steps of the altar, takes the monstrance containing the Blessed Sacrament in his hands, and solemnly and in silence makes with it the sign of the cross over the people. (Meanwhile, a bell is rung by an acolyte.)

177

‡THE DIVINE PRAISES

Blessed be God.
Blessed be His holy name.
Blessed be Jesus Christ, true God and true man.
Blessed be the name of Jesus.
Blessed be His most Sacred Heart.
Blessed be His most Precious Blood.
Blessed be Jesus in the most Holy Sacrament of the Altar.
Blessed be the Holy Ghost, the Paraclete.
Blessed be the great Mother of God, Mary most holy.
Blessed be her holy and Immaculate Conception.
Blessed be her glorious Assumption.
Blessed be the name of Mary, Virgin and Mother.
Blessed be St. Joseph, her most chaste spouse.
Blessed be God in His angels and in His saints.

After the Blessed Sacrament has been replaced in the tabernacle, all rise and sing:

PSALM 116

Laudate Dominum, omnes gentes: *
laudate eum, omnes populi.
Quoniam confirmata est super nos misericordia ejus: * et veritas Domini
manet in æternum.
Gloria Patri, etc.

O praise the Lord, all ye nations: praise
Him, all ye people.
For His mercy is confirmed upon us:
and the truth of the Lord endureth
forever.
Glory be to the Father, etc.

During the singing of the Sicut erat *of the* Gloria, *the celebrant and ministers retire; and thus ends the Benediction.*

Occasional Offices

THE BLESSING OF THE CANDLES

On the Feast of the Purification, February 2.

The priest, clad in a violet cope, or else without chasuble, proceeds to the Blessing of the Candles, placed on a table near the Epistle corner of the altar: and there standing, facing the altar, and with hands joined before his breast, the priest says:

Dominus vobiscum.
℞. Et cum spiritu tuo.

The Lord be with you.
℞. And with thy spirit.

Oremus.

Domine sancte, Pater omnipotens, æterne Deus, qui omnia ex nihilo creasti, et jussu tuo, per opera apum, hunc liquorem ad perfectionem cerei venire fecisti; et qui hodierna die petitionem justi Simeonis implesti: te humiliter deprecamur, ut has candelas ad usus hominum, et sanitatem corporum et animarum, sive in terra, sive in aquis, per invocationem tui sanctissimi nominis, et per intercessionem beatæ Mariæ semper Virginis, cujus hodie festa devote celebrantur, et per preces omnium sanctorum tuorum, bene ✠ dicere et sancti ✠ ficare digneris: et hujus plebis tuæ, quæ illas honorifice in manibus desiderat portare, teque cantando laudare, exaudias voces de cœlo sancto tuo, et de sede majestatis tuæ: et propitius sis omnibus clamantibus ad te, quos redemisti pretioso sanguine Filii tui. Qui tecum vivit et regnat, in unitate Spiritus Sancti Deus, per omnia sæcula sæculorum. ℞. Amen.

Let us pray.

O holy Lord, Father Almighty, eternal God, Who didst create all things from nothing, and by the labor of bees at Thy command hast brought this liquid to the perfection of wax; and Who on this day didst fulfill the petition of just Simeon: we humbly beseech Thee that by the invocation of Thy most holy name, and by the intercession of Blessed Mary, ever Virgin, whose festival we this day devoutly celebrate, and by the prayers of all Thy saints, Thou wouldst vouchsafe to bless ✠ and sanctify ✠ these candles for the service of men, and for the health of their bodies and souls, whether on land or water; and wouldst hear from Thy holy heaven, and from the throne of Thy Majesty, the voice of this Thy people, who desire reverently to bear them in their hands, and to praise Thee in song; and wouldst show mercy to all that call upon Thee, whom Thou hast redeemed with the Precious Blood of Thy Son. Who liveth and reigneth, etc. ℞. Amen.

Omnipotens, sempiterne Deus, qui hodierna die Unigenitum tuum, ulnis sancti Simeonis in templo sancto tuo suscipiendum præsentasti: tuam supplices deprecamur clementiam, ut has candelas, quas nos famuli tui, in tui nominis magnificentiam suscipientes, gestare cupimus luce accensas, bene ✠ dicere et sancti ✠ ficare, atque lumine supernæ benedictionis accendere digneris; quatenus eas tibi Domino Deo nostro offerendo digni, et sancto igne dulcissimæ caritatis tuæ succensi, in templo sancto gloriæ tuæ repræsentari mereamur. Per eundem Dominum, etc. ℟. Amen.

Almighty, everlasting God, Who on this day didst present Thine only begotten Son to be received by the arms of holy Simeon in Thy holy temple: we humbly beseech Thy loving kindness, that Thou wouldst vouchsafe to bless, ✠ sanctify, ✠ and kindle with the light of Thy heavenly benediction these candles, which we Thy servants desire to receive and carry lighted in honor of Thy name; to the end that by offering them to Thee, Our Lord God, we, being worthy to be inflamed with the holy fire of Thy sweetest charity, may deserve to be presented in the holy temple of Thy glory. Through the same Our Lord, etc. ℟. Amen.

Oremus.

Domine Jesu Christe, lux vera, quæ illuminas omnem hominem venientem in hunc mundum: effunde bene ✠ dictionem tuam super hos cereos, et sancti ✠ fica eos lumine gratiæ tuæ, et concede propitius, ut sicut hæc luminaria igne visibili accensa nocturnas depellunt tenebras, ita corda nostra invisibili igne, id est, Sancti Spiritus splendore illustrata, omnium vitiorum cæcitate careant: ut, purgato mentis oculo, ea cernere possimus, quæ tibi sunt placita, et nostræ saluti utilia; quatenus post hujus sæculi caliginosa discrimina, ad lucem indeficientem pervenire mereamur. Per te, Christe Jesu, Salvator mundi, qui in Trinitate perfecta vivis et regnas Deus, per omnia sæcula sæculorum. ℟. Amen.

Let us pray.

O Lord Jesus Christ, the true Light, that enlightenest every man who cometh into this world: pour forth Thy blessing ✠ upon these candles, and sanctify ✠ them with the light of Thy grace; and mercifully grant that as these lights, enkindles with visible fire, dispel the darkness of night, so our hearts, illumined by invisible fire, that is, the brightness of the Holy Ghost, may be free from the blindness of every vice; that, the eye of our minds being purified, we may discern those things which are pleasing to Thee and profitable to our salvation; so that, after the darksome perils of this world, we may be found worthy to arrive at the light that never faileth. Through Thee, Christ Jesus, Savior of the world, Who in perfect Trinity livest and reignest, etc. ℟. Amen.

Oremus.

Omnipotens, sempiterne Deus, qui per Moysen famulum tuum, purissimum olei liquorem ad luminaria ante conspectum tuum jugiter concinanda præparari jussisti: bene ✠ dictionis tuæ gratiam super hos cereos benignus infunde; quatenus sic administrent lumen exterius, ut, te donante, lumen Spiritus tui nostris non desit mentibus interius. Per Dominum, etc. ℞. Amen.

Oremus.

Domine Jesu Christe, qui hodierna die in nostræ carnis substantia inter homines apparens, a parentibus in templo es præsentatus; quem Simeon venerabilis senex, lumine Spiritus tui irradiatus, agnovit, suscepit, et benedixit: præsta propitius, ut ejusdem Spiritus Sancti gratia illuminati, atque edocti, te veraciter agnoscamus, et fideliter diligamus. Qui cum Deo Patre in unitate ejusdem Spiritus Sancti, vivis et regnas Deus, per omnia sæcula sæculorum. ℞. Amen.

Let us pray.

Almighty, everlasting God, Who by Thy servant Moses didst command the purest oil to be prepared for lamps to burn continually before Thee: graciously pour forth the grace of Thy blessing ✠ upon these candles; that as they afford us external light, so by Thy bounty the light of Thy Spirit may never be inwardly wanting to our minds. Through Our Lord Jesus Christ, etc. ℞. Amen.

Let us pray.

O Lord Jesus Christ, Who, appearing among men in the substance of our flesh, wast this day presented by Thy parents in the temple; Whom the venerable old man Simeon, illumined by the light of Thy Spirit, recognized, received, and blessed: mercifully grant that, enlightened and taught by the grace of the same Holy Spirit, we may truly acknowledge Thee, and faithfully love Thee. Who with God the Father, in the unity of the same Holy Spirit, livest and reignest God, world without end. ℞. Amen.

Here the priest, having put incense into the censer, sprinkles the candles three times with holy water, saying the Antiphon:

Asperges me, Domine, hyssopo, et mundabor; lavabis me, et super nivem dealbabor.

Thou shalt sprinkle me, O Lord, with hyssop, and I shall be cleansed; Thou shalt wash me, and I shall be made whiter than snow.

He then incenses the candles three times, and distributes them, first to the clergy, then to the laity, who receive them kneeling, and kissing the candle and the priest's hand. During the distribution, the choir sings:

Lumen ad revelationem gentium, et gloriam plebis tuæ Israel.

Light to enlighten the Gentiles, and glory of Thy people Israel.

℣. Nunc dimittis servum tuum, Domine, * secundum verbum tuum in pace.

℣. Now, O Lord, lettest Thou Thy servant depart in peace: according to Thy word.

℟. Lumen ad revelationem gentium, et gloriam plebis tuæ Israel.

℟. Light to enlighten the Gentiles, and glory of Thy people Israel.

℣. Quia viderunt oculi mei * salutare tuum.

℣. For mine eyes have seen: Thy salvation.

℟. Lumen ad revelationem gentium, et gloriam plebis tuæ Israel.

℟. Light to enlighten the Gentiles, and glory of Thy people Israel.

℣. Quod parasti * ante faciem omnium populorum.

℣. Which Thou hast prepared: in sight of all nations.

℟. Lumen ad revelationem gentium, et gloriam plebis tuæ Israel.

℟. Light to enlighten the Gentiles, and glory of Thy people Israel.

℣. Gloria Patri, et Filio, * et Spiritui Sancto.

℣. Glory be to the Father, and to the Son: and to the Holy Ghost.

℟. Lumen ad revelationem gentium, et gloriam plebis tuæ Israel.

℟. Light to enlighten the Gentiles, and glory of Thy people Israel.

℣. Sicut erat in principio, et nunc, et semper, * et in sæcula sæculorum. *Amen.*

℣. As it was in the beginning, is now, and ever shall be: world without end. *Amen.*

℟. Lumen ad revelationem gentium, et gloriam plebis tuæ Israel.

℟. Light to enlighten the Gentiles, and glory of Thy people Israel.

Then follows the Antiphon:

Exurge, Domine, adjuva nos, et libera nos propter nomen tuum.

Arise, O Lord, help us, and deliver us, for Thy name's sake.

Deus, auribus nostris audivimus: * patres nostri annuntiaverunt nobis.

We have heard with our ears, O God: our fathers have declared unto us.

℣. Gloria Patri, etc.

Ant. Exurge, Domine, adjuva nos, et libera nos propter nomen tuum.

Then the priest says:

Oremus.

[*If after* Septuagesima, *and not on a Sunday, the deacon adds:*

Flectamus genua.

℟. Levate.

Exaudi, quæsumus Domine, plebem tuam, et quæ extrinsecus annua tribuis devotione venerari, interius assequi gratiæ tuæ luce concede. Per Christum Dominum nostrum. ℟. Amen.

℣. Glory be to the Father, etc.

Ant. Arise, O Lord, help us, and deliver us, for Thy name's sake.

Let us pray.

Let us kneel.

℟. Arise.]

Hear Thy people, O Lord, we beseech Thee, and grant us to obtain those things inwardly by the light of Thy grace, which Thou grantest us outwardly to worship by this yearly devotion. Through Christ Our Lord. ℟. Amen.

Then follows the procession. The celebrant puts incense into the censer, after which the deacon, turning toward the people, sings:

℣. Procedamus in pace.

℣. Let us proceed in peace.

To which the choir answers:

℟. In nomine Christi. Amen.

℟. In the name of Christ, Amen.

The thurifer goes before with burning incense; then the subdeacon, vested, carrying the cross between two acolytes with lighted candles; the clergy follow according to their order; and lastly the celebrant, with the deacon at his left hand, all bearing lighted candles. They sing the following Antiphons:

Adorna thalamum tuum, Sion, et suscipe Regem Christum; amplectere Mariam, quæ est cœlestis porta: ipsa enim portat Regem gloriæ novi luminis: subsistit Virgo, adducens manibus filium ante luciferum genitum: quem accipiens Simeon in ulnas suas, prædicavit populis Dominum eum esse vitæ et mortis, et Salvatorem mundi.

Adorn thy chamber, O Sion, and receive Christ the King; in love consider Mary, who is the gate of heaven: for she bears the glorious King of the new light; remaining ever a Virgin, she brings in her hands the Son begotten before the daystar: Whom Simeon, receiving into his arms, proclaimed to the people to be the Lord of life and death, and the Savior of the world.

Responsum accepit Simeon a Spiritu Sancto, non visurum se mortem, nisi videret Christum Domini: et cum inducerent puerum in templum, accepit eum in ulnas suas, et benedixit Deum, et dixit: Nunc dimittis servum tuum, Domine, in pace.

℣. Cum inducerent puerum Jesum parentes ejus, ut facerent secundum consuetudinem legis pro eo, ipse accepit eum in ulnas suas.

Entering into the church, is sung:

Obtulerunt pro eo Domino par turturum, aut duos pullos columbarum: † sicut scriptum est in lege Domini.

℣. Postquam impleti sunt dies purgationis Mariæ secundum legem Moysi, tulerunt Jesum in Jerusalem, ut sisterent eum Domino.

Sicut scriptum est in lege Domini.

℣. Gloria Patri, et Filio, et Spiritui Sancto.

Sicut scriptum est in lege Domini.

Simeon received an answer from the Holy Ghost, that he should not see death before he had seen the Christ of the Lord; and when they brought the Child into the temple, he took Him in his arms, and blessed God, and said, Now, O Lord, lettest Thou Thy servant depart in peace.

℣. When His parents brought in the Child Jesus, to do for Him according to the custom of the law, he took Him in his arms.

They offered for Him to the Lord a pair of turtle doves, or two young pigeons: † as it is written in the law of the Lord.

℣. After the days of the purification of Mary, according to the Law of Moses, were past, they carried Jesus to Jerusalem, to present Him to the Lord.

As it is written in the law of the Lord.

℣. Glory be to the Father.

As it is written in the law of the Lord.

The procession being finished, the clergy put on white vestments for the Mass, and the candles are held lighted during the Gospel, and from the Elevation to the Communion.

✠ *THE BLESSING OF THE CANDLES AND OF THE THROATS, ON THE FEAST OF ST. BLASE*

Adjutorium nostrum in nomine Domini.

℞. Qui fecit cœlum et terram.

℣. Dominus vobiscum.

℞. Et cum spiritu tuo.

Our help is in the name of the Lord.

℞. Who hath made heaven and earth.

℣. The Lord be with you.

℞. And with thy spirit.

Oremus.

Omnipotens et mitissime Deus, qui omnium mundi rerum diversitates solo Verbo creasti, et ad hominum reformationem illud idem Verbum, per quod facta sunt omnia, incarnari voluisti: qui magnus es, et immensus, terribilis atque laudabilis, ac faciens mirabilia: pro cujus fidei confessione gloriosus Martyr et Pontifex Blasius, diversorum tormentorum genera non pavescens, martyrii palmam feliciter est adeptus: quique eidem, inter ceteras gratias, hanc prærogativam contulisti, ut, quoscumque gutturis morbos tua virtute curaret; majestatem tuam suppliciter exoramus, ut non inspectu reatus nostri, sed ejus placatus meritis et precibus, hanc ceræ creaturam bene ✠ dicere, ac sancti ✠ ficare tua venerabili pietate digneris, tuam gratiam infundendo; ut omnes, quorum colla per eam ex bona fide tacta fuerint, a quocumque gutturis morbo ipsius passionis meritis liberentur, et in Ecclesia sancta tua sani et hilares tibi gratiarum referant actiones, laudentque nomen tuum gloriosum, quod est benedictum in sæcula sæculorum.

Let us pray.

O Almighty and most loving God, Who by Thy Word only hast created all the various beings of the universe, and hast willed that, for man's restoration, the same Word, through Whom everything was made, should become incarnate; O God, Who art great and present everywhere, terrible and worthy of all praise, and dost wonders; for Whose holy religion the illustrious martyr and bishop Blase has dared many a torture and gloriously obtained a martyr's crown; O God, Who hast conferred upon him, among other favors, the special privilege of curing, through Thy power, every kind of throat disease, we humbly beg of Thy Majesty that, disregarding our sinfulness and being appeased by his merits and prayers, Thou vouchsafest to bless ✠ this wax and sanctify ✠ it in Thy kindness worthy of all praise, by pouring Thy grace hereinto; so that all those devoted servants whose necks it has touched, may, through the merits of his sufferings, be freed from every throat affliction, and in a sound body and with a heart full of joy, give thanks to Thee in Thy holy Church, and praise Thy glorious name,

Per Dominum nostrum Jesum Christum Filium tuum, qui tecum vivit et regnat in unitate Spiritus Sancti Deus, per omnia sæcula sæculorum. ℟. Amen.

which is blessed for all ages. Through Our Lord, Jesus Christ, Thy Son, Who liveth and reigneth, etc. ℟. Amen.

The priest sprinkles the candles with holy water; and then he places two of these candles in the shape of a cross, under the chin of every one of the people who are kneeling before the altar rail, and says at the same time:

Per intercessionem sancti Blasii, Episcopi et Martyris, liberet te Deus a malo gutturis, et a quolibet alio malo. In nomine Patris, et Filii, ✠ et Spiritus Sancti. ℟. Amen.

By the intercession of St. Blase, bishop and martyr, may God preserve thee from all throat trouble, and from all other evil. In the name of the Father, and of the Son, ✠ and of the Holy Ghost. ℟. Amen.

THE BLESSING OF THE ASHES

On Ash Wednesday.

Exaudi nos, Domine, quoniam benigna est misericordia tua: secundum multitudinem miserationum tuarum respice nos, Domine.

Hear us, O Lord, for Thy mercy is kind: look upon us, O Lord, according to the multitude of Thy tender mercies.

Salvum me fac Deus; quoniam intraverunt aquæ usque ad animam meam.

Save me, O God; for the waters are come in even unto my soul.

℣. Gloria Patri, etc.

℣. Glory be to the Father, etc.

The Antiphon Exaudi nos *is repeated. Then the priest, standing at the Epistle corner of the altar, says:*

℣. Dominus vobiscum.
℟. Et cum spiritu tuo.

℣. The Lord be with you.
℟. And with thy spirit.

Oremus.

Omnipotens, sempiterne Deus, parce pœnitentibus, propitiare supplicantibus: et mittere digneris sanctum Angelum tuum de cœlis, qui bene ✠ dicat et sancti ✠ ficet hos cineres, ut sint remedium salubre omnibus nomen sanctum tuum humiliter implorantibus ac semetipsos pro conscientia delictorum suorum accusantibus, ante conspectum divinæ clementiæ tuæ facinora sua deplorantibus, vel serenissimam pietatem tuam suppliciter, obnixeque flagitantibus: et præsta per invocationem sanctissimi nominis tui, ut quicumque per eos aspersi fuerint, pro redemptione peccatorum suorum, corporis sanitatem, et animæ tutelam percipiant. Per Christum Dominum nostrum. ℟. Amen.

Oremus.

Deus, qui non mortem, sed pœnitentiam desideras peccatorum: fragilitatem conditionis humanæ benignissime respice, et hos cineres, quos causa proferendæ humilitatis, atque promerendæ veniæ, capitibus nostris imponi decernimus, bene ✠ dicere pro tua pietate dignare; ut, qui nos cinerem esse, et ob pravitatis nostræ demeritum in pulverem reversuros cognoscimus, peccatorum omnium veniam, et præmia pœnitentibus repromissa, misericorditer consequi mereamur. Per Christum Dominum nostrum. ℟. Amen.

Let us pray.

Almighty, everlasting God, spare those who are penitent, be merciful to those who supplicate Thee, and vouchsafe to send Thy holy angel from heaven to bless ✠ and sanctify ✠ these ashes, that they may be a wholesome remedy to all who humbly implore Thy holy name, and, conscious of their sins, accuse themselves, deploring their crimes before Thy divine mercy, or humbly and earnestly calling upon Thy bountiful loving kindness; and grant, through the invocation of Thy most holy name, that all those whosoever shall be sprinkled with these ashes, for the remission of their sins, may receive both health of body and salvation of soul. Through Christ Our Lord. ℟. Amen.

Let us pray.

O God, Who desirest not the death but the repentance of sinners: graciously look down upon the frailty of human nature, and in Thy mercy vouchsafe to bless ✠ these ashes, which we design to place upon our heads in token of our humility, and to obtain forgiveness; that we, who know that we are but ashes, and for the demerits of our wickedness must return to dust, may deserve to obtain of Thy mercy the pardon of all our sins, and the rewards promised to the penitent. Through Christ Our Lord. ℟. Amen.

Oremus.

Deus, qui humilitatione flecteris, et satisfactione placaris: aurem tuæ pietatis inclina precibus nostris; et capitibus servorum tuorum, horum cinerum aspersione contactis, effunde propitius gratiam tuæ benedictionis: ut eos et spiritu compunctionis repleas, et quæ juste postulaverint, efficaciter tribuas; et concessa perpetuo stabilita, et intacta manere decernas. Per Christum Dominum nostrum. ℟. Amen.

Let us pray.

O God, Who art moved by humiliation, and by satisfaction appeased: incline the ear of Thy fatherly love unto our prayers, and mercifully pour forth upon the heads of Thy servants, sprinkled with these ashes, the grace of Thy blessing; that Thou mayest both fill them with the spirit of compunction, and effectually grant those things for which they have justly prayed; and ordain that what Thou hast granted may be established and remain unmoved forever. Through Christ Our Lord. ℟. Amen.

Oremus.

Omnipotens, sempiterne Deus, qui Ninivitis in cinere et cilicio pœnitentibus, indulgentiæ tuæ remedia præstitisti: concede propitius, ut sic eos imitemur habitu, quatenus veniæ prosequamur obtentu. Per Dominum nostrum, etc. ℟. Amen.

Let us pray.

Almighty and eternal God, Who didst grant the remedy of Thy pardon to the Ninivites doing penance in ashes and sackcloth: mercifully grant that we may so imitate their penance that we may follow them in obtaining forgiveness. Through Our Lord Jesus Christ, etc. ℟. Amen.

The priest sprinkles the ashes thrice with holy water, saying the Antiphon Asperges me, Domine, *and incenses them three times:*

Asperges me, Domine, hyssopo, et mundabor: lavabis me, et super nivem dealbabor.

Thou shalt sprinkle me, O Lord, with hyssop, and I shall be cleansed; Thou shalt wash me, and I shall be made whiter than snow.

The priest then puts the ashes on the foreheads of the people, saying:

Memento, homo, quia pulvis es, et in pulverem reverteris.

Remember, O man, that dust thou art, and into dust thou shalt return.

While the people are receiving the ashes, the following Antiphons are sung:

Immutemur habitu, in cinere et cilicio: jejunemus et ploremus ante Dominum: quia multum misericors est dimittere peccata nostra Deus noster.

Let us change our garments for ashes and sackcloth: let us fast and lament before the Lord: for our God is very merciful to forgive our sins.

Inter vestibulum et altare plorabunt sacerdotes ministri Domini, et dicent, Parce Domine, parce populo tuo: et ne claudas ora canentium te Domine.

Between the porch and the altar, the priests, the Lord's ministers, shall weep, and shall say: Spare, O Lord, spare Thy people: and shut not the mouths of those who sing to Thee, O Lord.

℞. Emendemus in melius, quæ ignoranter peccavimus: ne subito præoccupati die mortis, quæramus spatium pœnitentiæ, et invenire non possimus. † Attende, Domine, et miserere: quia peccavimus tibi.

℞. Let us change for the better in those things in which we have sinned through ignorance: lest we be suddenly overtaken by the day of death, and seek space for penance, and find it not: † Hear, O Lord, and have mercy: for we have sinned against Thee.

℣. Adjuva nos, Deus, salutaris noster: et propter honorem nominis tui, Domine, libera nos. Attende, Domine, et miserere: quia peccavimus tibi.

℣. Help us, O God our Savior: and for the honor of Thy name, O Lord, deliver us. Hear, O Lord, and have mercy: for we have sinned against Thee.

℣. Gloria Patri, etc. Attende, Domine, et miserere: quia peccavimus tibi.

℣. Glory be to the Father, etc. Hear, O Lord, and have mercy: for we have sinned against Thee.

When all have received the ashes, the priest says:

℣. Dominus vobiscum.
℞. Et cum spiritu tuo.

℣. The Lord be with you.
℞. And with thy spirit.

Oremus.
    Concede nobis, Domine, præsidia militiæ christianæ sanctis inchoare jejuniis: ut contra spiritales nequitias pugnaturi, continentiæ muniamur auxiliis. Per Christum Dominum nostrum. ℞. Amen.

Let us pray.
    Grant us, O Lord, to begin our Christian warfare with holy fasts; that, as we are about to fight against the spirits of wickedness, we may be defended by the aids of self-denial. Through Christ Our Lord. ℞. Amen.

Then follows the Mass.[20]

THE BLESSING OF CHILDREN WHEN THEY ARE PRESENTED IN THE CHURCH

The children being assembled, the boys and the girls in separate ranks, the priest, turning toward them, says:

Adjutorium nostrum in nomine Domini.

Our help is in the name of the Lord.

℟. Qui fecit cœlum et terram.

℟. Who hath made heaven and earth.

Then is said the Antiphon:

Laudate, pueri, Dominum, laudate nomen Domini.

Praise the Lord, ye children, praise ye the name of the Lord.

Then Psalm 112, beginning with the second verse:

Sit nomen Domini benedictum, * ex hoc nunc, et usque in sæculum.

Blessed be the name of the Lord: from this time forth, forevermore.

A solis ortu usque ad occasum, * laudabile nomen Domini.

From the rising up of the sun unto the going down of the same: the name of the Lord is worthy to be praised.

Excelsus super omnes Gentes Dominus, * et super cœlos gloria ejus.

The Lord is high above all nations: and His glory above the heavens.

Quis sicut Dominus Deus noster, qui in altis habitat, * et humilia respicit in cœlo et in terra?

Who is like unto the Lord our God, Who dwelleth on high: and regardeth the things that are lowly in heaven and on earth?

Suscitans a terra inopem, * et de stercore erigens pauperem:

Who raiseth up the needy from the earth: and lifteth the poor out of the dunghill;

Ut collocet eum cum principibus, * cum principibus populi sui.

That He may set him with the princes: even with the princes of His people.

---

[20] The offices of *Holy Week*, being of great length, are not given in this book. They are contained in full in the *Holy Week Book*, published by the Catholic Publication Society Co.

Qui habitare facit sterilem in domo, *
matrem filiorum lætantem.

Who maketh the barren woman to
dwell in her house: the joyful mother
of children.

Gloria Patri, etc.

Glory be to the Father, etc.

The Antiphon *is repeated:*

Laudate, pueri, Dominum, laudate nomen Domini.

Praise the Lord, ye children, praise ye
the name of the Lord.

The priest then says:

℣. Sinite parvulos venire ad me.

℣. Suffer the little children to come to
Me.

℟. Talium est enim regnum cœlorum.

℟. For of such is the kingdom of heaven.

℣. Angeli eorum

℣. Their angels

℟. Semper vident faciem Patris.

℟. Always behold the face of the Father.

℣. Nihil proficiat inimicus in eis.

℣. Let not the enemy prevail against
them.

℟. Et filius iniquitatis non apponat
nocere eis.

℟. Nor the son of iniquity draw nigh to
hurt them.

℣. Domine, exaudi orationem meam.

℣. O Lord, hear my prayer.

℟. Et clamor meus ad te veniat.

℟. And let my cry come unto Thee.

℣. Dominus vobiscum.

℣. The Lord be with you.

℟. Et cum spiritu tuo.

℟. And with thy spirit.

Oremus.

Domine Jesu Christe, qui parvulos tibi oblatos et ad te venientes complexus es, manusque super illos imponens benedixisti eis, atque dixisti: Sinite parvulos venire ad me, et nolite prohibere eos, talium est enim regnum cœlorum, et Angeli eorum semper vident faciem Patris mei; respice, quæsumus, ad puerorum præsentium innocentiam, et ad eorum parentum devotionem, et clementer eos hodie per ministerium nostrum bene ✠ dic; ut in tua gratia et misericordia semper proficiant, te sapiant, te diligant, te timeant, et mandata tua custodiant, et ad finem optatum feliciter perveniant: per te, Salvator mundi. Qui cum Patre et Spiritu Sancto vivis et regnas Deus in sæcula sæculorum. ℟. Amen.

Let us pray.

O Lord Jesus Christ, Who didst embrace little children who were brought unto Thee, and didst lay Thy hands upon them and bless them, saying: "Suffer the little children to come to Me, and forbid them not, for of such is the kingdom of heaven," and, "Their angels always behold the face of My Father": look down, we beseech Thee, upon the innocence of these little ones here present, and upon the devotion of their parents, and graciously bless ✠ them this day by our ministry; that in Thy grace and mercy they may ever grow in the knowledge, love, and fear of Thee, and in the keeping of Thy commandments, and may happily attain unto their wished-for end. Through Thee, O Savior of the world, Who with the Father and the Holy Ghost livest and reignest, etc. ℟. Amen.

Oremus.

Defende, quæsumus, Domine, beata Maria semper Virgine intercedente, istam ab omni adversitate familiam: et toto corde tibi prostratam, ab hostium propitius tuere clementer insidiis. Per Christum Dominum nostrum. ℟. Amen.

Let us pray.

Defend, we beseech Thee, O Lord, through the intercession of Blessed Mary, ever Virgin, this Thy family from all adversity; and, as in all humility they prostrate themselves before Thee, do Thou graciously protect them against all the snares of their enemies. Through Christ Our Lord. ℟. Amen.

Oremus.

Deus, qui ineffabili providentia sanctos Angelos tuos ad nostram custodiam mittere dignaris: largire supplicibus tuis; et eorum semper protectione defendi, et æterna societate gaudere. Per Christum Dominum nostrum. ℟. Amen.

Let us pray.

O God, Who, in Thine unspeakable providence, art pleased to send Thy holy angels to watch over us: mercifully grant unto Thy humble servants, both that we be always defended by their protection here, and rejoice forever in their company hereafter. Through Christ Our Lord. ℟. Amen.

Then the priest blesses the children in the form of a cross, saying:

Benedicat vos Deus, et custodiat corda vestra et intelligentias vestras, Pater, ✠ et Filius, et Spiritus Sanctus. ℟. Amen.

May God, the Father, and the Son, and the Holy Ghost, bless ✠ you, and keep your hearts and your minds. ℟. Amen.

He then sprinkles them with holy water in the form of a cross.

The Seven Penitential Psalms[21]

Ant. Remember not, O Lord, our offenses, nor those of our parents; nor take Thou revenge of our sins.

1. PSALM 6

O Lord, rebuke me not in Thine anger: nor chastise me in Thy wrath.

Have mercy on me, O Lord, for I am weak: heal me, O Lord, for my bones are troubled.

My soul also is troubled exceedingly: but Thou, O Lord, how long?

Turn Thee, O Lord, and deliver my soul: O save me for Thy mercy's sake.

For in death there is no one that is mindful of Thee: and who will give Thee thanks in hell?

I have labored in my groanings, every night will I wash my bed: and water my couch with my tears.

Mine eye is troubled through indignation: I have grown old amongst all mine enemies.

Depart from me, all ye workers of iniquity: for the Lord hath heard the voice of my weeping.

The Lord hath heard my supplication: the Lord hath received my prayer.

Let all mine enemies be put to shame, and be sore troubled: let them be turned back, and put to shame very speedily.

Glory be to the Father, etc.

2. PSALM 31

Blessed are they whose iniquities are forgiven: and whose sins are covered.

Blessed is the man to whom the Lord hath not imputed sin: and in whose spirit there is no guile.

Because I was silent, my bones grew old: whilst I cried out all the day long.

For day and night Thy hand was heavy upon me: I am turned in my anguish, whilst the thorn is fastened.

I have acknowledged my sin unto Thee: and mine iniquity I have not concealed.

I said, I will confess against myself mine iniquity unto the Lord: and Thou hast forgiven the wickedness of my sin.

For this shall everyone that is holy pray to Thee: in a seasonable time.

And yet in a flood of many waters: they shall not come nigh unto him.

Thou art my refuge from the trouble which hath encompassed me: my joy, deliver me from them that surround me.

---

[21]   It is a pious custom to recite the seven Penitential Psalms, respectively, by way of prayer against the seven deadly sins.

I will give thee understanding, and I will instruct thee in this way, in which thou
   shalt go; I will fix Mine eyes upon thee.

Be not as the horse and the mule: that have no understanding.

With bit and bridle bind fast their jaws: who come not near unto thee.

Many are the scourges of the sinner: but mercy shall encompass him that hopeth
   in the Lord.

Be glad in the Lord and rejoice, ye just: and be joyful, all ye that are right of heart.

Glory be to the Father, etc.

3. PSALM 37

Rebuke me not, O Lord, in Thine indignation: neither chasten me in Thy sore
displeasure.

For Thine arrows are fastened in me: and Thy hand presseth heavily upon me.

There is no health in my flesh, because of Thy wrath: there is no rest for my bones,
   because of my sins.

For mine iniquities are gone over my head: and as a heavy burden are become heavy
   upon me.

My sores have rotted and are corrupt: because of my foolishness.

I am become miserable, and am greatly bowed down: I went about sorrowful all
   the day long.

For my loins are filled with illusions; and there is no soundness in my flesh.

I am afflicted, and humbled exceedingly: I have roared with the groaning of my
   heart.

Lord, all my desire is before Thee: and my groaning is not hid from Thee.

My heart is troubled, my strength hath forsaken me: and the light of mine eyes
   itself is not with me.

My friends and my neighbors have drawn near: and stood against me.

And they that were near me stood afar off: and they that sought after my soul used
   violence.

They that sought my hurt spoke vain things: and thought upon deceits all the day
   long.

But I, as a deaf man, heard not: and I was as a dumb man that doth not open his
   mouth.

And I became as a man that heareth not: and that hath no reproofs in his mouth.

For in Thee, O Lord, have I hoped: Thou wilt hear me, O Lord my God.

For I said, Lest at any time mine enemies rejoice over me: and whilst my feet slip,
   they glory over me.

For I am ready for scourges: and my sorrow is continually before me.

For I will declare mine iniquity: and I will be thoughtful of my sin.

But mine enemies live, and are stronger than I: and they that hate me wrongfully
   are multiplied.

They that render evil for good have slandered me: because I followed goodness.

Forsake me not, O Lord my God: do not Thou depart from me.

Give heed unto my help, O Lord: Thou God of my salvation.

Glory be to the Father, etc.

4. PSALM 50

Miserere mei, Deus, * secundum magnam misericordiam tuam.

Have mercy upon me, O God: according to Thy great mercy.

Et secundum multitudinem miserationum tuarum, * dele iniquitatem meam.

And according to the multitude of Thy tender mercies: blot out my iniquity.

Amplius lava me ab iniquitate mea: * et a peccato meo munda me.

Wash me yet more from my iniquity: and cleanse me from my sin.

Quoniam iniquitatem meam ego cognosco: * et peccatum meum contra me est semper.

For I acknowledge my iniquity: and my sin is always before me.

Tibi soli peccavi, et malum coram te feci: * ut justificeris in sermonibus tuis, et vincas cum judicaris.

Against Thee only have I sinned, and done evil in Thy sight: that Thou mayest be justified in Thy words, and mayest overcome when Thou art judged.

Ecce enim in iniquitatibus conceptus sum: * et in peccatis concepit me mater mea.

For behold, I was conceived in iniquities: and in sins did my mother conceive me.

Ecce enim veritatem dilexisti: * incerta et occulta sapientiæ tuæ manifestasti mihi.

For behold, Thou hast loved truth: the secret and hidden things of Thy wisdom Thou hast made manifest unto me.

Asperges me hyssopo, et mundabor: * lavabis me, et super nivem dealbabor.

Thou shalt sprinkle me with hyssop, and I shall be cleansed: Thou shalt wash me, and I shall be made whiter than snow.

Auditui meo dabis gaudium et lætitiam: * et exultabunt ossa humiliata.

Thou shalt make me hear of joy and gladness: and the bones that were humbled shall rejoice.

Averte faciem tuam a peccatis meis: * et omnes iniquitates meas dele.

Turn away Thy face from my sins: and blot out all my iniquities.

Cor mundum crea in me, Deus: * et spiritum rectum innova in visceribus meis.

Create in me a clean heart, O God: and renew a right spirit within me.

Ne projicias me a facie tua: * et Spiritum Sanctum tuum ne auferas a me.

Cast me not away from Thy face: and take not Thy Holy Spirit from me.

Redde mihi lætitiam salutaris tui: * et spiritu principali confirma me.

Restore unto me the joy of Thy salvation: and strengthen me with a perfect spirit.

Docebo iniquos vias tuas: * et impii ad te convertentur.

I will teach the unjust Thy ways: and the wicked shall be converted unto Thee.

Libera me de sanguinibus, Deus, Deus salutis meæ: * et exultabit lingua mea justitiam tuam.

Deliver me from sins of blood, O God, Thou God of my salvation: and my tongue shall extol Thy justice.

Domine, labia mea aperies: * et os meum annuntiabit laudem tuam.

Thou shalt open my lips, O Lord: and my mouth shall declare Thy praise.

Quoniam si voluisses sacrificium, dedissem utique: * holocaustis non delectaberis.

For if Thou hadst desired sacrifice, I would surely have given it: with burnt offerings Thou wilt not be delighted.

Sacrificium Deo spiritus contribulatus: * cor contritum, et humiliatum, Deus, non despicies.

A sacrifice unto God is a troubled spirit: a contrite and humble heart, O God, Thou wilt not despise.

Benigne fac, Domine, in bona voluntate tua Sion, * ut ædificentur muri Jerusalem.

Deal favorably, O Lord, in Thy good will with Sion: that the walls of Jerusalem may be built up.

Tunc acceptabis sacrificium justitiæ, oblationes, et holocausta: * tunc imponent super altare tuum vitulos.

Then shalt Thou accept the sacrifice of justice, oblations, and whole burnt offerings: then shall they lay calves upon Thine altar.

Gloria Patri, etc.

Glory be to the Father, etc.

5. PSALM 101

Hear my prayer, O Lord: and let my cry come unto Thee.

Turn not away Thy face from me: in the day when I am in trouble, incline Thine ear unto me.

In what day soever I shall call upon Thee: O hearken unto me speedily.

For my days are vanished like smoke: and my bones are dried up like fuel for the fire.

I am smitten as grass, and my heart is withered: for I have forgotten to eat my bread.

Through the voice of my groaning: my bones have cleaved unto my flesh.

I am become like a pelican in the wilderness: and like a night raven in the house.

I have watched, and am become like a sparrow: that sitteth alone on the housetop.

Mine enemies reviled me all the day long: and they that praised me have sworn together against me.

For I have eaten ashes as it were bread: and mingled my drink with weeping.

Because of Thine indignation and wrath: for Thou hast lifted me up and cast me down.

My days have gone down like a shadow: and I am withered like the grass.

But Thou, O Lord, endurest forever: and Thy memorial unto all generations.

Thou shalt arise, and have mercy upon Sion: for it is time that Thou have mercy upon her; yea, the time is come.

For Thy servants have delighted in her stones: and they shall have pity on the earth thereof.

And the Gentiles shall fear Thy name, O Lord: and all the kings of the earth Thy glory.

For the Lord hath built up Sion: and He shall be seen in His glory.

He hath had regard unto the prayer of the lowly: and hath not despised their petition.

Let these things be written for another generation: and the people that shall be created shall praise the Lord;

For he hath looked down from His high and holy place: out of heaven hath the Lord looked upon the earth;

That He might hear the groaning of them that are in fetters: that He might deliver the children of the slain;

That they may declare the name of the Lord in Sion: and His praise in Jerusalem,

When the people assembled together: and the kings to serve the Lord.

He answered him in the way of his strength: Declare unto me the fewness of my days.

Call me not away in the midst of my days: Thy years are unto generation and generation.

Thou, Lord, in the beginning didst lay the foundation of the earth: and the heavens are the work of Thy hands.

They shall perish, but Thou endurest: and they all shall grow old as a garment.

And as a vesture shalt Thou change them, and they shall be changed: but Thou art the same, and Thy years shall not fail.

The children of Thy servants shall continue: and their seed shall be directed forever.

Glory be to the Father, etc.

6. PSALM 129

De profundis clamavi ad te, Domine: * Domine, exaudi vocem meam.

Out of the depths have I cried unto Thee, O Lord: Lord, hear my voice.

Fiant aures tuæ intendentes, * in vocem deprecationis meæ.

O let Thine ears consider well: the voice of my supplication.

Si iniquitates observaveris, Domine: * Domine, quis sustinebit?

If Thou, O Lord, wilt mark iniquities: Lord, who shall abide it?

Quia apud te propitiatio est: * propter legem tuam sustinui te, Domine.

For with Thee there is merciful forgiveness: and because of Thy law I have waited for Thee, O Lord.

Sustinuit anima mea in verbo ejus: * speravit anima mea in Domino.

My soul hath waited on His word: my soul hath hoped in the Lord.

A custodia matutina usque ad noctem: * speret Israel in Domino.

From the morning watch even until night: let Israel hope in the Lord.

Quia apud Dominum misericordia: * et copiosa apud eum redemptio.

For with the Lord there is mercy: and with Him is plenteous redemption.

Et ipse redimet Israel, * ex omnibus iniquitatibus ejus.

And He shall redeem Israel: from all his iniquities.

Gloria Patri, etc.

Glory be to the Father, etc.

7. PSALM 142

Hear my prayer, O Lord: give ear to my supplication in Thy truth: hearken unto me for Thy justice' sake.

And enter not into judgment with Thy servant: for in Thy sight shall no man living be justified.

For the enemy hath persecuted my soul: he hath brought my life down unto the ground.

He hath made me to dwell in darkness as those that have been long dead: and my spirit is vexed within me; my heart within me is troubled.

I remembered the days of old, I meditated on all Thy works: I have mused upon the works of Thy hands.

I stretched forth my hands unto Thee: my soul gaspeth unto Thee, as a land where no water is.

Hear me speedily, O Lord: my spirit hath fainted away.

Turn not away Thy face from me: lest I be like unto them that go down into the pit.

Make me to hear Thy mercy in the morning: for in Thee have I hoped.

Make me to know the way wherein I should walk: for to Thee have I lifted up my soul.

Deliver me from mine enemies, O Lord, unto Thee have I fled: teach me to do Thy will, for Thou art my God.

Thy good spirit shall lead me into the right land: for Thy name's sake, O Lord, Thou shalt quicken me in Thy justice.

Thou shalt bring my soul out of trouble: and in Thy mercy Thou shalt destroy mine enemies.

And Thou shalt destroy all them that afflict my soul: for I am Thy servant.

Glory be to the Father, etc.

Ant. Remember not, O Lord, our offenses, nor those of our parents; nor take Thou revenge of our sins.

The Litany of the Saints

Kyrie, eleison.
Christe, eleison.
Kyrie, eleison.
Christe, audi nos.
Christe, exaudi nos.

Lord, have mercy on us.
Christ, have mercy on us.
Lord, have mercy on us.
Christ, hear us.
Christ, graciously hear us.

Pater de cœlis, Deus, miserere nobis.
Fili, Redemptor mundi Deus,
Spiritus Sancte, Deus,
Sancta Trinitas, unus Deus,

God the Father of heaven, have mercy on us.
God the Son, Redeemer of the world,
God the Holy Ghost,
Holy Trinity, one God,

Sancta Maria,
Sancta Dei Genitrix,
Sancta Virgo virginum,
Sancte Michael,
Sancte Gabriel,
Sancte Raphael,
Omnes sancti Angeli et Archangeli, *orate pro nobis.*
Omnes sancti beatorum Spirituum ordines.

Holy Mary,
Holy Mother of God,
Holy Virgin of virgins,
St. Michael,
St. Gabriel,
St. Raphael,
All ye holy angels and archangels, pray for us.
All ye holy orders of blessed spirits,

Sancte Joannes Baptista.
Sancte Joseph.
Omnes sancti Patriarchæ et Prophetæ.

St. John the Baptist,
St. Joseph,
All ye holy patriarchs and prophets,

Sancte Petre, ora pro nobis.
Sancte Paule,
Sancte Andrea,
Sancte Jacobe,
Sancte Joannes,
Sancte Thoma,
Sancte Jacobe,

St. Peter, pray for us.
St. Paul,
St. Andrew,
St. James,
St. John,
St. Thomas,
St. James,

Sancte Philippe,	St. Philip,
Sancte Bartholomæe,	St. Bartholomew,
Sancte Matthæe,	St. Matthew,
Sancte Simon,	St. Simon,
Sancte Thaddæe,	St. Thaddeus,
Sancte Matthia,	St. Matthias,
Sancte Barnaba,	St. Barnabas,
Sancte Luca,	St. Luke,
Sancte Marce,	St. Mark,
Omnes sancti Apostoli et Evangelistæ, *orate pro nobis.*	All ye holy apostles and evangelists, pray for us.
Omnes sancti Discipuli Domini.	All ye holy disciples of the Lord,
Omnes sancti Innocentes.	All ye Holy Innocents,
Sancte Stephane, *ora pro nobis.*	St. Stephen, pray for us.
Sancte Laurenti.	St. Lawrence,
Sancte Vincenti.	St. Vincent,
Sancti Fabiane et Sebastiane, *orate pro nobis.*	Sts. Fabian and Sebastian, pray for us.
Sancti Joannes et Paule.	Sts. John and Paul,
Sancti Cosma et Damiane.	Sts. Cosmas and Damian,
Sancti Gervasi et Protasi.	Sts. Gervase and Protase,
Omnes sancti Martyres.	All ye holy martyrs,
Sancte Silvester, *ora pro nobis.*	St. Sylvester, pray for us.
Sancte Gregori,	St. Gregory,
Sancte Ambrosi,	St. Ambrose,
Sancte Augustine,	St. Augustine,
Sancte Hieronyme,	St. Jerome,
Sancte Martine,	St. Martin,
Sancte Nicolae,	St. Nicholas,
Omnes sancti Pontifices et Confessores, *orate pro nobis.*	All ye holy bishops and confessors, pray for us.
Omnes sancti Doctores.	All ye holy Doctors,

Sancte Antoni, *ora pro nobis.*　　St. Anthony, pray for us.
Sancte Benedicte,　　St. Benedict,
Sancte Bernarde,　　St. Bernard,
Sancte Dominice,　　St. Dominic,
Sancte Francisce,　　St. Francis,
Omnes sancti Sacerdotes et Levitæ,　　All ye holy priests and Levites, pray for
　　orate pro nobis.　　us.
Omnes sancti Monachi et Eremitæ.　　All ye holy monks and hermits,

Sancta Maria Magdalena, *ora pro nobis.*　　St. Mary Magdalen, pray for us.
Sancta Agatha,　　St. Agatha,
Sancta Lucia,　　St. Lucy,
Sancta Agnes,　　St. Agnes,
Sancta Cæcilia,　　St. Cecilia,
Sancta Catharina,　　St. Catherine,
Sancta Anastasia,　　St. Anastasia,
Omnes sanctæ Virgines et Viduæ, *orate*　　All ye holy virgins and widows, pray for
　　pro nobis.　　us.
Omnes Sancti et Sanctæ Dei, *intercedite*　　All ye holy saints of God, *make interces-*
　　pro nobis.　　*sion for us.*

Propitus esto, *parce nobis, Domine.*　　Be merciful, *spare us, O Lord.*
Propitius esto, *exaudi nos, Domine.*　　Be merciful, *graciously hear us, O Lord.*
Ab omni malo, *libera nos, Domine.*　　From all evil, deliver us, O Lord.
Ab omni peccato,　　From all sin,
Ab ira tua,　　From Thy wrath,[22]
A subitanea et improvisa morte,　　From sudden and unlooked-for death,
Ab insidiis diaboli,　　From the snares of the devil,
Ab ira, et odio, et omni mala voluntate,　　From anger, and hatred, and every evil
A spiritu fornicationis,　　will,
A fulgure et tempestate,　　From the spirit of fornication,
A morte perpetua.　　From lightning and tempest,
　　From everlasting death,

[22]　　Here, for the devotion of the Forty Hours, is inserted:

　　Ab imminentibus periculis,　　From dangers that threaten us,
　　A flagello terræmotus,　　From the scourge of earthquakes,
　　A peste, fame, et bello,　　From plague, famine, and war,

Per mysterium sanctæ Incarnationis tuæ,

Per Adventum tuum,

Per Nativitatem tuam,

Per Baptismum et sanctum Jejunium tuum,

Per Crucem et Passionem tuam,

Per Mortem et Sepulturam tuam,

Per sanctam Resurrectionem tuam,

Per admirabilem Ascensionem tuam,

Per adventum Spiritus Sancti Paracliti,

In die judicii,

Peccatores, te rogamus, audi nos.

Ut nobis parcas,

Ut nobis indulgeas,

Ut ad veram pœnitentiam nos perducere digneris,

Ut Ecclesiam tuam sanctam regere et conservare digneris,

Ut domnum Apostolicum et omnes ecclesiasticos ordines in sancta religione conservare digneris,

Ut inimicos sanctæ Ecclesiæ humiliare digneris,

Ut regibus et principibus christianis pacem et veram concordiam donare digneris,

Ut cuncto populo Christiano pacem et unitatem largiri digneris,

---

Through the mystery of Thy holy Incarnation,

Through Thy coming,

Through Thy birth,

Through Thy baptism and holy fasting,

Through Thy Cross and Passion,

Through Thy death and burial,

Through Thy holy Resurrection,

Through Thine admirable Ascension,

Through the coming of the Holy Ghost the Paraclete,

In the Day of Judgment,

We sinners *we beseech Thee, hear us.*

That Thou wouldst spare us,

That Thou wouldst pardon us,

That Thou wouldst bring us to true penance,

That Thou wouldst vouchsafe to govern and preserve Thy holy Church,

That Thou wouldst vouchsafe to preserve our Apostolic Prelate and all orders of the Church in holy religion,[23]

That Thou wouldst vouchsafe to humble the enemies of holy Church,

That Thou wouldst vouchsafe to give peace and true concord to Christian kings and princes,

That Thou wouldst vouchsafe to grant peace and unity to the whole Christian world,

---

[23] For the devotion of the Forty Hours, insert:

Ut Turcarum, et hæreticorum conatus reprimere et ad nihilum redigere digneris,

That Thou wouldst vouchsafe to check and bring to naught the attempts of all Turks and heretics,

‡Ut omnes errantes ad unitatem Ecclesiæ revocare, et infideles universos ad Evangelii lumen perducere digneris,

Ut nosmetipsos in tuo sancto servitio confortare et conservare digneris,

Ut mentes nostras ad cœlestia desideria erigas,

Ut omnibus benefactoribus nostris sempiterna bona retribuas,

Ut animas nostras, fratrum, propinquorum et benefactorum nostrorum ab æterna damnatione eripias,

Ut fructus terræ dare et conservare digneris,

Ut omnibus fidelibus defunctis requiem æternam donare digneris,

Ut nos exaudire digneris,

Fili Dei, te rogamus, audi nos.

Agnus Dei, qui tollis peccata mundi, *parce nobis, Domine.*
Agnus Dei, qui tollis peccata mundi, *exaudi nos, Domine.*
Agnus Dei, qui tollis peccata mundi, *miserere nobis.*
Christe, audi nos.
Christe, exaudi nos.

Kyrie, eleison.
Christe, eleison.
Kyrie, eleison.

‡That Thou wouldst bring back all the erring to the unity of the Church, and lead to the light of the gospel all infidels,

That Thou wouldst vouchsafe to confirm and preserve us in Thy holy service,

That Thou wouldst lift up our minds to heavenly desires,

That Thou wouldst render eternal blessings to all our benefactors,

That Thou wouldst deliver our souls and the souls of our brethren, relations, and benefactors, from eternal damnation,

That Thou wouldst vouchsafe to give and preserve the fruits of the earth,

That Thou wouldst vouchsafe to grant eternal rest to all the faithful departed,

That Thou wouldst vouchsafe graciously to hear us,

Son of God, we beseech Thee, hear us.

Lamb of God, Who takest away the sins of the world, *spare us, O Lord.*
Lamb of God, Who takest away the sins of the world, *graciously hear us, O Lord.*
Lamb of God, Who takest away the sins of the world, *have mercy on us.*
Christ, hear us.
Christ, graciously hear us.

Lord, have mercy on us.
Christ, have mercy on us.
Lord, have mercy on us.

Pater noster (*secreto*).
℣. Et ne nos inducas in tentationem.
℟. Sed libera nos a malo.

Our Father (*inaudibly*).
℣. And lead us not into temptation.
℟. But deliver us from evil.

PSALM 69

Deus, in adjutorium meum intende:
* Domine, ad adjuvandum me
festina.

Come unto my help, O God: O Lord,
make haste to help me.

Confundantur et revereantur, * qui
quærunt animam meam:

Let them be ashamed and put to confusion that seek after my soul:

Avertantur retrorsum, et erubescant, *
qui volunt mihi mala.

Let them be turned backward and blush
for shame: that wish me evil.

Avertantur statim erubescentes, * qui
dicunt mihi: Euge, euge.

Let them be presently turned away
blushing for shame: that say to me,
Aha, aha.

Exultent et lætentur in te omnes qui
quærunt te, * et dicant semper:
Magnificetur Dominus: qui dili-
gunt salutare tuum.

Let all those that seek Thee rejoice, and
be glad in Thee: and let such as love
Thy salvation say always, The Lord
be magnified.

Ego vero egenus, et pauper sum: *
Deus, adjuva me.

But I am poor and needy: help me, O
God.

Adjutor meus, et liberator meus es tu: *
Domine, ne moreris.

Thou art my helper and my deliverer: O
Lord, make no delay.

Gloria Patri, etc.

Glory be to the Father, etc.

℣. Salvos fac servos tuos.
℟. Deus meus, sperantes in te.

℣. Save Thy servants.
℟. O my God, who put their trust in
Thee.

℣. Esto nobis, Domine, turris
fortitudinis.
℟. A facie inimici.

℣. Be unto us, O Lord, a tower of
strength.
℟. From the face of the enemy.

℣. Nihil proficiat inimicus in nobis.
℟. Et filius iniquitatis non apponat
nocere nobis.

℣. Let not the enemy prevail against us.
℟. Nor the son of iniquity draw nigh to
hurt us.

℣. Domine, non secundum peccata nostra facias nobis.

℟. Neque secundum iniquitates nostras retribuas nobis.

℣. Oremus pro Pontifice nostro, N.

℟. Dominus conservet eum, et vivificet eum, et beatum faciat eum in terra, et non tradat eum in animam inimicorum ejus.

℣. Oremus pro benefactoribus nostris.

℟. Retribuere dignare, Domine, omnibus nobis bona facientibus propter nomen tuum vitam æternam. *Amen.*

℣. Oremus pro fidelibus defunctis.

℟. Requiem æternam dona eis, Domine; et lux perpetua luceat eis.

℣. Requiescant in pace.

℟. Amen.

℣. Pro fratribus nostris absentibus.

℟. Salvos fac servos tuos, Deus meus, sperantes in te.

℣. Mitte eis, Domine, auxilium de sancto.

℟. Et de Sion tuere eos.

℣. Domine, exaudi orationem meam.

℟. Et clamor meus ad te veniat.

℣. O Lord, deal not with us after our sins.

℟. Neither reward us according to our iniquities.

℣. Let us pray for our Sovereign Pontiff, N.

℟. The Lord preserve him and give him life, and make him blessed upon the earth; and deliver him not up to the will of his enemies.

℣. Let us pray for our benefactors.

℟. Vouchsafe, O Lord, to reward with eternal life all those who do us good, for Thy name's sake. *Amen.*

℣. Let us pray for the faithful departed.

℟. Eternal rest grant unto them, O Lord; and let perpetual light shine upon them.

℣. May they rest in peace.

℟. Amen.

℣. For our absent brethren.

℟ Save Thy servants, O my God, who put their trust in Thee.

℣. Send them help, O Lord, from Thy holy place.

℟. And defend them out of Sion.

℣. O Lord, hear my prayer.

℟. And let my cry come unto Thee.

Oremus.

Deus, cui proprium est misereri semper et parcere: suscipe deprecationem nostram; ut nos, et omnes famulos tuos, quos delictorum catena constringit, miseratio tuæ pietatis clementer absolvat.

Let us pray.[24]

O God, Whose property is always to have mercy and to spare: graciously receive our supplication; that we, and all Thy servants whom the chain of sin doth bind, may, by the compassion of Thy loving kindness, be mercifully absolved.

Exaudi, quæsumus Domine, supplicum preces, et confitentium tibi parce peccatis; ut pariter nobis indulgentiam tribuas benignus et pacem.

Graciously hear, we beseech Thee, O Lord, the prayers of Thy humble servants, and forgive the sins of those who confess to Thee; that, in Thy bounty, Thou mayest grant us both pardon and peace.

Ineffabilem nobis, Domine, misericordiam tuam clementer ostende: ut simul nos et a peccatis omnibus exuas, et a pœnis, quas pro his meremur, eripias.

Show forth upon us, O Lord, in Thy mercy, Thine unspeakable pity; that Thou mayest both loose us from all our sins, and deliver us from the punishments which we deserve for the same.

---

[24] *For the devotion of the Forty Hours, the following Collects are said:* Deus, qui nobis, *p. 177.*
From Advent to Christmas, Deus, qui de beatæ Mariæ, *p. 596.*
From Christmas to the Purification, Deus qui salutis æternæ, *pp. 58, 158.*
From the Purification to Advent, Concede nos, *p. 157.*
Then follows the Collect for the pope, as on p. 91, after which is said, Deus, refugium nostrum, *p. 589, and this prayer:*

Omnipotens, sempiterne Deus, in cujus manu sunt omnium potestates, et omnium jura regnorum, respice in auxilium Christianorum, ut gentes paganorum et hæreticorum, quæ in sua feritate et fraude confidunt, dexteræ tuæ potentia conterantur.

Almighty, everlasting God, in Whose hand are all the powers and all the rights of kingdoms, come to the assistance of Thy Christian people, that all pagan and heretical nations, who trust in their own violence and fraud, may be crushed by the might of Thy right hand.

Then follows the last Collect, Omnipotens, sempiterne Deus, *as on p. 62, with the Versicles, except that, in the last response but one, instead of the simple Amen, is said:*

℟. Et custodiat nos semper. Amen.

℟. And preserve us always. *Amen.*

Deus, qui culpa offenderis, pœnitentia placaris: preces populi tui supplicantis propitius respice; et flagella tuæ iracundiæ, quæ pro peccatis nostris meremur, averte.

O God, Who by sin art offended, and by penance appeased: look graciously down upon the prayers of Thy people making supplication to Thee, and turn away the scourges of Thy wrath, which for our sins we deserve.

Omnipotens sempiterne Deus, miserere famulo tuo Pontifici nostro N., et dirige eum secundum tuam clementiam in viam salutis æternæ: ut, te donante, tibi placita cupiat, et tota virtute perficiat.

Almighty, everlasting God, have mercy upon Thy servant N., our Sovereign Pontiff, and direct him, according to Thy mercy, in the way of everlasting salvation; that by Thy gift he may desire such things as please Thee, and may fulfill them with all his strength.

Deus, a quo sancta desideria, recta consilia, et justa sunt opera: da servis tuis illam, quam mundus dare non potest, pacem; ut et corda nostra mandatis tuis dedita, et hostium sublata formidine, tempora sint tua protectione tranquilla.

O God, from Whom are holy desires, right counsels, and just works: give unto Thy servants that peace which the world cannot give; that our hearts being given to the keeping of Thy commandments, and the fear of enemies being removed, our days, by Thy protection, may be peaceful.

Ure igne Sancti Spiritus renes nostros et cor nostrum, Domine: ut tibi casto corpore serviamus, et mundo corde placeamus.

Inflame, O Lord, our reins and our hearts with the fire of the Holy Ghost; that we may serve Thee with a chaste body, and please Thee with a pure mind.

Fidelium, Deus, omnium Conditor et Redemptor, animabus famulorum, famularum que tuarum remissionem cunctorum tribue peccatorum: ut indulgentiam, quam semper optaverunt, piis supplicationibus consequantur.

O God, the Creator and Redeemer of all the faithful, grant unto the souls of Thy servants and handmaids remission of all their sins; that through our pious supplications they may obtain the pardon which they have always desired.

Actiones nostras, quæsumus Domine, aspirando præveni, et adjuvando prosequere: ut cuncta nostra oratio et operatio a te semper incipiat, et per te cœpta finiatur.

Direct, we beseech Thee, O Lord, our actions by Thy inspiration, and further them with Thy continual help; that every prayer and work of ours may always begin from Thee, and through Thee be brought to an end.

Omnipotens sempiterne Deus, qui vivorum dominaris simul et mortuorum, omniumque misereris quos tuos fide et opere futuros esse prænoscis: te supplices exoramus; ut, pro quibus effundere preces decrevimus, quosque vel præsens sæculum adhuc in carne retinet, vel futurum jam exutos corpore suscepit, intercedentibus omnibus Sanctis tuis, pietatis tuæ clementia omnium delictorum suorum veniam consequantur. Per Dominum nostrum Jesum Christum Filium tuum, qui tecum vivit et regnat in unitate Spiritus Sancti Deus, etc. ℞. Amen.

Almighty, everlasting God, Who hast dominion over the living and the dead, and showest mercy unto all whom Thou foreknowest will be Thine by faith and works: we humbly beseech Thee that they for whom we have resolved to pour forth our prayers, whether this present world still detain them in the flesh, or the world to come hath already received them stripped of their bodies, may, by the grace of Thy fatherly love, and through the intercession of all the saints, obtain the remission of all their sins. Through Our Lord Jesus Christ, etc. ℞. Amen.

℣. Domine, exaudi orationem meam.
℞. Et clamor meus ad te veniat.

℣. O Lord, hear my prayer.
℞. And let my cry come unto Thee.

℣. Exaudiat nos omnipotens et misericors Dominus.
℞. Amen.

℣. May the Almighty and merciful Lord graciously hear us.
℞. Amen.

℣. Et fidelium animæ per misericordiam Dei requiescant in pace.
℞. Amen.

℣. And may the souls of the faithful departed, through the mercy of God, rest in peace.
℞. Amen.

𝔍nstructions and 𝔇evotions for Confession

ON THE SACRAMENT OF PENANCE

Penance is a Sacrament instituted by Jesus Christ, in which, by the ministry of the priest, actual sins are forgiven, and the conscience is released from the bonds by which it may be bound. In this Sacrament, also, the eternal punishment due to sin is remitted, and a part or the whole of the temporal punishment, according to the disposition of the penitent.

This holy and salutary institution is grounded on the words of Jesus Christ: "Amen I say to you, whatsoever you shall bind on earth, shall be bound also in heaven; and whatsoever you shall loose upon earth shall be loosed also in heaven" (Mt 18:18), and, "'As the Father hath sent Me, I also send you.' When He had said this, He breathed on them; and He said to them, 'Receive ye the Holy Ghost. Whose sins you shall forgive, they are forgiven them; and whose sins you shall retain, they are retained'" (Jn 20:21–23). In these words, Jesus Christ gave to His apostles, and to their lawful successors, power and authority to absolve from all sin those who sincerely repent of their offenses.

Hence we see the great necessity of this Sacrament; and the Council of Trent has decreed that it is not less necessary for salvation to those who have fallen into mortal sin after Baptism, than Baptism to those who have never been baptized. And although Penance may, at first sight, and in itself, seem to be a bitter and painful thing, yet, viewed in its fruits and consequences, it is full of consolation; and every Christian, as soon as he is conscious that he has fallen into a mortal sin, ought at once to have recourse to this fount of divine mercy.

The evil consequences of delay are manifold. 1) In the state of mortal sin, every other mortal sin committed renders our hearts still more hardened. 2) The commission of one mortal sin makes a second easier, and this leads to a third, and so on. 3) In the state of mortal sin, we lose the value of all the good works that we may do. They avail nothing for everlasting life. Neither alms, nor prayers, nor fasts, nor even martyrdom itself can profit us, if we have not repented of our sins. 4) Sin, continued in, shuts by degrees the door of divine mercy, until at last scarce any hope is left of obtaining pardon from God. Lastly, just as the longer a stain remains upon a garment, the more difficult it is to remove, so the longer the soul neglects to purify itself by Confession, the more difficult the work becomes, and the more intricate, on account of the number of sins and anxiety of mind, until at last even an experienced confessor may be unable to extricate the soul from its miserable state.

A PRAYER

To Implore the Divine Assistance in Order to Make a Good Confession

O Almighty and most merciful God, Who hast made me out of nothing, and redeemed me by the Precious Blood of Thine only Son; Who hast with so much patience borne with me to this day, notwithstanding all my sins and ingratitude; ever calling after me to return to Thee from the ways of vanity and iniquity, in which I have been quite wearied out in the pursuit of empty toys and mere shadows; seeking in vain to satisfy my thirst in unclean waters, and my hunger with husks of swine: behold, O most gracious Lord, I now sincerely desire to leave all these my evil ways, to forsake the region of death where I have so long lost myself, and to return to Thee, the Fountain of life. I desire, like the prodigal son, to enter seriously into myself, and with the like resolution to arise without delay, and to go home to my Father—though I am infinitely unworthy to be called His child—in hopes of meeting with the like reception from His most tender mercy. But, O my God, though I can go astray from Thee of myself, yet I cannot make one step toward returning to Thee, unless Thy divine grace move and assist me. This grace, therefore, I most humbly implore, prostrate in spirit before the throne of Thy mercy; I beg it for the sake of Jesus Christ, Thy Son, Who died upon the Cross for my sins; I know that Thou desirest not the death of a sinner, but that he may be converted and live; I know Thy mercies are above all Thy works; and I most confidently hope that as in Thy mercy Thou hast spared me so long, and hast now given me this desire of returning to Thee, so Thou wilt finish the work which Thou hast begun, and bring me to a perfect reconciliation with Thee.

I desire now to comply with Thy holy institution of the Sacrament of Penance; I desire to confess my sins with all sincerity to Thee and to Thy minister; and therefore I desire to know myself, and to call myself to an account by a diligent examination of my conscience. But, O my God, how miserably shall I deceive myself if Thou assist me not in this great work by Thy heavenly light. O then remove every veil that hides any of my sins from me, that I may see them all in their true colors, and may sincerely detest them. O let me no longer be imposed upon by the enemy of souls, or by my own self-love, so as to mistake vice for virtue, to hide myself from myself, or in any way to make excuses in sins.

But, O my good God, what will it avail me to know my sins, if Thou dost not also give me a hearty sorrow and repentance for them? Without this my sins will be all upon me still, and I shall be still Thine enemy and a child of hell. Thou dost require that contrite heart, without which there can be no reconciliation with Thee; and this heart none but Thyself can give. O then, dear Lord, grant it unto me at this time. Give me a lively faith, and a steadfast hope, in the Passion of my Redeemer; teach me to fear Thee and to love Thee. Give me, for Thy mercy's sake, a hearty sorrow for having offended so good a God. Teach me to detest my evil ways; to abhor all my past ingratitude; to hate myself now with a perfect hatred for my many treasons against Thee. O give me a full and a firm resolution to lead henceforward a new life; and unite me unto Thee with an eternal band of love which nothing in life or death may ever break.

Grant me also the grace to make an entire and sincere confession of all my sins, and to accept the confusion of it as a penance justly due to my transgressions. Let not the enemy prevail upon me to pass over anything through fear or shame; rather let me die than consent to so great an evil. Let no self-love deceive me, as I fear it has done too often. O grant that this confession may be good; and for the sake of Jesus Christ, Thy Son, Who died for me and for all sinners, assist me in every part of my preparation for it; that I may perform it with the same care and diligence as I should be glad to do at the hour of my death; that so, being perfectly reconciled to Thee, I may never offend Thee more. *Amen.*

PRAYERS BEFORE EXAMINATION OF CONSCIENCE

O Almighty God, Maker of heaven and earth, King of Kings, and Lord of Lords, Who hast made me out of nothing in Thine image and likeness, and hast redeemed me with Thine own blood; Whom I, a sinner, am not worthy to name, or call upon, or think of: I humbly pray Thee, I earnestly beseech Thee, to look mercifully on me, Thy wicked servant. Thou Who hadst mercy on the woman of Chanaan and Mary Magdalen; Thou Who didst spare the publican and the thief upon the cross, have mercy upon me. Thou art my hope and my trust; my guide and my succor; my comfort and my strength; my defense and my deliverance; my life, my health, and my resurrection; my light and my longing; my help and my protection. I pray and entreat Thee, help me and I shall be safe; direct me and defend me; strengthen me and comfort me; confirm me and gladden me; enlighten me and come unto me. Raise me from the dead; I am Thy creature, and the work of Thy hands. Despise me not, O Lord, nor regard my iniquities; but according to the multitude of Thy tender mercies have mercy upon me, the chief of sinners, and be gracious unto me. Turn Thou unto me, O Lord, and be not angry with me. I implore Thee, most compassionate Father, I pray Thee meekly, of Thy great mercy, to bring me to a holy death, and to true penance, to a perfect confession, and to worthy satisfaction for all my sins. *Amen.*

O Lord God, Who enlightenest every man who cometh into this world, enlighten my heart, I pray Thee, with the light of Thy grace, that I may fully know my sins, shortcomings, and negligences, and may confess them with that true sorrow and contrition of heart which I so much need. I desire to make full amends for all my sins, and to avoid them for the future to Thy honor and glory, and to the salvation of my soul, through Jesus Christ Our Lord. *Amen.*

I believe in Thee, O God, Father, Son, and Holy Ghost, my Creator, my Redeemer, and my Sanctifier; I believe that Thou art all-holy, just, and merciful. I believe that Thou art willing to pardon and to save me, if I repent and forsake my sins.

O my God, strengthen and increase my faith, and grant me the grace of a true repentance, for Jesus Christ's sake. *Amen.*

I hope in Thee, O my God, because Thou art Almighty, faithful, and long-suffering. I humbly trust that Thou wilt pardon my sins for the sake of Thy dear Son Jesus Christ, Who suffered and died for me upon the Cross; and that Thou wilt cleanse my sinful soul in His Precious Blood, and make me holy, and bring me safe to everlasting life.

O Lord, in Thee have I hoped, let me never be confounded. *Amen.*

I love Thee, O my God, above all things, because Thou hast been so good, so patient, so loving to me, notwithstanding all the sins by which I have so grievously offended Thee. I love Thee, O Blessed Jesus, my Savior, because Thou didst suffer so much for love of me, an ungrateful sinner, and didst die on the Cross for my salvation.

O make me love Thee more and more, and show my love to Thee by faithfully keeping Thy commandments all the days of my life. *Amen.*

O Mary Immaculate, Mother of Fair Love: obtain for me that love of God, which is so necessary for true contrition. *Amen.*

CONSIDERATIONS TO EXCITE CONTRITION

1. Place before yourself, as distinctly as you can, the sins which have come to your remembrance, and their circumstances.

2. Consider Who God is, against Whom you have sinned, how great, how good, how gracious to you; that He made you, that He gave His only Son to die for you, that He made you His child in Baptism, that He has loaded you with blessings and prepared heaven for you. Consider how patient He has been with you—how long-suffering in calling you and moving you to repent. Say: "O most loving God, O infinite Goodness, I repent of having offended Thee; behold me at Thy feet. O my Father, my Creator, my Benefactor, grant me the grace of a true repentance, and the blessing of a pardon, for Thy dear Son's sake."

3. Consider the infinite wickedness of sin. Say: "O my Savior, I behold Thee on the Cross, torn and wounded. Thy sacred body streaming with blood; this is the work of my sin. In Thy wounds, O my Savior, I read the greatness of the guilt and malice of my sins. By the greatness of Thy pains and sorrows, O my loving Redeemer, I measure the hatefulness of my offenses."

4. Consider the consequences of one mortal sin: that you might justly be now banished from God's presence forever for one single unrepented, deadly sin; how many have you not committed! Say: "O my God, how much do I owe Thee for not

cutting me off in the midst of my sins. Before I fell into sin, heaven was my home, my inheritance, my country, my blessed resting place; by sin, I have given up my title to the glory of the blessed. For the sake of sin, I have lost the love of Jesus, the sight of Mary, the communion with the blessed saints and with the angels. O my God, would that I had never offended Thee, would that I had never consented to sin. In pity behold me now at Thy feet, full of sorrow and compunction. I hate sin, which is accursed of Thee; I renounce all that would draw me away from Thee; I most bitterly repent my sin and folly, which would have deprived me forever of heaven if Thou hadst not mercifully brought me to repentance. I grieve that I have sinned against Thee, O my God, Who art all-good, all-bountiful, all-worthy of love. O Mary, conceived without sin, pray for us sinners, who have recourse to thee."

EXAMINATION OF CONSCIENCE

(*For the* Ten Commandments, *the* six precepts of the Church, *and the* seven capital sins *in full, see pp. 22 and 24*).

FIRST COMMANDMENT

Sins against this commandment are:

1. Those which detract from the honor and worship due to God; such as: neglect of prayer; superstitious practices; divination; consulting fortune-tellers; attaching undue importance to dreams, omens; tempting God by exposing one's self to danger of soul, life, or health, without grave cause; sacrilege; profane or superstitious use of blessed objects; profanation of places or things consecrated to God; receiving the holy Sacraments in a state of mortal sin.

2. Those against faith; such as: willfull doubt of any article of Faith; reading or circulating books or writings against Catholic belief or practice; joining in schismatical or heretical worship; denying one's religion; neglecting means of religious instruction.

3. Those against hope; such as: despair of God's mercy, or want of confidence in the power of His grace to support us in trouble or temptation; murmuring against God's providence; presuming on God's mercy, or on the supposed efficacy of certain pious practices, in order to continue in sin.

4. Those against charity; such as: willfully rebellious thoughts against God; boasting of sin; violating God's law, or omitting good works, through human respect.

SECOND COMMANDMENT

Sins against this commandment are:

All irreverence toward God's most holy name; such as: cursing and profane swearing; false, unlawful, and unnecessary oaths; membership in societies condemned by the Church; breaking or deferring lawful vows; irreverence in divine service, and in churches and holy places even when service is not going on.

THIRD COMMANDMENT

Sins against this commandment are:

Neglect to hear Mass on Sundays and holy days of obligation; working or making others work without necessity on such days.

FOURTH COMMANDMENT

Sins against this commandment are:

For children: All manner of anger or hatred against parents and other lawful superiors; provoking them to anger; grieving them; insulting them; neglecting them in their necessity; contempt of or disobedience to their lawful commands.

For parents: Hating their children; cursing them; giving scandal to them by cursing, drinking, etc.; allowing them to grow up in ignorance, idleness, or sin; showing habitual partiality, without cause; deferring their children's Baptism; neglecting to watch over their bodily health, their religious instruction, the company they keep, the books they read, etc.; failing to correct them when needful; being harsh or cruel in correction; sending children to Protestant and other dangerous schools.

For husbands and wives: Ill-usage; putting obstacles to the fulfillment of religious duties; want of gentleness and consideration in regard to each other's faults; unreasonable jealousy; neglect of household duties; sulkiness; injurious words.

For employers: Not allowing one's domestics reasonable time for religious duties and instruction; giving bad example to them, or allowing others to do so; withholding their lawful wages; not caring for them in sickness; dismissing them arbitrarily and without cause.

For the employed: Disrespect to employers; want of obedience in matters wherein one has bound one's self to obey; waste of time; neglect of work; waste of employer's property, by dishonesty, carelessness, or neglect.

For professional men and public officials: Culpable lack of the knowledge relating to duties of office or profession; neglect in discharging those duties; injustice or partiality; exorbitant fees.

For teachers: Neglecting the progress of those confided to their care; unjust, indiscreet, or excessive punishment; partiality; bad example, loose and false maxims.

For pupils: Disrespect; disobedience; stubbornness; idleness; waste of time.

For all: Contempt for the laws of our state and country, as well as of the Church; disobedience to lawful authority.

FIFTH COMMANDMENT

Sins against this commandment are:

Unjust taking of human life (and hence, indirectly and implicitly, any violence of thought, word, or act which may lead thereto); exposing life or limb to danger without reasonable cause; carelessness in leaving about poisons, dangerous drugs, weapons, etc.; desires of revenge; quarrels; fights; showing aversion or contempt for others; refusing to speak to them when addressed; ignoring offers of reconciliation, especially between relatives; cherishing an unforgiving spirit; raillery and ridicule; insults; irritating words and actions; sadness at another's prosperity; rejoicing over another's misfortune; jealousy at attentions shown to others; tyrannical behavior; inducing others to sin by word or example; gluttony; drunkenness; rash use of opiates; injury to health by overindulgence; giving drink to others, knowing that they will abuse it.

SIXTH AND NINTH COMMANDMENTS

The former forbids in action what the latter forbids in thought or desire. We shall not enter into details on this subject. It is a pitch which defiles. Those who sin against these two commandments know it well; those who do not should pray God that they may never learn. It is sufficient to remind penitents that each and every act, *if deliberate,* contrary to the holy virtue of purity—be it in thought or desire, in look, gesture, word, or deed—is a mortal sin, and as such must be mentioned in Confession intelligibly, yet modestly.

It will be further useful to remark that, in regard to sins of this kind, it is wrong to dwell too much on details; that we should be especially careful to take note of the avoidable *occasions* of our falls, and to direct our purpose of amendment to the keeping away from *them,* rather than to the making of vague, general resolutions about the future avoidance of the sin itself.

SEVENTH AND TENTH COMMANDMENTS

Sins against these commandments are:

Stealing (What value? What damage done to property or interests?), possession of ill-gotten goods; exorbitant prices; false weights and measures; cheating; adulteration of wares; careless or malicious injury to the property of others; cheating at play; appropriation of what is lent or found, without reasonable pains to return it, or to find its owner; concealment of fraud, theft, or damage, when in duty bound to give information; petty thefts; culpable delay in paying lawful debts, of restitution, when able to make it; neglect to make reasonable efforts and sacrifices in this matter, for example by gradually laying up the amount required.

EIGHTH COMMANDMENT

Sins against this commandment are:

Lying; perjury; frauds, public and private, such as at elections, etc.; malicious falsehoods; lies for unjust or bad ends; lies against character, especially if told publicly; revealing secrets; publishing discreditable secrets about others, *even if true;* refusing or delaying to restore the good name we have blackened; slander or detraction, and encouraging these in others; baseless accusations, groundless suspicions, rash judgments of others, in our own mind.

THE PRECEPTS OF THE CHURCH

1. Have I neglected, without good reason, to hear Mass on Sundays and holy days of obligation, and to keep those days holy by avoiding all servile work?

2. Have I failed to fast or abstain, without sufficient reason, on those days commanded to be so observed by the Church?

3, 4. Have I omitted to confess my mortal sins at least once a year, or to make my Easter duty?

5. Have I refused to contribute to the support of my pastor, according to my means?—gone to Mass Sunday after Sunday, without giving anything to the collections?

6. Have I entered into marriage, or aided anyone else to do so, without bans, or before a state official or a Protestant minister; or without dispensation within the forbidden degrees of kindred; or with any other known impediment?

AFTER EXAMINATION OF CONSCIENCE

O my God, I cry unto Thee with the prodigal: "Father, I have sinned against heaven and before Thee; I am no longer worthy to be called Thy son."

I have gone astray like a sheep that is lost. O seek Thy servant, for I have not forgotten Thy commandments.

Enter not into judgment with Thy servant, O Lord. O spare me for Thy mercy's sake.

Prove me, O God, and know my heart; examine me, and know my paths.

Thou Whose property is always to have mercy and to spare, O meet me in pity, embrace me in love, and forgive me all my sin.

I confess my sins unto Thee, O Christ, Healer of our souls, O Lord of life. Heal me, heal me of my spiritual sickness. Thou Who art long-suffering and of tender mercy; heal me, O Lord Christ.

Accept my supplications, O Thou Holy Spirit, unto Whom every heart is open, every desire known, and from Whom no secret is hid, and Who givest life to our souls; hear and answer, O Spirit of God.

O heavenly Father, Who willest not that any sinner should perish, give me true repentance for this my sin, that I perish not!

To what misery am I come by my own fault! O merciful God, pity and forgive me for Jesus' sake.

Thine eyes, O God, are as a flame of fire searching my inmost heart. O pardon my sin, for it is great!

Thou, God, seest me in all the foulness of my sins! Blessed Jesus, speak for me, plead for me, come between my soul and my offended God, that I perish not. *Amen.*

Here may be said the Miserere, *or any of the preceding* Penitential Psalms (*p. 194*).

PRAYER BEFORE CONFESSION

Accept my confession, O most loving, most gracious Lord Jesus Christ, on Whom alone my soul trusts for salvation. Grant me, I beseech Thee, contrition of heart, and give tears to mine eyes, that I may sorrow deeply for all my sins with humility and sincerity of heart.

O good Jesus, Savior of the world, Who gavest Thyself to the death of the Cross to save sinners, look on me, a miserable sinner who calls upon Thy name. Spare me, Thou that art my Savior, and pity my sinful soul; loose its chains, heal its sores. Lord Jesus, I desire Thee, I seek Thee, I long for Thee; show me the light of Thy countenance, and I shall be saved; send forth Thy light and Thy truth into my soul, to show me fully all the sins and shortcomings which I must still confess, and to aid and teach me to lay them bare without reserve and with a contrite heart; O Thou Who livest and reignest with God the Father, in the unity of the Holy Ghost, one God, world without end. *Amen.*

O most gracious Virgin Mary, beloved Mother of Jesus Christ, my Redeemer, intercede for me with Him. Obtain for me the full remission of my sins, and perfect amendment of life, to the salvation of my soul and the glory of His name. *Amen.*

I implore the same grace of thee, O my angel guardian; of you, my holy patrons, N. N.; of you, O blessed Peter and holy Magdalen, and of all the saints of God. Intercede for me a sinner, repenting of my sins, firmly resolving to confess them, and to avoid them for the future. *Amen.*

DIRECTIONS FOR CONFESSION

Approach the confessional in a humble and contrite spirit, and kneel down by your confessor. Then, making the sign of the cross, say, *Benedicite*, or, "Father, bless me, for I have sinned." After he has given the blessing, say the Confiteor,[25] in English or Latin, as far as the words, "through my most grievous fault"; then say, "Since my last confession, which was … ago, I accuse myself of …." Here name all the sins which you have recalled to mind since your last confession; and, in confessing them, be sure to observe these rules:

1. Let your confession be *entire*, that is do not knowingly conceal any one mortal sin; otherwise, so far from obtaining absolution, you do but add to your sins. State the kind of sins you have committed, and, as far as you can, their number; and mention any circumstances which you think would change the nature of your sins.

2. Let your confession be *pure*. Let everything be mentioned sincerely and exactly, without any disguise or dissimulation; let the certain things be mentioned as certain, the doubtful as doubtful. Avoid all excuses for yourself, either direct or indirect; and take the greatest care not to throw blame on anyone else, or to mention

---

[25] If many penitents are waiting for Confession, the Confiteor should be said before entering the confessional.

or hint at the name of any third person. Avoid all superfluous words and matter, and everything which does not directly concern the integrity of the confession. Be as concise as you can, consistently with fullness and candor.

3. Let your confession be *humble,* remembering that you are in an especial manner in the presence of God, from Whom, through His priest, you are seeking and expecting pardon. The thought of God at this moment will be your best protection against all false shame, insincere trifling, and affectation.

After you have confessed all your sins, according to these rules, say, "For these and all my other sins which I cannot now remember, I am heartily sorry, and humbly ask pardon of God, and penance and absolution of you, Father. Therefore I beseech Blessed Mary," etc., to the end of the Confiteor.

Then listen attentively and humbly to the direction and advice of your confessor, and be fully resolved to do whatever he bids you to do, either in the way of penance, or restitution, or reparation, or for the avoiding of sin in the future. While he is giving you absolution, devoutly bow your head, and with all possible fervor recite the following act of contrition:

O my God, I am heartily sorry for having offended Thee, and I detest all my sins, because I dread the loss of heaven and the pains of hell, but most of all because they offend Thee, my God, Who art all-good and deserving of all my love. I firmly resolve, with the help of Thy grace, to confess my sins, to do penance, and to amend my life.

THE RITUAL OF THE SACRAMENT OF PENANCE

THE FORM OF ABSOLUTION

When, therefore, the penitent is ready to be absolved, having first enjoined a salutary penance, the priest says:

Misereatur tui omnipotens Deus, et dimissis peccatis tuis, perducat te ad vitam æternam. Amen.

May Almighty God have mercy upon thee, and forgive thee thy sins, and bring thee unto life everlasting. Amen.

He then, with his right hand raised toward the penitent, says:

Indulgentiam, ✠ absolutionem, et remissionem peccatorum tuorum tribuat tibi omnipotens, et misericors Dominus. Amen.

May the Almighty and merciful Lord grant thee pardon, ✠ absolution, and forgiveness of thy sins. Amen.

Dominus noster Jesus Christus te absolvat: et ego auctoritate ipsius, te absolvo ab omni vinculo excommunicationis (suspensionis,) et interdicti, in quantum possum, et tu indiges. *Deinde* ego te absolvo a peccatis tuis, in nomine Patris, ✠ et Filii, et Spiritus Sancti. Amen.

May Our Lord Jesus Christ absolve thee; and I, by His authority, absolve thee from every bond of excommunication (suspension,) and interdict, inasmuch, as in my power lieth, and thou standest in need. *Finally,* I absolve thee from thy sins, in the name of the Father, ✠ and of the Son, and of the Holy Ghost. Amen.

(*If the penitent is a lay person, the word* suspension *is omitted.*)

Passio Domini nostri Jesu Christi, merita beatæ Mariæ Virginis, et omnium Sanctorum, quidquid boni feceris, et mali sustinueris, sint tibi in remissionem peccatorum, augmentum gratiæ, et præmium vitæ æternæ. Amen.

May the Passion of Our Lord Jesus Christ, the merits of the Blessed Virgin Mary and of all the saints, whatsoever thou shalt have done of good and borne of evil, be unto thee for remission of sins, increase of grace, and reward of life everlasting. Amen.

In frequent and shorter confessions, the prayer Almighty God have mercy upon thee, *etc., may be omitted; and it suffices to say:* May Our Lord Jesus Christ absolve thee, *etc., as far as* May the Passion of Our Lord, *etc.*

In danger of death, or any grave necessity, this brief form may be used:

Ego te absolvo ab omnibus censuris, et peccatis, in nomine Patris, ✠ et Filli, et Spiritus Sancti. Amen.

I absolve thee from all censures and sins, in the name of the Father, ✠ and of the Son, and of the Holy Ghost. Amen.

AFTER CONFESSION

1. As soon after Confession as you conveniently can, perform your penance, and renew your resolutions of avoiding all sin, and of adopting all the means for so doing, by avoiding the occasions and temptations of sin; and then you may have a perfect confidence, with devout thankfulness, that all your sins, through the mercy of God, are forgiven.

2. Consider how you can amend your life. This will be best done by fixing your attention on one or two of your more prominent defects of character, and directing your chief efforts to overcome these by such means as the following: 1) Conceive a strong desire to overcome these faults, frequently renew your resolution, and examine yourself particularly upon them. 2) When you commit them, punish

yourself in some way for it. 3) Endeavor always to have the thought of Christ present in your mind, and direct short prayers to Him, especially when you are attacked by temptations, or when you are necessarily exposed to the danger of sinning. 4) Meditate frequently on those subjects most calculated to excite your fears, hopes, and affections, as death and judgment, the love of God, His kindnesses to you, His promises, and the like. Be earnest and persevere with a good hope of victory, through the grace of Jesus Christ.

THANKSGIVING AFTER CONFESSION

O most merciful God, Who according to the multitude of Thy mercies dost so put away the sins of those who truly repent that Thou rememberest them no more: look graciously upon me, Thine unworthy servant, and accept my confession for Thy mercy's sake; receive my humble thanks, most loving Father, that of Thy great goodness Thou hast given me pardon for all my sins. O may Thy love and pity supply whatsoever has been wanting in the sufficiency of my contrition, and the fullness of my confession. And do Thou, O Lord, vouchsafe to grant me the help of Thy grace, that I may diligently amend my life and persevere in Thy service unto the end, through Jesus Christ Our Lord. *Amen.*

PSALM 102

Bless the Lord, O my soul: and let all that is within me bless His holy name.

Bless the Lord, O my soul: and forget not all His benefits.

Who forgiveth Thee all thine iniquities: Who healeth all thine infirmities.

Who redeemeth thy life from destruction: Who crowneth thee with mercy and compassion.

Who satisfieth thy desire with good things: thy youth shall be renewed like the eagle's.

The Lord doth mercies and judgment: for all that suffer wrong.

He hath made His ways known unto Moses: His will unto the children of Israel.

The Lord is full of compassion and mercy: long-suffering and plenteous in mercy.

He will not always be angry: neither will He threaten forever.

He hath not dealt with us after our sins: nor rewarded us according to our iniquities.

For as the heaven is high above the earth: so hath He strengthened His mercy toward them that fear Him.

As far as the east is from the west: so far hath He removed our iniquities from us.

As a father hath pity upon his children, so hath the Lord pity upon them that fear Him: for He knoweth whereof we are made.

He remembereth that we are but dust: man's days are as the grass, as the flower of the field so shall he flourish.

For the wind shall pass over it, and it shall not be: and one shall know its place no more.

But the mercy of the Lord is from everlasting to everlasting: upon them that fear Him;

And His justice upon children's children; unto such as keep His covenant;

And are mindful of His commandments: to do them.

The Lord hath prepared His throne in heaven: and His kingdom shall rule over all.

Bless the Lord, all ye His angels: ye that are mighty in strength, and fulfill His commandment, hearkening to the voice of His words.

Bless the Lord, all ye His hosts: ye ministers of His that do His will.

Bless the Lord, all ye His works: in every place of His dominion bless the Lord, O my soul.

Glory be to the Father, etc.

PSALM 15

Preserve me, O Lord, for in Thee have I put my trust: I have said to the Lord, Thou art my God, for Thou hast no need of my goods.

To the saints who are in His land: He hath made wonderful all my desires in them.

Their infirmities were multiplied: afterward they made haste.

I will not gather together their meetings for blood offerings: nor will I make mention of their names with my lips.

The Lord is the portion of my inheritance and of my cup: Thou art He that will restore my inheritance unto me.

The lines are fallen unto me in goodly places: for my inheritance is goodly unto me.

I will bless the Lord, Who hath given me understanding: moreover my reins also have corrected me even till night.

I set the Lord always in my sight: for He is at my right hand, that I be not moved

Therefore my heart hath been glad, and my tongue hath rejoiced: moreover my flesh also shall rest in hope.

For Thou wilt not leave my soul in hell: nor wilt Thou give Thy holy one to see corruption.

Thou hast made known unto me the ways of life: Thou shalt fill me with joy with Thy countenance: at Thy right hand are delights forevermore.

Glory be to the Father, etc.

PSALM 19

May the Lord hear thee in the day of trouble: may the name of the God of Jacob protect thee.

May He send thee help from the sanctuary: and defend thee out of Sion.

May He be mindful of all thy sacrifices: and may thy whole burnt offerings be made fat.

May He give unto thee according to thine own heart: and confirm all thy counsels.

We will rejoice in thy salvation: and in the name of our God we shall be exalted.

The Lord fulfill all thy petitions: now have I known that the Lord hath saved His anointed.

He will hear him from His holy heaven: the salvation of His right hand is powerful.

Some trust in chariots, and some in horses: but we will call upon the name of the Lord our God.

They are entangled and have fallen: but we are risen, and stand upright.

O Lord, save the king: and hear us in the day that we shall call upon Thee.

Glory be to the Father, etc.

PRAYER BEFORE PERFORMING SACRAMENTAL PENANCE[26]

And since I have so grievously insulted Thee, O most tender and loving God, by my manifold sins and negligences, I am ready now to make perfect satisfaction to Thy divine justice to the utmost of my ability. To this end I will faithfully and most reverently perform the penance appointed me by my confessor in Thy name; and would that I could perform it with so great devotion and love as to give Thee an honor and delight greater than the insult and outrage of my sins! And that this may be so, I unite and blend this my penance with all the works of satisfaction which Thy beloved Son accomplished during the three-and-thirty years of His life on earth, and in union with His fastings, His watchings, and His prayers, I offer Thee this my penance and my prayer. Look down, therefore, O most loving Father, upon me Thy most bounden debtor, now prostrate at Thy feet, desiring to make Thee adequate satisfaction and reparation for all the insults and injuries I have done Thee; and grant me strength and grace to say this prayer according to Thy most holy will. *Amen.*

Here perform your sacramental penance, and then say as follows:
O most holy Father, I offer Thee this my confession and my satisfaction in union with all the acts of penance which have ever been done to the glory of Thy holy name: beseeching Thee that Thou wouldst vouchsafe to accept it, and to render it availing through the merits of the Passion of Thy beloved Son, and through the intercession of the ever Blessed Virgin Mary, and of all Thy holy apostles, martyrs, confessors, and virgins. Whatever has been lacking to me in sincere and earnest preparation, in perfect contrition, in frank and clear confession, I commend to the most loving Heart of Thine only begotten Son, that Treasury of all good and of all grace, from Whose overflowing abundance all debts to Thee are fully acquitted; that, through it, all my negligences and defects in the reception of this holy Sacrament may be fully and perfectly supplied to Thine everlasting praise and glory: through Jesus Christ Our Lord, Who liveth and reigneth with Thee in the unity of the Holy Ghost, one God, world without end. *Amen.*

---

[26] St. Gertrude.

A PRAYER FOR THE PRIEST

O Lord Jesus Christ, bless, I beseech Thee, Thy servant who has now ministered to me in Thy name. Help me to remember his good counsel and advice, and to perform duly what he has rightly laid upon me. And grant him the abundance of Thy grace and favor, that his own soul may be refreshed and strengthened for Thy perfect service, and that he may come at last to the joy of Thy heavenly kingdom. Who livest and reignest with the Father and the Holy Ghost, ever one God, world without end. *Amen.*

PRAYERS FOR PARDON AND AMENDMENT

I.

O most sweet Lord Jesus Christ, I, an unworthy sinner, would beg Thee to be mindful of all the holy thoughts which have been Thine from eternity until now; above all, that one by which Thou, O eternal Word, didst will to become man.

Our Father, etc.

O most merciful Lord, I pray Thee, from the bottom of my heart, to pardon me all the vain, foul, and evil thoughts which, up to this hour, I have entertained, or in any way have caused others to entertain, against or besides Thy will.

Our Father, etc.

II.

O most compassionate Lord Jesus Christ, I, a miserable sinner, would beg Thee to be mindful of all the good and saving words which Thou didst ever speak when on earth.

Our Father, etc.

I humbly pray Thee, O good Jesus, to forgive me all the words which up to this hour I have uttered or caused others to utter against Thy holy will.

Our Father, etc.

III.

O most sweet Jesus Christ, I, an unworthy sinner, yet redeemed by Thy Precious Blood, would beg Thee to be mindful of all the good works which Thou wroughtest on the earth for our salvation. I beseech Thee, most compassionate Lord, pardon me whatsoever, by my ill deeds, I have at any time knowingly or unknowingly committed, or have caused others to commit, against Thy law and the glory of Thy name.

Our Father, etc.

And now, O most gracious Lord, direct and order all my thoughts, words, and works according to Thy good pleasure, and to the praise of Thy name; and conform them to the perfect pattern of Thy most holy life and conversation. I am Thine, and will be Thine, O Lord, in life and in death; into Thy hands I commend myself and all that I have.

Our Father, etc.

PRAYERS AGAINST THE SEVEN DEADLY SINS

1. Against pride.

O Lord Jesus Christ, Pattern of humility, Who didst empty Thyself of Thy glory, and take upon Thee the form of a servant: root out of us all pride and conceit of heart, that, owning ourselves miserable and guilty sinners, we may willingly bear contempt and reproaches for Thy sake, and, glorying in nothing but Thee, may esteem ourselves lowly in Thy sight. Not unto us, O Lord, but to Thy name be the praise, for Thy loving mercy and for Thy truth's sake. *Amen.*

2. Against covetousness.

O Lord Jesus Christ, Who though Thou wast rich yet for our sakes didst become poor, grant that all overeagerness and covetousness of earthly goods may die in us, and the desire of heavenly things may live and grow in us: keep us from all idle and vain expenditures, that we may always have to give to him that needeth, and that giving not grudgingly nor of necessity, but cheerfully, we may be loved of Thee, and be made through Thy merits partakers of the riches of Thy heavenly treasure. *Amen.*

3. Against lust.

O Lord Jesus Christ, Guardian of chaste souls, and Lover of purity, Who wast pleased to take our nature and to be born of an immaculate Virgin: mercifully look upon my infirmity. Create in me a clean heart, O God: and renew a right spirit within me; help me to drive away all evil thoughts, to conquer every sinful desire, and so pierce my flesh with the fear of Thee that, this worst enemy being overcome, I may serve Thee with a chaste body and please Thee with a pure heart. *Amen.*

4. Against anger.

O most meek Jesus, Prince of Peace, Who, when Thou wast reviled, reviled not, and on the Cross didst pray for Thy murderers: implant in our hearts the virtues of gentleness and patience, that, restraining the fierceness of anger, impatience, and resentment, we may overcome evil with good; for Thy sake, love our enemies; and, as children of our heavenly Father, seek Thy peace and evermore rejoice in Thy love. *Amen.*

5. *Against gluttony.*

O Lord Jesus Christ, Mirror of abstinence, Who, to teach us the virtue of abstinence, didst fast forty days and forty nights, grant that, serving Thee and not our own appetites, we may live soberly and piously with contentment, without greediness, gluttony, or drunkenness, that Thy will being our meat and drink, we may hunger and thirst after justice, and finally obtain from Thee that food which endureth unto life eternal. *Amen.*

6. *Against envy.*

O most loving Jesus, Pattern of charity, Who makest all the commandments of the law to consist in love toward God and toward man, grant to us so to love Thee with all our heart, with all our mind, and all our soul, and our neighbor for Thy sake, that the grace of charity and brotherly love may dwell in us, and all envy, harshness, and ill-will may die in us; and fill our hearts with love, kindness, and compassion, so that by constantly rejoicing in the happiness and success of others, by sympathizing with them in their sorrows, and putting away all harsh judgments and envious thoughts, we may follow Thee, Who art Thyself the true and perfect love. *Amen.*

7. *Against sloth.*

O Lord Jesus Christ, eternal Love, Who in the garden didst pray so long and so fervently that Thy sweat was, as it were, great drops of blood falling down to the ground: put away from us, we beseech Thee, all sloth and inactivity both of body and mind; kindle within us the fire of Thy love; strengthen our weakness, that whatsoever our hand is able to do we may do it earnestly, and that, striving heartily to please Thee in this life, we may have Thee hereafter as our reward exceedingly great. *Amen.*

SEVEN THANKSGIVINGS FOR THE SEVEN EFFUSIONS OF OUR LORD'S BLOOD (AGAINST THE SEVEN DEADLY SINS)

I.

O most humble Lord and Master, Jesus Christ, true God and true man, eternal praise and thanksgiving be to Thee, because in Thy tenderest age, on the eighth day of Thy mortal life, Thou didst vouchsafe to shed Thy precious and innocent blood for us, and as a true Son of Abraham to bear the pain of circumcision.

By this most holy shedding of Thy blood, I beg of Thee the grace of humility against all pride and worldly vanity.

Our Father, etc.

O Savior of the world, Who by Thy Cross and Precious Blood hast redeemed us: save us, and help us, we humbly beseech Thee, O Lord.

II.

O Thou Whose love is like the pelican's for her young, Jesus Christ, true God and true man, eternal praise and thanksgiving be to Thee, because in the garden, out of the exceeding anguish of Thy Heart, Thou didst pour forth a bloody sweat, and, wholly resigning Thyself to death, didst offer it to Thy Father.

By this most holy shedding of Thy blood, I ask of Thee the grace of liberality against all covetousness and avarice.

Our Father, etc.

O Savior of the world, Who by Thy Cross and Precious Blood hast redeemed us: save us, and help us, we humbly beseech Thee, O Lord.

III.

O most chaste Spouse, Jesus Christ, true God and true man, eternal praise and thanksgiving be to Thee, because Thou didst suffer Thyself to be mercilessly bound in Pilate's judgment hall, and Thy virgin flesh to be cruelly scourged and mangled.

By this most holy shedding of Thy blood, I implore of Thee the grace of chastity against all sensuality and lust.

Our Father, etc.

O Savior of the world, Who by Thy Cross and Precious Blood hast redeemed us: save us, and help us, we humbly beseech Thee, O Lord.

IV.

O most meek Lamb, Jesus Christ, true God and true man, eternal praise and thanksgiving be to Thee, because Thou didst suffer Thy sacred head to be crowned with piercing thorns and struck with a hard reed.

By this most holy shedding of Thy blood, I pray Thee for the grace of meekness against all anger and desire of revenge.

Our Father, etc.

O Savior of the world, Who by Thy Cross and Precious Blood hast redeemed us: save us, and help us, we humbly beseech Thee, O Lord.

V.

O most sweet Jesus Christ, Pattern of temperance and self-denial, true God and true man, eternal praise and thanksgiving be to Thee, because Thou didst allow Thy garments to be torn from Thy bleeding body both before and after the carrying of Thy Cross, which opened Thy wounds again, and caused them to bleed afresh.

By this most holy shedding of Thy blood, I beseech of Thee the grace of temperance and abstinence against all greediness and gluttony.

Our Father, etc.

O Savior of the world, Who by Thy Cross and Precious Blood hast redeemed us: save us, and help us, we humbly beseech Thee, O Lord.

VI.

O good and faithful Samaritan, Jesus Christ, true God and true man, eternal praise and thanksgiving be to Thee, because out of Thy burning love for us Thou didst suffer Thy sacred hands and feet to be pierced and nailed to the Cross for our Redemption.

By this most holy shedding of Thy blood, I beg of Thee the grace of brotherly love against all envy and jealousy.

Our Father, etc.

O Savior of the world, Who by Thy Cross and Precious Blood hast redeemed us: save us, and help us, we humbly beseech Thee, O Lord.

VII.

O most zealous High Priest, true God and true man, eternal praise and thanksgiving be to Thee, because Thou didst suffer Thy sacred side to be pierced, opened, and wounded with a spear.

By this most holy shedding of Thy blood, I earnestly pray Thee for the grace of holy zeal and fervor against all sloth and weariness in Thy service, and in every religious exercise.

Our Father, etc.

O Savior of the world, Who by Thy Cross and Precious Blood hast redeemed us: save us, and help us, we humbly beseech Thee, O Lord.

Instructions for Holy Communion

The Holy Eucharist is the true Body and Blood of Jesus Christ, true God and true man, under the appearances of bread and wine. "The bread which I will give," says Jesus Christ, "is My Flesh, for the life of the world" (Jn 6:52). And at His Last Supper, Jesus took bread, and blessed, and broke, and gave to His disciples, and said: Take and eat: THIS IS MY BODY. And He took the cup, and gave thanks, and gave to them, saying: Drink ye all of this. FOR THIS IS MY BLOOD of the New Testament which shall be shed for many, unto remission of sins" (Mt 26:26–28).

Our Blessed Redeemer, having thus instituted this adorable Sacrament, ordained His apostles priests of the New Law, and gave to them and their lawful successors power and authority to do what He had done—that is, to change bread and wine into His Body and Blood. This change (which the Church calls *transubstantiation*) is effected by these divine words of our Redeemer, "This is My Body," "This is My Blood," which the priest at the Consecration in the Mass pronounces in the name and Person of Jesus Christ. It is God Himself Who works this wonderful change by the ministry of His priest.

When, therefore, the words of Consecration are pronounced, we believe that the whole substance of the bread is changed into the substance of the Body, and the whole substance of the wine into the substance of the Blood, of Our Blessed Lord. And as Jesus Christ is now immortal, and cannot be divided, He is truly present, whole and entire, both God and man, under the appearance of bread and under the appearance of wine.

The method by which our salvation is graciously accomplished is by our personal union with our incarnate Lord and Savior Jesus Christ. He came to be the new Head of the human race, the Second Adam. He is the Vine of which we are the branches, the Head of the Body of which we are the members. We who have been baptized have been incorporated into Christ. A new life has been imparted to us. But the spiritual, supernatural life which He imparts needs, like our natural, physical life, to be fed and nourished; otherwise it will languish and be in danger of perishing. And Our Lord Jesus Christ has revealed to us that as He is the Source of this our true life, so He is Himself its Food and Sustenance. He tells us that we must definitely and personally appropriate Him: "He that eateth Me," He says, "the same also shall live by Me" (Jn 6:58).

He explains that we must be partakers of His sacred humanity, of His Flesh, and of His glorious life, once laid down for our sins, but now risen, and ascended, and ever presented as an atoning and acceptable sacrifice—the Blood of the New Testament. "Unless ye eat," He says, "the Flesh of the Son of Man, and drink His Blood, ye shall not have life in you. He who eateth My Flesh and drinketh My Blood hath everlasting life; and I will raise him up on the Last Day" (Jn 6:54–55).

The means whereby this most momentous feeding upon Christ is accomplished is the Sacrament of the Holy Eucharist. This is the means appointed by Our Blessed Lord Himself, and it is clear, therefore, that this Holy Sacrament must on no account be neglected where it may be had. If we willfully or carelessly refuse the means, we cannot expect to receive the grace.

"Let a man prove himself," says St. Paul, "and so let him eat of that bread and drink of the cup" (1 Cor 11:28). This proving one's self is the first and most necessary preparation for the Holy Communion, and consists in looking diligently into the state of one's soul, in order to discover what unworthy dispositions or sins may lie there concealed, and to apply a proper remedy to them by sincere repentance and Confession; lest otherwise, approaching the Holy of Holies with a soul defiled with the guilt of mortal sin, we become guilty of the Body and of the Blood of Christ, and receive judgment to ourselves, not discerning the Body of the Lord (see 1 Cor 11:27, 29). For this reason, we go to Confession before Communion, in order to clear our souls from the defilement of sin.

The person who is to receive the Blessed Sacrament must be also fasting from the previous midnight, by the command of the Church and by a most ancient and apostolical tradition ordaining that, in reference to so great a Sacrament, nothing should enter into the body of a Christian before the Body of Christ. The case of danger of approaching death is excepted, when the Blessed Sacrament is received by way of Viaticum.

Besides this preparation of Confession and fasting, the person who proposes to go to Communion must endeavor to attain the best possible devotion, in order to dispose his soul for more suitably receiving so great a Guest. To this end he is recommended:

1. To think well on the great work he has in hand; to consider attentively Who it is Whom he is going to receive, and how far he is from deserving such a favor; and to implore, with fervor and humility, God's grace and mercy. And this should be the subject of his meditations and prayers for some time beforehand, and more particularly the night before his Communion and the morning he receives.

2. To propose to himself a pure intention, namely the honor of God and the sanctification of his own soul; and, in particular, that by worthily receiving Christ in this heavenly Sacrament he may come to a happy union with Him, according to His words in the Gospel of St. John: "He who eateth My Flesh, and drinketh My Blood abideth in Me, and I in him" (6:57).

3. To meditate on the sufferings and death of his Redeemer; this Sacrament being instituted to this end, that we should "show the death of the Lord until He come" (1 Cor 11:26).

4. To prepare himself by acts of virtue, more especially of faith, hope, love, and humility; that so he may approach to his Lord with a firm belief of His Real Presence in this Sacrament, and of that great sacrifice which He heretofore offered upon the Cross for our Redemption, of which He here makes us partakers; with an

ardent affection of love to Him Who has loved us so much, and Who, out of pure love, gives Himself to us; and with a great sentiment of his own unworthiness and sins, joined with a firm confidence in the mercies of his Redeemer.

Here follow the forms of preparation for, and thanksgiving after, the Holy Communion, which are set forth in the Roman Missal. They should be used as *aids* to the exercise of our thoughts and the kindling of our affections, and not as substitutes for our own efforts. They point out the proper line of thought and subjects for reflection, and, if used carefully and meditatively, will be found of great assistance. But no forms, however perfect in themselves, would be good for us without much care and effort on our own parts. These forms are enlarged and extended somewhat, as a variety is useful for different minds, and also for the same mind at different times.

DEVOTIONS FOR HOLY COMMUNION

PREPARATION

Antiphon. Remember not, O Lord, our offenses.

PSALM 83

How lovely are Thy tabernacles, O Lord of hosts: my soul longeth and fainteth for the courts of the Lord.

My heart and my flesh have rejoiced in the living God.

For the sparrow hath found her a house: and the turtle a nest for herself, where she may lay her young:

Even Thine altars, O Lord of hosts: my King and my God.

Blessed are they that dwell in Thy house, O Lord: they shall praise Thee forever and ever.

Blessed is the man whose help is in Thee: in his heart he hath disposed to ascend by steps, in the vale of tears, in the place which he hath set.

For the lawgiver shall give a blessing: they shall go from strength to strength: the God of gods shall be seen in Sion.

O Lord God of hosts, hear my prayer: give ear, O God of Jacob.

Behold, O God, our protector: and look upon the face of Thy Christ.

For one day in Thy courts: is better than a thousand.

I had rather be despised in the house of my God, than to dwell in the tents of sinners.

For God loveth mercy and truth: the Lord will give grace and glory.

He will not withhold good things from them that walk in innocence: O Lord of hosts, blessed is the man that hopeth in Thee.

Glory be to the Father, etc.

PSALM 84

Thou hast blessed Thy land, O Lord: Thou hast turned away the captivity of Jacob.

Thou hast forgiven the iniquity of Thy people: Thou hast covered all their sins.

Thou hast softened all Thine anger: Thou hast turned away from the wrath of Thine indignation.

Convert us, O God our Savior: and turn away Thine anger from us.

Wilt Thou be angry with us forever: or wilt Thou stretch out Thy wrath from generation to generation?

Thou shalt turn again, O God, and quicken us: and Thy people shall rejoice in Thee.

Show us Thy mercy, O Lord: and grant us Thy salvation.

I will hearken what the Lord God shall say within me: for He will speak peace unto His people:

And unto His saints: and unto them that are converted in heart.

Surely His salvation is nigh unto them that fear Him: that glory may dwell in our land.

Mercy and truth have met together: justice and peace have kissed each other.

Truth is sprung out of the earth: and justice hath looked down from heaven.

For the Lord shall give goodness: and our earth shall yield her fruit.

Justice shall walk before Him: and shall set His steps in the way.

Glory be to the Father, etc.

PSALM 85

Incline Thine ear, O Lord, and hear me: for I am needy and poor.

Preserve my soul, for I am holy: O my God, save Thy servant, that trusteth in Thee.

Have mercy upon me, O Lord: for unto Thee have I cried all the day. Give joy to the soul of Thy servant, for unto Thee, O Lord, have I lifted up my soul.

For Thou, O Lord, art sweet and mild; and plenteous in mercy unto all that call upon Thee.

Give ear, O Lord, unto my prayer: and attend to the voice of my petition.

I have called upon Thee in the day of my trouble: for Thou hast heard me.

Among the gods there is none like unto Thee, O Lord: and there is none that can do works like unto Thy works.

All the nations whom Thou hast made shall come and worship before Thee, O Lord: and shall glorify Thy name.

For Thou art great, and doest wondrous things: Thou art God alone.

Lead me, O Lord, in Thy way, and I will walk in Thy truth: let my heart rejoice that it may fear Thy name.

I will praise Thee, O Lord my God, with my whole heart: and I will glorify Thy name forever.

For great is Thy mercy toward me: and Thou hast delivered my soul out of the lower hell.

O God, the wicked are risen up against me; and the assembly of the mighty have sought after my soul: and they have not set Thee before their eyes.

And Thou, O Lord, art a God full of compassion, and merciful: long-suffering, and of much mercy, and true.

O look upon me, and have mercy on me: give Thy strength unto Thy servant, and save the son of Thine handmaid.

Show me a token for good: that they who hate me may see, and be confounded: because Thou, O Lord, hast helped me, and hast comforted me.

Glory be to the Father, etc.

PSALM 115

I believed, and therefore did I speak: but I was humbled exceedingly.

I said in mine excess: All men are liars.

What shall I render unto the Lord: for all the things that He hath rendered unto me?

I will take the chalice of salvation; and call upon the name of the Lord.

I will pay my vows unto the Lord, in the presence of all His people: precious in the sight of the Lord is the death of His saints.

O Lord, I am Thy servant: I am Thy servant, and the son of Thine handmaid.

Thou hast broken my bonds in sunder: I will offer unto Thee the sacrifice of praise, and will call upon the name of the Lord.

I will pay my vows unto the Lord in the sight of all His people: in the courts of the house of the Lord, in the midst of thee, O Jerusalem.

Glory be to the Father, etc.

PSALM 129

Out of the depths have I cried unto Thee, O Lord: Lord, hear my voice.

O let Thine ears consider well: the voice of my supplication.

If Thou, O Lord, wilt mark iniquities: Lord, who shall abide it?

For with Thee there is merciful forgiveness: and because of Thy law I have waited for Thee, O Lord.

My soul hath waited on His word: my soul hath hoped in the Lord.

From the morning watch even until night: let Israel hope in the Lord.

For with the Lord there is mercy: and with Him is plenteous redemption.

And He shall redeem Israel: from all his iniquities.

Glory be to the Father, etc.

Ant. Remember not, O Lord, our offenses, nor those of our parents; neither take Thou revenge of our sins: Spare us, good Lord, spare Thy people whom Thou hast redeemed with Thy most Precious Blood, and be not angry with us forever.

Lord, have mercy.

Christ, have mercy.

Lord, have mercy.

Our Father (*inaudibly*).

℣. And lead us not into temptation.

℟. But deliver us from evil.

℣. I said: O Lord, be Thou merciful unto me.

℟. Heal my soul, for I have sinned against Thee.

℣. Return, O Lord, for a little space.

℟. And be entreated in favor of Thy servants.

℣. Let Thy mercy, O Lord, be upon us.

℟. As we have hoped in Thee.

℣. Let Thy priests be clothed with justice.

℟. And let Thy saints rejoice.

℣. From my secret sins cleanse me, O Lord.

℟. And from those of others spare Thy servant.

℣. O Lord, hear my prayer.

℟. And let my cry come unto Thee.

Let us pray.

O merciful Lord, incline Thine ears to our prayers, and enlighten our hearts by the grace of Thy Holy Spirit: that we may worthily receive Thy holy mysteries, and love Thee with an everlasting love.

O God, unto Whom every heart is open, every desire known, and from Whom no secret is hid: cleanse the thoughts of our hearts by the inspiration of Thy Holy Spirit, that we may perfectly love Thee and worthily praise Thee.

Inflame, O Lord, our reins and our hearts with the fire of the Holy Ghost: that we may serve Thee with a chaste body, and please Thee with a pure mind.

We pray Thee, O Lord, that the Comforter Who proceedeth from Thee may illumine our minds, and lead us, as Thy Son hath promised, into all truth.

May the power of Thy Holy Spirit, O Lord, be present with us to cleanse us from all evil and defend us from all adversities.

O God, Who didst teach the hearts of Thy faithful by the light of Thy Holy Spirit: grant us by the same Spirit to have a right judgment in all things, and evermore to rejoice in His holy comfort.

Visit, O Lord, we beseech Thee, and cleanse our consciences, that Thy Son, Our Lord Jesus Christ, when He cometh, may find in us a mansion prepared for Himself.

PRAYER OF ST. THOMAS
AQUINAS—TO BE SAID DAILY

Almighty, everlasting God, lo, I draw near to the Sacrament of Thine only begotten Son, Our Lord Jesus Christ. As sick, I approach to the Physician of life; unclean, to the Fountain of mercy; blind, to the Light of eternal brightness; poor and needy, to the Lord of heaven and earth. I implore Thee, therefore, out of the abundance of Thy boundless mercy, that Thou wouldst vouchsafe to heal my sickness, to wash my defilements, to enlighten my blindness, to enrich my poverty, and to clothe my nakedness; that I may receive the Bread of angels, the King of Kings, the Lord of Lords, with such reverence and humility, such contrition and devotion, such purity and faith, such purpose and intention, as is expedient for the health of my soul. Grant, I beseech Thee, that I may receive not only the Sacrament of the Body and Blood of the Lord, but also the whole grace and virtue of that Sacrament. O most merciful God, grant me so to receive the Body of Thine only begotten Son, Our Lord Jesus Christ, which He took of the Virgin Mary, that I may be found worthy to be incorporated into His Mystical Body, and accounted among His members. And, O most loving Father, grant that Whom now I purpose to receive under a veil I may at last behold with unveiled face, even Thy beloved Son, Who with Thee and the Holy Ghost ever liveth and reigneth, one God, world without end. *Amen.*

Sunday[27]

O great High Priest, the true Pontiff, Jesus Christ, Who didst offer Thyself to God the Father a pure and spotless Victim upon the altar of the Cross for us miserable sinners, and didst give us Thy Flesh to eat and Thy Blood to drink, and didst ordain this mystery in the power of Thy Holy Spirit, saying, "Do this for the commemoration of Me": I pray Thee, by the same Thy blood, the great price of our salvation; I pray Thee, by that wonderful and unspeakable love wherewith Thou deignedst so to love us, miserable and unworthy, as to wash us from our sins in Thine own blood: teach me, Thine unworthy servant, by Thy Holy Spirit, to approach so great a mystery with that reverence and honor, that devotion and fear, which is due and fitting. Make me, through Thy grace, always so to believe and understand, to conceive and firmly to hold, to think and to speak, of that exceeding mystery, as shall please Thee and be good for my soul.

Let Thy good Spirit enter my heart, and there be heard without utterance, and without the sound of words speak all truth. For Thy mysteries are exceeding deep, and covered with a sacred veil. For Thy great mercy's sake, grant me to approach Thy holy mysteries with a clean heart and a pure mind. Free my heart from all defiling and unholy, from all vain and hurtful thoughts. Fence me round about with the holy and faithful guard and mighty protection of Thy blessed angels, that the enemies

---

[27] These following eight prayers were authored by St. Ambrose.

of all good may go away ashamed. By the virtue of this mighty mystery, and by the hand of Thy holy angel, drive away from me and from all Thy servants the hard spirit of pride and vainglory, of envy and blasphemy, of impurity and uncleanness, of doubting and mistrust. Let them be confounded that persecute us; let them perish who are bent upon our ruin.

Monday

King of virgins and Lover of chastity and innocence, extinguish in my frame, by the dew of Thy heavenly blessing, the fuel of evil concupiscence, that so an equal purity of soul and body may abide in me. Mortify in my members the lusts of the flesh and all harmful emotions, and give me true and persevering chastity with Thine other gifts which please Thee in truth, so that I may with chaste body and pure heart offer unto Thee the sacrifice of praise. For with what contrition of heart and fountain of tears, with what reverence and awe, with what chastity of body and purity of soul, should that divine and heavenly sacrifice be celebrated, wherein Thy Flesh is indeed eaten, where Thy Blood is indeed drunk, wherein things lowest and highest, earthly and divine, are united, where the holy angels are present, and where Thou art in a marvelous and unspeakable manner both Sacrifice and Priest!

Tuesday

Who can worthily be present at this sacrifice, unless Thou, O God, makest him worthy? I know, O Lord, yea, truly do I know, and this do confess to Thy loving kindness, that I am unworthy to approach so great a mystery, by reason of my numberless sins and negligences, but I know, and truly with my own heart do I believe, and with my mouth confess, that Thou canst make me worthy, Who alone canst make that clean which proceedeth from that which is unclean, and sinners to be just and holy. By this Thine Almighty power I beseech Thee, O my God, to grant that I, a sinner, may assist at this sacrifice with fear and trembling, with purity of heart and plenteous tears, with spiritual gladness and heavenly joy. May my mind feel the sweetness of Thy most blessed presence, and the love of Thy holy angels, keeping watch around me.

Wednesday

Mindful then, O Lord, of Thy worshipful Passion, I approach Thine altar, sinner though I am, to join in offering unto Thee that sacrifice which Thou hast instituted and commanded to be offered in remembrance of Thee for our well-being. Receive it, I beseech Thee, O God most High, for Thy holy Church, and for the people whom Thou hast purchased with Thine own blood. Let not, through my unworthiness, the price of their salvation be wasted, whose saving Victim and Redemption Thou didst Thyself vouchsafe to be. Also behold in pity, O Lord, the sorrows of Thy people, which I bring before Thee; the perils of Thy servants; the sorrowful sighing of prisoners; the miseries of widows and orphans, and all that are desolate and bereaved; the necessities of strangers and travelers; the helplessness and sadness of the weak and sickly; the depressions of the languishing; the weakness of the aged and of children; the trials and aspirations of young men; and the vows of virgins.

Thursday

For Thou hast mercy upon all, O Lord, and hatest nothing that Thou hast made. Remember how frail our nature is, and that Thou art our Father and our God. Be not angry with us forever, and shut not up Thy tender mercies in displeasure. For it is not for our just works that we present our prayers before Thy face, but for the multitude of Thy tender mercies. Take away from us, O Lord, our iniquities, and mercifully kindle in us the fire of Thy Holy Spirit. Take away from us the heart of stone, and give us a heart of flesh, a heart to love and adore Thee, a heart to delight in, to follow, and to enjoy Thee. And we entreat Thy mercy, O Lord, that Thou wouldst look down graciously upon Thy family, as it pays its vows to Thy most holy name; and that the desire of none may be in vain, and the petitions of none unfulfilled, do Thou inspire our prayers, that they may be such as Thou delightest to hear and answer.

Friday

We pray Thee also, O Lord, holy Father, for the souls of the faithful departed: that this great Sacrament of Thy love may be to them health and salvation, joy and refreshment. O Lord, my God, grant them this day a great and abundant feast of Thee, the living Bread, Who camest down from heaven and givest life unto the world; even of Thy holy and blessed Flesh, the Lamb without spot, Who takest away the sins of the world; that Flesh, which was taken of the Blessed Virgin Mary, and conceived by the Holy Ghost; and of that Fountain of mercy which, by the soldier's lance, flowed from Thy most sacred side; that they be thereby fed and satisfied, refreshed and comforted, and may rejoice in Thy praise and in Thy glory. I pray Thy loving mercy, O Lord, that on the bread and wine to be offered unto Thee may descend the fullness of Thy blessing and the sanctification of Thy divinity. May there descend also the invisible and incomprehensible Majesty of Thy Holy Spirit, as it descended of old on the sacrifices of the fathers, which shall make these oblations Thy Body and Blood; and may this offering be acceptable unto Thee, through Him Who offered Himself a Sacrifice to Thee, O Father, even Jesus Christ, Thine only Son Our Lord.

Saturday

I entreat Thee also, O Lord, by this most holy mystery of Thy Body and Blood, wherewith we are daily fed, and cleansed, and sanctified in Thy Church, and are made partakers of the one supreme Divinity, grant unto me Thy holy virtues, that filled therewith I may draw near with a good conscience unto Thy holy altar, so that these heavenly mysteries may be made unto me salvation and life; for Thou hast said with Thy holy and blessed mouth: "The bread which I will give is My Flesh, for the life of the world. I am the living Bread which came down from heaven. If any man eat of this Bread, he shall live forever." O most sweet Bread, heal the palate of my heart, that I may taste the sweetness of Thy love. Heal it of all infirmities, that I may find sweetness in nothing out of Thee. O most pure Bread, having all delight and all savor, which ever refreshest us, and never failest, let my heart feed on Thee, and may my inmost soul be filled with the sweetness of Thy savor. The angels feed on Thee fully; let pilgrim man feed on Thee after his measure, so that, refreshed by this nourishment, he may not faint by the way. Holy Bread! Living Bread! Pure Bread! Who didst come down from heaven, and Who givest life to the world, enter into my heart and cleanse me from all impurity of flesh and spirit. Come into my soul; heal and cleanse me within and without; be the protection and continual health of my soul and body. Drive far from me all foes that lie in wait: let them flee afar off at the presence of Thy power; that, fortified by Thee without and within, I may by a straight way arrive at Thy kingdom, where, not as now in mysteries, but face-to-face, we shall behold Thee; when Thou shalt have delivered up the kingdom to God Thy Father, and shalt be God All in all. Then shalt Thou satisfy me with Thyself by a wondrous fullness, so that I shall never hunger nor thirst anymore forever. Who with the same God the Father, and the Holy Ghost, ever livest and reignest world without end. *Amen.*

Daily

O gracious Lord Jesus Christ, I, a sinner, nothing presuming on my own deserts, but trusting in Thy mercy and goodness, with fear and trembling approach to the table of Thy most sweet feast. For my heart and body are stained with many sins; my thoughts and lips not diligently guarded. Wherefore, O gracious God, O awful Majesty, in my extremity I turn to Thee, the Fount of mercy; to Thee I hasten to be healed, and take refuge under Thy protection; and Thee, before Whom as my Judge I cannot stand, I long for as my Savior. To Thee, O Lord, I show my wounds, to Thee I lay bare my shame. I know my sins are many and great, for which I am afraid. My trust is in Thy mercies, of which there is no end. Look therefore upon me with the eyes of Thy mercy, O Lord Jesus Christ, God and man, crucified for man; hearken unto me, whose trust is in Thee; have mercy upon me, who am full of sin and misery, O Thou Fount of mercy, that wilt never cease to flow. Hail, saving Victim, offered for me and all mankind on the Cross of suffering and shame. Hail, noble and Precious Blood, flowing from the wounds of my crucified Lord and Savior Jesus Christ, and washing away the sins of the whole world. Be mindful, O Lord, of Thy creature, whom Thou hast redeemed with Thine own blood. I repent that I have sinned; I desire to amend what I have done. Take therefore away from me, O most merciful Father, all my iniquities and sins: that, being cleansed both in body and soul, I may worthily taste the Holy of Holies; and grant that this holy feeding on Thy Body and Blood, of which, unworthy as I am, I purpose to partake, may be for the remission of my sins, and the perfect cleansing of all my offenses, for the driving away of all evil thoughts and the renewal of all holy desires, for the healthful bringing forth of fruit well-pleasing unto Thee, and the most sure protection of my soul and body against the wiles of all my enemies. *Amen.*

ACT OF CONTRITION

I desire, O my Savior, to humbly offer Thee the sacrifice of a troubled spirit and a contrite heart. I grieve from my inmost heart that I have ever offended Thee by my sins, Thee my God and my chief Good, Thee Who art so gracious to me, and so oft refreshest me in Thy Blessed Sacrament. I grieve especially for the sins of ... which Thou knowest, Thou Searcher of our hearts, and which I, a miserable sinner, do confess in the bitterness of my soul. Would that I had never offended Thee! Yet a contrite and humble heart, O God, Thou wilt not despise; Thou Who for love of us didst give to us Thine only begotten Son, to wash us from our sins in His own blood.

RESOLUTION OF AMENDMENT

I desire, O Lord, earnestly longing for the help of Thy grace, to renew all my baptismal vows to Thee, to renounce all that displeaseth Thee, and to walk more perfectly in newness of life. I renounce the devil and all his works and pomps, the glory of the world with all its covetous desires, all sinful excesses in things lawful, and whatever may lead my heart from Thee or hinder my duty toward Thee; also, I renounce all the sinful lusts of the flesh, with everything in thought, word, or deed, which displeaseth Thee, especially ..., from all which let it be Thy good pleasure to deliver me, and to turn the whole stream of my affections to the love of Thee, that Thy will and Thy love may be the sole rule and guide of my life, and I may love whatever Thou lovest, and hate whatever Thou hatest.

ACT OF FAITH

Of a truth I firmly believe, O good Jesus, and with lively faith confess, that Thou Thyself, equal to God the Father in glory and in power, true God and man, art verily and indeed present in this Sacrament. For Thou, the very Truth itself, hast said, "This is My Body, This is My Blood." I believe whatever the Son of God hath said. Nothing can be truer than this word of Him Who is the Truth. I do believe, Lord; help my unbelief, increase my faith.

ACT OF HOPE

O Christ Jesus, I am sinful dust and ashes, but Thou callest to Thee all who labor and are burdened, that Thou mayest refresh them. Art not Thou my Refuge? To whom else shall I go? Thou hast the words of eternal life. Thou alone canst comfort me in every trouble. Lord, I am weak and sick, but Thou art my salvation. Those who are well need not a physician, but those who are sick. Therefore I come to Thee, my Physician and my Refuge, hoping that this Communion may be to me the increase of faith, hope, and charity; a firm defense against the snares of my enemies; a help to the removal of the fault and defect of ..., and to the bringing forth of works well-pleasing unto Thee, especially ..., and a pledge of future glory. This is the hope and desire which I cherish in my heart, for Thou art compassionate and of tender mercy, and in all Thy promises most faithful.

ACT OF LOVE

O most sweet Savior, Jesus Christ, how great was Thy love, which drew Thee from the bosom of the Father to this vale of tears, to take our flesh and endure infinite miseries and wrongs, yea, even the death of the Cross, and that only for us miserable sinners and for our salvation. O how great was Thy love! Thou mightest have condemned us, and Thou didst rather choose to save us: we were guilty, and Thou, the sinless One, didst endure our punishment to set us free. Out of love it was that Thou camest down to take our flesh; and when about to depart from this world to the Father, Thou didst leave to us this Sacrament as a pledge of Thy love, that after a new and wondrous manner Thou mightest abide with us forever; Thou Whose delights are to be with the children of men. O Lord, how worthy art Thou of love, Who dost so much for love of us! Wherefore I will love Thee, O Lord, my Strength, my Refuge, and my Deliverer. O God, Thou art true Love! He that dwelleth in love dwelleth in Thee. I desire to receive Thee in this Sacrament, that I may be more firmly united with Thee in the bond of love. Who shall separate me from the love of Christ my Savior? O that neither life, nor death, nor any creature may have power to do so.

ACT OF HUMILITY

How dare I venture to approach to Thee, O Lord? Art not Thou, O God, my Lord, my Creator, my Redeemer, the King of heaven and earth? And who am I? A poor worm of earth, and what is yet more unworthy, so often a disobedient and ungrateful sinner against Thee! Of a truth, Lord, I am not worthy that Thou shouldst enter under my roof; yet remember, O Lord, that, although Thou wast Lord of all, yet didst Thou take upon Thee the form of a servant, and coming unto us didst converse familiarly with publicans and sinners; and lastly didst humble Thyself and become obedient unto death. Let that Thy humility move Thee, I beseech Thee, not to despise me, vile and worthless as I am, but graciously to come unto me, and mercifully to receive me, who come to Thee.

ACT OF REPARATION

O Lord, my God and Savior, Who, as Thou didst endure for our salvation the outrages of those who crucified Thee, so now deignest to bear with those who by careless or unworthy Communions approach and touch Thee, not discerning Thee, and endurest all irreverences rather than withhold Thy sacred presence from our altars: I bewail these indignities, and most earnestly desire to prevent, to the utmost of my power, whatever thus still grieves Thee. I beseech Thee, accept this sorrow and this desire as the only offering I can make in reparation of so great dishonor. O Lord, increase our faith, and preserve us from the least profanation of this adorable mystery, and kindle in me and in the hearts of all Thy people, especially of all who celebrate or assist in its ministration, such reverence and devotion that Thy most holy name may more and more be honored and glorified in this Sacrament of love. *Amen.*

ASPIRATIONS

O Lord Jesus, what great things hast Thou done, and what didst Thou suffered, out of the power of Thy boundless love toward me! But what return have I made? and what return shall I make?

I am sorry from the bottom of my heart that I have ever offended Thee, Who hast so greatly loved me.

I believe in Thee with a lively faith, O eternal Truth! Because Thou art Thyself God and man, my Lord and Savior.

I hope in Thee, O Lord, O only Hope, and true Salvation of my soul.

I love Thee, O my sovereign Good! O that I may love Thee above all things with my whole heart! O may the burning power of Thy love absorb me, that nothing may ever separate me from the love of Christ Jesus, my Savior!

For what have I in heaven but Thee? and besides Thee what do I desire upon earth?

As the hart panteth after the water-springs, so panteth my soul after Thee, O God.

What is man, that Thou art mindful of him? or the son of man that Thou visitest him?

Blessed is He Who cometh in the name of the Lord.

TO THE BLESSED VIRGIN

O most Blessed Virgin Mary, Mother of gentleness and mercy, I, a miserable and unworthy sinner, fly to thy protection with every sentiment of humility and love; and I implore of thy loving kindness that thou wouldst vouchsafe graciously to be near me, and all who throughout the whole Church are to receive the Body and Blood of thy Son this day, even as thou wert near thy sweetest Son as He hung bleeding on the Cross, that, aided by thy gracious help, we may worthily offer up a pure and acceptable sacrifice in the sight of the Holy and undivided Trinity. *Amen.*

TO ST. JOSEPH

Happy and blessed art thou, O Joseph, to whom it was given not only to see and to hear that God whom many kings desired to see, and saw not, to hear, and heard not; but also to bear Him in thine arms, to embrace Him, to clothe Him, and to guard and defend Him.

℣. Pray for us, O blessed Joseph.

℟. That we may be made worthy of the promises of Christ.

Let us pray.

O God, Who hast given unto us a royal priesthood, vouchsafe, we beseech Thee, that as blessed Joseph was found worthy to handle with his hands, and bear within his arms, Thine only begotten Son, born of the Virgin Mary, so may we be made fit, by cleanness of heart and innocency of works, to wait upon Thy holy altars; that we may worthily receive the most sacred Body and Blood of Thy Son, now in this present, and deserve to attain an everlasting reward in the world to come. Through the same Christ Our Lord. *Amen.*

DIRECTION OF THE INTENTION

I intend to assist at the Holy Sacrifice of the Mass, and to receive the Body and Blood of Our Lord Jesus Christ, according to the rite of the holy Roman Church, to the praise of Almighty God and of the whole court of heaven; for my benefit, and that of the whole Church on earth; for all those who have commended themselves unto my prayers, in general and in particular; and for the happy estate of the holy Roman Church. Amen.

Joy with peace, amendment of life, space for true repentance, the grace and comfort of the Holy Ghost, perseverance in good works, a contrite and humble heart, and a happy consummation of my life, grant unto me, O Almighty and merciful Lord. *Amen.*

[FOR THOSE WHO WISH TO PRAY IN THEIR OWN WORDS

Reflect on the events of the period since your last Communion. Consider:

WHAT YOU HAVE SPECIALLY TO BE THANKFUL FOR —

The mercies you have enjoyed.

(In home life; the love of friends; success in business, and the like; spiritual blessings, etc.)

Any troubles which have been averted.

(Dangers to which you have been exposed; causes of anxiety which have been removed, etc.)

Any sorrows or troubles which have fallen upon you.

(Trace God's hand in them, trusting that He has some merciful design in them, so that you can *thank* Him for them.)

WHAT YOU HAVE SPECIALLY TO PRAY FOR —

For the Church of Christ.

(The pope, the whole hierarchy, your own bishop, the clergy with whom you are specially concerned, missions, etc.)

For your country.

(The president and his counselors, Congress, the governor, etc.; national dangers to be averted, etc.)

For your relatives, friends, and acquaintances.

(Any who are sick or in sorrow; any for whom you desire God's guidance in religious or worldly affairs. Think whether anyone has any special claim upon you. Have you injured anyone? If so, have you made all the reparation in your power? Has anyone injured you, having thus a special need for your prayers? The souls in purgatory—have you to pray especially for some of these?)

For yourself.

(Sins to be forgiven. What are your chief temptations just now? What sins and faults do you most need aid against? What Christian virtues are you chiefly deficient in? Are there any business affairs, or undertakings of any kind, or expected events, upon which you desire to ask God's blessing? etc.)]

When the bell rings at the Domine, non sum dignus, *go up to the altar rail, and kneel there, with ungloved and folded hands. Renew with all possible fervor your contrition of heart, while the* Confiteor *is recited by the acolyte, and the* Misereatur *and* Indulgentiam *pronounced by the priest. When the Sacred Host is presented to you, receive it on your tongue lightly resting on the lower lip. Say in your heart the words which the priest uses:* The Body of Our Lord Jesus Christ preserve my soul unto life everlasting. *Retire to your place with recollection and holy modesty, and remain for some time kneeling, in silent communing with your heavenly Guest. Do not be too anxious to use your prayer book; it is far better for a while to meditate upon the sacred mysteries which you have received, using the unspoken sentiments of the soul. Let not this precious time be wasted, however; should attention flag and distractions arise, have immediate recourse to the following prayers.*

THANKSGIVING AFTER COMMUNION

Antiphon. Of the three children.

THE BENEDICITE

All ye works of the Lord, bless the Lord: praise and exalt Him above all forever.

O ye angels of the Lord, bless the Lord: bless the Lord, O ye heavens.

O all ye waters that are above the heavens, bless the Lord: bless the Lord, O all ye powers of the Lord.

O ye sun and moon, bless the Lord: bless the Lord, O ye stars of heaven.

O every shower and dew, bless ye the Lord: bless the Lord, O all ye spirits of God.

O ye fire and heat, bless the Lord: bless the Lord, O ye cold and heat.

O ye dews and hoarfrost, bless the Lord: bless the Lord, O ye frost and cold.

O ye ice and snow, bless the Lord: bless the Lord, O ye nights and days.

O ye light and darkness, bless the Lord: bless the Lord, O ye lightnings and clouds.

O let the earth bless the Lord: let it praise and exalt Him above all forever.

O ye mountains and hills, bless the Lord: bless the Lord, O all ye things that spring up in the earth.

O ye fountains, bless the Lord: bless the Lord, O ye seas and rivers.

O ye whales, and all that move in the waters, bless the Lord: bless the Lord, O all ye fowls of the air.

O all ye beasts and cattle, bless the Lord: bless the Lord, O ye sons of men.

O let Israel bless the Lord: let them praise and exalt Him above all forever.

O ye priests of the Lord, bless the Lord: bless the Lord, O ye servants of the Lord.

O ye spirits and souls of the just, bless the Lord: bless the Lord, O ye holy and humble of heart.

O Ananiah, Azariah, and Misael, bless ye the Lord: praise and exalt Him above all forever.

Let us bless the Father, and the Son, with the Holy Ghost: let us praise and exalt Him above all forever.

Blessed art Thou, O Lord, in the firmament of heaven: and worthy to be praised and glorified, and exalted above all forever.

PSALM 150

Praise the Lord in His holy places: praise Him in the firmament of His power.

Praise Him in His mighty acts: praise Him according to the multitude of His greatness.

Praise Him with the sound of the trumpet: praise Him with psaltery and harp.

Praise Him with timbrel and choir: praise Him with strings and organs.

Praise Him upon the high-sounding cymbals: praise Him upon cymbals of joy: let every spirit praise the Lord. Alleluia.

Glory be to the Father, etc.

Antiphon. Let us sing the song of the three children, which the holy souls sang in the fiery furnace, blessing the Lord.

Lord, have mercy.

Christ, have mercy.

Lord, have mercy.

Our Father (*inaudibly*).

℣. And lead us not into temptation.

℟. But deliver us from evil.

℣. Let all Thy works, O Lord, praise Thee.

℟. And let Thy saints bless Thee.

℣. The saints shall rejoice in glory.

℟. They shall be joyful in their beds.

℣. Not unto us, O Lord, not unto us.

℟. But unto Thy name give the glory.

℣. O Lord, hear my prayer.

℟. And let my cry come unto Thee.

Let us pray.

O God, Who for the three children didst assuage the flames of fire: mercifully grant that the flames of sin may not consume us Thy servants.

Direct, we beseech Thee, O Lord, our actions by Thy inspiration, and further them with Thy continual help; that every prayer and work of ours may always begin from Thee, and through Thee be brought to an end.

Vouchsafe, O Lord, to extinguish within us the flames of sin; Thou Who didst grant to blessed Lawrence grace to arise whole from his fiery torments. Through Christ Our Lord. *Amen.*

A PRAYER OF ST. THOMAS AQUINAS

Almighty and everlasting God, the Preserver of souls and the Redeemer of the world, look favorably upon me, Thy servant, prostrate before Thy Majesty, and most graciously accept this sacrifice at which, in honor of Thy name, I have been present, for the saving health of the faithful, living as well as departed, as also for all my sins and offenses. Take away Thine anger from me: grant Thy grace and mercy unto me; open unto me the gates of paradise; deliver me by Thy power from all evils; and whatever guilt I have of my own sinfulness incurred, do Thou graciously forgive; and make me so to preserve in Thy precepts in this world that I may be rendered worthy to be joined to the company of Thine elect; of Thine only gift, O my God, Whose blessed name, honor, and dominion endureth forever and ever. *Amen.*

I render thanks to Thee, O Lord, holy Father, everlasting God, Who hast vouchsafed, not for any merits of mine, but of Thy great mercy only, to feed me a sinner, Thine unworthy servant, with the precious Body and Blood of Thy Son, Our Lord Jesus Christ; and I pray that this Holy Communion may not be for my judgment and condemnation, but for my pardon and salvation. Let it be unto me an armor of faith and a shield of good purpose, a riddance of all vices, and a rooting out of all evil desires; an increase of love and patience, of humility and obedience, and of all virtues; a firm defense against the wiles of all my enemies, visible and invisible; a perfect quieting of all my impulses, fleshly and spiritual; a cleaving unto Thee, the one true God; and a blessed consummation of my end when Thou dost call. And I pray that Thou wouldst vouchsafe to bring me a sinner to that unspeakable feast where Thou, with Thy Son and Thy Holy Spirit, art to Thy holy ones true light, fullness of blessedness, everlasting joy, and perfect happiness. Through the same Christ Our Lord. *Amen.*

A PRAYER OF ST. BONAVENTURE

O most sweet Lord Jesus Christ, transfix the affections of my inmost soul with that most joyous and healthful wound of Thy love, with true, serene, holiest apostolic charity, that my soul may ever languish and melt with entire love and longing for Thee, that it may desire Thee, and faint for Thy courts, long to be dissolved and to be with Thee. Grant that my soul may hunger after Thee, the Bread of angels, the Refreshment of holy souls, our daily and supersubstantial Bread, Who hast all sweetness and savor, and the sweetness of every taste. Let my heart ever hunger after and feed upon Thee, upon Whom the angels desire to look, and my inmost soul be filled with the sweetness of Thy savor. May it ever thirst for Thee, the Fountain of life, the Source of wisdom and knowledge, the Fountain of eternal light, the Torrent of pleasure, the Richness of the house of God. May it ever yearn for Thee, seek Thee, find Thee, stretch toward Thee, attain to Thee, meditate upon Thee, speak of Thee, and do all things to the praise and glory of Thy holy name, with humility and discretion, with love and delight, with readiness and affection, with perseverance even unto the end. And be Thou ever my hope and my whole confidence; my riches; my delight, my pleasure, and my joy; my rest and tranquillity; my peace, my sweetness, and my fragrance; my sweet savor, my food and refreshment; my refuge and my help; my wisdom; my portion, my possession, and my treasure, in Whom my mind and my heart may ever remain fixed and firm, and rooted immovably, henceforth and forevermore. *Amen.*

O most holy, O most benign, O noble and glorious Virgin Mary, who wast worthy to bear in thy sacred womb the Creator of all, and at thy virginal breast to nourish Him Whose true, real, and most holy Body and Blood I, an unworthy sinner, have just now dared to receive: vouchsafe, I humbly beseech thee, to intercede with Him for me, a sinner; that whatsoever, by ignorance or neglect, by accident or irreverence, I have left undone, or have done amiss, in this unspeakably Holy Sacrifice, may be pardoned through thy prayers to the same Our Lord Jesus Christ, thy Son, Who with the Father and the Holy Ghost liveth and reigneth world without end. *Amen.*

ASPIRATIONS

Who art Thou, O Lord, and what am I?

Dost Thou come unto me, O King most High, even to the very lowest of Thy servants?

Behold, O Lord, I now have Thee, Who hast all things: I possess Thee, Who possessest all things and canst do all things; therefore, O my God and my All, do Thou wean my heart from all other things besides Thee, for in them there is nothing but vanity and weariness of spirit; on Thee alone may my heart be fixed; in Thee be my rest, for in Thee is my treasure, in Thee are sovereign truth, true happiness, and eternal life.

Let my soul, O Lord, feel the sweetness of Thy presence. May it taste how sweet Thou art, O Lord, that, drawn by love of Thee, it may seek for nothing wherein to rejoice out of Thee; for Thou art the Joy of my heart, and my God, and my portion forever.

Thou art the Physician of my soul, Who with Thine own stripes hast healed our sickness. I am that sick soul whom Thou camest from heaven to heal; heal my soul, therefore, for I have sinned against Thee.

Thou art the Good Shepherd, Who hast laid down Thy life for Thy sheep. Behold, I am that sheep which was lost, and yet Thou dost vouchsafe to feed me with Thy Body and Blood; lay me now upon Thy shoulders. What wilt Thou refuse me, Who hast given Thyself unto me? O be Thou my Shepherd, and I shall lack nothing in the green pasture wherein Thou feedest me, until I am brought to the pastures of eternal life.

O Thou true Light, which enlightenest every man who cometh into the world, enlighten mine eyes, that I sleep not in death.

O Fire continually burning, and never failing! behold how lukewarm and cold I am; O do Thou inflame my reins and my heart, that they may be on fire with the love of Thee. For Thou camest to send fire on the earth, and what wilt Thou but that it be kindled?

O King of heaven and earth, rich in pity! behold, I am poor and needy: Thou knowest what I most require; Thou alone art able to enrich and help me; help me, O God, and, out of the treasure of Thy goodness, succor Thou my needy soul.

O my Lord and my God! behold, I am Thy servant: give me understanding and kindle my affections, that I may know and do Thy will.

Thou art the Lamb of God, the Lamb without spot, Who takest away the sins of the world; take away from me whatever hurteth me and displeaseth Thee; and give me what Thou knowest to be pleasing to Thee and good for me.

Thou art my love and all my joy; Thou art my God and my All; Thou art the portion of my inheritance and of my cup; Thou art He that will restore my inheritance unto me.

O my God and my All! may the sweet and burning power of Thy love, I beseech Thee, so absorb my soul, that I may die unto the world for the love of Thee, Who for the love of me hast vouchsafed to die upon the Cross, O my God and my All.

Lord, if I had lived innocently, I could not have deserved to receive the crumbs that fall from Thy table. How great is Thy mercy, Who hast feasted me with the Bread of angels, with the Wine of virgins, with Manna from heaven!

O when shall I pass from this dark glass, from this veil of Sacraments, to the vision of Thy eternal light; from eating Thy Body, to beholding Thy face in Thy eternal kingdom?

Let not my sins crucify the Lord of life again; let it never be said of me, "The hand of him who betrayeth Me is with Me on the table."

O that I might love Thee as well as ever any creature loved Thee! Let me think nothing but Thee, desire nothing but Thee, enjoy nothing but Thee.

O Jesus, be a Jesus unto me. Thou art all things unto me. Let nothing ever please me but what savors of Thee and Thy miraculous sweetness.

Blessed be the mercies of Our Lord, Who of God is made unto me wisdom, and justice, and sanctification, and redemption. Let him who glorieth glory in the Lord. *Amen.*

Adore and Magnify the Lord

O Lord Jesus, sweetest Guest, mayest Thou have come happily to me, Thy poor and humble servant. Mayest Thou have entered in blessing under this mean and lowly roof. Blessed art Thou, O Lord, in the highest, for that Thou hast come into my heart. Thou Dayspring from on high. O King of peace, drive from my heart all vain and idle thoughts, that my soul may be able to imitate and to love Thee only, the Author of peace. For what besides Thee, O Thou peace, Thou calm and sweetness of my heart, should my soul seek for or desire?

Pray for Grace

Grant me Thy grace, most merciful Jesus, that it may be with me, and work with me, and continue with me even to the end. Grant me ever to will and to desire what is most pleasing unto Thee. Let Thy will be mine, and my will ever follow Thine in perfect agreement with it, that so I may neither choose nor reject, save what Thou choosest and rejectest.

Grant me to die to all that is in the world, and for love of Thee to be content to be despised and unknown in this life. Grant me, above all objects of desire, to rest in Thee, and to still my heart to perfect peace in Thee. For Thou art the true Peace of the heart, Thou art its only Rest, and out of Thee all is restless and unquiet. In this peace, that is in Thyself alone, my chief and eternal Good, may I lay down and take my rest. *Amen.*

Give Thanks

What shall I render unto Thee, O Lord Jesus, for all that Thou hast done unto me, and on this day especially? In Thy care for me Thou hast given me Thy Body for my food, and Thy Blood for my drink, and both for a pledge of future glory. Would that my lips might be opened, and my mouth filled with Thy praise, that I might sing of Thy glory and of Thy greatness all the day long, and tell of all Thy wondrous works. O my soul, magnify the Lord, from Whom thou hast received blessings so many and so great; and rejoice, my spirit, in God thy Savior: for He hath looked down on my lowliness; and the Mighty One hath done great things for me, and hath filled me, when hungry, with good things.

Let my words please Thee, O Lord; my joy shall be in Thee, and I will be exercised in Thy commandments. Hold Thou me by my right hand, and guide me by Thy will, that Thou mayest afterward receive me with Thy glory, for Thy mercy's sake. *Amen.*

Offer to God the Father His Son Jesus Christ

O most merciful Father, Who hast so loved me as to give me Thine only begotten Son for my food and drink, and with Him all things, look upon the face of Thine Anointed, in Whom Thou art well pleased. This Thy beloved Son, and with Him my heart, I offer and present to Thee for all the blessings Thou hast this day given me. Mayest Thou, O Father, be now well pleased in Him, and through Him turn away Thine indignation from me.

Behold the one Mediator between God and men, the man Christ Jesus, my Advocate and High Priest, Who intercedes for me. Him do I offer and plead before Thee, Who committed no sin, but bore the sins of the world, and by Whose stripes we are healed. Accept, therefore, O Holy Father, this immaculate Victim, to the honor and glory of Thy name, in thanksgiving for all Thy benefits bestowed upon me, in remission also of my sins, and supply of all my defects and shortcomings.

O Blessed Virgin, Mother of my God and Savior, recommend my petitions to thy Son. O all ye angels and saints, citizens of heaven, join also your prayers with mine. Ye stand always before the throne, and see Him face-to-face, Whom I here receive under veils. Be ever mindful of me, and obtain from Him and through Him that with you I may bless Him and love Him forever. *Amen.*

Offer Yourself to Christ

O Lord, for that I am Thy servant and the son of Thy handmaid, I therefore renounce the devil and all his works and pomps; all the vanity of this wicked world, and all the sinful lusts of the flesh. Thou alone art the God of my heart; Thou, O God, art my portion forever. Thou art the portion of my inheritance and of my cup. Thou art He that will restore my inheritance unto me. Do Thou therefore take for Thine own the whole powers of my soul, my memory, my intellect, and all my will. All that I am, and all that I have, Thou hast bestowed upon me: therefore I give back all to Thee, and surrender it to be wholly governed by Thy sovereign will. Grant me but grace to love Thee alone, and I am rich enough and ask no more.

Here may be said the Tantum ergo *(p. 472), the* Lauda Sion *(p. 475), the* Pange, lingua *(p. 472), or any other Hymn in honor of the Blessed Sacrament.*

A PRAYER

Behold, O kind and most sweet Jesus, I cast myself upon my knees in Thy sight, and with the most fervent desire of my soul I pray and beseech Thee that Thou wouldst impress upon my heart lively sentiments of faith, hope, and charity, with true repentance for my sins, and a firm desire of amendment, whilst with deep affection and grief of soul I ponder within myself and mentally contemplate Thy five most precious wounds; having before my eyes that which David spake in prophecy: "They have pierced My hands and feet; they have numbered all My bones."

The Devotion of the Forty Hours' Adoration

This devotion, known in Italy as the *Quarant'Ore*, continues for forty hours, in memory of the forty hours during which the body of Our Lord remained in the sepulchre. It was begun at Milan in 1534, and was introduced into Rome by St. Philip Neri in 1548, and sanctioned by Pope Clement VIII, who issued a solemn bull respecting it, November 25, 1592.

The devotion owes its origin to Fr. Joseph, a Capuchin friar at Milan. In the year 1534, the city of Milan was suffering all the horrors attendant on war, and was reduced almost to despair, when Fr. Joseph called upon the citizens to raise their eyes from the miseries around them, and look up to heaven for succor, assuring them, on the part of God, that if they would give themselves to fervent prayer for forty hours, their city and their country would be liberated from the devastations of their enemies. The citizens obeyed the call. The Forty Hours' prayer commenced in the cathedral, and was taken up by the other churches of the city in rotation. The people meanwhile attended with fervor at the appointed prayers, and approached with great devotion the Sacraments of Penance and the Holy Eucharist. Heaven did not delay to fulfill the assurance given by the pious servant of God; for, in a short time, the emperor Charles V and Francis, king of France, were seen at the gate of Milan arranging the articles of peace.

To promote this devotion, Pope Clement VIII granted a plenary indulgence to all such as, confessing their sins and receiving Holy Communion, should visit any church or chapel where this devotion was being performed.

To gain this indulgence, it is required 1) to visit the Blessed Sacrament once during the three days of Exposition; and 2) to receive Holy Communion on the day preceding, or on one of the three days, but not necessarily in the same church or chapel in which the Blessed Sacrament is exposed.

Pope Paul V also granted an indulgence of ten years and ten *quadragenæ* for every visit made to the Blessed Sacrament thus exposed.

These indulgences are applicable to the souls in purgatory.

The forms of prayers used in this devotion are: the Litany of the Saints, Collects, etc., as given on p. 201; to which may be added the Litany of the Holy Name (*p. 47*), [‡the Litany of the Sacred Heart (*p. 255*),] the Litany of the Blessed Virgin (*p. 50*), the *Miserere* (*p. 400*), and the *Te Deum* (*p. 133*).

VISIT TO THE BLESSED SACRAMENT

AN ACT OF ADORATION TO THE MOST HOLY TRINITY

I most humbly adore Thee, O uncreated Father, and Thee, O only begotten Son, and Thee, O Holy Ghost the Paraclete, one Almighty, everlasting and unchangeable God, Creator of heaven and earth, and of all things visible and invisible. I acknowledge in Thee a true and ineffable trinity of Persons, a true and indivisible unity of substance. I glorify Thee, O Almighty Trinity, one only Deity, my most compassionate Lord, my sweetest hope, my dearest light, my most desired repose, my joy, my life, and all my good. To Thy most merciful goodness I commend my soul and body; to Thy most sacred Majesty I wholly devote myself, and to Thy divine will I resign and yield myself eternally. All honor and glory be to Thee forever and ever. *Amen.*

O heavenly Father, O most forgiving Father, O Lord God, have mercy upon me a wretched sinner, have mercy upon all men. In fullest reparation, expiation, and satisfaction for all my iniquities and negligences, and for the sins of the whole world, and perfectly to supply the deficiency of my works, I offer unto Thee Thy beloved Son, Christ Jesus, in union with that sovereign charity with which Thou didst send Him to us, and didst give Him to us as our Savior. I offer His transcendent virtues, and all that He did and suffered for us. I offer His labors, sorrows, torments, and most Precious Blood. I offer the merits of the most Blessed Virgin Mary and of all Thy saints. Assist me, I beseech Thee, O most merciful Father, through the same Thy Son, by the power of Thy Holy Spirit. Have mercy on all unhappy sinners, and graciously call them back to the way of salvation. Grant to all the living pardon and grace, and to the faithful departed eternal light and rest. *Amen.*

O Holy Spirit, sweetest Comforter, Who proceedest from the Father and the Son in an ineffable manner, come, I beseech Thee, and enter into my heart. Purify and cleanse me from all sin, and sanctify my soul. Wash away its defilements, moisten its dryness, heal its wounds, subdue its stubbornness, melt its coldness, and correct its wanderings. Make me truly humble and resigned, that I may be pleasing unto Thee, and Thou mayest abide with me forever. O most blessed Light, O Light worthy of all love, enlighten me. O Joy of paradise, O Fount of purest delights, O my God, give Thyself to me, and kindle in my inmost soul the fire of Thy love. O my Lord, instruct, direct, and defend me in all things. Give me strength against all undue fears and a cowardly spirit; bestow upon me a right faith, a firm hope, and a sincere and perfect charity; and grant that I may ever do Thy most gracious will. *Amen.*

A PRAYER OF ST. ALPHONSUS LIGUORI

Lord Jesus Christ, Who, through the love which Thou bearest to men, dost remain with them, day and night, in this Sacrament, full of mercy and of love, expecting, inviting, and receiving all who come to visit Thee: I believe that Thou art present in the Sacrament of the Altar. From the abyss of my nothingness I adore Thee, and I thank Thee for all the graces which Thou hast bestowed upon me, particularly for having given me Thyself in this Sacrament, for having given me for my advocate Thy most holy Mother, Mary, and for having called me to visit Thee in this church. I pay my homage this day to Thy most loving Heart, and I do so, first, in thanksgiving for this great gift itself; secondly, as a reparation for all the injuries which Thou hast received from Thine enemies in this Sacrament; thirdly, I wish, by this visit, to adore Thee in all those places on earth where Thou art sacramentally present, and in which Thou art the least honored and the most abandoned. My Jesus, I love Thee with my whole heart. I am sorry for having hitherto so many times offended Thine infinite goodness. I purpose, with the assistance of Thy grace, nevermore to offend Thee; and, at this moment, miserable as I am, I consecrate my whole being to Thee. I give Thee my entire will, all my affections and desires, and all that I have. From this day forward do what Thou wilt with me, and with everything that belongs to me. I ask and desire only Thy holy love, the gift of final perseverance, and the perfect fulfillment of Thy will. I commend to Thee the souls in purgatory, particularly those who were most devoted to the most Blessed Sacrament and to the Blessed Virgin Mary; and I also commend to Thee all poor sinners. Finally, my dear Savior, I unite all my affections with the affections of Thy most loving Heart; and, thus united, I offer them to Thine eternal Father, and I entreat Him, in Thy name and for Thy sake, to accept and answer them. *Amen.*

The prayer Look down, O Lord (*p. 67*) *may be used here.*

Devotions to the Sacred Heart of Jesus

✝*LITANY OF THE SACRED HEART*

Kyrie, eleison.
Christe, eleison.
Kyrie, eleison.
Christe, audi nos.
Christe, exaudi nos.

Lord, have mercy on us.
Christ, have mercy on us.
Lord, have mercy on us.
Christ, hear us.
Christ, graciously hear us.

Pater de cœlis, Deus,
Fili, Redemptor mundi, Deus,
Spiritus Sancte, Deus,
Sancta Trinitas, unus Deus,

God the Father of heaven,
God the Son, Redeemer of the world,
God the Holy Ghost,
Holy Trinity, one God,

Cor Jesu, Filii Patris æterni,
Cor Jesu, in sinu Virginis Matris a Spiritu Sancto formatum,
Cor Jesu, Verbo Dei substantialiter unitum,
Cor Jesu, majestatis infinitæ,

Heart of Jesus, Son of the eternal Father,
Heart of Jesus, formed by the Holy Ghost in the womb of the Virgin Mother,
Heart of Jesus, substantially united to the Word of God,
Heart of Jesus, of infinite majesty,

Cor Jesu, templum Dei sanctum,
Cor Jesu, tabernaculum Altissimi,
Cor Jesu, domus Dei et porta, cœli,
Cor Jesu, fornax ardens caritatis,

Heart of Jesus, sacred Temple of God,
Heart of Jesus, Tabernacle of the most High,
Heart of Jesus, House of God and Gate of heaven,
Heart of Jesus, burning Furnace of charity,

Cor Jesu, justitiæ et amoris receptaculum,
Cor Jesu, bonitate et amore plenum,
Cor Jesu, virtutum omnium abysse,
Cor Jesu, omni laude dignissimum,

Heart of Jesus, Abode of justice and love,
Heart of Jesus, full of goodness and love,
Heart of Jesus, Abyss of all virtues,
Heart of Jesus, most worthy of all praise,

Cor Jesu, rex et centrum omnium cordium,

Heart of Jesus, King and Center of all hearts,

Cor Jesu, in quo sunt omnes thesauri sapientiæ et scientiæ,

Heart of Jesus, in which are all the treasures of wisdom and knowledge,

Cor Jesu, in quo habitat omnis plenitudo divinitatis,

Heart of Jesus, in which dwells all the fullness of the Divinity,

Cor Jesu, in quo Pater sibi bene complacuit,

Heart of Jesus, in which the Father was well pleased,

Cor Jesu, de cujus plenitudine omnes nos accepimus,

Heart of Jesus, of Whose fullness we have all received,

Cor Jesu, desiderium collium æternorum,

Heart of Jesus, Desire of the everlasting hills,

Cor Jesu, patiens et multæ misericordiæ,

Heart of Jesus, patient and most merciful,

Cor Jesu, dives in omnes qui invocant te,

Heart of Jesus, enriching all who invoke Thee,

Cor Jesu, fons vitæ et sanctitatis,

Heart of Jesus, Fountain of life and holiness,

Cor Jesu, propitiatio pro peccatis nostris,

Heart of Jesus, Propitiation for our sins,

Cor Jesu, saturatum opprobriis,

Heart of Jesus, loaded down with opprobrium,

Cor Jesu, attritum propter scelera nostra,

Heart of Jesus, bruised for our offenses,

Cor Jesu, usque ad mortem obediens factum,

Heart of Jesus, obedient unto death,

Cor Jesu, lancea perforatum,

Heart of Jesus, pierced with a lance,

Cor Jesu, fons totius consolationis,

Heart of Jesus, Source of all consolation,

Cor Jesu, vita et resurrectio nostra,

Heart of Jesus, our Life and Resurrection,

Cor Jesu, pax et reconciliatio nostra,

Heart of Jesus, our Peace and Reconciliation,

Cor Jesu, victima peccatorum,

Heart of Jesus, Victim for sin,

Cor Jesu, salus in te sperantium,

Heart of Jesus, Salvation of those who trust in Thee,

Cor Jesu, spes in te morientium,

Heart of Jesus, Hope of those who die in Thee,

Cor Jesu, deliciæ Sanctorum omnium,

Heart of Jesus, Delight of all the saints,

Agnus Dei, qui tollis peccata mundi,
parce nobis, Domine.
Agnus Dei, qui tollis peccata mundi,
exaudi nos, Domine.
Agnus Dei, qui tollis peccata mundi,
miserere nobis.

℣. Jesu, mitis et humilis Corde.
℟. Fac cor nostrum secundum Cor
tuum.

Oremus.
Omnipotens sempiterne Deus,
respice in Cor dilectissimi Filii tui,
et in laudes et satisfactiones, quas in
nomine peccatorum tibi persolvit,
iisque misericordiam tuam petentibus tu veniam concede placatus,
in nomine ejusdem Filii tui Jesu
Christi. Qui tecum vivit et regnat in
sæcula sæculorum. ℟. Amen.

Lamb of God, Who takest away the sins
of the world, *spare us, O Lord.*
Lamb of God, Who takest away the
sins of the world, *graciously hear us,
O Lord.*
Lamb of God, Who takest away the sins
of the world, *have mercy on us.*

℣. Jesus meek and humble of heart.
℟. Make our hearts like unto Thine.

Let us pray.
O Almighty and eternal God, look
upon the Heart of Thy dearly beloved Son, and upon the praise and
satisfaction He offers Thee in the
name of sinners, and through their
merit grant pardon to us who implore Thy mercy, in the name of Thy
Son, Jesus Christ, Who liveth and
reigneth with Thee, world without
end. ℟. Amen.

☦ACT OF SOLEMN CONSECRATION
TO THE SACRED HEART

(Read by the priest on the feast of the Kingship of Our Lord)

Most sweet Jesus, Redeemer of the human race, look down upon us, humbly prostrate before Thy altar. We are Thine, and Thine we wish to be; but, to be more surely
united with Thee, behold each one of us freely consecrates himself today to Thy
most Sacred Heart. Many indeed have never known Thee; many, too, despising Thy
precepts, have rejected Thee. Have mercy on them all, most merciful Jesus, and draw
them to Thy Sacred Heart. Be Thou King, O Lord, not only of the faithful who
have never forsaken Thee, but also of the prodigal children who have abandoned
Thee; grant that they may quickly return to their Father's house lest they die of
wretchedness and hunger. Be Thou King of those who are deceived by erroneous
opinions, or whom discord keeps aloof, and call them back to the harbor of truth
and unity of faith, so that soon there may be but one flock and one Shepherd. Be
Thou King of all those who are still involved in the darkness of idolatry or Islamism,
and refuse not to draw them into the light and Kingdom of God. Turn Thine eyes
of mercy toward the children of that race, once Thy Chosen People. Of old they
called upon themselves the blood of the Savior; may it now descend upon them a

laver of redemption and of life. Grant, O Lord, to Thy Church, assurance of freedom and immunity from harm; give peace and order to all nations, and make the earth resound from pole to pole with one cry: Praise to the divine Heart that wrought our salvation; to it be glory and honor forever. Amen.

AN ACT OF REPARATION TO THE SACRED HEART OF JESUS

O Jesus, only Son of the living God, Who, by an incomprehensible effect of Thy love, wast pleased to be made man, to be born in a stable, to live amidst labors and sufferings, to die upon a Cross, and to leave us, as a perpetual pledge of Thy tenderness, Thine own Body and Blood for the nourishment of our souls, in the ineffable Sacrament of the Eucharist: Thou beholdest at Thy feet a criminal covered with confusion, who comes, in the spirit of union with all the associates in the adoration of Thy divine Heart, humbly to confess his ingratitude, his iniquities, and those of all other men, that he may make reparation for them as far as in him lies.

Alas! O loving Jesus, we have sinned against heaven and before Thee. What hath Thy most Sacred Heart not suffered on our part in the course of Thy sacred life, in Thy bitter Passion, and from the moment that Thou hast dwelt amongst us in the Sacrament of Thy love! O with how much bitterness, opprobrium, and grief have we deluged Thy divine Heart! Pardon; mercy; O adorable Heart of Jesus! mercy for me, mercy for all men, and for our land in particular!

I detest, with all the sincerity of my soul, and with the most profound and bitter grief, everything which hath ever offended Thee in myself or in others; I detest it for the love Thou deservest, and which is supremely due unto Thee. O that I could efface with my tears, and wash away with my blood, the injuries which we have done unto Thee. O that I could repay Thee, by my repentance, by my works, and by my love, all the glory, honor, and satisfaction of which Thou hast been robbed by the injuries and outrages that have been committed against Thee! Accept at least the earnest desire with which Thou inspirest me.

Vouchsafe, O Heart infinitely rich in mercy, to light again in my heart and that of all men the sacred fire which Thou camest to kindle upon the earth. Let it purify them, let it inflame them, let it make of them one heart with Thy Heart. Pour down, I beseech Thee, Thy most precious and abundant benedictions on Thy holy Church, and those who govern it; on this diocese, on this region, and on all those who are united with us in devotion to Thy Sacred Heart. O Heart of Jesus, live, reign in all hearts, for time and for eternity. *Amen.*

‡ANOTHER ACT OF REPARATION TO THE SACRED HEART OF JESUS

(Read by the priest on the feast of the Sacred Heart)

O sweet Jesus, Whose overflowing charity for men is requited by so much forgetfulness, negligence, and contempt, behold us prostrate before Thy altar eager to repair by a special act of homage the cruel indifference and injuries, to which Thy loving Heart is everywhere subject.

Mindful alas! that we ourselves have had a share in such great indignities, which we now deplore from the depths of our hearts, we humbly ask Thy pardon and declare our readiness to atone by voluntary expiation not only for our personal offenses, but also for the sins of those, who, straying far from the part of salvation, refuse in their obstinate infidelity to follow Thee, their Shepherd and Leader, or, renouncing the vows of their Baptism, have cast off the sweet yoke of Thy law.

We are now resolved to expiate each and every deplorable outrage committed against Thee; we are determined to make amends for the manifold offenses against Christian modesty in unbecoming dress and behavior, for all the foul seductions laid to ensnare the feet of the innocent, for the frequent violation of Sundays and holy days, and the shocking blasphemies uttered against Thee and Thy saints. We wish also to make amends for the insults to which Thy Vicar on earth and Thy priests are subjected, for the profanation, by conscious neglect or terrible acts of sacrilege, of the very Sacrament of Thy divine love; and lastly for the public crimes of nations who resist the rights and the teaching authority of the Church which Thou hast founded.

Would, O divine Jesus, we were able to wash away such abominations with our blood. We now offer, in reparation for these violations, of Thy divine honor, the satisfaction Thou didst once make to Thy eternal Father on the Cross and which Thou dost continue to renew daily on our altars; we offer it in union with the acts of atonement of Thy Virgin Mother and all the saints and of the pious faithful on earth; and we sincerely promise to make recompense, as far as we can with the help of Thy grace, for all neglect of Thy great love and for the sins we and others have committed in the past. Henceforth we will live a life of unwavering faith, of purity of conduct, of perfect observance of the precepts of the gospel and especially that of charity. We promise to the best of our power to prevent others from offending Thee and to bring as many as possible to follow Thee.

O loving Jesus, through the intercession of the Blessed Virgin Mary our model in reparation, deign to receive the voluntary offering we make of this act of expiation; and, by the crowning gift of perseverance, keep us faithful unto death in our duty and the allegiance we owe to Thee, so that we may all one day come to that happy home, where Thou with the Father and the Holy Ghost livest and reignest God, world without end. Amen.

AN ACT OF CONSECRATION TO THE SACRED HEART OF JESUS

To Thee, O Sacred Heart of Jesus, do I devote and offer up my life, my thoughts, my words, my actions, and my sufferings. May my whole being be no longer employed but in loving and serving and glorifying Thee. O Sacred Heart, be Thou henceforth the sole Object of my love, the Protector of my life, the Pledge of my salvation, and my Refuge at the hour of my death. Plead for me, O blessed and adorable Heart, at the bar of divine justice, and screen me from the anger which my sins deserve. Imprint Thyself like a Seal upon my heart, that I may never be separated from Thee. May my name also be ever engraven upon Thee, and may I ever be consecrated to Thy glory, ever burning with the flames of Thy love, and entirely penetrated with it for all eternity. This is all my desire, to live in Thee. One thing have I sought of the Lord, and this will I seek, that I may dwell in the Heart of my Lord all the days of my life.

A PRAYER TO THE ETERNAL FATHER

O eternal Father, let me offer up unto Thy mercy the Sacred Heart of Thy dearly beloved Son, even as He offered Himself up a Sacrifice to Thy justice.

Accept, on my behalf, all the thoughts, sentiments, affections, motions, and all the actions of this Sacred Heart; they are mine, because it was immolated for me; they are mine, because for the future I am resolved to admit nothing into my heart but what hath place in Thine. Receive, then, O God, the merits of this Sacred Heart in satisfaction for my sins, and in thanksgiving for all the benefits conferred upon me. Receive them, O Lord, as so many motives for granting my petitions. Give me, O Lord, for their sake, all the graces I need, but especially the gift of final perseverance. Receive them as so many acts of love, adoration, and praise, which I now offer to Thy divine Majesty. This Sacred Heart, this Heart alone, can love, honor, and glorify Thee as Thou deservest. *Amen.*

A PRAYER TO THE SACRED HEART OF JESUS, IN THE BLESSED SACRAMENT OF THE ALTAR

How boundless, O Jesus, is Thy love! Thou hast prepared for me, of Thy most precious Body and Blood, a divine banquet, wherein Thou dost give Thyself to me without reserve. What hath urged Thee to this excess of love? Nothing but Thine own most loving Heart. O adorable Heart of Jesus, Furnace of divine love, receive my soul into the wounds of Thy most sacred Passion, that, in this school of charity, I may learn to make a return of love to that God Who hath given me such wonderful proofs of His love. *Amen.*

Jesus, meek and humble of heart,

Make my heart like unto Thine!

O sweetest Heart of Jesus, I implore
That I may ever love Thee more and more!

O Heart of Jesus, burning with love of me, inflame my heart with the love of Thee!

O Sacred Heart of Jesus, mayest Thou be known, loved, and adored throughout all the world!

O Heart of my dear Redeemer, may the love of Thy friends supply all the injuries and neglects which Thou sustainest!

The Stations of the Cross

This devotion arose first in Jerusalem, among the Christians who dwelt there, out of veneration for those sacred spots which were sanctified by the sufferings of our divine Redeemer. From the Holy City this devout exercise was introduced into Europe. When, in 1342, the Franciscan Fathers established their house in Jerusalem, and undertook the custody of the sacred places of the Holy Land, they began to spread throughout the Catholic world the devotion of the Way of the Cross.

This excellent devotion has met with the repeated approvals of the Holy See, and is enriched with many indulgences; to gain them, it is necessary to meditate, according to individual ability, on the Passion and death of Our Lord Jesus Christ, and to go from one station to another, if the space and number of persons will admit.

METHOD OF PRACTICING THIS EXERCISE[28]

Let each one, kneeling before the high altar, make an act of contrition, and form the intention of gaining the indulgences, whether for himself or for the souls in purgatory, Then say:

My Lord Jesus Christ, Thou hast made this journey to die for me with love unutterable, and I have so many times unworthily abandoned Thee; but now I love Thee with my whole heart, and because I love Thee I repent sincerely for having ever offended Thee. Pardon me, my God, and permit me to accompany Thee on this journey. Thou goest to die for love of me; I wish also, my beloved Redeemer, to die for love of Thee. My Jesus, I will live and die always united to Thee.

Dear Jesus, Thou dost go to die
For very love of me:
Ah! let me bear Thee company;
I wish to die with Thee.[29]

‡At the Cross her station keeping,
Stood the mournful Mother weeping,
Close to Jesus to the last.

---

[28]   Composed by St. Alphonsus Liguori, A.D. 1787.
[29]   While passing from one station to another, a verse of the *Stabat Mater* (p. 462) is frequently sung.

FIRST STATION

JESUS IS CONDEMNED TO DEATH.
℣. We adore Thee, O Christ, and we bless Thee.
℟. Because by Thy holy Cross Thou hast redeemed the world.

Consider how Jesus, after having been scourged and crowned with thorns, was unjustly condemned by Pilate to die on the Cross.

My adorable Jesus, it was not Pilate; no, it was my sins that condemned Thee to die. I beseech Thee, by the merits of this sorrowful journey, to assist my soul in her journey toward eternity. I love Thee, my beloved Jesus; I love Thee more than myself. I repent with my whole heart of having offended Thee. Never permit me to offend Thee again. Grant that I may love Thee always, and then do with me what Thou wilt.

Our Father. Hail Mary. Glory be to the Father.

Dear Jesus, Thou dost go to die
For very love of me:
Ah! let me bear Thee company;
I wish to die with Thee.

‡Through her heart, His sorrow sharing,
All His bitter anguish bearing,
Now at length the sword had passed!

SECOND STATION

JESUS IS MADE TO BEAR HIS CROSS.

℣. We adore Thee, O Christ, and we bless Thee.
℟. Because by Thy holy Cross Thou hast redeemed the world.

Consider how Jesus, in making this journey with the Cross on His shoulders, thought of us, and for us offered to His Father the death He was about to undergo.

My most beloved Jesus, I embrace all the tribulations Thou hast destined for me until death. I beseech Thee, by the merits of the pain Thou didst suffer in carrying Thy Cross, to give me the necessary help to carry mine with perfect patience and resignation. I love Thee, Jesus my love. I repent of having offended Thee. Never permit me to offend Thee again. Grant that I may love Thee always, and then do with me what Thou wilt.

Our Father. Hail Mary. Glory be to the Father.

Dear Jesus, Thou dost go to die
For very love of me:

Ah! let me bear Thee company;
I wish to die with Thee.

‡O how sad and sore distressed,
Was that Mother highly blessed
Of the sole begotten One.

THIRD STATION
JESUS FALLS THE FIRST TIME UNDER HIS CROSS.

℣. We adore Thee, O Christ, and we bless Thee.
℟. Because by Thy holy Cross Thou hast redeemed the world.

Consider this first fall of Jesus under His Cross. His flesh was torn by the scourges, His head crowned with thorns, and He had lost a great quantity of blood. He was so weakened that He could scarcely walk, and yet He had to carry this great load upon His shoulders. The soldiers struck Him rudely, and thus He fell several times in His journey.

My Jesus, it is not the weight of the Cross, but of my sins, which has made Thee suffer so much pain. Ah! by the merits of this first fall, deliver me from the misfortune of falling into mortal sin. I love Thee, O my Jesus, with my whole heart. I repent of having offended Thee. Never permit me to offend Thee again. Grant that I may love Thee always, and then do with me what Thou wilt.

Our Father. Hail Mary. Glory be to the Father.

Dear Jesus, Thou dost go to die
For very love of me:
Ah! let me bear Thee company;
I wish to die with Thee.

‡Christ above in torment hangs,
She beneath beholds the pangs
Of her dying, glorious Son.

FOURTH STATION
JESUS MEETS HIS ATFLICTED MOTHER.

℣. We adore Thee, O Christ, and we bless Thee.
℟. Because by Thy holy Cross Thou hast redeemed the world.

Consider the meeting of the Son and the Mother, which took place on this journey. Jesus and Mary looked at each other, and their looks became as so many arrows to wound those hearts which loved each other so tenderly.

My most loving Jesus, by the sorrow that Thou didst experience in this meeting, grant me the grace of a truly devoted love for Thy most holy Mother. And thou, my Queen, who wast overwhelmed with sorrow, obtain for me, by thy intercession, a continual and tender remembrance of the Passion of thy Son. I love Thee, Jesus my love. I repent of having offended Thee. Never permit me to offend Thee again. Grant that I may love Thee always, and then do with me what Thou wilt.

Our Father. Hail Mary. Glory be to the Father.

Dear Jesus, Thou dost go to die
For very love of me:
Ah! let me bear Thee company;
I wish to die with Thee.

‡Is there one who would not weep,
Whelmed in miseries so deep,
Christ's dear Mother to behold?

FIFTH STATION

THE CYRENIAN HELPS JESUS TO CARRY HIS CROSS.

℣. We adore Thee, O Christ, and we bless Thee.
℟. Because by Thy holy Cross Thou hast redeemed the world.

Consider how the Jews, seeing that at each step Jesus from weakness was on the point of expiring, and fearing that He would die on the way, when they wished Him to die the ignominious death of the Cross, constrained Simon the Cyrenian to carry the Cross behind Our Lord.

My most beloved Jesus, I will not refuse the Cross as the Cyrenian did; I accept it—I embrace it. I accept in particular the death Thou hast destined for me, with all the pains which may accompany it; I unite it to Thy death—I offer it to Thee. Thou hast died for love of me; I will die for love of Thee, and to please Thee. Help me by Thy grace. I love Thee, Jesus my love. I repent of having offended Thee. Never permit me to offend Thee again. Grant that I may love Thee always, and then do with me what Thou wilt.

Our Father. Hail Mary. Glory be to the Father.

Dear Jesus, Thou dost go to die
For very love of me:
Ah! let me bear Thee company;
I wish to die with Thee.

‡Can the human heart refrain
From partaking in her pain
In that Mother's pain untold.

SIXTH STATION
VERONICA WIPES THE FACE OF JESUS.

℣. We adore Thee, O Christ, and we bless Thee.
℟. Because by Thy holy Cross Thou hast redeemed the world.

Consider how the holy woman named Veronica, seeing Jesus so afflicted, and His face bathed in sweat and blood, presented Him with a towel, with which He wiped His adorable face, leaving on it the impression of His holy countenance.

My most beloved Jesus, Thy face was beautiful before, but in this journey it has lost all its beauty, and wounds and blood have disfigured it. Alas! my soul also was once beautiful, when it received Thy grace in Baptism; but I have disfigured it since by my sins. Thou alone, my Redeemer, canst restore it to its former beauty. Do this by Thy Passion. O Jesus, I repent of having offended Thee. Never permit me to separate myself from Thee again. Grant that I may love Thee always, and then do with me what Thou wilt.

Our Father. Hail Mary. Glory be to the Father.

Dear Jesus, Thou dost go to die
For very love of me:
Ah! let me bear Thee company;
I wish to die with Thee.

‡Bruised, derided, cursed, defiled,
She beheld her tender Child,
All with bloody scourges rent.

SEVENTH STATION
JESUS FALLS THE SECOND TIME.

℣. We adore Thee, O Christ, and we bless Thee.
℟. Because by Thy holy Cross Thou has redeemed the world.

Consider the second fall of Jesus under the Cross—a fall which renews the pain of all the wounds of the head and members of our afflicted Lord.

My most gentle Jesus, how many times Thou hast pardoned me, and how many times have I fallen again, and begun again to offend Thee! Oh! by the merits of this new fall, give me the necessary helps to persevere in Thy grace until death. Grant that, in all temptations which assail me, I may always commend myself to Thee. I love Thee, Jesus my love, with my whole heart. I repent of having offended Thee. Never permit me to offend Thee again. Grant that I may love Thee always, and then do with me what Thou wilt.

Our Father. Hail Mary. Glory be to the Father.

Dear Jesus, Thou dost go to die
For very love of me:
Ah! let me bear Thee company;
I wish to die with Thee.

‡For the sins of His own nation
Saw Him hang in desolation
Till His spirit forth He sent.

EIGHTH STATION
JESUS SPEAKS TO THE WOMEN OF JERUSALEM.

℣. We adore Thee, O Christ, and we bless Thee.
℟. Because by Thy holy Cross Thou hast redeemed the world.

Consider how those women wept with compassion at seeing Jesus in such a pitiable state, streaming with blood, as He walked along. But Jesus said to them: "Weep not for Me, but for your children."

My Jesus, laden with sorrows, I weep for the offenses I have committed against Thee, because of the pains they have deserved, and still more because of the displeasure they have caused Thee, Who hast loved me so much. It is Thy love, more than the fear of hell, which causes me to weep for my sins. My Jesus, I love Thee more than myself. I repent of having offended Thee. Never permit me to offend Thee again. Grant that I may love Thee always; and then do with me what Thou wilt.

Our Father. Hail Mary. Glory be to the Father.

Dear Jesus, Thou dost go to die
For very love of me:
Ah! let me bear Thee company;
I wish to die with Thee.

‡O thou Mother! Font of love,
Touch my spirit from above,
Make my heart with Thine accord.

NINTH STATION
JESUS FALLS THE THIRD TIME.

℣. We adore Thee, O Christ, and we bless Thee.
℟. Because by Thy holy Cross Thou hast redeemed the world.

Consider the third fall of Jesus Christ. His weakness was extreme, and the cruelty of His executioners excessive, who tried to hasten His steps when He had scarcely strength to move.

Ah, my outraged Jesus, by the merits of the weakness Thou didst suffer in going to Calvary, give me strength sufficient to conquer all human respect, and all my wicked passions, which have led me to despise Thy friendship. I love Thee, Jesus my love, with my whole heart. I repent of having offended Thee. Never permit me to offend Thee again. Grant that I may love Thee always, and then do with me what Thou wilt.

Our Father. Hail Mary. Glory be to the Father.

Dear Jesus, Thou dost go to die
For very love of me:
Ah! let me bear Thee company;
I wish to die with Thee.

‡Make me feel as thou hast felt;
Make my soul to glow and melt
With the love of Christ my Lord.

TENTH STATION
JESUS IS STRIPPED OF HIS GARMENTS.

℣. We adore Thee, O Christ, and we bless Thee.
℟. Because by Thy holy Cross Thou hast redeemed the world.

Consider the violence with which the executioners stripped Jesus. His inner garments adhered to His torn flesh, and they dragged them off so roughly that the skin came with them. Compassionate your Savior thus cruelly treated, and say to Him:

My innocent Jesus, by the merits of the torment Thou hast felt, help me to strip myself of all affection to things of earth, in order that I may place all my love in Thee, Who art so worthy of my love. I love thee, O Jesus, with my whole heart. I repent of having offended Thee. Never permit me to offend Thee again. Grant that I may love Thee always, and then do with me what Thou wilt.

Our Father. Hail Mary. Glory be to the Father.

Dear Jesus, Thou dost go to die
For very love of me:
Ah! let me bear Thee company;
I wish to die with Thee.

‡Holy Mother! pierce me through,
In my heart each wound renew
Of my Savior crucified.

ELEVENTH STATION

JESUS IS NAILED TO THE CROSS.

℣. We adore Thee, O Christ, and we bless Thee.
℟. Because by Thy holy Cross Thou hast redeemed the world.

Consider how Jesus, after being thrown on the Cross, extended His hands, and offered to His eternal Father the sacrifice of His life for our salvation. These barbarians fastened Him with nails, and then, raising the Cross, allowed Him to die with anguish on this infamous gibbet.

My Jesus! loaded with contempt, nail my heart to Thy feet, that it may ever remain there, to love Thee, and never quit Thee again. I love Thee more than myself. I repent of having offended Thee. Never permit me to separate myself from Thee again. Grant that I may love Thee always, and then do with me what Thou wilt.

Our Father. Hail Mary. Glory be to the Father.

Dear Jesus, Thou dost go to die
For very love of me:
Ah! let me bear Thee company;
I wish to die with Thee.

‡Let me share with thee His pain,
Who for all my sins was slain,
Who for me in torment died.

TWELFTH STATION

JESUS DIES ON THE CROSS.

℣. We adore Thee, O Christ, and we bless Thee.
℟. Because by Thy holy Cross Thou hast redeemed the world.

Consider how thy Jesus, after three hours' agony on the Cross, consumed at length with anguish, abandons Himself to the weight of His body, bows His head, and dies.

My dying Jesus, I kiss devoutly the Cross on which Thou didst die for love of me. I have merited by my sins to die a miserable death, but Thy death is my hope. Ah, by the merits of Thy death, give me grace to die, embracing Thy feet, and burning with love of Thee. I commit my soul into Thy hands. I love Thee with my whole heart. I repent of ever having offended Thee. Never permit me to offend Thee again. Grant that I may love Thee always, and then do with me what Thou wilt.

Our Father. Hail Mary. Glory be to the Father.

Dear Jesus, Thou dost go to die
For very love of me:
Ah! let me bear Thee company;
I wish to die with Thee.

‡Let me mingle tears with thee,
Mourning Him Who mourned for me,
All the days that I may live.

THIRTEENTH STATION
JESUS IS TAKEN DOWN FROM THE CROSS.

℣. We adore Thee, O Christ, and we bless Thee.
℟. Because by Thy holy Cross Thou hast redeemed the world.

Consider how, after the death of Our Lord, two of His disciples, Joseph and Nicodemus, took Him down from the Cross, and placed Him in the arms of His afflicted Mother, who received Him with unutterable tenderness, and pressed Him to her bosom.

O Mother of sorrow, for the love of this Son, accept me for thy servant, and pray to Him for me. And Thou, my Redeemer, since Thou hast died for me, permit me to love Thee; for I wish but Thee, and nothing more. I love Thee, my Jesus, and I repent of ever having offended Thee. Never permit me to offend Thee again. Grant that I may love Thee always, and then do with me what Thou wilt.

Our Father. Hail Mary. Glory be to the Father.

Dear Jesus, Thou dost go to die
For very love of me:
Ah! let me bear Thee company;
I wish to die with Thee.

‡By the Cross with thee to stay;
There with thee to weep and pray,
Is all I ask of thee to give.

FOURTEENTH STATION

JESUS IS PLACED IN THE SEPULCHRE.

℣. We adore Thee, O Christ, and we bless Thee.
℟. Because by Thy holy Cross Thou hast redeemed the world.

Consider how the disciples carried the body of Jesus to bury it, accompanied by His holy Mother, who arranged it in the sepulchre with her own hands. They then closed the tomb, and all withdrew.

Ah, my buried Jesus, I kiss the stone that encloses Thee. But Thou didst rise again the third day. I beseech Thee by Thy Resurrection, make me rise glorious with Thee at the Last Day, to be always united with Thee in heaven, to praise Thee and love Thee forever. I love Thee, and I repent of ever having offended Thee. Never permit me to offend Thee again. Grant that I may love Thee always; and then do with me what Thou wilt.

Our Father. Hail Mary. Glory be to the Father.

Dear Jesus, Thou dost go to die
For very love of me:
Ah! let me bear Thee company;
I wish to die with Thee.

‡Virgin of all virgins best!
Listen to my fond request;
Let me share thy grief divine.

After this, return to the high altar, and say the Our Father, *the* Hail Mary, *and the* Glory be to the Father *five times, in honor of the Passion of Jesus Christ, to gain the other indulgences granted to those who recite them.*

The Devotion of the Seven Words upon the Cross

Come unto my help, O God.
℟. O Lord, make haste to help me.
Glory be to the Father, etc.

The First Word
FATHER, FORGIVE THEM, FOR THEY KNOW NOT WHAT THEY DO.

℣. We adore Thee, O Christ, and we bless Thee.
℟. Because by Thy holy Cross Thou hast redeemed the world.

O beloved Jesus, Who for the love of me didst agonize on the Cross that Thou mightest pay by Thy sufferings the debt due to my sins, and didst open Thy divine mouth to obtain my pardon from eternal Justice: have mercy on all the faithful in their agony, and on me also when I shall be in that extremity, and, through the merits of Thy most Precious Blood shed for our salvation, give us so lively a sorrow for our sins that we may breathe out our souls into the bosom of Thine infinite mercy.
Glory be to the Father (*three times*).
℣. Have mercy on us, O Lord.
℟. Have mercy on us.
O my God, I believe in Thee, I hope in Thee, I love Thee, and I repent of having offended Thee by my sins.

The Second Word
THIS DAY THOU SHALT BE WITH ME IN PARADISE.

℣. We adore Thee, O Christ, and we bless Thee.
℟. Because by Thy holy Cross Thou hast redeemed the world.

O beloved Jesus, Who for the love of me didst agonize on the Cross, and with such readiness and bounty didst respond to the faith of the Good Thief, who in the midst of Thy humiliation acknowledged Thee to be the Son of God: O Thou Who didst assure him of paradise, have mercy on all the faithful in their agony, and on me also when I shall be in that extremity, and, through the merits of Thy most Precious Blood, revive in our souls a faith so firm and constant that it may not waver at any suggestion of the devil, so that we also may obtain the blessed reward of heaven.
Glory be to the Father (*three times*).
℣. Have mercy on us, O Lord.

℟. Have mercy on us.

O my God, I believe in Thee, I hope in Thee, I love Thee, and I repent of having offended Thee by my sins.

The Third Word

BEHOLD THY SON; BEHOLD THY MOTHER.

℣. We adore Thee, O Christ, and we bless Thee.
℟. Because by Thy holy Cross Thou hast redeemed the world.

O beloved Jesus, Who for the love of me didst agonize on the Cross, and, forgetting Thy sufferings, didst leave us as a pledge of Thy love Thine own most holy Mother, that through her we might confidently have recourse to Thee in our greatest need: have mercy on all the faithful in their agony, and on me also when I shall be in that extremity, and, through the interior martyrdom of this Thy dear Mother, awaken in our hearts a firm hope in the infinite merits of Thy most Precious Blood, that we may avoid the eternal damnation which our sins have deserved.

Glory be to the Father (*three times*).

℣. Have mercy on us, O Lord.

℟. Have mercy on us.

O my God, I believe in Thee, I hope in Thee, I love Thee, and I repent of having offended Thee by my sins.

The Fourth Word

MY GOD! MY GOD! WHY HAST THOU FORSAKEN ME?

℣. We adore Thee, O Christ, and we bless Thee.
℟. Because by Thy holy Cross Thou hast redeemed the world.

O beloved Jesus, Who for the love of me didst agonize on the Cross, and, heaping suffering on suffering, didst endure with infinite patience not only Thy many bodily tortures, but the most heavy affliction of spirit through the dereliction of Thine eternal Father: have mercy on all the faithful in their agony, and on me also when I shall be in that extremity, and, through the merits of Thy most Precious Blood, give us grace to suffer with true patience all the pains and afflictions of our agony, that, uniting them with Thine, we may be partakers of Thy glory in paradise.

Glory be to the Father (*three times*).

℣. Have mercy on us, O Lord.

℟. Have mercy on us.

O my God, I believe in Thee, I hope in Thee, I love Thee, and I repent of having offended Thee by my sins.

The Fifth Word

I THIRST.

℣. We adore Thee, O Christ, and we bless Thee.
℟. Because by Thy holy Cross Thou hast redeemed the world.

O beloved Jesus, Who didst agonize on the Cross for the love of me, and Who, not satisfied with all the ignominy and suffering, wouldst willingly have suffered yet more, so that all men might be saved—as was clearly proved when all the torrents of Thy Passion would not allay the thirst of Thy tender Heart: have mercy on all the faithful in their agony, and on me also when I shall be in that extremity, and, through the merits of Thy most Precious Blood, enkindle such a fire of charity in our hearts as may cause them to burn with the desire of uniting themselves to Thee for all eternity.

Glory be to the Father (*three times*).

℣. Have mercy on us, O Lord.
℟. Have mercy on us.

O my God, I believe in Thee, I hope in Thee, I love Thee, and I repent of having offended Thee by my sins.

The Sixth Word

IT IS CONSUMMATED.

℣. We adore Thee, O Christ, and we bless Thee.
℟. Because by Thy holy Cross Thou hast redeemed the world.

O beloved Jesus, Who for the love of me didst agonize on the Cross, and from that throne of truth didst announce the completion of the work of our Redemption, through which, from being the children of wrath and perdition, we have become the children of God and the heirs of heaven: have mercy on all the faithful in their agony, and on me also when I shall be in that extremity, and, through the merits of Thy most Precious Blood, detach us entirely from the world and from ourselves, and at the moment of our agony, give us grace sincerely to offer Thee the sacrifice of our life in expiation of our sins.

Glory be to the Father (*three times*).

℣. Have mercy on us, O Lord.
℟. Have mercy on us.

O my God, I believe in Thee, I hope in Thee, I love Thee, and I repent of having offended Thee by my sins.

The Seventh Word

FATHER, INTO THY HANDS I COMMEND MY SPIRIT.

℣. We adore Thee, O Christ, and we bless Thee.
℟. Because by Thy holy Cross Thou hast redeemed the world.

O beloved Jesus, Who didst agonize on the Cross for the love of me, and Who, in completing this great sacrifice, didst accept the will of Thine eternal Father, by resigning Thy spirit into His hands, and then bowing Thy head and dying: have mercy on all the faithful in their agony, and on me also when I shall be in that extremity, and, through the merits of Thy most Precious Blood, give us, in our agony, an entire conformity to the divine will, that we may be ready either to live or die according as it shall best please Thee, desiring nothing but the accomplishment of Thy blessed will in us.

Glory be to the Father (*three times*).
℣. Have mercy on us, O Lord.
℟. Have mercy on us.
O my God, I believe in Thee, I hope in Thee, I love Thee, and I repent of having offended Thee by my sins.

A PRAYER TO OUR BLESSED LADY OF SORROWS

O holy Mother, most afflicted by the bitter sorrow which thou didst endure at the foot of the Cross during the three hours' agony of Jesus: vouchsafe to assist all of us, the children of thy sorrows, in our last agony, that, through thine intercession, we may pass from the bed of death to form a crown for thee in heavenly paradise.

Hail Mary (*three times*).
O Mary, Mother of grace,
Mother of mercy,
Protect us from the enemy,
And receive us at the hour of death.
℣. From sudden and unlooked-for death,
℟. O Lord, deliver us.
℣. From the snares of the devil,
℟. O Lord, deliver us.
℣. From everlasting death,
℟. O Lord, deliver us.

Let us pray.
O God, Who for the salvation of mankind didst give an example and a help in the Passion and death of Thy Son: grant, we beseech Thee, that in the hour of our death we may experience the effects of this Thy charity, and deserve to be partakers

in the glory of Him our Redeemer, through the same Jesus Christ, Our Lord. ℟.
Amen.

Jesus, Mary, and Joseph, I give you my heart and my soul.
Jesus, Mary, and Joseph, assist me in my last agony.
Jesus, Mary, and Joseph, may I breathe forth my soul in peace with you.

The Rosary of the Blessed Virgin Mary

The devotion called the Rosary consists of fifteen *Pater Nosters* and *Glorias*, and one hundred and fifty *Ave Marias*, to be recited on indulgenced beads. It is divided into three parts, each containing five *decades*, or tens; a decade consisting of one *Pater*, ten *Aves*, and one *Gloria*.[30] To each of these decades is assigned one of the principal mysteries of the life of our Savior or of His Blessed Mother, as matter of meditation, whereon the mind is to exercise itself while at prayer, and therefore it is prefixed to every decade.

The fifteen mysteries, as we have said, are divided into three parts — namely five joyful, five sorrowful, and five glorious mysteries. Now, the method consists in raising corresponding affections in the will during the recital of each decade, such as the devotion of each one may suggest: for example, in the first part, sentiments of *joy* for the coming of our Redeemer; in the second, of *compassion* for the sufferings of Our Lord, and *contrition* for our sins, which were the occasion of them; in the third, of *thanksgiving* for the exaltation and glory of our Savior and His Blessed Mother, hoping through the merits of His Passion, and her intercession, to be made partakers of their glory. To assist the mind in this exercise, a short meditation and prayer are usually given to be used before and after each decade. In order to say the Rosary well, we should not be satisfied with merely pronouncing the words of the prayers, or with a vague and general reflection on the mysteries; but we should endeavor to acquire the habit of reciting them with great attention and reverence, at the same time dwelling in a vivid manner upon the different mysteries. In order to do this the better, it is sometimes the custom, in addition to the short meditation on the mystery (which is usually read before the recital of each decade, and which contains, either expressed or understood, a prayer for the particular virtue to which it has relation), to subjoin a short ejaculation in reference to the subject of the mystery, which may be inserted after the holy name of Jesus in the *Hail Mary*, or to divide the meditation into ten points, one for each *Ave*. The reading of the meditation, ejaculation, or prayer are only pious practices to assist in the more devout recitation of the Rosary, which consists essentially only in the recitation of the vocal prayers while the mind dwells upon the subject of the mystery contemplated.

---

[30]   It is customary to preface these prayers with the *Apostles' Creed*, one *Pater*, three *Aves*, and one *Gloria*, as in the chaplet introduced by St. Bridget of Sweden.

THE FORM OF BLESSING ROSARIES

PROPER TO THE ORDER OF PREACHERS

The priest, vested in surplice and white stole, says:

Adjutorium nostrum in nomine Domini.

℟. Qui fecit cœlum et terram.

℣. Domine, exaudi orationem meam.

℟. Et clamor meus ad te veniat.

℣. Dominus vobiscum.

℟. Et cum spiritu tuo.

Our help is in the name of the Lord.

℟. Who hath made heaven and earth.

℣. O Lord, hear my prayer.

℟. And let my cry come unto Thee.

℣. The Lord be with you.

℟. And with thy spirit.

Oremus.

Omnipotens et misericors Deus, qui propter eximiam charitatem tuam, qua dilexisti nos, Filium tuum unigenitum, Dominum nostrum Jesum Christum, de cœlis in terram descendere, et de Beatissimæ Virginis Mariæ Dominæ nostræ utero sacratissimo, Angelo nuntiante, carnem suscipere, crucemque ac mortem subire, et tertia die gloriose a mortuis resurgere voluisti, ut nos eriperes de potestate diaboli: obsecramus immensam clementiam tuam; ut hæc signa Rosarii, in honorem et laudem ejusdem Genitricis Filii tui ab Ecclesia tua fideli dicata, bene ✠ dicas et sancti ✠ fices, eisque tantam infundas virtutem Spiritus ✠ Sancti, ut, quicumque horum quodlibet secum portaverit, atque in domo sua reverenter tenuerit, et in eis ad te, secundum hujus sanctæ Societatis instituta, divina contemplando mysteria devote oraverit, salubri et perseveranti devotione abundet,

Let us pray.

Almighty and most merciful God, Who out of the wondrous love whereby Thou hast loved us, that Thou mightest deliver us from the power of the devil, didst will that Thine only begotten Son, Our Lord Jesus Christ, should come down upon earth, and at the message of an angel take flesh from the most sacred womb of Our Lady, Blessed Mary, and undergo the death of the Cross, and the third day rise gloriously from the dead: we implore Thine abounding mercy that Thou wouldst bless ✠ and sanctify ✠ these rosaries, dedicated by Thy faithful Church to the honor and praise of the same Mother of Thy Son, and wouldst so abundantly pour forth upon them the power of the Holy ✠ Ghost that whosoever shall carry them about their persons, and shall reverently keep them in their homes, and shall devoutly pray unto Thee, contemplating, according to the institutes of this holy Society, the divine mysteries thereupon, may abound in sound and lasting devotion,

sitque consors et particeps omnium gratiarum, privilegiorum, et indulgentiarum, quæ eidem Societati per sanctam Sedem Apostolicam concessa fuerunt, ab omni hoste visibili et invisibili semper et ubique in hoc sæculo liberetur, et in exitu suo ab ipsa Beatissima Virgine Maria Dei Genitrice tibi plenus bonis operibus præsentari mereatur. Per eundem Dominum nostrum Jesum Christum, Filium tuum, qui tecum vivit et regnat in unitate Spiritus Sancti Deus, per omnia sæcula sæculorum. ℟. Amen.

and may be sharers and partakers in all the graces, privileges, and indulgences which have been granted to the same Society by the Holy Apostolic See; may at all times and in all places be delivered from every foe, visible and invisible, in this present world, and may finally at the hour of death, full of all good works, be found worthy to be presented unto Thee by the same most Blessed Virgin Mary, Mother of God. Through the same Our Lord Jesus Christ, etc. ℟. Amen.

The priest then sprinkles the rosaries with holy water.

A METHOD OF RECITING THE ROSARY OF THE BLESSED VIRGIN MARY

In the name of the Father, ✠ and of the Son, and of the Holy Ghost. *Amen.*

℣. Thou shalt open my lips, O Lord.

℟. And my mouth shall show forth Thy praise.

℣. Come unto my help, O God.

℟. O Lord, make haste to help me.

℣. Glory be to the Father, and to the Son, and to the Holy Ghost.

℟. As it was in the beginning, is now, and ever shall be, world without end. Amen. Alleluia.

[*From* Septuagesima *to* Easter, *for* Alleluia *say,* Praise to Thee, O Lord, King of eternal glory.]

[*At the Cross say the Apostles' Creed:* I believe in God, etc. *On the three small beads say: 1st,* I salute thee, Daughter of God the Father; obtain for us the gift of a firm faith. Hail Mary, etc. *2nd,* I salute thee, Mother of God the Son; obtain for us the gift of constant hope. Hail Mary, etc. *3rd,* I salute thee, Spouse of God the Holy Ghost; obtain for us the gift of an ardent charity. Hail Mary, etc.]

THE FIVE JOYFUL MYSTERIES

For Mondays and Thursdays; the Sundays of Advent and those from the Epiphany until Lent.

I. *The Annunciation.*

Let us contemplate, in this mystery, how the angel Gabriel saluted Our Blessed Lady with the title, *Full of grace,* and declared unto her the Incarnation of Our Lord and Savior Jesus Christ.

Our Father. Hail Mary (*ten times*). Glory be to the Father.

Let us pray.

O holy Mary, Queen of virgins, through the most high mystery of the Incarnation of thy beloved Son, Our Lord Jesus Christ, wherein our salvation was begun, obtain for us, through thy most holy intercession, light to understand the greatness of the benefit He hath bestowed upon us, in vouchsafing to become our Brother, and in giving thee, His own beloved Mother, to be our Mother also. *Amen.*

II. *The Visitation.*

Let us contemplate, in this mystery, how the Blessed Virgin Mary, understanding from the angel that her cousin St. Elizabeth had conceived, went with haste into the mountains of Judea to visit her, and remained with her three months.

Our Father. Hail Mary (*ten times*). Glory be to the Father.

Let us pray.

O holy Virgin, spotless Mirror of humility, by that exceeding love which moved thee to visit thy holy cousin St. Elizabeth, obtain for us, through thine intercession, that our hearts being visited by thy divine Son, and freed from all sin, we may praise and thank Him forever. *Amen.*

III. *The Birth of Jesus Christ in Bethlehem.*

Let us contemplate, in this mystery, how the Blessed Virgin Mary, when the time of the delivery was come, brought forth our Redeemer, Jesus Christ, at midnight, and laid Him in a manger, because there was no room for Him in the inns of Bethlehem.

Our Father. Hail Mary (*ten times*). Glory be to the Father.

Let us pray.

O pure Mother of God, through thy virginal and most joyful delivery, whereby thou gavest to the world thine only Son, our Savior, obtain for us, we beseech thee, through thine intercession, the grace to lead such pure and holy lives in this world that we may become worthy to sing, without ceasing, the mercies of thy Son, and His benefits to us by thee. *Amen.*

IV. The Presentation of Our Lord in the Temple.

Let us contemplate, in this mystery, how the Blessed Virgin Mary, on the day of her purification, presented the Child Jesus in the temple, where holy Simeon, giving thanks to God, with great devotion received Him into his arms.

Our Father. Hail Mary (*ten times*). Glory be to the Father.

Let us pray.

O holy Virgin, most admirable example and pattern of obedience, who didst present the Lord of the temple in the temple of God, obtain for us, of thy blessed Son, that, with holy Simeon and devout Anna, we may praise and glorify Him forever. *Amen.*

V. The Finding of the Child Jesus in the Temple.

Let us contemplate, in this mystery, how the Blessed Virgin Mary, after having lost her beloved Son in Jerusalem, sought Him for the space of three days; and at length found Him in the temple, sitting in the midst of the doctors, hearing them, and asking them questions.

Our Father. Hail Mary (*ten times*). Glory be to the Father.

Let us pray.

O most Blessed Virgin, more than martyr in thy sufferings, and yet the comfort of such as are afflicted: by that unspeakable joy wherewith thy soul was filled when at length thou didst find thy dearly beloved Son in the temple, teaching in the midst of the doctors, obtain of Him that we may so seek Him and find Him in His holy Catholic Church as nevermore to be separated from Him. *Amen.*

Hail, holy Queen, *with ℣. and ℟., and Prayer (p. 77); or* Prayer of Rosary Sunday (*p. 619*).

THE FIVE SORROWFUL MYSTERIES

For Tuesdays and Fridays; and the Sundays in Lent.

I. The Prayer and Bloody Sweat of Our Blessed Savior in the Garden.

Let us contemplate, in this mystery, how Our Lord Jesus was so afflicted for us in the Garden of Gethsemane that His body was bathed in a bloody sweat, which ran down in great drops to the ground.

Our Father. Hail Mary (*ten times*). Glory be to the Father.

Let us pray.

O holy Virgin, more than martyr, by that ardent prayer which our beloved Savior poured forth to His heavenly Father, vouchsafe to intercede for us, that, our passions being subjected to the obedience of reason, we may always, and in all things, conform and subject ourselves to the holy will of God. *Amen.*

II. *The Scourging of Our Blessed Lord at the Pillar.*

Let us contemplate, in this mystery, how Our Lord Jesus Christ was most cruelly scourged in the house of Pilate; the number of stripes inflicted upon Him being, it is said, about five thousand.

Our Father. Hail Mary (*ten times*). Glory be to the Father.

Let us pray.

O Mother of God, Fountain of patience, through those stripes thy only and dearly beloved Son vouchsafed to suffer for us, obtain of Him for us grace to mortify our rebellious senses, to avoid the occasions of sin, and to be ready to suffer everything rather than offend God. *Amen.*

III. *The Crowning of Our Blessed Savior with Thorns.*

Let us contemplate, in this mystery, how those cruel ministers of Satan plaited a crown of thorns, and cruelly pressed it on the sacred head of Our Lord Jesus Christ.

Our Father. Hail Mary (*ten times*). Glory be to the Father.

Let us pray.

O Mother of our eternal Prince, the King of glory, by those sharp thorns wherewith His sacred head was pierced, we beseech thee to obtain, through thine intercession, that we may be delivered from all emotions of pride, and escape that shame which our sins deserve at the Day of Judgment. *Amen.*

IV. *Jesus Carrying His Cross.*

Let us contemplate, in this mystery, how Our Lord Jesus Christ, being sentenced to die, bore, with most amazing patience, the Cross which was laid upon Him for His greater torment and ignominy.

Our Father. Hail Mary (*ten times*). Glory be to the Father.

Let us pray.

O holy Virgin, model of patience, by the most painful carrying of the Cross, in which thy Son, Our Lord Jesus Christ, bore the heavy weight of our sins, obtain for us of Him, through thine intercession, courage and strength to follow His steps, and bear our cross after Him to the end of our lives. *Amen.*

V. *The Crucifixion of Our Lord Jesus Christ.*

Let us contemplate, in this mystery, how Our Lord Jesus Christ, being come to Mount Calvary, was stripped of His clothes, and His hands and feet were cruelly nailed to the Cross, in the presence of His most afflicted Mother.

Our Father. Hail Mary (*ten times*). Glory be to the Father.

Let us pray.

O holy Mary, Mother of God, as the body of thy beloved Son was for us stretched upon the Cross, so may we offer up our souls and bodies to be crucified with Him, and our hearts to be pierced with grief at His most bitter Passion; and thou, O most sorrowful Mother, graciously vouchsafe to help us, by thy all-powerful prayers, to accomplish the work of our salvation. *Amen.*

Hail, holy Queen, etc. (*p. 77*); *or* Prayer (*p. 619*).

THE FIVE GLORIOUS MYSTERIES

For Wednesdays and Saturdays; and the Sundays from Easter until Advent.

I. *The Resurrection of Our Lord from the Dead.*

Let us contemplate, in this mystery, how Our Lord Jesus Christ, triumphing gloriously over death, rose again the third day, immortal and impassible.

Our Father. Hail Mary (*ten times*). Glory be to the Father.

Let us pray.

O glorious Virgin Mary, by that unspeakable joy thou didst receive in the Resurrection of thy divine Son, we beseech thee obtain for us of Him that our hearts may never go astray after the false joys of this world, but may be wholly employed in seeking the true and solid joys of heaven. *Amen.*

II. *The Ascension of Christ into Heaven.*

Let us contemplate, in this mystery, how Our Lord Jesus Christ, forty days after His Resurrection, ascended into heaven, attended by angels, in the sight of His most holy Mother and His holy apostles and disciples.

Our Father. Hail Mary (*ten times*). Glory be to the Father.

Let us pray.

O Mother of God, Consoler of the afflicted, as thy beloved Son, when He ascended into heaven, lifted up His hands and blessed His apostles, as He departed from them; so vouchsafe, most holy Mother, to lift up thy pure hands to Him on our behalf, that we may enjoy the benefits of His blessing, and of thine, here on earth, and hereafter in heaven. *Amen.*

III. *The Descent of the Holy Ghost upon the Apostles.*

Let us contemplate, in this mystery, how the Lord Jesus Christ, being seated on the right hand of God, sent, as He had promised, the Holy Ghost upon His apostles, who, after He had ascended, returned to Jerusalem, and continued in prayer and supplication, waiting for the fulfillment of His promise.

Our Father. Hail Mary (*ten times*). Glory be to the Father.

Let us pray.

O sacred Virgin, Tabernacle of the Holy Ghost, we beseech thee to obtain, by thine intercession, that this Comforter, Whom thy beloved Son sent down upon His apostles, filling them thereby with spiritual joy, may teach us in this world the true way of salvation, and make us to walk in the way of virtue and good works. *Amen.*

IV. *The Assumption of the Blessed Virgin Mary into Heaven.*

Let us contemplate, in this mystery, how the glorious Virgin, twelve years after the Resurrection of her Son, passed out of this world unto Him, and was by Him taken up into heaven, attended by the holy angels.

Our Father. Hail Mary (*ten times*). Glory be to the Father.

Let us pray.

O holy Virgin, who, entering the heavenly mansions, didst fill the angels with joy and man with hope: vouchsafe to intercede for us at the hour of our death, that, being delivered from the illusions and temptations of the devil, we may joyfully pass out of this earthly estate to enjoy the happiness of eternal life. *Amen.*

V. *The Coronation of the Blessed Virgin Mary in Heaven.*

Let us contemplate, in this mystery, how the glorious Virgin Mary was, to the great jubilee and exultation of the whole court of heaven, crowned by her Son with the brightest diadem of glory.

Our Father. Hail Mary (*ten times*). Glory be to the Father.

Let us pray.

O glorious Queen of all the heavenly host, we beseech thee to accept these prayers, which, as a crown of roses, we offer at thy feet; and grant, most gracious Lady, that, by thy intercession, our souls may be inflamed with so ardent a desire of seeing thee so gloriously crowned, that it may never die within us until it shall be changed into the happy fruition of thy blessed sight. *Amen.*

Hail, holy Queen, etc. (*p. 77*); *or* Prayer (*p. 619*).

A PRAYER ASCRIBED TO ST. BERNARD

Memorare, O piissima Virgo Maria, non esse auditum a sæculo quemquam ad tua currentem præsidia, tua implorantem auxilia, tua petentem suffragia, esse derelictum. Ego, tali animatus confidentia, ad te, Virgo virginum, Mater, curro, ad te venio; coram te gemens peccator assisto. Noli, Mater Verbi, verba mea despicere, sed audi propitia et exaudi. *Amen.*

Remember, O most loving Virgin Mary, that never was it known that anyone who fled to thy protection, implored thy help, and sought thine intercession, was left forsaken. Inspired with this confidence, I fly unto thee, O Virgin of virgins, my Mother. To thee I come; before thee I stand, sinful and sorrowful. O Mother of the Word, despise not my words, but graciously hear and grant my prayer. *Amen.*

☦PRAYER OF ST. ALOYSIUS GONZAGA

O Domina mea, sancta Maria, in tuam benedictam fidem, ac singularem custodiam, et in sinum misericordiæ tuæ, hodie et quotidie, et in hora exitus mei, animam meam et corpus meum tibi commendo; omnem spem et consolationem meam, omnes angustias et miserias meas, vitam et finem vitæ meæ tibi committo; ut per tuam sanctissimam intercessionem, et per tua merita, omnia mea dirigantur et disponantur opera, secundum tuam tuique Filii voluntatem. *Amen.*

O holy Mary, my mistress, into thy blessed trust and special custody, and into the bosom of thy mercy I this day, every day, and in the hour of my death, commend my soul and my body: to thee I commit all my anxieties and miseries, my life and the end of my life, that by thy most holy intercession and by thy merits all my actions may be directed and disposed according to thy will and that of thy Son. *Amen.*

285

The Scapular

OF THE CONFRATERNITY OF OUR LADY OF MT. CARMEL

The Scapular, or Little Habit of the Blessed Virgin, is composed of two small square pieces of brown cloth, connected by two cords, and designed to be worn over the shoulders under the ordinary clothing. It was, according to a most authentic tradition, given by Our Blessed Lady herself, as a pledge of her love and patronage, to St. Simon Stock, general of the Carmelites, on the 16th of July, A.D. 1251.

THE FORM OF RECEIVING A PERSON INTO THE CONFRATERNITY OF MT. CARMEL,

AND OF BLESSING AND BESTOWING THE SCAPULAR, OR LITTLE HABIT OF THE SAME.

NOTE. — *The* italicized *words, or endings of words, occurring in the text, are those which must be varied according to sex.*

The postulant kneels before the priest, who is vested in surplice and white stole, and the priest says:

Suscepimus, Deus, misericordiam tuam in medio templi tui; secundum nomen tuum, Deus, sic et laus tua in fines terræ; justitia plena est dextera tua.

We have received Thy mercy, O God, in the midst of Thy temple; according to Thy name, O God, so also is Thy praise unto the ends of the earth; Thy right hand is full of justice.

Kyrie eleison.
Christe eleison.
Kyrie eleison.
Pater noster (*secreto*).

Lord, have mercy.
Christ, have mercy.
Lord, have mercy.
Our Father (*inaudibly*).

℣. Et ne nos inducas in tentationem.
℟. Sed libera nos a malo.
℣. Salv*um* fac *servum tuum*,
℟. Deus meus, sperantem in te.

℣. And lead us not into temptation
℟. But deliver us from evil.
℣. Save Thy *servant*,
℟. O my God, who putteth *his* trust in Thee.

℣. Mitte ei, Domine, auxilium de sancto,

℟. Et de Sion tuere *eum*.

℣. Nihil proficiat inimicus in *eo*.

℟. Et filius iniquitatis non apponat nocere *ei*.

℣. Domine, exaudi orationem meam.

℟. Et clamor meus ad te veniat.

℣. Dominus vobiscum.

℟. Et cum spiritu tuo.

Oremus.

Suscipiat te Christus in numero fidelium suorum; et nos, licet indigni, te suscipimus in orationibus nostris. Concedat tibi Deus per Unigenitum suum mediatorem Dei et hominum, tempus bene vivendi, locum bene agendi, constantiam bene perseverandi, et ad æternæ vitæ hereditatem feliciter perveniendi; et sicut nos hodie fraterna charitas spiritualiter jungit in terris, ita divina pietas, quæ dilectionis est auctrix et amatrix, nos cum fidelibus suis conjungere dignetur in cœlis. Per eundem Christum Dominum nostrum. ℟. Amen.

℣. Adjutorium nostrum in nomine Domini,

℟. Qui fecit cœlum et terram.

℣. Sit nomen Domini benedictum

℟. Ex hoc nunc et usque in sæculum.

℣. Domine, exaudi orationem meam.

℟. Et clamor meus ad te veniat.

℣. Dominus vobiscum.

℟. Et cum spiritu tuo.

℣. Send *him* help, O Lord, from Thy holy place,

℟. And defend *him* out of Sion.

℣. Let not the enemy prevail against *him*,

℟. Nor the son of iniquity draw nigh to hurt *him*.

℣. O Lord, hear my prayer.

℟. And let my cry come unto Thee.

℣. The Lord be with you.

℟. And with thy spirit.

Let us pray.

May Christ receive thee into the number of His faithful people; and we, though unworthy, receive thee into fellowship in our prayers. May God, through His only begotten, the Mediator between God and man, grant thee time for right-living, space for well-doing, steadfastness for truly persevering, and for happily attaining unto the inheritance of everlasting life; and as brotherly love doth now spiritually join us together on earth, so may the fatherly love of God, the Author and Nourisher of all love, vouchsafe to number us among His faithful in heaven. Through the same Christ Our Lord. ℟. Amen.

℣. Our help is in the name of the Lord,

℟. Who hath made heaven and earth.

℣. Blessed be the name of the Lord

℟. From this time forth forevermore.

℣. O Lord, hear my prayer.

℟. And let my cry come unto Thee.

℣. The Lord be with you.

℟. And with thy spirit.

Oremus.

Æterne Pater, et Omnipotens Deus, qui Unigenitum tuum vestem nostræ mortalitatis induere voluisti: obsecramus immensam tuæ largitatis bene✠dictionem in hoc genus effluere vestimenti, quod sancti Patres ad innocentiæ et humilitatis indicium a renuntiantibus sæculo gestari sanxerunt, et sic ipsum bene✠dicere digneris; ut quicumque eo usus fuerit induere mereatur ipsum Dominum nostrum Jesum Christum Filium tuum, qui tecum vivit et regnat in unitate Spiritus Sancti Deus, per omnia sæcula sæculorum. ℟. Amen.

Let us pray.

Everlasting Father and Almighty God, Who didst will that Thine only begotten should put on the garment of our mortal nature: we humbly beseech Thee that upon this form of garment, which, as a sign of innocence and humility, the holy fathers appointed to be worn by those renouncing the world, Thou wouldst pour the boundless riches of Thy benediction, ✠ and therewith bless ✠ the same; to the end that whosoever shall be clad in it may also be found worthy to put on Our Lord Jesus Christ Himself, Thy Son, Who liveth and reigneth, etc. ℟. Amen.

Oremus.

Suppliciter te, Domine, rogamus, ut super hunc habitum *servo tuo* imponendum bene✠dictio tua benigna descendat, ut sit bene✠dictus, atque divina virtute procul pellantur hostium nostrorum visibilium et invisibilium tela nequissima. ℟. Amen.

Let us pray.

We humbly beseech Thee, O Lord, that Thy gracious blessing ✠ may descend upon this habit, now to be bestowed upon Thy *servant*, that it may be blessed, ✠ and that the wicked darts of all our enemies, visible and invisible, may be driven far from us by the power of God. ℟. Amen.

The priest sprinkles the scapular with holy water, and, placing it upon the shoulders of the postulant, says:

Accipe, *vir* devot*e*, hunc habitum benedictum, precans Sanctissimam Virginem, ut ejus meritis illum perferas sine macula, et te ab omni adversitate defendat, atque ad vitam perducat æternam. ℟. Amen.

Receive, devout *man*, this blessed habit; and pray the most holy Virgin that by her merits thou mayest bear it without stain, and that she may guard thee from all adversity, and bring thee unto life everlasting. ℟. Amen.

Adesto Domine supplicationibus nostris, et *hunc* famul*um tuum, quem* Sodalitati sanctæ Religionis Carmelitarum sociamus, perpetua tribue firmitate corroborari, ut perseveranti proposito, in omni sanctitate tibi valeat famulari.

Be favorable, O Lord, unto our supplications, and grant that this Thy *servant*, whom we now receive into the Sodality of the holy Carmelite Order, may be strengthened by Thy continual help; that with abiding purpose *he* may serve Thee in all holiness of life.

Protege, Domine, famul*um tuum* subsidiis pacis, et Beatæ Mariæ semper Virginis patrociniis confidentem a cunctis hostibus redde secur*um.*

Shield, O Lord, this Thy *servant* with the shelter of Thy peace, and as *he* trusts in the protecting care of Blessed Mary ever Virgin, do Thou make *him* fearless of all enemies.

Bene✠dicat te conditor cœli et terræ Deus omnipotens, qui te eligere dignatus est ad Beatissimæ Virginis Mariæ de monte Carmelo Societatem et Confraternitatem; quam precamur, ut in hora obitus tui conterat caput serpentis, qui tibi est adversarius, et tandem tamquam victor palmam, et coronam sempiternæ hœreditatis consequaris. Per Christum Dominum nostrum. ℟. Amen.

Almighty God, the Creator of heaven and earth, bless ✠ thee, He Who hath vouchsafed to call thee unto the Society and Confraternity of Blessed Mary of Mount Carmel; let us beseech her, therefore, that in the hour of thy death she may bruise the head of the serpent, thine adversary, and that finally thou mayest attain unto the palm of victory and the crown of inheritance everlasting. Through Christ Our Lord. ℟. Amen.

[*If only the scapular is to be blessed, the priest begins at the* ℣. Adjutorium nostrum, *and continues to the prayer* Suppliciter *inclusive.*]

Then the priest sprinkles the recipient with holy water, and continues:

Ego auctoritate, qua fungor, et mihi concessa, recipio te ad Confraternitatem sacræ Religionis Carmelitarum, et investio, ac participem te facio omnium bonorum spiritualium ejusdem Ordinis. In nomine Patris, ✠ et Filii, et Spiritus Sancti. Amen.

By the authority which I exercise, and which is granted unto me, I receive thee into the Confraternity of the holy Carmelite Order; and I invest thee and make thee a partaker in all the spiritual goods of the same order. In the name of the Father, ✠ and of the Son, and of the Holy Ghost. Amen.

✝Devotions to St. Joseph

THE LITANY OF ST. JOSEPH

Kyrie, eleison.	Lord, have mercy on us.
Christe, eleison.	*Christ, have mercy on us.*
Kyrie, eleison.	Lord, have mercy on us.
Christe, audi nos.	Christ, hear us.
Christe, exaudi nos.	*Christ, graciously hear us.*

Pater de cœlis, Deus, miserere nobis.	God the Father of heaven, have mercy on us.
Fili, Redemptor mundi, Deus,	
Spiritus Sancte, Deus,	God, the Son, Redeemer of the world,
Sancta Trinitas, unus Deus,	God, the Holy Ghost,
	Holy Trinity, one God,

Sancta Maria, ora pro nobis.	Holy Mary, pray for us.
Sancte Joseph,	St. Joseph,
Proles David inclyta,	Illustrious scion of David,
Lumen Patriarcharum,	Light of patriarchs,

Dei Genitricis sponse,	Spouse of the Mother of God,
Custos pudice Virginis,	Chaste guardian of the Virgin,
Filii Dei nutricie,	Foster-father of the Son of God,
Christi defensor sedule,	Watchful defender of Christ,

Almæ Familiæ præses,	Head of the Holy Family,
Joseph justissime,	Joseph most just,
Joseph castissime,	Joseph most chaste,
Joseph prudentissime,	Joseph most prudent,

Joseph fortissime,	Joseph most valiant,
Joseph obedientissime,	Joseph most obedient,
Joseph fidelissime,	Joseph most faithful,
Speculum patientiæ,	Mirror of patience,

Amator paupertatis,	Lover of poverty,
Exemplar opificum,	Model of workmen,
Domesticæ vitæ decus,	Glory of home life,
Custos virginum,	Guardian of virgins,

Familiarum columen,
Solatium miserorum,
Spes ægrotantium,
Patrone morientium,

Terror dæmonum,
Protector sanctæ Ecclesiæ,

Agnus Dei, qui tollis peccata mundi,
parce nobis, Domine.
Agnus Dei, qui tollis peccata mundi,
exaudi nos, Domine.
Agnus Dei, qui tollis peccata mundi,
miserere nobis.

℣. Constituit eum dominum domus
suæ.
℟. Et principem omnis possessionis
suæ.

Oremus.
Deus, qui ineffabili providentia beatum Joseph sanctissimæ Genitricis tuæ sponsum eligere dignatus es: præsta, quæsumus; ut, quem protectorem veneramur in terris, intercessorem habere mereamur in cœlis: Qui vivis et regnas in sæcula sæculorum. ℟. Amen.

Pillar of families,
Solace of the afflicted,
Hope of the sick,
Patron of the dying,

Terror of demons,
Protector of holy Church,

Lamb of God, Who takest away the sins
of the world, *spare us, O Lord.*
Lamb of God, Who takest away the
sins of the world, *graciously hear us,
O Lord.*
Lamb of God, Who takest away the sins
of the world, *have mercy on us.*

℣. He made him lord over His houses.
℟. And the ruler of all His possessions.

Let us pray.
O God, Who in Thine ineffable providence didst vouchsafe to choose blessed Joseph to be the spouse of Thy most holy Mother: grant, we beseech Thee, that we may have him for an intercessor in heaven, whom we venerate as our protector on earth. Who livest and reignest, world without end. ℟. Amen.

PRAYER TO ST. JOSEPH

(*To be said during the month of October, after the recitation of the Rosary*)
To thee, O blessed Joseph, we have recourse in our affliction, and, having implored the help of thy thrice-holy spouse, we now with hearts filled with confidence earnestly beg thee also to take us under thy protection. By that charity wherewith thou wert united to the immaculate Virgin Mother of God, and by that fatherly love with which thou didst cherish the Child Jesus, we beseech thee and we humbly pray that thou wilt look down with gracious eye upon that inheritance which Jesus Christ purchased by His Blood, and wilt succor us in our need by thy power and strength.

Defend, O most watchful guardian of the Holy Family, the chosen offspring of Jesus Christ. Keep from us, O most loving father, all blight of error and corruption.

Aid us from on high, most valiant defender, in this conflict with the powers of darkness; and even as of old thou didst rescue the Child Jesus from the peril of His life, so now defend God's holy Church from the snares of the enemy and from all adversity. Shield us ever under thy patronage, that, following thy example and strengthened by thy help, we may live a holy life, die a happy death, and attain to everlasting bliss in heaven. Amen.

‡Devotions to St. Thérèse of the Child Jesus

"THE LITTLE FLOWER"

COLLECT

O Lord, Who hast said, Unless ye become as little children, ye shall not enter the kingdom of heaven, grant, we beseech Thee, that in humility and simplicity of heart we may so follow the virgin blessed Thérèse, as to obtain reward everlasting: Who livest and reignest world without end. Amen.

PRAYER TO HER

Thou, servant of God, St. Thérèse of the Child Jesus, who in thy dying moments didst say, I will spend my heaven in doing good upon earth, hasten to let fall upon me a shower of roses that I too may be inflamed with that fire of love which burned so brilliantly in thy breast and which brought thee so gloriously to the arms of Jesus, my Lord and my God. Amen.

LITANY OF ST. THÉRÈSE, THE LITTLE FLOWER OF JESUS

Lord, have mercy on us.
Christ, have mercy on us.
Lord, have mercy on us.
Christ, hear us.
Christ, graciously hear us.

God, the Father of heaven, have mercy on us.
God, the Son, Redeemer of the world,
God, the Holy Ghost,
Holy Trinity, one God,

Holy Mary, pray for us.
Our Lady of Victory,
St. Thérèse, servant of God,
St. Thérèse, victim of the merciful love of God,
St. Thérèse, spouse of Jesus,
St. Thérèse, gift of heaven,
St. Thérèse, remarkable in childhood,
St. Thérèse, an example of obedience,

St. Thérèse, resigned to the divine will of God,
St. Thérèse, lover of peace,
St. Thérèse, lover of patience,
St. Thérèse, lover of gentleness,
St. Thérèse, heroic in sacrifices,
St. Thérèse, generous in forgiving,
St. Thérèse, benefactress of the needy,
St. Thérèse, lover of Jesus,
St. Thérèse, devoted to the Holy Face,
St. Thérèse, consumed with divine love of God,
St. Thérèse, advocate of extreme cases,
St. Thérèse, persevering in prayer,
St. Thérèse, a powerful advocate with God,
St. Thérèse, showering roses,
St. Thérèse, doing good upon earth,
St. Thérèse, answering all prayers,
St. Thérèse, lover of holy chastity,
St. Thérèse, lover of voluntary poverty,
St. Thérèse, lover of obedience,
St. Thérèse, burning with zeal for God's glory,
St. Thérèse, inflamed with the Spirit of love,
St. Thérèse, child of benediction,
St. Thérèse, perfect in simplicity,
St. Thérèse, so remarkable for trust in God,
St. Thérèse, gifted with unusual intelligence,
St. Thérèse, never invoked without some answer,
St. Thérèse, teaching us the sure way,
St. Thérèse, victim of divine Love,

Lamb of God, Who takest away the sins of the world, *spare us, O Lord.*
Lamb of God, Who takest away the sins of the world, *graciously hear us, O Lord.*
Lamb of God, Who takest away the sins of the world, *have mercy on us.*
St. Thérèse, the Little Flower of Jesus, *pray for us.*

Let us pray.
   O God, Who didst inflame with Thy Spirit of love the soul of Thy servant Thérèse of the Child Jesus, grant that we also may love Thee and may make Thee much loved. Amen.

𝔍nstruction on the 𝔖acraments in 𝔊eneral

By *Sacrament* is meant an outward sign of inward grace, or a sacred and mysterious sign and ceremony ordained by Christ to convey grace to our souls.

The Sacraments may be compared to channels which convey water from a fountainhead, and the soul to a vessel which one carries to these channels to be filled. The fountain, abounding with water, courses through the channels and fills every vessel which is applied thereto, as far as it can hold; the larger the vessel, the greater the quantity of water it will contain. So the larger the capacity of the soul (which capacity depends upon the soul's dispositions), the greater the portion of grace which it receives through the heavenly channels of the Sacraments. But the conditions required in the receiver are by no means *productive* of the efficacy of the Sacraments. Take the example of light and heat: fire is not lacking in burning power because it cannot act on incombustible materials; nor are the windows of a room the cause of light, though necessary to give it admission.

The *Church* has never instituted, and could not institute, any Sacrament—this is a power reserved to God Himself. He alone is the Fountain of grace: He alone can appoint the channels by which that grace is conveyed to our souls. Since, therefore, as a fact, He has appointed those channels—and no others—which we call Sacraments, by those only can we ordinarily obtain that special grace. Hence it follows that no power on earth can *change* what was ordained by Jesus Christ in the outward forms of the Sacraments, without destroying them entirely; for if any change is made in what He ordained, it is no longer the *same form* to which grace is annexed, and consequently ceases to be a Sacrament.

The Passion of Christ is the rich and exhaustless source from which the grace of every Sacrament is derived; for each grace was purchased for us at the price of our divine Redeemer's blood.

There are seven Sacraments: **Baptism, Confirmation, Penance, Holy Eucharist, Extreme Unction, Holy Orders, and Matrimony.**

Special Instructions on each Sacrament will be found in their proper places. Of these Sacraments, some *give* sanctifying grace, and others *increase* it in our souls. Those that give sanctifying grace are *Baptism* and *Penance*; they are called *Sacraments of the dead*, because they take away sin, which is the death of the soul, and give grace, which is its life. Those that increase sanctifying grace in the soul are *Confirmation, Holy Eucharist, Extreme Unction, Holy Orders*, and *Matrimony*; these are called *Sacraments of the living*, because those who receive them worthily are already living the life of grace. They should be received, therefore, in a state of grace; anyone receiving the Sacraments of the living in mortal sin incurs the additional guilt of sacrilege. The Sacraments of *Baptism, Confirmation*, and *Holy Orders* imprint what is called a *character* upon the soul—a spiritual mark which remains forever—and hence they can be received but once.

Besides the sanctifying grace common to all the Sacraments, God has annexed to each a particular *sacramental* grace, which is a special help to enable us to perform the duties and attain the end for which each Sacrament was instituted—for example 1) Shortly after we come into the world we are made the children of God by *Baptism.* 2) As we grow up we are fortified for the combats against our spiritual enemies which we have to undergo, and are made soldiers of Christ, by *Confirmation.* 3) The *Holy Eucharist* is the daily Bread which feeds and nourishes our souls to everlasting life. 4) If unhappily we fall in the spiritual conflict, *Penance* is the remedy which restores life to the soul. 5) In *Matrimony,* special graces are provided to sanctify and assuage the cares of the married state. 6) *Holy Orders* keeps up the succession of pastors in the Church, and enables them faithfully to discharge their sacred functions. 7) When the Christian soul is on the verge of eternity, it is strengthened and comforted by the refreshing graces of *Extreme Unction,* so that the Christian warrior may not be vanquished at the last.

The Sacrament of Baptism

EXPLANATION OF THE CEREMONIES

The ceremonies used by the Church in the administration of Baptism are very ancient. St. Basil mentions many of them, which, he says, are of apostolical tradition: as the consecration of the water, and of the oil used in the anointings, the renunciation of Satan and his works, and the profession of faith. St. Augustine mentions the sign of the cross, the imposition of hands, and the custom of giving salt to the catechumens. St. Ambrose speaks of the ceremony of touching the ears and nostrils with spittle, with the words, "Be opened."

These ceremonies have a twofold signification. They are outward signs of that which the Holy Spirit operates inwardly in the souls of those that receive the Sacrament; and they also admonish them of that which they ought to do, and represent to them the obligations they contract.

The priest is vested in a white surplice, as denoting innocence, and successively uses two stoles, one violet, the other white. The violet color signifies the unhappy state to which sin has reduced mankind. After the exorcisms, the priest puts on the white stole, as the symbol of the innocence conferred by the Sacrament.

Addressing himself to the godfather and godmother, he asks the *name* by which the child is to be called. A name is given, says St. Charles Borromeo, to show that the person is dedicated to the service of Jesus Christ. This name, the Council of Trent teaches, should be that of some saint, in order that, by bearing the same name, the person may be excited to imitate his virtues and sanctity; and that, while endeavoring to imitate him, he may invoke him and pray to him, in the confident hope that he will be his patron and advocate, for the safety of his body and the salvation of his soul.

The wretched state to which sin has reduced the human race is still further intimated by the priest's breathing three times on the person to be baptized, which is done to drive away the devil, as by the Holy Ghost, Who is the Spirit or Breath of God. It also expresses the contempt which Christians have of him, and the ease with which he may be put to flight, like a straw with a puff of wind.

After having put to flight the tyrant who holds in captivity everyone that cometh into the world, the priest imprints on the person to be baptized the seal of a very different Master. He signs him with the sign of the cross on the forehead and on the breast, that Christ, Who was crucified for our sins, may take possession of him—on the forehead, to signify that a Christian must never be ashamed to make open profession of the Faith of his crucified Savior; and on the breast, to signify that the love of Jesus Christ, and a readiness to obey all His divine commandments and to share in His sufferings, ought constantly to reside in his heart.

The priest, as God's representative, then lays his hand on the head of the person to be baptized, to denote possession in the name of the Almighty.

He then blesses the salt, to purify it from the malignant influences of the evil spirit; and puts a few grains of this salt, thus blessed, into the mouth of the person to be baptized. The salt is the symbol of wisdom, as when St. Paul says: "Let your speech be always with grace seasoned with salt" (Col 4:6). Salt is also a preservative against corruption. This ceremony, then, signifies that the person baptized must make known to the world the sweet savor of the law of God, by the good example of a virtuous and holy conversation; and show by all his works that it is the doctrine of Christ that preserves the soul from corruption, and establishes a firm hope of the resurrection of the body.

Having thus communicated to the person to be baptized the wisdom of Christ and the relish for divine things, the priest peremptorily commands the wicked spirit to depart, and never attempt to deprive him of this precious gift, in the solemn words of the ancient exorcism; then, making the sign of the cross, he says: "And this sign of the holy Cross which we place upon *his* forehead, do thou, accursed devil, never dare to violate."

After this the priest lays the end of his stole, the symbol of his authority, upon the person to be baptized, and introduces him into the church. Being come therein, the priest, jointly with the person to be baptized, or, if it be an infant, with the godfather and godmother, recites aloud the Lord's Prayer and the Apostles' Creed. He then again exorcises the unclean spirit, and commands him to depart in the name and by the power of the most Blessed Trinity.

The next is a ceremony deeply significative. We read in the Gospel (see Mk 7:32–35) that Our Lord cured one that was deaf and dumb by touching his tongue and his ears with spittle, saying, *Ephpheta*—"Be opened." Man, in his natural state, is spiritually both deaf and dumb. Therefore the Church, the Spouse of Jesus Christ and the depository of His power, follows His example; and the priest of the Church, taking spittle from his mouth, touches therewith the ears and the nostrils of the person to be baptized, repeating the same miraculous word, as if to signify the necessity of having the senses of the soul open to the truth and grace of God.

Then follows the solemn renunciation of Satan and of his works and pomps. After which the priest anoints the person to be baptized on the breast and between the shoulders, making the sign of the cross. This outward unction represents the inward anointing of the soul by divine grace, which, like a sacred oil, penetrates our hearts, heals the wounds of our souls, and fortifies them against our passions and concupiscences. The anointing of the breast signifies the necessity of fortifying the heart with heavenly courage, that we may act manfully and do our duty in all things. The anointing between the shoulders signifies the necessity of the like grace, in order to bear and support all the adversities and crosses of this mortal life. The oil is a symbol also of the sweetness of the yoke of Christ.

The moment having arrived at which another human being is to become the child of God and a member of the Mystical Body of Christ; the priest, to denote that sorrow is about to be changed into joy, changes his stole, and instead of the violet puts on a white one.

Then follows the Profession of Faith, after which the Sacrament of regeneration is thus administered: while the godfather and godmother both hold or touch their godchild, the priest pours the baptismal water on the child's head three times, in the form of a cross, repeating the sacramental words in such manner that the three pourings of the water concur with the pronouncing of the three names of the divine Persons. The water is poured three times, while the words are pronounced but once, to show that the three Persons unite in the regeneration of man in holy Baptism. The godparents hold or touch their godchild, to signify that they answer for him, or that they engage to put him in mind of his vow and promise.

Then the priest anoints the person baptized on the crown of the head, in the form of a cross, with holy chrism, compounded of oil and balsam. This ceremony is of apostolical tradition, and signifies: 1st. That the person baptized is solemnly consecrated to the service of God, and made a living temple of the Holy Ghost. 2nd. That by Baptism he is made partaker with Christ, the great *Anointed* of God, and has a share in His unction and grace. 3rd. That he is anointed to be king, priest, and prophet; and therefore that, as king, he must have dominion over his passions; as priest, he must offer himself unceasingly to God as a living sacrifice for an odor of sweetness; as prophet, he must declare by his life the rewards of the world to come.

After the anointing, the priest puts upon the head of the baptized a white linen cloth, now used instead of the white garment with which the new Christian used anciently to be clothed in Baptism, to signify the purity and innocence which we receive in Baptism, and which we must take care to preserve till death.

Lastly, the priest puts a lighted candle into the hand of the person baptized, or of the godfather; which ceremony is derived from the parable of the virgins, "who taking their lamps went forth to meet the bridegroom" (Mt 25:1); and is intended to remind the person baptized that, being now a child of light, he must walk as a child of light, and keep the lamp of faith ever burning with the oil of charity and good works, for the glory of God and the edification of his neighbor; so that, whenever the Lord shall come, he may be found prepared, and may go in with Him into the eternal life of His heavenly kingdom.

THE BAPTISM OF INFANTS

By special permission of the Holy See, this form is used in the United States for the Baptism of adults also.

NOTE.—The italicized words, or endings of words, occurring in the text, are those which must be varied according to sex or number.

Sacerdos. N., quid petis ab Ecclesia Dei?

Priest. N., what dost thou ask of the Church of God?

Resp. Fidem.

Sponsor. Faith.

S. Fides quid tibi præstat?

P. What doth faith bring thee to?

℞. Vitam æternam.

S. Life everlasting.

S. Si igitur vis ad vitam ingredi, serva mandata. Diliges Dominum Deum tuum ex toto corde tuo, et ex tota anima tua, et ex tota mente tua, et proximum tuum sicut teipsum.

P. If, therefore, thou wilt enter into life, keep the commandments. Thou shalt love the Lord thy God with all thy heart, and with all thy soul, and with all thy mind, and thy neighbor as thyself.

The priest then gently breathes thrice upon the face of the infant, and says once:

Exi ab *eo*, immunde spiritus, et da locum Spiritui Sancto Paraclito.

Depart from *him*, thou unclean spirit, and give place to the Holy Ghost the Paraclete.

After that, he makes with his thumb the sign of the cross upon the forehead and upon the breast of the infant, saying:

Accipe signum crucis tam in fronte, ✠ quam in corde; ✠ sume fidem cœlestium præceptorum, et talis esto moribus, ut templum Dei jam esse possis.

Receive the sign of the cross both upon the forehead ✠ and also upon the heart; ✠ take unto thyself the faith of the heavenly precepts, and be in thy manners such that now thou mayest be the temple of God.

Oremus.

Preces nostras, quæsumus, Domine, clementer exaudi: et *hunc* elect*um tuum,* N., crucis Dominicæ impressione signat*um,* perpetua virtute custodi: ut magnitudinis gloriæ tuæ rudimenta serva*ns,* per custodiam mandatorum tuorum, ad regenerationis gloriam pervenire mere*a*tur. Per Christum Dominum nostrum. ℟. Amen.

Let us pray.

Mercifully hear our prayers, O Lord, we beseech Thee; and with Thy perpetual power guard *this* Thine elect, N., signed with the seal of the cross of the Lord: that, being faithful to these ordinances of Thy great Majesty, *he* may, by keeping Thy commandments, deserve to attain the glory of regeneration. Through Christ Our Lord. ℟. Amen.

He then lays his hand upon the infant's head, and says:

Oremus.

Omnipotens, sempiterne Deus, Pater Domini nostri Jesu Christi, respicere dignare super *hunc* famu-l*um tuum,* N., *quem* ad rudimenta fidei vocare dignatus es: omnem cæcitatem cordis ab *eo* expelle: disrumpe omnes laqueos Satanæ, quibus fuer*at* colligat*us;* aperi *ei,* Domine, januam pietatis tuæ, ut signo sapientiæ tuæ imbut*us,* omnium cupiditatum fœtoribus care*at,* et ad suavem odorem præceptorum tuorum læt*us* tibi in Ecclesia tua deservi*at,* et profici*at* de die in diem. Per eundem Christum Dominum nostrum. ℟. Amen.

Let us pray.

Almighty, everlasting God, Father of Our Lord Jesus Christ, look graciously down upon *this* Thy *servant,* N., whom Thou hast graciously called unto the beginnings of the faith: drive out from *him* all blindness of heart: break all the toils of Satan wherewith *he* was held: open unto *him,* O Lord, the gate of Thy loving kindness, that, being impressed with the sign of Thy wisdom, *he* may be free from the foulness of all wicked desires, and, in the sweet odor of Thy precepts, may joyfully serve Thee in Thy Church, and grow in grace from day to day. Through the same Christ Our Lord. ℟. Amen.

The priest then blesses the salt, which, after it has been once blessed, may serve for the same purpose on other occasions.

THE BLESSING OF THE SALT

Exorcizo te, creatura salis, in nomine Dei Patris ✠ omnipotentis, et in charitate Domini nostri Jesu ✠ Christi, et in virtute Spiritus ✠ Sancti. Exorcizo te per Deum ✠ vivum, per Deum ✠ verum, per Deum ✠ sanctum, per Deum ✠ qui te ad tutelam humani generis procreavit, et populo venienti ad credulitatem per servos suos consecrari præcepit, ut in nomine sanctæ Trinitatis efficiaris salutare sacramentum ad effugandum inimicum. Proinde rogamus te, Domine Deus noster, ut hanc creaturam salis sanctificando ✠ sanctifices, et benedicendo ✠ benedicas, ut fiat omnibus accipientibus perfecta medicina, permanens in visceribus eorum, in nomine ejusdem Domini nostri Jesu Christi, qui venturus est judicare vivos et mortuos, et sæculum per ignem. ℟. Amen.

I exorcise thee, creature of salt, in the name of God, the Father ✠ Almighty, and in the love of Our Lord Jesus ✠ Christ, and in the power of the Holy ✠ Ghost. I exorcise thee by the living ✠ God, by the true ✠ God, by the all-holy ✠ God, by the God ✠ Who hath created thee for a preservation of the human race, and hath appointed thee to be consecrated by His servants for the people coming unto faith, that in the name of the Holy Trinity thou mayest become a saving sacrament to put the enemy to flight. Wherefore we pray Thee, O Lord our God, that sanctifying ✠ Thou mayest sanctify this creature of salt, and blessing ✠ Thou mayest bless it, that unto all who receive it it may become a perfect cure, abiding in their hearts, in the name of the same Our Lord Jesus Christ, Who shall come to judge the living and the dead and the world by fire. ℟. Amen.

He then puts a little of the blessed salt into the mouth of the infant, saying:

N., Accipe sal sapientiæ: propitiatio sit tibi in vitam æternam. ℟. Amen.

N., receive the salt of wisdom; may it be to thee a propitiation unto everlasting life. ℟. Amen.

S. Pax tecum.
℟. Et cum spiritu tuo.

P. Peace be with thee.
℟. And with thy spirit.

Oremus

Deus patrum nostrorum, Deus universæ conditor veritatis, te supplices exoramus, ut *hunc* famul*um tuum*, N., respicere digneris propitius, et hoc primum pabulum salis gustan*tem*, non diutius esurire permittas, quo minus cibo exple*a*tur cœlesti, quatenus *sit* semper spiritu ferve*ns*, spe gaude*ns*, tuo semper nomini servie*ns*. Perduc *eum*, Domine, quæsumus, ad novæ regenerationis lavacrum, ut cum fidelibus tuis promissionum tuarum æterna præmia consequi mere*a*tur. Per Christum Dominum nostrum. ℞. Amen.

Let us pray.

O God of our fathers, O God the Author of all truth, vouchsafe, we humbly beseech Thee, to look graciously down upon *this* Thy *servant,* N., and as *he* tastes this first nutriment of salt, suffer *him* no longer to hunger for want of heavenly food, to the end that *he* may be always fervent in spirit, rejoicing in hope, always serving Thy name. Lead *him*, O Lord, we beseech Thee, to the laver of the new regeneration, that, together with Thy faithful, *he* may deserve to attain the everlasting rewards of Thy promises. Through Christ Our Lord. ℞. Amen.

Exorcizo te, immunde spiritus, in nomine Patris, ✠ et Filii, ✠ et Spiritus ✠ Sancti, ut exeas, et recedas ab *hoc* famulo Dei N. Ipse enim tibi imperat, maledicte damnate, qui pedibus super mare ambulavit, et Petro mergenti dexteram porrexit.

I exorcise thee, thou unclean spirit, in the name of the Father, ✠ and of the Son, ✠ and of the Holy ✠ Ghost, that thou go forth and depart from *this servant* of God, N.; for He Himself commands thee, accursed outcast, He Who walked upon the sea, and stretched forth to sinking Peter His right hand.

Ergo, maledicte diabole, recognosce sententiam tuam, et da honorem Deo vivo et vero, da honorem Jesu Christo Filio ejus, et Spiritui Sancto, et recede ab *hoc* famul*o* Dei N., quia *istum* sibi Deus et Dominus noster Jesus Christus ad suam sanctam gratiam, et benedictionem, fontemque baptismatis vocare dignatus est.

Therefore, accursed devil, acknowledge thy sentence, and give honor unto the true and living God; give honor unto Jesus Christ, His Son, and unto the Holy Ghost; and depart from *this servant* of God, N., because *him* hath God and Our Lord Jesus Christ vouchsafed to call unto His holy grace, and blessing, and the font of Baptism.

Here he makes with his thumb the sign of the cross upon the infant's forehead, saying:

Et hoc signum sanctæ crucis ✠ quod nos fronti ejus damus, tu, maledicte diabole, numquam audeas violare. Per eundem Christum Dominum nostrum. ℟. Amen.

And this sign of the holy Cross, ✠ which we place upon *his* forehead, do thou, accursed devil, never dare to violate. Through the same Christ Our Lord. ℟. Amen.

Immediately laying his hand upon the infant's head, he says:

Oremus.

Æternam, ac justissimam pietatem tuam deprecor, Domine sancte, Pater omnipotens, æterne Deus, Auctor luminis et veritatis, super *hunc* famul*um tuum,* N., ut digneris *eum* illuminare lumine intelligentiæ tuæ: munda *eum,* et sanctifica: da *ei* scientiam veram, ut dign*us* gratia baptismi tui effect*us,* tene*at* firmam spem, consilium rectum, doctrinam sanctam. Per Christum Dominum nostrum. ℟. Amen.

Let us pray.

O holy Lord, Father Almighty, eternal God, Author of light and truth, I implore Thine everlasting and most just goodness upon *this* Thy *servant,* N., that Thou wouldst vouchsafe to enlighten *him* with the light of Thy wisdom: cleanse *him* and sanctify *him:* give unto *him* true knowledge, that, being made worthy of the grace of Thy Baptism, *he* may hold firm hope, right counsel, holy doctrine. Through Christ Our Lord. ℟. Amen.

After this, the priest lays the end of his stole upon the infant, and admits him into the church, saying:

Ingred*ere* in templum Dei, ut habe*as* partem cum Christo in vitam æternam. ℟. Amen.

Enter *thou* into the temple of God, that *thou* may*est* have part with Christ unto life everlasting. ℟. Amen.

When they have entered the church, the priest, as he proceeds to the font, says in a loud voice along with the sponsors:

Credo in Deum, Patrem omnipotentem, Creatorem cœli et terræ. Et in Jesum Christum, Filium ejus unicum, Dominum nostrum: qui conceptus est de Spiritu Sancto, natus ex Maria Virgine, passus sub Pontio Pilato, crucifixus, mortuus, et sepultus: descendit ad inferos; tertia die resurrexit a mortuis; ascendit ad cœlos; sedet ad dexteram Dei Patris omnipotentis: inde venturus est judicare vivos et mortuos. Credo in Spiritum Sanctum, sanctam Ecclesiam Catholicam, Sanctorum communionem, remissionem peccatorum, carnis resurrectionem, vitam æternam. Amen.

I believe in God, the Father Almighty, Creator of heaven and earth; and in Jesus Christ, His only Son, Our Lord: Who was conceived by the Holy Ghost, born of the Virgin Mary, suffered under Pontius Pilate, was crucified; died, and was buried. He descended into hell; the third day He arose again from the dead; He ascended into heaven, sitteth at the right hand of God the Father Almighty; from thence He shall come to judge the living and the dead. I believe in the Holy Ghost, the holy Catholic Church, the communion of saints, the forgiveness of sins, the resurrection of the body, and the life everlasting. Amen.

Pater noster, qui es in cœlis, sanctificetur nomen tuum: adveniat regnum tuum: fiat voluntas tua, sicut in cœlo et in terra. Panem nostrum quotidianum da nobis hodie: et dimitte nobis debita nostra, sicut et nos dimittimus debitoribus nostris. Et ne nos inducas in tentationem; sed libera nos a malo. Amen.

Our Father, Who art in heaven, hallowed be Thy name: Thy kingdom come: Thy will be done on earth as it is in heaven. Give us this day our daily bread: and forgive us our trespasses as we forgive those who trespass against us. And lead us not into temptation; but deliver us from evil. Amen.

And then, before he reaches the baptistery, he says:

THE EXORCISM

Exorcizo te, omnis spiritus immunde, in nomine Dei Patris ✠ omnipotentis, et in nomine Jesu Christi Filii ejus, ✠ Domini et Judicis nostri, et in virtute Spiritus ✠ Sancti, ut discedas ab *hoc* plasma*te* Dei N., *quod* Dominus noster ad templum sanctum suum vocare dignatus est, ut fi*at* templ*um* Dei vivi, et Spiritus Sanctus habitet in *eo.* Per eundem Christum Dominum nostrum, qui venturus est judicare vivos et mortuos, et sæculum per ignem. ℟. Amen.

I exorcise thee, every unclean spirit, in the name of God the Father ✠ Almighty, and in the name of Jesus Christ, His Son, ✠ Our Lord and Judge, and in the power of the Holy ✠ Ghost, that thou depart from *this creature* of God, N., which Our Lord hath deigned to call unto His holy temple, that *it* may be made the templ*e* of the living God, and that the Holy Ghost may dwell therein. Through the same Christ Our Lord, Who shall come to judge the living and the dead, and the world by fire. ℟. Amen.

Then the priest wets his thumb with spittle from his mouth, and touches the ears and nostrils of the infant. And in touching first the right ear and then the left, he says:

Ephpheta, quod est, Adaperire.

Ephpheta, that is to say, Be opened.

Then he touches the nostrils, saying:

In odorem suavitatis.

For a savor of sweetness.

And he adds:

Tu autem effugare, diabole; appropinquabit enim judicium Dei.

And do thou, O devil, begone! for the judgment of God is at hand.

He then interrogates the person to be baptized, by name, saying:

N., Abrenuntias Satanæ?
℟. Abrenuntio.
S. Et omnibus operibus ejus?
℟. Abrenuntio.
S. Et omnibus pompis ejus?
℟. Abrenuntio.

N., dost thou renounce Satan?
Sponsor. I do renounce him.
P. And all his works?
℟. I do renounce them.
P. And all his pomps?
℟. I do renounce them.

The priest then dips his thumb into the oil of catechumens, and anoints the infant upon the breast and between the shoulders, in the form of a cross, saying:

Ego te linio ✚ oleo salutis, in Christo Jesu Domino nostro, ut habeas vitam æternam. ℞. Amen.

I anoint thee ✚ with the oil of salvation in Christ Jesus, Our Lord, that thou mayest have life everlasting. ℞. Amen.

(Here he puts aside the violet stole, and puts on another of white color.)

Next with cotton, or something similar, he wipes his thumb and the places anointed. And he interrogates the person to be baptized by name, the sponsor answering:

N., Credis in Deum Patrem omnipotentem, Creatorem cœli et terræ?

N., dost thou believe in God, the Father Almighty, Creator of heaven and earth?

℞. Credo.

℞. I do believe.

S. Credis in Jesum Christum, Filium ejus unicum, Dominum nostrum, natum et passum?

P. Dost thou believe in Jesus Christ, His only Son, Our Lord, Who was born, and Who suffered for us?

℞. Credo.

℞. I do believe.

S. Credis et in Spiritum Sanctum, sanctam Ecclesiam Catholicam, Sanctorum communionem, remissionem peccatorum, carnis resurrectionem, et vitam æternam?

P. Dost thou also believe in the Holy Ghost, the holy Catholic Church, the communion of saints, the remission of sins, the resurrection of the body, and the life everlasting?

℞. Credo.

℞. I do believe.

Then, pronouncing the name of the person to be baptized, the priest says:

N., vis baptizari?
℞. Volo.

N., wilt thou be baptized?
Sponsor. I will.

Then the godfather or the godmother, or both (if both are admitted), holding the infant, the priest takes the baptismal water in a small vessel or pitcher, and from it pours thrice upon the infant's head in the form of a cross; and at the same time, pronouncing the words once only, distinctly and attentively he says:

N., ego te baptizo in nomine ✠ Patris [*fundat primo*], et Filii ✠ [*fundat secundo*], et Spiritus ✠ Sancti [*fundat tertio*].

N., I baptize thee in the name ✠ of the Father [*he pours the first time*], and of the Son ✠ [*he pours the second time*], and of the Holy ✠ Ghost [*he pours the third time*].

He then dips his thumb in the holy chrism, anoints the infant upon the crown of the head in the form of a cross, saying:

Deus omnipotens, Pater Domini nostri Jesu Christi, qui te regeneravit ex aqua et Spiritu Sancto, quique dedit tibi remissionem omnium peccatorum, ipse te ✠ liniat chrismate salutis in eodem Christo Jesu Domino nostro in vitam æternam. ℟. Amen.

May Almighty God, the Father of Our Lord Jesus Christ, He Who hath regenerated thee by water and the Holy Ghost, and given thee remission of all thy sins, anoint thee ✠ with the chrism of salvation, in the same Christ Jesus Our Lord, unto life everlasting. ℟. Amen.

S. Pax tibi.
℟. Et cum spiritu tuo.

P. Peace be with thee.
℟. And with thy spirit.

Then with cotton, or something similar, he wipes his thumb and the place anointed, and puts upon the head of the infant a white linen cloth, saying:

Accipe vestem candidam, quam immaculatam perferas ante tribunal Domini nostri Jesu Christi, ut habeas vitam æternam. ℟. Amen.

Receive this white garment, which mayest thou bear without stain before the judgment seat of Our Lord Jesus Christ, that thou mayest have life everlasting. ℟. Amen.

Afterward, he gives the infant or the godfather a lighted candle, saying:

Accipe lampadem ardentem, et irreprehensibilis custodi baptismum tuum: serva Dei mandata, ut cum Dominus venerit ad nuptias, possis occurrere ei una cum omnibus sanctis in aula cœlesti, habeasque vitam æternam, et vivas in sæcula sæculorum. ℟. Amen.

Receive this burning light, and keep thy Baptism so as to be without blame: keep the commandments of God, that when the Lord shall come to the nuptials, thou mayest meet Him together with all the saints in the heavenly court, and mayest have eternal life, and live forever and ever. ℟. Amen.

Lastly, he says:

N., vade in pace, et Dominus sit tecum.   N., go in peace, and the Lord be with
  ℟. Amen.   thee. ℟. Amen.

A PRAYER FOR ONE LATELY BAPTIZED

O Lord our God, our true Life, Who by the font of Baptism dost illuminate the baptized with heavenly radiance, Who hast vouchsafed to Thy *servant* by water and the Holy Ghost remission of all *his* sins, lay Thy mighty hand upon *him*, and protect *him* with the power of Thy goodness; preserve *him* from losing the earnest of glory; be pleased to bring *him* to eternal life and to the vision of Thyself; for Thou art our Sanctification, and to Thee, Father, Son, and Holy Ghost, do we render praise and thanksgiving, now and forever, world without end. *Amen.*

A RENEWAL OF BAPTISMAL VOWS

Most Holy Trinity, Father, Son, and Holy Ghost, one God, I mourn and lament my most sinful neglect of the sacred promise and vow which was made in my name at my Baptism. I lament my long-continued transgressions, my ingratitude, my coldness and hardness of heart. O Lord, Who art the great Searcher of hearts, and from Whom no secrets are hid, in Thy presence I do most freely, fully, and unfeignedly, from henceforth and forevermore, repent of and renounce all my sins; I resolve, to the utmost of the power Thou givest me, to resist all the temptations of the devil, the world, and the flesh, so that I may never willingly be led by them. I do firmly believe, and will, by Thy help, continue in the belief of all the articles of the Christian Faith; and I am resolved, in all sincerity of heart, to keep Thy holy will and commandments, and to persevere, through the help of Thy grace, to the end of my life. Enlighten and strengthen me, O God, by Thy Holy Spirit, to perform this my vow and covenant. Preserve me as a living and faithful member of Thy Church, a dutiful and dear child of God, and an inheritor of the kingdom of heaven; that through Thy mercy I may in Thy good time obtain the end of my faith, even the salvation of my soul. *Amen.*

The Reception of Converts

THE MODE OF RECEIVING THE PROFESSION OF FAITH OF CONVERTS TO THE CATHOLIC CHURCH, ACCORDING TO THE FORM PRESCRIBED BY THE SACRED CONGREGATION OF THE HOLY OFFICE, THE 20th OF JULY, 1859

When heretics are converted, inquiry must first be made concerning the validity of their former Baptism. If, therefore, it should be found, after diligent examination, either that Baptism had not been conferred at all, or else conferred improperly, they must be baptized anew. But if, upon investigation, there remains a reasonable doubt of the validity of their former Baptism, then it should be repeated conditionally, after the form for the *Baptism of Adults,* when that is required. If, on the other hand, the former Baptism was valid, then the converts should simply make their *Abjuration* or *Profession of Faith.* There are three ways, therefore, of reconciling heretics to the Church:

I. If Baptism is conferred absolutely, neither abjuration nor absolution follows; since all the past is wiped away by the Sacrament of regeneration.

II. If Baptism is repeated conditionally, the following order is to be observed: 1st. The *Abjuration* or *Profession of Faith.* 2nd. *Conditional Baptism.* 3rd. *Sacramental Confession* with conditional absolution.

III. When, finally, the former Baptism is held to be valid, the *Abjuration* or *Profession of Faith* alone is received, followed by the *Absolution from Censures.* If, however, the convert strongly desires that the rites which were omitted in his former Baptism shall be now supplied, the priest shall gratify his pious desire. He ought, however, in this case to use the form *for Adults,* if required, and to make the necessary changes caused by the former valid Baptism.

The priest, vested in surplice and violet stole, seats himself at the Epistle side of the altar, if the Blessed Sacrament is reserved in the tabernacle, otherwise before the middle of the altar; and before him kneels the convert, who, touching the Book of Gospels with his right hand, makes his *Profession of Faith,* as below. (If he cannot read, the priest slowly reads for him the Profession, which he distinctly pronounces together with the priest.)

PROFESSION OF FAITH

I, N. N., having before my eyes the holy Gospels, which I touch with my hand, and knowing that no one can be saved without that Faith which the holy, catholic, apostolic Roman Church holds, believes, and teaches, against which I grieve that I have greatly erred, inasmuch as I have held and believed doctrines opposed to her teaching—

I now, with grief and contrition for my past errors, profess that I believe the holy, catholic, apostolic Roman Church to be the only and true Church established on earth by Jesus Christ, to which I submit myself with my whole heart. I believe all the articles that she proposes to my belief, and I reject and condemn all that she rejects and condemns, and I am ready to observe all that she commands me. And, especially, I profess that I believe:

One only God in three divine Persons, distinct from, and equal to, each other—that is to say, the Father, the Son, and the Holy Ghost;

The Catholic doctrine of the Incarnation, Passion, death, and Resurrection of Our Lord Jesus Christ; and the personal union of the two natures, the divine and the human; the divine Maternity of the most holy Mary, together with her most spotless virginity;

The true, real, and substantial Presence of the Body and Blood, together with the Soul and Divinity of Our Lord Jesus Christ, in the most holy Sacrament of the Eucharist;

The seven Sacraments instituted by Jesus Christ for the salvation of mankind—that is to say, Baptism, Confirmation, Eucharist, Penance, Extreme Unction, Order, Matrimony;

Purgatory, the resurrection of the dead, everlasting life;

The primacy, not only of honor but also of jurisdiction, of the Roman Pontiff, successor of St. Peter, Prince of the Apostles, Vicar of Jesus Christ;

The veneration of the saints and of their images; the authority of the apostolic and ecclesiastical traditions, and of the Holy Scriptures, which we must interpret and understand only in the sense which our holy mother the Catholic Church has held and does hold;

And everything else that has been defined and declared by the sacred canons and by the general councils, and particularly by the holy Council of Trent, and delivered, defined, and declared by the general Council of the Vatican, especially concerning the primacy of the Roman Pontiff, and his infallible teaching authority.

With a sincere heart, therefore, and with unfeigned faith, I detest and abjure every error, heresy, and sect opposed to the said holy, catholic, and apostolic Roman Church. So help me God, and these His holy Gospels, which I touch with my hand.

Afterward, the convert still kneeling, the priest sitting, says:
Psalm 50, p. 196.

Or else:
Psalm 129, p. 234.

NOTE. —The italicized *words, or endings of words, occurring in the text, are those which must be varied according to sex.*

Then the priest, standing, says:

Kyrie, eleison.	Lord, have mercy.
℟. Christe, eleison.	℟. Christ, have mercy.
℣. Kyrie, eleison. Pater noster (*secreto*).	℣. Lord, have mercy. Our Father (*inaudibly*).
℣. Et ne nos inducas in tentationem.	℣. And lead us not into temptation.
℟. Sed libera nos a malo.	℟. But deliver us from evil.
℣. Salv*um* fac *servum tuum.*	℣. Save Thy *servant.*
℟. Deus meus, sperantem in te.	℟. O my God, who putteth *his* trust in Thee.
℣. Domine, exaudi orationem meam.	℣. O Lord, hear my prayer.
℟. Et clamor meus ad te veniat.	℟. And let my cry come unto Thee.
℣. Dominus vobiscum.	℣. The Lord be with you.
℟. Et cum spiritu tuo.	℟. And with thy spirit.

Oremus.

Deus, cui proprium est misereri semper et parcere: suscipe deprecationem nostram, ut *hunc* famul*um tuum, quem* excommunicationis catena constringit, miseratio tuæ pietatis clementer absolvat. Per Dominum nostrum Jesus Christum Filium tuum, qui tecum vivit et regnat in unitate Spiritus Sancti, Deus, per omnia sæcula sæculorum. ℟. Amen.

Let us pray.

O God, Whose property is always to have mercy and to spare: graciously receive our supplication, that this Thy *servant,* whom the bonds of excommunication do hold a prisoner, the compassion of Thy loving kindness may now mercifully absolve. Through Our Lord Jesus Christ, Thy Son, Who liveth and reigneth with Thee, in the unity of the Holy Ghost, one God, world without end. ℟. Amen.

Then the priest, sitting, and turned toward the kneeling convert, absolves him from his heresy, saying:

Auctoritate apostolica, qua fungor in hac parte, absolvo te a vinculo excommunicationis quam (forsan) incurristi, et restituo te sacrosanctis Ecclesiæ Sacramentis, communioni et unitati fidelium, in nomine Patris, ✠ et Filii, et Spiritus Sancti. Amen.

By the Apostolic authority, which I here do exercise, I absolve thee from the bond of excommunication which (perchance)[31] thou hast incurred; and I restore thee to the holy Sacraments of the Church, and to the communion and unity of the faithful, in the name of the Father, ✠ and of the Son, and of the Holy Ghost. Amen.

---

[31] In doubt whether the penitent has incurred excommunication or no, the priest shall insert this word *perchance.*

In fine, the priest enjoins upon the new convert some salutary penance—for example prayers, visits to churches, and the like.

The Sacrament of Confirmation

"When the apostles had heard that Samaria had received the Word of God, they sent to them Peter and John, who, when they were come, prayed for them, that they might receive the Holy Spirit. For as yet He was come upon none of them; but they were only baptized into the name of the Lord Jesus. Then they laid their hands on them, and they received the Holy Spirit" (Acts 8:14–17).

INSTRUCTIONS

1. Confirmation is a Sacrament by which the faithful, who have already been made children of God by their Baptism, receive the Holy Ghost by the prayer and the imposition of the hands of the bishops, the successors of the apostles, in order to their being made strong and perfect Christians and valiant soldiers of Jesus Christ. It is called *Confirmation* from its effect, which is to *confirm* or *strengthen* those that receive it in the profession of the true Faith; to give them such courage and resolution as to be willing rather to die than turn from it; and to arm them in general against all their spiritual enemies.

2. This Sacrament was designed and instituted by Our Lord for all Christians, and consequently is a *divine ordinance.*

3. The principal effects of this Sacrament are a fortifying grace in order to strengthen the soul against all the visible and invisible enemies of the Faith; and a certain dedication and consecration of the soul by the Holy Ghost, the mark of which dedication and consecration is left in the soul as a *character*, which can never be effaced.

4. Hence this Sacrament can be received but once, and it would be a sacrilege to attempt to receive it a second time; for which reason also the faithful are bound to take extreme care to come to this Sacrament duly disposed, lest, if they should be so unhappy as to receive it in mortal sin, they should receive their own condemnation, and run the risk of being deprived forever of its grace.

5. Now, the dispositions which the Christian must bring with him to receive worthily the Sacrament of Confirmation are: a *purity of conscience,* at least from all mortal sin; for which reason he ought to go to Confession before he is confirmed, for the Holy Ghost will not come to a soul in which Satan reigns by mortal sin; secondly, a sincere desire of giving himself up to the Holy Ghost, to follow the influence of His divine grace, to be His temple forever, and, by His assistance, to fulfill all the obligations of a soldier of Christ.

6. Hence a Christian ought to prepare himself for this Sacrament by fervent prayer, as we find the apostles prepared themselves for the receiving of the Holy Ghost. "All these were persevering with one mind in prayer," says St. Luke (1:14—speaking of the ten days that passed between the Ascension of Our Lord and Pentecost). How happy shall they be who, like them, prepare themselves for the Holy Ghost by these spiritual exercises!

7. The obligations which accompany the *character* of Confirmation, and which a Christian takes upon himself when he receives this Sacrament, are: to bear a loyal and perpetual allegiance to the great King in Whose service he enlists himself as a soldier; to be true to His standard, the Cross of Christ, the mark of which he receives on his forehead; to fight His battles against His enemies, the world, the flesh, and the devil; to be faithful unto death; and rather to die than desert from the service, or go over to the enemy by willfull sin—in fine, to live up to the glorious character of a soldier of Christ, and to maintain that interior purity and sanctity which becomes the temple of the Holy Ghost, by a life of prayer and a life of love. Where the *character* of our Confirmation, when we shall bring it before the judgment seat of Christ, shall be found to have been accompanied with such a life as this, it will shine most gloriously in our souls for all eternity; but if, instead of living up to it, we should be found to have been deserters and rebels, and to have violated this sacred *character* by a life of sin, it will certainly rise up in judgment against us, it will condemn us at the bar of divine justice, it will cast us deeper into the bottomless pit, and be a mark of eternal ignominy and reproach to our souls amongst the damned.

THE CEREMONIES EXPLAINED

The *chrism* used in Confirmation is a sacred unguent, composed of oil of olives and balsam, solemnly blessed by the bishop on Maundy Thursday. The outward anointing of the forehead with chrism represents the inward anointing of the soul, in this Sacrament, with the Holy Ghost. The *oil*, whose properties are to strengthen and invigorate the limbs, to assuage pain, and the like, represents the like spiritual effects of the grace of the Sacrament in the soul, penetrating and diffusing itself throughout all her powers; oil also, being a smooth and mild substance, represents that spirit of meekness and patience under the cross which is one principal effect of Confirmation. The *balsam* fitly represents the fortifying grace received in Confirmation, by which our souls are preserved from corruption after our sins have been destroyed by the Sacrament of Baptism; also, being of a sweet smell, it represents the good odor or sweet savor of Christian virtues and an innocent life, with which we are to edify our neighbors after having received this Sacrament.

The anointing of the forehead is made in the form of a cross, because the virtue of this Sacrament, as all other graces, comes through the merits of the sacrifice of the death of Jesus Christ; and to show that, being now confirmed in His service and enlisted as His soldiers, we should never be ashamed of our Master, but boldly profess ourselves disciples of a crucified Savior and members of His Church, in spite of all the world may do against us, either by ridicule or persecution.

The bishop gives the person confirmed a gentle stroke on the cheek, to teach him that, being now a soldier of Jesus Christ, he must fight manfully against all his enemies; suffer patiently all kinds of affronts and injuries for his faith; and bear with meekness all crosses and trials, for the sake and for the glory of his Lord and Master.

In giving him this gentle stroke, the bishop says, "Peace be with thee," to signify that the true peace of God, which as St. Paul says, "surpasseth all understanding" (Phil 4:7), is chiefly to be found in suffering patiently for Christ's sake; and also to encourage him to do so by the hope of reward, according to Our Lord's promise: "Learn of Me, because I am meek and lowly in heart, and you shall find rest for your souls" (Mt 11:29).

Persons usually take a new name at Confirmation, which ought to be the name of some saint, whom they choose for their particular patron.

A PRAYER FOR ONE ABOUT TO BE CONFIRMED

Almighty and eternal God, Who hast vouchsafed to regenerate Thy *servant* in holy Baptism by water and the Holy Ghost, perfect the work Thou hast begun in *him*. Strengthen *him* with Thy sevenfold gifts: the Spirit of *wisdom*, that *he* may despise the perishable things of this world, and love the things that are eternal; the Spirit of *understanding*, to enlighten *him* and give *him* a more perfect knowledge of the mysteries of the Faith; the Spirit of *counsel*, that *he* may make a right choice in things belonging to *his* eternal salvation; the Spirit of *fortitude*, that *he* may overcome all temptations; the Spirit of *knowledge*, that *he* may know Thy will; the Spirit of true *piety*, that *he* may be faithful and devout in Thy service; and the Spirit of Thy holy *fear*, that *he* may be filled with a loving reverence, and may fear in any way to displease Thee. Seal *him* through Thy mercy with the seal of a disciple of Jesus Christ unto life eternal; and grant, O Lord, that bearing the Cross on *his* forehead, *he* may bear it also in *his* heart, so that boldly confessing Thee before men, *he* may be found worthy to be one day reckoned in the number of Thine elect: through Jesus Christ Our Lord. *Amen.*

(*This prayer may be used also by the candidate.*)

The bishop, wearing over his rochet an amice, stole, and cope of white, and having a miter on his head, proceeds to the faldstool, before the middle of the altar, or has it placed for him in some other convenient place, and sits thereon, with his back to the altar and his face toward the people, holding his crosier in his left hand. He washes his hands, still sitting; then, laying aside his miter, he arises, and standing with his face toward the persons to be confirmed, and having his hands joined before his breast (the persons to be confirmed kneeling, and having their hands also joined before their breasts), he says:

Spiritus Sanctus superveniat in vos, et virtus Altissimi custodiat vos a peccatis. R̸. Amen.

May the Holy Ghost descend upon you, and may the power of the Most High preserve you from sins. R̸. Amen.

Then, signing himself with the sign of the cross, from his forehead to his breast, he says:

℣. Adjutorium nostrum in nomine Domini.

℟. Qui fecit cœlum et terram.

℣. Domine, exaudi orationem meam.

℟. Et clamor meus ad te veniat.

℣. Dominus vobiscum.

℟. Et cum spiritu tuo.

℣. Our help is in the name of the Lord.

℟. Who hath made heaven and earth.

℣. O Lord, hear my prayer.

℟. And let my cry come unto Thee.

℣. The Lord be with you.

℟. And with thy spirit.

Then, with hands extended toward those to be confirmed, he says:

Oremus.

Omnipotens, sempiterne Deus, qui regenerare dignatus es hos famulos tuos ex aqua, et Spiritu Sancto, quique dedisti eis remissionem omnium peccatorum, emitte in eos septiformem Spiritum tuum Sanctum Paraclitum de cœlis.

Let us pray.

Almighty and eternal God, Who hast vouchsafed to regenerate these Thy servants by water and the Holy Ghost, and hast given unto them forgiveness of all their sins: send forth from heaven upon them Thy sevenfold Spirit, the holy Comforter.

℟. Amen.

℣. Spiritum sapientiæ et intellectus.

℟. Amen.

℣. Spiritum consilii et fortitudinis.

℟. Amen.

℣. Spiritum scientiæ et pietatis.

℟. Amen.

Adimple eos spiritu timoris tui, et consigna eos signo crucis ✠ Christi, in vitam propitiatus æternam. Per eundem Dominum nostrum Jesum Christum Filium tuum, qui tecum vivit et regnat in unitate ejusdem Spiritus Sancti Deus, per omnia sæcula sæculorum.

℟. Amen.

℟. Amen.

℣. The Spirit of wisdom and understanding.

℟. Amen.

℣. The Spirit of counsel and fortitude.

℟. Amen.

℣. The Spirit of knowledge and piety.

℟. Amen.

Fill them with the spirit of Thy fear, and sign them with the sign of the cross ✠ of Christ, in Thy mercy, unto life eternal. Through the same Our Lord Jesus Christ, Thy Son, Who liveth and reigneth with Thee in the unity of the same Holy Ghost, God, world without end.

℟. Amen.

The bishop, sitting on the faldstool, or, if the number of persons to be confirmed requires it, standing, with his miter on his head, confirms them, arranged in rows and kneeling in order. He inquires separately the name of each person to be confirmed, who is presented to him by the godfather or godmother, kneeling; and having dipped the end of the thumb of his right hand in chrism, he says:

N., signo te signo crucis, ✠

N., I sign thee with the sign of the cross, ✠

Whilst saying these words he makes the sign of the cross, with his thumb, on the forehead of the person to be confirmed, and then says:

Et confirmo te chrismate salutis. In no- mine Patris, ✠ et Filii, ✠ et Spiritus ✠ Sancti. ℞. Amen.

And I confirm thee with the chrism of salvation. In the name of the Father, ✠ and of the Son, ✠ and of the Holy ✠ Ghost. ℞. Amen.

Then he strikes him gently on the cheek, saying:

Pax tecum.

Peace be with thee.

When all have been confirmed, the bishop wipes his hands with breadcrumbs, and washes them over a basin. In the meantime, the following Antiphon is sung or read by the clergy:

Confirma hoc, Deus, quod operatus es in nobis, a templo sancto tuo, quod est in Jerusalem.
℣ Gloria Patri, etc.

Confirm, O God, that which Thou hast wrought in us, from Thy holy temple which is in Jerusalem.
℣. Glory be to the Father, etc.

Then the Antiphon Confirm, O God *is repeated; after which the bishop, laying aside his miter, rises up, and standing toward the altar, with his hands joined before his breast, says:*

Ostende nobis, Domine, misericordiam tuam.
℞. Et salutare tuum da nobis.
℣. Domine, exaudi orationem meam.
℞. Et clamor meus ad te veniat.
℣. Dominus vobiscum.
℞. Et cum spiritu tuo.

O Lord, show Thy mercy upon us.
℞. And grant us Thy salvation.
℣. O Lord, hear my prayer.
℞. And let my cry come unto Thee.
℣. The Lord be with you.
℞. And with thy spirit.

Then, with his hands still joined before his breast, and all the persons confirmed devoutly kneeling, he says:

Oremus.

Deus, qui Apostolis tuis Sanctum dedisti Spiritum, et per eos, eorum-que successores, cæteris fidelibus tradendum esse voluisti; respice propitius ad humilitatis nostræ famulatum, et præsta; ut eorum corda, quorum frontes sacro chris-mate delinivimus, et signo sanctæ crucis signavimus, idem Spiritus Sanctus in eis superveniens, tem-plum gloriæ suæ dignanter inhab-itando perficiat. Qui, cum Patre et eodem Spiritu Sancto, vivis et regnas Deus, in sæcula sæculorum. ℞. Amen.

Let us pray.

O God, Who didst give to Thine apostles the Holy Ghost, and didst ordain that by them and their suc-cessors He should be given to the rest of the faithful; look mercifully upon our unworthy service; and grant that the hearts of those whose foreheads we have anointed with holy chrism, and signed with the sign of the holy cross, may, by the same Holy Spirit coming down upon them, and graciously abiding within them, be made the temple of His glory. Who, with the Father and the same Holy Ghost, livest and reignest, God, world without end. ℞. Amen.

Then he says:

Ecce sic benedicetur omnis homo, qui timet Dominum.

Behold, thus shall every man be blessed that feareth the Lord.

And turning to the persons confirmed, he makes over them the sign of the cross, saying:

Benedicat ✠ vos Dominus ex Sion, ut videatis bona Jerusalem omnibus diebus vitæ vestræ, et habeatis vitam æternam. ℞. Amen.

May the Lord ✠ bless you out of Sion, that you may see the good things of Jerusalem all the days of your life, and may have life everlasting. ℞. Amen.

PRAYERS FOR THE SEVEN GIFTS OF THE HOLY GHOST

The Spirit of Wisdom

Come, O Blessed Spirit of *wisdom,* and reveal to my soul the mysteries of heavenly things, their exceeding greatness, and power, and beauty. Teach me to love them above and beyond all the passing joys and satisfactions of earth. Show me the way by which I may be able to attain to them, and possess them, and hold them hereafter, mine own forever. *Amen.*

The Spirit of Understanding

Come, O Blessed Spirit of *understanding,* enlighten my mind, that I may perceive and embrace all the mysteries of the deep things of God; that in the end I may be found worthy in Thy light clearly to see the eternal Light, and may come unto a perfect knowledge of Thee, and of the Father, and of the Son. *Amen.*

The Spirit of Counsel

Come, O Blessed Spirit of *counsel,* help and guide me in all my ways, that I may always do Thy holy will. Incline my heart to that which is good, turn it away from all that is evil, and direct me by the straight path of Thy commandments to that goal of eternal life for which I long. *Amen.*

The Spirit of Fortitude

Come, O Blessed Spirit of *fortitude,* uphold my soul in every time of trouble or adversity. Sustain all my efforts after holiness; strengthen my weakness, give me courage against all the assaults of my enemies, that I may never be overcome, and separated from Thee, my God, my chiefest Good. *Amen.*

The Spirit of Knowledge

Come, O Blessed Spirit of *knowledge,* grant that I may perceive and know the will of the Father; show me the nothingness of earthly things, that I may know their vanity, and use them only for Thy glory, and my own salvation, looking ever beyond them to Thee, and Thy eternal great rewards. *Amen.*

The Spirit of Piety

Come, O Blessed Spirit of *piety,* possess my heart, incline it to a true faith in Thee, to a holy love of Thee, my God, that with my whole soul I may seek Thee, and find Thee my best, my truest joy. *Amen.*

The Spirit of the Fear of the Lord

Come, O Blessed Spirit of holy *fear*, penetrate my inmost heart, that I may set Thee, my Lord and God, before my face forever; and shun all things that can offend Thee, so that I may be made worthy to appear before the pure eyes of Thy divine Majesty in the heaven of heavens, where Thou livest and reignest in the unity of the ever Blessed Trinity, God, world without end. *Amen.*

PRAYER FOR THE TWELVE FRUITS OF THE HOLY GHOST

O Holy Spirit, eternal Love of the Father and of the Son, grant me to taste the sweetness of Thy loving kindness: the fruit of *charity*, that I may love Thee above all things, and my neighbor as myself; the fruit of *joy*, that I may be filled with a holy consolation; the fruit of *peace*, that I may enjoy inward tranquility of soul; the fruit of *patience*, that I may not be discouraged by delay, but may persevere in prayer; the fruit of *benignity*, that I may be kind and considerate to all men; the fruit of *goodness*, that I may be ever ready to do good to all; the fruit of *long-suffering*, that I may humbly submit to everything that is opposed to my own desires; the fruit of *mildness*, that I may subdue every rising of evil temper, and, so far from offering the least injury, may never return the greatest; the fruit of *faith*, that I may rightly receive the word of truth, and walk in it; the fruit of *modesty*, that I may be holy in my thoughts, watchful in my words, and grave in all my behavior; the fruit of *continency*, that, using Thy creatures to Thy glory, I may keep my body in subjection; the fruit of *chastity*, that, with a pure body and a clean heart, I may adore and please Thee to my life's end; so that, having served Thee faithfully here on earth, I may attain in Christ Jesus to praise Thee eternally in heaven, with the Father and the Son, three Persons, one glorious and eternal God, to Whom be glory now and evermore. Amen.

ON THE ANNIVERSARY OF CONFIRMATION

Thanks be unto Thee, O my God, for all Thy infinite goodness, and especially for that love that Thou hast showed unto me at my Confirmation. I give Thee thanks that Thou didst then send down Thy Holy Spirit into my soul with all His gifts and graces. O may He take full possession of me forever: may His divine unction cause my face to shine: may His heavenly *wisdom* reign in my heart, His *understanding* enlighten my darkness, His *counsel* guide me, His *fortitude* strengthen me, His *knowledge* instruct me, His *piety* make me fervent, His divine *fear* keep me from all evil. Drive from my soul, O Lord, all that may defile it. Give me grace to be Thy faithful soldier, that, having fought the good fight of faith, I may be brought to the crown of everlasting life, for the merits of Thy dearly beloved Son, our Savior, Jesus Christ. *Amen.*

The Sacrament of Matrimony

INSTRUCTIONS

The holy state of Matrimony was instituted by Almighty God in the beginning of the world, and under the law of nature had a particular blessing annexed to it. "God created man to His own image: to the image of God He created them: male and female He created them. And God blessed them, saying: Increase and multiply, and fill the earth" (Gn 1:27–28). Under the Mosaic Law, the Almighty more distinctly announced its dignity and obligations. Afterward, under the Christian Law, our divine Redeemer sanctified this state still more, and from a natural and civil contract raised Matrimony to the dignity of a Sacrament. And St. Paul declared it to be a representation of that sacred union which Jesus Christ had formed with His spouse the Church. "This mystery is great, but I say in Christ, and in the Church" (Eph 5:32).

Seeing, therefore, that this state is so very holy, and instituted for such great and holy ends, and, moreover, that it has so great a grace annexed to it (when the Sacrament of Matrimony is worthily received) as to put the married couple into the way of being happy both in this world and in the world to come, they who intend to enter into this state ought to proceed with the greatest prudence and make the best possible preparation, that they may obtain these precious and abundant graces from Almighty God.

1. They ought to enter into this holy state with the pure intention of promoting the honor and glory of God, and the sanctification of their own souls.

2. They ought to select a person of their own religion; experience shows that a want of union in faith between husband and wife is frequently attended with the worst consequences, both to themselves and to their children. A Catholic cannot, without special dispensation, lawfully marry a person of another religion; and if, for good reason, such marriage is permitted, the Catholic party cannot enter into an agreement that any of the children shall be brought up in any other than the Catholic Faith, and the non-Catholic party must make beforehand a positive and solemn promise: 1st, that no obstacle of any kind shall be put in the way of the practice of all Catholic duties by the Catholic party; and, 2nd, that all the children who shall be born to them shall be baptized and brought up as Catholics.

3. They must obtain the pardon of their sins by worthily approaching the Sacrament of Penance, and then sanctify their marriage by the fervent reception of the Holy Communion.

4. The Marriage should be celebrated *in the morning,* and with a *Nuptial Mass.* That this is the constant and universal and emphatic desire of holy Church, the following quotations from the decrees and from the pastoral letter of the Third Plenary Council of Baltimore very clearly show:

"Let those who have the care of souls take every occasion earnestly to exhort the faithful to the keeping of that pious and praiseworthy custom of the Church whereby Marriages are celebrated, not in the nighttime, but during Mass, and accompanied by the *Nuptial Blessing*.... This custom is held to be not merely a commendable but quite a necessary one, now in these present days, when the foes of religion are leaving nothing untried in their efforts to deprive, if possible, Holy Matrimony of all sanctity, and of all likeness to a Sacrament, and to degrade it to the level of a mere civil contract."[32]

"Let them enter into Marriage only through worthy and holy motives, with the blessings of religion, especially with the blessing of the *Nuptial Mass*."[33]

5. They ought frequently to reflect on their duties and obligations as inculcated in the Word of God.

St. Paul, strongly inculcating these duties by the great example of Christ and His Church, says:

"Let women be subject to their husbands, as to the Lord; because man is head of the woman, as Christ is Head of the Church; Himself is Savior of His Body. But as the Church is subject to Christ, so also women to their husbands in all things. Husbands, love your wives, as Christ also hath loved the Church, and delivered Himself up for it.... So, also, the men ought to love their wives as their own bodies. He who loveth his wife, loveth himself. For no man ever hated his own flesh, but he nourisheth and cherisheth it, as also Christ the Church.... For this cause man shall leave his father and mother, and shall cleave to his wife, and they two shall be one flesh. This mystery is great, but I say in Christ, and in the Church. Nevertheless, let you also severally each love his wife, as he loveth himself: and let the wife fear her husband" (Eph 5:22–33).

IMPEDIMENTS TO MARRIAGE

From the earliest ages, holy Church has annexed certain conditions to the matrimonial contract, which are called *impediments*. They are of two kinds: 1) *annulling impediments*, or those which, without special dispensation, make a marriage null and void from the beginning; 2) *prohibitory impediments*, which, without dispensation, make a marriage unlawful and sinful, though not invalid.

I. THE ANNULLING IMPEDIMENTS

1. *Consanguinity*. This forbids marriage between third cousins or any nearer degree of kindred.

2. *Affinity*. By this it is forbidden to marry the third cousin, or any nearer blood-relation, of a deceased husband or wife. *Spiritual affinity* is a species of relationship, contracted by means of the Sacraments of Baptism and Confirmation, whereby parents cannot marry the sponsors of the child, or the person who baptized it; nor can sponsors marry their godchildren.

[32] Decrees, no. 125.
[33] Pastoral Letter, p. 87.

3. *Public honesty.* This prohibits marriage with a parent, child, brother, or sister of a person with whom a valid *engagement to marry* has existed.

4. *Crime.* Persons (of whom one at least must be already married) who are guilty of homicide or adultery with a view to a subsequent marriage cannot marry each other.

5. *Difference of worship.* This renders marriage null and void between a baptized and an unbaptized person.

6. *Vows.* This makes marriage impossible to all persons who have made solemn vows by entering into a religious order; and to all the orders of the clergy, from subdeacons upward.

7. *Clandestinity.* Wherever the decree of the Council of Trent concerning Matrimony has been published, marriage between two Catholics is not only unlawful but invalid without the presence of the parish priest and two witnesses. This decree is in force in the following places in the United States: 1) The Province of New Orleans. 2) The Province of San Francisco, and Utah Territory, except the part lying east of the Colorado River. 3) The Province of Santa Fe, except the northern part of Colorado Territory. 4) The Diocese of Vincennes. 5) The city of St. Louis, and the parishes of St. Genevieve, St. Ferdinand, and St. Charles in the Diocese of St. Louis. 6) The parishes of Kaskaskia, Cahokia, French Village, and Prairie du Rocher, in the Diocese of Alton.

8. *The bond of a previous marriage.* This is an impediment which death alone can remove. "What, therefore, God hath joined together let not man put asunder" (Mt 19:6). No court, no judge, no legislature, no power on earth, can break the bond which unites husband and wife. For certain just causes, especially for the crime of adultery, they may *live separately,* but they are still married and cannot marry again. Let it be remembered that no so-called divorce, no guilt, no desertion, can ever sever the marriage bond. Nothing but a *certain knowledge* of the death of one party can make it lawful for the other to marry.

II. THE PROHIBITORY IMPEDIMENTS

1. *A simple vow* to preserve chastity, to enter the priesthood or into a religious order.

2. *A previous valid engagement* to marry any person.

3. Impediments arising from a *prohibition of the Church*, such as: 1) the *solemnization* of marriage (in other words, to marry with outward pomp and festivity) during Advent or Lent. 2) *Mixed marriages*—the union of a Catholic with one who is not a Catholic. (See paragraph 2 in "Instructions" above.)

4. The *non-consent of parents*, when consent is withheld for good and just reasons.

In addition to these, there are a few other impediments which are not generally likely to occur. With regard to all such matters, it is very important to consult the priest when arranging for the marriage.

THE PUBLICATION OF THE BANNS

In order to place a check upon clandestine marriages, to discover any impediments which may exist, to prevent deceptions and surprises, to afford parents and others interested an opportunity to interpose, if needful, and in order to procure the prayers of the faithful that God may give light, grace, and prosperity to the contracting parties, the Council of Trent has decreed that "the promise of marriage be published on three successive Sundays or holy days, at the principal Mass, by the parish priest of the parties."[34]

This is a very important law, and imposes very serious obligations. Bishops can, and for good and sufficient reason do, dispense with this law. Catholics should remember that it is a mortal sin to marry unless such dispensation is procured or the banns published in regular form. There can be no doubt that if anyone knows of an impediment in the way of a proposed marriage, he is in duty bound to reveal it.

PRAYER OF ONE ABOUT TO BE MARRIED

O gracious Father, Who dost bless us by Thy bounty, pardon us by Thy mercy, support and guide us by Thy grace, and govern us by Thy providence: I give Thee humble and hearty thanks for all the mercies which I have received at Thy hands in time past. And now, since Thou hast called me to the holy estate of Marriage, be pleased to be with me in my entering into it and passing through it, that it may not be a state of temptation or sorrow to me by occasion of my sins or infirmities, but of holiness and comfort, of love and dutifulness, as Thou hast intended it to be to all that love and fear Thy holy name. *Amen.*

Here may be said Psalm 121 (*p. 162*).

THE RITUAL FOR THE CELEBRATION OF MATRIMONY

The priest, vested in a surplice and white stole (but vested as for Mass, yet without maniple, if the Nuptial Mass is to follow), attended by an acolyte holding a vessel of holy water, asks, in the vernacular, in the hearing of two or three witnesses, the man and the woman separately, as follows, concerning their consent. And first he asks the bridegroom, who must stand at the right hand of the bride:

N., wilt thou take N. here present, for thy lawful wife, according to the rite of our holy Mother the Church?
℞. I will.

---

[34] Session 24.

Then the priest asks the bride:
N., wilt thou take N. here present, for thy lawful husband, according to the rite of our holy Mother the Church?
℟. I will.

The consent of one is not sufficient; it should be expressed by both, and there should be some sensible sign thereof. Having obtained this mutual consent, the priest bids the man and woman join their right hands.

[*In places where it is customary, the man and woman pledge themselves one to the other as follows, repeating these words after the priest:*
The man first says:

I, N. N., take thee, N. N., for my lawful wife, to have and to hold, from this day forward, for better, for worse, for richer, for poorer, in sickness and in health, until death do us part.

Then the woman says after the priest:
I, N. N., take thee, N. N., for my lawful husband, to have and to hold, from this day forward, for better, for worse, for richer, for poorer, in sickness and in health, until death do us part.]

The priest then says:

Ego conjungo vos in matrimonium, in nomine Patris, ✠ et Filii, et Spiritus Sancti. Amen.	I join you together in Marriage, in the name of the Father, ✠ and of the Son, and of the Holy Ghost. Amen.

He then sprinkles them with holy water.

This done, the priest blesses the ring, saying:

Adjutorium nostrum in nomine Domini.	Our help is in the name of the Lord.
℟. Qui fecit cœlum et terram.	℟. Who hath made heaven and earth.
℣. Domine, exaudi orationem meam.	℣. O Lord, hear my prayer.
℟. Et clamor meus ad te veniat.	℟. And let my cry come unto Thee.
℣. Dominus vobiscum.	℣. The Lord be with you.
℟. Et cum spiritu tuo.	℟. And with thy spirit.

Oremus.

Benedic, ✠ Domine, anulum hunc, quem nos in tuo nomine benedicimus, ✠ ut quæ eum gestaverit, fidelitatem integram suo sponso tenens, in pace et voluntate tua permaneat, atque in mutua charitate semper vivat. Per Christum Dominum nostrum. ℟. Amen.

Let us pray.

Bless, ✠ O Lord, this ring, which we bless ✠ in Thy name, that she who shall wear it, keeping faith unchanged with her husband, may abide in peace and obedience to Thy will, and ever live in mutual love. Through Christ Our Lord. ℟. Amen.

Then the priest sprinkles the ring with holy water, in the form of a cross; and the bridegroom, having received the ring from the hand of the priest, places it on the third finger of the left hand of the bride.

[In some places the bridegroom says after the priest:
With this ring I thee wed, and I plight unto thee my troth.]

The priest then says:

In nomine Patris, ✠ et Filii, et Spiritus Sancti. Amen.

In the name of the Father, ✠ and of the Son, and of the Holy Ghost. Amen.

This done, the priest adds:

℣. Confirma hoc, Deus, quod operatus es in nobis.

℟. A templo sancto tuo, quod est in Jerusalem.

℣. Confirm, O God, that which Thou hast wrought in us.

℟. From Thy holy temple which is in Jerusalem.

℣. Kyrie, eleison.
℟. Christe, eleison.
℣. Kyrie, eleison. Pater noster (*secreto*).

℣. Lord, have mercy.
℟. Christ, have mercy.
℣. Lord, have mercy. Our Father (*inaudibly*).

℣. Et ne nos inducas in tentationem.
℟. Sed libera nos a malo.
℣. Salvos fac servos tuos,
℟. Deus meus, sperantes in te.

℣. And lead us not into temptation.
℟. But deliver us from evil.
℣. Save Thy servants,
℟. O my God, who put their trust in Thee.

℣. Mitte eis, Domine, auxilium de sancto.
℟. Et de Sion tuere eos.
℣. Esto eis, Domine, turris fortitudinis.

℣. Send them help, O Lord, from Thy holy place.
℟. And defend them out of Sion.
℣. Be unto them, O Lord, a tower of strength

℟. A facie inimici.

℟. From the face of the enemy.

℣. Domine, exaudi orationem meam.

℟. Et clamor meus at te veniat.

℣. Dominus vobiscum.

℟. Et cum spiritu tuo.

Oremus.

Respice, quæsumus, Domine, super hos famulos tuos: et institutis tuis, quibus propagationem humani generis ordinasti, benignus assiste; ut qui te auctore junguntur, te auxiliante serventur. Per Christum Dominum nostrum. ℟. Amen.

℣. O Lord, hear my prayer.

℟. And let my cry come unto Thee.

℣. The Lord be with you.

℟. And with thy spirit.

Let us pray.

Look down, we beseech Thee, O Lord, upon these Thy servants, and graciously protect this Thine ordinance, whereby Thou hast provided for the propagation of mankind; that those who are joined together by Thine authority may be preserved by Thy help. Through Christ Our Lord. ℟. Amen.

After this, if the Nuptial Benediction is to be given, the Mass is said pro Sponso et Sponsa, *as below; at which the newly married parties are present, kneeling at the altar rail (or on faldstools, according to custom), the man on the right, and the woman on the left.*

THE MASS FOR THE BRIDEGROOM AND BRIDE

[*For the* Ordinary of the Mass, *see p. 86.*]

THE INTROIT.

Deus Israel conjungat vos: et ipse sit vobiscum, qui misertus est duobus unicis: et nunc, Domine, fac eos plenius benedicere te.

℣. Beati omnes qui timent Dominum: qui ambulant in viis ejus.

℣. Gloria Patri, etc.

Deus Israel conjungat vos: et ipse sit vobiscum, qui misertus est duobus unicis: et nunc, Domine, fac eos plenius benedicere te.

May the God of Israel join you together: and may He be with you Who was merciful to two only children: and now, O Lord, make them bless Thee more fully.

℣. Blessed are all they that fear the Lord: that walk in His ways.

℣. Glory be to the Father, etc.

May the God of Israel join you together: and may He be with you Who was merciful to two only children: and now, O Lord, make them bless Thee more fully.

THE COLLECT.

Exaudi nos, omnipotens et misericors Deus: ut quod nostro ministratur officio, tua benedictione potius impleatur. Per Dominum nostrum Jesum Christum, etc.

Graciously hear us, Almighty and merciful God, that what is performed by our ministry may be abundantly filled with Thy blessing. Through Our Lord Jesus Christ, etc.

THE EPISTLE. Eph 5:22–33.

Fratres: Mulieres viris suis subditæ sint, sicut Domino: quoniam vir caput est mulieris: sicut Christus caput est Ecclesiæ: Ipse, salvator corporis ejus. Sed sicut Ecclesia subjecta est Christo, ita et mulieres viris suis in omnibus. Viri, diligite uxores vestras, sicut et Christus dilexit Ecclesiam, et seipsum tradidit pro ea, ut illam sanctificaret, mundans lavacro aquæ in verbo vitæ, ut exhiberet ipse sibi gloriosam Ecclesiam, non habentem maculam, aut rugam, aut aliquid hujusmodi, sed ut sit sancta et immaculata. Ita et viri debent diligere uxores suas, ut corpora sua. Qui suam uxorem diligit, seipsum diligit. Nemo enim unquam carnem suam odio habuit: sed nutrit, et fovet eam, sicut et Christus Ecclesiam: quia membra sumus corporis ejus, de carne ejus, et de ossibus ejus. Propter hoc relinquet homo patrem et matrem suam, et adhærebit uxori suæ: et erunt duo in carne una. Sacramentum hoc magnum est, ego autem dico in Christo, et in Ecclesia. Verumtamen et vos singuli, unusquisque uxorem suam, sicut seipsum diligat: uxor autem timeat virum suum.

Let women be subject to their husbands, as to the Lord; because man is head of the woman, as Christ is Head of the Church: Himself is Savior of His Body. But as the Church is subject to Christ, so also women to their husbands in all things. Husbands, love your wives, as Christ also hath loved the Church, and delivered Himself up for it, that He might sanctify it, cleansing it with the laver of water in the word of life, that He Himself might present to Himself a glorious Church, not having spot or wrinkle, or any such thing, but that it may be holy, and without blemish. So also the men ought to love their wives, as their own bodies. He who loveth his wife, loveth himself. For no man ever hated his own flesh, but he nourisheth and cherisheth it, as also Christ the Church: for we are members of His body, of His flesh, and of His bones. For this cause man shall leave his father and mother, and shall cleave to his wife, and they two shall be one flesh. This mystery is great, but I say in Christ, and in the Church. Nevertheless, let you also severally each love his wife as he loveth himself; and let the wife fear her husband.

THE GRADUAL.

Uxor tua sicut vitis abundans in lateri-bus domus tuæ.	Thy wife shall be as a fruitful vine on the walls of thy house.
℣. Filii tui sicut novellæ olivarum in circuitu mensæ tuæ.	℣. Thy children as olive plants round about thy table.
Alleluia, alleluia. ℣. Mittat vobis Dominus auxilium de sancto: et de Sion tueatur vos. Alleluia.	Alleluia, alleluia. ℣. May the Lord send you help from the sanctuary, and defend you out of Sion. Alleluia.

After Septuagesima, *instead of* Alleluia *and* ℣. *is said the*

TRACT.

Ecce sic benedicetur omnis homo, qui timet Dominum.	Behold, thus shall every man be blessed that feareth the Lord.
℣. Benedicat tibi Dominus ex Sion: et videas bona Jerusalem omnibus die-bus vitæ tuæ.	℣. May the Lord bless thee out of Sion; and mayest thou see the good things of Jerusalem all the days of thy life.
℣. Et videas filios filiorum tuorum: pax super Israel.	℣. And mayest thou see thy children's children: peace upon Israel.

At Eastertide *the* Gradual *is omitted, and in its place is said:*

Alleluia, Alleluia.	Alleluia, Alleluia.
℣. Mittat vobis Dominus auxilium de sancto: et de Sion tueatur vos. Alleluia.	℣. May the Lord send you help from the sanctuary: and defend you out of Sion. Alleluia.
℣. Benedicat vobis Dominus ex Sion: qui fecit cœlum et terram. Alleluia.	℣. May the Lord bless you out of Sion: Who hath made heaven and earth. Alleluia.

THE GOSPEL. Mt 19:3–6.

In illo tempore: Accesserunt ad Jesum Pharisæi tentantes eum, et dicentes: Si licet homini dimittere uxorem suam quacumque ex causa? Qui respondens, ait eis: Non legistis, quia qui fecit hominem ab initio, masculum et feminam fecit eos? et dixit: Propter hoc dimittet homo patrem et matrem, et adhærebit uxori suæ, et erunt duo in carne una. Itaque jam non sunt duo, sed una caro. Quod ergo Deus conjunxit, homo non separet.

At that time there came to Jesus the Pharisees, tempting Him, and saying: Is it lawful for a man to put away his wife for every cause? And He answered and said to them: Have ye not read, that He Who made man from the beginning, made them male and female? and said: For this cause shall a man leave father and mother, and shall cleave to his wife, and the two shall be one flesh. Therefore, now they are not two, but one flesh. What therefore God hath joined together, let not man put asunder.

THE OFFERTORY.

In te speravi, Domine: dixi: Tu es Deus meus: in manibus tuis tempora mea.

In Thee, O Lord, have I put my trust: I said, Thou art my God: my lot is in Thy hands.

THE SECRET PRAYER.

Suscipe, quæsumus, Domine, pro sacra connubii lege munus oblatum: et, cujus largitor es operis, esto dispositor. Per Dominum nostrum Jesum Christum, etc.

Receive, we beseech Thee, O Lord, the gift which we here offer up in behalf of Thy holy law of Marriage: and as Thou art the Giver of the work, be Thou also the Disposer thereof. Through Our Lord Jesus Christ, etc.

After the Pater noster *the priest standing at the Epistle side of the altar, and turning toward the bridegroom and bride, who kneel before the altar, says over them the following prayers:*

Oremus.

Propitiare, Domine, supplicationibus nostris, et institutis tuis, quibus propagationem humani generis ordinasti, benignus assiste: ut, quod te auctore jungitur, te auxiliante servetur. Per Dominum nostrum Jesus Christum, etc. ℟. Amen.

Let us pray.

Be favorable, O Lord, unto our prayers, and graciously protect Thine ordinance, whereby Thou hast provided for the propagation of mankind; that what is now joined together by Thine authority may be preserved by Thy help. Through Our Lord Jesus Christ, etc. ℟. Amen.

Oremus.

Deus, qui potestate virtutis tuæ de nihilo cuncta fecisti: qui dispositis universitatis exordiis, homini ad imaginem Dei facto, ideo inseparabile mulieris adjutorium condidisti, ut femineo corpori de virili dares carne principium, docens quod ex uno placuisset institui, numquam licere disjungi: Deus, qui tam excellenti mysterio conjugalem copulam consecrasti, ut Christi et Ecclesiæ sacramentum præsignares in fœdere nuptiarum: Deus, per quem mulier jungitur viro, et societas principaliter ordinata, ea benedictione donatur, quæ sola nec per originalis peccati pœnam, nec per diluvii est ablata sententiam: respice propitius super hanc famulam tuam, quæ maritali jungenda consortio, tua se expetit protectione muniri: sit in ea jugum dilectionis, et pacis: fidelis et casta nubat in Christo, imitatrixque sanctarum permaneat feminarum:

Let us pray.

O God, Who by the might of Thy power didst make all things out of nothing; Who, when the foundations of the world were laid, and man was made in the image of God, didst so ordain the inseparable aid of woman, as to give her body its origin from that of man: teaching thereby that what it had pleased Thee to fashion out of one could never be lawfully put asunder: O God, Who hast consecrated wedlock to so excellent a mystery, that in the marriage covenant Thou wouldst foreshow the mysterious union of Christ with His Church: O God, by Whom woman is joined to man, and that union, established in the beginning, is gifted with a blessing, which alone was not taken away, either in punishment of Original Sin, or by the sentence of the Flood: look graciously down upon this Thy handmaid, now about to be joined in marriage, who heartily desires to be strengthened by Thy protection: may it be to her a yoke of love and peace; faithful and chaste may she marry in Christ, and be a follower of holy matrons;

sit amabilis viro suo, ut Rachel: sapiens, ut Rebecca: longæva et fidelis, ut Sara: nihil in ea ex actibus suis ille auctor prævaricationis usurpet; nexa fidei, mandatisque permaneat; uni thoro juncta, contactus illicitos fugiat; muniat infirmitatem suam robore disciplinæ: sit verecundia gravis, pudore venerabilis, doctrinis cælestibus erudita: sit fœcunda in sobole, sit probata et innocens: et ad beatorum requiem, atque ad cœlestia regna perveniat: et videant ambo filios filiorum suorum, usque in tertiam et quartam generationem, et ad optatam perveniant senectutem. Per eundem Dominum nostrum Jesum Christum, Filium tuum, qui tecum vivit et regnat in unitate Spiritus Sancti Deus, per omni sæcula sæculorum. Amen.

may she be pleasing to her husband like Rachel, wise like Rebecca, long-lived and faithful like Sarah. In none of her deeds may that first author of transgression have any share; may she abide firmly knit unto the faith and the commandments; joined in one union, may she remain ever constant thereto; may she fortify her weakness by the strength of a chastened life; in shamefacedness be grave, in modesty worthy of respect, in heavenly doctrines learned; may she be fruitful in offspring; may she be approved and blameless; and attain unto the rest of the blessed, and unto the heavenly kingdom; that they both see their children's children unto the third and fourth generation, and arrive at a happy old age. Through the same Our Lord Jesus Christ Thy Son, Who liveth and reigneth with Thee in the unity of the Holy Ghost, God, world without end. ℞. Amen.

THE COMMUNION.

Ecce sic benedicetur omnis homo, qui timet Dominum: et videas filios filiorum tuorum: pax super Israel.

Behold, thus shall every man be blessed that feareth the Lord: and mayest thou see thy children's children: peace upon Israel.

THE POSTCOMMUNION.

Quæsumus, omnipotens Deus: instituta providentiæ tuæ pio favore comitare; ut, quos legitima societate connectis, longæva pace custodias. Per Dominum nostrum Jesum Christum, etc.

We beseech Thee, O God Almighty, to accompany with Thy gracious favor what Thy providence hath ordained; and preserve in continual peace those whom Thou hast joined in lawful union. Through Our Lord Jesus Christ, etc.

After the Benedicamus Domino, *the priest turns toward the bridegroom and bride, and says:*

Deus Abraham, Deus Isaac, et Deus Jacob sit vobiscum: et ipse adimpleat benedictionem suam in vobis: ut videatis filios filiorum vestrorum usque ad tertiam et quartam generationem, et postea vitam æternam habeatis sine fine: adjuvante Domino nostro Jesu Christo, qui cum Patre et Spiritu Sancto vivit et regnat Deus, per omnia sæcula sæculorum. ℟. Amen.	May the God of Abraham, the God of Isaac, and the God of Jacob be with you, and may He fulfill His blessing upon you; that you may see your children's children unto the third and fourth generation; and may afterward have everlasting life, without end, by the help of Our Lord Jesus Christ, Who, with the Father and the Holy Ghost, liveth and reigneth God world without end. ℟. Amen.

He then sprinkles them with holy water. Afterward, bowing down before the altar, he says the Placeat, *gives the Blessing, and ends the Mass as usual.*

THE MANNER OF ASSISTING AT MIXED MARRIAGES

The priest, having obtained the proper dispensation for the marriage of a Catholic with a non-Catholic, should assure himself that the Catholic party shall not in anywise be impeded in the practice of the Catholic religion; that there shall be no probable danger of perversion; that the Catholic party shall endeavor with all earnestness to bring the non-Catholic spouse to the knowledge of the Truth; and that all children which may bless the union shall be baptized and brought up in the Catholic Faith.

The ceremony of a mixed marriage is not to be performed in a church, but usually in some convenient room in the rectory (or elsewhere, by special permission of the ordinary). No sacred vestment may be used, nor prayer said, nor blessing given. The priest, about to assist at such marriage, first asks the man concerning his consent, as follows:
N., wilt thou take N., here present, for thy lawful wife?
℟. I will.

Then the priest asks the woman:
N., wilt thou take N., here present, for thy lawful husband?
℟. I will.

Then, with right hands joined, they pledge themselves each to the other, repeating these words after the priest:
The man first says:

I, N. N., take thee, N. N., for my lawful wife, to have and to hold, from this day forward, for better, for worse, for richer, for poorer, in sickness and in health, until death do us part.

Then the woman says:
I, N. N., take thee, N. N., for my lawful husband, to have and to hold, from this day forward, for better, for worse, for richer, for poorer, in sickness and in health, until death do us part.

This done, the priest says:
By the authority committed to me, I pronounce you united in the bonds of Matrimony.

The bridegroom then places the ring on the third finger of the left hand of the bride, saying after the priest:
With this ring I thee wed, and I plight unto thee my troth.

Afterward the priest may, at his discretion, address some suitable remarks to the married couple: recalling to their minds the indissoluble nature of the marriage bond; the peculiar sanctity of this estate; the harmony and mutual love which should prevail therein; and especially the solicitude which each should manifest to know the will of God, that, by constantly and faithfully fulfilling the same, they may attain unto everlasting salvation.

A HUSBAND'S PRAYER

O gracious Father, Maker and Preserver of heaven and earth, Who in the beginning didst institute Matrimony, thereby foreshadowing the mystical union of the Church with our Savior Christ, Who, in the time of His ministry upon earth, did honor marriage with His first miracle: enable me, I pray Thee, by Thy grace to live in holiness and purity with the wife whom Thou hast given me. Mortify in me all violence of earthly passion, all selfishness and inconsiderateness (*here name any besetting sin which may be a hindrance to you*), that I may love her as Christ loved His Church, cherish and comfort her as my own body, and have as great care for her happiness as for my own. Grant that we may live in peace, without contention; in unity, without discord. [Give us, O Lord, discreet hearts and understanding minds, to bring up our children in Thy faith and fear, that they may be obedient to Thee and to Thy commandments, and to all that Thou requirest of them in duty toward their parents.] And give us, O Lord, a competency of estate, to maintain ourselves and our family according to that rank and calling wherein Thou hast placed us, without excess or vainglory, in singleness and pureness of heart. Grant this for Jesus Christ's sake, to Whom with Thee and the Holy Ghost, be all honor and glory, now and forever. *Amen.*

A WIFE'S PRAYER

O merciful Lord God, Who in the beginning didst take Eve out of the side of Adam and didst give her to him as a helpmate: give me grace to live worthy of the honorable estate of Matrimony to which Thou hast called me, that I may love my husband with a pure and chaste love, acknowledging him as my head, and truly reverencing and obeying him in all good things; that thereby I may please him, and live with him in all Christian quietness. Keep me from all worldliness and vanity. Help me, O Lord, that I may, under him, prudently and discreetly guide and govern his household. Let no fault of mine aggravate any sins by which he may be especially tempted; enable me to soothe him in perplexity, to cheer him in difficulty, to refresh him in weariness, and, as far as may be, to advise him in doubt. [Give me understanding so to fulfill my part in the education of our children, that they may be our joy in this world and our glory in the next.] Grant that our perfect union here may be the beginning of the still more perfect and blissful union hereafter in Thy kingdom; and this I pray through Jesus Christ Our Lord. *Amen.*

A PRAYER TO BE SAID BY HUSBAND OR WIFE

O merciful God, we humbly beseech Thee to send Thy blessing continually upon us, and to make us thankful for all that Thou hast already vouchsafed unto us; and as Thou hast made us one in the mystical grace of Matrimony, grant that we may be also inwardly of one heart and of one mind, paying due honor one to another, united in love to Thee and to each other in Thee; living together in peace and holiness, as faithful members of Thy Church, denying ourselves, and being a mutual help, comfort, and support to each other, all the days of our life. [Give us grace to train our children in Thy faith and fear.] Bless us with health and strength, if it be Thy will, and with whatever else Thy good providence shall see to be best for our souls and bodies. Fit and prepare us day by day for our departure hence, that we may together inherit eternal life in Thy heavenly kingdom. Through the merits of Jesus Christ, Our Lord and Savior. *Amen.*

A PARENT'S PRAYER

Almighty God, the Father and Maker of us all, Who of Thy blessing and goodness hast vouchsafed to make me a father [*or* mother] of children: be pleased to accept my hearty thanksgiving and devout praise for the same; grant me Thy heavenly grace and assistance so to train up my children in Thy faith, fear, and love that as they advance in years they may grow in grace and may hereafter be found in the number of Thine elect. Through Jesus Christ Our Lord. *Amen.*

The Blessing of Women after Childbirth
COMMONLY CALLED
THE CHURCHING OF WOMEN

If, according to a pious and praiseworthy custom, a woman, after childbirth, wishes to come to the church to give thanks to God for her safe delivery, and to ask the priest's blessing, he, vested in surplice and white stole, and attended by an acolyte carrying the holy-water sprinkler, will proceed to the door of the church. While the woman kneels there, holding a lighted candle in her hand, the priest sprinkles her with holy water, and then says:

Adjutorium nostrum in nomine Domini.	Our help is in the name of the Lord.
℟. Qui fecit cœlum et terram.	℟. Who hath made heaven and earth.
Ant. Hæc accipiet.	*Ant.* She shall receive.

PSALM 23

Domini est terra, et plenitudo ejus: orbis terrarum, et universi qui habitant in eo.	The earth is the Lord's, and the fullness thereof: the world and all they that dwell therein.
Quia ipse super maria fundavit eum: et super flumina præparavit eum.	For He hath founded it upon the seas: and hath prepared it upon the rivers.
Quis ascendet in montem Domini? aut quis stabit in loco sancto ejus?	Who shall ascend into the mountain of the Lord: or who shall stand in His holy place?
Innocens manibus et mundo corde, qui non accepit in vano animam suam, nec juravit in dolo proximo suo.	He that hath clean hands and a pure heart: who hath not taken his soul in vain, nor sworn deceitfully to his neighbor.
Hic accipiet benedictionem a Domino: et misericordiam a Deo, salutari suo.	He shall receive a blessing from the Lord; and mercy from God his Savior.
Hæc est generatio quærentium eum, quærentium faciem Dei Jacob.	This is the generation of them that seek Him: of them that seek the face of the God of Jacob.

Attollite portas, principes, vestras, et elevamini, portæ æternales: et introibit Rex gloriæ.

Lift up your gates, O ye princes, and be ye lifted up, O eternal gates: and the King of glory shall enter in.

Quis est iste Rex gloriæ? Dominus fortis et potens: Dominus potens in prælio.

Who is this King of glory? the Lord strong and mighty: the Lord mighty in battle.

Attollite portas, principes, vestras, et elevamini, portæ æternales: et introibit Rex gloriæ.

Lift up your gates, O ye princes, and be ye lifted up, O eternal gates: and the King of glory shall enter in.

Quis est iste Rex gloriæ? Dominus virtutum, ipse est Rex gloriæ.

Who is this King of glory? the Lord of hosts, He is the King of glory.

Gloria Patri, etc.

Glory be to the Father, etc.

Ant. Hæc accipiet benedictionem a Domino, et misericordiam a Deo salutari suo; quia hæc est generatio quærentium Dominum.

Ant. She shall receive a blessing from the Lord, and mercy from God her Savior; for this is the generation of them that seek the Lord.

Then, reaching the end of the stole into the woman's hand, the priest introduces her into the church, saying:

Ingredere in templum Dei, adora Filium beatæ Mariæ Virginis, qui tibi fœcunditatem tribuit prolis.

Enter thou into the temple of God, adore the Son of the Blessed Virgin Mary, Who hath given thee fruitfulness of offspring

She, having entered, kneels before the altar, and prays, giving thanks to God for the benefits bestowed upon her; and the priest says:

Kyrie, eleison.
Christe, eleison.
Kyrie, eleison.
Pater noster (*secreto*).

Lord, have mercy.
Christ, have mercy.
Lord, have mercy.
Our Father (*inaudibly*).

℣. Et ne nos inducas in tentationem.
℟. Sed libera nos a malo.
℣. Salvam fac ancillam tuam, Domine,
℟. Deus meus, sperantem in te.

℣. And lead us not into temptation.
℟. But deliver us from evil.
℣. O Lord, save Thy handmaid,
℟. O my God, who putteth her trust in Thee.

℣. Mitte ei, Domine, auxilium de sancto.

℟. Et de Sion tuere eam.

℣. Nihil proficiat inimicus in ea.

℟. Et filius iniquitatis non apponat nocere ei.

℣. Domine, exaudi orationem meam.

℟. Et clamor meus ad te veniat.

℣. Dominus vobiscum.

℟. Et cum spiritu tuo.

Oremus.

Omnipotens sempiterne Deus, qui per beatæ Mariæ Virginis partum fidelium parientium dolores in gaudium vertisti: respice propitius super hanc famulam tuam, ad templum sanctum tuum pro gratiarum actione lætam accedentem, et præsta; ut post hanc vitam, ejusdem beatæ Mariæ meritis et intercessione, ad æternæ beatitudinis gaudia cum prole sua pervenire mereatur. Per Christum Dominum nostrum. ℟. Amen.

℣. Send her help, O Lord, from Thy holy place.

℟. And defend her out of Sion.

℣. Let not the enemy prevail against her.

℟. Nor the son of iniquity draw nigh to hurt her.

℣. O Lord, hear my prayer.

℟. And let my cry come unto Thee.

℣. The Lord be with you.

℟. And with thy spirit.

Let us pray.

Almighty, everlasting God, Who, through the delivery of the Blessed Virgin Mary, hast turned the pains of the faithful at childbirth into joy: look mercifully on this Thy handmaid, who cometh in gladness to Thy temple to offer up her thanks: and grant that after this life, through the merits and intercession of the same Blessed Mary, she may be found worthy to attain, together with her offspring, unto the joys of everlasting happiness. Through Christ Our Lord. ℟. Amen.

The priest then sprinkles her with holy water in the form of a cross, saying:

Pax et benedictio Dei omnipotentis, Patris, ✠ et Filii, et Spiritus Sancti, descendat super te, et maneat semper. ℟. Amen.

The peace and blessing of God Almighty, the Father, ✠ and the Son, and the Holy Ghost, descend upon thee, and remain with thee always. ℟. Amen.

THANKSGIVING AFTER CHILDBIRTH

Gracious God, by Whose providence we are made, Who formest us in secret, Who beholdest us when we are yet imperfect, and in Whose book all shall be written: I humbly beseech Thee to accept this my acknowledgment of Thy power, and to receive this my most hearty praise and thanksgiving, which I now offer to Thy divine Majesty, for Thy favor and goodness toward me. Behold, O Lord, what Thine own hands have fashioned; and grant that this infant, which Thou hast made by

Thy power, may be preserved by Thy goodness, and, through the grace of Thy holy Baptism, may be made a living member of Thy Church and be carefully brought up to serve Thee in all piety and honesty. Through the merits of Thy dearly beloved Son, Jesus Christ Our Lord. Amen.

Devotions for the Sick

RULES FOR A SICK PERSON

1. Receive your sickness from the hands of your heavenly Father dealing with you as with a child.

2. Look on it as a loving correction for your sins, and as a summons to prepare more carefully for death.

3. Practice the virtues of patience and submission to the will of God; deepen your repentance and offer yourself to God to suffer, if it pleases Him, still greater pains; give thanks for the blessings you enjoy.

4. In any dangerous illness, let your first care be to send for a priest.

5. Engage your friends to give you timely notice if your illness be dangerous, and not to flatter you with false hopes of recovery.

6. Make the best use of the time you have; admit but few visitors; let your conversation be as little as may be of worldly matters.

7. Settle your temporal affairs, in order to give yourself more entirely to spiritual matters.

8. Meditate often on Our Lord's Passion.

9. Bear in mind St. Augustine's words: "However innocent your life may have been, no Christian ought to venture to die in any other state than that of a penitent."

PRAYER IN THE BEGINNING OF SICKNESS

O heavenly Father, Who in Thy wisdom knowest what is best for me, glory be to Thee. Lord, if it seem good in Thy sight, remove from me this sickness which I now feel seizing upon me, that I may employ my health to Thy glory, and praise Thy name. But if Thou art pleased it should grow on me, I willingly submit to Thy afflicting hand, for Thou art wont to chasten those whom Thou dost love, and Thou hast promised not to lay on me any more than Thou wilt enable me to bear. I know, O my God, that Thou sendest this sickness on me for my good, even to humble and to prove me; O grant that it may not fail to work that saving effect in me. O Lord, create in me a true sorrow for all my past sins, a firm faith in Thee, and sincere resolutions of amendment for the time to come. Deliver me from all fretfulness and impatience, and give me an entire resignation to Thy divine will: O suffer not my sickness to take away my senses, and do Thou continually supply my thoughts with holy ejaculations. Lord, bless all the means that are used for my recovery, and restore me to health, if it be Thy will, in Thy good time; but if Thou hast appointed otherwise for me, Thy blessed will be done. O wean my affections from all things of earth, and fill me with ardent desires after heaven: Lord, fit me for Thyself, and then call me, when Thou pleasest, to that joy unspeakable and full of glory; for the sake of Thine only Son, Jesus Christ, my Lord and Savior. *Amen.*

A DAILY PRAYER

O Almighty God, behold I receive this sickness, with which Thou art pleased to visit me, as coming from Thy fatherly hand. It is Thy will that it should be thus with me. Thy will be done on earth, as it is in heaven. May this sickness be to the honor of Thy holy name and for the good of my soul. For these ends I here offer myself to Thee with entire submission; to suffer what Thou pleasest, as long as Thou pleasest, and in what manner Thou pleasest: for I am Thy creature and Thy child, who have most ungratefully offended Thee. I have truly deserved Thy chastisement, and far more than Thou layest on me, but, O Lord, rebuke me not in Thine indignation, neither chasten me in Thy sore displeasure. Look upon my weakness, and be merciful unto me, for Thou knowest whereof I am made. Thou rememberest that I am but dust; deal not with me therefore after my sins, nor reward me according to mine iniquities; but according to the multitude of Thy tender mercies have compassion upon me. Assist me, I pray Thee, with Thy heavenly grace, and give me strength, that I may be able to bear with Christian patience all the pains, uneasiness, and trials of my sickness. Preserve me from all temptations so far as Thou seest fit, and be Thou my defense against all the assaults of the enemy, that I may in nowise offend Thee; and if it be Thy will that this sickness should be my last, I beg of Thee so to direct me by Thy grace that I may in no way neglect or be deprived of those Sacraments which Thou hast ordained for the good of my soul, to prepare it for its passage into eternity; so that, being cleansed from all my sins, I may put my whole trust in Thee, and love Thee above all things; and that finally, through the merits of the Passion and death of Thy Son, I may be admitted into the company of the blessed, there to praise Thee forever, through the same Jesus Christ Our Lord. *Amen.*

ACTS OF MOST NECESSARY VIRTUES FOR THE SICK

Act of Resignation

Lord, I accept this sickness from Thy fatherly hands; I entirely resign myself to Thy blessed will, whether it be for life or death. Not my will, but Thine be done; Thy will be done on earth, as it is in heaven.

Act of Submission

Lord, I submit to all the pains and uneasiness of this my illness: my sins have deserved infinitely more. Thou art just, O Lord, and Thy judgment is right.

Act of Self-Oblation

Lord, I offer up to Thee all that I now suffer, or may have to suffer, to be united to the sufferings of my Savior, and to be sanctified by His Passion.

Act of Adoration

I adore Thee, O my God and my All, as my First Beginning and my Last End; I desire to pay Thee the best homage that I am able, and to bow down all the powers of my soul to Thee.

Act of Praise

Lord, I desire to praise Thee forever, in sickness as well as in health; I desire to join my heart and voice with the whole Church of heaven and earth, in blessing Thee forever.

Act of Thanksgiving

I give Thee thanks, O Lord, from the bottom of my heart, for all the mercies and blessings which Thou hast bestowed upon me and on Thy whole Church through Jesus Christ Thy Son; above all, because Thou hast loved me from all eternity, and hast sent Thy Son to redeem me with His Precious Blood. O let not that blood be shed for me in vain.

Act of Faith

Lord, I believe all those heavenly truths which Thou hast revealed, and which Thy holy Catholic Church believes and teaches. Thou art the sovereign Truth, Who canst neither deceive nor be deceived. Thou hast promised Thy Spirit of truth to guide Thy Church into all truth. In this faith I resolve, through Thy grace, both to live and die. O Lord, strengthen and increase this my faith.

Act of Hope

O my God, all my hope is in Thee! Through Jesus Christ, my Redeemer, through His Passion and death, I hope for mercy, grace, and salvation from Thee. In Thee, O Lord, have I put my trust: let me never be confounded. O sweet Jesus, receive me into Thine arms in this day of my distress; hide me in Thy wounds, bathe my soul in Thy Precious Blood.

Act of Love

I love Thee, O my God, with my whole heart and soul, above all things: at least I desire so to love Thee. O come now and take full possession of my soul, and teach me to love Thee forever. I desire to depart, and to be with Christ. O when will Thy kingdom come? O Lord, when wilt Thou perfectly reign in all hearts? When shall sin be no more?

Act of Love of One's Neighbor

I desire to love my neighbor with perfect charity for the love of Thee. I forgive from my heart all who have in any way offended or injured me, and I ask pardon of all whom I have in any way offended or injured.

Act of Contrition

Have mercy upon me, O God, according to Thy great mercy: and according to the multitude of Thy tender mercies blot out my iniquity. O who will give water to my head, and a fountain of tears to my eyes, that, day and night, I may bewail my sins? O that I had never offended so good a God! O that I had never sinned! Happy those souls that have always preserved their baptismal innocence! Lord, be merciful to me a sinner; holy Jesus, Son of the living God, have mercy upon me.

Act of Commendation to God

I commend my soul to God my Maker, Who created me from nothing; to Jesus Christ my Savior, Who redeemed me with His blood; to the Holy Ghost, Who sanctified me in Baptism. Into Thy hands, O Lord, I commend my spirit.

Act of Renunciation of Evil

I renounce, from this moment and for all eternity, the devil and all his works and pomps. I abhor all his suggestions and temptations. Suffer not, O Lord, this mortal enemy of my soul to have any power over me, either now or at my last hour. Let Thy holy angels ever keep me and defend me against all the powers of darkness.

O holy Mary, Mother of God, who wert present beneath the Cross at the death of thy beloved Son Jesus, obtain for me the grace of a happy death. Hail Mary, etc.

Glorious St. Michael, prince of the heavenly host, intercede for me at the hour of my death.

O holy guardian angel, to whose care God, in His mercy, has committed me, stand by me at the last hour; protect me against all the powers of darkness; defend me from all my enemies; and conduct my soul to the mansions of bliss.

O all ye blessed angels and saints of God, assist me by your intercession in the passage from time to eternity. *Amen.*

A PRAYER FOR PATIENCE

Remember, O most pitying Father, what this frail and feeble work of Thy hands can bear without fainting; nothing, indeed, of itself, but all things in Thee, if strengthened by Thy grace. Wherefore grant me strength, that I may suffer and endure; patience alone I ask. Lord, give me this, and behold my heart is ready, O God, my heart is ready to receive whatsoever shall be laid upon me; may it even be a consolation to me that, afflicting me with pain, Thou sparest not here, that Thou mayest spare hereafter. Grant, O Lord, that in my patience I may possess my soul; to that end may I often look upon the face of Christ Thy Son, that as He hath suffered such terrible things in the flesh, I may endeavor to be armed with the same mind. Wherefore I commit my strength unto Thee, O Lord; for Thou art my Strength and my Refuge; Thou dost uphold my life. Behold, O Lord, now am I in the midst of the fire, and how long I shall be there Thou knowest. Keep me, Thou Who didst preserve unhurt the three children in the furnace of fire, and bring me safe out of this trial when it shall please Thee, as Thou didst deliver them, that I also may bless Thee with all Thy creatures forever. *Amen.*

A PRAYER IN SUFFERING

O Lord Jesus Christ, accept my sufferings which I desire to unite with Thine. Sanctify this affliction, so that every pang I feel may purify my soul and bring it nearer to Thee, to be made more one with Thee; grant that I may welcome the sufferings which will make me more like to Thee.

O my Lord, stand Thou by me with Thy supporting grace; sanctify each pang, sustain my weakness. And then order for me what Thou pleasest. Come now to my help, O Lord, and so purify my soul that I may be spared the last, the eternal suffering; let me fly to the embrace of Thy love forever.

Lord Jesus, hast Thou not invited all that labor and are burdened to come to Thee for refreshment? Behold now Thy servant, afflicted and oppressed, comes to Thee for help; relieve me, I beseech Thee, Thou Who art infinite in mercy.

O Thou Who hast comforted the martyrs in their torments, and refreshed them with heavenly sweetness on the rack and in the fire, renew Thy mercies to me Thine unworthy servant; defend me against all temptation, suffer not the enemy to take advantage of me, but grant me Thy heavenly strength, the fullness of Thy grace and peace. *Amen.*

Ejaculation

O Lord, by Thy Cross and Passion strengthen me; Lord, let this cup pass from me; nevertheless, not my will but Thine be done. *Amen.*

PRAYERS FOR A GOOD DEATH

O Lord Jesus, God of goodness, and Father of mercies, I draw nigh to Thee with a contrite and humble heart; to Thee I recommend the last hour of my life, and that judgment which awaits me afterward.

Merciful Jesus, have mercy on me.

When my feet, benumbed with death, shall admonish me that my mortal course is drawing to an end,

Merciful Jesus, have mercy on me.

When my hands, cold and trembling, shall no longer be able to clasp the crucifix, and, against my will, shall let it fall on my bed of suffering,
Merciful Jesus, have mercy on me.
When mine eyes, dim and troubled at the approach of death, shall fix themselves on Thee, my last and only support,
Merciful Jesus, have mercy on me.
When my lips, pale and trembling, shall pronounce for the last time Thine adorable name,
Merciful Jesus, have mercy on me.
When my face, pale and livid, shall inspire the beholders with pity and dismay; when my hair, bathed in the sweat of death, and stiffening on my head, shall forebode mine approaching end,
Merciful Jesus, have mercy on me.
When mine ears, soon to be forever shut to the discourse of men, shall be open to that irrevocable decree which is to fix my doom for all eternity,
Merciful Jesus, have mercy on me.
When my imagination, agitated by dreadful specters, shall be sunk in an abyss of anguish; when my soul, affrighted with the sight of my iniquities and the terrors of Thy judgments, shall have to fight against the angel of darkness, who will endeavor to conceal Thy mercies from mine eyes, and plunge me into despair,
Merciful Jesus, have mercy on me.
When my poor heart, oppressed with suffering and exhausted by its continual struggles with the enemies of its salvation, shall feel the pangs of death,
Merciful Jesus, have mercy on me.
When the last tear, the forerunner of my dissolution, shall drop from mine eyes, receive it as a sacrifice of expiation for my sins; grant that I may expire the victim of penance; and then, in that dreadful moment,
Merciful Jesus, have mercy on me.
When my friends and relations, surrounding my bed, shall be moved with compassion for me, and invoke Thy clemency in my behalf,
Merciful Jesus, have mercy on me.
When I shall have lost the use of my senses, when the world shall have vanished from my sight, when mine agonizing soul shall feel the pangs of death,
Merciful Jesus, have mercy on me.
When my last sighs shall force my soul from my body, accept them as signs of a loving impatience to come to Thee,
Merciful Jesus, have mercy on me.
When my soul, trembling on my lips, shall bid farewell to the world, and leave my body lifeless, pale, and cold, receive this separation as a homage which I willingly pay to Thy divine Majesty, and in that last moment of my mortal life,
Merciful Jesus, have mercy on me.

When at length my soul, admitted to Thy presence, shall first behold the splendor of Thy Majesty, reject it not, but receive me into Thy bosom, where I may forever sing Thy praises; and in that moment when eternity shall begin for me,
Merciful Jesus, have mercy on me.

Let us pray.
O God, Who hast doomed all men to die, but hast concealed from all the hour of their death: grant that I may pass my days in the practice of holiness and justice, and that I may be made worthy to quit this world in the peace of a good conscience and in the embrace of Thy love. Through Christ Our Lord. *Amen.*

O Mary, conceived without sin, pray for us who have recourse to thee. O Refuge of sinners, O Mother of those in their agony, forsake us not in the hour of our death, but obtain for us perfect sorrow, sincere contrition, remission of our sins, a worthy reception of the most holy Viaticum, the strengthening power of the Sacrament of Extreme Unction; that we may present ourselves without fear before the throne of that Judge Who is both just and merciful, our God and our Redeemer. *Amen.*

Jesus, Mary, and Joseph, I give you my heart and my soul.
Jesus, Mary, and Joseph, assist me in my last agony.
Jesus, Mary, and Joseph, may I breathe forth my soul in peace with you.

THANKSGIVING FOR RECOVERY

Glory be to Thee, O heavenly Father, for the sickness Thou hast in mercy sent me. Lord, the stripes Thou didst lay on me were the stripes of love; glory be to Thee. Before I was humbled I did wickedly; but now will I keep Thy word. It is good for me that Thou hast humbled me, that I might learn Thine ordinances.

Glory be to Thee, O Lord, glory be to Thee, for delivering me from the terrors of death, and restoring me to my health again; glory be to Thee. I called upon the Lord in my trouble, and the Lord heard me. I shall not die, but live and declare the works of the Lord. Bless the Lord, therefore, O my soul: as long as I have my life, which at first God gave me, and which He has now restored to me, I will sing praises unto my God.

O Lord God, Who hast in Thy tender mercy prolonged my days in this world, give me grace to spend this life which Thou hast now lengthened, in Thy service. O give me grace to perform all my resolutions of new obedience, and so to live in the filial fear of Thee all the remainder of my time, that I may at last die at peace with myself, at peace with the whole world, and at peace with Thee; for the sake of Thy dearly beloved Son, Our Lord and Savior.

Our Father. Hail Mary. Glory be to the Father.

May the blessing of God Almighty, the Father, ✠ the Son, and the Holy Ghost, descend upon me and all belonging to me, and dwell in my heart and be with me in my going out and coming in, now and forever. *Amen.*

PRAYER FOR A SICK PERSON BEFORE RECEIVING HOLY VIATICUM

O Father of mercies, and God of all consolation, behold I Thy creature, made after Thine image and redeemed by the blood of Thy only begotten Son, appear before Thee my Creator; by Whom and for Whom I was created, by Whose grace I have hitherto lived; unto Whom henceforth, so long as Thou seest good, I would wish to live; for Whom, and in Whom, I desire to die; I humbly adore Thee, Whom my soul desireth and longeth for; I cry to Thee, Whom alone I love above all things, O Thou my Rest, my Hope, my Love, my Desire, my heart's only Good.

O most loving Father, although I am the least of all Thy children, yea, unworthy to be called Thy child, because I have not honored Thee as a Father, yet I come to Thee with full confidence, and throw myself upon the breast and into the arms of Thy most sweet love and mercy, grieving from my inmost soul that I have ever forsaken Thee, my God, the Fountain of all good; that I have departed from Thee, my most loving Father; and have forgotten Thee, Who, as though there were none else to care for, every moment rememberest me. O that I had never offended Thee, my God and my All; accept at least this the ardent wish and desire of my inmost heart; look Thou upon me, and be merciful unto me now in the time of pity; Thou knowest, O Lord, that I love Thee, or desire to love Thee, more than myself, more than all that claims or can claim my love. I know Whom I have believed, and that Thou art able to keep that which I have committed to Thee: I know, too, that a contrite and humble heart, O God, Thou wilt not despise.

I hope, O Lord, that Thou wilt never cast me away from Thy presence, Thou Who dost so lovingly invite us to Thyself, saying: "Come unto Me, all ye that labor and are heavy burdened, and I will refresh you." Behold, I come, O Lord; Thou that castest not out any that come to Thee, receive me according to Thy word, and I shall live, and let me not be disappointed of my hope.

I give Thee infinite thanks because Thou hast vouchsafed to think of me so lovingly from all eternity, for creating me in time after Thine image, and, when the fullness of time was come, for redeeming me by the blood of Thine only begotten Son, for sparing me so often when sinning, and calling me so often out of the darkness of sin into Thy marvelous light.

What reward shall I give unto Thee, Lord Jesus, for Thy toilsome life and most bitter death, for vouchsafing so often to feed me with Thy Body and Thy Blood? What return shall I make unto Thee for all the benefits Thou hast bestowed upon me, O beloved Spouse of my soul? The deep of my nothingness and my misery calleth on the deep of Thy goodness and Thy boundless love, because of Thy wounds:

in them is all my hope and my confidence: through them, and the boundless ocean of Thy love that flows from them, I come in confidence to Thee, wretched though I am, and poor and naked; for Thou art rich toward all, and my goods are as nothing unto Thee. I will take cheerfully at Thy hand the cup of salvation which Thou givest me to drink, bitter though it be, and I will drink it with Thee, Who didst drain it first for me when Thou didst so earnestly thirst for my salvation. I will call upon the name of the Lord, and offer to Thee the sacrifice of thanksgiving. O that in return for this I could embrace Thee with all the love of the heavenly company, angels and saints, and, above all, of Blessed Mary, Thine Immaculate Mother; and that, with the voices and affections of all Thy creatures, I could praise and magnify Thy name.

Accept, Lord, my heart as a burnt offering; I give it all to Thee; I give Thee mine eyes, to see Thee alone and all things in Thee; mine ears, to hear Thy Word; my mouth, my lips and tongue, to be filled with Thy praise, and to sing of Thy glory and of Thy greatness all the day long; my hands, to be stretched forth in prayer to Thee in heaven, or in alms to the poor, and to do Thy will; my feet, to be led into the way of peace; all my members, that they may say, "Lord, who is like unto Thee?" Bless the Lord, O my soul, and let all that is within me bless His holy name: bless the Lord, O my soul, and forget not all His benefits. I now freely surrender all these earthly things, for in Thee alone I have all things: I renounce myself, for I am Thine: I live, yet not I, but Thou, Christ Jesus, livest in me. I love Thee with all my heart, with all my mind, with all my soul, and with all my strength. *Amen.*

The Holy Viaticum

The Viaticum is the Holy Eucharist administered with the intention of preparing the sick for death. This Blessed Sacrament is indeed the Bread of life, of which every good Christian frequently partakes during health; but when the soul is about to pass from the body, there arises a new and peculiar obligation of receiving it. This obligation is founded on the abundant graces which this Holy Sacrament, above all the rest, is capable of imparting, and which are at that time so necessary. It is the safeguard that must preserve the soul on its journey to heaven; it is the pledge of immortal glory. "He who eateth this Bread shall live forever" (Jn 6:59). And so urgent is the obligation of receiving it at the approach of death, that the Church dispenses with her rule in behalf of those who are dangerously sick, and allows them to communicate after having broken their fast. The sick person will therefore use his best endeavor to make a worthy preparation for this Blessed Sacrament.

Before the priest arrives, the following things should be made ready in the sickroom: 1) a table, covered with a clean, white cloth; and upon it 2) at least one candlestick, holding a blessed candle lighted; 3) a crucifix; 4) two small glasses, one containing holy water, and the other pure fresh water (for the ablution after Communion); and 4) a tablespoon (with which the priest administers the ablution to the sick person).

The priest bearing the Blessed Sacrament should be met at the door by some-one holding a lighted candle, who should go before him to the place prepared. All should then retire, while the Confession of the sick person is being heard, and return immediately thereafter to assist at the giving of the Holy Communion: remaining kneeling and spending the time in prayer.

NOTE. — The italicized words, or endings of words, occurring in the text, are those which must be varied according to sex or number.

The priest, on entering the sick person's room with the Blessed Sacrament, says:

Pax huic domui.	Peace be unto this house.
℟. Et omnibus habitantibus in ea.	℟. And unto all who dwell therein.

Then, placing the Holy Sacrament, with the corporal, on a table, when the candles have been lighted, he adores upon his knees, all present doing likewise; after which he takes holy water, and sprinkles the sick person and the bed, saying:

Asperges me, Domine, hyssopo, et mundabor: lavabis me, et super nivem dealbabor.

Thou shalt sprinkle me, O Lord, with hyssop, and I shall be cleansed: Thou shalt wash me, and I shall be made whiter than snow.

Miserere mei, Deus, secundum magnam misericordiam tuam.

Have mercy upon me, O God, according to Thy great mercy.

Gloria Patri, et Filio, et Spiritui Sancto. Sicut erat in principio, et nunc, et semper, et in sæcula sæculorum. Amen.

Glory be to the Father, and to the Son, and to the Holy Ghost. As it was in the beginning, is now, and ever shall be, world without end. Amen.

Then is repeated the Antiphon, Thou shalt sprinkle me, *etc.*

Afterward:

Adjutorium nostrum in nomine Domini.

Our help is in the name of the Lord.

℟. Qui fecit cœlum et terram.

℟. Who hath made heaven and earth.

℣. Domine, exaudi orationem meam.

℣. O Lord, hear my prayer.

℟. Et clamor meus ad te veniat.

℟. And let my cry come unto Thee.

℣. Dominus vobiscum.

℣. The Lord be with you.

℟. Et cum spiritu tuo.

℟. And with thy spirit.

Oremus

 Exaudi nos, Domine sancte, Pater omnipotens, æterne Deus: et mittere digneris sanctum Angelum tuum de cœlis, qui custodiat, foveat, protegat, visitet, atque defendat omnes habitantes in hoc habitaculo. Per Christum Dominum nostrum. ℞. Amen.

Let us pray.

 Hear us, O holy Lord, Father Almighty, everlasting God; and vouchsafe to send Thy holy angel from heaven, to guard, cherish, protect, visit, and defend all those that dwell in this house. Through Christ Our Lord. ℞. Amen.

The priest then approaches the sick person, to learn if he be properly disposed to receive the Holy Viaticum, and whether he wishes to make a confession. If so, he hears the confession and gives absolution. (The Confession should, however, have been made beforehand, unless necessity demanded otherwise.) Then, the Confiteor *having been recited by the sick person, or by another in his name, the priest says:*

Misereatur tui omnipotens Deus, et dimissis peccatis tuis, perducat te ad vitam æternam. ℞. Amen.

May Almighty God have mercy upon thee, and forgive thee thy sins, and bring thee unto life everlasting. ℞. Amen.

Indulgentiam, ✚ absolutionem, et remissionem peccatorum tuorum tribuat tibi omnipotens, et misericors Dominus. ℞. Amen.

May the Almighty and merciful Lord grant thee pardon, ✚ absolution, and remission of thy sins. ℞. Amen.

Then, making a genuflection, he takes the Blessed Sacrament from the pyx, and, raising it, shows it to the sick person, saying:

Ecce Agnus Dei, ecce qui tollit peccata mundi.

Behold the Lamb of God, behold Him Who taketh away the sins of the world.

And thrice in the accustomed manner:

Domine, non sum dignus, ut intres sub tectum meum, sed tantum dic verbo, et sanabitur anima mea.

Lord, I am not worthy that Thou shouldst enter under my roof; but only say the word, and my soul shall be healed.

And the sick person should at least once, in a low tone, say the same words together with the priest; then the priest, giving the Holy Eucharist to the sick person, says:

Accipe, *frater,* Viaticum corporis Domini nostri Jesu Christi, qui te custodiat ab hoste maligno, et perducat in vitam æternam. Amen.

Receive, *brother,* the Viaticum of the Body of Our Lord Jesus Christ; may He preserve thee from the wicked enemy, and bring thee unto life everlasting. Amen.

[But if Communion is not given in the way of Viaticum, *he says the ordinary words:*

Corpus Domini nostri Jesu Christi custodiat animam tuam in vitam æternam. Amen.

The Body of Our Lord Jesus Christ preserve thy soul unto life everlasting. Amen.]

If death be imminent and there be danger in delay, then all the other prayers are partly or wholly ommitted; and the Confiteor *being said, the* Viaticum *is administered at once.*

The priest then washes his fingers in silence, and the ablution is given to the sick person; after which the priest says:

℣. Dominus vobiscum.

℟. Et cum spiritu tuo.

℣. The Lord be with you.

℟. And with thy spirit.

Oremus.

Domine sancte, Pater omnipotens, æterne Deus, te fideliter deprecamur, ut accipienti *fratri* nostro sacrosanctum Corpus Domini nostri Jesu Christi Filii tui, tam corpori, quam animæ prosit ad remedium sempiternum. Qui tecum vivit et regnat in unitate Spiritus Sancti, Deus, per omnia sæcula sæculorum. ℟. Amen.

Let us pray.

O holy Lord, Father Almighty, eternal God, we earnestly beseech Thee that the most sacred Body of Our Lord Jesus Christ, Thy Son, which our *brother* hath now received, may be to *him* an eternal remedy both of body and soul. Who liveth and reigneth with Thee, in the unity of the Holy Ghost, one God, world without end. ℟. Amen.

After this prayer, if any particle of the Blessed Sacrament remains, the priest genuflects, rises, and, taking the Blessed Sacrament in its receptacle, he makes with it the sign of the cross over the sick person, in silence. If no particle remains, the priest blesses with his hand, in the usual manner.

PRAYER AFTER COMMUNICATING

Glory be to Thee, O Christ, Who hast vouchsafed to visit and refresh my poor soul with Thy sweetness. Now O Lord, lettest Thou Thy servant depart in peace, according to Thy word, for mine eyes have seen Thy salvation. I hold Thee now, my Love and Sweetness, and will not let Thee go: I gladly bid farewell to the world and all therein; and now I come with joy, my God, to Thee. Henceforth nothing, O good Jesus, shall part me from Thee: I am joined to Thee, O Christ; I will live in Thee and die in Thee, and if Thou wilt, abide in Thee forever. Now I live, yet not I, but Christ liveth in me. I am weary of my life; I desire to depart and to be with Christ; to me, to live is Christ, and to die is gain. I will fear no evil as I walk through the valley of the shadow of death, for Thou, O Lord, art with me: as the heart panteth after the water-springs, so panteth my soul after Thee, O God; my soul hath thirsted after the strong living God; when shall I come and appear before the face of God? Bless me, most loving Jesus, and let me now depart in peace, for I am Thine; and I will never let Thee go forever. O that I were now joined to Thee in a blessed union forever! O that I were wholly taken up, wholly absorbed and buried in Thee! O that my soul, resting sweetly in Thy arms, were altogether taken up in Thee, and blissfully enjoyed Thee, my loving God! What more have I to do with the world, my most loving Jesus? Behold, there is none upon earth that I desire besides Thee. Into Thy hands, Lord Jesus, I commend my spirit. Receive me, my Love and Sweetness, that it may be well with me forever, and that I may gently lay me down in peace in Thee, and take my rest. *Amen.*

The Sacrament of Extreme Unction

Our Lord and Savior Jesus Christ, in His tender solicitude for those whom He has redeemed by His Precious Blood, has been pleased to institute another Sacrament to help us at that most important hour on which eternity depends—the hour of death. This Sacrament is called Extreme Unction, or the Last Anointing.

Of this Sacrament St. James the apostle thus speaks: "Is any man sick among you? Let him call in the priests of the Church, and let them pray over him, anointing him with oil in the name of the Lord: and the prayer of faith shall save the sick man and the Lord will raise him up: and if he be in sins, they shall be forgiven him" (5:14–15) These words show the great and salutary graces bestowed by this Sacrament.

The priest, in administering this Sacrament, anoints the five principal senses of the body—the eyes, the ears, the nostrils, the lips, the hands—and the feet, because these may have been employed, during life, in offending God. At each anointing he pronounces these words: "Through this holy unction, and of His most tender mercy, may the Lord pardon thee whatsoever sins thou hast committed by sight, hearing," etc.

The sick person should endeavor to prepare himself to receive this Sacrament by acts of sincere contrition for all his sins, by great confidence in the tender mercies of his Redeemer, and by a perfect resignation of himself to the holy will of God.

A PRAYER BEFORE EXTREME UNCTION

O Lord, Who hast mercifully provided remedies for all our necessities; grant me Thy grace so to use them that my soul may receive all those good effects which Thou didst intend in their institution. I desire now to be anointed, as Thou hast commanded by Thine apostle. Grant, I beseech Thee, that by this holy unction, and the prayers of the Church, I may partake of that spirit with which Christ suffered on the Cross, for Thy glory, and for the destruction of sin. Give me true patience to support all the pains and trouble of my sickness; give me an inward strength to resist all the temptations of the enemy; give me grace for the pardon of all my failings; give me that true light, by which I may be conducted through the shadow of death to eternal happiness; and if my health be expedient for Thy glory, let this be the means to restore it. Behold, I approach to this holy ordinance with a firm faith and confidence in Thy goodness, that Thou wilt not forsake me in this time of my distress; but that Thou wilt fortify me with Thy grace, and defend me from all evil, and prepare my soul for a happy eternity. *Amen.*

THE MANNER OF ADMINISTERING THE SACRAMENT OF EXTREME UNCTION

NOTE. — The italicized words, or endings of words, occurring in the text, are those which must be varied according to sex.

On arriving at the place where the sick man lies, the priest, with the holy oil, entering the chamber, says:

Pax huic domui.

℞. Et omnibus habitantibus in ea.

Peace be unto this house.

℞. And unto all who dwell therein.

Then, after placing the oil on a table, being vested in a surplice and violet stole, he offers the sick man a crucifix piously to kiss; after which he sprinkles both the chamber and the bystanders with holy water in the form of a cross, saying the Asperges.

Asperges me, Domine, hyssopo, et mundabor: lavabis me, et super nivem dealbabor.

Thou shalt sprinkle me, O Lord, with hyssop, and I shall be cleansed: Thou shalt wash me, and I shall be made whiter than snow.

Miserere mei, Deus, secundum magnam misericordiam tuam.

Have mercy upon me, O God, according to Thy great mercy.

Gloria Patri, et Filio, et Spiritui Sancto. Sicut erat in principio, et nunc, et semper, et in sæcula sæculorum. Amen.

Glory be to the Father, and to the Son, and to the Holy Ghost. As it was in the beginning, is now, and ever shall be, world without end. Amen.

Then he says:

Adjutorium nostrum in nomine Domini.

℞. Qui fecit cœlum et terram.

℣. Dominus vobiscum.

℞. Et cum spiritu tuo.

Our help is in the name of the Lord.

℞. Who hath made heaven and earth.

℣. The Lord be with you.

℞. And with thy spirit.

Oremus.

Introeat, Domine Jesu Christe, domum hanc sub nostræ humilitatis ingressu, æterna felicitas, divina prosperitas, serena lætitia, charitas fructuosa, sanitas sempiterna: effugiat ex hoc loco accessus dæmonum, adsint angeli pacis, domumque hanc deserat omnis maligna discordia. Magnifica, Domine, super nos nomen sanctum tuum; et benedic ✠ nostræ conversationi: sanctifica nostræ humilitatis ingressum, qui sanctus et qui pius es, et permanes cum Patre et Spiritu Sancto in sæcula sæculorum. Amen.

Oremus, et deprecemur Dominum nostrum Jesum Christum, ut benedicendo benedicat ✠ hoc tabernaculum, et omnes habitantes in eo et det eis angelum bonum custodem, et faciat eos sibi servire, ad considerandum mirabilia de lege sua: avertat ab eis omnes contrarias potestates: eripiat eos ab omni formidine, et ab omni perturbatione, ac sanos in hoc tabernaculo custodire dignetur: Qui cum Patre et Spiritu Sancto vivit et regnat Deus in sæcula sæculorum. Amen.

Let us pray.

May there enter, O Lord Jesus Christ, into this house, at the entrance of our lowliness, everlasting happiness, heaven-sent prosperity, peaceful gladness, fruitful charity, abiding health: may the devils fear to approach this place, may the angels of peace be present therein, and may all wicked strife depart from this house. Magnify, O Lord, upon us Thy holy name, and bless ✠ our ministry: hallow the entrance of our lowliness. Thou Who art holy and compassionate, and abidest with the Father and the Holy Ghost world without end. Amen.

Let us pray and beseech Our Lord Jesus Christ, that blessing He may bless ✠ this abode, and all who dwell therein, and give unto them a good angel for their keeper, and make them serve Him, so as to behold wondrous things out of His law. May He ward off from them all adverse powers: may He deliver them from all fear and from all disquiet, and vouchsafe to keep in health them that dwell in this house. Who, with the Father and the Holy Ghost, liveth and reigneth God world without end. Amen.

Oremus.

Exaudi nos, Domine sancte, Pater
omnipotens, æterne Deus: et mittere digneris sanctum Angelum
tuum de cœlis, qui custodiat, foveat,
protegat, visitet, atque defendat
omnes habitantes in hoc habitaculo.
Per Christum Dominum nostrum.
Amen.

Let us pray.

Hear us, O holy Lord, Father
Almighty, everlasting God, and
vouchsafe to send Thy holy angel
from heaven, to guard, cherish, protect, visit, and defend all those that
dwell in this house. Through Christ
Our Lord. Amen.

(*These prayers, if time will not permit, may be either wholly or in part omitted.*) *After which is said the* Confiteor, *etc., as at p. 32.*

(*Before the priest begins to anoint the sick person, he admonishes the bystanders to pray for him; and, when it is convenient to do so, they recite for him the* Penitential Psalms [*p. 194*], *with Litanies or other prayers, while the priest is administering the Sacrament of Extreme Unction.*) *Then he says:*

In nomine Patris, ✠ et Filii, ✠ et
Spiritus ✠ Sancti, extinguatur in
te omnis virtus diaboli per imposi-
tionem manuum nostrarum, et per
invocationem [‡gloriosæ et sanctæ
Dei Genitricis Virginis Mariæ,
ejusque inclyti Sponsi Joseph, et]
omnium sanctorum Angelorum,
Archangelorum, Patriarcharum,
Prophetarum, Apostolorum,
Martyrum, Confessorum,
Virginum, atque omnium simul
Sanctorum. Amen.

In the name of the Father, ✠ and of the
Son, ✠ and of the Holy ✠ Ghost,
may all the power of the devil be ex-
tinguished in thee, by the laying on
of our hands, and by the invocation
of [‡the glorious and ever Blessed
Virgin Mary, Mother of God, of her
chaste spouse, St. Joseph, and] all
holy angels, archangels, patriarchs,
prophets, apostles, martyrs, confessors, virgins, and of the whole company of the saints. Amen.

Then, dipping his thumb in the holy oil, he anoints the sick person, in the form of a cross, on the parts mentioned below, using the words of the form as follows:

On the eyes.

Per istam sanctam unctionem ✠ et
suam piissimam misericordiam, indulgeat tibi Dominus quidquid per
visum deliquisti. Amen.

Through this holy unction ✠ and of His
most tender mercy, may the Lord
pardon thee whatsoever sins thou
hast committed by sight. Amen.

(With cotton he wipes the anointed parts.)

On the ears.

Per istam sanctam unctionem ✠ et suam piissimam misericordiam, indulgeat tibi Dominus quidquid per auditum deliquisti. Amen.

Through this holy unction ✠ and of His most tender mercy, may the Lord pardon thee whatsoever sins thou hast committed by hearing. Amen.

On the nostrils.

Per istam sanctam unctionem ✠ et suam piissimam misericordiam, indulgeat tibi Dominns quidquid per odoratum deliquisti. Amen.

Through this holy unction ✠ and of His most tender mercy, may the Lord pardon thee whatsoever sins thou hast committed by smell. Amen.

On the mouth, the lips being closed.

Per istam sanctam unctionem ✠ et suam piissimam misericordiam, indulgeat tibi Dominus quidquid per gustum et locutionem deliquisti. Amen.

Through this holy unction ✠ and of His most tender mercy, may the Lord pardon thee whatsoever sins thou hast committed by taste and speech. Amen.

On the hands.

Per istam sanctam unctionem ✠ et suam piissimam misericordiam, indulgeat tibi Dominus quidquid per tactum deliquisti. Amen.

Through this holy unction ✠ and of His most tender mercy, may the Lord pardon thee whatsoever sins thou hast committed by touch. Amen.

On the feet.

Per istam sanctam unctionem ✠ et suam piissimam misericordiam, indulgeat tibi Dominus quidquid per gressum deliquisti. Amen.

Through this holy unction ✠ and of His most tender mercy, may the Lord pardon thee whatsoever sins thou hast committed by thy footsteps. Amen.

This done, the priest says:

Kyrie, eleison.	Lord, have mercy.
Christe, eleison.	Christ, have mercy.
Kyrie, eleison.	Lord, have mercy.
Pater noster (*secreto*).	Our Father (*inaudibly*).

Et ne nos inducas in tentationem.
And lead us not into temptation.

℟. Sed libera nos a malo.
℟. But deliver us from evil.

℣. Salv*um* fac *servum tuum.*
℣. Save Thy *servant.*

℟. Deus meus, sperantem in te.
℟. O my God, who putteth *his* trust in Thee.

℣. Mitte ei, Domine, auxilium de sancto.
℣. Send *him* help, O Lord, from Thy holy place.

℟. Et de Sion tuere *eum.*
℟. And defend *him* out of Sion.

℣. Esto ei, Domine, turris fortitudinis.
℣. Be unto *him,* O Lord, a tower of strength.

℟. A facie inimici.
℟. From the face of the enemy.

℣. Nihil proficiat inimicus in *eo.*
℣. Let not the enemy prevail against *him.*

℟. Et filius iniquitatis non apponat nocere ei.
℟. Nor the son of iniquity draw nigh to hurt *him.*

℣. Domine, exaudi orationem meam.
℣. O Lord, hear my prayer.

℟. Et clamor meus ad te veniat.
℟. And let my cry come unto Thee.

℣. Dominus vobiscum.
℣. The Lord be with you.

℟. Et cum spiritu tuo.
℟. And with thy spirit.

Oremus.
Let us pray.

Domine Deus, qui per Apostolum tuum Jacobum locutus es: Infirmatur quis in vobis? inducat presbyteros Ecclesiæ, et orent super eum, ungentes eum oleo in nomine Domini: et oratio fidei salvabit infirmum, et alleviabit eum Dominus: et si in peccatis sit, remittentur ei:

Lord God, Who hast spoken by Thine apostle James, saying: Is any man sick among you? Let him call in the priests of the Church, and let them pray over him, anointing him with oil in the name of the Lord: and the prayer of faith shall save the sick man, and the Lord will raise him up; and if he be in sins, they shall be forgiven him:

cura, quæsumus, Redemptor noster, gratia Sancti Spiritus languores istius infir*mi*, ejusque sana vulnera, et dimitte peccata, atque dolores cunctos mentis et corporis ab *eo* expelle, plenamque interius et exterius sanitatem misericorditer redde, ut, ope misericordiæ tuæ restitut*us*, ad pristina reparetur officia: Qui cum Patre et eodem Spiritu Sancto vivis et regnas Deus, in sæcula sæculorum. Amen.

Oremus.

Respice, quæsumus, Domine, famul*um tuum*, N., infirmitate sui corporis fatiscentem, et animam refove, quam creasti: ut, castigationibus emendat*us*, se tua sentiat medicina salvat*um*. Per Christum Dominum nostrum. Amen.

Oremus.

Domine sancte, Pater omnipotens, æterne Deus, qui benedictionis tuæ gratiam ægris infundendo corporibus, facturam tuam multiplici pietate custodis: ad invocationem tui nominis benignus assiste; ut famul*um tuum* ab ægritudine liberat*um*, et sanitate donat*um* dextera tua erigas, virtute confirmes, potestate tuearis, atque Ecclesiæ tuæ sanctæ, cum omni desiderata prosperitate, restituas. Per Christum Dominum nostrum. Amen.

cure, we beseech Thee, O our Redeemer, by the grace of the Holy Ghost, the ailments of this sick *man*; heal *his* wounds, and forgive *his* sins; drive out from *him* all pains of body and mind, and mercifully restore to *him* full health, both inwardly and outwardly: that, having recovered by the help of Thy loving kindness, *he* may be enabled to return to *his* former duties. Who, with the Father and the same Holy Ghost, livest and reignest God, world without end. Amen.

Let us pray.

Look down, O Lord, we beseech Thee, upon Thy *servant*, N., languishing through bodily ailment, and refresh the soul which Thou hast created, that, being bettered by Thy chastisements, *he* may feel *himself* saved by Thy healing. Through Christ Our Lord. Amen.

Let us pray.

O holy Lord, Father Almighty, eternal God, Who, by shedding Thy gracious blessing upon our failing bodies, dost preserve, by Thy manifold goodness, the work of Thy hands: graciously draw near at the invocation of Thy name, that, having freed Thy *servant* from sickness, and bestowed health upon *him,* Thou mayest raise *him* up by Thy right hand, strengthen *him* by Thy might, defend *him* by Thy power, and restore *him* to Thy holy Church, with all the prosperity *he* desires. Through Christ Our Lord. Amen.

Lastly, the priest may add some short and salutary admonitions, according to the condition of the sick person, whereby he may be strengthened to die in the Lord, and to put to flight all the temptations of the evil one.

A PRAYER AFTER EXTREME UNCTION

O God, by Whom I have been created, redeemed, and sanctified; Who hast preserved me from many dangers, both of soul and body; Who hast nourished me with the adorable Sacrament of Thy Body and Blood, and granted me the grace to receive the rites of Thy Church, in preference to so many others who are carried off by sudden death; for these and all other blessings which I have received from Thee, I give Thee most humble and hearty thanks. And I beseech Blessed Mary, and all the saints and angels, with me and for me, to give thanks unto Thee for all Thy mercies. To Thee I resign my heart. Into Thy hands, O Lord, I commend my spirit. Receive me, O dear Jesus, in Thy mercy, into those loving arms, which were extended on the Cross for my redemption, and admit me into the embraces of Thine infinite love. I desire not to be freed from my pains, since Thou knowest what is best for me. Suffer me never to murmur; but grant me patience to bear whatever Thou wilt, and as long as Thou wilt. Should it be Thy will to inflict greater punishments on my weak body and languishing soul than those which I now suffer, my heart is ready, O Lord, to accept them, and to suffer in whatever manner and whatever measure may be most conformable to Thy divine will.

This one grace I most humbly beg of Thee, that I may die the death of the just, and be admitted, after the sufferings and tribulations of this transitory and sinful life, into the kingdom of Thy glory, there to see and enjoy Thee in the company of the blessed for a never-ending eternity. *Amen.*

The Visitation of the Sick

NOTE. — The italicized *words, or endings of words, occurring in the text, are those which must be varied according to sex.*

The following prayers are left entirely to the discretion of the priest. According to the time and the condition of the sick person, they may be said whole or in part, or altogether omitted. The priest, entering the room in which the sick person lies, first says:
Peace be unto this house.
℟. And to all who dwell therein.

Then he sprinkles the sick person and the bed and the room with holy water, saying the Antiphon, Thou shalt sprinkle me, *etc.*
Thou shalt sprinkle me, O Lord, with hyssop, and I shall be cleansed: Thou shalt wash me, and I shall be made whiter than snow.

   Have mercy upon me, O God, according to Thy great mercy.

   Glory be to the Father, and to the Son, and to the Holy Ghost. As it was in the beginning, is now, and ever shall be, world without end. Amen.

   Ant. Thou shalt sprinkle me, O Lord, with hyssop, and I shall be cleansed: Thou shalt wash me, and I shall be made whiter than snow.

He then administers to the sick person as circumstances require. Which done, or before he leaves the sickroom, he may say over the sick person any one of the first four Penitential Psalms *(p. 194) or the Psalm* Qui habitat *(p. 54), adding the* Glory be to the Father *at the end. He then says:*
Lord, have mercy.
℟. Christ, have mercy.
℣. Lord, have mercy. Our Father (*inaudibly*).
℣. And lead us not into temptation.
℟. But deliver us from evil.
℣. Save thy *servant.*
℟. O my God, who putteth *his* trust in Thee.
℣. Send *him* help, O Lord, from Thy holy place.
℟. And defend *him* out of Sion.
℣. Let not the enemy prevail against *him,*
℟. Nor the son of iniquity draw nigh to hurt *him.*
℣. Be unto *him,* O Lord, a tower of strength,
℟. From the face of the enemy.
℣. The Lord bring strength unto *him.*
℟. Upon *his* bed of pain.
℣. O Lord, hear my prayer.

℟. And let my cry come unto Thee.

℣. The Lord be with you.

℟. And with thy spirit.

Let us pray.

O God, Whose property is always to have mercy and to spare: graciously receive our supplication, that we, and this Thy *servant*, whom the chains of sin do hold in bondage, may by the compassion of Thy loving kindness be mercifully absolved.

O God, the one only remedy for human infirmity, show forth upon this Thy sick *servant* the power of Thine aid, that, strengthened by the might of Thy tender mercy, *he* may be found worthy to be restored whole unto Thy holy Church.

Grant, O Lord God, we beseech Thee, that this Thy *servant* may rejoice in continual health of body and mind; and, through the glorious intercession of Blessed Mary, ever Virgin, be freed from *his* present sorrow, and enjoy eternal gladness. Through Christ Our Lord. ℟. Amen.

The blessing of God Almighty, the Father, ✠ the Son, and the Holy Ghost, descend upon thee and remain with thee always. ℟. Amen.

He then sprinkles the sick person with holy water.

The priest may also say the psalms, Gospels, and prayers which follow, according to the exigency of the time and the wish of the sick person.

PSALM 6

O Lord, rebuke me not in Thine anger: nor chastise me in Thy wrath.

Have mercy on me, O Lord, for I am weak: heal me, O Lord, for my bones are troubled.

My soul also is troubled exceedingly: but Thou, O Lord, how long?

Turn Thee, O Lord, and deliver my soul: O save me for Thy mercy's sake.

For in death there is no one that is mindful of Thee: and who will give Thee thanks in hell?

I have labored in my groanings, every night will I wash my bed: and water my couch with my tears.

Mine eye is troubled through indignation: I have grown old amongst all mine enemies.

Depart from me, all ye workers of iniquity: for the Lord hath heard the voice of my weeping.

The Lord hath heard my supplication: the Lord hath received my prayer.

Let all mine enemies be put to shame, and be sore troubled: let them be turned back, and put to shame very speedily.

Glory be to the Father, etc.

℣. The Lord be with you.
℟. And with thy spirit.
℣. The continuation of the holy Gospel according to Matthew.
℟. Glory be to Thee, O Lord.

When the priest says, The continuation, *etc., he makes the sign of the cross in the usual manner upon his forehead, mouth, and breast; and also upon the sick man, if he cannot do thus for himself.*

(*But if the sick person is a woman, and unable to make the crosses upon herself, let them be made by some other woman. And likewise in all such instances.*)

Matthew 8:5–13

And on His entering into Capharnaum, a centurion came to Him, beseeching Him, and saying: Lord, my servant lieth at home sick of the palsy, and is grievously tormented. And Jesus saith to him: I will come and heal him. And the centurion making answer, said: Lord, I am not worthy that Thou shouldst enter under my roof; but only say the word, and my servant shall be healed. For I also am a man subject to authority, having soldiers under me; and I say to one: Go, and he goeth; and to another: Come, and he cometh; and to my servant: Do this, and he doeth it. And Jesus, hearing this, marveled, and said to those who followed Him: Truly, I say to you, I have not found so great faith in Israel. And I say to you, that many shall come from the East and the West, and shall recline at table with Abraham, and Isaac, and Jacob, in the kingdom of heaven. But the children of the kingdom shall be cast out into the outer darkness; there shall be wailing and gnashing of teeth. And Jesus said to the centurion: Go, and as thou hast believed, be it done to thee. And the servant was healed at the same hour.

Let us pray.
    Almighty and eternal God, the everlasting Health of them that believe: hear us for Thy sick *servant,* N., for whom we implore the aid of Thy pitying mercy, that, with *his* bodily health restored, *he* may give thanks to Thee in Thy church. Through Christ Our Lord. ℟. Amen.

Psalm 15

Preserve me, O Lord, for in Thee have I put my trust: I have said to the Lord, Thou
    art my God, for Thou hast no need of my goods.
To the saints who are in His land: He hath made wonderful all my desires in them.
Their infirmities were multiplied: afterward they made haste.

I will not gather together their meetings for blood offerings: nor will I make mention of their names with my lips.

The Lord is the portion of my inheritance and of my cup: Thou art He that will restore my inheritance unto me.

The lines are fallen unto me in goodly places: for my inheritance is goodly unto me.

I will bless the Lord, Who hath given me understanding: moreover my reins also have corrected me even till night.

I set the Lord always in my sight: for He is at my right hand, that I be not moved.

Therefore my heart hath been glad, and my tongue hath rejoiced: moreover my flesh also shall rest in hope.

For Thou wilt not leave my soul in hell: nor wilt Thou give Thy holy one to see corruption.

Thou hast made known unto me the ways of life: Thou shalt fill me with joy with Thy countenance: at Thy right hand are delights forevermore.

Glory be to the Father, etc.

℣. The Lord be with you.
℟. And with thy spirit.
℣. The continuation of the holy Gospel according to Mark.
℟. Glory be to Thee, O Lord.

Mark 16:14–18

At that time: Jesus appeared to the Eleven, as they were at table, and upbraided them with their unbelief and hardness of heart, because they did not believe those who had seen Him after He was risen again. And He said to them: Go ye into the whole world, and preach the gospel to every creature. He that believeth and is baptized shall be saved, but he that believeth not shall be condemned. And these signs shall follow those who believe: in My name they shall cast out devils; they shall speak with new tongues; they shall take up serpents; and if they drink any deadly thing, it shall not hurt them; they shall lay their hands upon the sick, and they shall recover.

Let us pray.

O God of the heavenly virtues, who from the bodies of men drivest forth all sickness and all infirmity by the power of Thy word: draw graciously nigh unto this Thy *servant*, N., that with weakness put to flight, and health and strength continually renewed, *he* may ever bless Thy holy name. ℟. Amen.

Psalm 19

May the Lord hear thee in the day of trouble: may the name of the God of Jacob protect thee.

May He send thee help from the sanctuary: and defend thee out of Sion.

May He be mindful of all thy sacrifices: and may thy whole burnt offerings be made fat.

May He give unto thee according to thine own heart: and confirm all thy counsels.

We will rejoice in thy salvation: and in the name of our God we shall be exalted.

The Lord fulfill all thy petitions: now have I known that the Lord hath saved His anointed.

He will hear him from His holy heaven: the salvation of His right hand is powerful.

Some trust in chariots, and some in horses: but we will call upon the name of the Lord our God.

They are entangled and have fallen: but we are risen, and stand upright.

O Lord, save the king: and hear us in the day that we shall call upon Thee.

Glory be to the Father, etc.

℣. The Lord be with you.

℟. And with thy spirit.

℣. The continuation of the holy Gospel according to Luke.

℟. Glory be to Thee, O Lord.

Luke 4:38–40.

At that time: Jesus rising up out of the synagogue, went into the house of Simon: and Simon's mother-in-law was taken with a great fever, and they besought Him for her. And standing over her, He commanded the fever, and it left her: and immediately she arose and ministered to them. And after sunset, all they who had any sick with various diseases brought them to Him: and He laid His hands on every one of them, and healed them.

Let us pray.

O holy Lord, Father Almighty, everlasting God, Who by the inpouring of the dignity of Thy power strengthenest the weakness of man's estate, that our bodies and minds may be quickened by the saving remedies of Thy loving kindness: graciously incline unto this Thy *servant*, that, every strait of bodily infirmity being done away, the grace of former health may in *him* be perfectly restored. ℟. Amen.

Psalm 85

Incline Thine ear, O Lord, and hear me: for I am needy and poor.

Preserve my soul, for I am holy: O my God, save Thy servant, that trusteth in Thee.

Have mercy upon me, O Lord: for unto Thee have I cried all the day. Give joy to the soul of Thy servant, for unto Thee, O Lord, have I lifted up my soul.

For Thou, O Lord, art sweet and mild; and plenteous in mercy unto all that call upon Thee.

Give ear, O Lord, unto my prayer: and attend to the voice of my petition.

I have called upon Thee in the day of my trouble: for Thou hast heard me.

Among the gods there is none like unto Thee, O Lord: and there is none that can do works like unto Thy works.

All the nations whom Thou hast made shall come and worship before Thee, O Lord: and shall glorify Thy name.

For Thou art great, and doest wondrous things: Thou art God alone.

Lead me, O Lord, in Thy way, and I will walk in Thy truth: let my heart rejoice that it may fear Thy name.

I will praise Thee, O Lord my God, with my whole heart: and I will glorify Thy name forever.

For great is Thy mercy toward me: and Thou hast delivered my soul out of the lower hell.

O God, the wicked are risen up against me; and the assembly of the mighty have sought after my soul: and they have not set Thee before their eyes.

And Thou, O Lord, art a God full of compassion, and merciful: long-suffering, and of much mercy, and true.

O look upon me, and have mercy on me: give Thy strength unto Thy servant, and save the son of Thine handmaid.

Show me a token for good: that they who hate me may see, and be confounded: because Thou, O Lord, hast helped me, and hast comforted me.

Glory be to the Father, etc.

℣. The Lord be with you.

℟. And with thy spirit.

℣. The continuation of the holy Gospel according to John.

℟. Glory be to Thee, O Lord.

John 5:1–14.

At that time there was a feast of the Jews, and Jesus went up to Jerusalem. Now there is at Jerusalem a pool, Probatica, which in Hebrew is named Bethsaida, having five porches. In these lay a great multitude of infirm, blind, lame, withered, waiting for the stirring of the water. For an angel of the Lord descended at certain times into the pool, and the water was stirred; and he who went down first into the pond after the stirring of the water, was cured of whatever disease he had. And a certain man was there, who had an infirmity eight-and-thirty years. When Jesus saw him as he lay, and knew that he had been so a long time, He saith to him, Wilt thou be healed? The infirm man answered Him, Sir, I have no man, when the water is stirred, to put me into the pool; for whilst I am coming, another goeth down before me. Jesus saith to him, Arise, take up thy bed, and walk; and immediately the man was healed, and he took up his bed and walked. And on that day was the Sabbath. The Jews therefore said to him who had been healed, It is the Sabbath; it is not lawful for thee to take up thy bed. He answered them, He Who healed me, He said to me, Take up thy bed and walk. They asked him therefore: Who is that man Who said to thee, Take up thy bed and walk? But he who was healed knew not who it was; for Jesus had gone aside from the crowd standing in the place. Afterward, Jesus findeth him in the temple, and saith to him, Behold, thou art healed; sin no more, lest something worse befall thee.

Let us pray.

Look Thou down, O Lord, we beseech Thee, upon Thy *servant*, grievously stricken with bodily infirmity; and refresh the soul which Thou hast created, that, being bettered by Thy chastisements, *he* may without ceasing feel *himself* saved by Thy healing. Through Christ Our Lord. ℞. Amen.

Psalm 90

He that dwelleth in the help of the Most High: shall abide under the protection of the God of heaven.

He shall say unto the Lord: Thou art my upholder, and my refuge: my God, in Him will I hope.

For He hath delivered me from the snare of the hunters; and from the sharp word.

He shall overshadow thee with His shoulders: and under His wings shalt thou trust.

His truth shall compass thee with a shield: thou shalt not be afraid for the terror of the night;

For the arrow that flieth in the day; for the plague that walketh in the darkness; for the assault of the evil one in the noonday.

A thousand shall fall at thy side, and ten thousand at thy right hand: but it shall not come nigh thee

But with thine eyes shalt thou behold: and shalt see the reward of the wicked.

For Thou, O Lord, art my hope: thou hast made the Most High thy refuge.

There shall no evil approach unto thee: neither shall the scourge come nigh thy dwelling.

For He hath given His angels charge over thee: to keep thee in all thy ways.

In their hands they shall bear thee up: lest haply thou dash thy foot against a stone.

Thou shalt walk upon the asp and the basilisk: the lion and the dragon shalt thou trample underfoot.

Because he hath hoped in Me, I will deliver him: I will protect him because he hath known My name.

He shall cry unto Me, and I will hear him: I am with him in trouble, I will deliver him, and I will glorify him.

I will fill him with length of days: and will show him My salvation.

Glory be to the Father, etc.

Let us pray.

Almighty, everlasting God, look graciously down upon the sickness of this Thy *servant*: and stretch forth the right hand of Thy majesty to help and defend *him*. Through Christ Our Lord. ℞. Amen.

At the end of this prayer the priest places his right hand upon the head of the sick person, and says:
They shall lay their hands upon the sick, and they shall recover. May Jesus, the Son of Mary, the Lord and Redeemer of the world, through the merits and intercession of His holy apostles Peter and Paul, and all His saints, be favorable and gracious unto thee. Amen.

He then says:
℣. The Lord be with you.
℞. And with thy spirit.
℣. The beginning of the holy Gospel according to John.
℞. Glory be to Thee, O Lord.

John 1:1–14

In the beginning was the Word, and the Word was with God, and the Word was God. This was in the beginning with God. All things were made through Him, and without Him was made nothing that was made: in Him was life, and the life was the light of men: and the light shineth in darkness, and the darkness did not comprehend it.

There was a man sent from God, whose name was John. This one came for a witness, to testify concerning the light, that all might believe through him. He was not the light, but he was to testify concerning the light. The true Light, which enlighteneth every man, cometh into this world.

He was in the world, and the world was made through Him, and the world knew Him not. He came to His own possessions, and His own people received Him not. But to as many as received Him He gave power to become children of God, to those who believe in His name, who are born not of blood, nor of the will of the flesh, nor of the will of man, but of God. AND THE WORD WAS MADE FLESH, and dwelt among us; and we saw His glory, the glory as of the only begotten of the Father, full of grace and truth.

He then blesses the sick person, adding:
The blessing of God Almighty, the Father, ✠ the Son, and the Holy Ghost, descend upon thee and remain with thee always. ℞. Amen.

He then sprinkles the sick person with holy water.

If there are many sick in the same room, all the above prayers are said in the plural number. And all can be abbreviated at the will of the priest.

The Last Blessing and Plenary Indulgence

As the hour of death approaches—that hour on which so much depends—the pious Christian should fervently prepare to receive the last blessing and plenary indulgence granted to those who are near their end. For Our Lord Jesus Christ promised to St. Peter the keys of the kingdom of heaven; assuring him that whatever he should bind on earth should be bound also in heaven, and whatever he should loose on earth should be loosed also in heaven (see Mt 16:19). By this power of binding and loosing, derived from St. Peter to his successors, and by them specially communicated to the pastors of souls, the latter are authorized to grant a plenary indulgence, together with a solemn blessing, to all such as are in or near their last agony. But then the dying Christian should remember well that, in order to receive the benefit of this plenary indulgence and blessing, it is requisite that he concur on his part, by renouncing and detesting all his sins, both known and unknown, mortal and venial; by accepting with patience and resignation whatever he may have yet to suffer, and offering up his pains and death, in union with the sufferings and death of his Redeemer, in satisfaction for his sins.

To this end the Church directs the priest who ministers to the sick person to put him in mind frequently to invoke the name of Jesus, and to exhort him:

1. That he firmly believe all the articles of the Faith, and whatever the holy Roman Catholic and apostolic Church believes and teaches.

2. That he confidently hope that Our Lord Jesus Christ, in His boundless compassion, will have mercy on him; and that, by the merits of His most holy Passion, and through the intercession of the Blessed Virgin Mary and all the saints, he will obtain everlasting life.

3. That he love the Lord God with all his heart, and that he desire to love Him more and more perfectly, with that love wherewith all the saints and blessed in heaven love Him.

4. That, for the love of God, he grieve from the heart for all offenses whatsoever that he has committed against God and his neighbor.

5. That, for the love of God, he forgive from the heart his enemies, and all that have in any way injured him and done him wrong.

6. That he beg forgiveness of those whom he has at any time offended in word or deed.

7. That he patiently endure all the pains and discomfort of sickness, for God's sake, in penance for his sins.

8. That if God shall vouchsafe to restore him to his bodily health, he resolve henceforth, to the best of his power, to guard against sin, and to keep His commandments.

9. That, as far as he is able, he should say such prayers as these:

Have mercy upon me, O God, according to Thy great mercy.—In Thee, O Lord, have I hoped: let me never be confounded.—Into Thy hands, O Lord, I commend my spirit: Thou hast redeemed me, O Lord God of truth.—Come unto my help, O God: O Lord, make haste to help me.—O Lord, be Thou unto me a God, a Protector.—O God, be merciful to me a sinner.—O sweetest Lord Jesus Christ, by the power of Thy most holy Passion, receive me into the number of Thine elect.—O Lord Jesus Christ, receive my spirit.—O Mary, Mother of grace, Mother of mercy, do thou protect me from the enemy, and receive me at the hour of death.—O holy angel of God, assist me as my guardian.—O all ye holy angels, and all ye saints, intercede for me, and hasten to my aid.

FORM OF BESTOWING THE APOSTOLIC BLESSING AND THE PLENARY INDULGENCE AT THE HOUR OF DEATH

NOTE.—The italicized *words, or endings of words, occurring in the text, are those which must be varied according to sex.*

The priest having faculties to bestow this Apostolic Blessing *enters the house, and says:*

Pax huic domui.	Peace be unto this house.
℟. Et omnibus habitantibus in ea.	℟. And unto all who dwell therein.

After which he sprinkles the sick person, the room, and the bystanders, with holy water in the form of a cross, saying the Asperges.

Asperges me, Domine, hyssopo, et mundabor: lavabis me, et super nivem dealbabor.

Thou shalt sprinkle me, O Lord, with hyssop, and I shall be cleansed: Thou shalt wash me, and I shall be made whiter than snow.

Miserere mei, Deus, secundum magnam misericordiam tuam.

Have mercy upon me, O God, according to Thy great mercy.

Gloria Patri, et Filio, et Spiritui Sancto. Sicut erat in principio, et nunc, et semper, et in sæcula sæculorum. Amen.

Glory be to the Father, and to the Son, and to the Holy Ghost. As it was in the beginning, is now, and ever shall be, world without end. Amen.

Ant. Asperges me, Domine, hyssopo, et mundabor: lavabis me, et super nivem dealbabor.

Ant. Thou shalt sprinkle me, O Lord, with hyssop, and I shall be cleansed: Thou shalt wash me, and I shall be made whiter than snow.

He then hears the Confession of the sick person; or if that be not necessary, bids him at least make an act of contrition, and, if time allows, briefly instructs him concerning the efficacy and power of this blessing. The priest then exhorts him to bear his sufferings patiently, as an expiation for the sins of the past; to offer himself wholly to God prepared cheerfully to accept whatever may be His holy will; and to be ready to undergo death itself as a payment of the penalty due to his sins. Then, with consoling words, the priest bids him have great confidence in God, and to be assured that he will attain, through the riches of His exceeding bounty, a remission of temporal punishment, and the reward of everlasting life. The priest then says:

Adjutorium nostrum in nomine Domini.

Our help is in the name of the Lord.

℞. Qui fecit cœlum et terram.

℞. Who hath made heaven and earth.

Ant. Ne reminiscaris, Domine, delicta famu*li tui* neque vindictam sumas de peccatis ejus.

Ant. Remember not, O Lord, the offenses of Thy *servant*, neither take Thou revenge of *his* sins.

Kyrie, eleison.
Christe, eleison.
Kyrie, eleison.
Pater noster (*secreto*).

Lord, have mercy.
Christ, have mercy.
Lord, have mercy.
Our Father (*inaudibly*).

℣. Et ne nos inducas in tentationem.
℞. Sed libera nos a malo.
℣. Salv*um* fac *servum tuum*.
℞. Deus meus, sperantem in te.

℣. And lead us not into temptation.
℞. But deliver us from evil.
℣. Save Thy *servant*.
℞ O my God, who putteth *his* trust in Thee.

℣. Domine, exaudi orationem meam.
℞. Et clamor meus ad te veniat.
℣. Dominus vobiscum.
℞. Et cum spiritu tuo.

℣. O Lord, hear my prayer.
℞. And let my cry come unto Thee.
℣. The Lord be with you.
℞. And with thy spirit.

Oremus.

Clementissime Deus, Pater miseri-
cordiarum, et Deus totius consolationis, qui neminem vis perire in te
credentem, atque sperantem: secundum multitudinem miserationum
tuarum respice propitius famul*um*
tuum N., *quem* tibi vera fides, et spes
Christiana commendant. Visita *eum*
in salutari tuo, et per Unigeniti tui
passionem et mortem, omnium ei
delictorum suorum remissionem, et
veniam clementer indulge; ut ejus
anima in hora exitus sui te judicem
propitiatum inveniat, et in sanguine
ejusdem Filii tui ab omni macula
abluta, transire ad vitam mereatur
perpetuam. Per eundem Christum
Dominum nostrum. ℟. Amen.

Let us pray.

O most gracious God, Father of
mercies and God of all comfort,
Who wouldest not that any should
perish who believeth and trusteth in
Thee, according to the multitude of
Thy tender mercies, look favorably
upon Thy *servant* N., whom the
true faith and hope of Christ do
commend unto Thee. Visit *him* in
Thy saving power; and through the
Passion and death of Thine Only-
begotten, graciously grant unto *him*
pardon and remission of all *his* sins;
that *his* soul at the hour of its departure may find Thee a most merciful
Judge; and, cleansed from every stain
in the blood of the same, Thy Son,
may be found worthy to pass to life
everlasting. Through the same Christ
Our Lord. ℟. Amen.

Then the Confiteor *being repeated by an attendant clergyman, or by the priest himself,
the priest says the* Misereatur, *etc., and then proceeds thus.*[35]

Dominus noster Jesus Christus, Filius
Dei vivi, qui beato Petro Apostolo
suo dedit potestatem ligandi, atque
solvendi, per suam piissimam misericordiam recipiat confessionem
tuam, et restituat tibi stolam pri-
mam, quam in baptismate recepisti:
et ego facultate mihi ab Apostolica
Sede tributa, indulgentiam plenar-
iam et remissionem omnium peccatorum tibi concedo: In nomine
Patris, ✠ et Filii, et Spiritus Sancti.
Amen.

May Our Lord Jesus Christ, Son of the
living God, Who gave to His blessed
apostle Peter the power of binding
and loosing; of His most tender
mercy receive thy confession, and restore unto thee that first robe which
thou didst receive in Baptism; and
I, by the power committed to me by
the Apostolic See, grant thee a plenary indulgence and remission of all
thy sins. In the name of the Father,
✠ and of the Son, and of the Holy
Ghost. *Amen.*

---

[35]   ‡In case of necessity, this prayer alone may be said.

Per sacrosancta humanæ reparationis mysteria, remittat tibi omnipotens Deus omnes præsentis et futuræ vitæ pœnas, paradisi portas aperiat, et ad gaudia sempiterna perducat. *Amen.*	Through the most sacred mysteries of man's Redemption may God Almighty remit unto thee the pains of the present and the future life, open to thee the gates of paradise, and bring thee to everlasting joys. *Amen.*
Benedicat te omnipotens Deus, Pater, ✠ et Filius, et Spiritus Sanctus. *Amen.*	May God Almighty bless thee; the Father, ✠ and the Son, and the Holy Ghost. *Amen.*

EJACULATIONS TO JESUS SUFFERING

FOR THE SICK AND DYING

Good Jesus! Physician of souls and bodies; make my sickness a healing medicine to my soul; soothe by Thy presence each ache and pain; hallow my suffering by Thine all-holy suffering; teach me to unite my sufferings with Thine, to be hallowed by Thine.

Lord, offer all my sufferings to Thy Father, as Thou didst offer all Thine agonies to Him.

O good Jesus, crucified for us; nail my will to Thy Cross, for love of Thee.

Good Jesus, give me a deep love for Thee, that nothing may be too hard for me to bear from Thee.

Good Jesus, Who hast borne the Cross for me, what cross willest Thou that I should bear for Thee?

Thou knowest, Lord, that I am all weakness; teach me to bear my cross. Bear it for me, bear it in me.

Lord, strengthen me to bear my cross patiently, humbly, lovingly. If I sink under it, look on me and raise me up. Give what Thou commandest, and command what Thou willest. Only by Thine all-holy Cross and Passion, sanctify my cross to me, and keep me Thine forever.

Good Jesus, nailed motionless by Thy sacred hands and feet for love of me; keep me still, motionless, unmoved, unshaken, cleaving fast to Thee.

O good Jesus, my God, and my All, keep me ever near Thee, let nothing for a moment separate me from Thee.

Good Jesus, to Thee I flee; hide me in Thy sacred side.

O good Jesus, Who keepest Thine own under the shadow of Thy wings; teach me to flee to Thee, and hide me from all evil.

O good Jesus, shelter me from the evil one, shed Thy dew upon me to calm my soul, and dwell in me fully, that I may wholly love Thee.

Good Jesus, Strength of the weary, Rest of the restless; by the weariness and unrest of Thy sacred Cross, come to me who am weary that I may rest in Thee.

Lord, if Thou increase my pain, increase also my patience. Thou knowest my weakness.

Good Jesus, Who hast borne so patiently with me; make me wholly patient for love of Thee.

O good Jesus, obedient unto death, even the death of the Cross for me; good Jesus, mocked and blasphemed for love of us; make me truly humble for love of Thee.

O blessed Jesus, into Thy hands I commend my soul and my body, to live or to die as seemeth good to Thee, and to Thine infinite mercy; for Thou hast redeemed me, O Lord, Thou God of truth!

Good Lord, teach me to judge myself as Thou judgest. Make me more ashamed of sin than of all besides: yet not so ashamed as not quickly to come to Thee, O all-merciful, all-loving Lord.

Good Jesus! by Thy loneliness in the Garden, by the desolation Thou didst will to come over Thee, sanctify mine.

Good Jesus, Who alone orderest all things well, I cast myself wholly upon Thine infinite undeserved love; I trust Thee with my all: myself, and all whom I love, and all which I desire, my present and my future, my hopes and my fears, my time and my eternity, my joys and my sorrows. Deal with me as Thou willest, and knowest best; only bind me safe to Thine everlasting love.

Good Jesus! Who didst give Thyself for me, give Thyself to me; make me wholly Thine, that I may deeply love Thee.

Good Jesus! stripped naked, racked, reviled, forsaken, motionless on the Cross for love of me; help me to bear all pain meekly, in humble love of Thee. Strip me, empty me of myself, to fill me with love of Thee.

Good Jesus, lead me, that I may follow Thee; hold me, that I may cling fast to Thee; teach me, that I may choose Thee alone; keep me, that I may be Thine forever.

Jesus, most tender, Thou hast been very tender to me; make me very tender to all and of all who are Thine, for the love of Thy most tender love.

O good Jesus, Who hast so loved us; pour Thy love into my soul, that I may love Thee intensely, and all besides in and for Thee. *Amen.*

O eternal Father! I am Thy most unworthy servant, whom Thou hast so loved that Thou gavest Thy dearly beloved Son to die for me. Deal mercifully with Thy servant in this hour, lest that Precious Blood be shed for me in vain. For what profit is there to me in my Savior's blood, if I go down to corruption?

O Jesus Christ, I am like that lost sheep whom Thou didst seek so diligently, and set it on Thy shoulders to bring it home again. Thou art the Good Shepherd, Who didst lay down Thy life for Thy sheep. Oh! seek Thy servant, for I have gone astray like a sheep that is lost. Let not that roaring lion, that goeth about seeking whom he may devour, snatch me and tear me from Thee; save me upon the Cross, take me into Thy loved embrace and draw my soul to Thee; receive me good Jesus, of Thy mercy; receive my soul in peace.

Enlighten mine eyes, O good Jesus, that I sleep not in death; lest mine enemy say, I have prevailed against him.

O Lord Jesus Christ, Son of the living God, set Thy Passion, Cross, and death, between Thy judgment and my soul.

O good Jesus, remember not my old sins, but have mercy upon me and that soon, for I am come to great misery.

O most sweet Lord Jesus Christ, for the honor and virtue of Thy blessed Passion, bid me be written among the number of Thine elect.

Enter not into judgment with Thy servant, most compassionate Jesus, for in Thy sight shall no man living be justified.

One thing have I asked of the Lord, this will I seek after: that I may dwell in the house of the Lord all the days of my life.

Bring my soul out of prison, that I may give thanks unto Thy name: lo, the just wait for me till Thou recompense me.

Oh! establish me according to Thy word, that I may live, and let me not be disappointed of my hope. *Amen.*

PRAYER FOR THE FAITHFUL IN THEIR AGONY

O most merciful Jesus, Lover of souls; I pray Thee, by the agony of Thy most Sacred Heart, and by the sorrows of Thy Immaculate Mother, cleanse in Thine own blood the sinners of the whole world who are now in their agony and who are to die this day. *Amen.*

Heart of Jesus, once in agony, pity the dying.

RECOMMENDATION OF A DEPARTING SOUL

NOTE. — The italicized words, or endings of words, (or those in Roman *throughout the* responses *of the Litany) occurring in the text, are those which must be varied according to sex.*

The priest, vested in surplice and violet stole, enters the room of the dying person, saying:

Pax huic domui.	Peace be unto this house.
℟. Et omnibus habitantibus in ea.	℟. And unto all who dwell therein.

He then sprinkles the dying person, the chamber, and the bystanders, with holy water in the form of a cross, saying the Asperges.

Asperges me, Domine, hyssopo, et mundabor: lavabis me, et super nivem dealbabor.	Thou shalt sprinkle me, O Lord, with hyssop, and I shall be cleansed: Thou shalt wash me, and I shall be made whiter than snow.
Miserere mei, Deus, secundum magnam misericordiam tuam.	Have mercy upon me, O God, according to Thy great mercy.
Gloria Patri, et Filio, et Spiritui Sancto. Sicut erat in principio, et nunc, et semper, et in sæcula sæculorum. Amen.	Glory be to the Father, and to the Son, and to the Holy Ghost. As it was in the beginning, is now, and ever shall be, world without end. Amen.
Ant. Asperges me, Domine, hyssopo, et mundabor: lavabis me, et super nivem dealbabor.	*Ant.* Thou shalt sprinkle me, O Lord, with hyssop, and I shall be cleansed: Thou shalt wash me, and I shall be made whiter than snow.

He next presents a crucifix to the dying persom to be kissed, and exhorts him to look forward to everlasting life; leaving the crucifix before him, that, beholding it, he may be encouraged to hope for eternal salvation. Then, having lighted a candle, the priest kneels, and with the bystanders devoutly recites the Shorter Litany, *as follows:*

THE LITANY FOR THE DYING

Kyrie, eleison.	Lord, have mercy.
Christe, eleison.	*Christ, have mercy.*
Kyrie, eleison.	Lord, have mercy.
Sancta Maria, *ora pro eo.*	Holy Mary, *pray for* him.
Omnes sancti Angeli et Archangeli, *orate pro eo.*	All ye holy angels and archangels,
Sancte Abel, *ora pro eo.*	Holy Abel,
Omnis chorus Justorum,	All ye choirs of the just,
Sancte Abraham,	Holy Abraham,

Sancte Joannes Baptista,	St. John the Baptist,
Sancte Joseph,	St. Joseph,
Omnes sancti Patriarchæ et Prophetæ, *orate* eo.	All ye holy patriarchs and prophets,
Sancte Petre, *ora pro* eo.	St. Peter, pray for us.
Sancte Paule,	St. Paul,
Sancte Andrea,	St. Andrew,
Sancte Joannes,	St. John,
Omnes sancti, Apostoli et Evangelistæ, *orate pro* eo.	All ye holy apostles and evangelists, pray for us.
Omnes sancti Discipuli Domini, *orate pro* eo.	All ye holy disciples of the Lord,
Omnes sancti Innocentes, *orate pro* eo.	All ye Holy Innocents,
Sancte Stephane, *ora pro* eo.	St. Stephen, pray for us.
Sancte Laurenti, *ora pro* eo.	St. Lawrence,
Omnes sancti Martyres, *orate pro* eo.	All ye holy martyrs,
Sancte Silvester, *ora pro* eo.	St. Sylvester, pray for us.
Sancte Gregori, *ora pro* eo.	St. Gregory,
Sancte Augustine, *ora pro* eo.	St. Augustine,
Omnes sancti Pontifices et Confessores, *orate pro* eo.	All ye holy bishops and confessors, pray for us.
Sancte Benedicte, *ora pro* eo.	St. Benedict,
Sancte Francisce, *ora pro* eo.	St. Francis,
Sancte Camille, *ora pro* eo.	All ye holy priests and Levites, pray for us.
Sancte Joannes de Deo,	
Omnes sancti Monachi et Eremitæ, *orate pro* eo.	All ye holy monks and hermits,
Sancta Maria Magdalena, *ora pro* eo.	St. Mary Magdalen,
Sancta Lucia, *ora pro* eo.	St. Lucy,
Omnes sanctæ Virgines et Viduæ, *orate pro* eo.	All ye holy virgins and widows,
Omnes Sancti et Sanctæ Dei, *intercedite pro* eo.	All ye holy saints of God, *make intercession for* him.

Propitius esto, *parce ei, Domine.*
Propitius esto, *libera* eum, *Domine.*
Propitius esto *libera* eum, *Domine.*

Be merciful, *spare* him, *O Lord.*
Be merciful, *O Lord, deliver* him.
Be merciful, *O Lord, deliver* him.

Ab ira tua,
A periculo mortis,
A mala morte,
A pœnis inferni,

From Thy wrath,
From the peril of death,
From an evil death,
From the pains of hell,

Ab omni malo,
A potestate diaboli,
Per Nativitatem tuam,
Per Crucem et Passionem tuam,

From all evil,
From the power of the devil,
Through Thy birth,
Through Thy Cross and Passion,

Per Mortem et Sepulturam tuam,
Per gloriosam Resurrectionem tuam,
Per admirabilem Ascensionem tuam,
Per gratiam Spiritus Sancti Paracliti,

Through Thy death and burial,
Through Thy glorious Resurrection,
Through Thine admirable Ascension,
Through the grace of the Holy Ghost
the Paraclete,

In die judicii,
Peccatores, *te rogamus, audi nos.*
Ut ei parcas, *te rogamus, audi nos.*

In the Day of Judgment,
We sinners, we *beseech Thee, hear us.*
That Thou spare *him, we beseech Thee,
hear us.*

Kyrie, eleison.
Christe, eleison.
Kyrie, eleison.

Lord, have mercy.
Christ, have mercy.
Lord, have mercy.

Then, while the soul is in the agony of its departure, the priest recites the following prayers:

Proficiscere, anima christiana, de hoc mundo, in nomine Dei Patris omnipotentis, qui te creavit: in nomine Jesu Christi Filii Dei vivi, qui pro te passus est: in nomine Spiritus Sancti, qui in te effusus est: [‡in nomine gloriosæ et Sanctæ Dei Genitricis Virginis Mariæ; in nomine beati Joseph, inclyti ejusdem Virginis Sponsi:] in nomine Angelorum et Archangelorum: in nomine Thronorum et Dominationum: in nomine Principatuum et Potestatum: in nomine [‡Virtutum,] Cherubim et Seraphim: in nomine Patriarcharum et Prophetarum: in nomine sanctorum Apostolorum et Evangelistarum: in nomine sanctorum Martyrum et Confessorum: in nomine sanctorum Monachorum et Eremitarum: in nomine sanctarum Virginum et omnium Sanctorum et Sanctarum Dei. Hodie sit in pace locus tuus, et habitatio tua in sancta Sion. Per eundem Christum Dominum nostrum. ℟. Amen.

Go forth, O Christian soul, from this world, in the name of God the Father Almighty, Who created thee; in the name of Jesus Christ, Son of the living God, Who suffered for thee; in the name of the Holy Ghost, Who was poured forth upon thee; [‡in the name of the glorious and ever Blessed Virgin Mary, Mother of God; in the name of St. Joseph, chaste spouse of the same Virgin;] in the name of the angels and archangels; in the name of the thrones and dominations; in the name of the principalities and powers; in the name of the [‡heavenly forces,] cherubim, and seraphim; in the name of the patriarchs and prophets; in the name of the holy apostles and evangelists; in the name of the holy martyrs and confessors; in the name of the holy monks and hermits; in the name of the holy virgins and of all the saints of God: may thy place be this day in peace, and thine abode in holy Sion. Through the same Christ Our Lord. ℟. Amen.

Deus misericors, Deus clemens, Deus, qui secundum multitudinem miserationum tuarum peccata pœnitentium deles, et præteritorum criminum culpas venia remissionis evacuas: respice propitius super *hunc* famul*um tuum* N., et remissionem omnium peccatorum suorum, tota cordis confessione poscentem, depracatus exaudi. Renova in *eo*, piissime Pater, quidquid terrena fragilitate corruptum, vel quidquid diabolica fraude violatum est: et unitati corporis Ecclesiæ membrum redemptionis annecte. Miserere, Domine, gemituum, miserere lacrymarum ejus: et non habentem fiduciam, nisi in tua misericordia, ad tuæ Sacramentum reconciliationis admitte. Per Christum Dominum nostrum. ℟. Amen.

O merciful God, O gracious God, O God, Who, according to the multitude of Thy tender mercies, blottest out the sins of the penitent, and graciously remittest the guilt of past offenses; look favorably upon this Thy *servant* N., and in Thy mercy hear *him* as *he* craves, with heartfelt confession, the remission of all *his* sins. Renew within *him*, O most loving Father, whatsoever hath been corrupted through human frailty, or violated through the deceit of the devil; and associate *him* as a member redeemed to the unity of the body of Thy Church. Have pity, Lord, on *his* groanings; have pity on *his* tears; and admit *him*, who hath no hope save in Thy mercy, to the Sacrament of Thy reconciliation. Through Christ Our Lord. ℟. Amen.

Commendo te omnipotenti Deo, charissime *frater*, et ei, cujus es creatura, committo; ut, cum humanitatis debitum morte interveniente persolveris, ad Auctorem tuum, qui te de limo terræ formaverat, revertaris. Egredienti itaque animæ tuæ de corpore splendidus Angelorum cœtus occurrat: judex Apostolorum tibi senatus adveniat: candidatorum tibi Martyrum triumphator exercitus obviet: liliata rutilantium te Confessorum turma circumdet: jubilantium te Virginum chorus excipiat: et beatæ quietis in sinu Patriarcharum te complexus astringat:

I commend thee to Almighty God, dearly beloved *brother*, and commit thee to Him Whose creature thou art; that, when thou shalt have paid the debt of humanity by passing through death, thou mayest return to thy Maker, Who formed thee from the dust of the earth. When, therefore, thy soul goeth forth from thy body, may the glorious company of angels meet thee; may the council of the apostles who shall judge the world greet thee; may the triumphant army of white-robed martyrs come out to welcome thee; may the band of shining confessors, crowned with lilies, encircle thee; may the choir of joyous virgins receive thee; and unto the bosom of blessed rest may the embrace of the patriarchs clasp thee;

[‡sanctus Joseph, morientium Patronus dulcissimus, in magnam spem te erigat: sancta Dei Genitrix Virgo Maria suos benigna oculos ad te converta:] mitis, atque festivus Christi Jesu tibi aspectus appareat, qui te inter assistentes sibi jugiter interesse decernat. Ignores omne, quod horret in tenebris, quod stridet in flammis, quod cruciat in tormentis. Cedat tibi teterrimus Satanas cum satellitibus suis: in adventu tuo te comitantibus Angelis contremiscat, atque in æternæ noctis chaos immane diffugiat. Exurgat Deus, et dissipentur inimici ejus: et fugiant qui oderunt eum, a facie ejus. Sicut deficit fumus, deficiant: sicut fluit cera a facie ignis, sic pereant peccatores a facie Dei: et justi epulentur, et exultent in conspectu Dei. Confundantur igitur et erubescant omnes tartareæ legiones, et ministri Satanæ iter tuum impedire non audeant. Liberet te a cruciatu Christus, qui pro te crucifixus est. Liberet te ab æterna morte Christus, qui pro te mori dignatus est. Constituat te Christus Filius Dei vivi intra paradisi sui semper amœna virentia, et inter oves suas te verus ille Pastor agnoscat. Ille ab omnibus peccatis tuis te absolvat, atque ad dexteram suam in electorum suorum et sorte constituat. Redemptorem tuum facie ad faciem videas,

[‡may St. Joseph, most consoling patron of the dying, lift thee up in holy hope; may Mary, the holy Mother of God, mercifully turn her eyes upon thee;] gentle and joyful may the face of Jesus Christ appear to thee, and may He award thee a place among those who stand before Him forever. Mayest thou never know aught of the terror of darkness, the gnashing of teeth in the flames, the agonies of torment. May Satan most foul, with his wicked crew, give way before thee; may he tremble at thy coming with the angels that attend thee, and flee away into the vast chaos of eternal night. Let God arise, and let His enemies be scattered; and let them that hate Him flee from before His face. As smoke vanisheth, so let them vanish away; as wax melteth before the fire, so let the wicked perish at the presence of God; and let the just feast and rejoice before God. May, then, all the legions of hell be confounded and put to shame, nor may the ministers of Satan dare to hinder thy way. May Christ, Who was crucified for thee, deliver thee from torment. May Christ, Who vouchsafed to die for thee, deliver thee from everlasting death. May Christ, the Son of the living God, place thee within the green pastures of His paradise, and may He, the true Shepherd, acknowledge thee as one of His sheep. May He absolve thee from all thy sins, and set thee at His right hand in the portion of His elect. Mayest thou behold thy Redeemer face-to-face;

et præsens semper assistens, manifestissimam beatis oculis aspicias veritatem. Constitut*us* igitur inter agmina beatorum, contemplationis divinæ dulcedine potiaris in sæcula sæculorum. ℟. Amen.

and, standing ever before Him, gaze with blessed eyes on the Truth made manifest. And set thus among the choirs of the blessed, mayest thou enjoy the sweetness of divine contemplation forevermore. ℟. Amen.

Suscipe, Domine, *servum tuum* in locum sperandæ sibi salvationis a misericordia tua. ℟. Amen.

Receive, O Lord, Thy *servant* into the place of salvation, which *he* hopes for from Thy mercy. ℟. Amen.

Libera, Domine, animam *servi tui* ex omnibus periculis inferni, et de laqueis pœnarum, et ex omnibus tribulationibus. ℟. Amen.

Deliver, O Lord, the soul of Thy *servant* from all the dangers of hell, and from the bonds of its punishments, and from all tribulations. ℟. Amen.

Libera, Domine, animam *servi tui* sicut liberasti Henoch et Eliam de communi morte mundi. ℟. Amen.

Deliver, O Lord, the soul of Thy *servant*, as Thou didst deliver Henoch and Elias from the common death of the world. ℟. Amen.

Libera, Domine, animam *servi tui* sicut liberasti Noe de diluvio. ℟. Amen.

Deliver, O Lord, the soul of Thy *servant*, as Thou didst deliver Noah from the Flood. ℟. Amen.

Libera, Domine, animam *servi tui* sicut liberasti Abraham de Ur Chaldæorum. ℟. Amen.

Deliver, O Lord, the soul of Thy *servant*, as Thou didst deliver Abraham from Ur of the Chaldeans. ℟. Amen.

Libera, Domine, animam *servi tui* sicut liberasti Job de passionibus suis. ℟. Amen.

Deliver, O Lord, the soul of Thy *servant*, as Thou didst deliver Job from his sufferings. ℟. Amen.

Libera, Domine, animam *servi tui* sicut liberasti Isaac de hostia, et de manu patris sui Abrahæ. ℟. Amen.

Deliver, O Lord, the soul of Thy *servant*, as Thou didst deliver Isaac from being sacrificed by the hand of his father Abraham. ℟. Amen.

Libera, Domine, animam *servi tui* sicut liberasti Loth de Sodomis, et de flamma ignis. ℟. Amen.

Deliver, O Lord, the soul of Thy *servant*, as Thou didst deliver Lot from Sodom and from the flame of fire. ℟. Amen.

Libera, Domine, animam *servi tui* sicut liberasti Moysen de manu Pharaonis regis Ægyptiorum. ℞. Amen.

Libera, Domine, animam *servi tui* sicut liberasti Danielem de lacu leonum. ℞. Amen.

Libera, Domine, animam *servi tui* sicut liberasti tres pueros de camino ignis ardentis, et de manu regis iniqui. ℞. Amen.

Libera, Domine, animam *servi tui* sicut liberasti Susannam de falso crimine. ℞. Amen.

Libera, Domine, animam *servi tui* sicut liberasti David de manu Regis Saul, et de manu Goliæ. ℞. Amen.

Libera, Domine, animam *servi tui* sicut liberasti Petrum et Paulum de carceribus. ℞. Amen.

Et sicut beatissimam Theclam Virginem et Martyrem tuam de tribus atrocissimis tormentis liberasti, sic liberare digneris animam hujus *servi tui*, et tecum facias in bonis congaudere cœlestibus. ℞. Amen.

Deliver, O Lord, the soul of Thy *servant*, as Thou didst deliver Moses from the hands of Pharaoh, king of the Egyptians. ℞. Amen.

Deliver, O Lord, the soul of Thy *servant*, as Thou didst deliver Daniel from the lions' den. ℞. Amen.

Deliver, O Lord, the soul of Thy *servant*, as Thou didst deliver the three children from the burning fiery furnace, and from the hand of a wicked king. ℞. Amen.

Deliver, O Lord, the soul of Thy *servant*, as Thou didst deliver Susanna from a false accusation. ℞. Amen.

Deliver, O Lord, the soul of Thy *servant*, as Thou didst deliver David from the hand of King Saul and from the hand of Goliath. ℞. Amen.

Deliver, O Lord, the soul of Thy *servant*, as Thou didst deliver Peter and Paul out of prison. ℞. Amen.

And as Thou didst deliver Thy most blessed virgin and martyr, Thecla, from three most cruel torments, so vouchsafe to deliver the soul of this Thy *servant*, and make it to rejoice with Thee in the bliss of heaven. ℞. Amen.

Commendamus tibi, Domine, animam *famuli tui,* N., precamurque te, Domine Jesu Christe, Salvator mundi, ut, propter quam ad terram misericorditer descendisti, Patriarcharum tuorum sinibus insinuare non renuas. Agnosce, Domine, creaturam tuam, non a diis alienis creatam, sed a te solo Deo vivo et vero: quia non est alius Deus præter te, et non est secundum opera tua. Lætifica, Domine, animam ejus in conspectu tuo, et ne memineris iniquitatum ejus antiquarum, et ebrietatum, quas suscitavit furor, sive fervor mali desiderii. Licet enim peccaverit, tamen Patrem, et Filium, et Spiritum Sanctum non negavit, sed credidit, et zelum Dei in se habuit, et Deum, qui fecit omnia, fideliter adoravit.

We commend unto Thee, O Lord, the soul of Thy *servant,* N., and we beseech Thee, O Lord Jesus Christ, Savior of the world, that Thou wouldst not refuse to place in the bosom of Thy patriarchs a soul for whose sake Thou didst mercifully come down upon earth. Acknowledge, O Lord, Thy creature, made, not by strange gods, but by Thee, the only living and true God: for there is no other God besides Thee, and none that doeth according to Thy works. Make glad *his* soul, O Lord, with Thy presence, and remember not *his* old sins, and the excesses which wrath or heat of evil desire may have aroused. For though *he* has sinned, *he* has not denied the Father, and the Son, and the Holy Ghost; but has believed, and has had a zeal for God, and has faithfully worshipped God, the Creator of all things.

Delicta juventutis, et ignorantias ejus, quæsumus, ne memineris, Domine; sed secundum magnam misericordiam tuam memor esto illius in gloria claritatis tuæ. Aperiantur ei cœli, collætentur illi Angeli. In regnum tuum, Domine, *servum tuum* suscipe. Suscipiat *eum* sanctus Michael Archangelus Dei, qui militiæ cœlestis meruit principatum. Veniant illi obviam sancti Angeli Dei, et perducant *eum* in civitatem cœlestem Jerusalem. Suscipiat *eum* beatus Petrus Apostolus, cui a Deo claves regni cœlestis traditæ sunt. Adjuvet *eum* sanctus Paulus Apostolus, qui dignus fuit esse vas electionis. Intercedat pro *eo* sanctus Joannes electus Dei Apostolus, cui revelata sunt secreta cœlestia. Orent pro *eo* omnes sancti Apostoli, quibus a Domino data est potestas ligandi, atque solvendi. Intercedant pro *eo* omnes Sancti et Electi Dei, qui pro Christi nomine tormenta in hoc sæculo sustinuerunt: ut vinculis carnis exut*us*, pervenire mereatur ad gloriam regni cœlestis, præstante Domino nostro Jesu Christo, qui, cum Patre et Spiritu Sancto, vivis et regnas in sæcula sæculorum. ℟. Amen.

Remember not, O Lord, we beseech Thee, the sins of *his* youth nor *his* ignorances; but, according to Thy great mercy, be mindful of *him* in the brightness of Thy glory. May the heavens be opened unto *him,* may the angels rejoice with *him.* Into Thy kingdom, O Lord, receive Thy *servant.* May St. Michael, archangel of God, prince of the heavenly host, receive *him.* May the holy angels of God come forth to meet *him,* and lead *him* into the heavenly city, Jerusalem. May blessed Peter the apostle, to whom were given by God the keys of the kingdom of heaven, receive *him.* May St. Paul the apostle, who was counted worthy to be a vessel of election, assist *him.* May St. John, the chosen apostle of God, to whom were revealed the secrets of heaven, intercede for *him.* May all the holy apostles, to whom the Lord gave the power of binding and loosing, pray for *him.* May all the saints and elect of God, who, in this world, suffered torments for the name of Christ, intercede for *him:* that, being loosed from the bonds of the flesh, *he* may come to the glory of the heavenly kingdom, through the grace of Our Lord Jesus Christ, Who, with the Father and the Holy Ghost, liveth and reigneth, world without end. ℟. Amen.

[✝Clementissima Virgo Dei Genitrix Maria, mærentium piissima consolatrix, *famuli* N. spiritum Filio suo commendet, ut, hoc materno interventu, terrores mortis non timeat, sed desideratam cœlestis patriæ mansionem, ea comite, læt*us* adeat. ℞. Amen.

[✝May the most clement Virgin Mary, Mother of God, loving consoler of the afflicted, commend to her divine Son the soul of this her *servant* N., so that, through her maternal intercession, our dying *brother* may be freed from the terrors of death and in her company joyfully enter the desired heavenly home. ℞. Amen.

Ad te confugio, Sancte Joseph, Patrone morientium, tibique, in cujus beato transitu vigiles adstiterunt Jesus et Maria, per hoc utrumque carissimum pignus, animam hujus *famuli* N., in extremo agone laborantem, enixe commendo, ut ab insidiis diaboli, et a morte perpetua, te protegente, liberetur, et ad gaudia æterna pervenire mereatur. Per eundem Christum Dominum nostrum. ℞. Amen.]

We fly to thee, St. Joseph, patron of the dying, and we earnestly commend to thee, whom Jesus and Mary assisted at thy happy death by this twofold pledge most dear, the soul of this thy *servant* N., now in *his* last agony, so that, under thy protection, *he* may be freed from the snares of the devil and from everlasting death, thus reaching the eternal joys of heaven. Through the same Christ Our Lord. ℞. Amen.]

Here, if the soul still linger, may be read the seventeenth chapter of St. John's Gospel, and the Passion of Our Lord, *according to St. John.*

PRAYER TO OUR LORD JESUS CHRIST

To be said by the dying person, or by another for him.

℣. Adoramus te, Christe, et benedicimus tibi.

℟. Quia per sanctam crucem tuam redemisti mundum.

Deus, qui pro redemptione mundi voluisti nasci, circumcidi, a Judæis reprobari, a Juda traditore osculo tradi, vinculis alligari, sicut agnus innocens ad victimam duci, atque conspectibus Annæ, Caiphæ, Pilati, et Herodis indecenter offerri, a falsis testibus accusari, flagellis et opprobriis vexari, sputis conspui, spinis coronari, colaphis cædi, arundine percuti, facie velari, vestibus exui, cruci clavis affigi, in cruce levari, inter latrones deputari, felle et aceto potari, et lancea vulnerari: Tu, Domine, per has sanctissimas pœnas tuas, quas ego indignus recolo, et per sanctam crucem et mortem tuam, libera me (*vel* famul*um tuum* N.) a pœnis inferni, et perducere digneris, quo perduxisti latronem tecum crucifixum. Qui cum Patre et Spiritu Sancto vivis et regnas in sæcula sæculorum. ℟. Amen.

℣. We adore Thee, O Christ, and we bless Thee.

℟. Because by Thy holy Cross Thou hast redeemed the world.

O God, Who for the Redemption of the world didst vouchsafe to be born, to be circumcised, to be rejected by the Jews, to be betrayed with a kiss by the traitor Judas, to be bound with cords, to be led as an innocent lamb to the slaughter, and in the sight of Annas, Caiphas, Pilate, and Herod, to be treated with indignity, to be accused by false witnesses, to be afflicted with scourges and reproaches, to be spit upon, to be crowned with thorns, to be beaten with blows, to be struck with a reed, to have Thy face veiled, to be stripped of Thy garments, to be nailed to the Cross and raised high thereon, to be ranked among thieves, to be offered gall and vinegar to drink, and to be pierced with a lance: Do Thou, O Lord, by these Thy most holy pains, which I, though unworthy, now call to mind, and by Thy holy Cross and death, deliver me (*or* this Thy *servant*, N.) from the pains of hell, and vouchsafe to lead me (*or him*) whither Thou didst lead the Good Thief who was crucified with Thee. Who, with the Father and the Holy Ghost, ever livest and reignest, world without end. ℟. Amen.

The following psalms may also be said:

Psalm 117

Confitemini Domino quoniam bonus: * quoniam in sæculum misericordia ejus.

O praise the Lord, for He is good: for His mercy endureth forever.

Dicat nunc Israel, quoniam bonus: * quoniam in sæculum misericordia ejus.

Let Israel now say, that He is good: that His mercy endureth forever.

Dicat nunc domus Aaron: * quoniam in sæculum misericordia ejus.

Let the house of Aaron now say: that His mercy endureth forever.

Dicant nunc qui timent Dominum: * quoniam in sæculum misericordia ejus.

Let them that fear the Lord now say: that His mercy endureth forever.

De tribulatione invocavi Dominum: * et exaudivit me in latitudine Dominus.

In my trouble I called upon the Lord: and the Lord heard me, and set me at large.

Dominus mihi adjutor: * non timebo quid faciat mihi homo.

The Lord is my helper: I will not fear what man can do unto me.

Dominus mihi adjutor: * et ego despiciam inimicos meos.

The Lord is my helper: and I will look down upon mine enemies.

Bonum est confidere in Domino, * quam confidere in homine.

It is better to trust in the Lord: than to put confidence in man.

Bonum est sperare in Domino, * quam sperare in principibus.

It is better to trust in the Lord: than to put confidence in princes.

Omnes gentes circuierunt me: * et in nomine Domini, quia ultus sum in eos.

All nations compassed me round about: and in the name of the Lord have I been revenged upon them.

Circumdantes circumdederunt me: * et in nomine Domini, quia ultus sum in eos.

Surrounding me, they compassed me about: and in the name of the Lord have I been revenged upon them.

Circumdederunt me sicut apes, et ex-arserunt sicut ignis in spinis: * et in nomine Domini, quia ultus sum in eos.

They gathered about me like bees, and burned like fire among thorns: and in the name of the Lord I have been revenged upon them.

Impulsus eversus sum ut caderem: * et Dominus suscepit me.

I was sore pressed, and overthrown that I might fall: but the Lord held me up.

Fortitudo mea, et laus mea Dominus: * et factus est mihi in salutem.

The Lord is my strength and my praise: and He is become my salvation.

Vox exultationis, et salutis: * in taber-naculis justorum.

The voice of joy and salvation: is in the tabernacles of the just.

Dextera Domini fecit virtutem: dextera Domini exaltavit me, * dextera Domini fecit virtutem.

The right hand of the Lord hath done mightily; the right hand of the Lord hath exalted me: the right hand of the Lord hath wrought strength.

Non moriar, sed vivam; * et narrabo opera Domini.

I shall not die, but live: and shall declare the works of the Lord.

Castigans castigavit me Dominus: * et morti non tradidit me.

The Lord hath chastened and corrected me: but He hath not given me over unto death.

Aperite mihi portas justitiæ, ingressus in eas confitebor Domino: * hæc porta Domini, justi intrabunt in eam.

Open unto me the gates of justice; I will go into them, and give praise unto the Lord: this is the gate of the Lord: the just shall enter into it.

Confitebor tibi quoniam exaudisti me: * et factus es mihi in salutem.

I will praise Thee, for Thou hast heard me: and art become my salvation.

Lapidem, quem reprobaverunt ædi-ficantes: * hic factus est in caput anguli.

The stone which the builders rejected: the same is become the head of the corner.

A Domino factum est istud: * et est mi-rabile in oculis nostris.

This is the Lord's doing: and it is won-derful in our eyes.

Hæc est dies, quam fecit Dominus: * exultemus, et lætemur in ea.

This is the day which the Lord hath made: let us be glad and rejoice in it.

O Domine, salvum me fac, O Domine,
bene prosperare: * benedictus qui
venit in nomine Domini.

O Lord, save me; O Lord, give good
success: Blessed be he that cometh
in the name of the Lord.

Benediximus vobis de domo Domini: *
Deus Dominus, et illuxit nobis.

We have blessed you out of the house of
the Lord: The Lord is God, and He
hath shone upon us.

Constituite diem solemnem in conden-
sis, * usque ad cornu altaris.

Appoint a solemn day, with shady
boughs: even unto the horn of the
altar.

Deus meus es tu, et confitebor tibi: *
Deus meus es tu, et exaltabo te.

Thou art my God, and I will praise Thee:
Thou art my God, and I will exalt
Thee.

Confitebor tibi quoniam exaudisti me, *
et factus es mihi in salutem.

I will praise Thee, for Thou hast heard
me: and art become my salvation.

Confitemini Domino quoniam bonus:
* quoniam in sæculum misericordia
ejus.

O praise ye the Lord, for He is good: for
His mercy endureth forever.

Gloria Patri, etc.

Glory be to the Father, etc.

Psalm 118

Beati immaculati in via, * qui ambulant
in lege Domini.

Blessed are the undefiled in the way:
who walk in the law of the Lord.

Beati qui scrutantur testimonia ejus, *
in toto corde exquirunt eum.

Blessed are they that search His testimonies: that seek Him with their whole
heart.

Non enim qui operantur iniquitatem *
in viis ejus ambulaverunt.

For they that work iniquity: have not
walked in His ways.

Tu mandasti * mandata tua custodiri
nimis.

Thou hast commanded that Thy commandments be kept most diligently.

Utinam dirigantur viae meae * ad cus-
todiendas justificationes tuas!

O that my ways may be so directed: that
I may keep Thine ordinances.

Tunc non confundar, * cum perspexero in omnibus mandatis tuis.

Then shall I not be confounded: when I shall have regard to all Thy commandments.

Confitebor tibi in directione cordis, * in eo quod didici judicia justitiae tuae.

I will praise Thee with uprightness of heart: when I shall have learned the judgments of Thy justice.

Justificationes tuas custodiam; * non me derelinquas usquequaque.

I will keep Thine ordinances: O forsake me not utterly.

In quo corrigit adolescentior viam suam? * in custodiendo sermones tuos.

By what doth a young man correct his way? even by keeping Thy words.

In toto corde meo exquisivi te; * ne repellas me a mandatis tuis.

With my whole heart have I sought after Thee: let me not stray from Thy commandments.

In corde meo abscondi eloquia tua, * ut non peccem tibi.

Thy words have I hidden within my heart: that I may not sin against Thee.

Benedictus es, Domine; * doce me justificationes tuas.

Blessed art Thou, O Lord: O teach me Thine ordinances.

In labiis meis * pronuntiavi omnia judicia oris tui.

With my lips have I declared: all the judgments of Thy mouth.

In via testimoniorum tuorum delectatus sum, * sicut in omnibus divitiis.

I have had delight in the way of Thy testimonies: even as in all riches.

In mandatis tuis exercebor, * et considerabo vias tuas.

I will meditate on Thy commandments: and I will consider Thy ways.

In justificationibus tuis meditabor: * non obliviscar sermones tuos.

I will think upon Thine ordinances: I will not forget Thy words.

Gloria Patri, etc.

Glory be to the Father, etc.

THREE DEVOUT PRAYERS USEFUL FOR THE DYING

To be recited with three Our Fathers, *and three* Hail Marys *in the agony of death. First is said:*
Lord, have mercy. Christ, have mercy. Lord, have mercy.
Our Father. Hail Mary.

Let us pray.
O Lord Jesus Christ, by Thy most sacred agony and by the prayer which Thou didst pour forth for us on the Mount of Olives, where Thy sweat became as drops of blood running down upon the earth, I beseech Thee to offer up the many drops of Thy bloody sweat, which in Thy fearful anguish Thou didst most abundantly shed for us, and graciously to present them to Thy Almighty Father, to be set against the many sins of this Thy *servant* N., and mercifully deliver *him* in this hour of *his* death from all the pains and sufferings which *he* fears *he* may justly have deserved for *his* sins. Who with the Father and the Holy Ghost, livest and reignest, God, world without end. ℟. Amen.

A second time is said:
Lord, have mercy. Christ, have mercy. Lord, have mercy.
Our Father, Hail Mary.

O Lord Jesus Christ, Who didst vouchsafe to die upon the Cross for us, I beseech Thee to offer up to Thy Almighty Father all the bitter pains and sufferings which Thou didst endure for us upon the Cross, especially in that hour when Thy most holy soul quitted Thy most sacred body; and present them in behalf of this Thy *servant* N., and deliver *him* in this hour of death from all the pains and sufferings which *he* fears *he* may justly have deserved for *his* sins. Who with the Father and the Holy Ghost, livest and reignest God, world without end. ℟. Amen.

A third time is said:
Lord, have mercy. Christ, have mercy. Lord, have mercy.
Our Father, Hail Mary.

O Lord Jesus Christ, Who by the mouth of Thy prophet hast said: "With everlasting love I have loved thee: therefore have I drawn thee graciously": I beseech Thee to offer up this same love which drew Thee down from heaven to earth there to endure all the bitterness of Thy Passion and present it to Thy Almighty Father for the soul of this Thy *servant* N., and deliver *him* from all the pains and sufferings which *he* fears *he* has deserved for *his* sins. And save *his* soul in this hour of *his* departure. Open unto *him* the gates of life, and make *him* to rejoice with Thy saints in glory everlasting. And do Thou, O most merciful Lord Jesus Christ, Who hast redeemed us by Thy most Precious Blood, have mercy on the soul of this Thy *servant*, and vouchsafe to introduce *him* into the ever green and pleasant places of paradise, that *he* may live unto Thee in undivided love, and never be separated from Thee and Thine elect. Who with the Father and the Holy Ghost ever livest and reignest God, world without end. ℟. Amen.

THE LAST AGONY

When the soul is about to depart from the body, then more than ever ought they who are by to pray earnestly around the dying person's bed; and if he be unable to speak, the holy name of Jesus *should constantly be invoked, and such words as the following again and again repeated in his ear:*
Into Thy hands, O Lord, I commend my spirit.—O Lord Jesus Christ, receive my spirit.—Holy Mary, pray for me.—O Mary, Mother of grace, Mother of mercy, do thou protect me from the enemy, and receive me at the hour of death.—[‡St. Joseph, pray for me.—St. Joseph, in company with the Blessed Virgin thy spouse, open to me the bosom of divine mercy.

Jesus, Mary, Joseph, to you I commend my heart and my soul.
Jesus, Mary, Joseph, assist me in my last agony.
Jesus, Mary, Joseph, let me depart and rest with you in peace.]

When the soul has departed, the following Responsory *may be said:*

Subvenite, Sancti Dei, occurrite, Angeli Domini, †Suscipientes animam ejus, †Offerentes eam in conspectu Altissimi.

Come to *his* assistance, ye saints of God, come forth to meet *him*, ye angels of the Lord: †Receiving *his* soul: †Offering it in the sight of the most High.

℣. Suscipiat te Christus, qui vocavit te, et in sinum Abrahæ Angeli deducant te.
℟. Suscipientes, etc.

℣. May Christ receive thee, Who hath called thee, and may the angels bear thee into Abraham's bosom.
℟. Receiving, etc.

℣. Requiem æternam dona ei, Domine, et lux perpetua luceat ei.
℟. Offerentes, etc.

℣. Eternal rest grant unto *him*, O Lord, and let perpetual light shine upon *him.*
℟. Offering, etc.

℣. Kyrie, eleison.
℟. Christe, eleison.

℣. Lord, have mercy.
℟. Christ, have mercy.

℣. Kyrie, eleison. Pater noster (*secreto*).

℣. Et ne nos inducas in tentationem.
℞. Sed libera nos a malo.

℣. Requiem æternam dona ei, Domine.
℞. Et lux perpetua luceat ei.

℣. A porta inferi,
℞. Erue, Domine, animam ejus.

℣. Requiescat in pace.
℞. Amen.

℣. Domine, exaudi orationem meam.
℞. Et clamor meus ad te veniat.

℣. Dominus vobiscum.
℞. Et cum spiritu tuo.

Oremus.

Tibi, Domine, commendamus animam famu*li tui* N., ut defunct*us* sæculo tibi vivat: et quæ per fragilitatem humanæ conversationis peccata commisit, tu venia misericordissimæ pietatis absterge. Per Christum Dominum nostrum. ℞. Amen.

℣. Lord, have mercy. Our Father (*inaudibly*).

℣. And lead us not into temptation.
℞. But deliver us from evil.

℣. Eternal rest grant unto *him*, O Lord.
℞. And let perpetual light shine upon *him*.

℣. From the gate of hell,
℞. Deliver *his* soul, O Lord.

℣. May *he* rest in peace.
℞. Amen.

℣. O Lord hear my prayer.
℞. And let my cry come unto thee.

℣. The Lord be with you.
℞. And with thy spirit.

Let us pray.

To Thee, O Lord, do we commend the soul of Thy *servant* N., that being dead to the world *he* may live unto Thee; and whatsoever sins *he* has committed through the frailty of *his* mortal nature, do Thou, by the pardon of Thy most merciful love, wash away. ℞. Amen.

Meanwhile, according to the custom of the place, let the passing-bell *be rung, reminding all who hear it to pray for the Christian soul. Then let the body be decently laid out, with lighted candles near. Let a small cross be placed upon the breast, between the hands, or else let the hands themselves be folded one upon another, in the form of a cross. The body is sprinkled with holy water, and thenceforward until the time of burial, let all who are present pray for the repose of the departed soul.*

PRAYERS FOR THE USE OF MOURNERS

O Almighty God, Who knowest the weakness and frailty of our nature: we beseech Thee to give unto us, Thy servants, whom Thou hast stricken with this sorrow, such measure of Thy grace as shall enable us to bear it with humility, resignation, and submission to Thy divine will. Grant that no impatient murmuring or repining thoughts may find a place in our hearts: that we may not sorrow as those who have no hope. Let not our grief exceed the bounds of reason and religion; but so temper it, we beseech Thee, with the consolations of Thy Holy Spirit, that whatever we may want in outward consolation, we may find in the inward rest of perfect submission to Thy holy will, and unshaken trust in Thy loving mercy; through Jesus Christ Our Lord. *Amen.*

Almighty and most merciful Father, Who lovest those whom Thou chastiseth, and turnest away Thine anger from us, look down in pity upon our distress and sorrow, and grant that the affliction which it has pleased Thee to bring on us may be a means of drawing us nearer to Thee. Strengthen us, O Lord, that we may not languish in fruitless and unavailing sorrow, but, by the assistance of Thy Holy Spirit, may truly repent, meekly submit, and effectually be comforted; that we may obtain that peace which the world cannot give, and pass the rest of our life in humble resignation and cheerful obedience. Teach us to set our affections on things above, not on things of earth; on those joys which never fade, the pleasures that are at Thy right hand forevermore. *Amen.*

O Almighty God, Judge of the living and the dead, so fit and prepare us, we beseech Thee, by Thy grace, for that last account which we must one day give; that, when the time of our appointed change shall come, we may look up to Thee with joy and comfort, and may at last be received together with *him* whom Thou hast now taken from us, and with all that are near and dear to us, into that place of rest and peace where Thou shalt Thyself wipe away all tears from all eyes and where all our troubles and sorrows shall have an end, through the merits and for the sake of Jesus Christ, our Blessed Savior and Redeemer. *Amen.*

AN ACT OF FAITH. TAKEN FROM HOLY SCRIPTURE

I believe, O God, that my time is in Thy hand.

That going through the vale of misery, I may draw waters with joy out of the fountains of salvation.

That they that sow in tears shall reap in joy.

That blessed are they that mourn, for they shall be comforted.

That in all our affliction Christ is afflicted, and that the angel of His presence saveth us.

That in the evening weeping may have place, but in the morning gladness.

That Christ will not leave us orphans.

That as one whom his mother caresseth, so will the Lord comfort us.

That our present tribulation, which is momentary and light, worketh for us above measure exceedingly an eternal weight of glory.

That as a father hath pity upon his children, so hath the Lord pity upon us.

That a Sabbath rest remaineth for the people of God.

That He healeth the broken in heart, and bindeth up their bruises.

That His good Spirit shall lead us into the right land.

That the God of all consolation comforteth us in all our tribulation: that we ourselves also may be able to comfort those who are in all tribulation, by the comfort with which we ourselves are comforted by God.

That she who is a widow indeed and desolate, let her trust in God, and continue in supplications and prayers night and day.

That we have a great cloud of witnesses above us.

That in our Father's house there are many mansions.

That He hath there prepared a place for us.

That though we should walk in the midst of the shadow of death we fear no evils, for He is with us.

That God is our God unto eternity, and forever and ever: He shall rule us forevermore.

That death is swallowed up in victory.

That we may not sorrow as others who have no hope.

That this corruptible must put on incorruption, and this mortal put on immortality.

That as by a man came death, so by a man came the Resurrection of the dead.

That Christ will reform our vile bodies conformably to His glorious body.

That if our earthly house, this tent, be destroyed, we have a building from God, a house not built with hands, everlasting in the heavens.

That what is mortal shall be swallowed up by life.

That we shall be like Christ, because we shall see Him as He is.

That His saints in paradise shall not hunger nor thirst anymore: for the Lamb that is in the midst of the throne will rule them, and lead them to the fountains of the waters of life.

That God shall wipe away all tears from our eyes: and death shall be no more, nor mourning, nor wailing, nor sorrow shall be anymore, for the former things are passed away.

That heaven and earth will pass away, but His words will not pass away.

That He cometh quickly. Amen. Come, Lord Jesus. *Amen.*

PRAYERS IN GREAT SORROW

O most Mighty, most merciful Father, have mercy on me; have mercy on me, good Lord. O do Thou bear me up, succor me, strengthen me in my hour of tribulation. Thou hast smitten me to the dust. Thou hast sorely afflicted me; my heart fainteth within me, I am brought very low. I know not, O Lord, how to bear such sorrow: I am overwhelmed with grief. I fly to Thee for help, for Thou alone canst give me help. Help me, O Father, help me, and that soon; help me for Thy mercies' sake. Make haste to help me for Thy dear Son's sake, Jesus Christ Our Lord. *Amen.*

O Almighty God, I fall down before Thee in the agony of my soul. Thou hast taken my beloved one from mine eyes, I have none to help me, my heart is desolate. O comfort me, for I am very greatly troubled. Teach me, O God, in this awful hour of affliction, in this great bereavement, in this most bitter day, to have patience and Christian resignation. Teach me to bow meekly to Thy will, that my affliction may not utterly break me down, that I may be able to bear it. Thou knowest my sufferings, my sorrows, my tears; look upon me and succor me. Enable me to bear this weight of trial, for of myself I am unable to bear it. O pity me, good Lord; pity me, most gracious Father: for Christ's sake turn Thou Thy face toward me, and mercifully accept my prayer. *Amen.*

O Lord God, Who correctest those whom Thou dost love, teach me in this sore trial, this dark day of very heavy chastisement, to know Thy love. Lord, I believe that Thou lovest me; help Thou mine unbelief. Teach me to see Thy love, though Thou seemest to turn Thy face from me. Increase Thy love toward me, O God, now that Thou hast smitten me, lest I be consumed; have pity upon me, speak consolation to my soul. Give me of Thy comfort, for what can I do, whither can I turn, O Lord? Thou only, Who hast afflicted, can comfort me; I have none besides Thee. I come to Thee in my loneliness, my desolation of heart, my anguish. Hold Thou me up; give me of Thy love; I kneel at Thy feet, I cast myself down before Thee; weeping do I beseech Thee to receive my prayer for Jesus' sake. *Amen.*

PRAYER TO OUR LADY OF PITY

Kneeling at thy holy feet, O gracious Queen of heaven! we offer thee our deepest reverence. We confess that thou art the Daughter of the eternal Father, the Mother of the divine Word, and the Spouse of the Holy Ghost. Full of grace, of virtue, and of heavenly gifts, thou art the chaste temple of the Holy Trinity. With thee are treasured God's mercies, and thou, too, dost dispense them. And since thy loving Heart is filled with charity, sweetness, and tender compassion for us poor sinners, we call thee Mother of Holy Pity. With the greatest trust, then, do we come to thee in this our sorrow and distress. We beg that thou wouldst make us confide in thy love, by granting us [*Here mention your request*], if it be God's will, and for the welfare of our souls. Cast, then, thine eyes of pity upon us and upon all our kindred. That we may not perish, shield us from the attacks of the world, the flesh, and the devil, that continually assail us. Remember, O fondest of mothers, that we are thy children, purchased with the Precious Blood of thy divine Son. Pray, without ceasing, that the adorable Trinity may give us the grace ever to be victorious over the devil, the world, and our unhallowed passions; that grace by which the just grow in holiness, sinners are converted, and heresy destroyed; by which the unbeliever is enlightened, and the Jews brought to the true religion. Bestow upon us this boon, O most pure Virgin, through the infinite bounty of the most High, through the merits of thy Son, by the care with which thou didst nourish Him, by the devotion with which thou didst serve Him, by the love with which thou didst cherish Him, by thy tears and anguish endured in His holy Passion. Obtain for us the great favor that the whole world may be made one people and one Church, which shall give thanks, praise, and glory to the most Holy Trinity, and to thee who art its mediator.

May the power of the Father, the wisdom of the Son, and the virtue of the Holy Ghost, grant us this blessing. *Amen.*

Our Father. Hail Mary.

The Burial of the Dead

[The parts within brackets refer to solemn obsequies.]

NOTE. — *The* italicized *words, or endings of words,* (*or those in* Roman *throughout the* responses *of the Litany*) *occurring in the text, are those which must be varied according to sex.*

The priest, being vested in a surplice and black stole, (*or in a cope also,*) *meets the corpse at the church door. Standing at its feet, he sprinkles it with holy water, and then says the Antiphon:*

Si iniquitates observaveris, Domine;
  Domine, quis sustinebit?

If Thou, O Lord, wilt mark iniquities;
  Lord, who shall abide it?

PSALM 129

De profundis clamavi ad te, Domine: *
  Domine, exaudi vocem meam.

Out of the depths have I cried unto
  Thee, O Lord: Lord, hear my voice.

Fiant aures tuæ intendentes, * in vocem
  deprecationis meæ.

O let Thine ears consider well: the voice
  of my supplication.

Si iniquitates observaveris, Domine: *
  Domine, quis sustinebit?

If Thou, O Lord, wilt mark iniquities:
  Lord, who shall abide it?

Quia apud te propitiatio est: * et propter legem tuam sustinui te, Domine.

For with Thee there is merciful forgiveness: and because of Thy law I have
  waited for Thee, O Lord.

Sustinuit anima mea in verbo ejus: *
  speravit anima mea in Domino.

My soul hath waited on His word: my
  soul hath hoped in the Lord.

A custodia matutina usque ad noctem:
  * speret Israel in Domino.

From the morning watch even until
  night: let Israel hope in the Lord.

Quia apud Dominum misericordia: * et
  copiosa apud eum redemptio.

For with the Lord there is mercy: and
  with Him is plenteous redemption.

Et ipse redimet Israel, * ex omnibus
  iniquitatibus ejus.

And He shall redeem Israel: from all his
  iniquities.

After each Psalm is said:

Requiem æternam dona ei, Domine; et lux perpetua luceat ei.

Eternal rest grant unto *him,* O Lord; and let perpetual light shine upon *him.*

Ant. Si iniquitates observaveris, Domine: Domine, quis sustinebit?

Ant. If Thou, O Lord, wilt mark iniquities; Lord, who shall abide it?

The body is then borne into the Church, meanwhile the priest recites the following:

Ant. Exultabunt Domino ossa humiliata.

Ant. The bones that were humbled shall rejoice in the Lord.

PSALM 50

Miserere mei, Deus, * secundum magnam misericordiam tuam.

Have mercy upon me, O God: according to Thy great mercy.

Et secundum multitudinem miserationum tuarum, * dele iniquitatem meam.

And according to the multitude of Thy tender mercies: blot out my iniquity.

Amplius lava me ab iniquitate mea: * et a peccato meo munda me.

Wash me yet more from my iniquity: and cleanse me from my sin.

Quoniam iniquitatem meam ego cognosco: * et peccatum meum contra me est semper.

For I acknowledge my iniquity: and my sin is always before me.

Tibi soli peccavi, et malum coram te feci: * ut justificeris in sermonibus tuis, et vincas cum judicaris.

Against Thee only have I sinned, and done evil in Thy sight: that Thou mayest be justified in Thy words, and mayest overcome when Thou art judged.

Ecce enim in iniquitatibus conceptus sum: * et in peccatis concepit me mater mea.

For behold, I was conceived in iniquities: and in sins did my mother conceive me.

Ecce enim veritatem dilexisti: * incerta et occulta sapientiæ tuæ manifestasti mihi.

For behold, Thou hast loved truth: the secret and hidden things of Thy wisdom Thou hast made manifest unto me.

Asperges me hyssopo, et mundabor: * lavabis me, et super nivem
dealbabor.

Thou shalt sprinkle me with hyssop, and
I shall be cleansed: Thou shalt wash
me, and I shall be made whiter than
snow.

Auditui meo dabis gaudium et lætitiam:
* et exultabunt ossa humiliata.

Thou shalt make me hear of joy and
gladness: and the bones that were
humbled shall rejoice.

Averte faciem tuam a peccatis meis: * et
omnes iniquitates meas dele.

Turn away Thy face from my sins: and
blot out all my iniquities.

Cor mundum crea in me, Deus: * et
spiritum rectum innova in visceribus meis.

Create in me a clean heart, O God: and
renew a right spirit within me.

Ne projicias me a facie tua: * et
Spiritum Sanctum tuum ne auferas
a me.

Cast me not away from Thy face: and
take not Thy Holy Spirit from me.

Redde mihi lætitiam salutaris tui: * et
spiritu principali confirma me.

Restore unto me the joy of Thy salvation:
and strengthen me with a perfect
spirit.

Docebo iniquos vias tuas: * et impii ad
te convertentur.

I will teach the unjust Thy ways: and the
wicked shall be converted unto Thee.

Libera me de sanguinibus, Deus, Deus
salutis meæ: * et exultabit lingua
mea justitiam tuam.

Deliver me from sins of blood, O God,
Thou God of my salvation: and my
tongue shall extol Thy justice.

Domine, labia mea aperies: * et os
meum annuntiabit laudem tuam.

Thou shalt open my lips, O Lord: and
my mouth shall declare Thy praise.

Quoniam si voluisses sacrificium, dedissem utique: * holocaustis non
delectaberis.

For if Thou hadst desired sacrifice, I
would surely have given it: with
burnt offerings Thou wilt not be
delighted.

Sacrificium Deo spiritus contribulatus:
* cor contritum, et humiliatum,
Deus, non despicies.

A sacrifice unto God is a troubled spirit:
a contrite and humble heart, O God,
Thou wilt not despise.

Benigne fac, Domine, in bona voluntate tua Sion, * ut ædificentur muri
Jerusalem.

Deal favorably, O Lord, in Thy good
will with Sion: that the walls of
Jerusalem may be built up.

Tunc acceptabis sacrificium justitiæ, oblationes, et holocausta: * tunc imponent super altare tuum vitulos.

Then shalt Thou accept the sacrifice of justice, oblations, and whole burnt offerings: then shall they lay calves upon Thine altar.

Requiem æternam dona ei, Domine; et lux perpetua luceat ei.

Eternal rest grant unto *him*, O Lord; and let perpetual light shine upon *him*.

Ant. Exultabunt Domino ossa humiliata.

Ant. The bones that were humbled shall rejoice in the Lord.

Then is said the Subvenite.

Subvenite, Sancti Dei, occurrite, Angeli Domini, †Suscipientes animam ejus, †Offerentes eam in conspectu Altissimi.

Come to *his* assistance, ye saints of God, come forth to meet *him*, ye angels of the Lord: †Receiving *his* soul: †Offering it in the sight of the Most High.

℣. Suscipiat te Christus, qui vocavit te, et in sinum Abrahæ Angeli deducant te.
℟. Suscipientes, etc.

℣. May Christ receive thee, Who hath called thee, and may the angels bear thee into Abraham's bosom.
℟. Receiving, etc.

℣. Requiem æternam dona ei, Domine, et lux perpetua luceat ei.

℣. Eternal rest grant unto *him*, O Lord, and let perpetual light shine upon *him*.

℟. Offerentes, etc.

℟. Offering, etc.

℣. Kyrie, eleison.
℟. Christe, eleison.
℣. Kyrie, eleison. Pater noster (*secreto*).

℣. Lord, have mercy.
℟. Christ, have mercy.
℣. Lord, have mercy. Our Father (*inaudibly*).

V. Et ne nos inducas in tentationem.
R. Sed libera nos a malo.

℣. And lead us not into temptation.
℟. But deliver us from evil.

℣. Requiem æternam dona ei, Domine.
℟. Et lux perpetua luceat ei.

℣. Eternal rest grant unto *him*, O Lord.
℟. And let perpetual light shine upon *him*.

℣. A porta inferi,
℟. Erue, Domine, animam ejus.

℣. From the gate of hell,
℟. Deliver *his* soul, O Lord.

℣. Requiescat in pace.
℟. Amen.

℣. May *he* rest in peace.
℟. Amen.

℣. Domine, exaudi orationem meam.
℟. Et clamor meus ad te veniat.

℣. O Lord hear my prayer.
℟. And let my cry come unto thee.

℣. Dominus vobiscum.
℟. Et cum spiritu tuo.

℣. The Lord be with you.
℟. And with thy spirit.

Oremus.

Tibi, Domine, commendamus an-imam famu*li tui* N., ut defunc*tus* sæculo tibi vivat: et quæ per fra-gilitatem humanæ conversationis peccata commisit, tu venia miseri-cordissimæ pietatis absterge. Per Christum Dominum nostrum. ℟. Amen.

Let us pray.

To Thee, O Lord, do we commend the soul of Thy *servant* N., that be-ing dead to the world *he* may live unto Thee; and whatsoever sins *he* has committed through the frailty of *his* mortal nature, do Thou, by the pardon of Thy most merciful love, wash away. ℟. Amen.

The bier is then set at the head of the nave of the church, with the feet of the corpse, if a lay person, toward the altar, but with the head turned thereto if a priest. Lighted candles are placed about the bier, and forthwith (when it is to be said) is begun the [Mass for the Dead, *p. 422.*[36]

[*At Solemn Funerals, the choir chants before the Mass:*

THE OFFICE OF THE DEAD
MATINS

THE INVITATORY

The King, unto Whom all live: O come, let us worship Him.
℟. The King, unto Whom all live: O come, let us worship Him.

PSALM 94

O come, let us exult in the Lord; let us rejoice before God our Savior; let us come into His presence with thanksgiving:, and rejoice before Him with psalms.
The King, unto Whom all live: O come, let us worship Him.

---

[36]   When neither Office nor Mass is said, pass on to p. 428.

For the Lord is a great God, and a great King above all gods; for the Lord doth not repel His people, for in His hand are all the ends of the earth; and the heights of the mountains He beholdeth also.

O come, let us worship Him.

For the sea is His, and He made it, and His hands formed the dry land; O come, let us worship and fall down; and weep before the Lord that made us, for He is the Lord our God; and we are the people of His pasture, and the sheep of His hand.

The King, unto Whom all live: O come, let us worship Him.

Today, if ye shall hear His voice, harden not your hearts, as in the provocation, and in the day of temptation in the wilderness; where your fathers tempted Me, proved Me, and saw My works.

O come, let us worship Him.

Forty years long was I offended with that generation, and said, They do always err in their heart, and they have not known My ways: so I swear in My wrath that they shall not enter into My rest.

The King, unto Whom all live: O come, let us worship Him.

Eternal rest grant unto them, O Lord, and let perpetual light shine upon them.

O come, let us worship Him.

The King, unto Whom all live: O come, let us worship Him.

THE FIRST NOCTURN.[37]

Ant. Direct, O Lord my God, my way in Thy sight.

PSALM 5

Give ear, O Lord, unto my words; understand my cry.

Hearken unto the voice of my prayer: O my King and my God.

For unto Thee will I pray, O Lord: in the morning: Thou shalt hear my voice.

In the morning I will stand before Thee, and will see: for Thou art not a God that willest iniquity.

Neither shall the wicked dwell near Thee: nor shall the unjust abide before Thine eyes.

Thou hatest all the workers of iniquity: Thou wilt destroy all that speak a lie.

The bloody and the deceitful man: the Lord will abhor.

But as for me I will come into Thy house in the multitude of Thy mercy: in Thy fear will I worship toward Thy holy temple.

Lead me, O Lord, in Thy justice: because of mine enemies direct my way in Thy sight.

For there is no truth in their mouth: their heart is vain.

---

[37] When only one Nocturn of Matins is said, this *First Nocturn* is usually taken.

Their throat is an open sepulchre, they dealt deceitfully with their tongues; judge them, O God.

Let them fall from their devices; according to the multitude of their iniquities cast them out: for they have provoked Thee, O Lord.

But let all them that hope in Thee be glad: they shall rejoice forever, and Thou shalt dwell in them.

And all they that love Thy name shall glory in Thee: for Thou wilt bless the just.

O Lord, Thou hast crowned us: as with a shield of Thy good will.

Eternal rest, etc.

Ant. Direct, O Lord my God, my way in Thy sight.

Ant. Turn Thee, O Lord, and deliver my soul; for in death there is no one that is mindful of Thee.

PSALM 6

O Lord, rebuke me not in Thine anger: nor chastise me in Thy wrath.

Have mercy on me, O Lord, for I am weak: heal me, O Lord, for my bones are troubled.

My soul also is troubled exceedingly: but Thou, O Lord, how long?

Turn Thee, O Lord, and deliver my soul: O save me for Thy mercy's sake.

For in death there is no one that is mindful of Thee: and who will give Thee thanks in hell?

I have labored in my groanings, every night will I wash my bed: and water my couch with my tears.

Mine eye is troubled through indignation: I have grown old amongst all mine enemies.

Depart from me, all ye workers of iniquity: for the Lord hath heard the voice of my weeping.

The Lord hath heard my supplication: the Lord hath received my prayer.

Let all mine enemies be put to shame, and be sore troubled: let them be turned back, and put to shame very speedily.

Eternal rest, etc.

Ant. Turn Thee, O Lord, and deliver my soul; for in death there is no one that is mindful of Thee.

Ant. Lest at any time he seize upon my soul like a lion; while there is no one to redeem me, nor to save.

PSALM 7

O Lord my God, in Thee have I put my trust: save me from all them that persecute
me, and deliver me.

Lest at any time he seize upon my soul like a lion: while there is no one to redeem
me, nor to save.

O Lord my God, if I have done this thing: if there be iniquity in my hands:

If I have made a return to them that did evils to me: let me deservedly fall empty
before mine enemies.

Let the enemy pursue my soul, and take it, and tread down my life on the earth:
and bring down my glory to the dust.

Rise up, O Lord, in Thine anger: and be Thou exalted in the borders of mine enemies.

And arise, O Lord my God, in the precept which Thou hast commanded: and a
congregation of people shall surround Thee.

And for their sakes return Thou on high: the Lord judgeth the people.

Judge me, O Lord, according to my justice: and according to my innocence in me.

The wickedness of sinners shall be brought to naught, and Thou shalt direct the just:
O God Who searchest the hearts and reins.

Just is my help from the Lord: Who saveth the upright of heart.

God is a just Judge, strong and patient: Is He angry every day?

Except ye be converted, He will brandish His sword: He hath bent His bow, and
made it ready.

And in it He hath prepared the instruments of death: He hath made ready His
arrows for them that burn.

Behold, he hath been in travail with injustice: he hath conceived sorrow, and brought
forth iniquity.

He hath opened a pit and dug it: and he is fallen into the hole that he hath made.

His sorrow shall be turned on his own head: and his wickedness shall come down
upon his own pate.

I will give glory to the Lord according to His justice: and will sing to the name of
the Lord most High.

Eternal rest, etc.

Ant. Lest at any time he seize upon my soul like a lion; while there is no one to
redeem me, nor to save.

℣. From the gate of hell.

℟. Deliver their souls, O Lord.

Our Father (*inaudibly*).

THE FIRST LESSON. Jb 7:16–21.

Spare me, O Lord, for my days are nothing. What is a man that Thou shouldst
magnify him? or why dost Thou set Thy heart upon him? Thou visitest him early in

the morning, and Thou provest him suddenly. How long wilt Thou not spare me, nor suffer me to swallow down my spittle? I have sinned, what shall I do to Thee, O Keeper of men? Why hast Thou set me opposite to Thee, and I am become burdensome to myself? Why dost Thou not remove my sin, and why dost Thou not take away mine iniquity? Behold, now I shall sleep in the dust: and if Thou seek me in the morning, I shall not be.

℟. I believe my Redeemer liveth, and that in the Last Day I shall rise from the earth: †And in my flesh I shall see God my Savior.

℣. Whom I myself shall see, and not another, and mine eyes shall behold. And in my flesh, etc.

THE SECOND LESSON. Jb 10:1–7.

My soul is weary of my life, I will let go my speech against myself, I will speak in the bitterness of my soul. I will say to God: Do not condemn me: tell me why Thou judgest me so. Doth it seem good to Thee that Thou shouldst crush me, and oppress me, the work of Thy own hands, and help the counsel of the wicked? Hast Thou eyes of flesh: or seest Thou as man seeth? Are Thy days as the days of man, and are Thy years as the times of men: that Thou shouldst inquire after my iniquity, and search after my sin? And Thou knowest that I have done no wicked thing, whereas there is no man that can deliver out of Thy hand.

℟. Thou Who didst raise the dead Lazarus from the grave: †Do Thou, O Lord, grant them rest and a place of forgiveness.

℣. Thou Who art to come to judge the living and the dead, and the world by fire. Do Thou, O Lord, etc.

THE THIRD LESSON. Jb 10:8–12.

Thy hands have made me, and fashioned me wholly round about, and dost Thou thus cast me down headlong on a sudden? Remember, I beseech Thee, that Thou hast made me as the clay, and Thou wilt bring me into dust again. Hast Thou not pressed me out as milk, and curdled me like cheese? Thou hast clothed me with skin and flesh: Thou hast put me together with bones and sinews: Thou hast granted me life and mercy, and Thy visitation hath preserved my spirit.

℟. O Lord, when Thou shalt come to judge the earth, where shall I hide myself from the face of Thy wrath? †For I have sinned greatly in my life.

℣. I dread my misdeeds, and blush before Thee: condemn me not, when Thou shalt come to judge. For I have sinned greatly in my life.

℣. Eternal rest grant unto them, O Lord, and let perpetual light shine upon them. For I have, etc.

Here Lauds *(p. 415) are recited when only the First Nocturn is said.*

THE SECOND NOCTURN

Ant. He hath set me in a place of pasture.

PSALM 22

The Lord ruleth me, and I shall want nothing: He hath set me in a place of pasture.

He hath brought me to the waters of refreshment: He hath converted my soul.

He hath led me on the paths of justice: for His own name's sake.

For though I should walk in the midst of the shadow of death, I fear no evils: for Thou art with me.

Thy rod and Thy staff: they have comforted me.

Thou hast prepared a table before me: against them that afflict me.

Thou hast anointed my head with oil: and my cup which inebriateth me, how goodly it is!

And Thy mercy will follow me: all the days of my life.

And that I may dwell in the house of the Lord: unto length of days.

Eternal rest, etc.

Ant. He hath set me in a place of pasture.

Ant. Remember not, O Lord, the sins of my youth, and mine ignorances.

PSALM 24

To Thee, O Lord, have I lifted up my soul. In Thee, O my God, I put my trust; let me not be ashamed.

Neither let mine enemies laugh at me: for none that wait on Thee shall be confounded.

Let all them be confounded: that transgress without cause.

Show me Thy ways, O Lord: and teach me Thy paths.

Direct me in Thy truth, and teach me: for Thou art God my Savior, and on Thee have I waited all the day long.

Call to remembrance, O Lord, Thy compassion: and Thy mercies which are of old.

Remember Thou not the sins of my youth, and mine ignorances:

According to Thy mercy remember Thou me: for Thy goodness's sake, O Lord.

The Lord is sweet and righteous: therefore He will give a law to sinners in the way.

The meek will He guide in judgment: the gentle He will teach His ways.

All the ways of the Lord are mercy and truth: unto such as seek after His covenant and His testimonies.

For Thy name's sake, O Lord, Thou wilt pardon my sin: for it is great.

Who is the man that feareth the Lord? He hath appointed him a law in the way he hath chosen.

His soul shall dwell in good things: and his seed shall inherit the land.

The Lord is a support to them that fear Him: and His covenant that it may be manifest unto them.

Mine eyes are ever toward the Lord: for He shall pluck my feet out of the snare.

Look Thou upon me, and have mercy on me: for I am alone and poor.

The troubles of my heart are multiplied: deliver me out of my necessities.

Look upon my lowliness and my labor: and forgive me all my sins.

Consider mine enemies, for they are multiplied: and have hated me with an unjust hatred.

Keep Thou my soul, and deliver me: I shall not be ashamed, for I have hoped in Thee.

The innocent and the upright have cleaved unto me: because I have waited on Thee.

Deliver Israel, O God: out of all his troubles.

Eternal rest, etc.

Ant. Remember not, O Lord, the sins of my youth, and mine ignorances.

Ant. I believe that I shall see the good things of the Lord in the land of the living.

PSALM 26

The Lord is my light and my salvation: whom shall I fear?

The Lord is the protector of my life: of whom shall I be afraid?

Whilst the wicked draw near against me: to eat my flesh.

Mine enemies that trouble me: have themselves been weakened, and have fallen.

If armies in camp should stand together against me: my heart shall not fear.

If battle should rise up against me: in this will I be confident.

One thing have I asked of the Lord, this will I seek after: that I may dwell in the house of the Lord all the days of my life.

That I may see the delight of the Lord: and may visit His temple.

For He hath hidden me in His tabernacle: in the day of evils, He hath protected me in the secret place of His tabernacle.

He hath set me up upon a rock: and now He hath lifted up my head above mine enemies.

I have gone round and have offered up in His tabernacle a sacrifice of praise: I will sing and speak praise unto the Lord.

Hear, O Lord, my voice, with which I have cried unto Thee: have mercy on me, and hear me.

My heart hath said to Thee: My face hath sought Thee: Thy face, O Lord, will I seek.

Hide not Thy face from me: turn not in Thy wrath from Thy servant.

Be Thou my helper, forsake me not: neither despise me, O God my Savior.

For my father and my mother have forsaken me: but the Lord hath taken me up.

Set me, O Lord, a law in Thy way: and guide me in the right path, because of mine enemies.

Deliver me not over to the will of them that trouble me: for unjust witnesses have risen up against me, and iniquity hath lied to itself.

I believe that I shall see the good things of the Lord in the land of the living.

Wait on the Lord, do manfully, and let thy heart take courage: and wait thou on the Lord.

Eternal rest, etc.

Ant. I believe that I shall see the good things of the Lord in the land of the living.

℣. May the Lord set them with princes.

℟. Even with the princes of His people.

Our Father (*inaudibly*).

THE FOURTH LESSON. Jb 13:22-28.

Do Thou answer me: how many are my iniquities and sins; make me know my crimes and offenses. Why hidest Thou Thy face, and thinkest me Thy enemy? Against a leaf that is carried away with the wind Thou showest Thy power; and Thou pursuest dry stubble. For Thou writest bitter things against me, and consumest me for the sins of my youth. Thou hast put my feet in the stocks, and Thou observest all my paths, and considerest the steps of my feet: who am to be consumed as rottenness, and as a garment that is moth-eaten.

℟. Remember me, O God, because my life is as a breath: †Nor may the sight of man behold me.

℣. Out of the depths have I cried unto Thee, O Lord: Lord, hear my voice.

Nor may, etc.

THE FIFTH LESSON. Jb 14:1-6.

Man born of a woman, living for a short time, is filled with many miseries. He cometh forth like a flower, and is destroyed, and fleeth as a shadow, and never continueth in the same state. And dost Thou think it meet to open Thy eyes upon such a one, and to bring him into judgment with Thee? Who can make him clean that is conceived of unclean seed? Is it not Thou only? The days of man are short, and the number of his months is with Thee: Thou hast appointed his bounds, which cannot be passed. Depart a little from him, that he may rest, until his wished-for day come, as that of the hireling.

℟. Woe is me, O Lord, because I have sinned greatly in my life: What shall I do, wretch that I am? Whither shall I fly but unto Thee, O my God? †Have mercy on me when Thou comest at the latter day.

℣. My soul is sore troubled; but Thou, O Lord, succor it.

Have mercy on me, etc.

410

THE SIXTH LESSON. Jb 14:13–16.

Who will grant me this, that Thou mayest protect me in hell, and hide me till Thy wrath pass, and appoint me a time when Thou wilt remember me? Shall man that is dead, thinkest Thou, live again? all the days, in which I am now in warfare, I expect until my change come. Thou wilt call me, and I will answer Thee: to the work of Thy hands Thou wilt reach out Thy right hand. Thou indeed hast numbered my steps, but spare my sins.

℟. Remember not my sins, O Lord: †When Thou shalt come to judge the world by fire.

℣. Direct, O Lord my God, my way in Thy sight.

When, etc.

℣. Eternal rest grant unto them, O Lord, and let perpetual light shine upon them.

When, etc.

Here Lauds (*p. 415*) *are recited when only the second Nocturn is said.*

THE THIRD NOCTURN

Ant. Be pleased, O Lord, to deliver me; look down, O Lord, to help me.

PSALM 39

With expectation I waited for the Lord: and He was attentive unto me.

And He heard my prayers: and brought me out of the pit of misery, and out of the miry clay.

He set my feet also upon a rock: and directed my steps.

And He put a new song into my mouth: even a hymn unto our God.

Many shall see it, and shall fear: and they shall hope in the Lord.

Blessed is the man whose trust is in the name of the Lord; and who hath not had regard to vanities and lying follies.

Many are Thy wonderful works which Thou hast done, O Lord my God; and in Thy thoughts there is none that is like unto Thee.

I have declared, and I have spoken: they are multiplied above number.

Sacrifice and offering Thou didst not desire: but ears Thou hast perfected unto me.

Burnt offering, and sin offering Thou didst not require: then said I, Behold I come.

In the head of the book it is written of me that I should do Thy will: O my God, I have desired it, and Thy law is in the midst of my heart.

I have declared Thy justice in the great congregation: lo, I will not restrain my lips: O Lord, Thou knowest it.

I have not hid Thy justice within my heart: I have declared Thy truth and Thy salvation.

I have not concealed Thy mercy and Thy truth: from the great assembly.

Withhold not Thou Thy tender mercies from me, O Lord: Thy mercy and Thy truth have always upheld me.

For evils without number have surrounded me: mine iniquities have overtaken me, and I was not able to see.

They are multiplied above the hairs of my head: and my heart hath failed me.

Be pleased, O Lord, to deliver me: look down, O Lord, to help me.

Let them be confounded and ashamed together: that seek after my soul to take it away.

Let them be turned backward, and put to shame: that wish me evil.

Let them at once be put to confusion: that say unto me, Aha, aha.

Let all those that seek Thee rejoice and be glad in Thee: and let such as love Thy salvation say always, The Lord be praised.

But as for me I am poor and needy; but the Lord is careful for me.

Thou art my helper and my protector: O my God, make no delay.

Eternal rest, etc.

Ant. Be pleased, O Lord, to deliver me; look down, O Lord, to help me.

Ant. Heal my soul, O Lord, for I have sinned against Thee.

PSALM 40

Blessed is he that considereth the needy and poor: the Lord will deliver him in the evil day.

The Lord preserve him, and give him life, and make him blessed upon the earth: and deliver him not up to the will of his enemies.

The Lord help him on his bed of sorrow: Thou hast turned all his bed in his sickness.

I said: O Lord, be Thou merciful unto me: heal my soul, for I have sinned against Thee.

Mine enemies have spoken evil against me: When shall he die, and his name perish?

And if he came in to see me, he spoke vain things: his heart gathered together iniquity to itself.

He went out: and spoke to the same purpose.

All mine enemies whispered together against me: against me have they devised evils.

They sent forth an unjust word against me: Shall he that sleepeth rise again no more?

For even the man of my peace, in whom I trusted, who ate my bread: hath greatly sought to overthrow me.

But do Thou, O Lord, have mercy upon me, and raise me up again: and I will requite them.

By this I know that Thou hast wished well to me: because mine enemy shall not rejoice over me.

But Thou hast upheld me because of mine innocence: and Thou hast set me before Thy face forever.

Blessed be the Lord, the God of Israel: from eternity and to eternity. Amen, amen.

Eternal rest, etc.

Ant. Heal my soul, O Lord, for I have sinned against Thee.

Ant. My soul hath thirsted after the living God; when shall I come, and appear before the face of God?

PSALM 41

As the hart panteth after the water-springs: so panteth my soul after Thee, O God.

My soul hath thirsted after the strong living God; when shall I come, and appear before the face of God?

My tears have been my bread day and night: whilst it is said to me daily, Where is thy God?

These things I remembered, and I poured out my soul in me: for I shall go over into the place of the wonderful tabernacle, even unto the house of God.

With the voice of joy and praise: the noise of one feasting.

Why art thou sad, O my soul? and why dost thou disquiet me?

Hope thou in God, for I will yet praise Him: Who is the salvation of my countenance, and my God.

My soul is troubled within myself: therefore will I remember Thee from the land of Jordan and Hermoniim, from the little hill.

Deep calleth on deep: at the noise of Thy floodgates.

All Thy waves and Thy billows: have passed over me.

In the daytime the Lord hath commanded His mercy: and a song to Him in the night.

With me is prayer to the God of my life: I will say unto God, Thou art my support.

Why hast Thou forgotten me: and why go I mourning whilst mine enemy afflicteth me?

Whilst my bones are broken: mine enemies who trouble me have reproached me.

Whilst they say to me day by day: Where is thy God?

Why art thou cast down, O my soul? and why dost thou disquiet me?

Hope thou in God, for I will yet praise Him: Who is the salvation of my countenance, and my God.

Eternal rest, etc.

Ant. My soul hath thirsted after the living God; when shall I come, and appear before the face of God?

℣. Deliver not unto beasts the souls that praise Thee.

℟. And forget not the souls of Thy poor forever.

Our Father (*inaudibly*).

THE SEVENTH LESSON. Jb 17:1–3, 11–15.

My spirit is wasted: my days are shortened; and only the grave remaineth for me. I have not sinned, and my eye abideth in bitterness. Deliver me, O Lord, and set me beside Thee, and let any man's hand fight against me. My days have passed away; my thoughts are broken off, tormenting my heart. They have turned night into day; and after darkness I hope for light again. If I wait, hell is my house; and I have made my bed in darkness. I have said to rottenness: Thou art my father; to worms: My mother and my sister. Where is now then my expectation, and who considereth my patience?

℞. Forasmuch as I sin daily, and repent not, the fear of death troubleth me: †Because in hell there is no redemption, have mercy upon me, O God, and save me.

℣. O God, save me in Thy name, and in Thy power deliver me.

Because in hell, etc.

THE EIGHTH LESSON. Jb 19:20–27.

The flesh being consumed, my bone cleaveth to my skin: and nothing but lips are left about my teeth. Have pity on me, have pity on me, at least ye my friends; because the hand of the Lord hath touched me. Why do ye persecute me as God, and glut yourselves with my flesh? Who will grant me that my words may be written? Who will grant me that they may be marked down in a book, with an iron stile, and on a plate of lead, or else be graven with an instrument on the rock? For I know that my Redeemer liveth; and on the Last Day I shall rise out of the earth: and I shall be clothed again with my skin, and in my flesh I shall see my God. Whom I myself shall see, and my eyes shall behold, and not another: this, my hope, is laid up in my bosom.

℞. Judge me not, O Lord, according to my works, for I have done nothing worthy in Thy sight; therefore I beseech Thy Majesty: †That Thou, O God, mayest blot out my iniquity.

℣. Wash me, O Lord, yet more from my injustice, and cleanse me from my sin.

That Thou, O God, etc.

THE NINTH LESSON. Jb 10:18–22.

Why didst Thou bring me forth out of the womb? O that I had been consumed, that eye might not see me! I should have been as if I had not been, carried from the womb to the grave. Shall not the fewness of my days be ended shortly? Suffer me, therefore, that I may lament my sorrow a little: before I go and return no more, to a land that is dark and covered with the mist of death: a land of misery and darkness, where the shadow of death, and no order, but everlasting horror dwelleth.

℟. Deliver me, O Lord, from the ways of hell, Thou Who didst break the gates of brass in sunder, and didst visit hell, and give light therein: †That they who were in the pains of darkness might behold Thee.

℣. Crying, and saying: Thou art come, O our Redeemer.

That they, etc.

℣. Eternal rest grant unto them, O Lord, and let perpetual light shine upon them.

That they, etc.

Here Lauds *follow immediately, when only the preceding Nocturn has been said.*

When the three Nocturns have been said, the Responsory *to the ninth Lesson is as follows:*

Libera me, Domine, de morte æterna, in die ilia tremenda, †Quando cœli movendi sunt et terra: †Dum veneris judicare sæculum per ignem.

Deliver me, O Lord, from eternal death in that awful day: †When the heavens and the earth shall be shaken: †When Thou shalt come to judge the world by fire.

℣. Tremens factus sum ego, et timeo, dum discussio venerit, atque ventura ira.

℣. I am seized with fear and trembling, until the trial shall be at hand, and the wrath to come.

Quando, etc.

When the heavens, etc.

℣. Dies illa, dies iræ, calamitatis et miseriæ, dies magna et amara valde.

℣. That day, a day of wrath, of wasting, and of misery, a great day, and exceeding bitter.

Dum veneris, etc.

When Thou shalt come, etc.

℣. Requiem æternam dona eis, Domine, et lux perpetua luceat eis.

℣. Eternal rest grant unto them, O Lord, and let perpetual light shine upon them.

℟. Libera me, etc.

℟. Deliver me, etc.

LAUDS

Ant. The bones that were humbled shall rejoice in the Lord.

PSALM 50

Have mercy upon me, O God: according to Thy great mercy.

And according to the multitude of Thy tender mercies: blot out my iniquity.

Wash me yet more from my iniquity: and cleanse me from my sin.

For I acknowledge my iniquity: and my sin is always before me.

Against Thee only have I sinned, and done evil in Thy sight: that Thou mayest be justified in Thy words, and mayest overcome when Thou art judged.

For behold, I was conceived in iniquities: and in sins did my mother conceive me.

For behold, Thou hast loved truth: the secret and hidden things of Thy wisdom Thou hast made manifest unto me.

Thou shalt sprinkle me with hyssop, and I shall be cleansed: Thou shalt wash me, and I shall be made whiter than snow.

Thou shalt make me hear of joy and gladness: and the bones that were humbled shall rejoice.

Turn away Thy face from my sins: and blot out all my iniquities.

Create in me a clean heart, O God: and renew a right spirit within me.

Cast me not away from Thy face: and take not Thy Holy Spirit from me.

Restore unto me the joy of Thy salvation: and strengthen me with a perfect spirit.

I will teach the unjust Thy ways: and the wicked shall be converted unto Thee.

Deliver me from sins of blood, O God, Thou God of my salvation: and my tongue shall extol Thy justice.

Thou shalt open my lips, O Lord: and my mouth shall declare Thy praise.

For if Thou hadst desired sacrifice, I would surely have given it: with burnt offerings Thou wilt not be delighted.

A sacrifice unto God is a troubled spirit: a contrite and humble heart, O God, Thou wilt not despise.

Deal favorably, O Lord, in Thy good will with Sion: that the walls of Jerusalem may be built up.

Then shalt Thou accept the sacrifice of justice, oblations, and whole burnt offerings: then shall they lay calves upon Thine altar.

Eternal rest, etc.

Ant. The bones that were humbled shall rejoice in the Lord.

Ant. O hear my prayer, O Lord; unto Thee shall all flesh come.

PSALM 64

A hymn becometh Thee, O God, in Sion: and unto Thee shall the vow be paid in Jerusalem.

O hear my prayer: unto Thee shall all flesh come.

The words of the wicked have prevailed against us: and Thou wilt pardon our transgressions.

Blessed is he whom Thou has chosen, and taken to Thee: he shall dwell in Thy courts.

We shall be filled with the good things of Thy house: holy is Thy temple, wonderful in justice.

Hear us, O God our Savior, Who art the hope of all the ends of the earth, and in the sea afar off.

Thou Who preparest the mountains by Thy strength, being girded with power: Who troublest the depth of the sea, the noise of its waves.

The Gentiles shall be troubled, and they that dwell in the uttermost borders shall be afraid at Thy signs: Thou shalt make the outgoings of the morning and of the evening to be joyful.

Thou hast visited the earth, and hast watered it plenteously: Thou hast copiously enriched it.

The river of God is filled with water, Thou hast prepared their food: for so is its preparation.

Fill up plentifully the streams thereof, multiply its fruits: it shall spring up and rejoice in its showers.

Thou shalt bless the crown of the year of Thy goodness: and Thy fields shall be filled with plenty.

The beautiful places of the wilderness shall grow fat: and the hills shall be girded about with joy.

The rams of the flock are clothed, and the vales shall abound with corn; they shall shout, yea, they shall sing a hymn.

Eternal rest, etc.

Ant. O hear my prayer, O Lord; unto Thee shall all flesh come.

Ant. Thy right hand hath upheld me, O Lord.

PSALM 62

O God, my God, to Thee do I watch at break of day. For Thee my soul hath thirsted: for Thee my flesh longeth, O how exceedingly!

In a desert and pathless land where no water is: so have I come before Thee in Thy holy place, that I might see Thy power and Thy glory.

For Thy mercy is better than life: my lips shall praise Thee.

Thus will I bless Thee all my life long: and in Thy name I will lift up my hands.

Let my soul be filled as with marrow and fatness: and my mouth shall praise Thee with joyful lips.

If I have remembered Thee upon my bed, on Thee will I meditate in the morning; because Thou hast been my helper.

And I will rejoice under the covert of Thy wings: my soul hath cleaved unto Thee: Thy right hand hath upheld me.

But they have sought my soul in vain: they shall go into the lower parts of the earth:

They shall be delivered into the hands of the sword: they shall be the portions of foxes.

But the king shall rejoice in God, all they that swear by Him shall be praised: because the mouth of them that speak wicked things is stopped.

PSALM 66

God be merciful unto us, and bless us: cause the light of His countenance to shine upon us, and have mercy on us.

That we may know Thy way upon earth: Thy salvation in all nations.

Let the people praise Thee, O God: let all the people praise Thee.

O let the nations be glad and rejoice: for Thou dost judge the people with justice, and govern the nations upon earth.

Let the people praise Thee, O God: let all the people praise Thee: the earth hath yielded her fruit.

May God, even our own God, bless us, may God bless us: and may all the ends of the earth fear Him.

Eternal rest, etc.

Ant. Thy right hand hath upheld me, O Lord.

Ant. From the gate of hell deliver my soul, O Lord.

THE SONG OF HEZECHIAH. Is 38:10–20.

I said, In the midst of my days: I shall go to the gates of hell.

I sought for the residue of my years; I said, I shall not see the Lord God in the land of the living.

I shall behold man no more: nor the inhabitant of rest.

My generation is at an end; and it is rolled away from me: as a shepherd's tent.

My life is cut off as by a weaver; whilst I was yet but beginning He cut me off: from morning even to night Thou wilt make an end of me.

I hoped till morning: as a lion so hath He broken all my bones.

From morning even to night Thou wilt make an end of me: I cry like a young swallow, I moan like a dove.

My eyes are weakened: looking upward.

Lord, I suffer violence, answer Thou for me: What shall I say, or what shall He answer for me, whereas He Himself hath done it?

I will recount to Thee all my years: in the bitterness of my soul.

O Lord, if man's life be such, and the life of my spirit be in such things as these, Thou wilt correct me, and make me live! Behold, for peace is my bitterness most bitter.

But Thou hast delivered my soul, that it should not perish: Thou hast cast all my sins behind Thy back.

For hell will not thank Thee, neither will death praise Thee: nor will they that go down into the pit look for Thy truth.

The living, the living, he shall give praise to Thee, as I do this day: the father shall make Thy truth known to the children.

O Lord, save me: and we will sing our psalms all the days of our life in the house of the Lord.

Eternal rest, etc.

Ant. From the gate of hell deliver my soul, O Lord.

Ant. Let every spirit praise the Lord.

PSALM 148

Praise ye the Lord from the heavens: praise Him in the heights.

Praise Him, all ye His angels: praise ye Him, all His hosts.

Praise Him, O ye sun and moon: praise Him, all ye stars and light.

Praise Him, O ye heaven of heavens: and let all the waters that are above the heavens praise the name of the Lord.

For He spake, and they were made: He commanded, and they were created.

He hath established them forever, and for ages of ages: He hath made a decree, and it shall not pass away.

Praise the Lord from the earth: ye dragons, and all ye deeps.

Fire and hail; snow and ice: and stormy winds, which fulfill His word.

Mountains and all hills: fruitful trees and all cedars:

Beasts and all cattle: creeping things and feathered fowls:

Kings of the earth, and all people: princes and all judges of the earth:

Young men and maidens, old men and children, let them praise the name of the Lord: for His name alone is exalted.

His praise is above heaven and earth: and He hath exalted the horn of His people.

A song of praise to all His saints: to the children of Israel, a people drawing nigh unto Him.

PSALM 149

Sing unto the Lord a new song: let His praise be in the Church of the saints.

Let Israel rejoice in Him that made him: and let the children of Sion be joyful in their King.

Let them praise His name in the choir: let them sing unto Him with timbrel and psaltery:

For the Lord is well pleased with His people: and He will exalt the meek unto salvation.

The saints shall rejoice in glory: they shall be joyful in their beds.

The high praises of God shall be in their mouth: and two-edged swords in their hands:

To execute vengeance upon the nations: and chastisements among the people:
To bind their kings with fetters: and their nobles with chains of iron.
To execute upon them the judgment that is written: this glory have all His saints.

PSALM 150

Praise the Lord in His holy places: praise Him in the firmament of His power.
Praise Him in His mighty acts: praise Him according to the multitude of His
greatness.
Praise Him with the sound of the trumpet: praise Him with psaltery and harp.
Praise Him with timbrel and choir: praise Him with strings and organs.
Praise Him upon the high-sounding cymbals; praise Him upon cymbals of joy: let
every spirit praise the Lord.
Eternal rest, etc.

Ant. Let every spirit praise the Lord.
℣. I heard a voice from heaven saying unto me:
℟. Blessed are the dead who die in the Lord.

Ant. I am the Resurrection and the Life: he that believeth in Me, although he be
dead, shall live; and everyone who liveth, and believeth in Me, shall never die.

THE *BENEDICTUS*, OR SONG OF
ZACHARY. Lk 1:68–79.

Benedictus Dominus, Deus Israel, * quia visitavit, et fecit redemptionem plebis suæ:

Blessed be the Lord God of Israel: for He hath visited and wrought redemption for His people:

Et erexit cornu salutis nobis: * in domo David, pueri sui:

And raised up for us a horn of salvation: in the house of David His servant:

Sicut locutus est per os sanctorum, * qui a sæculo sunt, prophetarum ejus:

As He spake by the mouth: of His holy prophets of old:

Salutem ex inimicis nostris, * et de manu omnium, qui oderunt nos:

Deliverance from our enemies: and from the hand of all who hate us:

Ad faciendam misericordiam cum patribus nostris; * et memorari testamenti sui sancti.

To perform mercy to our fathers: and to remember His holy covenant.

Jusjurandum, quod juravit ad Abraham, patrem nostrum, * daturum se nobis:	The oath which He swore to Abraham our father: that He would grant us:
Ut sine timore, de manu inimicorum nostrorum liberati, * serviamus illi.	That being delivered out of the hand of our enemies: we may serve Him without fear.
In sanctitate, et justitia coram ipso, * omnibus diebus nostris.	In holiness and justice before Him: all our days.
Et tu, puer, Propheta Altissimi vocaberis: * præibis enim ante faciem Domini parare vias ejus:	And thou, child, shalt be called the prophet of the Most High: for thou shalt go before the face of the Lord, to prepare His ways:
Ad dandam scientiam salutis plebi ejus: * in remissionem peccatorum eorum:	To give knowledge of salvation to His people: unto remission of their sins:
Per viscera misericordiæ Dei nostri: * in quibus visitavit nos, oriens ex alto:	Through the tender mercy of our God: in which the Dayspring from on high hath visited us:
Illuminare his, qui in tenebris, et in umbra mortis sedent: * ad dirigendos pedes nostros in viam pacis.	To enlighten those who sit in darkness, and in the shade of death: to direct our feet into the way of peace.
Requiem æternam, etc.	Eternal rest, etc.

Ant. I am the Resurrection and the Life: he that believeth in Me, although he be dead, shall live; and everyone who liveth, and believeth in Me, shall never die.

Then are said the following prayers, all kneeling:
Our Father (*inaudibly*).

℣. And lead us not into temptation.
℟. But deliver us from evil.
℣. From the gate of hell.
℟. Deliver *his* soul, O Lord.
℣. May *he* rest in peace.
℟. Amen.
℣. O Lord, hear my prayer.
℟. And let my cry come to Thee.

℣. The Lord be with you.
℟. And with thy spirit.

Let us pray.

Absolve, we beseech Thee, O Lord, the soul of Thy *servant* N. from every bond of sin; that, in the glory of the resurrection, among Thy saints and elect *he* may rise again unto newness of life. Through Christ Our Lord. ℟. Amen.

During the singing of Lauds *the celebrant and his ministers prepare for the* Mass. (*See the* Ordinary of the Mass, *p. 86, for everything not here noted.*)

THE MASS FOR THE DEAD

ON THE DAY OF DECEASE OR BURIAL

THE INTROIT.

Requiem æternam dona eis, Domine: et lux perpetua luceat eis.	Eternal rest grant unto them, O Lord, and let perpetual light shine upon them.
Te decet hymnus, Deus in Sion, et tibi reddetur votum in Jerusalem: exaudi orationem meam, ad te omnis caro veniet.	A hymn becometh Thee, O God in Sion; and unto Thee shall the vow be paid in Jerusalem: O hear my prayer; unto Thee shall all flesh come.
Requiem æternam, etc.	Eternal rest, etc.

THE COLLECT.

Deus, cui proprium est misereri semper et parcere, te supplices exoramus pro anima *famuli tui* N., quam hodie de hoc sæculo migrare jussisti: ut non tradas eam in manus inimici, neque obliviscaris in finem, sed jubeas eam a sanctis Angelis suscipi, et ad patriam paradisi perduci; ut, quia in te speravit et credidit, non pœnas inferni sustineat, sed gaudia æterna possideat. Per Dominum nostrum Jesum Christum, etc.

O God, Whose property is always to have mercy and to spare, we humbly beseech Thee for the soul of Thy *servant* N., which Thou hast this day commanded to depart out of this world: that Thou deliver it not into the hands of the enemy, nor forget it unto the end; but command it to be received by Thy holy angels, and conducted into paradise, its true country; that, as in Thee it hath hoped and believed, it may not suffer the pains of hell, but may take possession of eternal joys. Through Our Lord Jesus Christ, etc.

THE EPISTLE. 1 Thes 4:12–17.

Fratres: Nolumus vos ignorare de dormientibus, ut non contristemini, sicut et cæteri, qui spem non habent. Si enim credimus quod Jesus mortuus est, et resurrexit: ita et Deus eos, qui dormierunt per Jesum, adducet cum eo. Hoc enim vobis dicimus in verbo Domini, quia nos, qui vivimus, qui residui sumus in adventum Domini, non præveniemus eos, qui dormierunt. Quoniam ipse Dominus in jussu, et in voce Archangeli, et in tuba Dei descendet de cœlo: et mortui, qui in Christo sunt, resurgent primi. Deinde nos, qui vivimus, qui relinquimur, simul rapiemur cum illis in nubibus obviam Christo in aëra, et sic semper cum Domino erimus. Itaque consolamini invicem in verbis istis.

Brethren: We will not have you ignorant concerning those who sleep, that ye sorrow not, as even the others who have no hope. For if we believe that Jesus died and rose again, so also those who are asleep through Jesus, God will bring with Him. For this we say to you on the word of the Lord, that we who are alive, who remain to the coming of the Lord, shall not precede those who are asleep. For the Lord Himself, with command, and with the voice of an archangel, and with the trumpet of God, shall come down from heaven: and the dead who are in Christ shall rise first. Then we who are alive, who are left, shall be caught up with them in the clouds to meet Christ in the air, and so we shall be always with the Lord. Therefore comfort one another with these words.

THE GRADUAL.

Requiem æternam dona eis, Domine: et lux perpetua luceat eis.

Eternal rest grant unto them, O Lord, and let perpetual light shine upon them.

℣. In memoria æterna erit justus: ab auditione mala non timebit.

℣. The just man shall be in everlasting remembrance; he shall not be afraid for evil tidings.

THE TRACT.

Absolve, Domine, animas omnium fidelium defunctorum ab omni vinculo delictorum.

Absolve, O Lord, the souls of all Thy faithful departed from every bond of sin.

℣. Et gratia tua illis succurrente, mereantur evadere judicium ultionis.

℣. And by the help of Thy grace may they be enabled to escape the judgment of vengeance.

℣. Et lucis æternæ beatitudine perfrui.

℣. And enjoy the blessedness of light eternal.

THE SEQUENCE.

Dies iræ, dies ilia,
Solvet sæclum in favilla:
Teste David cum Sibylla.

Day of wrath, O day of mourning,
Lo, the world in ashes burning—
Seer and Sibyl gave the warning.

Quantus tremor est futurus,
Quando judex est venturus,
Cuncta stricte discussurus!

O what fear man's bosom rendeth,
When from heaven the Judge
    descendeth,
On Whose sentence all dependeth!

Tuba mirum spargens sonum
Per sepulcra regionum,
Coget omnes ante thronum.

Wondrous sound the trumpet flingeth,
Through earth's sepulchres it ringeth,
All before the throne it bringeth.

Mors stupebit, et natura,
Cum resurget creatura,
Judicanti responsura.

Death is struck, and Nature quaking,
All creation is awaking—
To its Judge an answer making.

Liber scriptus proferetur,
In quo totum continetur,
Unde mundus judicetur.

Lo, the Book, exactly worded,
Wherein all hath been recorded—
Thence shall judgment be awarded.

Judex ergo cum sedebit,
Quidquid latet, apparebit:
Nil inultum remanebit.

When the Judge His seat attaineth,
And each hidden deed arraigneth,
Nothing unavenged remaineth.

Quid sum miser tunc dicturus?
Quem patronum rogaturus,
Cum vix justus sit securus?

What shall I, frail man, be pleading?
Who for me be interceding
When the just are mercy needing?

Rex tremendæ majestatis,
Qui salvandos salvas gratis,
Salva me, fons pietatis.

King, of majesty tremendous,
Who dost free salvation send us,
Fount of pity, then befriend us.

Recordare, Jesu pie,
Quod sum causa tuæ viæ:
Ne me perdas illa die.

Think, kind Jesu, my salvation
Caused Thy wondrous Incarnation—
Leave me not to reprobation.

Quærens me, sedisti lassus:
Redemisti crucem passus:
Tantus labor non sit cassus.

Faint and weary Thou hast sought me,
On the Cross of suffering bought me;
Shall such grace be vainly brought me?

Juste Judex ultionis,
Donum fac remissionis
Ante diem rationis.

Righteous Judge of retribution,
Grant Thy gift of absolution
Ere that Reck'ning Day's conclusion.

Ingemisco, tanquam reus,
Culpa rubet vultus meus:
Supplicanti parce, Deus.

Guilty, now I pour my moaning,
All my shame with anguish owning:
Spare, O God, Thy suppliant groaning.

Qui Mariam absolvisti,
El latronem exaudisti,
Mihi quoque spem dedisti.

Thou the sinful Mary savest,
Thou the dying thief forgavest,
And to me a hope vouchsafest.

Preces meæ non sunt dignæ:
Sed tu bonus fac benigne,
Ne perenni cremer igne.

Worthless are my prayers and sighing,
Yet, good Lord, in grace complying,
Rescue me from fires undying.

Inter oves locum præsta,
Et ab hœdis me sequestra,
Statuens in parte dextra.

With Thy favored sheep O place me;
Nor among the goats abase me,
But to Thy right hand upraise me.

Confutatis maledictis,
Flammis acribus addictis:
Voca me cum benedictis.

While the wicked are confounded,
Doomed to flames of woe unbounded,
Call me, with Thy saints surrounded.

Oro supplex, et acclinis,
Cor contritum quasi cinis:
Gere curam mei finis.

Low I kneel, with heart-submission;
See, like ashes, my contrition—
Help me in my last condition.

Lacrymosa dies illa,
Qua resurget ex favilla
Judicandus homo reus.

Ah, that day of tears and mourning,
From the dust of earth returning,
Man for judgment must prepare him—

Huic ergo parce, Deus:
Pie Jesu Domine,
Dona eis requiem.
Amen.

Spare, O God, in mercy spare him.
Lord, Who didst our souls redeem,
Grant a blessed requiem.
Amen.

THE GOSPEL. Jn 11:21–27.

In illo tempore: Dixit Martha ad Jesum: Domine, si fuisses hic, frater meus non fuisset mortuus: sed et nunc scio, quia quæcumque poposceris a Deo, dabit tibi Deus. Dicit illi Jesus: Resurget frater tuus. Dicit ei Martha: Scio, quia resurget in resurrectione in novissimo die. Dixit ei Jesus: Ego sum resurrectio et vita: qui credit in me, etiam si mortuus fuerit, vivet: et omnis qui vivit, et credit in me, non morietur in æternum. Credis hoc? Ait illi: Utique, Domine, ego credidi, quia tu es Christus Filius Dei vivi, qui in hunc mundum venisti.

At that time: Martha said to Jesus: Lord, if Thou hadst been here, my brother had not died. But now also I know that whatever Thou wilt ask of God, God will give Thee. Jesus saith to her: Thy brother will rise again. Martha saith to Him: I know that he will rise again in the resurrection at the Last Day. Jesus said to her: I am the Resurrection and the Life: he that believeth in Me, although he be dead, shall live: and everyone who liveth, and believeth in Me, shall never die. Believest thou this? She saith to Him: Yea, Lord, I believe that Thou art the Christ, the Son of the living God, Who art come into this world.

THE OFFERTORY.

Domine Jesu Christe, Rex gloriæ, libera animas omnium fidelium defunctorum de pœnis inferni, et de profundo lacu: libera eas de ore leonis, ne absorbeat eas tartarus, ne cadant in obscurum: sed signifer sanctus Michael repræsentet eas in lucem sanctam: †Quam olim Abrahæ promisisti, et semini ejus.

O Lord Jesus Christ, King of glory, deliver the souls of all the faithful departed from the pains of hell, and from the depths of the pit: deliver them from the mouth of the lion, lest hell swallow them up, lest they fall into darkness; but, let the standard-bearer, St. Michael, bring them into the holy light. †Which Thou didst promise of old to Abraham, and to his seed.

℣. Hostias et preces tibi, Domine, laudis offerimus: tu suscipe pro animabus illis, quarum hodie memoriam facimus: fac eas, Domine, de morte transire at vitam.

℣. We offer Thee, O Lord, a sacrifice of praise and prayers: do Thou accept them in behalf of those souls whom we this day commemorate. Grant, O Lord, that they may pass from death to life.

Quam olim Abrahæ promisisti et semini ejus.

Which Thou didst promise of old to Abraham, and to his seed.

THE SECRET PRAYER.

Propitiare, quæsumus, Domine, animæ *famuli tui* N., pro qua hostiam laudis tibi immolamus, majestatem tuam suppliciter deprecantes: ut per hæc piæ placationis officia, pervenire mereatur ad requiem sempiternam. Per Dominum nostrum Jesum Christum, etc.

Be merciful, we beseech Thee, O Lord, to the soul of Thy *servant* N., for which we offer Thee the sacrifice of praise; humbly beseeching Thy Majesty, that, by these offices of loving reconciliation, it may be found worthy to attain everlasting rest. Through Our Lord Jesus Christ, etc.

THE COMMUNION.

Lux æterna luceat eis, Domine: †Cum Sanctis tuis in æternum: quia pius es.

May light eternal shine upon them, O Lord: †With Thy saints forever, because Thou art merciful.

℣. Requiem æternam dona eis, Domine: et lux perpetua luceat eis.

Eternal rest grant unto them, O Lord, and let perpetual light shine upon them.

Cum Sanctis, etc.

With Thy saints, etc.

THE POSTCOMMUNION.

Præsta, quæsumus, omnipotens Deus, ut anima *famuli tui* N., quæ hodie de hoc sæculo migravit, his sacrificiis purgata, et a peccatis expedita, indulgentiam pariter et requiem capiat sempiternam. Per Dominum nostrum Jesum Christum, etc.

Grant, we beseech Thee, Almighty God, that the soul of Thy *servant* N., which has this day departed out of this world, being purified by this sacrifice, and delivered from sins, may receive both pardon and eternal rest. Through Our Lord Jesus Christ, etc.

After Mass the celebrant, having put off the chasuble and maniple, receives a cope of black color. The subdeacon takes the processional cross, and places himself at the head of the corpse with the cross, between two acolytes with their candlesticks and lighted candles. The celebrant, with the deacon and other ministers, places himself at the feet of the corpse, opposite the cross. An acolyte holds the Ritual before the celebrant, who says the following Prayer:]

In less solemn funerals, where the Office *and* Mass *are omitted, the priest, after reciting the* Subvenite, *etc., (p. 402), begins at once the following prayer:*

Non intres in judicium cum servo tuo, Domine, quia nullus apud te justificabitur homo, nisi per te omnium peccatorum ei tribuatur remissio. Non ergo eum, quæsumus, tuo judicialis sententia premat, quem tibi vera supplicatio fidei Christianæ commendat: sed, gratia tua illi succurrente, mereatur evadere judicium ultionis, qui dum viveret, insignitus est signaculo Sanctæ Trinitatis: Qui vivis et regnas in sæcula sæculorum. ℟. Amen.

Enter not into judgment with Thy servant, O Lord, for in Thy sight shall no man be justified, unless through Thee remission of all his sins be granted unto him. Let not, therefore, we beseech Thee, the sentence of Thy judgment weigh heavily upon him whom the true supplication of Christian Faith doth commend unto Thee: but, by the succor of Thy grace, may he be found worthy to escape the judgment of vengeance, who, while he lived, was sealed with the seal of the Holy Trinity: Who livest and reignest, world without end. ℟. Amen.

Then is said or sung the Responsory, Libera me.

Libera me, Domine, de morte æterna, in die ilia tremenda, †Quando cœli movendi sunt et terra: †Dum veneris judicare sæculum per ignem.

Deliver me, O Lord, from eternal death in that awful day: †When the heavens and the earth shall be shaken: †When Thou shalt come to judge the world by fire.

℣. Tremens factus sum ego, et timeo, dum discussio venerit, atque ventura ira.

℣. I am seized with fear and trembling, until the trial shall be at hand, and the wrath to come.

Quando, etc.

When the heavens, etc.

℣. Dies illa, dies iræ, calamitatis et miseriæ, dies magna et amara valde.

℣. That day, a day of wrath, of wasting, and of misery, a great day, and exceeding bitter.

Dum veneris, etc.

When Thou shalt come, etc.

℣. Requiem æternam dona eis, Domine, et lux perpetua luceat eis.

℣. Eternal rest grant unto them, O Lord, and let perpetual light shine upon them.

℟. Libera me, etc.

℟. Deliver me, etc.

Whilst the above Responsory *is being sung, the priest puts incense into the censer. At the end of the* Responsory *is said:*

Kyrie, eleison.
Christe, eleison.
Kyrie, eleison.
Pater noster (*secreto*).

Lord, have mercy.
Christ, have mercy.
Lord, have mercy.
Our Father (*inaudibly*).

Meanwhile, the priest receives the sprinkler from the assistant, and, having made a low bow to the crucifix, goes round the bier, and sprinkles the corpse thrice on each side; then, returning to his place, he receives the censer from the assistant, and in like manner goes round the bier, and incenses the corpse in the same way as he sprinkled it; then, having returned the censer to the assistant, he says:

℣. Et ne nos inducas in tentationem.
℟. Sed libera nos a malo.

℣. And lead us not into temptation.
℟. But deliver us from evil.

℣. A porta inferi,
℟. Erue, Domine, animam ejus.

℣. From the gate of hell,
℟. Deliver *his* soul, O Lord.

℣. Requiescat in pace.
℟. Amen.

℣. Domine, exaudi orationem meam.
℟. Et clamor meus ad te veniat.

℣. Dominus vobiscum.
℟. Et cum spiritu tuo.

Oremus.

Deus, cui proprium est misereri semper et parcere: te supplices exoramus pro anima *famuli tui* N., quam hodie de hoc sæculo migrare jussisti, ut non tradas eam in manus inimici, neque obliviscaris in finem, sed jubeas eam a sanctis Angelis suscipi, et ad patriam Paradisi perduci; ut, quia in te speravit et credidit, non pœnas inferni sustineat, sed gaudia æterna possideat. Per Christum Dominum nostrum. ℟. Amen.

℣. May *he* rest in peace.
℟. Amen.

℣. O Lord, hear my prayer.
℟. And let my cry come unto Thee.

℣. The Lord be with you.
℟. And with thy spirit.

Let us pray.

O God, Whose property is always to have mercy and to spare, we humbly beseech Thee for the soul of Thy *servant* N., which Thou hast this day commanded to depart out of this world: that Thou deliver it not into the hands of the enemy, nor forget it unto the end; but command it to be received by Thy holy angels, and conducted into paradise, its true country; that, as in Thee it hath hoped and believed, it may not suffer the pains of hell, but may take possession of eternal joys. Through Christ Our Lord. ℟. Amen.

(If the deceased was a priest, the word priest *is added to the name expressed in the prayer.)*

After this, the body is borne to the grave, if it is to be buried then; meanwhile is said or sung:

In paradisum deducant te Angeli: in tuo adventu suscipiant te Martyres, et perducant te in civitatem sanctam Jerusalem. Chorus Angelorum te suscipiat, et cum Lazaro quondam paupere æternam habeas requiem.

May the angels lead thee into paradise; at thy coming may the martyrs receive thee, and bring thee into the holy city, Jerusalem. May the choir of angels receive thee, and with Lazarus, once a beggar, mayest thou have eternal rest.

On reaching the grave, if it be not blessed, the priest blesses it, as follows:

Oremus.

Let us pray.

Deus, cujus miseratione animæ fidelium requiescunt, hunc tumulum benedicere ✠ dignare, eique Angelum tuum sanctum deputa custodem: et quorum quarumque corpora hic sepeliuntur, animas eorum ab omnibus absolve vinculis delictorum, ut in te semper cum Sanctis tuis sine fine lætentur. Per Christum Dominum nostrum. ℞. Amen.

O God, in Whose tender mercy the souls of the faithful departed are at rest, vouchsafe to bless ✠ this grave, and assign thereto Thy holy angel as its keeper; and absolve from all the bonds of sin the souls of those whose bodies are here buried, that with Thy saints they may ever rejoice in Thee to all eternity. Through Christ Our Lord. ℞. Amen.

The prayer being said, the priest sprinkles with holy water, and afterward incenses the body of the deceased and the grave. But if the body is not buried then, the Responsory In paradisum *is omitted (and also the* Blessing of the Grave, *if it be already blessed). The Office then continues as follows:*

Ego sum.

I am.

The Benedictus *is then said.*

Benedictus Dominus, Deus Israel, * quia visitavit, et fecit redemptionem plebis suæ:

Blessed be the Lord God of Israel: for He hath visited and wrought redemption for His people:

Et erexit cornu salutis nobis: * in domo David, pueri sui:

And raised up for us a horn of salvation: in the house of David His servant:

Sicut locutus est per os sanctorum, * qui a sæculo sunt, prophetarum ejus:

As He spake by the mouth: of His holy prophets of old:

Salutem ex inimicis nostris, * et de manu omnium, qui oderunt nos:

Deliverance from our enemies: and from the hand of all who hate us:

Ad faciendam misericordiam cum patribus nostris; * et memorari testamenti sui sancti.

To perform mercy to our fathers: and to remember His holy covenant.

Jusjurandum, quod juravit ad Abraham, patrem nostrum, * daturum se nobis:

The oath which He swore to Abraham our father: that He would grant us:

Ut sine timore, de manu inimicorum nostrorum liberati, * serviamus illi.	That being delivered out of the hand of our enemies: we may serve Him without fear.
In sanctitate, et justitia coram ipso, * omnibus diebus nostris.	In holiness and justice before Him: all our days.
Et tu, puer, Propheta Altissimi vocaberis: * præibis enim ante faciem Domini parare vias ejus:	And thou, child, shalt be called the prophet of the most High: for thou shalt go before the face of the Lord, to prepare His ways:
Ad dandam scientiam salutis plebi ejus: * in remissionem peccatorum eorum:	To give knowledge of salvation to His people: unto remission of their sins:
Per viscera misericordiæ Dei nostri: * in quibus visitavit nos, oriens ex alto:	Through the tender mercy of our God: in which the Dayspring from on high hath visited us:
Illuminare his, qui in tenebris, et in umbra mortis sedent: * ad dirigendos pedes nostros in viam pacis.	To enlighten those who sit in darkness, and in the shade of death: to direct our feet into the way of peace.

After which:

Requiem æternam, etc.

Ant. Ego sum resurrectio et vita: qui credit in me, etiam si mortuus fuerit, vivet: et omnis qui vivit et credit in me, non morietur in æternum.

Eternal rest, etc.

Ant. I am the Resurrection and the Life: he that believeth in Me, although he be dead, shall live: and everyone who liveth, and believeth in Me, shall never die.

Then is said:

Kyrie, eleison.	Lord, have mercy.
Christe, eleison.	Christ, have mercy.
Kyrie, eleison.	Lord, have mercy.
Pater noster (*secreto*).	Our Father (*inaudibly*).

In the meantime the priest sprinkles the corpse.

℣. Et ne nos inducas in tentationem.	℣. And lead us not into temptation.
℟. Sed libera nos a malo.	℟. But deliver us from evil.
℣. A porta inferi,	℣. From the gate of hell,
℟. Erue, Domine, animam ejus.	℟. Deliver *his* soul, O Lord,

℣. Requiescat in pace.
℟. Amen.

℣. Domine, exaudi orationem meam.
℟. Et clamor meus ad te veniat.

℣. Dominus vobiscum.
℟. Et cum spiritu tuo.

Oremus.

Fac, quæsumus, Domine, hanc cum *servo* tu*o* defunct*o* misericordiam, ut factorum suorum in pœnis non recipiat vicem, *qui* tuam in votis tenuit voluntatem: ut sicut hic *eum* vera fides junxit fidelium turmis; ita illic *eum* tua miseratio societ angelicis choris. Per Christum Dominum nostrum. ℟. Amen.

℣. Requiem æternam dona ei, Domine.
℟. Et lux perpetua luceat ei.

℣. Requiescat in pace.
℟. Amen.

℣. Anima ejus, et animæ omnium fidelium defunctorum, per misericordiam Dei, requiescant in pace.
℟. Amen.

℣. May *he* rest in peace.
℟. Amen.

℣. O Lord, hear my prayer.
℟. And let my cry come unto Thee.

℣. The Lord be with you.
℟. And with thy spirit.

Let us pray.

Grant, O Lord, we beseech Thee, this mercy unto Thy *servant* deceased, that, having in desire kept Thy will, *he* may not suffer in requital of *his* deeds: and as a true Faith joined *him* unto the company of Thy faithful here below, so may Thy tender mercy give *him* place above, among the angel choirs. Through Christ Our Lord. ℟. Amen.

℣. Eternal rest grant unto *him*, O Lord.
℟. And let perpetual light shine upon *him*.

℣. May *he* rest in peace.
℟. Amen.

℣. May *his* soul, and the souls of all the faithful departed, through the mercy of God, rest in peace.
℟. Amen.

THE BURIAL OF CHILDREN

When a baptized child shall have departed this life before coming to the use of reason, the body shall be dressed as befits his age, and flowers shall be laid upon it, in token of purity and virginity. The priest, vested in surplice and white stole, first sprinkles the body with holy water, and says the first words of the Antiphon:
Sit nomen Domini.

Blessed be the name of the Lord.

PSALM 112

Laudate, pueri, Dominum: * laudate nomen Domini.	Praise the Lord, ye children: praise ye the name of the Lord.
Sit nomen Domini benedictum: * ex hoc nunc, et usque in sæculum.	Blessed be the name of the Lord: from this time forth forevermore.
A solis ortu usque ad occasum, * laudabile nomen Domini.	From the rising up of the sun unto the going down of the same: the name of the Lord is worthy to be praised.
Excelsus super omnes gentes Dominus: * et super cœlos gloria ejus.	The Lord is high above all nations: and His glory above the heavens.
Quis sicut Dominus Deus noster, qui in altis habitat * et humilia respicit in cœlo et in terra?	Who is like unto the Lord our God, Who dwelleth on high: and regardeth the things that are lowly in heaven and on earth?
Suscitans a terra inopem: * et de stercore erigens pauperem:	Who raiseth up the needy from the earth: and lifteth the poor out of the dunghill;
Ut collocet eum cum principibus: * cum principibus populi sui.	That He may set him with the princes: even with the princes of His people.
Qui habitare facit sterilem in domo: * matrem filiorum lætantem.	Who maketh the barren woman to dwell in her house: the joyful mother of children.

followed by Glory be to the Father, etc. *Then the Antiphon is said entire:*

Sit nomen Domini benedictum, ex hoc nunc et usque in sæculum.	Blessed be the name of the Lord: from this time forth for evermore.

If the body is borne to the church, is said, according to the space of time:
PSALMS 118 (p. 390); 148, 149, 150 (p. 419).

On arriving at the church the priest says:

Ant. Hic accipiet.	*Ant.* He shall receive.

PSALM 23

Domini est terra, et plenitudo ejus: orbis terrarum, et universi qui habitant in eo.	The earth is the Lord's, and the fullness thereof: the world and all they that dwell therein.
Quia ipse super maria fundavit eum: et super flumina præparavit eum.	For He hath founded it upon the seas: and hath prepared it upon the rivers.
Quis ascendet in montem Domini? aut quis stabit in loco sancto ejus?	Who shall ascend into the mountain of the Lord: or who shall stand in His holy place?
Innocens manibus et mundo corde, qui non accepit in vano animam suam, nec juravit in dolo proximo suo.	He that hath clean hands and a pure heart: who hath not taken his soul in vain, nor sworn deceitfully to his neighbor.
Hic accipiet benedictionem a Domino: et misericordiam a Deo, salutari suo.	He shall receive a blessing from the Lord; and mercy from God his Savior.
Hæc est generatio quærentium eum, quærentium faciem Dei Jacob.	This is the generation of them that seek Him: of them that seek the face of the God of Jacob.
Attollite portas, principes, vestras, et elevamini, portæ æternales: et introibit Rex gloriæ.	Lift up your gates, O ye princes, and be ye lifted up, O eternal gates: and the King of glory shall enter in.
Quis est iste Rex gloriæ? Dominus fortis et potens: Dominus potens in prælio.	Who is this King of glory? the Lord strong and mighty: the Lord mighty in battle.
Attollite portas, principes, vestras, et elevamini, portæ æternales: et introibit Rex gloriæ.	Lift up your gates, O ye princes, and be ye lifted up, O eternal gates: and the King of glory shall enter in.
Quis est iste Rex gloriæ? Dominus virtutum, ipse est Rex gloriæ.	Who is this King of glory? the Lord of hosts, He is the King of glory.
Gloria Patri, etc.	Glory be to the Father, etc.

Ant. Hic accipiet benedictionem a Domino, et misericordiam a Deo salutari suo: quia hæc est generatio quærentium Dominum.

Ant. He shall receive a blessing from the Lord, and mercy from God his Savior, for this is the generation of them that seek the Lord.

Then is said:

Kyrie, eleison.
Christe, eleison.
Kyrie, eleison.
Pater noster (*secreto*).

Lord, have mercy.
Christ, have mercy.
Lord, have mercy.
Our Father (*inaudibly*).

Meanwhile, he sprinkles the body.

℣. Et ne nos inducas in tentationem.
℟. Sed libera nos a malo.

℣. And lead us not into temptation.
℟. But deliver us from evil.

℣. Me autem propter innocentiam suscepisti.
℟. Et confirmasti me in conspectu tuo in æternum.

℣. As for me, Thou hast received me because of mine innocence.
℟. And hast set me before Thy face forever.

℣. Dominus vobiscum.
℟. Et cum spiritu tuo.

℣. The Lord be with you.
℟. And with thy spirit.

Oremus.

Omnipotens et mitissime Deus, qui omnibus parvulis renatis fonte baptismatis, dum migrant a sæculo, sine ullis eorum meritis vitam illico largiris æternam, sicut animæ hujus parvuli hodie credimus te fecisse: fac nos, quæsumus, Domine, per intercessionem beatæ Mariæ semper Virginis et omnium Sanctorum tuorum, his purificatis tibi mentibus famulari, et in Paradiso cum beatis parvulis perenniter sociari. Per Christum Dominum nostrum. ℟. Amen.

Let us pray.

Almighty and most merciful God, Who, when little children born again at the font of Baptism depart this world, dost forthwith, without any desert of theirs, bestow upon them life everlasting, as we believe Thou hast done this day to the soul of this little child: grant us, we beseech Thee, O Lord, through the intercession of Blessed Mary ever Virgin, and of all Thy saints, to serve Thee here with pure minds, and to be forever united to the blessed little ones in paradise. Through Christ Our Lord. ℟. Amen.

While the body is borne to the grave, and even if it be not then buried, is said the first word of the Antiphon:

Juvenes.   Young men.

PSALM 148

Laudate Dominum de cœlis: * laudate eum in excelsis.

Praise ye the Lord from the heavens: praise Him in the heights.

Laudate eum, omnes angeli ejus: * laudate eum, omnes virtutes ejus.

Praise Him, all ye His angels: praise ye Him, all His hosts.

Laudate eum, sol et luna: * laudate eum, omnes stellæ et lumen.

Praise Him, O ye sun and moon: praise Him, all ye stars and light.

Laudate eum, cœli cœlorum: * et aquæ omnes quæ super cœlos sunt, laudent nomen Domini.

Praise Him, O ye heaven of heavens: and let all the waters that are above the heavens praise the name of the Lord.

Quia ipse dixit, et facta sunt: * ipse mandavit, et creata sunt.

For He spake, and they were made: He commanded, and they were created.

Statuit ea in æternum, et in sæculum sæculi: * præceptum posuit, et non præteribit,

He hath established them forever, and for ages of ages: He hath made a decree, and it shall not pass away.

Laudate Dominum de terra, * dracones et omnes abyssi.

Praise the Lord from the earth: ye dragons, and all ye deeps.

Ignis, grando, nix, glacies, spiritus procellarum: * quæ faciunt verbum ejus:

Fire and hail; snow and ice: and stormy winds, which fulfill His word.

Montes, et omnes colles: * ligna fructifera, et omnes cedri.

Mountains and all hills: fruitful trees and all cedars:

Bestiæ, et universa pecora: * serpentes, et volucres pennatæ:

Beasts and all cattle: creeping things and feathered fowls:

Reges terræ et omnes populi: * principes, et omnes judices terræ.

Kings of the earth, and all people: princes and all judges of the earth:

Juvenes et virgines: senes cum juniori-
bus laudent nomen Domini: * quia
exaltatum est nomen ejus solius.

Young men and maidens, old men and
children, let them praise the name
of the Lord: for His name alone is
exalted.

Confessio ejus super cælum et terram: *
et exaltavit cornu populi sui.

His praise is above heaven and earth:
and He hath exalted the horn of His
people.

Hymnus omnibus sanctis ejus: * filiis
Israel, populo appropinquanti sibi.

A song of praise to all His saints: to the
children of Israel, a people drawing
nigh unto Him.

Ant. Juvenes et virgines, senes cum ju-
nioribus laudent nomen Domini.

Ant. Young men and maidens, old men
and children, let them praise the
name of the Lord.

Then is said:

Kyrie, eleison.
Christe, eleison.
Kyrie, eleison.
Pater noster (*secreto*).

Lord, have mercy.
Christ, have mercy.
Lord, have mercy.
Our Father (*inaudibly*).

℣. Et ne nos inducas in tentationem.
℟. Sed libera nos a malo.

℣. And lead us not into temptation.
℟. But deliver us from evil.

℣. Sinite parvulos venire ad me.
℟. Talium est enim regnum cœlorum.

℣. Suffer the little children to come to
Me.
℟. For of such is the kingdom of heaven.

℣. Dominus vobiscum.
℟. Et cum spiritu tuo.

℣. The Lord be with you.
℟. And with thy spirit.

Oremus.

Omnipotens sempiterne Deus, sanctæ puritatis amator, qui animam hujus parvuli ad cœlorum regnum hodie misericorditer vocare dignatus es: digneris etiam, Domine, ita nobiscum misericorditer agere ut meritis tuæ sanctissimæ passionis, et intercessione beatæ Mariæ semper Virginis et omnium Sanctorum tuorum, in eodem regno nos cum omnibus Sanctis et Electis tuis semper facias congaudere. Qui vivis et regnas, cum Deo Patre, in unitate Spiritus Sancti Deus, per omnia sæcula sæculorum. ℟. Amen.

Let us pray.

Almighty, everlasting God, Lover of holy purity, Who of Thy mercy hast this day vouchsafed to call the soul of this little one unto the kingdom of heaven: vouchsafe also, O Lord, to deal with us with the like mercy, that, by the merits of Thy most holy Passion, and by the intercession of Blessed Mary ever Virgin, and of all Thy saints, Thou mayest make us to rejoice in the same kingdom with all Thy saints and elect. Who livest and reignest with God the Father, in the unity of the Holy Ghost, God, world without end. ℟. Amen.

Then the priest sprinkles the body (as also the grave) with holy water, and incenses it; after which it is buried.

Lastly, when he returns from the burial to the church, he says the Song of the Three Children, Benedicite, *with the* Gloria Patri *at the end. This* Antiphon *is said before and after:*

Benedicite Dominum, omnes electi ejus: agite dies lætitiæ, et confitemini illi.

Bless the Lord, all ye His elect, keep days of gladness and give praise unto Him.

The Benedicite.

Benedicite, omnia opera Domini, Domino: * laudate et superexaltate eum in sæcula.

All ye works of the Lord, bless the Lord: praise and exalt Him above all forever.

Benedicite, angeli Domini, Domino: * benedicite, cœli, Domino.

O ye angels of the Lord, bless the Lord: bless the Lord, O ye heavens.

Benedicite, aquæ omnes, quæ super cœlos sunt, Domino: * benedicite, omnes virtutes Domini, Domino.

O all ye waters that are above the heavens, bless the Lord: bless the Lord, O all ye powers of the Lord.

Benedicite, sol et luna, Domino: * benedicite, stellæ cœli, Domino.

O ye sun and moon, bless the Lord: bless the Lord, O ye stars of heaven.

Benedicite, omnis imber et ros, Domino: * benedicite, omnes spiritus Dei, Domino.

O every shower and dew, bless ye the Lord: bless the Lord, O all ye spirits of God.

Benedicite, ignis et æstus, Domino: * benedicite, frigus et æstus, Domino.

O ye fire and heat, bless the Lord: bless the Lord, O ye cold and heat.

Benedicite, rores et pruina, Domino: * benedicite, gelu et frigus, Domino.

O ye dews and hoarfrost, bless the Lord: bless the Lord, O ye frost and cold.

Benedicite, glacies et nives, Domino: * benedicite, noctes et dies, Domino.

O ye ice and snow, bless the Lord: bless the Lord, O ye nights and days.

Benedicite, lux et tenebræ, Domino: * benedicite, fulgura et nubes, Domino.

O ye light and darkness, bless the Lord: bless the Lord, O ye lightnings and clouds.

Benedicat terra Dominum: * laudet et superexaltet eum in sæcula.

O let the earth bless the Lord: let it praise and exalt Him above all forever.

Benedicite, montes et colles, Domino: * benedicite, universa germinantia in terra, Domino.

O ye mountains and hills, bless the Lord: bless the Lord, O all ye things that spring up in the earth.

Benedicite, fontes, Domino: * benedicite, maria et flumina, Domino.

O ye fountains, bless the Lord: bless the Lord, O ye seas and rivers.

Benedicite, cete, et omnia quæ moventur in aquis, Domino: * benedicite, omnes volucres cœli, Domino.

O ye whales, and all that move in the waters, bless the Lord: bless the Lord, O all ye fowls of the air.

Benedicite, omnes bestiæ et pecora, Domino: * benedicite, filii hominum, Domino.

O all ye beasts and cattle, bless the Lord: bless the Lord, O ye sons of men.

Benedicat Israel Dominum: * laudet et superexaltet eum in sæcula.

O let Israel bless the Lord: let them praise and exalt Him above all forever.

Benedicite, sacerdotes Domini, Domino: * benedicite, servi Domini, Domino.

O ye priests of the Lord, bless the Lord: bless the Lord, O ye servants of the Lord.

Benedicite, spiritus et animæ justorum, Domino: * benedicite, sancti et humiles corde, Domino.

O ye spirits and souls of the just, bless the Lord: bless the Lord, O ye holy and humble of heart.

Benedicite, Anania, Azaria, Misael, Domino: * laudate et superexaltate eum in sæcula.

O Ananiah, Azariah, and Misael, bless ye the Lord: praise and exalt Him above all forever.

Benedicamus Patrem et Filium cum Sancto Spiritu: * laudemus et super-exaltate eum in sæcula.

Let us bless the Father, and the Son, with the Holy Ghost: let us praise and exalt Him above all forever.

Benedictus es, Domine, in firmamento cœli: * et laudabilis, et gloriosus, et superexaltatus in sæcula.

Blessed art Thou, O Lord, in the firmament of heaven: and worthy to be praised and glorified, and exalted above all forever.

Gloria Patri, etc.

Glory be to the Father, etc.

Benedicite Dominum, omnes electi ejus: agite dies lætitiæ, et confitemini illi.

Bless the Lord, all ye His elect, keep days of gladness and give praise unto Him.

Having arrived in the church, the priest says before the altar:

℣. Dominus vobiscum.
℟. Et cum spiritu tuo.

℣. The Lord be with you.
℟. And with thy spirit.

Oremus.

Deus, qui miro ordine Angelorum ministeria hominumque dispensas: concede propitius; ut a quibus tibi ministrantibus in cœlo semper assistitur, ab his in terra vita nostra muniatur. Per Christum Dominum nostrum. ℟. Amen.

Let us pray.

O God, Who dost dispose the services of angels and men in a wonderful order, mercifully grant that as Thy holy angels always minister before Thee in heaven, so by them we may be protected in our life on earth. Through Christ Our Lord. ℟. Amen.

VARIOUS PRAYERS FOR THE DEAD

For a deceased pope

O God, by Whose inscrutable appointment Thy servant N. (*here express his name*) was numbered among the chief bishops: grant, we beseech Thee, that he, who was Vicar of thine only begotten Son on earth, may receive a place among Thy holy pontiffs who have entered into everlasting blessedness.

For a deceased bishop or priest

O God, Who didst raise Thy servant N. (*here express his name*) to the dignity of bishop (*or* priest) in the apostolic priesthood: grant, we beseech Thee, that he may be forever united to the company of the same.

Another prayer for a deceased bishop

Grant, we beseech Thee, O Lord, that the soul of Thy servant Bishop N. (*here express his name*), which Thou hast taken from the toilsome conflict of this world, may have fellowship among Thy saints.

For a deceased priest

O Lord, we pray Thee that the soul of Thy priest, Thy servant N. (*here express his name*), which, while he abode in this world, Thou didst adorn with sacred gifts, may ever rejoice in a glorious seat in heaven.

For a man deceased

O Lord, incline Thine ear unto the prayers whereby we humbly call upon Thee to show mercy unto the soul of Thy servant N. (*here express his name*), which Thou hast commanded to depart out of this life; that it may please Thee to set him in a place of peace and light, and give him a part with Thy saints.

For a woman deceased

Lord, we beseech Thee, in the tenderness of Thy great mercy, to have pity upon the soul of Thy handmaid N. (*here express her name*); cleanse her from all defilements which have stained this mortal body, and give her inheritance in everlasting salvation.

For deceased parents

O God, Who hast commanded us to honor our father and mother, look in the tenderness of Thy mercy upon the *souls* of my *father and mother,* and forgive *them* *their* sins, and grant unto me the joy of seeing *them* again in the glorious light of everlasting life.

For deceased brethren, relations, and benefactors

O God, the Bestower of forgiveness and the Lover of human salvation: we beseech Thee of Thy tender love to grant that the brethren of our congregation, with their relations and benefactors who have passed out of this life, by the intercession of Blessed Mary ever Virgin, and all Thy saints, may come to the fellowship of eternal bliss.

For a dead friend

Help us, O God of our salvation, and at the prayers of Mary, the most Blessed Mother of God, ever Virgin, let the soul of Thy servant have a place in the light of everlasting blessedness.

For benefactors

Have mercy, O Lord, we beseech Thee, upon the souls of all our departed benefactors, and in return for the benefits which they bestowed upon us on earth let them obtain an eternal reward in heaven.

For those we are bound to pray for

Grant, we beseech Thee, O Lord our God, that the souls of Thy servants and handmaidens, the commemoration of whom we keep with special reverence, and for whom we are bidden and are bound to pray, and the souls of all our benefactors, relations, and connections, and all the faithful, may rest in the bosom of Thy saints; and hereafter, in the resurrection from the dead, may please Thee in the land of the living.

For one overtaken by sudden death

Almighty and merciful God, in Whose hand is the lot of man, absolve the soul of Thy servant, we beseech Thee, from all sins; that although surprised by sudden death he may not lose the benefit of the repentance which he desired.

For those who repose in a cemetery

O God, in Whose tender mercy the souls of the faithful are at rest, of Thy favor give unto the souls of all Thy servants and handmaidens, who here and everywhere sleep in Christ, pardon of sin; that they, being absolved from all guilt, may evermore rejoice with Thee. Through Our Lord Jesus Christ, Thy Son, Who liveth and reigneth with Thee, in the unity of the Holy Ghost, God, world without end. *Amen.*

Hymns and Sequences for the Church's Seasons

1. MORNING HYMN.[38]

Jam lucis orto sidere	The star of morn to night succeeds;
Deum precemur supplices,	We therefore meekly pray,
Ut in diurnis actibus	May God, in all our words and deeds,
Nos servet a nocentibus.	Keep us from harm this day.
Linguam refrænans temperet,	May He in love restrain us still
Ne litis horror insonet:	From tones of strife and words of ill,
Visum fovendo contegat,	And wrap around and close our eyes
Ne vanitates hauriat.	To earth's absorbing vanities.
Sint pura cordis intima,	May wrath and thoughts that gender shame
Absistat et vecordia:	Ne'er in our breasts abide,
Carnis terat superbiam	And painful abstinences tame
Potus cibique parcitas.	Of wanton flesh the pride;
Ut cum dies abscesserit,	So when the weary day is o'er,
Noctemque sors reduxerit,	And night and stillness come once more,
Mundi per abstinentiam	Blameless and clean from spot of earth
Ipsi canamus gloriam.	We may repeat with reverent mirth—
Deo Patri sit gloria,	To God the Father glory be,
Ejusque soli Filio,	And to His only Son,
Cum Spiritu Paraclito,	And to the Spirit, one and three,
Nunc et per omne sæculum.	While endless ages run.
Amen.	Amen.

2. THE THIRD HOUR, TERCE.

Nunc, Sancte nobis Spiritus,	Come, Holy Ghost, with God the Son,
Unum Patri cum Filio,	And God the Father, ever one;
Dignare promptus ingeri	Shed forth Thy grace within our breast,
Nostro refusus pectori.	And dwell with us, a ready Guest.

---

[38]   Translation by Cardinal Newman.

Os, lingua, mens, sensus, vigor
Confessionem personent;
Flammescat igne caritas,
Accendat ardor proximos.

By every power, by heart and tongue,
By act and deed, Thy praise be sung:
Inflame with perfect love each sense,
That others' souls may kindle thence.

Præsta, Pater piisime,
Patrique compar Unice,
Cum Spiritu Paraclito
Regnans per omne sæculum.
Amen.

O Father, that we ask be done,
Through Jesus Christ, Thine only Son,
Who, with the Holy Ghost and Thee,
Shall live and reign eternally.
Amen.

3. THE SIXTH HOUR, SEXT.

Rector potens, verax Deus,
Qui temperas rerum vices,
Splendore mane illuminas,
Et ignibus meridiem:

O God of truth, O Lord of might,
Who orderest time and change aright,
Brightening the morn with golden
    gleams,
Kindling the noonday's fiery beams:

Exstingue flammas litium,
Aufer calorem noxium,
Confer salutem corporum,
Veramque pacem cordium.

Quench Thou in us the flames of strife,
From passion's heat preserve our life,
Our bodies keep from perils free,
And give our souls true peace in Thee.

Præsta, Pater piisime,
Patrique compar Unice,
Cum Spiritu Paraclito
Regnans per omne sæculum.
Amen.

Almighty Father, hear our cry
Through Jesus Christ Our Lord most
    High,
Who, with the Holy Ghost and Thee,
Doth live and reign eternally.
Amen.

4. THE NINTH HOUR, NONE.

Rerum, Deus, tenax vigor,
Immotus in te permanens,
Lucis diurnæ tempora
Successibus determinans:

O God, creation's secret force,
Thyself unmov'd, all motion's source,
Who, from the morn till evening's ray,
Through all its changes guid'st the day:

Largire lumen vespere,
Quo vita nusquam decidat;
Sed præmium mortis sacræ
Perennis instet gloria.

Grant us, when this short life is past,
The glorious evening that shall last:
That, by a holy death attain'd,
Eternal glory may be gain'd.

Præsta, Pater piisime,
Patrique compar Unice,
Cum Spiritu Paraclito
Regnans per omne sæculum.
Amen.

O Father, that we ask be done,
Through Jesus Christ, Thine only Son,
Who, with the Holy Ghost and Thee,
Shall live and reign eternally.
Amen.

5. VESPER HYMN.[39]

Lucis Creator optime,
Lucem dierum proferens,
Primordiis lucis novæ
Mundi parans originem:

Father of lights, by Whom each day
Is kindled out of night,
Who, when the heavens were made,
   didst lay
Their rudiments in light;

Qui mane junctum vesperi
Diem vocari præcipis:
Illabitur tetrum chaos,
Audi preces cum fletibus.

Thou, Who didst bind and blend in one
The glistening morn and evening pale,
Hear Thou our plaint, when light is
   gone,
And lawlessness and strife prevail.

Ne mens gravata crimine,
Vitæ sit exul munere,
Dum nil perenne cogitat,
Seseque culpis illigat.

Hear, lest the whelming weight of crime
Wreck us with life in view;
Lest thoughts and schemes of sense and
   time
Earn us a sinner's due.

Cœleste pulset ostium:
Vitale tollat præmium:
Vitemus omne noxium:
Purgemus omne pessimum.

So may we knock at heaven's door,
And strive the immortal prize to win,
Continually and evermore
Guarded without and pure within.

Præsta, Pater piissime,
Patrique compar unice,
Cum Spiritu Paraclito
Regnans per omne sæculum.
Amen.

Grant this, O Father, only Son,
And Spirit, God of grace,
To Whom all worship shall be done
In every time and place.
Amen.

℣. Dirigatur, Domine, oratio mea.
℟. Sicut incensum in conspectu tuo.

℣. Let my prayer, O Lord, be directed.
℟. As incense in Thy sight.

---

[39]   Translation by Cardinal Newman.

6. COMPLINE, OR EVENING HYMN.[40]

Te lucis ante terminum,	Now that the daylight dies away.
Rerum Creator poscimus,	By all Thy grace and love,
Ut pro tua clementia	Thee, Maker of the world, we pray
Sis præsul et custodia.	To watch our bed above.
Procul recedant somnia,	Let dreams depart and phantoms fly,
Et noctium phantasmata;	The offspring of the night;
Hostemque nostrum comprime,	Keep us, like shrines, beneath Thine eye,
Ne polluantur corpora.	Pure in our foes' despite.
Præsta, Pater piisime,	This grace on Thy redeemed confer,
Patrique compar Unice,	Father, coequal Son,
Cum Spiritu Paraclito	And Holy Ghost, the Comforter,
Regnans per omne sæculum.	Eternal Three in One.
Amen.	Amen.

7. ADVENT, AT VESPERS.

Creator alme siderum,	Creator of the stars of night,
Æterna lux credentium,	Thy people's everlasting light,
Jesu, Redemptor omnium,	Jesu, Redeemer, save us all,
Intende votis supplicum.	And hear Thy servants when they call.
Qui dæmonis ne fraudibus	Thou, grieving that the ancient curse
Periret orbis, impetu	Should doom to death a universe,
Amoris actus, languidi	Hast found the med'cine, full of grace,
Mundi medela factus es.	To save and heal a ruin'd race.
Commune qui mundi nefas	Thou cam'st, the Bridegroom of the
Ut expiares, ad Crucem	Bride,
E Virginis sacrario	As drew the world to evening tide,
Intacta prodis victima.	Proceeding from a virgin shrine,
	The spotless Victim all divine.
Cujus potestas gloriæ,	At Whose dread name, majestic now,
Nomenque cum primum sonat,	All knees must bend, all hearts must
Et cœlites et inferi	bow;
Tremente curvantur genu.	And things celestial Thee shall own,
	And things terrestrial, Lord alone.

---

[40] Translation by Cardinal Newman.

Te deprecamur ultimæ
Magnum diei Judicem,
Armis supernæ gratiæ
Defende nos ab hostibus.

O Thou Whose coming is with dread,
To judge the living and the dead,
Preserve us, while we dwell below,
From ev'ry insult of the foe.

Virtus, honor, laus, gloria
Deo Patri cum Filio,
Sancto simul Paraclito,
In sæculorum sæcula.
Amen.

To Him Who comes the world to free,
To God the Son, all glory be:
To God the Father, as is meet,
To God the Blessed Paraclete.
Amen.

8. ADVENT HYMN.

Veni, veni, Emmanuel!
Captivum solve Israel,
Qui gemit in exilio,
Privatus Dei Filio.
Gaude! gaude! Emmanuel
Nascetur pro te, Israel.

Draw nigh, draw nigh, Emmanuel,
And ransom captive Israel,
That mourns in lonely exile here
Until the Son of God appear.
Rejoice! rejoice! Emmanuel
Shall be born for thee, O Israel!

Veni, O Jesse virgula!
Ex hostis tuos ungula,
De specu tuos tartari
Educ, et antro barathri.
Gaude! gaude! Emmanuel
Nascetur pro te, Israel

Draw nigh, O Jesse's Rod, draw nigh,
To free us from the enemy;
From hell's infernal pit to save,
And give us victory o'er the grave.
Rejoice! rejoice! Emmanuel
Shall be born for thee, O Israel!

Veni, veni, O Oriens!
Solare nos adveniens:
Noctis depelle nebulas,
Dirasque noctis tenebras.
Gaude! gaude! Emmanuel
Nascetur pro te, Israel.

Draw nigh, Thou Orient, Who shalt
        cheer
And comfort by Thine Advent here,
And banish far the brooding gloom
Of sinful night and endless doom.
Rejoice! rejoice! Emmanuel
Shall be born for thee, O Israel!

Veni, clavis Davidica!
Regna reclude cœlica,
Fac iter tutum superum,
Et claude vias inferum.
Gaude! gaude! Emmanuel
Nascetur pro te, Israel.

Draw nigh, draw nigh, O David's Key,
The heavenly Gate will ope to Thee;
Make safe the way that leads on high,
And close the path to misery.
Rejoice! rejoice! Emmanuel
Shall be born for thee, O Israel!

Veni, veni, Adonai!
Qui populo in Sinai
Legem dedisti vertice,
In majestate gloriæ.
Gaude! gaude! Emmanuel
Nascetur pro te, Israel.
Amen.

Draw nigh, draw nigh, O Lord of
   Might,
Who to Thy tribes from Sinai's height
In ancient time didst give the law,
In cloud, and majesty, and awe.
Rejoice! rejoice! Emmanuel
Shall be born for thee, O Israel!
Amen.

9. ADVENT.

"Drop dew, ye heavens, from above, and let the clouds rain the Just One: let the earth be opened, and bud forth a Savior" (Is 45:8).

†Rorate cœli desuper, et nubes pluant Justum.

†Drop dew, ye heavens, from above, and let the clouds rain the Just One.

Ne irascaris Domine, ne ultra memineris iniquitatis: ecce civitas Sancti facta est deserta: Sion deserta facta est: Jerusalem desolata est: domus sanctificationis tuæ et gloriæ tuæ, ubi laudaverunt te patres nostri.
Rorate, etc.

Be not very angry, O Lord, and remember no longer our iniquity: behold, Thy holy city is become deserted: Sion is become a desert: Jerusalem is desolate: the house of Thy sanctification and of Thy glory, where our fathers praised Thee.
Drop dew, etc.

Peccavimus, et facti sumus tanquam immundus nos, et cecidimus quasi folium universi: et iniquitates nostræ quasi ventus abstulerunt nos: abscondisti faciem tuam a nobis, et allisisti nos in manu iniquitatis nostræ.
Rorate, etc.

We have sinned, and are become as unclean: and we have all fallen as a leaf, and our iniquities like the wind have carried us away: Thou hast hidden Thy face from us, and hast crushed us in the hand of our iniquity.
Drop dew, etc.

Vide, Domine, afflictionem populi tui, et mitte quem missurus es: emitte Agnum dominatorem terræ, de petra deserti, ad montem filiæ Sion: ut auferat ipse jugum captivitatis nostræ.

Rorate, etc.

Behold, O Lord, the affliction of Thy people, and send forth Him Who is to come: send forth the Lamb, the Ruler of the earth, from Petra of the desert, to the mount of the daughter of Sion: that He may take away the yoke of our captivity.
Drop dew, etc.

Consolamini, consolamini, popule meus: cito veniet salus tua: quare mœrore consumeris? quia innovavit te dolor: salvabo te, noli timere, ego enim sum Dominus Deus tuus, Sanctus Israel, redemptor tuus.

Rorate, etc.

Be comforted, be comforted, My people: thy salvation cometh quickly: Why with grief art thou consumed? for sorrow hath stricken thee: I will save thee, fear not: for I am the Lord thy God, the Holy One of Israel, thy Redeemer.
Drop dew, etc.

10. THE GREAT ANTIPHONS.

The following Great Antiphons *are said entire before and after the* Magnificat, *from the 17th to the 23rd of December, inclusive. If the Vespers are of a double, the great Antiphon is said after the prayer of the feast, for the Commemoration of Advent.*

Antiphon for the 17th of December

O Sapientia, quæ ex ore Altissimi pro-diisti, attingens a fine usque ad fi-nem, fortiter suaviterque disponens omnia: veni ad docendum nos viam prudentiæ.

O Wisdom that comest out of the mouth of the Most High, that reachest from one end to another, and dost mightily and sweetly or-der all things: come to teach us the way of prudence!

Antiphon for the 18th of December

O Adonai, et dux domus Israel, qui Moysi in igne flammæ rubi ap-paruisti, et ei in Sina legem dedisti: veni ad redimendum nos in brachio extento.

O Adonai, and Ruler of the house of Israel, Who didst appear unto Moses in the burning bush, and gavest him the Law in Sinai: come to redeem us with an outstretched arm!

Antiphon for the 19th of December

O Radix Jesse, qui stas in signum pop-ulorum, super quem continebunt reges os suum, quem Gentes depre-cabuntur: veni ad liberandum nos, jam noli tardare.

O Root of Jesse, which standest for an ensign of the people, at Whom the kings shall shut their mouths, Whom the Gentiles shall seek: come to deliver us, make no tarrying.

Antiphon for the 20th of December

O Clavis David, et sceptrum domus Israel; qui aperis, et nemo claudit; claudis, et nemo aperit: veni, et educ vinctum de domo carceris, sedentem in tenebris, et umbra mortis.

O Key of David, and Scepter of the house of Israel; that openeth and no man shutteth; and shutteth and no man openeth: come to bring out the prisoner from the prison, and them that sit in darkness, and in the shadow of death.

Antiphon for the 21st of December

O Oriens, splendor lucis æternæ, et sol justitiæ: veni, et illumina sedentes in tenebris, et umbra mortis.

O Dayspring, Brightness of the everlasting light, Sun of Justice: come to give light to them that sit in darkness and in the shadow of death!

Antiphon for the 22nd of December

O Rex gentium, et desideratus earum, lapisque angularis, qui facis utraque unum: veni, et salva hominem, quem de limo formasti.

O King of the Gentiles, yea, and Desire thereof; O Cornerstone, that makest of two one: come to save man, whom Thou hast made of the dust of the earth!

Antiphon for the 23rd of December

O Emmanuel, rex et legifer noster, expectatio Gentium, et Salvator earum: veni ad salvandum nos, Domine, Deus noster.

O Emmanuel, our King and our Lawgiver, Longing of the Gentiles; yea, and Salvation thereof: come to save us, O Lord our God!

11. CHRISTMAS, AT VESPERS.

Jesu, Redemptor omnium,
Quem lucis ante originem
Parem paternæ gloriæ
Pater supremus edidit.

Jesu! Redeemer of the world!
Who, ere the earliest dawn of light,
Wast from eternal ages born,
Immense in glory as in might:

Tu lumen, et splendor Patris,
Tu spes perennis omnium,
Intende quas fundunt preces
Tui per orbem servuli.

Immortal Hope of all mankind!
In Whom the Father's face we see,
Hear Thou the prayers Thy people pour
This day throughout the world to Thee.

Memento, rerum Conditor,
Nostri quod olim corporis,
Sacrata ab alvo Virginis
Nascendo, formam sumpseris.

Remember, O Creator Lord!
That in the Virgin's sacred womb
Thou wast conceived, and of her flesh
Didst our mortality assume.

Testatur hoc præsens dies,	This ever-blest recurring day
Currens per anni circulum,	Its witness bears that all alone,
Quod solus e sinu Patris	From Thy own Father's bosom forth,
Mundi salus adveneris.	To save the world Thou camest down.

Hunc astra, tellus, æquora, 　　　　O day to which the seas and sky,
Hunc omne, quod cœlo subest, 　　And earth and heaven, glad welcome
Salutis Auctorem novæ 　　　　　　　　sing;
Novo salutat cantico. 　　　　　　　O day which healed our misery,
　　　　　　　　　　　　　　　And brought on earth salvation's King!

Et nos, beata quos sacri 　　　　　We too, O Lord, who have been
Rigavit unda sanguinis, 　　　　　　　　cleansed
Natalis ob diem tui 　　　　　　　In Thy own fount of blood divine,
Hymni tributum solvimus. 　　　　Offer the tribute of sweet song
　　　　　　　　　　　　　　　On this blest natal day of Thine.

Jesu, tibi sit gloria, 　　　　　　O Jesu! born of Virgin bright,
Qui natus es de Virgine, 　　　　　Immortal glory be to Thee;
Cum Patre, et almo Spiritu 　　　Praise to the Father infinite,
In sempiterna sæcula. 　　　　　　And Holy Ghost eternally.
Amen. 　　　　　　　　　　　　Amen.

12. CHRISTMASTIDE.

Adeste, fideles, 　　　　　　　　Ye faithful, approach ye
Læti, triumphantes; 　　　　　　Joyfully triumphing;
Venite, venite in Bethlehem: 　　O come ye, O come ye to Bethlehem;
Natum videte 　　　　　　　　　Come and behold ye
Regem Angelorum: 　　　　　　Born the King of angels:
†Venite, adoremus, 　　　　　　†O come, let us adore Him,
Venite, adoremus, 　　　　　　　O come, let us adore Him,
Venite adoremus Dominum. 　　O come, let us adore Him, Christ the
　　　　　　　　　　　　　　　Lord.

Deum de Deo, 　　　　　　　　God of God eternal;
Lumen de Lumine, 　　　　　　Light from Light proceeding;
Gestant puellæ viscera: 　　　　Lo, He deigns in the Virgin's womb to
Deum verum, 　　　　　　　　　lie,
Genitum non factum: 　　　　　Very God, yea,
Venite adoremus, etc. 　　　　　Not made but begotten:
　　　　　　　　　　　　　　　O come, let us adore, etc.

Cantet nunc Io
Chorus Angelorum;
Cantet nunc aula cœlestium,
Gloria in excelsis Deo:
Venite adoremus, etc.

Ergo qui natus
Die hodierna,
Jesu, tibi sit gloria:
Patris æterni
Verbum caro factum;
Venite adoremus, etc.
Amen.

All ye choirs of angels,
Come, alleluia! sing,
Sing all ye citizens of heaven above,
Glory to God in the highest heavens:
O come, let us adore, etc.

Yea, Lord, we greet Thee,
Born this happy morning:
O Jesus, now to Thee be glory given,
Word of the Father,
In our flesh appearing:
O come, let us adore, etc.
Amen.

13. THE HOLY INNOCENTS, AT VESPERS.

Salvete, flores martyrum,
Quos lucis ipso in limine
Christi insecutor sustulit,
Ceu turbo nascentes rosas.

Vos prima Christi victima,
Grex immolatorum tener,
Aram sub ipsam simplices
Palma et coronis luditis.

Jesu, tibi sit gloria,
Qui natus es de Virgine,
Cum Patre et almo Spiritu,
In sempiterna sæcula.
Amen.

Lovely flowers of martyrs, hail!
Smitten by the tyrant foe
On life's threshold—as the gale
Strews the roses ere they blow.

First to bleed for Christ, sweet lambs!
What a simple death ye died!
Sporting with your wreaths and palms
At the very altar-side!

Honor, glory, virtue, merit,
Be to Thee, O Virgin's Son,
With the Father and the Spirit,
While eternal ages run.
Amen.

14. THE EPIPHANY, AT VESPERS.

Crudelis Herodes, Deum
Regem venire quid times?
Non eripit mortalia,
Qui regna dat cœlestia.

O cruel Herod! why thus fear
Thy King and God, Who comes below?
No earthly crown comes He to take,
Who heavenly kingdoms doth bestow.

Ibant Magi, quam viderant,
Stellam sequentes præviam:
Lumen requirunt lumine:
Deum fatentur munere.

The wiser Magi see the star,
And follow as it leads before;
By its pure ray they seek the Light,
And with their gifts that Light adore.

Lavacra puri gurgitis
Cœlestis Agnus attigit:
Peccata, quæ non detulit,
Nos abluendo sustulit.

Behold at length the heavenly Lamb
Baptized in Jordan's sacred flood;
There consecrating by His touch
Water to cleanse us in His blood.

Novum genus potentiæ:
Aquæ rubescunt hydriæ,
Vinumque jussa fundere,
Mutavit unda originem.

But Cana saw her glorious Lord
Begin His miracles divine;
When water, reddening at His word,
Flowed forth obedient in wine.

Jesu, tibi sit gloria,
Qui apparuisti gentibus,
Cum Patre, et almo Spiritu,
In sempiterna sæcula.
Amen.

To Thee, O Jesu, Who Thyself
Hast to the Gentile world displayed,
Praise, with the Father evermore,
And with the Holy Ghost, be paid.
Amen.

‡THE HOLY FAMILY (*First Sunday after Epiphany*).

O Lux beata cœlitum
Et summa spes mortalium,
Jesu, o cui domestica
Arrisit orto caritas:

O highest Hope of mortals,
Blessed Light of saints above,
O Jesu, on whose boyhood
Home smiled with kindly love;

Maria, dives gratia,
O sola quæ casto potes
Fovere Jesum pectore,
Cum lacte donans oscula:

And then whose bosom nursed Him,
O Mary, highly graced,
Whose breast gave milk to Jesus,
Whose arms Thy God embraced;

Tuque ex vetustis patribus
Delecte custos Virginis
Dulci patris quem nomine
Divina Proles invocat:

And Thou of all men chosen
To guard the Virgin's fame,
To whom God's Son refused not
A father's gracious name;

De stirpe Jesse nobili
Nati in salutem gentium,
Audite nos qui supplices
Vestras ad aras sistimus.

Born for the nation's healing,
Of Jesse's lineage high,
Behold His suppliants kneeling,
O hear the sinners' cry!

Dum sol redux ad vesperum
Rebus nitorem detrahit,
Nos hic manentes intimo
Ex corde vota fundimus.

Qua vestra sedes floruit
Virtutis omnis gratia,
Hanc detur in domesticis
Referre posse moribus.

Jesu, tuis obediens
Qui factus es parentibus,
Cum Patre summo ac Spiritu
Semper tibi sit gloria.
Amen.

The sun returned to evening,
Dusks all the twilight air,
We, lingering here before you,
Pour out our heartfelt prayer.

Your home was as a garden
Made glad with fairest flowers;
May life thus blossom sweetly
In every home of ours.

Jesus, to Thee be glory,
The Maiden-Mother's Son,
With Father and with Spirit
While endless ages run.
Amen.

15. THE CONVERSION OF ST. PAUL, AT VESPERS (*January 25*).

Egregie doctor Paule, mores instrue,
Et nostra tecum pectora in cœlum
      trahe;
Velata dum meridiem cernat Fides,
Et solis instar sola regnet Charitas.

Sit Trinitati sempiterna gloria,
Honor, potestas, atque jubilatio,
In unitate, quæ gubernat omnia,
Per universa æternitatis sæcula.
Amen.

Lead us, great teacher, Paul, in wisdom's
      ways,
And lift our hearts with thine to heaven's
      high throne:
Till faith beholds the clear meridian
      blaze,
And sunlike in the soul reigns charity
      alone.

Praise, blessing, majesty, through endless
      days,
Be to the Trinity immortal given;
Who in pure unity profoundly sways
Eternally all things alike in earth and
      heaven.
Amen.

16. LENT, AT VESPERS.

Audi, benigne Conditor,	O Maker of the world, give ear!
Nostras preces cum fletibus,	Accept the prayer, and own the tear,
In hoc sacro jejunio	Toward Thy seat of mercy sent,
Fusas quadragenario.	In this most holy fast of Lent.
Scrutator alme cordium,	Each heart is manifest to Thee:
Infirma tu scis virium:	Thou knowest our infirmity:
Ad te reversis exhibe	Forgive Thou then each soul that fain
Remissionis gratiam.	Would seek to Thee, and turn again.
Multum quidem peccavimus,	Our sins are manifold and sore;
Sed parce confitentibus:	But pardon them that sin deplore;
Ad nominis laudem tui	And, for Thy name's sake, make each
Confer medelam languidis.	soul,
	That feels and owns its languor, whole.
Concede nostrum conteri	So mortify we every sense
Corpus per abstinentiam;	By grace of outward abstinence,
Culpæ ut relinquant pabulum	That from each stain and spot of sin
Jejuna corda criminum.	The soul may keep her fast within.
Præsta, beata Trinitas,	Grant, O Thou Blessed Trinity,
Concede, simplex Unitas;	Grant, O essential Unity,
Ut fructuosa sint tuis	That this our fast of forty days
Jejuniorum munera.	May work our profit and Thy praise.
Amen.	Amen.

17. LENT.

Ex more docti mystico	Now, with the slow revolving year,
Servemus hoc jejunium,	Again the fast we greet
Deno dierum circulo,	Which in its mystic circle moves
Ducto quater notissimo.	Of forty days complete.
Lex et Prophetæ primitus	That fast, by law and prophet taught,
Hoc prætulerunt, postmodum	By Jesus Christ restored;
Christus sacravit, omnium	Jesus, of seasons and of times
Rex atque Factor temporum.	The Maker and the Lord.

Utamur ergo parcius
Verbis, cibis, et potibus,
Somno, jocis, et arctius
Perstemus in custodia.

Vitemus autem noxia,
Quæ subruunt mentes vagas,
Nullumque demus callidi
Hostis locum tyrannidi.

Flectamus iram vindicem,
Ploremus ante Judicem,
Clamemus ore supplici,
Dicamus omnes cernui.

Nostris malis offendimus
Tuam, Deus, clementiam:
Effunde nobis desuper
Remissor indulgentiam.

Memento quod sumus tui,
Licet caduci plasmatis:
Ne des honorem nominis
Tui, precamur, alteri.

Laxa malum, quod fecimus,
Auge bonum, quod poscimus:
Placere quo tandem tibi
Possimus hic, et perpetim.

Præsta, beata Trinitas,
Concede, simplex Unitas,
Ut fructuosa sint tuis
Jejuniorum munera.
Amen.

Henceforth more sparing let us be
Of food, of words, of sleep;
Henceforth beneath a stricter guard
The roving senses keep;

And let us shun whatever things
Distract the careless heart;
And let us shut our souls against
The tyrant tempter's art;

And weep before the Judge, and strive
His vengeance to appease;
Saying to Him with contrite voice
Upon our bended knees:

Much have we sinned, O Lord! and still
We sin each day we live;
Yet look in pity from on high,
And of Thy grace forgive.

Remember that we still are Thine,
Though of a fallen frame;
And take not from us in Thy wrath
The glory of Thy name.

Undo past evil; grant us, Lord,
More grace to do aright;
So may we now and ever find
Acceptance in Thy sight.

Blest Trinity in Unity!
Vouchsafe us, in Thy love,
To gather from these fasts below
Immortal fruit above.
Amen.

18. PASSION SUNDAY.

Vexilla Regis prodeunt:
Fulget Crucis mysterium,
Qua vita mortem pertulit,
Et morte vitam protulit.

The royal banners forward go;
The Cross shines forth in mystic glow;
Where He in flesh, our flesh Who
    made,
Our sentence bore, our ransom paid:

Quæ, vulnerata lanceæ
Mucrone diro, criminum
Ut nos lavaret sordibus,
Manavit unda et sanguine.

Where deep for us the spear was dyed,
Life's torrent rushing from His side,
To wash us in that precious flood
Where mingled water flowed, and blood.

Impleta sunt quæ concinit
David fideli carmine,
Dicendo nationibus:
Regnavit a ligno Deus.

Fulfilled is all that David told
In true prophetic song of old;
Amidst the nations, God, saith he,
Hath reigned and triumphed from the
   Tree.

Arbor decora et fulgida,
Ornata Regis purpura,
Electa digno stipite
Tam sancta membra tangere.

O Tree of beauty, Tree of light!
O Tree with royal purple dight!
Elect on whose triumphal breast
Those holy limbs should find their rest:

Beata, cujus brachiis
Pretium pependit sæculi,
Statera facta corporis,
Tulitque prædam tartari.

On whose dear arms, so widely flung,
The weight of this world's ransom hung:
The price of humankind to pay,
And spoil the spoiler of his prey:

O Crux ave, spes unica,
Hoc Passionis tempore
Piis adauge gratiam,
Reisque dele crimina.

O Cross, our one reliance, hail!
This holy Passiontide avail
To give fresh merit to the saint,
And pardon to the penitent.

Te, fons salutis, Trinitas,
Collaudet omnis spiritus:
Quibus Crucis victoriam
Largiris, adde præmium.
Amen.

To Thee, eternal Three in One,
Let homage meet by all be done:
Whom by the Cross Thou dost restore,
Preserve and govern evermore!
Amen.

19. PASSIONTIDE.

Pange, lingua, gloriosi
Lauream certaminis,
Et super crucis trophæo
Dic triumphum nobilem,
Qualiter Redemptor orbis
Immolatus vicerit.

Sing, my tongue, the glorious battle
With completed victory rife:
And above the Cross's trophy
Tell the triumph of the strife:
How the world's Redeemer conquered
By surrendering of His life.

Da parentis protoplasti
Fraude Factor condolens,
Quando pomi noxialis
In necem morsu ruit,
Ipse lignum tunc notavit,
Damna ligni ut solveret.

Hoc opus nostræ salutis
Ordo depoposcerat,
Multiformis proditoris
Ars ut artem falleret,
Et medelam ferret inde
Hostis unde læserat.

Quando venit ergo sacri
Plenitudo temporis,
Missus est ab arce Patris
Natus orbis Conditor,
Atque ventre virginali
Carne amictus prodiit.

Vagit infans inter arcta
Conditus præsepia
Membra pannis involuta
Virgo mater alligat:
Et Dei manus, pedesque
Stricta cingit fascia.

Lustra sex qui jam peregit
Tempus implens corporis,
Sponte libera Redemptor
Passioni deditus,
Agnus in crucis levatur
Immolandus stipite.

Felle potus ecce languet
Spina, clavi, lancea;
Mite corpus perforatur,
Unda manat, et cruor;
Terra, pontus, astra, mundus,
Quo lavantur flumine.

God his Maker, sorely grieving
That the first-made Adam fell
When he ate the fruit of sorrow,
Whose reward was death and hell,
Noted then this wood, the ruin
Of the ancient wood to quell.

For the work of our salvation
Needs would have His order so;
And the multiform deceiver's
Art by art would overthrow,
And from thence would bring the
    med'cine
Whence the insult of the foe.

Wherefore, when the sacred fullness
Of th' appointed time was come,
This world's Maker left His Father,
Sent the heav'nly mansion from,
And proceeded, God incarnate,
Of the Virgin's holy womb.

Weeps the Infant in the manger
That in Bethlehem's stable stands;
And His limbs the Virgin Mother
Doth compose in swaddling bands,
Meekly thus in linen folding
Of her God the feet and hands.

Thirty years among us dwelling,
His appointed time fulfilled,
Born for this, He meets His Passion,
For that this He freely willed:
On the Cross the Lamb is lifted,
Where His lifeblood shall be spilled.

He endured the nails, the spitting,
Vinegar, and spear, and reed;
From that holy body broken
Blood and water forth proceed:
Earth, and stars, and sky, and ocean
By that flood from stain are freed.

Crux fidelis! inter omnes
Arbor una nobilis!
Silva talem nulla profert
Fronde, flore, germine:
Dulce ferrum, dulce lignum,
Dulce pondus sustinent.

Flecte ramos, arbor alta,
Tensa laxa viscera,
Et rigor lentescat ille
Quem dedit nativitas,
Et superni membra Regis
Tende miti stipite.

Sola digna tu fuisti
Ferre mundi victimam
Atque portum præparare
Arca mundo naufrago,
Quem sacer cruor perunxit
Fusus Agni corpore.

Sempiterna sit beatæ
Trinitati gloria;
Æqua Patri, Filioque,
Par decus Paraclito:
Unius Trinique nomen
Laudet universitas.
Amen.

Faithful Cross! above all other
One and only noble Tree!
None in foliage, none in blossom,
None in fruit thy peers may be:
Sweetest wood and sweetest iron!
Sweetest weight is hung on thee!

Bend thy boughs, O Tree of glory!
Thy relaxing sinews bend;
For a while the ancient rigor,
That thy birth bestowed, suspend:
And the King of heav'nly beauty
On thy bosom gently tend!

Thou alone wast counted worthy
This world's ransom to uphold;
For a shipwrecked race preparing
Harbor, like the ark of old,
With the sacred blood anointed
From the smitten Lamb that rolled.

To the Trinity be glory
Everlasting, as is meet;
Equal to the Father, equal
To the Son and Paraclete:
Trinal Unity, Whose praises
All created things repeat.
Amen.

20. PASSIONTIDE.

Stabat Mater dolorosa
Juxta crucem lacrymosa,
Dum pendebat Filius.
Cujus animam gementem,
Contristatam et dolentem,
Pertransivit gladius.

At the Cross her station keeping,
Stood the mournful Mother weeping,
Close to Jesus to the last;
Through her Heart, His sorrow sharing,
All His bitter anguish bearing,
Lo! the piercing sword had passed!

O quam tristis et afflicta
Fuit illa benedicta
Mater Unigeniti!
Quæ mœrebat, et dolebat
Pia Mater dum videbat
Nati pœnas inclyti.

Quis est homo qui non fleret,
Matrem Christi si videret
In tanto supplicio?
Quis non posset contristari,
Christi Matrem contemplari
Dolentem cum Filio?

Pro peccatis suæ gentis
Vidit Jesum in tormentis,
Et flagellis subditum.
Vidit suum dulcem Natum
Moriendo desolatum,
Dum emisit spiritum.

Eia, Mater, fons amoris,
Me sentire vim doloris
Fac ut tecum lugeam.
Fac, ut ardeat cor meum
In amando Christum Deum,
Ut sibi complaceam.

Sancta Mater, istud agas,
Crucifixi fige plagas
Cordi meo valide.
Tui Nati vulnerati,
Tam dignati pro me pati,
Pœnas mecum divide.

Fac me tecum pie flere,
Crucifixo condolere,
Donec ego vixero.
Juxta Crucem tecum stare,
Et me tibi sociare
In planctu desidero.

O how sad, and sore distressed,
Now was she, that Mother Blessed
Of the sole begotten One;
Woe-begone, with heart's prostration,
Mother meek, the bitter Passion
Saw she of her glorious Son.

Who could mark, from tears refraining,
Christ's dear Mother uncomplaining,
In so great a sorrow bowed?
Who, unmoved, behold her languish
Underneath His Cross of anguish,
'Mid the fierce, unpitying crowd?

For His people's sins rejected,
She her Jesus, unprotected,
Saw with thorns, with scourges rent;
Saw her Son from judgment taken,
Her beloved in death forsaken,
Till His Spirit forth He sent.

Fount of love and holy sorrow,
Mother! may my spirit borrow
Somewhat of thy woe profound;
Unto Christ, with pure emotion,
Raise my contrite heart's devotion,
Love to read in every wound.

Those five wounds on Jesus smitten,
Mother! in my heart be written,
Deep as in thine own they be:
Thou, my Savior's Cross who bearest,
Thou, thy Son's rebuke who sharest,
Let me share them both with thee!

In the Passion of my Maker
Be my sinful soul partaker,
Weep till death, and weep with thee;
Mine with thee be that sad station,
There to watch the great salvation
Wrought upon the atoning Tree.

Virgo virginum præclara,
Mihi jam non sis amara:
Fac me tecum plangere.
Fac ut portem Christi mortem,
Passionis fac consortem,
Et plagas recolere.

Virgin thou of virgins fairest,
May the bitter woe thou sharest
Make on me impression deep:
Thus Christ's dying may I carry,
With Him in His Passion tarry,
And His wounds in memory keep.

Fac me plagis vulnerari,
Fac me Cruce inebriari,
Et cruore Filii.
Flammis ne urar succensus,
Per te, Virgo, sim defensus
In die judicii.

May His wounds transfix me wholly,
May His Cross and lifeblood holy
Ebriate my heart and mind;
Thus inflamed with pure affection,
In the Virgin's Son protection
May I at the judgment find.

Christe, cum sit hinc exire,
Da per Matrem me venire
Ad palmam victoriæ.
Quando corpus morietur,
Fac ut animæ donetur
Paradisi gloria.
Amen.

When in death my limbs are failing,
Let Thy Mother's prayer prevailing
Lift me, Jesus! to Thy throne;
To my parting soul be given
Entrance through the gate of heaven,
There confess me for Thine own.
Amen.

21. PALM SUNDAY, AT THE PROCESSION.

Gloria, laus, et honor tibi sit, Rex,
	Christe, Redemptor:
Cui puerile decus prompsit Hosanna
	pium.

To Thee, O Christ, be glory, praises loud,
To Thee, Hosanna, cried the Jewish
	crowd.

Israel es tu Rex, Davidis et inclyta
	proles:
Nomine qui in Domini, Rex benedicte
	venis.
℟. Gloria, laus, etc.

We Israel's monarch, David's Son
	proclaim:
Thou com'st, blest King, in God's most
	holy name.
℟. To Thee, etc.

Cœtus in excelsis te laudat cœlicus
	omnis,
Et mortalis homo, et cuncta creata
	simul.
℟. Gloria, laus, etc.

Angels and men in one harmonious
	choir
To sing Thy everlasting praise conspire.
℟. To Thee, etc.

Plebs Hebræa tibi cum palmis obvia venit:
Cum prece, voto, hymnis, adsumus ecce tibi.
℟. Gloria, laus, etc.

Thee Israel's children met with conquering palms;
To Thee our vows we pay in loudest psalms.
℟. To Thee, etc.

Hi tibi passuro solvebant munia laudis:
Nos tibi regnanti pangimus ecce melos.
℟. Gloria, laus, etc.

For Thee on earth with boughs they strewed the ways:
To Thee in heaven we sing melodious praise.
℟. To Thee, etc.

Hi placuere tibi, placeat devotio nostra:
Rex bone, Rex clemens, cui bona cuncta placent.
℟. Gloria, laus, etc.
Amen.

Accept this tribute, which to Thee we bring,
As Thou didst theirs, O good and gracious King.
℟. To Thee, etc.
Amen.

22. EASTER, SEQUENCE AT MASS.

Victimæ paschali laudes
Immolent Christiani.
Agnus redemit oves:
Christus innocens Patri

Unto the Paschal Victim bring,
Christians, your thankful offering.
The Lamb redeemed the flock,
So Christ the spotless, without guile,

Reconciliavit peccatores.
Mors et vita duello
Conflixere mirando:
Dux vitæ mortuus,

To God did sinners reconcile
In wondrous deadly shock
Lo! death and life contend and strive;
The Lord of life, Who died, doth reign and live.

Regnat vivus.
Dic nobis, Maria,
Quid vidisti in via?
Sepulchrum Christi viventis,

What thou sawest, Mary, say,
As thou wentest on the way.
I saw the grave which could not Christ retain;
I saw His glory as He rose again;

Et gloriam vidi resurgentis:
Angelicos testes,
Sudarium et vestes.
Surrexit Christus spes mea:

I saw th' angelic witnesses around;
The napkin and the linen clothes I found.
Yea, Christ my hope is risen, and He
Will go before you into Galilee.

Præcedet vos in Galilæam.
Scimus Christum surrexisse
A mortuis vere:
Tu nobis, victor Rex, miserere.
Amen. Alleluia.

We know that Christ indeed has risen
from the grave:
Hail, Thou King of victory!
Have mercy, Lord, and save.
Amen. Alleluia.

‡EASTERTIDE.

Alleluia, alleluia, alleluia
O filii et filiæ,
Rex cœlestis, Rex gloriæ,
Morte surrexit hodie,
alleluia.

Alleluia, alleluia, alleluia
Young men and maids rejoice and sing,
The King of heaven, the glorious King,
This day from death rose triumphing,
alleluia.

Et mane prima sabbati,
Ad ostium monumenti
Accesserunt discipuli,
alleluia.

On Sunday morn, by break of day,
His dear disciples haste away
Unto the tomb, wherein He lay,
alleluia.

Et Maria Magdalene,
Et Jacobi et Salome,
Venerunt corpus ungere,
alleluia.

Nor Magdalen, nor Salome,
Nor James's mother now delay
To embalm His precious corpse
straightway,
alleluia.

In albis sedens Angelus,
Prædixit mulieribus:
In Galilæa est Dominus,
alleluia.

An angel clothed in white they see,
When thither come; and thus spoke he:
"The Lord is gone to Galilee,"
alleluia.

Ex Joannes Apostolus
Cucurrit Petro citius,
Monumento venit prius,
alleluia.

The dear beloved apostle John
Much swifter than St. Peter run,
And first arrived at the tomb,
alleluia.

Discipulis adstantibus,
In medio stetit Christus,
Dicens: Pax vobis omnibus,
alleluia.

While in a room the apostles were,
In midst of them Christ did appear,
And said: "Peace be unto all here,"
alleluia.

Ut intellexit Didymus Quia surrexerat Jesus, Remansit fere dubius, alleluia.	When Didymus had heard it said That Christ was risen from the dead, His feeble faith yet staggered, alleluia.
Vide, Thoma, vide latus, Vide pedes, vide manus, Noli esse incredulus, alleluia.	"O Thomas, view My side and see The wounds in hands and feet that be; Renounce thy incredulity," alleluia.
Quando Thomas Christi latus, Pedes vidit atque manus, Dixit: Tu es Deus meus, alleluia.	When Thomas Jesus had surveyed, And on His wounds his fingers laid; "Thou art my Lord and God," he said, alleluia.
Beati qui non viderunt, Et firmiter crediderunt, Vitam æternam habebunt, alleluia.	"Blessed are they who have not seen, And yet whose faith entire hath been," Them endless life from death shall screen, alleluia.
In hoc festo sanctissimo Sit laus et jubilatio, Benedicamus Domino, alleluia.	On this most solemn feast let's raise Our hearts to God in hymns of praise, And let us bless the Lord always, alleluia.
De quibus nos humillimas, Devotas atque debitas Deo dicamus gratias, alleluia.	Our grateful thanks to God let's give In humble manner, while we live, For all the favors we receive, alleluia.

23. EASTER, AT VESPERS.

No Hymn is sung, but instead the following Antiphon:

Hæc dies, quam fecit Dominus; ex-
    ultemus, et lætemur in ea.
	This is the day which the Lord hath
	    made: let us be glad and rejoice
	    therein.

24. LOW SUNDAY, AT VESPERS

Ad regias agni dapes,
Stolis amicti candidis,
Post transitum maris Rubri,
Christo canamus Principi.

Now at the Lamb's high royal feast
In robes of saintly white we sing,
Through the Red Sea in safety brought
By Jesus our immortal King.

Divina cujus Charitas
Sacrum propinat sanguinem,
Almique membra corporis
Amor sacerdos immolat.

O depth of love! for us He drinks
The chalice of His agony;
For us a Victim on the Cross
He meekly lays Him down to die.

Sparsum cruorem postibus
Vastator horret angelus:
Fugitque divisum mare;
Merguntur hostes fluctibus.

And as the avenging angel passed
Of old the blood-besprinkled door;
As the cleft sea a passage gave,
Then closed to whelm th' Egyptians o'er:

Jam Pascha nostrum Christus est,
Paschalis idem victima,
Et pura puris mentibus
Sinceritatis azyma.

So Christ, our paschal Sacrifice,
Has brought us safe all perils through;
While for unleavened bread we need
But heart sincere and purpose true.

O vera cœli victima,
Subjecta cui sunt tartara,
Soluta mortis vincula,
Recepta vitæ præmia.

Hail, purest Victim heaven could find
The powers of hell to overthrow!
Who didst the chains of death destroy;
Who dost the prize of life bestow.

Victor, subactis inferis,
Trophæa Christus explicat;
Cœloque aperto, subditum
Regem tenebrarum trahit.

Hail, Victor Christ! hail, risen King!
To Thee alone belongs the crown,
Who hast the heavenly gates unbarred,
And dragged the prince of darkness
down.

Ut sis perenne mentibus
Paschale Jesu gaudium,
A morte dira criminum
Vitæ renatos libera.

O Jesu! from the death of sin
Keep us, we pray; so shalt Thou be
The everlasting paschal Joy
Of all the souls new-born in Thee.

Deo Patri sit gloria,
Et Filio qui a mortuis
Surrexit, ac Paraclito
In sempiterna sæcula.
Amen.

Now to the Father, and the Son
Who rose from death, be glory given,
With Thee, O holy Comforter,
Henceforth by all in earth and heaven.
Amen.

25. ASCENSIONTIDE, AT VESPERS.

Salutis humanæ Sator,
Jesu, voluptas cordium,
Orbis redempti Conditor,
Et casta lux amantium.

Qua victus es clementia,
Ut nostra ferres crimina?
Mortem subires innocens,
A morte nos ut tolleres?

Perrumpis infernum chaos;
Vinctis catenas detrahis;
Victor triumpho nobili
Ad dexteram Patris sedes.

Te cogat indulgentia,
Ut damna nostra sarcias,
Tuique vultus compotes
Dites beato lumine.

Tu dux ad astra, et semita,
Sis meta nostris cordibus,
Sis lacrymarum gaudium,
Sis dulce vitæ præmium.
Amen.

O Thou pure Light of souls that love!
True Joy of every human breast!
Sower of life's immortal seed!
Our Maker, and Redeemer blest!

What wondrous pity Thee o'ercame
To make our guilty load Thine own,
And, sinless, suffer death and shame,
For our transgressions to atone!

Thou, bursting Hades open wide,
Didst all the captive souls unchain;
And thence to Thy dread Father's side
With glorious pomp ascend again.

O still may pity Thee compel
To heal the wounds of which we die;
And take us in Thy light to dwell,
Who for Thy blissful Presence sigh.

Be Thou our Guide; be Thou our Goal;
Be Thou our Pathway to the skies:
Our Joy when sorrow fills the soul;
In death our everlasting Prize.
Amen.

26. WHITSUNTIDE, AT VESPERS.

Veni, Creator Spiritus,
Mentes tuorum visita,
Imple superna gratia,
Quæ tu creasti pectora.

Qui diceris Paraclitus,
Altissimi donum Dei,
Fons vivus, ignis, charitas,
Et spiritalis unctio.

Come, Holy Ghost, Creator, come,
From Thy bright heavenly throne!
Come, take possession of our souls,
And make them all Thine own!

Thou Who art called the Paraclete,
Best Gift of God above,
The living Spring, the living Fire,
Sweet Unction, and true Love!

Tu septiformis munere,
Digitus paternæ dexteræ,
Tu rite promissum Patris,
Sermone ditans guttura.

Thou Who art sevenfold in Thy grace,
Finger of God's right hand,
His Promise, teaching little ones
To speak and understand!

Accende lumen sensibus:
Infunde amorem cordibus:
Infirma nostri corporis
Virtute firmans perpeti.

O guide our minds with Thy blest light,
With love our hearts inflame,
And with Thy strength, which ne'er
    decays,
Confirm our mortal frame.

Hostem repellas longius,
Pacemque dones protinus:
Ductore sic te prævio
Vitemus omne noxium.

Far from us drive our hellish foe,
True peace unto us bring,
And through all perils guide us safe
Beneath Thy sacred wing.

Per te sciamus da Patrem,
Noscamus atque Filium,
Teque utriusque Spiritum
Credamus omni tempore.

Through Thee may we the Father know,
Through Thee the Eternal Son,
And Thee the Spirit of them both—
Thrice-blessèd Three in One.

Deo Patri sit gloria,
Et Filio qui a mortuis
Surrexit, ac Paraclito,
In sæculorum sæcula.
Amen.

Now to the Father, and the Son
Who rose from death, be glory given,
With Thee, O holy Comforter,
Henceforth by all in earth and heaven.
Amen.

27. WHITSUNTIDE, SEQUENCE AT MASS.

Veni sancte Spiritus,
Et emitte cœlitus
Lucis tuæ radium.

Come, Thou holy Paraclete,
And from Thy celestial seat
Send Thy light and brilliancy:

Veni pater pauperum,
Veni dator munerum,
Veni lumen cordium.

Father of the poor, draw near,
Giver of all gifts, be here:
Come, the soul's true Radiancy:

Consolator optime,
Dulcis hospes animæ,
Dulce refrigerium.

Come, of Comforters the best,
Of the soul the sweetest Guest,
Come in toil refreshingly:

In labore requies,
In æstu temperies,
In fletu solatium.

Thou in labor Rest most sweet,
Thou art Shadow from the heat,
Comfort in adversity.

O lux beatissima,	O Thou Light most pure and blest,
Reple cordis intima	Shine within the inmost breast
Tuorum fidelium.	Of Thy faithful company.
Sine tuo numine,	Where Thou art not, man hath naught;
Nihil est in homine,	Every holy deed and thought
Nihil est innoxium.	Comes from Thy divinity.
Lava quod est sordidum,	What is soilèd, make Thou pure;
Riga quod est aridum,	What is wounded, work its cure;
Sana quod est saucium.	What is parchèd, fructify;
Flecte quod est rigidum,	What is rigid, gently bend;
Fove quod est frigidum,	What is frozen, warmly tend;
Rege quod est devium.	Strengthen what goes erringly.
Da tuis fidelibus,	Fill Thy faithful, who confide
In te confidentibus,	In Thy power to guard and guide,
Sacrum septenarium.	With Thy sevenfold mystery.
Da virtutis meritum,	Here Thy grace and virtue send;
Da salutis exitum,	Grant salvation in the end,
Da perenne gaudium.	And in heaven felicity.
Amen. Alleluia.	Amen. Alleluia.

28. TRINITY SUNDAY, AT VESPERS.

Jam sol recedit igneus:	Now doth the fiery sun decline—
Tu, lux perennis, Unitas,	Thou, Unity eternal! shine;
Nostris, beata Trinitas,	Thou, Trinity, Thy blessings pour,
Infunde amorem cordibus.	And make our hearts with love run o'er.
Te mane laudum carmine,	Thee in the hymns of morn we praise;
Te deprecamur vespere;	To Thee our voice at eve we raise;
Digneris ut te supplices	O grant us, with Thy saints on high,
Laudemus inter cœlites.	Thee through all time to glorify.
Patri, simulque Filio,	Praise to the Father, with the Son
Tibique, Sancte Spiritus,	And Holy Spirit, Three in One;
Sicut fuit, sit jugiter	As ever was in ages past,
Sæclum per omne gloria.	And shall be so while ages last.
Amen.	Amen.

29. CORPUS CHRISTI, AT VESPERS.

Pange, lingua, gloriosi
Corporis mysterium,
Sanguinisque pretiosi,
Quem in mundi pretium
Fructus ventris generosi
Rex effudit gentium.

Now, my tongue, the mystery telling
Of the glorious Body sing,
And the Blood, all price excelling,
Which the Gentiles' Lord and King,
In a Virgin's womb once dwelling,
Shed for this world's ransoming.

Nobis datus, nobis natus
Ex intacta Virgine,
Et in mundo conversatus,
Sparso verbi semine,
Sui moras incolatus
Miro clausit ordine.

Given for us, and condescending
To be born for us below,
He with men in converse blending
Dwelt the seed of truth to sow,
Till He closed with wondrous ending
His most patient life of woe.

In supremæ nocte cœnæ
Recumbens cum fratribus,
Observata lege plene
Cibis in legalibus,
Cibum turbæ duodenæ
Se dat suis manibus.

That last night at supper lying,
'Mid the twelve His chosen band,
Jesus, with the law complying
Keeps the feast its rites demand;
Then, more precious Food supplying,
Gives Himself with His own hand.

Verbum caro, panem verum
Verbo carnem efficit;
Fitque sanguis Christi merum;
Et si sensus deficit,
Ad firmandum cor sincerum
Sola fides sufficit.

Word made flesh, true bread He maketh
By His Word His Flesh to be;
Wine, His Blood; which whoso taketh
Must from carnal thoughts be free;
Faith alone, though sight forsaketh,
Shows true hearts the mystery.

Tantum ergo Sacramentum
Veneremur cernui:
Et antiquum documentum
Novo cedat ritui:
Præstet fides supplementum
Sensuum defectui.

Therefore we, before Him bending,
This great Sacrament revere;
Types and shadows have their ending,
For the newer rite is here;
Faith, our outward sense befriending,
Makes our inward vision clear.

Genitori, Genitoque
Laus et jubilatio,
Salus, honor, virtus quoque
Sit et benedictio:
Procedenti ab utroque
Compar sit laudatio.
Amen.

Glory let us give, and blessing,
To the Father and the Son,
Honor, laud, and praise addressing,
And eternal benison.
Holy Ghost, from both progressing,
Equal laud to Thee be done.
Amen.

30. CORPUS CHRISTI, AT MATINS.

Sacris solemniis juncta sint gaudia
Et ex præcordiis sonent præconia;
Recedant vetera, nova sint omnia,
Corda, voces et opera.

Let this our solemn feast
With holy joys be crowned,
And from each loving breast
The voice of gladness sound;
Let ancient things depart,
And all be new around,
In every act and voice and heart.

Noctis recolitur cœna novissima,
Qua Christus creditur agnum et azyma
Dedisse fratribus, juxta legitima
Priscis indulta patribus.

Remember we that eve,
That supper last and dread,
When Christ, as we believe,
The lamb and leavenless bread
Unto His brethren brought,
And thus the Law obeyed
Of old time to the fathers taught.

Post agnum typicum, expletis epulis,
Corpus Dominicum datum discipulis,
Sic totum omnibus, quod totum
    singulis,
Ejus fatemur manibus.

But when the Law's repast
Was o'er, the type complete,
To His disciples last
The Lord His Flesh to eat,
The whole to all, no less
The whole to each, doth mete,
With His own hand, as we confess.

Dedit fragilibus corporis ferculum,
Dedit et tristibus sanguinis poculum,
Dicens, Accipite quod trado vasculum,
Omnes ex eo bibite.

He gave the weak and frail
His Body for their food,
The sad for their regale
The chalice of His Blood,
And said—Take ye of this,
My cup with life imbued;
O drink ye all this draught of bliss!

Sic sacrificium istud instituit,
Cujus officium committi voluit
Solis presbyteris, quibus sic congruit,
Ut sumant, et dent cæteris.

He ordered in this wise
Our holy offering
To be the sacrifice
Which priests alone should bring:
For whom is meet and fit
That they should eat of it,
And in their turn to others give.

Panis Angelicus fit panis hominum:
Dat panis cœlicus figuris terminum;
O res mirabilis! manducat Dominum
Pauper, servus et humilis.

Lo! Angels' Bread is made
The Bread of mortal man;
Shows forth this heavenly Bread
The ends which types began;
O wondrous boon indeed!
Upon his Lord now can
A poor and humble servant feed!

Te trina Deitas unaque poscimus,
Sic nos tu visita, sicut te colimus:
Per tuas semitas duc nos quo tendimus,
Ad lucem, quam inhabitas.
Amen.

Thee, Deity Triune
Yet One, we meekly pray
O visit us right soon,
As we our homage pay;
And in Thy footsteps bright
Conduct us on our way
To where Thou dwell'st in cloudless
    light.
Amen.

31. CORPUS CHRISTI, AT LAUDS.

Verbum supernum prodiens,
Nec Patris linquens dexteram,
Ad opus suum exiens,
Venit ad vitæ vesperam.

The Word of God proceeding forth,
Yet leaving not the Father's side,
And going to His work on earth,
Had reached at length life's eventide.

In mortem a discipulo
Suis tradendus æmulis,
Prius in vitæ ferculo
Se tradidit discipulis.

By a disciple to be given
To rivals for His blood athirst,
Himself, the very Bread of heaven,
He gave to His disciples first.

Quibus sub bina specie
Carnem dedit et sanguinem,
Ut duplicis substantiæ
Totum cibaret hominem.

He gave Himself in either kind,
His precious Flesh, His precious Blood;
Of flesh and blood is man combined,
And He of man would be the Food.

Se nascens dedit socium,
Convescens in edulium,
Se moriens in pretium,
Se regnans dat in præmium.

In birth, man's fellow man was He:
His Meat, while sitting at the board;
He died, his Ransomer to be;
He reigns, to be his great Reward.

O salutaris hostia,
Quæ cœli pandis ostium:
Bella premunt hostilia,
Da robur, fer auxilium.

O saving Victim, slain to bless,
Who op'st the heavenly gate to all:
The attacks of many a foe oppress:
Give strength in strife, and help in fall.

Uni, trinoque Domino
Sit sempiterna gloria,
Qui vitam sine termino
Nobis donet in patria.
Amen.

To God, the Three in One, ascend
All thanks and praise forevermore;
He grants the life that shall not end,
Upon the heavenly country's shore.
Amen.

32. CORPUS CHRISTI, PROCESSIONAL.

Lauda Sion Salvatorem,
Lauda Ducem et Pastorem,
In hymnis et canticis.
Quantum poses, tantum aude;
Quia major omni laude,
Nec laudare sufficis.

Praise high thy Savior, Sion, praise,
With hymns of joy and holy lays,
Thy Guide and Shepherd true.
Dare all thou canst, yea, take thy fill
Of praise and adoration, still
Thou fail'st to reach His due.

Laudis thema specialis,
Panis vivus et vitalis
Hodie proponitur.
Quem in sacræ mensa cœnæ
Turbæ fratrum duodenæ
Datum non ambigitur:

A special theme for thankful hearts,
The Bread that lives, and life imparts,
Today is duly set;
Which, at the solemn festal board,
Was dealt around when, with their Lord,
His chosen Twelve were met.

Sit laus plena, sit sonora,
Sit jucunda, sit decora
Mentis jubilatio.
Dies enim solemnis agitur,
In qua mensæ prima recolitur
Hujus institutio.

Full be the praise, and sweetly sounding,
With joy and reverence abounding,
The soul's glad festival.
This is the day of glorious state,
When of that feast we celebrate
The high original.

In hac mensa novi Regis,
Novum pascha novæ legis
Phase vetus terminat.
Vetustatem novitas,
Umbram fugat veritas,
Noctem lux eliminat.

'Tis here our King makes all things new,
And living rules and offerings true
Absorb each legal rite;
Before the new retreats the old,
And life succeeds to shadows cold,
And day displaces night.

Quod in cœna Christus gessit,
Faciendum hoc expressit
In sui memoriam.
Docti sacris institutis,
Panem, vinum in salutis
Consecramus hostiam.

His faithful followers Christ hath bid
To do what at the feast He did,
For sweet remembrance' sake;
And, gifted through His high
    commands,
Of bread and wine their priestly hands
A saving Victim make.

Dogma datur Christianis,
Quod in carnem transit panis,
Et vinum in sanguinem.
Quod non capis, quod non vides,
Animosa firmat fides
Præter rerum ordinem.

O Truth to Christian love displayed,
The bread His very Body made,
His very Blood the wine;
Nor eye beholds, nor thought conceives,
But dauntless faith the change believes
Wrought by a power divine.

Sub diversis speciebus,
Signis tantum, et non rebus,
Latent res eximiæ.
Caro cibus, sanguis potus:
Manet tamen Christus totus
Sub utraque specie.

Beneath two differing species
(Signs only, not their substances)
Lie mysteries deep and rare.
His Flesh the meat, the drink His
    Blood,
Yet Christ entire, our heavenly Food,
Beneath each kind is there.

A sumente non concisus,
Non confractus, non divisus,
Integer accipitur.
Sumit unus, sumunt mille,
Quantum isti, tantum ille,
Nec sumptus consumitur.

And they who of the Lord partake
Nor sever Him, nor rend, nor break:
All gain, and naught is lost;
The boon now one, now thousands
    claim,
Yet one and all receive the same—
Receive, but ne'er exhaust.

Sumunt boni, sumunt mali:
Sorte tamen inæquali
Vitæ vel interitus.
Mors est malis, vita bonis,
Vide paris sumptionis
Quam sit dispar exitus.

Fracto demum Sacramento,
Ne vacilles, sed memento,
Tantam esse sub fragmento
Quantum toto tegitur.
Nulla rei fit scissura;
Signi tantum fit fractura;
Qua nec status nec statura
Signati minuitur.

Ecce panis Angelorum,
Factus cibus viatorum:
Vere panis filiorum:
Non mittendus canibus.
In figuris præsignatur,
Cum Isaac immolatur:
Agnus Paschæ deputatur,
Datur manna patribus.

Bone Pastor, panis vere,
Jesu, nostri miserere:
Tu nos pasce, nos tuere,
Tu nos bona fac videre
In terra viventium.
Tu qui cuncta scis et vales,
Qui nos pascis hic mortales:
Tuos ibi commensales,
Cohæredes et sodales
Fac sanctorum civium.
Amen. Alleluia.

The gift is shared by all, yet tends,
In bad and good, to differing ends
Of blessing or of woe;
What death to some, salvation brings
To others: lo! from common springs
What various issues flow!

Nor be thy faith confounded, though
The Sacrament be broke, for know,
The life which in the whole doth glow
In every part remains;
No force the Substance can divide
Which those meek forms terrestial hide:
The sign is broke; the Signified
Nor change nor loss sustains.

The Bread of angels, lo! is sent
For weary pilgrims' nourishment;
The children's Bread, not to be spent
On worthless dogs profane;
In types significant portrayed,
Young Isaac on the altar laid,
And paschal offerings duly made,
And manna's fruitful rain.

O Thou Good Shepherd, very Bread,
Jesu, on us Thy mercy shed;
Sweetly feed us,
Gently lead us,
Till of Thy fullness us Thou give
Safe in the land of those that live.
Thou Who can'st all, and all dost know,
Thou Who dost feed us here below,
Grant us to share
Thy banquet there,
Coheirs and partners of Thy love
With the blest citizens above.
Amen. Alleluia.

‡THE KINGSHIP OF OUR LORD
(*Last Sunday of October*).[41]

Te sæculorum Principem,
Te, Christe, Regem Gentium,
Te mentium, Te cordium
Unum fatemur arbitrum.

Thee, Prince of all the centuries,
Thee, Christ, the King of all mankind,
Sole Ruler of the heart and mind,
Thee we confess on bended knees.

Scelesta turba clamitat:
Regnare Christum nolumus:
Te nos ovantes omnium
Regem supremum dicimus.

But wicked clamors we recall:
"The Christ shall never o'er us reign!"
Therefore again and yet again
We hail Thee: "King Supreme o'er all!"

O Christe, Princeps pacifer, Mentes re-
belles subjice:
Tuoque amore devios,
Ovile in unum congrega.

O Christ, the Prince Who bringest
peace,
Make all rebellious wiles obey:
By love compel the sheep that stray
Thy one true sheepfold to increase.

Ad hoc cruenta ab arbore
Pendes apertis brachiis,
Diraque fossum cuspide
Cor igne flagraus exhibes.

For this, upon Thy Cross of shame
Embracing arms Thou stretchest wide:
For this, the spearhead found Thy side
To show Thy Heart with love aflame:

Ad hoc in aris abderis
Vini dapisque imagine,
Fundens salutem filiis
Transverberato pectore.

For this, upon the altar stone
Hiding 'neath imaged Bread and Wine,
From out that pierced breast of Thine,
Thou pourest grace upon Thine own.

Te nationum Præsides
Honore tollant publico,
Colant magistri, judices,
Leges et artes exprimant.

Thee let his nations' rulers bless
And public honorings decree,
Let teachers, judges, worship Thee;
Let laws and arts Thy reign express!

Submissa regum fulgeant
Tibi dicata insignia:
Mitique sceptro patriam
Domosque subde civium.

Before Thee let all standards fall
To rise with prouder glorying:
Beneath Thy gentle scepter bring
The homes and fatherlands of all!

---

[41]   Msgr. Henry's translation.

Jesu, tibi sit gloria,
Qui sceptra mundi temperas,
Cum Patre, et almo Spiritu,
In sempiterna sæcula.
Amen.

To Thee, O Jesus, ruling o'er
Earth's rulers all, be glory meet,
With Father and the Paraclete,
Throughout the ages evermore.
Amen.

33. THE MOST HOLY NAME OF JESUS
(*Second Sunday after Epiphany*).

Jesu, dulcis memoria,
Dans vera cordis gaudia:
Sed super mel, et omnia,
Ejus dulcis præsentia.

Jesus! the very thought of Thee
With sweetness fills my breast;
But sweeter far Thy face to see,
And in Thy presence rest.

Nil canitur suavius,
Nil auditur jucundius,
Nil cogitatur dulcius,
Quam Jesus Dei Filius.

Nor voice can sing, nor heart can frame,
Nor can the memory find
A sweeter sound than that blest name,
O Savior of mankind!

Jesu, spes pœnitentibus,
Quam pius es petentibus!
Quam bonus te quærentibus!
Sed quid invenientibus!

O Hope of every contrite heart,
O Joy of all the meek,
To those who fall how kind Thou art!
How good to those who seek!

Nec lingua valet dicere,
Nec littera exprimere:
Expertus potest credere
Quid sit Jesum diligere.

But what to those who find? Ah! this
Nor tongue nor pen can show;
The love of Jesus, what it is,
None but His loved ones know.

Sis, Jesu, nostrum gaudium,
Qui es futurus præmium:
Sit nostra in te gloria,
Per cuncta semper sæcula.
Amen.

Jesus, our only Joy be Thou,
As Thou our Prize wilt be;
Jesus, be Thou our Glory now,
Our Hope, our Victory.
Amen.

34. THE PATRONAGE OF ST. JOSEPH
(*Third Sunday after Easter*).

Te, Joseph, celebrent agmina cœlitum,
Te cuncti resonent Christiadum chori,
Qui clarus meritis, junctus es inclytæ
Casto fœdere Virgini.

Joseph, pure spouse of that immortal
  Bride
Who shines in ever-virgin glory bright,
Thy praise let all the earth reechoing
  send
Back to the realms of light.

Almo cum tumidam germine conjugem
Admirans, dubio tangeris anxius,
Afflatu superi Flaminis angelus
Conceptum puerum docet.

Thee, when sore doubts of thine affi-
  anced wife
Had filled thy righteous spirit with
  dismay,
An angel visited, and, with blest words,
Scattered thy fears away.

Tu natum Dominum stringis, ad
  exteras
Ægypti profugum tu sequeris plagas;
Amissum Solymis quæris, et invenis,
Miscens gaudia fletibus.

Thine arms embraced thy Maker newly
  born,
With Him to Egypt's desert didst thou
  flee;
Him in Jerusalem didst seek and find;
O day of joy to thee!

Post mortem reliquos sors pia consecrat,
Palmamque emeritos gloria suscipit:
Tu vivens, superis par, frueris Deo,
Mira sorte beatior.

Not until after death their blissful crown
Others obtain; but unto thee was given
In thine own lifetime to enjoy thy God,
As do the blest in heaven.

Nobis, summa Trias, parce precantibus,
Da Joseph meritis sidera scandere:
Ut tandem liceat nos tibi perpetim
Gratum promere canticum.
Amen.

Grant us, great Trinity, for Joseph's sake,
The heights of immortality to gain:
There with glad tongues Thy praise to
  celebrate
In one eternal strain.
Amen.

35. THE NATIVITY OF ST. JOHN
THE BAPTIST (*June 24*).

Ut[42] queant laxis *re*sonare fibris
*Mi*ra gestorum *fa*muli tuorum
*Sol*ve polluti *la*bii reatum,
*Sa*ncte *Jo*annes.

O that once more, to sinful men
    descending,
Thou from polluted lips their chains
    wert rending,
So, holy John, might worthy hymns
    ascending
Tell of thy wonders.

Nuntius celso veniens Olympo
Te patri magnum fore nasciturum,
Nomen, et vitæ seriem gerendæ
Ordine promit.

Lo! from the hill of heaven's eternal
    glory
Comes a bright herald to thy father
    hoary,
Gives thee thy name, thy birth and won-
    drous story
Truly foretelling.

Ille promissi dubius superni
Perdidit promptæ modulos loquelæ:
Sed reformasti genitus peremptæ
Organa vocis.

But, while the heavenly word he
    disbelieveth,
Lo! all his power of ready utt'rance
    leaveth,
Till by thy birth his tongue again
    receiveth
Power of speaking.

Ventris obstruso recubans cubili
Senseras Regem thalamo manentem;
Hinc parens nati meritis uterque
Abdita pandit.

Thou, while thy mother's womb was thee
    containing,
Knewest thy King, in secret still
    remaining;
Thus was each parent through her child
    obtaining
Knowledge of mysteries.

---

[42]   The first verse of this hymn is of interest to musicians, as the initial syllables of each line (marked in *italics*) are those chosen by Guido of Arezzo for the musical scale.

Sit decus Patri, genitæque Proli,
Et tibi, compar utriusque Virtus,
Spiritus semper, Deus unus omni
Temporis ævo.
Amen.

Father and Son, to Thee be adoration;
Spirit of both, to Thee like veneration;
Praise to the one true God of our
    salvation,
Ever and ever.
Amen.

36. STS. PETER AND PAUL (*June 29*).

Decora lux æternitatis, auream
Diem beatis irrigavit ignibus,
Apostolorum quæ coronat Principes,
Reisque in astra liberam pandit viam.

Bathed in eternity's all-beauteous beam,
And opening into heaven a path
    sublime,
Welcome the golden day which heralds
    in
The apostolic chiefs, whose glory fills all
    time!

Mundi Magister atque cœli Janitor,
Romæ parentes arbitrique gentium,
Per ensis ille, hic per crucis victor
    necem
Vitæ senatum laureati possident.

Peter and Paul, the fathers of great
    Rome!
Now sitting in the Senate of the skies!
One by the cross, the other by the sword,
Sent to their thrones on high, and life's
    eternal prize.

O Roma felix, quæ duorum Principum
Es consecrata glorioso sanguine!
Horum cruore purpurata cæteras
Excellis orbis una pulchritudines.

O happy Rome! whom that most glori-
    ous blood
Forever consecrates while ages flow:
Thou, thus empurpled art more beautiful
Than all that doth appear most beautiful
    below.

Sit Trinitati sempiterna gloria,
Honor, potestas, atque jubilatio,
In unitate, quæ gubernat omnia,
Per universa sæculorum sæcula.
Amen.

Praise, blessing, majesty, through endless
    days,
Be to the Trinity immortal given;
Who, in pure Unity, profoundly sways
Eternally all things alike in earth and
    heaven.
Amen.

37. THE MOST PRECIOUS BLOOD
(*First Sunday of July*).

Festivis resonent compita vocibus
Cives lætitiam frontibus explicent,
Tædis flammiferis ordine prodeant
Instructi pueri et senes.

Forth let the long procession stream,
And through the streets in order wend;
Let the bright waving line of torches
    gleam,
The solemn chant ascend;

Quem dura moriens Christus in arbore
Fudit multiplici vulnere sanguinem,
Nos facti memores dum colimus, decet
Saltem fundere lacrymas.

While we, with tears and sighs
    profound,
That memorable blood record
Which, stretched on His hard Cross,
    from many a wound
The dying Jesus poured.

Humano generi pernicies gravis
Adami veteris crimine contigit:
Adami integritas et pietas novi
Vitam reddidit omnibus.

By the first Adam's fatal sin
Came death upon the human race;
In this New Adam doth new life begin,
And everlasting grace.

Clamorem validum summus ab æthere
Languentis Geniti si Pater audiit,
Placari potius sanguine debuit,
Et nobis veniam dare.

For scarce the Father heard from heaven
The cry of His expiring Son,
When in that cry our sins were all
    forgiven,
And boundless pardon won.

Hoc quicumque stolam sanguine
    proluit,
Abstergit maculas; et roseum decus,
Quo fiat similis protinus Angelis
Et Regi placeat, capit.

Henceforth, whoso in that dear blood
Washeth shall lose his every stain:
And in immortal roseate beauty robed,
An angel's likeness gain.

A recto instabilis tramite postmodum
Se nullus retrahat, meta sed ultima
Tangatur tribuet nobile præmium,
Qui cursum Deus adjuvat.

Only run thou with courage on
Straight to the goal set in the skies;
He Who assists thy course will give thee
    soon
The everlasting prize.

Nobis propitius sis, Genitor potens,
Ut, quos unigenæ Sanguine Filii
Emisti, et placido Flamine recreas,
Cœli ad culmina transferas.
Amen.

Father supreme! vouchsafe that we,
For whom Thine only Son was slain,
And whom thy Holy Spirit sanctifies,
May heavenly joys attain.
Amen.

38. THE TRANSFIGURATION (*August 6*).

Quicumque Christum quæritis,
Oculos in altum tollite:
Illic licebit visere
Signum perennis gloriæ.

All ye who seek, in hope and love,
For your dear Lord, look up above:
Where, traced upon the azure sky,
Faith may a glorious form descry.

Illustre quiddam cernimus,
Quod nesciat finem pati,
Sublime, celsum, interminum,
Antiquius cœlo et chao.

Lo! on the trembling verge of light
A something all divinely bright:
Immortal, infinite, sublime!
Older than chaos, space, or time:

Hic ille Rex est Gentium
Populique Rex judaici,
Promissus Abrahæ patri
Ejusque in ævum semini.

Hail, Thou the Gentiles' mighty Lord!
All hail, O Israel's King adored!
To Abraham sworn in ages past,
And to his seed while earth shall last.

Hunc, et prophetis testibus,
Iisdemque signatoribus,
Testator et Pater jubet
Audire nos et credere.

To Thee the prophets witness bear;
Of Thee the Father doth declare
That all who would His glory see
Must hear and must believe in Thee.

Jesu, tibi sit gloria,
Qui te revelas parvulis,
Cum Patre, et almo Spiritu,
In sempiterna sæcula.
Amen.

To Jesus from the proud concealed,
But evermore to babes revealed,
All glory with the Father be,
And Holy Ghost, eternally.
Amen.

39. THE SEVEN SORROWS OF THE BLESSED VIRGIN (*Third Sunday in September*).

O quot undis lacrymarum,
Quo dolore volvitur,
Luctuosa de cruento
Dum revulsum stipite,
Cernit ulnis incubantem
Virgo Mater filium.

Os suave, mite pectus,
Et latus dulcissimum,
Dexteramque vulneratam,
Et sinistram sauciam,
Et rubras cruore plantas
Ægra tingit lacrymis.

Centiesque milliesque
Stringit arctis nexibus
Pectus illud et lacertos,
Illa figit vulnera,
Sicque tota colliquescit
In doloris osculis.

Eia, Mater, obsecramus
Per tuas has lacrymas,
Filiique triste funus,
Vulnerumque purpuram,
Hunc tui cordis dolorem
Conde nostris cordibus.

Esto Patri, Filioque,
Et Coævo Flamini,
Esto summæ Trinitati
Sempiterna gloria;
Et perennis laus honorque,
Hoc et omni sæculo.
Amen.

What a sea of tears and sorrow
Did the soul of Mary toss
To and fro upon its billows,
While she wept her bitter loss;
In her arms her Jesus holding,
Torn but newly from the Cross!

O that mournful Virgin Mother!
See her tears how fast they flow
Down upon His mangled body,
Wounded side, and thorny brow;
While His hands and feet she kisses,
Picture of immortal woe!

Oft and oft His arms and bosom
Fondly straining to her own;
Oft her pallid lips imprinting
On each wound of her dear Son,
Till at last, in swoons of anguish,
Sense and consciousness are gone.

Gentle Mother, we beseech thee,
By thy tears and trouble sore,
By the death of thy dear Offspring,
By the bloody wounds He bore,
Touch our hearts with that true sorrow
Which afflicted thee of yore.

To the Father everlasting,
And the Son Who reigns on high,
With the coeternal Spirit,
Trinity in Unity,
Be salvation, honor, blessing,
Now and through eternity.
Amen.

‡THE SEVEN SORROWS OF THE BLESSED VIRGIN.[43]

Jam toto subitus vesper eat polo,
Et sol attonitum præcipitet diem,
Dum sævæ recolo ludibrium necis,
Divinamque catastrophen.

Now let the darkling eve
Mount suddenly on high,
The sun affrighted reave
His splendors from the sky,
While I in silence grieve
O'er His mocked agony
And His divine catastrophe.

Spectatrix aderas supplicio, Parens,
Malis uda, gerens cor adamantinum,
Natus funerea pendulus in cruce
Altos dum gemitus dabat.

Grief-drenched, thou dost appear
With Heart of adamant,
O Mother; and dost hear
The Great Hierophant,
Upon His wooden bier
Locked in the arms of Death,
Utter in groans His parting breath.

Pendens ante oculos Natus, atrocibus
Sectus verberibus, Natus hiantibus
Fossus vulneribus, quot penetrantibus
Te confixit aculeis!

What lookest thou upon,
Mangled and bruised and torn!
And, 'tis the very Son
Thy yearning breast hath borne!
Surely each breaking moan
And each deep-mouthed wound
Its fellow in thy Heart hath found!

Eheu! Sputa, alapæ, verbera, vulnera,
Clavi, fel, aloe, spongia, lancea
Sitis, spina, cruor, quam varia pium
Cor pressere tyrannide!

Surely, His taunts and woes
The scourge, head-ripping thorn,
The spitting and the blows,
The gall, the lance, the scorn—
Surely, each torment throws
A poison dart at thee,
Crushed by their manifold tyranny.

Cunctis interea stas generosior,
Virgo, Martyribus: prodigio novo,
In tantis moriens non moreris, Parens,
Diris fixa doloribus.

Yet thou with patient mien
Beneath His Cross dost stand,
Nobler in this, I ween,
Than all His martyr band:
A thousand deaths, O Queen,
Upon thy spirit life,
Yet thou, O marvel! dost not die.

---

[43]   Msgr. Henry's translation.

486

Sit summæ Triadi gloria, laus, honor,
A qua suppliciter, sollicita prece,
Posco virginei roboris æmulas
Vires rebus in asperis.
Amen.

O Holy Trinity,
Let earth and heaven raise
Their song of laud to Thee
The while my spirit prays;
When evil comes to me,
The strength do Thou impart
That erst upheld Thy Mother's Heart!
Amen.

40. ST. MICHAEL, ARCHANGEL (*September 29*).

Te, splendor et virtus Patris,
Te vita, Jesu, cordium,
Ab ore qui pendent tuo,
Laudamus inter Angelos.

O Jesu! Life-spring of the soul!
The Father's Power, and Glory bright!
Thee with the angels we extol:
From Thee they draw their life and light.

Tibi mille densa millium
Ducum corona militat;
Sed explicat victor crucem
Michael salutis signifer.

Thy thousand thousand hosts are spread
Embattled o'er the azure sky:
But Michael bears Thy standard dread,
And lifts the mighty Cross on high.

Draconis hic dirum caput
In ima pellit tartara,
Ducemque cum rebellibus
Cœlesti ab arce fulminat.

He in that sign the rebel powers
Did with their dragon prince expel;
And hurled them, from the heaven's
    high towers,
Down like a thunderbolt to hell.

Contra ducem superbiæ
Sequamur hunc nos Principem,
Ut detur ex Agni throno
Nobis corona gloriæ.

Grant us with Michael still, O Lord,
Against the prince of pride to fight;
So may a crown be our reward
Before the Lamb's pure throne of light.

Patri, simulque Filio,
Tibique Sancte Spiritus,
Sicut fuit, sit jugiter,
Sæclum per omne gloria.
Amen.

Now to the Father, and the Son
And Holy Ghost, all glory be,
As ever was in ages gone,
And shall be so eternally.
Amen.

41. THE HOLY GUARDIAN ANGELS (*October 2*).

Custodes hominum psalimus angelos,
Naturæ fragili quos Pater addidit
Cœlestis comites, insidiantibus
Ne succumberet hostibus.

Nam quod corruerit proditor angelus,
Concessis merito pulsus honoribus,
Ardens invidia pellere nititur,
Quos cœlo Deus advocat.

Huc custos igitur pervigil advola,
Avertens patria de tibi credita
Tam morbos animi, quam requiescere
Quidquid non sinit incolas.

Sanctæ sit Triadi laus pia jugiter,
Cujus perpetuo numine machina
Triplex hæc regitur, cujus in omnia
Regnat gloria sæcula.
Amen.

Praise those ministers celestial
Whom the dread Father chose
To be the guardians of our nature frail
Against our scheming foes.

For, since that from this glory in the
skies
The apostate angel fell,
Burning with envy, evermore he tries
To drown our souls in hell.

Then hither, watchful spirit, bend thy
wing,
Our country's guardian blest!
Avert her threatening ills, expel each
thing
That hindereth her rest.

Praise to the glorious Trinity, Whose
strength
This mighty fabric sways;
Whose glory spreads beyond the utmost
length
Of everlasting days.
Amen.

‡THE MOST HOLY ROSARY OF THE BLESSED VIRGIN[44] (*First Sunday in October*).

Te gestientem gaudiis,
Te sauciam doloribus,
Te jugi amictam gloria,
O Virgo Mater, pangimus.

Ave, redundans gaudio
Dum concipis dum visitas,
Et edis, offers, invenis,
Mater beata, Filium.

Ave, dolens, et intimo
In corde agonem, verbera,
Spinas, crucemque Filii
Perpessa; princeps martyrum.

Ave, in triumphis Filii,
In ignibus Paracliti
In regni honore et lumine,
Regina fulgens gloria.

Venite, gentes, carpite
Ex his rosas mysteriis,
Et pulchri amoris inclytæ
Alatri coronas nectite.

Jesu, tibi sit gloria.
Qui natus es de Virgine,
Cum Patre et almo Spiritu
In sempiterna sæcula.
Amen.

The gladness of thy Motherhood,
The anguish of thy suffering,
The glory now that crowns thy brow,
O Virgin Mother, we would sing.

Hail, Blessed Mother, full of joy,
In thy consent thy visit too;
Joy in the birth of Christ on earth,
Joy in Him lost and found anew.

Hail sorrowing in His agony—
The blows, the thorns that pierced His
   brow;
The heavy wood, His shameful Rood—
Yea! Queen and chief of martyrs thou.

Hail, in the triumph of Thy Son,
The quickening flames of Pentecost;
Shining a Queen in light serene
When all the world is tempest tost.

O come, ye nations, roses bring,
Called from these mysteries divine,
And for the Mother of your King,
With loving hands your chaplets twine.

We lay our homage at Thy feet,
Lord Jesus, Thou the Virgin's Son,
With Father and with Paraclete,
Reigning while endless ages run.
Amen.

---

[44] Dom Hunter-Blair's translation.

42. ST. RAPHAEL, ARCHANGEL (*October 24*).

Tibi, Christe, splendor Patris,	Jesu, Brightness of the Father!
Vita, virtus cordium:	Life and Strength of all who live!
In conspectu angelorum	In the presence of the angels,
Votis, vocis psallimus:	Glory to Thy name we give,
Alternantes concrepando	And Thy wondrous praise rehearse,
Melos damus vocibus.	Singing in alternate verse.
Collaudamus venerantes,	Hail, too, ye angelic powers!
Omnes cœli principes,	Hail, ye thrones celestial!
Sed præcipue fidelem	Hail, physician of salvation,
Medicum et comitem	Guide of life, blest Raphael!
Raphaelem, in virtute	Who the foe of all mankind
Alligantem dæmonem.	Didst in links of iron bind.
Quo custode procul pelle,	O may Christ, by thy protection,
Rex Christe piissime,	Shelter us from harm this day;
Omne nefas inimici,	Keep us pure in flesh and spirit,
Mundo corde et corpore:	Save us from the enemy;
Paradiso redde tuo	And vouchsafe us, of His grace,
Nos sola clementia.	In His paradise a place.
Gloriam Patri melodis	Glory to th' Almighty Father
Personemus vocibus:	Sing we now in anthems sweet;
Gloriam Christo canamus,	Glory to the great Redeemer,
Gloriam Paraclito;	Glory to the Paraclete;
Qui trinus et unus Deus	Three in One, and One in Three,
Extat ante sæcula. Amen.	Throughout all eternity.
	Amen.

43. THE MATERNITY OF THE BLESSED VIRGIN (*Second Sunday in October*).

Cœlo Redemptor prætulit	The Savior left high heaven to dwell
Felicis alvum Virginis,	Within the Virgin's womb,
Ubi caduca membra	And there arrayed Himself in flesh,
Mortale corpus induit.	Our Victim to become.

Hæc Virgo nobis edidit
Nostræ salutis auspicem,
Qui nos redemit sanguine,
Pœnas crucemque pertulit.

She unto us divinely bore
Salvation's King and God,
Who died for us upon the Cross,
Who saves us in His blood.

Spes læta nostro e pectore
Pellat timores anxios:
Hæc quippe nostras lacrymas,
Precesque defert Filio.

She too our joyful hope shall be,
And drive away all fears,
Offering for us to her dear Son
Our contrite sighs and tears.

Voces parentis excipit,
Votisque natus annuit:
Hanc quisque semper diligat,
Rebusque in arctis invocet.

That Son, He hears His Mother's prayer,
And grants, ere it be said;
Be ours to love her and invoke
In every strait her aid.

Sit Trinitati gloria,
Quæ Matris intactum sinum
Ditavit almo germine,
Laus sit per omne sæculum.
Amen.

Praise to the glorious Trinity
While endless times proceed,
Who in that bosom, pure of stain,
Sowed such immortal Seed.
Amen.

44. ALL SAINTS (*November 1*).

Placare, Christe, servulis,
Quibus Patris clementiam
Tuæ ad Tribunal gratiæ
Patrona Virgo postulat.

O Christ, Thy guilty people spare!
Lo, bending at Thy gracious throne,
Thy Virgin Mother pours her prayer,
Imploring pardon for her own.

Et vos, beata per novem
Distincta gyros agmina,
Antiqua cum præsentibus,
Futura damna pellite.

Ye angels, happy evermore!
Who in your circles nine ascend,
As ye have guarded us before,
So still from harm our steps defend.

Apostoli cum Vatibus,
Apud severum Judicem
Veris reorum fletibus
Exposcite indulgentiam.

Ye prophets and apostles high!
Behold our penitential tears;
And plead for us when death is nigh,
And our all-searching Judge appears.

Vos, purpurati Martyres,
Vos candidati præmio
Confessionis, exules
Vocate nos in patriam.

Ye martyrs all! a purple band,
And confessors, a white-robed train:
O call us to our native land,
From this our exile, back again.

Chorea casta Virginum,
Et quos eremus incolas
Transmisit astris Cœlitum
Locate nos in sedibus.

And ye, O choirs of virgins chaste,
Receive us to your seats on high,
With hermits whom the desert waste
Sent up of old into the sky.

Auferte gentem perfidam
Credentium de finibus,
Ut unus omnes unicum
Ovile nos Pastor regat.

Drive from the flock, O spirits blest!
The false and faithless race away;
That all within one fold may rest,
Secure beneath one Shepherd's sway.

Deo Patri sit gloria,
Natoque Patris unico,
Sancto simul Paraclito,
In sempiterna sæcula.
Amen.

To God the Father glory be,
And to His sole begotten Son;
The same, O Holy Ghost, to Thee,
While everlasting ages run.
Amen.

45. THE COMMON OF APOSTLES AND EVANGELISTS.

Exultet orbis gaudiis:
Cœlum resultet laudibus:
Apostolorum gloriam
Tellus et astra concinunt.

Now let the earth with joy resound,
And highest heaven reecho round;
Nor heaven nor earth too high can raise
The great apostles' glorious praise.

Vos, sæculorum Judices,
Et vera mundi lumina!
Votis precamur cordium,
Audite voces supplicum.

O ye who, throned in glory dread,
Shall judge the living and the dead!
Lights of the world forevermore!
To you the suppliant prayer we pour.

Qui templa cœli clauditis,
Serasque verbo solvitis,
Nos a reatu noxios
Solvi jubete, quæsumus.

Ye close the sacred gates on high;
At your command apart they fly:
O loose us from the guilty chain
We strive to break, and strive in vain.

Præcepta quorum protinus
Languor salusque sentiunt:
Sanate mentes languidas;
Augete nos virtutibus.

Sickness and health your voice obey;
At your command they go or stay:
O then from sin our souls restore;
Increase our virtues more and more.

Ut, cum redibit Arbiter
In fine Christus sæculi,
Nos sempiterni gaudii
Concedat esse compotes.

So when the world is at its end,
And Christ to judgment shall descend,
May we be called those joys to see,
Prepared from all eternity.

Patri, simulque Filio,
Tibique, Sancte Spiritus,
Sicut fuit, sit jugiter
Sæclum per omne gloria.
Amen.

Praise to the Father, with the Son,
And Holy Spirit, Three in One;
As ever was in ages past,
And shall be so while ages last.
Amen.

46. THE COMMON OF APOSTLES AND EVANGELISTS, AT EASTERTIDE.

Tristes erant Apostoli
De Christi acerbo funere,
Quem morte crudelissima
Servi necarant impii.

When Christ, by His own servants slain,
Had died upon the bitter Cross,
The apostles, of their joy bereft,
Were weeping their dear Master's loss:

Sermone verax Angelus
Mulieribus prædixerat:
Mox ore Christus gaudium
Gregi feret fidelium.

Meanwhile an angel at the tomb
To holy women hath foretold,
"The faithful flock with joy shall soon
Their Lord in Galilee behold."

Ad anxios Apostolos
Currunt statim dum nuntiæ,
Illæ micantis obvia
Christi tenent vestigia.

Who, as they run the news to bring,
Lo, straightway Christ Himself they
    meet,
All radiant bright with heavenly light,
And, falling, clasp His sacred feet.

Galilææ ad alta montium
Se conferunt Apostoli,
Jesuque, voti compotes,
Almo beantur lumine.

To Galilee's lone mountain height
The apostolic band retire,
There, blest with their dear Savior's sight,
Enjoy in full their souls' desire.

Ut sis perenne mentibus
Paschale, Jesu, gaudium,
A morte dira criminum
Vitæ renatos libera.

O Jesu, from the death of sin
Keep us, we pray; so shalt Thou be
The everlasting paschal Joy
Of all the souls newborn in Thee.

Deo Patri sit gloria,
Et Filio, qui a mortuis
Surrexit, ac Paraclito,
In sempiterna sæcula.
Amen.

To God the Father, with the Son
Who from the grave immortal rose,
And Thee, O Paraclete, be praise,
While age on endless ages flows.
Amen.

47. THE COMMON OF ONE MARTYR.

Deus, tuorum militum
Sors, et corona, præmitum,
Laudes canentes Martyris
Absolve nexu criminis.

Hic nempe mundi gaudia,
Et blanda fraudum pabula
Imbuta felle deputans,
Perventi ad cœlestia.

Pœnas cucurrit fortiter,
Et sustulit viriliter,
Fundensque pro te sanguinem,
Æterna dona possidet.

Ob hoc precatu supplici
Te poscimus, piissime:
In hoc triumpho Martyris
Dimitte noxam servulis.

Laus et perennis gloria
Patri sit, atque Filio,
Sancto simul Paraclito,
In sempiterna sæcula.
Amen.

O God, Thy soldiers' Crown and Guard,
And their exceeding great Reward,
From all transgressions set us free,
Who sing Thy martyr's victory.

The pleasures of the world he spurned,
From sin's pernicious lures he turned;
He knew their joys imbued with gall:
And thus he reached Thy heavenly hall.

For Thee through many a woe he ran,
In many a fight he played the man;
For Thee his blood he dared to pour,
And thence hath joy forevermore.

We therefore pray Thee, full of love,
Regard us from Thy throne above:
On this Thy martyr's triumph-day
Wash every stain of sin away.

O Father, that we ask be done,
Through Jesus Christ, Thine only Son:
Who, with the Holy Ghost and Thee,
Shall live and reign eternally.
Amen.

48. THE COMMON OF MANY MARTYRS.

Sanctorum meritis inclyta gaudia
Pangamus socii, gestaque fortia:
Gliscens fert animus promere cantibus
Victorum genus optimum.

The merits of the saints,
Blessèd forevermore,
Their love that never faints,
The toils they bravely bore—
For these the Church today
Pours forth her joyous lay:
These victors win the noblest bay.

Hi sunt, quos fatue mundus abhorruit;
Hunc fructu vacuum, floribus aridum,
Contempsere tui nominis asseclæ,
Jesu Rex bone Cœlitum.

They, whom this world of ill,
While it yet held, abhorred:
Its withering flowers that still
They spurned with one accord:
They knew them short-lived all,
And followed at Thy call,
King Jesu, to Thy heavenly hall.

Hi pro te furias atque minas truces
Calcarunt hominum, sævaque verbera:
His cessit lacerans fortiter ungula,
Nec carpsit penetralia.

For Thee all pangs they bare,
Fury and mortal hate,
The cruel scourge to tear,
The hook to lacerate;
But vain their foes' intent:
For, every torment spent,
Their valiant spirits stood unbent.

Cæduntur gladiis more bidentium:
Non murmur resonat, non quærimonia;
Sed corde impavido mens bene conscia
Conservat patientiam.

Like sheep their blood they poured:
And without groan or tear
They bent before the sword
For that their King most dear:
Their souls, serenely blest,
In patience they possessed,
And looked in hope toward their rest.

Quæ vox, quæ poterit lingua retexere
Quæ tu Martyribus munera præparas?
Rubri nam fluido sanguine fulgidis
Cingunt tempora laureis.

What tongue may here declare,
Fancy or thought descry,
The joys Thou dost prepare
For these Thy saints on high?
Empurpled in the flood
Of their victorious blood,
They won the laurel from their God.

Te, summa O Deitas, unaque, poscimus,
Ut culpas abigas, noxia subtrahas,
Des pacem famulis, ut tibi gloriam
Annorum in seriem canant.
Amen.

To Thee, O Lord most High,
One in Three Persons still,
To pardon us we cry,
And to preserve from ill:
Here give Thy servants peace,
Hereafter glad release,
And pleasures that shall never cease.
Amen.

49. THE COMMON OF MARTYRS, EASTERTIDE.

Rex gloriose Martyrum,
Corona confitentium,
Qui respuentes terrea
Perducis ad cœlestia:

Aurem benignam protinus
Intende nostris vocibus:
Trophæa sacra pangimus:
Ignosce quod deliquimus.

Tu vincis inter Martyres,
Parcisque Confessoribus:
Tu vince nostra crimina,
Largitor indulgentiæ.

Deo Patri sit gloria,
Et Filio qui a mortuis
Surrexit, ac Paraclito
In sempiterna sæcula.
Amen.

All-glorious King of martyrs Thou,
Crown of confessors here below;
Whom, casting earthly joys away,
Thou guidest to celestial day:

O quickly bend a gracious ear
To this our suppliant voice of prayer;
As we their sacred triumphs chant,
Forgiveness to our errors grant.

In martyrs, victory is Thine;
In Thy confessors, mercies shine:
Then conquer, Lord, our wickedness,
And us with loving pardon bless.

Now to the Father, and the Son
Who rose from death, all glory be,
With Thee, O holy Comforter,
Henceforth through all eternity.
Amen.

50. THE COMMON OF CONFESSORS.

Iste Confessor Domini, colentes
Quem pie laudant populi per orbem,
Hac die lætus meruit beatas
Scandere sedes.

This is the day when Jesu's true
  confessor,
Whose happy festal here His people
  keep,
Hasting with joy to dwell with Him the
  Blesser,
Climbed heaven's steep.

(If it be not the day of his death, the first verse is as follows:)

Iste Confessor Domini, colentes
Quem pie laudant populi per orbem,
Hac die lætus meruit supremos
Laudis honores.

Safe now forever, Jesu's true confessor,
Whose happy festal here His people
  keep,
Doth of his labors for his mighty Blesser
Rich harvest reap.

Qui pius, prudens, humilis, pudicus,
Sobriam duxit sine labe vitam,
Donec humanos animavit auræ
Spiritus artus.

Gentle was he, wise, pure, and
    lowly-hearted,
Sober and modest, ever foe to strife,
While in his frame there flowed as yet
    unparted
Currents of life.

Cujus ob præstans meritum, frequenter
Ægra quæ passim jacuere membra,
Viribus morbi domitis, saluti
Restituuntur.

Ofttimes hath He Whose face he sees
    in heaven,
Being entreated for His servant's sake,
To us on earth the same for healer given
Sick whole to make.

Noster hinc illi chorus obsequentem
Concinit laudem, celebresque palmas;
Ut piis ejus precibus juvemur
Omne per ævum.

Wherefore our choir, in thankfulness
    adoring,
Lifteth its voice with melody of laud,
While he on high for us his prayer is
    pouring
Unto his God.

Sit salus illi, decus atque virtus,
Qui super cœli solio coruscans,
Totius mundi seriem gubernat
Trinus et unus.
Amen.

Glory and honor, virtue and salvation
Be unto Him, Who, in His might
    divine,
Ruleth supremely over all creation,
One and yet Trine.
Amen.

51. THE COMMON OF VIRGINS.

Jesu, corona Virginum,
Quem Mater illa concipit.
Quæ sola Virgo parturit,
Hæc vota clemens accipe.

Jesus, the virgins' Crown, do Thou
Accept us, as in prayer we bow;
Born of that Virgin whom alone
The Mother and the maid we own.

Qui pergis inter lilia,
Septus choreis Virginum,
Sponsus decorus gloria,
Sponsisque reddens præmia.

Amongst the lilies Thou dost feed,
With virgin choirs accompanied;
With glory decked, the spotless brides
Whose bridal gifts Thy love provides.

Quocumque tendis, Virgines
Sequuntur, atque laudibus
Post te canentes cursitant,
Hymnosque dulces personant.

They, whereso'er Thy footsteps bend,
With hymns and praises still attend;
In blessèd troops they follow Thee,
With dance, and song, and melody.

Te deprecamur supplices,
Nostris ut addas sensibus
Nescire prorsus omnia
Corruptionis vulnera.

We pray Thee therefore to bestow
Upon our senses here below
Thy grace, that so we may endure,
From taint of all corruption pure.

Virtus, honor, laus, gloria
Deo Patri cum Filio,
Sancto simul Paraclito,
In sæculorum sæcula.
Amen.

All laud to God the Father be:
All laud, eternal Son, to Thee:
All laud, as is forever meet,
To God the holy Paraclete.
Amen.

52. THE COMMON OF HOLY WOMEN.

Fortem virili pectore
Laudemus omnes fœminam,
Quæ sanctitatis gloria
Ubique fulget inclyta.

High let us all our voices raise
In that heroic woman's praise
Whose name, with saintly glory bright,
Shines in the starry realms of light.

Hæc sancto amore saucia,
Dum mundi amorem noxium
Horrescit, ad cœlestia
Iter peregit arduum.

Filled with a pure celestial glow,
She spurned all love of things below;
And heedless here on earth to stay,
Climbed to the skies her toilsome way.

Carnem domans jejuniis,
Dulcique mentem pabulo
Orationis nutriens,
Cœli potitur gaudiis.

With fasts her body she subdued,
But filled her soul with prayer's sweet
    food;
In other worlds she tastes the bliss
For which she left the joys of this.

Rex Christe, virtus fortium,
Qui magna solus efficis,
Hujus precatu quæsumus
Audi benignus supplices.

O Christ, the Strength of all the strong,
To Whom all our best deeds belong!
Through her prevailing prayers on high
In mercy hear Thy people's cry.

Deo Patri sit gloria,
Ejusque soli Filio,
Cum Spiritu Paraclito,
Nunc et per omne sæculum.
Amen.

To God the Father, with the Son,
And Holy Spirit, Three in One,
Be glory while the ages flow,
From all above and all below.
Amen.

53. THE COMMON OF THE
DEDICATION OF A CHURCH.

Cœlestis Urbs Jerusalem,
Beata pacis visio,
Quæ celsa de viventibus
Saxis ad astra tolleris,
Sponsæque ritu cingeris
Mille Angelorum millibus.

O sorte nupta prospera,
Dotata Patris gloria,
Respersa Sponsi gratia,
Regina formosissima,
Christo jugata Principi,
Cœli corusca civitas.

Hic margaritis emicant,
Patentque cunctis ostia:
Virtute namque prævia
Mortalis illuc ducitur,
Amore Christi percitus
Tormenta quisquis sustinet.

Scalpri salubris ictibus,
Et tunsione plurima,
Fabri polita malleo
Hanc saxa molem construunt,
Aptisque juncta nexibus
Locantur in fastigio.

Decus Parenti debitum
Sit usquequaque Altissimo,
Natoque Patris unico,
Et inclyto Paraclito,
Cui laus, potestas, gloria
Æterna sit per sæcula.
Amen.

Blessèd city, heavenly Salem,
Vision dear of peace and love,
Who, of living stones upbuilded,
Art the joy of heaven above,
And, with angel cohorts circled,
As a bride to earth dost move!

From celestial realms descending,
Ready for the nuptial bed,
To His presence, decked with jewels,
By her Lord shall she be led;
All her streets, and all her bulwarks,
Of pure gold are fashionèd.

Bright with pearls her portal glitters!
It is open evermore;
And, by virtue of His merits,
Thither faithful souls may soar
Who, for Christ's dear name, in this
    world
Pain and tribulation bore.

Many a blow and biting sculpture
Polished well those stones elect,
In their places now compacted
By the heavenly Architect,
Who therewith hath willed forever
That His palace should be decked.

Laud and honor to the Father;
Laud and honor to the Son;
Laud and honor to the Spirit,
Ever Three, and ever One:
Consubstantial, coeternal,
While unending ages run.
Amen.

54. THE COMMON OF ALL FEASTS OF
THE BLESSED VIRGIN MARY.

Ave maris stella,
Dei Mater alma,
Atque semper virgo,
Felix cœli porta.

Sumens illud Ave
Gabrielis ore,
Funda nos in pace,
Mutans Hevæ nomen.

Solve vincla reis,
Profer lumen cæcis,
Mala nostra pelle,
Bona cuncta posce.

Monstra te esse matrem,
Sumat per te preces,
Qui pro nobis natus
Tulit esse tuus.

Virgo singularis,
Inter omnes mitis,
Nos culpis solutos,
Mites fac et castos.

Vitam præsta puram,
Iter para tutum,
Ut videntes Jesum,
Semper collætemur.

Sit laus Deo Patri,
Summo Christo decus,
Spiritui Sancto,
Tribus honor unus.
Amen.

Hail, bright Star of ocean,
God's own Mother blest,
Ever-sinless Virgin,
Gate of heavenly rest!

Taking that sweet Ave
Which from Gabriel came,
Peace confirm within us,
Changing Eva's name.

Break the captive's fetters;
Light on blindness pour;
All our ills expelling,
Every bliss implore.

Show thyself a Mother;
May the Word divine,
Born for us thine Infant,
Hear our prayers through thine.

Virgin all excelling,
Mildest of the mild,
Freed from guilt, preserve us
Meek and undefiled;

Keep our life all spotless,
Make our way secure,
Till we find in Jesus
Joy forevermore.

Through the highest heaven
To the Almighty Three,
Father, Son, and Spirit,
One same glory be.
Amen.

55. FOR THE BENEDICTION OF
THE BLESSED SACRAMENT.

Ave, verum Corpus, natum
Ex Maria Virgine,
Vere passum, immolatum
In cruce pro homine.

Hail to Thee, true Body, sprung
From the Virgin Mary's womb!
The same that on the Cross was hung,
And bore for man the bitter doom!

Cujus latus perforatum
Unda fluxit et sanguine,
Esto nobis prægustatum,
Mortis in examine.

Thou Whose side was pierced, and
    flowed
Both with water and with blood,
Suffer us to taste of Thee
In our life's last agony.

O Clemens, O Pie,
O Dulcis Jesu, Fili Mariæ.
Amen.

O kind, O loving One!
O sweet Jesus! Mary's Son!
Amen.

Adoro te devote, latens Deitas,
Quæ sub his figuris vere latitas;
Tibi se cor meum totum subjicit,
Quia te contemplans totum deficit.

Humbly I adore Thee, hidden Deity,
Which beneath these symbols art con-
    cealed from me:
Wholly in submission Thee my spirit
    hails,
For in contemplating Thee it wholly
    fails.

Visus, tactus, gustus, in te fallitur,
Sed auditu solo tuto creditur:
Credo quidquid dixit Dei Filius:
Nil hoc verbo veritatis verius.

Seeing, touching, tasting, all are here
    deceived,
But by hearing only safely 'tis believed:
I believe whatever God's own Son
    averred:
Nothing can be truer than Truth's very
    Word.

In cruce latebat sola Deitas,
At hic latet simul et Humanitas:
Ambo tamen credens atque confitens,
Peto quod petivit latro pœnitens.

On the Cross Thy Godhead only was
    concealed,
Here not e'en Thy manhood is to sight
    revealed:
But in both believing and confessing,
    Lord,
Ask I what the dying thief of Thee
    implored.

Plagas, sicut Thomas, non intueor,
Deum tamen meum te confiteor.
Fac me tibi semper magis credere,
In te spem habere, te diligere.

I do not, like Thomas, see Thy wounds
    appear,
But with him confess my Lord and God
    is here.
Grant this faith in me may evermore
    increase,
And my hope in Thee, and love, may
    never cease.

O memoriale mortis Domini!
Panis vivus, vitam præstans homini!
Præsta meæ menti de te vivere,
Et te illi semper dulce sapere.

O thrice-blest Memorial of my dying
    Lord.
This true Bread of life doth life to man
    afford;
Grant, O Lord, my soul may ever feed
    on Thee,
And Thy taste of all things to it sweetest
    be.

Pie Pelicane, Jesu Domine,
Me immundum munda tuo sanguine,
Cujus una stilla salvum facere
Totum mundum quit ab omni scelere.

Victim for Thy people, Jesu, Lord and
    God,
Cleanse me, wretched sinner, in Thy
    Precious Blood—
Blood whereof one drop for humankind
    outpoured
Might from all transgression have the
    world restored.

Jesu, quem velatum nunc aspicio,
Oro, fiat illud, quod tam sitio,
Ut, te revelata cernens facie,
Visu sim beatus tuæ gloriæ.
Amen.

Jesu, Whom in this life veilèd I behold,
Grant what my soul thirsts for with de-
    sire untold;
O may I, beholding Thine unveilèd
    grace,
Rest in blissful vision of Thine open face.
Amen.

The following is usually sung after each verse:

Ave Jesu, Pastor fidelium;
Adauge fidem omnium in te
    credentium.

Jesus, eternal Shepherd, hear our cry:
Increase the faith of all whose souls on
    Thee rely.

O quam suavis est, Domine, Spiritus tuus! qui ut dulcedinem tuam in filios demonstrares, pane suavissimo, de cœlo præstito, esurientes reples bonis, fastidiosos divites dimittens inanes. Alleluia.

O sacrum Convivium, in quo Christus sumitur; recolitur memoria passionis ejus; mens impletur gratia, et futuræ gloriæ nobis pignus datur. Alleluia.

O how gracious, O Lord, is Thy Spirit! Who, to show Thy sweetness to Thy children, by the sweetest Food from heaven, dost fill the hungry with good things, and sendest the proud rich empty away. Alleluia.

O sacred Banquet, wherein Christ is received; the memory of His Passion is renewed, the mind is filled with grace, and the pledge of future glory is given unto us. Alleluia.

The Proper Of The Mass

*For Sundays and
Principal Feasts*

The Proper of the Mass

FOR THE SUNDAYS AND PRINCIPAL FEASTS OF THE YEAR

Note. — *When a feast of greater rank falls upon a Sunday, the Mass is of the feast; the Collect of the Sunday is said after the Collect of the day, and the Gospel of the Sunday is read at the end of Mass, in place of the usual Gospel of St. John. Commemorations other than those proper to Sundays have been omitted here.*

FIRST SUNDAY OF ADVENT

INTROIT. To Thee, O Lord, have I lifted up my soul; in thee, O my God, I put my trust; let me not be ashamed; neither let mine enemies laugh at me: for none that wait on Thee shall be confounded.

Show me Thy ways, O Lord, and teach me Thy paths.

Glory be to the Father, etc.

To Thee, O Lord, etc. (*Thus the* Introit *is always repeated.*)

COLLECT. O Lord, we pray Thee, raise up Thy power, and come; that by Thy protection we may deserve to be rescued from the threatening dangers of our sins, and to be saved by Thy deliverance. Who livest and reignest, etc. *Amen.*

EPISTLE. Rom 13:11–14. Brethren: Knowing the time that it is now the hour for us to awake from sleep. For now our salvation is nearer than when we first believed. The night is far spent, and the day is at hand; let us therefore cast off the works of darkness, and put on the armor of light. As in the day let us walk becomingly; not in banquetings and drunkenness, not in chambering and wantonness, not in contention and jealousy. But put ye on the Lord Jesus Christ.

GRADUAL. None of them that wait on Thee shall be confounded O Lord. Show, O Lord, Thy ways to me, and teach me Thy paths. Alleluia, alleluia. Show us, O Lord, Thy mercy: and grant us Thy salvation. Alleluia.

GOSPEL. Lk 21:25–33. At that time: Jesus said to His disciples: There will be signs in the sun, and moon, and stars; and on the earth distress of nations, by reason of the confusion of the sound of the sea and of the waves, men withering away for fear and expectation of the things which are coming upon the world. For the powers of the heavens will be shaken. And then they will see the Son of Man coming on a cloud with great power and majesty. But when these things begin to come to pass, look up, and lift up your heads: because your redemption is at hand. And He spake to them a similitude: See the fig tree, and all the trees; when they now shoot forth their fruit, ye know that summer is nigh. So also, when ye shall see these things come to pass, know that the Kingdom of God is at hand. Truly, I say to you, this generation will not pass away till all things be fulfilled. Heaven and earth will pass away, but My words will not pass away.

OFFERTORY. To Thee have I lifted up my soul: in Thee, O my God, I put my trust, let me not be ashamed: neither let my enemies laugh at me: for none of them that wait on Thee shall be confounded.

SECRET. May these sacred mysteries, O Lord, cleanse us by their mighty power, and make us to approach with greater purity to Him Who is their source. Through Our Lord Jesus Christ, etc. *Amen.*

COMMUNION. The Lord will give goodness: and our earth shall yield her fruit.

POSTCOMMUNION. May we receive Thy mercy in the midst of Thy temple, O Lord: that we may anticipate with due honor the coming solemnities of our renewal. Through Our Lord Jesus Christ, etc. *Amen.*

SECOND SUNDAY OF ADVENT

INTROIT. People of Sion, behold the Lord shall come to save the nations; and the Lord shall make the glory of His voice to be heard in the joy of your heart.

Give ear, O Thou that rulest Israel: Thou that leadest Joseph like a sheep.

Glory be to the Father, etc.

COLLECT. Stir up our hearts, O Lord, to make ready the ways of Thine only begotten Son, that by His coming we may be worthy to serve Thee with purified minds. Through the same Our Lord Jesus Christ, etc. *Amen.*

EPISTLE. Rom 15:4–13. Brethren: Whatever things were written, were written for our instruction; that, through patience and the consolation of the Scriptures, we may have hope. Now the God of patience and of comfort grant you to be of one mind one toward another, according to Jesus Christ: that unanimously with one mouth ye may honor God, and the Father of Our Lord Jesus Christ; wherefore receive one another, as Christ also received you to the glory of God. For I say that Christ Jesus was minister of circumcision for the truth of God, to confirm the promises of the fathers. But that the Gentiles glorify God for mercy, as it is written: Therefore will I praise Thee among the Gentiles, O Lord, and will sing to Thy name. And again He saith: Rejoice, ye Gentiles, with His people. And again: Praise the Lord, all ye Gentiles; and glorify Him, all ye people. And again Isaiah said: There shall be a root of Jesse, and He who shall rise up to rule the Gentiles, in Him the Gentiles shall hope. Now the God of hope fill you with all joy and peace in believing: that ye may abound in hope and in the power of the Holy Spirit.

GRADUAL. Out of Sion the loveliness of His beauty: God shall come manifestly. Gather ye together His saints to Him; who have set His covenant before sacrifices. Alleluia, alleluia. I rejoiced at the things that were said to me: We shall go into the house of the Lord. Alleluia.

GOSPEL. Mt 11:2–10. At that time: When John in the prison had heard of the works of Christ, he sent two of his disciples, and said to Him: Art Thou He Who should come, or must we look for another? And Jesus answered and said to them: Go and relate to John what ye hear and see. The blind see, the lame walk, lepers are cleansed, the deaf hear, the dead rise again, the poor have the gospel preached to them. And happy is he who shall not be scandalized in Me. And as they departed, Jesus began to speak to the crowds concerning John: What went you out into the desert to see? a reed shaken by the wind? But what went ye out to see? a man clothed in soft garments? Behold, they who are clothed in soft garments are in the palaces of kings. But what went ye out to see? a prophet? Yea, I tell you, and more than a prophet; for this is he of whom it is written: Behold, I send My messenger before Thy face, who shall prepare Thy way before Thee.

OFFERTORY. O God, turning, Thou wilt bring us life; and Thy people shall rejoice in Thee: show us, O Lord, Thy mercy, and grant us Thy salvation.

SECRET. Be appeased, we beseech Thee, O Lord, by the prayers and sacrifices of our humility; and whereas we have no merits to plead in our favor, do Thou succor us by Thy protection. Through Our Lord Jesus Christ, etc. *Amen.*

COMMUNION. Arise, O Jerusalem, and stand on high: and behold the joy that cometh to thee from thy God.

POSTCOMMUNION. Having been filled with the food of spiritual nourishment, we humbly beseech Thee, O Lord, that by the participation of this mystery Thou wouldst teach us to despise earthly things, and love those that are heavenly. Through Our Lord Jesus Christ, etc. *Amen.*

THIRD SUNDAY OF ADVENT

INTROIT. Rejoice in the Lord always; again I say, rejoice. Let your moderation be known to all men; the Lord is nigh. Be anxious about nothing; but in everything by prayer let your petitions be made known to God.

Thou hast blessed Thy land, O Lord: Thou hast turned away the captivity of Jacob.

Glory be to the Father, etc.

COLLECT. O Lord, we beseech Thee, mercifully incline Thine ears unto our prayers, and enlighten the darkness of our minds by the grace of Thy heavenly visitation. Who livest and reignest, etc. *Amen.*

EPISTLE. Phil 4:4–7. Brethren: Rejoice in the Lord always: again I say, rejoice. Let your moderation be known to all men: the Lord is nigh. Be anxious about nothing, but in everything by prayer and supplication, with thanksgiving, let your petitions be made known to God. And may the peace of God, which surpasseth all understanding, guard your hearts and minds in Christ Jesus Our Lord.

GRADUAL. Thou, O Lord, that sittest upon the cherubim, stir up Thy might, and come. Give ear, O Thou that rulest Israel. Thou that leadest Joseph like a sheep. Alleluia, alleluia. Stir up thy might, O Lord, and come to save us. Alleluia.

GOSPEL. Jn 1:19–28. At that time: The Jews sent from Jerusalem priests and Levites to him, to ask him: Who art thou? And he confessed, and denied not; but confessed: I am not the Christ. And they asked him: What then? Art thou Elias? And he said: I am not. Art thou the prophet? And he answered: No. They said therefore to him: Who art thou, that we may give an answer to those who sent us? What sayest thou of thyself? He said: I am the voice of one crying in the wilderness: Make straight the way of the Lord, as said the prophet Isaias. And they who were sent were of the Pharisees. And they asked him, and said to him: Why then dost thou baptize, if thou art not Christ, nor Elias, nor the prophet? John answered them, saying: I baptize in water; but in the midst of you standeth One Whom ye know not. It is He Who, though coming after me, is preferred before me; the latchet of Whose shoe I am not worthy to loose. These things were done in Bethany, beyond the Jordan, where John was baptizing.

OFFERTORY. Thou hast blessed Thy land, O Lord; Thou hast turned away the captivity of Jacob: Thou hast forgiven the iniquity of Thy people.

SECRET. May the sacrifice of our devotion, we beseech Thee, O Lord, be continually offered unto Thee; that it may both attain the end for which Thou didst institute this sacred mystery, and wonderfully work in us Thy salvation. Through Our Lord Jesus Christ, etc. *Amen.*

COMMUNION. Say: to the fainthearted, take courage, and fear not: behold, our God will come and save us.

POSTCOMMUNION. We implore, O God, Thy clemency, that these divine helps having expiated our sins, may prepare us for the approaching festival. Through Our Lord Jesus Christ, etc. *Amen.*

FOURTH SUNDAY OF ADVENT

‡*N. B. — Should this Sunday fall on Dec. 24, the Mass will be of the Vigil of Christmas (as below) with Commemoration of the Sunday, only the Gospel of the Sunday will not be read at the end.*

INTROIT. Drop dew, ye heavens, from above, and let the clouds rain the Just One; let the earth be opened, and bud forth a Savior.

The heavens show forth the glory of God, and the firmament declareth the works of His hands.

Glory be to the Father, etc.

COLLECT. O Lord, we pray Thee, raise up Thy power, and come, and with great might succor us; that, by the aid of Thy grace, that which is hindered by our sins may be quickened by Thy merciful forgiveness. Who livest and reignest, etc. *Amen.*

EPISTLE. 1 Cor 4:1–5. Brethren: Let a man so regard us as ministers of Christ, and stewards of the mysteries of God. Here now it is required in stewards, that a man be found faithful. But to me it is of the least account to be judged by you, or by the day of man: but neither do I judge myself. For I am not conscious to myself of anything; yet am I not hereby justified: but He that judgeth me is the Lord. Therefore judge not before the time, until the Lord come, Who both will bring to light the hidden things of darkness, and will make manifest the counsels of hearts: and then shall every man have praise from God.

GRADUAL. The Lord is nigh unto all them that call upon Him, to all that call upon Him in truth. My mouth shall speak the praise of the Lord; and let all flesh bless His holy name. Alleluia, alleluia. Come, O Lord, and do not delay; forgive the sins of Thy people Israel. Alleluia.

GOSPEL. Lk 3:1–6. In the fifteenth year of the reign of Tiberius Cæsar, Pontius Pilate being procurator of Judea, and Herod being tetrarch of Galilee, and Philip his brother being tetrarch of Iturea and the country of Trachonitis, and Lysanias being tetrarch of Abilina, under the high priests Annas and Caiphas, the word of the Lord came to John, the son of Zachariah, in the desert. And he came into all the country about the Jordan, preaching the baptism of penance, for the remission of sins, as it is written in the book of the sayings of Isaias the prophet: A voice of one crying in the desert: Prepare ye the way of the Lord, make straight His paths. Every valley shall be filled, and every mountain and hill shall be made low: and what is crooked shall be made straight, and the rough way smooth. And all flesh shall see the salvation of God.

OFFERTORY. Hail, Mary, full of grace, the Lord is with thee, blessed art thou among women, and blessed is the fruit of thy womb.

SECRET. Favorably regard, we beseech Thee, O Lord, these present sacrifices, that they may profit us both unto devotion and salvation. Through Our Lord Jesus Christ, etc. *Amen.*

COMMUNION. Behold a Virgin shall conceive, and bring forth a Son, and His name shall be called Emmanuel.

POSTCOMMUNION. Having received Thy gifts, we beseech Thee, O Lord, that with the frequent use of this mystery the effect of our salvation may increase. Through Our Lord Jesus Christ, etc. *Amen.*

‡VIGIL OF THE NATIVITY OF OUR LORD

INTROIT. This day shall you know that the Lord will come, and save us; and in the morning you shall see His glory.

The earth is the Lord's, and the fullness thereof: the world, and all they that dwell therein.

Glory be to the Father, etc.

COLLECT. O God, Who dost gladden us with the yearly expectation of our Redemption, grant that we, who now joyfully receive Thine only begotten Son as our Redeemer, may also, without fear, behold Him coming as our Judge, Our Lord Jesus Christ, Thy Son, Who with Thee, etc. *Amen.*

EPISTLE. Rom 1:1–6. Paul, a servant of Jesus Christ, called to be an apostle, separated unto the gospel of God, which He had promised before, by His prophets, in the Holy Scriptures, concerning His Son, Who was made to Him of the seed of David, according to the flesh, Who was predestinated the Son of God in power, according to the spirit of sanctification, by the Resurrection of Our Lord Jesus Christ from the dead; by Whom we have received grace and apostleship for obedience to the Faith, in all nations, for His name; among whom are you also the called of Jesus Christ Our Lord.

GRADUAL. This day you shall know that the Lord will come and save us: and in the morning you shall see His glory. Give ear, O Thou that rulest Israel: Thou that leadest Joseph like a sheep: Thou that sittest on the Cherubim, shine forth Ephraim, Benjamin, and Manasses. Alleluia, alleluia. Tomorrow shall the iniquity of the earth be abolished; and the Savior of the world shall reign over us. Alleluia.

GOSPEL. Mt 1:18–21. When the Mother of Jesus, Mary, was espoused to Joseph, before they came together, she was found with Child, of the Holy Ghost. Whereupon Joseph her husband, being a just man, and not willing publicly to expose her, was minded to put her away privately. But while he thought on these things, behold the angel of the Lord appeared to him in his sleep, saying: Joseph, son of David, fear not to take unto thee Mary thy wife, for that which is conceived in her is of the Holy Ghost; and she shall bring forth a Son: and thou shalt call His name Jesus. For He shall save His people from their sins.

OFFERTORY. Lift up your gates, O ye princes, and be ye lifted up, O eternal gates; and the King of glory shall enter in.

SECRET. Grant, we beseech Thee, O Lord, that even as we anticipate the adorable birthday of Thy Son, so may we joyfully receive His eternal gifts: Who with Thee liveth, etc. *Amen.*

COMMUNION. The glory of the Lord shall be revealed; and all flesh shall see the salvation of our God.

POSTCOMMUNION. Grant, we beseech Thee, O Lord, that the celebration of the birth of Thine only begotten Son may give us fresh life: He Whose heavenly mystery is our food and drink. Through the same Our Lord Jesus Christ, etc. *Amen.*

THE NATIVITY OF OUR LORD, OR CHRISTMAS

FIRST MASS

INTROIT. The Lord hath said unto Me: Thou art My Son, this day have I begotten Thee.

Why have the Gentiles raged, and the people devised vain things?

Glory be to the Father, etc.

COLLECT. O God, Who hast made this most sacred night to shine forth with the brightness of the true Light; grant, we beseech Thee, that we may enjoy His happiness in heaven, the mystery of Whose light we have known upon earth. Who liveth and reigneth, etc. *Amen.*

EPISTLE. Ti 2:11–15. Dearly beloved: The grace of God our Savior hath appeared to all men, instructing us that denying impiety and worldly lusts we should live soberly, and justly, and piously in this world, waiting for the blessed hope and coming of the glory of our great God and Savior Jesus Christ, Who gave Himself for all, that He might redeem us from all iniquity, and cleanse for Himself an acceptable people, zealous of good works. These things speak and exhort: in Christ Jesus Our Lord.

GRADUAL. With Thee is the principality in the day of Thy strength, in the brightness of the saints; from the womb before the daystar I begot Thee. The Lord said to my Lord: Sit Thou at my right hand, until I make Thine enemies Thy footstool. Alleluia, alleluia. The Lord hath said to Me: Thou art My Son, this day have I begotten Thee. Alleluia.

GOSPEL. Lk 2:1–14. At that time: A decree went forth from Augustus Cæsar that the whole world should be enrolled. This first enrollment was made by Cyrinus, the governor of Syria. And all went to be enrolled, every one into his own city. And Joseph also went up from Galilee, from the city of Nazareth, into Judea to the city of David, which is called Bethlehem, because he was of the house and family of David, to be enrolled with Mary his espoused wife, who was with Child. And it came to pass that while they were there the days for her delivery were completed. And she brought forth her firstborn Son, and swathed Him and laid Him in a manger: because there was no room for them in the inn. And there were in the same country shepherds watching, and keeping the night watches over their flock. And behold, an angel of the Lord stood by them, and the brightness of God shone round them, and they feared greatly. And the angel said to them: Fear not; for behold, I bring you good news of great joy, which will be to all the people; for this day is born to you in the city of David a Savior, Who is Christ the Lord. And this shall be a sign to you. Ye shall find a Babe swathed and lying in a manger. And suddenly there was with the angel a multitude of the heavenly host, praising God, and saying: Glory to God on high: and on earth peace to men of good will.

OFFERTORY. Let the heavens rejoice, and let the earth be glad before the face of the Lord, because He cometh.

SECRET. May the offering of this day's festival be pleasing to Thee, O Lord, we beseech Thee: that by Thy grace, through this sacred intercourse, we may be found like unto Him in Whom our nature is united to Thee. Who liveth and reigneth, etc. *Amen.*

COMMUNION. In the brightness of the saints, from the womb before the daystar I begot Thee.

POSTCOMMUNION. Grant us, we beseech Thee, O Lord our God, that we, who rejoice in celebrating by these mysteries the Nativity of Our Lord Jesus Christ, may deserve by a worthy conduct to attain unto fellowship with Him. Who liveth and reigneth, etc. *Amen.*

SECOND MASS

INTROIT. A light shall shine upon us this day: for Our Lord is born to us; and He shall be called Wonderful, God, the Prince of Peace, the Father of the world to come; of Whose kingdom there shall be no end.

The Lord hath reigned, He is clothed with beauty: the Lord is clothed with strength, and hath girded Himself.

Glory be to the Father, etc.

COLLECT. Grant, we beseech Thee, Almighty God, that we, who are filled with the new light of Thy incarnate Word, may show forth in our works that which by faith shineth in our minds. Through the same Our Lord Jesus Christ, etc. *Amen.*

EPISTLE. Ti 3:4–7. Dearly beloved: The goodness and kindness of our Savior God appeared: not by works of justice done by us, but according to His mercy He saved us by the laver of regeneration and renewing of the Holy Spirit, Whom He hath poured forth upon us abundantly through Jesus Christ our Savior, that being justified by His grace we may be heirs according to hope of eternal life: in Christ Jesus Our Lord.

GRADUAL. Blessed is He that cometh in the name of the Lord; the Lord is God, and He hath shone upon us. This is the Lord's doing, and it is wonderful in our eyes. Alleluia, alleluia. The Lord hath reigned, He is clothed with beauty; the Lord is clothed with strength, and hath girded Himself with power. Alleluia.

GOSPEL. Lk 2:15–20. At that time: The shepherds said to one another: Let us go over to Bethlehem, and see this thing which is come to pass, which the Lord hath showed us. And they came in haste; and found Mary and Joseph, and the Babe lying in the manger. And when they had seen it, they understood the thing which had been spoken to them concerning this Child. And all who heard wondered; and at the things which were told them by the shepherds. But Mary kept all these words, pondering in her heart. And the shepherds returned, glorifying and praising God for all that they had heard and seen as it was told to them.

OFFERTORY. God hath established the world, which shall not be moved, Thy throne, O God, is prepared from of old; Thou art from everlasting.

SECRET. May our gifts, we beseech Thee, O Lord, be agreeable to the mysteries of this day's nativity, and may they ever give unto us peace: that, as He Who was born as man shone with the light of the Godhead, so these fruits of the earth may bestow on us what is divine. Through the same Our Lord Jesus Christ, etc. *Amen.*

COMMUNION. Rejoice greatly, O daughter of Sion, shout for joy O daughter of Jerusalem: behold thy King comes, the Holy, and the Savior of the world.

POSTCOMMUNION. May we, O Lord, always receive new life from this Sacrament, which reneweth to us the memory of that wonderful birth which destroyed the old man. Through the same Our Lord Jesus Christ, etc. *Amen.*

THIRD MASS

INTROIT. A Child is born for us, and a Son is given to us; Whose government is upon His shoulder; and His name shall be called the Angel of great counsel.

Sing unto the Lord a new song; for He hath done wonderful things.

Glory be to the Father, etc.

COLLECT. Grant, we beseech Thee, Almighty God, that the new birth of Thine only begotton Son in the flesh may deliver us who are held by the old bondage under the yoke of sin. Through the same Our Lord Jesus Christ, etc. *Amen.*

EPISTLE. Heb 1:1–12. God, Who formerly spoke to the fathers by the prophets, at different times and in various ways: lastly in these days hath spoken to us by His Son, Whom He hath appointed heir of all things, by Whom also He made the world: Who being the brightness of His glory, and the impression of His substance, and upholding all things by the word of His power, which He made a purification of sins, sitteth on the right hand of the Majesty on high: being made so much greater than the angels, as He hath inherited a more excellent name than they. For to which of the angels did He ever say: Thou art My Son, this day have I begotten Thee? And again: I will be to Him a Father, and He shall be to me a Son? And when He bringeth again the First-begotten into the world, He saith: And let all the angels of God adore Him. And of the angels indeed He saith: Who maketh His angels spirits, and His ministers a flame of fire. But to the Son: Thy throne, O God, is forever and ever; the scepter of Thy kingdom is a scepter of right. Thou hast loved justice and hated iniquity; therefore God, Thy God, hath anointed Thee with the oil of gladness above Thy partners. And: Thou, O Lord, in the beginning didst found the earth: and the heavens are works of Thine hands. They shall perish, but Thou shalt remain, and they all shall grow old as a garment: and as a vesture Thou shalt change them and they shall be changed: but Thou art the selfsame, and Thy years shall not fail.

GRADUAL. All the ends of the earth have seen the salvation of our God; sing joyfully to God all the earth. The Lord hath made known His salvation; He hath revealed His justice in the sight of the Gentiles. Alleluia, alleluia. A sanctified day hath shone upon us; come ye Gentiles, and adore the Lord; for this day a great light hath descended upon the earth. Alleluia.

GOSPEL. Jn 1:1–14. In the beginning was the Word, and the Word was with God, and the Word was God. This was in the beginning with God. All things were made through Him: and without Him was made nothing that was made. In Him was life, and the life was the light of men: and the light shineth in darkness, and the darkness did not comprehend it. There was a man sent from God, whose name was John. This one came for a witness, to testify concerning the light, that all might believe through him. He was not the light, but he was to testify concerning the light. The true light, which enlighteneth every man, cometh into this world. He was in the world, and the world was made through Him, and the world knew Him not. He came to His own possessions, and His own people received Him not. But to as many as received Him, He gave power to become children of God, to those who believe in His name: who are born, not of blood, nor of the will of the flesh, nor the will of man, but of God. AND THE WORD WAS MADE FLESH (*here all kneel*), and dwelt among us, and we saw His glory, the glory as of the only begotten of the Father: full of grace and truth.

OFFERTORY. Thine are the heavens, and Thine is the earth: the world and the fullness thereof Thou hast founded: justice and judgment are the preparation of Thy throne.

SECRET. The gifts we offer do Thou, O Lord, sanctify by the new birth of Thine only begotten Son, and cleanse us from the stains of our sins. Through the same Our Lord Jesus Christ, etc. *Amen.*

COMMUNION. All the ends of the earth have seen the salvation of our God.

POSTCOMMUNION. Grant, we beseech Thee, Almighty God, that as the Savior of the world, born this day, is the Author of a divine birth for us, so He may also be Himself the Giver of immortality. Who liveth and reigneth, etc. *Amen.*

LAST GOSPEL. Mt 2:1–12. When Jesus was born in Bethlehem of Juda, in the days of King Herod, behold Magians came from eastern parts to Jerusalem, saying: Where is He that is born King of the Jews? for we have seen His star in the East, and we are come to worship Him. And King Herod, hearing this, was troubled, and all Jerusalem with him. And assembling together all the chief priests, and the scribes of the people, he inquired of them where the Christ should be born. And they said to him: In Bethlehem of Juda: for so it is written by the prophet: And thou, Bethlehem, land of Juda, art not the least among the princes of Juda: for out of thee shall come forth a Leader, Who shall rule My people Israel. Then Herod, privately calling the Magians, ascertained from them the time when the star appeared to them. And sent them to Bethlehem, and said: Go, and diligently inquire after the Child, and when ye have found Him, bring back word to me, that I also may go and worship Him. When they had heard the king, they departed: and behold, the star which they had seen in the East went before them, till it came and stood over the place where the Child was. And seeing the star, they rejoiced with very great joy. And having entered into the house, they found the Child with Mary His Mother, and fell down and worshipped Him (*here all kneel*). And opening their treasures they offered Him gifts: gold, frankincense, and myrrh. And being warned of God in a dream, that they should not return to Herod, they went back another way into their own country.

SUNDAY WITHIN THE OCTAVE OF CHRISTMAS

INTROIT. While all things were in quiet silence, and the night was in the midst of her course, Thy Almighty Word, O Lord, came down from heaven, from Thy royal throne.

The Lord hath reigned, He is clothed with beauty: the Lord is clothed with strength, and hath girded Himself.

Glory be to the Father, etc.

COLLECT. O Almighty and everlasting God, do Thou order all our actions in conformity with Thy good pleasure, that, through the name of Thy beloved Son, we may worthily abound in good works. Through the same Our Lord Jesus Christ, etc. *Amen.*

EPISTLE. Gal 4:1–7. Brethren: As long as the heir is a child, he differeth nothing from a servant, although he is lord of all; but he is under tutors and governors, until the time appointed by the father: so we also, when we were children, were serving under the elements of the world. But when the fullness of time came, God sent His Son made of a woman, made under the law, to redeem those who were under the law, that we might receive the adoption of sons. And because ye are sons, God hath sent the Spirit of His Son into your hearts, crying: Abba, Father. Therefore he is no more a servant, but a son; and if a son, heir also through God.

GRADUAL. Thou art beautiful above the sons of men; grace is poured abroad in Thy lips. My heart hath uttered a good word, I speak my works to the king; my tongue is the pen of a scrivener that writeth swiftly. Alleluia, alleluia. The Lord hath reigned. He is clothed with beauty: the Lord is clothed with strength, and hath girded Himself with might. Alleluia.

GOSPEL. Lk 2:33–40. At that time: Joseph and Mary the Mother of Jesus were wondering at the things spoken concerning Him. And Simeon blessed them, and said to Mary His Mother: Behold, He is set for the fall and rising of many in Israel, and for a sign which will be opposed: And a sword shall pierce thine own soul, that the thoughts of many hearts may be revealed. And there was one Anna, a prophetess, the daughter of Phanuel, of the tribe of Aser: she was far advanced in years, and had lived with her husband seven years from her virginity. And she was a widow until eighty-four years; and departed not from the temple, but, by fastings and prayers, worshipped night and day. Now she, at the same hour, coming in, gave praise to the Lord; and spake of Him to all who were looking for the redemption of Israel. And after they had performed all things according to the law of the Lord, they returned into Galilee, to their own city, Nazareth. And the Child grew, and became strong, full of wisdom: and the grace of God was in Him.

OFFERTORY. God hath established the world which shall not be moved: Thy throne, O God, is prepared from of old; Thou art from everlasting.

SECRET. Grant, we beseech Thee, Almighty God, that the offering made in the sight of Thy Majesty may obtain for us the grace of loving devotion and the reward of a blessed immortality. Through Our Lord Jesus Christ, etc. *Amen.*

COMMUNION. Take the Child and His Mother, and go into the land of Israel: for they are dead who sought the life of the Child.

POSTCOMMUNION. By the operation of this mystery, O Lord, may our sins be purged away, and our just desires fulfilled. Through Our Lord Jesus Christ, etc. *Amen.*

NEW YEAR'S DAY

THE CIRCUMCISION OF OUR LORD

INTROIT. A Child is born for us, and a Son is given to us; Whose government is upon His shoulder; and His name shall be called the Angel of great counsel.

Sing unto the Lord a new song; for He hath done wonderful things.

Glory be to the Father, etc.

COLLECT. O God, Who by the fruitful virginity of Blessed Mary hast given unto mankind the rewards of eternal salvation: grant, we beseech Thee, that we may feel that she intercedes for us, through whom we have been made worthy to receive the Author of life, Our Lord Jesus Christ, Thy Son. Who with Thee, etc. *Amen.*

EPISTLE. Ti 2:11–15. Dearly beloved: The grace of God our Savior hath appeared to all men, instructing us that denying impiety and worldly lusts we should live soberly, and justly, and piously in this world, waiting for the blessed hope and coming of the glory of our great God and Savior Jesus Christ, Who gave Himself for all, that He might redeem us from all iniquity, and cleanse for Himself an acceptable people, zealous of good works. These things speak and exhort: in Christ Jesus Our Lord.

GRADUAL. All the ends of the earth have seen the salvation of our God; sing joyfully to God all the earth. The Lord hath made known His salvation; He hath revealed His justice in the sight of the Gentiles. Alleluia, alleluia. A sanctified day hath shone upon us; come ye Gentiles, and adore the Lord; for this day a great light hath descended upon the earth. Alleluia.

GOSPEL. Lk 2:21. At that time: After eight days were past that the Child should be circumcised, His name was called Jesus, so called by the angel before He was conceived in the womb.

OFFERTORY. Thine are the heavens, and Thine is the earth: the world and the fullness thereof Thou hast founded: justice and judgment are the preparation of Thy throne.

SECRET. The gifts we offer do Thou, O Lord, sanctify by the new birth of Thine only begotten Son, and cleanse us from the stains of our sins. Through the same Our Lord Jesus Christ, etc. *Amen.*

COMMUNION. All the ends of the earth have seen the salvation of our God.

POSTCOMMUNION. May this Communion, O Lord, purge us from guilt; and through the intercession of Blessed Mary, the Virgin-Mother of God, make us partakers of Thy heavenly remedy. Through the same Our Lord Jesus Christ, etc. *Amen.*

THE VIGIL OF THE EPIPHANY

INTROIT. While all things were in quiet silence, and the night was in the midst of her course, Thy Almighty Word, O Lord, came down from heaven, from Thy royal throne.

The Lord hath reigned, He is clothed with beauty: the Lord is clothed with strength, and hath girded Himself.

Glory be to the Father, etc.

COLLECT. O Almighty and everlasting God, do Thou order all our actions in conformity with Thy good pleasure, that, through the name of Thy beloved Son, we may worthily abound in good works. Through the same Our Lord Jesus Christ, etc. *Amen.*

EPISTLE. Gal 4:1–7. Brethren: As long as the heir is a child, he differeth nothing from a servant, although he is lord of all; but he is under tutors and governors, until the time appointed by the father: so we also, when we were children, were serving under the elements of the world. But when the fullness of time came, God sent His Son made of a woman, made under the law, to redeem those who were under the law, that we might receive the adoption of sons. And because ye are sons, God hath sent the Spirit of His Son into your hearts, crying: Abba, Father. Therefore he is no more a servant, but a son; and if a son, heir also through God.

GRADUAL. Thou art beautiful above the sons of men; grace is poured abroad in Thy lips. My heart hath uttered a good word, I speak my works to the king; my tongue is the pen of a scrivener that writeth swiftly. Alleluia, alleluia. The Lord hath reigned. He is clothed with beauty: the Lord is clothed with strength, and hath girded Himself with might. Alleluia.

GOSPEL. Mt 2:19–23. At that time: When Herod was dead, behold an angel of the Lord appeared in a dream to Joseph, in Egypt, saying: Arise, and take the Child and His Mother, and go into the land of Israel: for they who sought the life of the Child are dead. And he arose and took the Child and His Mother, and came into the land of Israel. But hearing that Archelaus reigned in Judea, in the room of Herod his father, he was afraid to go thither: and being warned in a dream, retired into the country of Galilee. And coming, he dwelt in a city called Nazareth, that what was said by the prophets might be fulfilled: He shall be called a Nazarene.

OFFERTORY. God hath established the world which shall not be moved: Thy throne, O God, is prepared from of old; Thou art from everlasting.

SECRET. Grant, we beseech Thee, Almighty God, that the offering made in the sight of Thy Majesty may obtain for us the grace of loving devotion and the reward of a blessed immortality. Through Our Lord Jesus Christ, etc. *Amen.*

COMMUNION. Take the Child and His Mother, and go into the land of Israel: for they are dead who sought the life of the Child.

POSTCOMMUNION. By the operation of this mystery, O Lord, may our sins be purged away, and our just desires fulfilled. Through Our Lord Jesus Christ, etc. *Amen.*

THE EPIPHANY OF OUR LORD

INTROIT. Behold the Lord the Ruler is come; and a kingdom is in His hand, and power and dominion.

Give to the king Thy judgment, O God; and Thy justice unto the king's son. Glory be to the Father, etc.

COLLECT. O God, Who by the leading of a star didst on this day manifest Thine only begotten Son to the Gentiles: mercifully grant that we, who know

Thee now by faith, may be brought to the contemplation of Thy glorious Majesty. Through the same Our Lord Jesus Christ, etc. *Amen.*

LESSON. Is 60:1–6. Arise, be enlightened, O Jerusalem: for thy light is come, and the glory of the Lord is risen upon thee. For behold, darkness shall cover the earth, and a mist the peoples: but the Lord shall arise upon thee, and His glory shall be seen on thee. And the Gentiles shall walk in thy light, and kings in the brightness of thy rising. Lift up thy eyes round about, and see: all these are gathered together, they are come to thee: thy sons shall come from afar, and thy daughters shall rise up at thy side. Then shalt thou see, and abound, and thy heart shall wonder and be enlarged, when the multitude of the sea shall be converted to thee, the strength of the Gentiles shall come to thee. The multitude of camels shall cover thee, the dromedaries of Madian and Epha: all they from Saba shall come, bringing gold and frankincense, and showing forth praise to the Lord.

GRADUAL. All they from Saba shall come bringing gold and frankincense, and showing forth praise to the Lord. Arise and be enlightened, O Jerusalem, for the glory of the Lord is risen upon thee. Alleluia, alleluia. We have seen His star in the East: and are come with gifts to adore the Lord. Alleluia.

GOSPEL. Mt 2:1–12. When Jesus was born in Bethlehem of Juda, in the days of King Herod, behold Magians came from eastern parts to Jerusalem, saying: Where is He that is born King of the Jews? for we have seen His star in the East, and we are come to worship Him. And King Herod, hearing this, was troubled, and all Jerusalem with him. And assembling together all the chief priests, and the scribes of the people, he inquired of them where the Christ should be born. And they said to him: In Bethlehem of Juda: for so it is written by the prophet: And thou, Bethlehem, land of Juda, art not the least among the princes of Juda: for out of thee shall come forth a Leader, Who shall rule My people Israel. Then Herod, privately calling the Magians, ascertained from them the time when the star appeared to them. And sent them to Bethlehem, and said: Go, and diligently inquire after the Child, and when ye have found Him, bring back word to me, that I also may go and worship Him. When they had heard the king, they departed: and behold, the star which they had seen in the East went before them, till it came and stood over the place where the Child was. And seeing the star, they rejoiced with very great joy. And having entered into the house, they found the Child with Mary His Mother, and fell down and worshipped Him (*here all kneel*). And opening their treasures they offered Him gifts: gold, frankincense, and myrrh. And being warned of God in a dream, that they should not return to Herod, they went back another way into their own country.

OFFERTORY. The kings of Tharsis and the Islands shall offer gifts: the kings of the Arabians and of Saba shall bring presents: and all the kings of the earth shall adore Him; all nations shall serve Him.

SECRET. Graciously regard, O Lord, we beseech Thee, the gifts of Thy Church, in which are offered now no longer gold, frankincense, and myrrh, but He Whom those mystic offerings signified is immolated and received, even Jesus Christ Thy Son Our Lord. Who liveth and reigneth, etc. *Amen.*

COMMUNION. We have seen His star in the East, and are come with gifts to adore the Lord.

POSTCOMMUNION. Grant, we beseech Thee, Almighty God, that what we celebrate with solemn office we may attain by the understanding of a purified mind. Through Our Lord Jesus Christ, etc. *Amen.*

‡SUNDAY WITHIN THE OCTAVE OF EPIPHANY
FEAST OF THE HOLY FAMILY

INTROIT. Let the father of the Just One exult with joy; let Thy father and Thy Mother rejoice; and let her that bore Thee be glad.

How lovely are Thy tabernacles, O Lord of hosts: my soul longeth and fainteth for the courts of the Lord.

Glory be to the Father, etc.

COLLECT. O Lord Jesus Christ, Who, becoming subject to Mary and Joseph didst sanctify the home life by singular virtues; by the help of both, do Thou grant that we may be taught by the example of Thy Holy Family, and have fellowship with it forevermore: Who livest and reignest, etc. *Amen.*

EPISTLE. Col 3:12–17. Brethren: Put ye on, as the elect of God, holy and beloved, bowels of compassion, kindness, humility, modesty, patience; bearing with one another, and forgiving one another, if any man hath a complaint against anyone; as even the Lord hath forgiven you, so ye also. But above all these things, put on charity, which is the bond of perfection; and let the peace of Christ reign in your hearts, in which also ye are called in one body; and be ye thankful. Let the word of Christ dwell in you abundantly, in all wisdom; teaching and admonishing one another in psalms, hymns, and spiritual songs, in grace, singing in your hearts to God. All whatever ye do in word, or in work, all things in the name of the Lord Jesus Christ, giving thanks to God and the Father through Jesus Christ Our Lord.

GRADUAL. One thing have I asked of the Lord, this will I seek after: that I may dwell in the house of the Lord all the days of my life. Blessed are they that dwell in Thy house, O Lord: they shall praise Thee forever and ever. Alleluia, alleluia. Verily Thou art a hidden King, the God of Israel, the Savior. Alleluia.

GOSPEL. Lk 2:42–52. When Jesus was twelve years old, they went up to Jerusalem, according to the custom of the feast, and when they had completed the days, as they returned, the Child Jesus remained behind in Jerusalem, and His parents knew it not. And thinking that He was in the company, they came a day's journey, and sought Him among their kindred and acquaintance. And not finding Him, they returned to Jerusalem, seeking Him. And it came to pass that after three days they found Him in the temple, sitting in the midst of the doctors, hearing them and asking them questions. And all who heard Him were astonished at His wisdom, and His answers. And when they saw Him they were amazed. And His

Mother said to Him: Child, why hast Thou done so to us? Behold, Thy father and I were seeking Thee sorrowing. And He said to them: Why did ye seek Me? Did ye not know that I must be about My Father's business? And they understood not the word which He spake to them. And He went down with them, and came to Nazareth: and He was subject to them. And His Mother kept all these things in her heart. And Jesus advanced in wisdom and age, and favor with God and men.

OFFERTORY. The parents of Jesus carried Him to Jerusalem to present Him to the Lord.

SECRET. We offer to Thee, O Lord, an atoning Victim, humbly entreating that through the intercession of the Virgin Mother of God and blessed Joseph, Thou wouldst strongly establish our families in Thy peace and grace. Through the same Our Lord Jesus Christ, etc. *Amen.*

COMMUNION. Jesus went down with them, and came to Nazareth: and was subject to them.

POSTCOMMUNION. Let us whom Thou dost refresh by Thy heavenly Sacraments, O Lord, ever follow the example of Thy Holy Family; that at the hour of our death Thy glorious Virgin Mother and blessed Joseph may be near us, and we may be found worthy to be received by Thee into eternal dwellings: Who livest and reignest, etc. *Amen.*

FIRST SUNDAY AFTER EPIPHANY

INTROIT. Upon a high throne I saw a man sitting, Whom a multitude of angels adore singing together: Behold Him the name of Whose empire is forever and ever.

Sing joyfully unto God, all the earth: serve ye the Lord with gladness.

Glory be to the Father, etc.

COLLECT. O Lord, we beseech Thee, receive, of Thy heavenly mercy, the prayers of Thy people who call upon Thee; and grant that they may both perceive what things they ought to do, and also may have power to fulfill the same. Through Our Lord Jesus Christ, etc. *Amen.*

EPISTLE. Rom 12:1–5. Brethren: I beseech you, by the mercy of God, that ye present your bodies a living victim, holy, well pleasing to God, your rational worship. And be not conformed to this world, but be ye reformed in the newness of your mind: that ye may prove what is the good, and acceptable, and perfect will of God. For I say, by the grace which is given me, to all who are among you: not to think more highly than it behooveth to think; but to think soberly, and according as God hath dealt to every one the measure of faith. For as we have many members in one body, but all the members have not the same office; so we, being many, are one body in Christ, and every one members one of another: in Christ Jesus Our Lord.

GRADUAL. Blessed be the Lord, the God of Israel, Who alone doth wonderful things from the beginning. Let the mountains receive peace for Thy people and the hills justice. Alleluia, alleluia. Sing joyfully to God, all the earth. Serve ye the Lord with gladness. Alleluia.

GOSPEL. Lk 2:42–52. When Jesus was twelve years old, they went up to Jerusalem, according to the custom of the feast, and when they had completed the days, as they returned, the Child Jesus remained behind in Jerusalem, and His parents knew it not. And thinking that He was in the company, they came a day's journey, and sought Him among their kindred and acquaintance. And not finding Him, they returned to Jerusalem, seeking Him. And it came to pass that after three days they found Him in the temple, sitting in the midst of the doctors, hearing them and asking them questions. And all who heard Him were astonished at His wisdom, and His answers. And when they saw Him they were amazed. And His Mother said to Him: Child, why hast Thou done so to us? Behold, Thy father and I were seeking Thee sorrowing. And He said to them: Why did ye seek Me? Did ye not know that I must be about My Father's business? And they understood not the word which He spake to them. And He went down with them, and came to Nazareth: and He was subject to them. And His Mother kept all these things in her heart. And Jesus advanced in wisdom and age, and favor with God and men.

OFFERTORY. Sing joyfully to God all the earth, serve ye the Lord with gladness: come in before His presence with exceeding great joy.

SECRET. May the sacrifice which is offered to Thee, O Lord, always quicken and protect us. Through Our Lord Jesus Christ, etc. *Amen.*

COMMUNION. Son why hast Thou done so to us? I and Thy father have sought Thee sorrowing. How is it that you sought Me? Did you not know that I must be about My Father's business?

POSTCOMMUNION. Grant, we humbly beseech Thee, Almighty God, that those whom Thou refreshest with Thy Sacraments may serve Thee worthily by a life well-pleasing to Thee. Through Our Lord Jesus Christ, etc. *Amen.*

SECOND SUNDAY AFTER EPIPHANY
FEAST OF THE HOLY NAME OF JESUS

INTROIT. At the name of Jesus every knee should bend of those that are in heaven, on earth, and under the earth; and every tongue should confess that the Lord Jesus Christ is in the glory of God the Father.

O Lord, Our Lord, how admirable is Thy name in the whole earth!

Glory be to the Father, etc.

COLLECT. O God Who hast appointed Thine only begotten Son to be the Savior of mankind, and hast commanded that His name should be called Jesus: mercifully grant that we may enjoy in heaven the blessed vision of Him Whose holy name we worship on earth. Through the same Our Lord Jesus Christ, etc. *Amen.*

COLLECT OF THE SUNDAY. Almighty and everlasting God, Who dost govern all things in heaven and earth: mercifully hear the prayers of Thy people, and grant us Thy peace in our days. Through Our Lord Jesus Christ, etc. *Amen.*

LESSON. Acts 4:8–12. In those days: Peter, filled with the Holy Ghost, said to them: Ye rulers of the people and ancients, hear: If we this day are examined concerning the good deed done to the infirm man, by what means he hath been made whole, be it known to you all, and to all the people of Israel, that by the name of Our Lord Jesus Christ of Nazareth, Whom ye crucified, Whom God hath raised from the dead, by Him this man standeth here before you whole. This is the Stone which was rejected by you the builders, which is become the Head of the corner; neither is there salvation in any other. For there is no other name under heaven given among men, by which we must be saved.

GRADUAL. Save us, O Lord our God, and gather us from among the nations: that we may give thanks to Thy holy name, and may glory in Thy praise. Thou, O Lord, art our Father and Redeemer, Thy name is from eternity. Alleluia, alleluia. My mouth shall speak the praise of the Lord, and let all flesh bless His holy name. Alleluia.

GOSPEL. Lk 2:21. At that time: After eight days were past that the Child should be circumcised, His name was called Jesus, so called by the angel before He was conceived in the womb.

OFFERTORY. I will praise Thee, O Lord my God with my whole heart, and I will glorify Thy name forever; for Thou, O Lord, art sweet and mild, and plenteous in mercy to all that call upon Thee, alleluia.

SECRET. May Thy blessing, by which all creatures live, hallow, we beseech Thee, most merciful God, this our sacrifice which we offer to Thee to the glory of the name of Thy Son Our Lord Jesus Christ, that it may please Thy Majesty and bring Thee praise, and avail us unto salvation. Through the same Our Lord Jesus Christ, etc. *Amen.*

SECRET OF THE SUNDAY. Sanctify, O Lord, the gifts we offer: and cleanse us from the stains of our sins. Through Our Lord Jesus Christ, etc. *Amen.*

COMMUNION. All the nations Thou hast made shall come and adore before Thee, O Lord; and they shall glorify Thy name: for Thou art great, and dost wonderful things: Thou art God alone, alleluia.

POSTCOMMUNION. Almighty and eternal God, Who hast created and redeemed us: mercifully hear our prayers; and vouchsafe to accept with a favorable and gracious countenance the sacrifice of the saving Victim, which we have offered to Thy Majesty, in honor of the name of Thy Son, Our Lord Jesus Christ: that Thy grace being infused into us, through the glorious name of Jesus, as a pledge of our eternal predestination, we may rejoice that our names are written in heaven. Through the same Our Lord Jesus Christ, etc. *Amen.*

POSTCOMMUNION OF THE SUNDAY. May the efficacy of Thy power, O Lord, be increased in us; that, being fed with Thy divine Sacraments, we may, through Thy bounty, be prepared to receive what they promise. Through Our Lord Jesus Christ, etc. *Amen.*

LAST GOSPEL. Jn 2:1–11. At that time: There was a wedding in Cana of Galilee: and the Mother of Jesus was there. And Jesus also was invited, and His disciples, to the wedding. And the wine failing, the Mother of Jesus saith to Him:

They have no wine. And Jesus saith to her: Woman, what is that to me and to thee? My hour is not yet come. His Mother saith to the waiters: Whatever He shall say to you, do ye. Now six stone pitchers were set there, after the manner of the purifying of the Jews, containing two or three measures apiece. Jesus saith to them: Fill the pitchers with water. And they filled them up to the brim. And Jesus saith to them: Draw out now, and carry to the master of the feast. And they carried it. And when the master of the feast had tasted the water made wine, and knew not whence it was, but the waiters who drew the water knew, the master of the feast calleth the bridegroom, and saith to him: Every man at first setteth forth good wine, and when men have well drunk, then that which is inferior: but thou hast kept the good wine until now. This beginning of miracles did Jesus in Cana of Galilee, and manifested His glory, and His disciples believed in Him.

THIRD SUNDAY AFTER EPIPHANY

INTROIT. Adore God, all ye His angels: Sion heard, and was glad; and the daughters of Juda rejoiced.

The Lord hath reigned; let the earth rejoice; let the multitude of the isles be glad. Glory be to the Father, etc.

COLLECT. Almighty and everlasting God, mercifully look upon our infirmities, and stretch forth the right hand of Thy Majesty to help and defend us. Through Our Lord Jesus Christ, etc. *Amen.*

EPISTLE. Rom 12:16–21. Brethren: Be not wise in your own conceit. Render to no man evil for evil: provide good things not only before God, but also before all men. If it be possible, as much as is in you, have peace with all men. Do not revenge yourselves, dearly beloved, but give place unto wrath: for it is written: Vengeance is Mine; I will repay, saith the Lord. But if thine enemy hunger, feed him; if he thirst, give him drink: for doing this, thou shalt heap coals of fire upon his head. Be not overcome by evil, but overcome evil with good.

GRADUAL. The Gentiles shall fear Thy name, O Lord, and all the kings of the earth, Thy glory. For the Lord hath built up Sion, and He shall be seen in His majesty. Alleluia, alleluia. The Lord hath reigned, let the earth rejoice: let many islands be glad. Alleluia.

GOSPEL. Mt 8:1–13. At that time: When Jesus was come down from the mountain, great crowds followed Him. And behold, a leper came and worshipped Him, saying: Lord, if Thou wilt, Thou canst make me clean. And Jesus stretching forth His hand, touched him, saying: I will; be thou made clean. And forthwith his leprosy was cleansed. And Jesus saith to him: See thou tell no man: but go, show thyself to the priest, and offer the gift which Moses commanded for a testimony to them. And on His entering into Capharnaum, a centurion came to Him, beseeching Him, and saying: Lord, my servant lieth at home sick of the palsy, and is grievously tormented. And Jesus saith to him: I will come and heal him. And the centurion making answer, said: Lord, I am not worthy that Thou shouldst enter under my roof;

but only say the word, and my servant shall be healed. For I also am a man subject to authority, having soldiers under me; and I say to one: Go, and he goeth; and to another: Come, and he cometh; and to my servant: Do this, and he doeth it. And Jesus, hearing this, marveled, and said to those who followed Him: Truly, I say to you, I have not found so great faith in Israel. And I say to you, that many shall come from the East and the West, and shall recline at table with Abraham, and Isaac, and Jacob, in the kingdom of heaven. But the children of the kingdom shall be cast out into the outer darkness; there shall be wailing and gnashing of teeth. And Jesus said to the centurion: Go, and as thou hast believed, be it done to thee. And the servant was healed at the same hour.

OFFERTORY. The right hand of the Lord hath wrought strength, the right hand of the Lord hath exalted me: I shall not die, but live, and shall declare the works of the Lord.

SECRET. May these offerings, O Lord, we beseech Thee, cleanse us from our sins, and sanctify the bodies and minds of Thy servants for the celebration of this sacrifice. Through Our Lord Jesus Christ, etc. *Amen.*

COMMUNION. They all wondered at these things, which proceeded from the mouth of God.

POSTCOMMUNION. We beseech Thee, O Lord, that we, to whom Thou vouchsafest the enjoyment of so great mysteries, may be fitted truly to receive the benefits thereof. Through Our Lord Jesus Christ, etc. *Amen.*

FOURTH SUNDAY AFTER EPIPHANY

INTROIT. Adore God, all ye His angels: Sion heard, and was glad; and the daughters of Juda rejoiced.

COLLECT. O God, Who knowest us to be set in the midst of so great dangers that, by reason of the frailty of our nature, we cannot stand: grant to us health of mind and body, that those things which we suffer for our sins we may by Thine aid overcome. Through Our Lord Jesus Christ, etc. *Amen.*

EPISTLE. Rom 13:8–10. Brethren: Owe no man anything, but to love one another; for he who loveth the neighbor hath fulfilled the law. For: thou shalt not commit adultery; thou shalt not kill; thou shalt not steal; thou shalt not bear false witness; thou shalt not covet: and if there be any other commandment, it is comprised in this word: Thou shalt love thy neighbor as thyself. The love of the neighbor worketh no evil. Love, therefore, is the fulfilling of the law.

GRADUAL. The Gentiles shall fear Thy name, O Lord, and all the kings of the earth, Thy glory. For the Lord hath built up Sion, and He shall be seen in His majesty. Alleluia, alleluia. The Lord hath reigned, let the earth rejoice: let many islands be glad. Alleluia.

GOSPEL. Mt 8:23–27. At that time: When Jesus entered into the boat, His disciples followed Him. And behold, a great storm arose at sea, so that the boat was covered with the waves, but He was asleep. And His disciples came to Him, and awaked Him, saying: Lord, save us, we perish. And Jesus saith to them: Why are ye fearful, O ye of little faith? Then rising up, He commanded the winds and the sea, and a great calm ensued. But the men wondered, saying: What a One is this, for the winds and the sea obey Him?

OFFERTORY. The right hand of the Lord hath wrought strength, the right hand of the Lord hath exalted me: I shall not die, but live, and shall declare the works of the Lord.

SECRET. Grant, we beseech Thee, Almighty God, that the offering of this sacrifice may ever purify our frailty and protect it from all evil. Through Our Lord Jesus Christ, etc. *Amen.*

COMMUNION. They all wondered at these things, which proceeded from the mouth of God.

POSTCOMMUNION. May Thy gifts, O God, detach us from all earthly pleasures, and ever refresh and strengthen us with heavenly food. Through Our Lord Jesus Christ, etc. *Amen.*

FIFTH SUNDAY AFTER EPIPHANY

INTROIT. Adore God, all ye His angels: Sion heard, and was glad; and the daughters of Juda rejoiced.

COLLECT. Keep, O Lord, we beseech Thee, Thy family by Thy continual mercy; that they who lean only upon the hope of Thy heavenly grace may evermore be defended by Thy protection. Through Our Lord Jesus Christ, etc. *Amen.*

EPISTLE. Col 3:12–17. Brethren: Put ye on, as the elect of God, holy and beloved, bowels of compassion, kindness, humility, modesty, patience; bearing with one another, and forgiving one another, if any man hath a complaint against anyone; as even the Lord hath forgiven you, so ye also. But above all these things, put on charity, which is the bond of perfection; and let the peace of Christ reign in your hearts, in which also ye are called in one body; and be ye thankful. Let the word of Christ dwell in you abundantly, in all wisdom; teaching and admonishing one another in psalms, hymns, and spiritual songs, in grace, singing in your hearts to God. All whatever ye do in word, or in work, all things in the name of the Lord Jesus Christ, giving thanks to God and the Father through Jesus Christ Our Lord.

GRADUAL. The Gentiles shall fear Thy name, O Lord, and all the kings of the earth, Thy glory. For the Lord hath built up Sion, and He shall be seen in His majesty. Alleluia, alleluia. The Lord hath reigned, let the earth rejoice: let many islands be glad. Alleluia.

GOSPEL. Mt 13:24–30. At that time: Jesus spoke this parable to the multitudes: The kingdom of heaven is likened to a man who sowed good seed in his field. But while the men were asleep, his enemy came and sowed cockle among the wheat, and went away. And when the blade sprang up and brought forth fruit, then appeared also the cockle. And the servants of the householder came and said to him: Sir, didst thou not sow good seed in thy field? Whence then hath it cockle?

And he said to them: An enemy hath done this. And the servants said to him: Wilt thou that we go and gather it up? And he said: No, lest in gathering up the cockle ye root up the wheat also with it. Let both grow together until the harvest, and in the time of the harvest I will say to the reapers: Gather up first the cockle, and bind it in bundles to burn, but the wheat gather into my barn.

OFFERTORY. The right hand of the Lord hath wrought strength, the right hand of the Lord hath exalted me: I shall not die, but live, and shall declare the works of the Lord.

SECRET. We offer to Thee, O Lord, the sacrifice of propitiation: that Thou mayest mercifully absolve us from our sins, and mayest deign Thyself direct our inconstant hearts. Through Our Lord Jesus Christ, etc. *Amen.*

COMMUNION. They all wondered at these things, which proceeded from the mouth of God.

POSTCOMMUNION. We beseech Thee, Almighty God, that we may receive the effect of that salvation, of which in these mysteries we have received a pledge. Through Our Lord Jesus Christ, etc. *Amen.*

SIXTH SUNDAY AFTER EPIPHANY

INTROIT. Adore God, all ye His angels: Sion heard, and was glad; and the daughters of Juda rejoiced.

COLLECT. Grant us, we beseech Thee, O Almighty God, ever to think such things as are reasonable, and, in every word and work of ours, to do that which is pleasing in Thy sight. Through Our Lord Jesus Christ, etc. *Amen.*

EPISTLE. 1 Thes 1:2–10. Brethren: We give thanks to God always for you all, making remembrance of you in our prayers, without ceasing, being mindful of the work of your faith, and labor, and charity, and the endurance of the hope of Our Lord Jesus Christ, before our God and Father: knowing, brethren, beloved of God, your election; because our gospel to you was not in word only, but also in power, and in the Holy Spirit, and in much fullness, as ye know what manner of men we were among you for your sake. And ye became followers of us and of the Lord; having received the word in much tribulation, with joy of the Holy Spirit: so that ye became a model to all who believe in Macedonia and Achaia. For from you the Word of the Lord was spread abroad, not only in Macedonia and Achaia, but also in every place your faith, which is toward God, hath gone forth: so that we have no need to say anything. For they themselves relate of us what manner of entrance we had among you; and how ye turned to God from idols, to serve the living and true God, and to wait for His Son from heaven (Whom He raised from the dead), Jesus, Who hath delivered us from the wrath to come.

GRADUAL. The Gentiles shall fear Thy name, O Lord, and all the kings of the earth, Thy glory. For the Lord hath built up Sion, and He shall be seen in His majesty. Alleluia, alleluia. The Lord hath reigned, let the earth rejoice: let many islands be glad. Alleluia.

GOSPEL. Mt 13:31–35. At that time: Jesus spake this parable to the multitudes: The kingdom of heaven is like to a grain of mustard, which a man took and sowed in his field: which indeed is the least of all seeds: but when it is grown up, it is greater than all herbs, and becometh a tree; so that the birds of the air come and lodge in the branches thereof. Another parable He spake to them: The kingdom of heaven is like to leaven, which a woman took and hid in three measures of meal, until the whole was leavened. All these things Jesus spake to the crowds in parables: and without parables He did not speak to them: that what was spoken by the prophet might be fulfilled, when he saith: I will open My mouth in parables. I will utter things hidden from the foundation of the world.

OFFERTORY. The right hand of the Lord hath wrought strength, the right hand of the Lord hath exalted me: I shall not die, but live, and shall declare the works of the Lord.

SECRET. May this oblation, O God, we beseech Thee, cleanse, renew, govern, and protect us. Through Our Lord Jesus Christ, etc. *Amen.*

COMMUNION. They all wondered at these things, which proceeded from the mouth of God.

POSTCOMMUNION. Being fed, O Lord, with heavenly delights, we beseech Thee that we may ever hunger after those things by which we truly live. Through Our Lord Jesus Christ, etc. *Amen.*

SEPTUAGESIMA

INTROIT. The groanings of death surrounded me, the sorrows of hell encompassed me: and in my affliction I called upon the Lord, and He heard my voice from His holy temple.

I will love Thee, O Lord, my strength: the Lord is my rock, my refuge, and my deliverer.

Glory be to the Father, etc.

COLLECT. O Lord, we beseech Thee, graciously hear the prayers of Thy people: that we, who are justly afflicted for our sins, may be mercifully delivered by Thy goodness, for the glory of Thy name. Through Our Lord Jesus Christ, etc. *Amen.*

EPISTLE. 1 Cor 9:24–10:5. Brethren: Know ye not that they who run in the race-ground, all run indeed, but one receiveth the prize? So run that ye may obtain. And everyone who striveth for the mastery refraineth himself from all things, and they, indeed, that they may receive a perishable crown: but we, an imperishable. I therefore so run, not as an uncertainty; I so fight, not as one beating the air. But I chastise my body, and bring it under subjection, lest perhaps, when I have preached to others, I myself become a reprobate. For I would not have you ignorant, brethren, that our fathers were all under the cloud, and all passed through the sea, and all were baptized unto Moses in the cloud, and in the sea; and all did eat the same spiritual food, and all drank the same spiritual drink (and they drank of the spiritual rock which followed them: and the rock was Christ). But with the most of them God was not well pleased.

GRADUAL. The helper in due time, in tribulation: let them trust in Thee, who know Thee: for Thou dost not forsake them that seek Thee, O Lord. For the poor man shall not be forgotten to the end: the patience of the poor shall not perish forever: arise, O Lord, let not man be strengthened.

GOSPEL. Mt 20:1–16. At that time: Jesus spoke to His disciples this parable: The kingdom of heaven is like to a householder, who went out early in the morning to hire laborers into his vineyard. And having agreed with the laborers for a shilling a day, he sent them into his vineyard. And going out about the third hour, he saw others standing idle in the marketplace. And he said to them: Go ye also into my vineyard, and I will give you what is just. And they went. And again he went out about the sixth and the ninth hour, and did in like manner. But about the eleventh he went out, and found others standing, and saith to them: Why stand ye here all the day idle? They say to him: Because no one hath hired us. He saith to them: Go ye also into my vineyard. And when evening was come, the lord of the vineyard saith to his steward: Call the laborers, and pay them their hire, beginning from the last even to the first. When therefore they who had come about the eleventh hour came forward, they received each one a shilling. But when the first also came, they thought that they should receive more; and they also received each one a shilling. And when they received it, they murmured against the householder, saying: These last have worked one hour, and thou hast made them equal to us, who have borne the burden of the day, and the burning heat. But he answered and said to one of them: Friend, I do thee no wrong: Didst thou not agree with me for a shilling? Take what is thine and go. It is my will also to give to this last even as to thee. Is it not lawful for me to do what I will? Is thine eye evil, because I am good? So shall the last be first, and the first last. For many are called, but few are chosen.

OFFERTORY. It is good to give praise to the Lord, and to sing to Thy name, O most High.

SECRET. Receive, we beseech Thee, O Lord, our gifts and prayers: and both cleanse us by these heavenly mysteries, and graciously hear us. Through Our Lord Jesus Christ, etc. *Amen.*

COMMUNION. Make Thy face to shine upon Thy servant, and save me in Thy mercy: let me not be confounded, O Lord, for I have called upon Thee.

POSTCOMMUNION. May Thy faithful, O God, be strengthened by Thy gifts; that partaking of them, they may still desire them, and, desiring them, may constantly receive them. Through Our Lord Jesus Christ, etc. *Amen.*

SEXAGESIMA

INTROIT. Arise, why sleepest Thou, O Lord? arise, and cast us not off forever: Why turnest Thou away Thy face and forgettest our trouble? Our belly hath cleaved unto the earth: arise, O Lord, help us and deliver us.

We have heard with our ears, O God; our fathers have declared unto us. Glory be to the Father, etc.

COLLECT. O God, Who seest that we put not our trust in anything that we do: mercifully grant that, through the protection of the Doctor of the Gentiles, we may be defended against all adversity. Through Our Lord Jesus Christ, etc. *Amen.*

EPISTLE. 2 Cor 11:19–12:9. Brethren: Ye willingly suffer the foolish, whereas ye yourselves are wise. For ye suffer if anyone bring you into bondage, if a man devour you, if a man take, if a man exalt himself, if a man strike you on the face. I speak according to dishonor, as though we had been weak in this respect. Wherein if anyone is bold (I speak foolishly), I am bold also. They are Hebrews; I also. They are Israelites; I also. They are the seed of Abraham; I also. They are ministers of Christ (I speak as foolish); I more so: in many more labors, in prisons more frequently, in stripes above measure, in deaths often. From the Jews I received five times forty stripes save one. Thrice I was beaten with rods; once I was stoned; thrice I suffered shipwreck; a night and a day have I been in the deep; in journeyings often, perils of rivers, perils of robbers, perils from my nation, perils from the Gentiles, perils in the city, perils in the wilderness, perils in the sea, perils among false brethren; in labor and distress, in watchings often, in hunger and thirst, in fastings often, in cold and nakedness; besides the things that are without, my daily charge, the care of all the churches. Who is weak, and I am not weak? Who is scandalized, and I do not burn? If I must glory, I will glory in the things which concern my weakness. God, even the Father of Our Lord Jesus Christ, Who is blessed forever, knoweth that I do not lie. At Damascus, the governor of King Aretas guarded the city of the Damascenes to apprehend me; and through a window, in a basket, was I let down by the wall, and so I escaped his hands. If I must glory (it is not indeed expedient); but I will come to the visions and revelations of the Lord. I know a man in Christ, above fourteen years ago (whether in the body, I know not, or whether out of the body, I know not; God knoweth), such a one caught up to the third heaven. And I know such a man (whether in the body or out of the body, I know not; God knoweth), that he was caught up into paradise; and heard secret words, which it is not allowed for man to utter. For such a one I will glory: but for myself I will not glory, but in mine infirmities. For, although I would glory, I shall not be foolish; for I will say the truth; but I forbear, lest any man should esteem me beyond what he seeth in me, or heareth something from me. And lest the greatness of the revelation should lift me up, a thorn in my flesh, an angel of Satan, was given me to buffet me. For which cause I besought the Lord thrice, that it might depart from me. And He said to me: My grace is sufficient for thee; for power is perfected in weakness. Gladly, therefore, will I glory in mine infirmities, that the power of Christ may dwell in me.

GRADUAL. Let the Gentiles know that God is Thy name: Thou alone art the most High over all the earth. O my God, make them like a wheel, and as stubble before the wind.

GOSPEL. Lk 8:4–15. At that time: When a great crowd was gathered together, and they hastened to Him out of the cities, He spake by a similitude: The sower went out to sow his seed. And as he sowed, some fell by the wayside, and it was trodden down, and the birds of the air ate it up. And some fell on the rock, and as soon as it had sprung up, it withered away, because it had no moisture. And some fell among thorns, and the thorns, growing up with it, choked it. And some fell on good ground, and sprang up, and yielded fruit a hundredfold. Saying these things, He cried out: He who hath ears to hear, let him hear. And His disciples asked Him what this parable might be. And He said to them: To you it is given to know the mystery of the Kingdom of God, but to the rest in parables; that seeing, they may not see, and hearing, they may not understand. Now the parable is this: The seed is the word of God. And those by the wayside are they who hear; then the devil cometh, and taketh the word out of their heart, lest believing they should be saved. Now those upon the rock are they who, when they hear, receive the word with joy: and these have no root, for they believe for a while, and in time of temptation they fall away. And that which fell among the thorns are they who, when they have heard, go forth and are choked with cares and riches and pleasures of life, and bring no fruit to maturity. But that on the good ground are they who in a good and excellent heart, hearing the word, retain it, and bring forth fruit in patience.

OFFERTORY. Perfect Thou my goings in Thy paths, that my footsteps be not moved: incline Thine ear, and hear my words: show forth Thy wonderful mercies, Thou Who savest them that trust in Thee, O Lord.

SECRET. May the sacrifice offered to Thee, O Lord, ever enliven and protect us. Through Our Lord Jesus Christ, etc. *Amen.*

COMMUNION. I will go in to the altar of God: to God Who giveth joy to my youth.

POSTCOMMUNION. Grant, we humbly beseech Thee, Almighty God, that those whom Thou refreshest with Thy Sacraments may serve Thee worthily by a life well-pleasing to Thee. Through Our Lord Jesus Christ, etc. *Amen.*

QUINQUAGESIMA

INTROIT. Be Thou unto me a God, a protector, and a place of refuge, to save me; for Thou art my strength and my refuge: and for Thy name's sake Thou wilt be my leader, and wilt nourish me.

In Thee, O Lord, have I hoped, let me never be confounded: deliver me in Thy justice, and set me free.

Glory be to the Father, etc.

COLLECT. O Lord, we beseech Thee, graciously hear our prayers; that we, being loosed from all chains of our sins, may by Thee be defended against all adversity. Through Our Lord Jesus Christ, etc. *Amen.*

EPISTLE. 1 Cor 13:1–13. Brethren: If I speak with the tongues of men and of angels, and have not charity, I am become as sounding brass, or a tinkling cymbal.

And if I have prophecy, and know all the mysteries and all knowledge, and if I have all faith, so as to remove mountains, and have not charity, I am nothing. And if I should distribute all my goods to feed the poor, and if I should deliver my body to be burned, and have not charity, it profiteth me nothing. Charity is patient, is kind: charity envieth not; dealeth not perversely; is not puffed up; is not ambitious; seeketh not her own; is not provoked to anger; thinketh no evil; rejoiceth not in iniquity, but rejoiceth with the truth; beareth all things, believeth all things, hopeth all things, endureth all things. Charity never falleth away, whether prophecies shall be made void, or tongues shall cease, or knowledge be made void. For we know in part, and we prophesy in part. But when that which is perfect is come, that which is in part shall be done away. When I was a child, I spake as a child, I understood as a child, I thought as a child: but when I became a man, I put away childish things. We now see through a glass darkly; but then, face-to-face. Now I know in part; but then I shall know even as I am known. And now remain faith, hope, charity, these three; but the greatest of these three is charity.

GRADUAL. Thou art the God that alone dost wonders; Thou hast made Thy power known among the nations. With Thine arm Thou hast redeemed Thy people, the children of Israel and of Joseph.

GOSPEL. Lk 18:31–43. At that time: Jesus took to Him the Twelve and said to them: Behold, we are going up to Jerusalem, and all things will be accomplished which were written by the prophets concerning the Son of Man. For He will be delivered up to the Gentiles, and mocked, and scourged, and spit upon. And after they have scourged Him, they will put Him to death, and the third day He will rise again. And they understood none of these things, and this word was hidden from them, and they understood not the things which were said. Now it came to pass, as He drew near to Jericho, that a certain blind man sat by the wayside, begging. And when he heard the multitude passing by, he asked what it meant. And they told him that Jesus of Nazareth was passing by. And he cried out, saying: Jesus, Son of David, have mercy on me. And they who went before, rebuked him, charging him to be silent. But he cried out much more: Son of David, have mercy on me. And Jesus stopped and commanded him to be brought to Him. And when he was come near, He asked him, saying: What wilt thou that I do for thee? And he said: Lord, that I may receive my sight. And Jesus said to him: Receive thy sight: thy faith hath made thee whole. And immediately he received his sight, and followed Him, glorifying God. And all the people, when they saw it, gave praise to God.

OFFERTORY. Blessed art Thou O Lord, teach me Thy justifications: with my lips I have pronounced all the judgments of Thy mouth.

SECRET. May these offerings, O Lord, we beseech Thee, cleanse us from our sins, and sanctify the bodies and minds of Thy servants for the celebration of this sacrifice. Through Our Lord Jesus Christ, etc. *Amen.*

COMMUNION. They did eat, and were filled exceedingly, and the Lord gave them their desire: they were not defrauded of that which they craved.

POSTCOMMUNION. We beseech Thee, Almighty God, that we who have received celestial food may be defended by it against all adversities. Through Our Lord Jesus Christ, etc. *Amen.*

ASH WEDNESDAY

(*For the* Blessing of the Ashes *see p. 186.*)

INTROIT. Thou hast mercy upon all, O Lord, and hatest none of the things which Thou hast made, overlooking the sins of men that they may repent, and sparing them; for Thou art the Lord our God.

Have mercy on me, O God, have mercy on me; for my soul trusteth in Thee.

Glory be to the Father, etc.

COLLECT. Grant, O Lord, unto Thy faithful people that they may begin the solemn service of fasting with due piety, and with tranquil devotion perform the same. Through Our Lord Jesus Christ, etc. *Amen.*

LESSON. Jl 2:12–19. Thus saith the Lord: Be converted to Me with all your heart, with fasting, and with weeping, and with mourning. And rend your hearts and not your garments, and turn to the Lord your God; for He is gracious and merciful, patient and rich in mercy, and ready to repent of the evil. Who knoweth but He will turn and forgive, and leave a blessing behind Him, and sacrifice and libation to the Lord your God? Blow the trumpet in Sion: sanctify a fast; call a solemn assembly; gather together the people; sanctify the congregation; assemble the ancients; gather together the little ones, and them that suck at the breasts; let the bridegroom go forth from his bed, and the bride out of her bridechamber. Between the porch and the altar the priests, the Lord's ministers, shall weep, and shall say: Spare, O Lord, spare Thy people; and give not Thine inheritance to reproach, that the heathens should rule over them. Why should they say among the nations: Where is their God? The Lord hath been zealous for His land, and hath spared His people. And the Lord answered, and said to His people: Behold, I will send you corn, and wine, and oil, and ye shall be filled with them; and I will no more make you a reproach among the nations, saith the Lord Almighty.

GRADUAL. Have mercy on me, O God, have mercy on me: for my soul trusteth in Thee. He hath sent from heaven, and delivered me; He hath made them a reproach that trod upon me.

GOSPEL. Mt 6:16–21. At that time: Jesus said to His disciples: When ye fast, be not of a sad countenance, as the hypocrites. For they disfigure their faces, that to men they may appear to fast. Truly I say to you, they have got their reward. But thou, when thou fastest, anoint thy head, and wash thy face: that thou appear not to men to fast, but to thy Father, Who is in secret: and thy Father, Who seeth in secret, will repay thee. Lay not up for yourselves treasures on earth, where rust and moth consume, and where thieves break through and steal. But lay up for yourselves treasures in heaven; where neither rust nor moth doth consume, and where thieves do not break through nor steal. For where thy treasure is, there is thy heart also.

OFFERTORY. I will extol Thee, O Lord, for Thou hast upheld me; and hast not made mine enemies to rejoice over me: O Lord, I have cried to Thee, and Thou hast healed me.

SECRET. Fit us, we beseech Thee, O Lord, to offer worthily to Thee these gifts, by which we celebrate the opening of this venerable mystery. Through Our Lord Jesus Christ, etc. *Amen.*

COMMUNION. He who shall meditate upon the law of the Lord, day and night, shall bring forth his fruit in due season.

POSTCOMMUNION. May the Sacraments which we have received, O Lord, afford us support: that our fasts may be pleasing to Thee, and be a healing remedy to us. Through Our Lord Jesus Christ, etc. *Amen.*

PRAYER OVER THE PEOPLE. Incline, O Lord, the ear of Thy mercy unto Thy people prostrate before Thy Majesty; that, as we have been refreshed by Thy divine gift, we may ever be sustained by heavenly aids. Through Our Lord Jesus Christ, etc. *Amen.*

FIRST SUNDAY IN LENT

INTROIT. He shall call upon Me, and I will hear him; I will deliver him, and glorify him; I will fill him with length of days.

He that dwelleth in the help of the Most High shall abide under the protection of the God of heaven.

Glory be to the Father, etc.

COLLECT. O God, Who dost every year purify Thy Church by the fast of forty days: grant unto this Thy family that what things they strive to obtain at Thy hand by abstinence, they may turn to profit by good works. Through Our Lord Jesus Christ, etc. *Amen.*

EPISTLE. 2 Cor 6:1–10. Brethren: We do exhort, that ye receive not the grace of God in vain. For He saith: In an acceptable time I have heard thee, and in the day of salvation I have helped thee. Behold, now is the acceptable time: behold, now is the day of salvation. Giving no offense to anyone, that our ministry may not be blamed: but in all let us present ourselves as ministers of God in much patience, in tribulations, in necessities, in distresses, in stripes, in prisons, in tumults, in labors, in watchings, in fastings, in chastity, in knowledge, in long-suffering, in sweetness, in the Holy Spirit, in charity unfeigned, in the word of truth, in the power of God; by the armor of justice on the right hand and on the left, by glory and dishonor, by evil report and good report; as deceivers and true; as unknown and known; as dying, and behold we live; as chastened, and not killed; as sorrowful, yet always rejoicing; as needy, yet enriching many: as having nothing, and possessing all things.

GRADUAL. God hath given His angels charge over thee, to keep thee in all thy ways. In their hands they shall bear thee up, lest at any time thou dash thy foot against a stone.

GOSPEL. Mt 4:1–11. At that time: Jesus was led by the Spirit into the desert, to be tempted by the devil. And when He had fasted forty days and forty nights, afterward He was hungry. And the tempter came and said to Him: If Thou art the Son of God, command that these stones be made bread. But He answered and said: It is written: Not by bread alone doth man live, but by every word that proceedeth from the mouth of God. Then the devil took Him up into the holy city, and set Him upon the pinnacle of the temple, and said to Him: If Thou art the Son of God, cast Thyself down: for it is written: He hath given His angels charge over Thee, and in their hands they shall bear Thee up, lest Thou dash Thy foot against a stone. Jesus said to him: It is written again: Thou shalt not tempt the Lord thy God. Again the devil took Him up into a very high mountain, and showed Him all the kingdoms of the world, and their glory, and said to Him: All these will I give Thee, if Thou wilt fall down and worship me. Then Jesus saith to him: Begone, Satan, for it is written: The Lord thy God shalt thou worship, and Him only shalt thou serve. Then the devil left Him; and behold, angels came and ministered to Him.

OFFERTORY. The Lord will overshadow thee with His shoulders, and under His wings thou shalt trust: His truth shall compass thee with a shield.

SECRET. We solemnly offer the sacrifice of the beginning of Lent, beseeching Thee, O Lord, that while we refrain from carnal feasting, we may likewise abstain from harmful pleasures. Through Our Lord Jesus Christ, etc. *Amen.*

COMMUNION. The Lord will overshadow thee with His shoulders, and under His wings thou shalt trust: His truth shall compass thee with a shield.

POSTCOMMUNION. May the holy oblation of Thy Sacrament refresh us, O Lord, and purifying us from our old life, make us pass on to the fellowship of Thy saving mystery. Through Our Lord Jesus Christ, etc. *Amen.*

SECOND SUNDAY IN LENT

INTROIT. Call to remembrance, O Lord, Thy compassion and Thy mercies, which are of old: lest at any time our enemies rule over us: deliver us, O God of Israel, from all our tribulations.

To Thee, O Lord, have I lifted up my soul: in Thee, O my God, I put my trust; let me not be ashamed.

Glory be to the Father, etc.

COLLECT. Almighty God, Who seest that we have no power of ourselves: keep us both inwardly and outwardly; that we may be defended from all adversities which may happen to the body, and from all evil thoughts which may hurt the soul. Through Our Lord Jesus Christ, etc. *Amen.*

EPISTLE. 1 Thes 4:1–7. Brethren: We ask and beseech you by the Lord Jesus, that as ye have received from us how ye ought to walk, and please God, so also ye would walk, that ye may abound the more. For ye know what commands I gave you by the Lord Jesus. For this is the will of God, your sanctification; that ye abstain from fornication; that every one of you know how to possess his vessel in sanctification and honor, not in the passion of lust, even as the Gentiles, who know not God; and that no man overreach, or circumvent his brother in the matter; because the Lord is the Avenger of all those things, as we have told you before, and testified. For God hath not called us to uncleanness, but to holiness: in Christ Jesus Our Lord.

GRADUAL. The troubles of my heart are multiplied; deliver me from my necessities, O Lord. See my abjection and my labor, and forgive all my sins.

GOSPEL. Mt 17:1–9. At that time: Jesus taketh with Him Peter and James, and John his brother, and bringeth them up on a high mountain apart; and was transfigured before them. And His face shone as the sun, and His garments became white as snow. And behold, there appeared to them Moses and Elias talking with Him. And Peter answered and said to Jesus: Lord, it is good for us to be here; if Thou wilt, let us make here three tents, one for Thee, and one for Moses, and one for Elias. And while he was yet speaking, behold a bright cloud overshadowed them. And lo! a voice from the cloud, saying: This is My beloved Son, in Whom I am well pleased; hear ye Him. And when the disciples heard it, they fell on their face, and were very much afraid. And Jesus came and touched them, and said to them: Arise, and fear not. And when they lifted up their eyes, they saw no one, but Jesus alone. And as they came down from the mountain, Jesus charged them, saying: Tell the vision to no man, till the Son of Man be risen from the dead.

OFFERTORY. I will meditate on Thy commandments which I have loved exceedingly: and I will lift up my hands to Thy commandments, which I have loved.

SECRET. Favorably regard, we beseech Thee, O Lord, these present sacrifices, that they may profit us both unto devotion and salvation. Through Our Lord Jesus Christ, etc. *Amen.*

COMMUNION. Understand my cry: hearken to the voice of my prayer, O my King and my God: for to Thee will I pray, O Lord.

POSTCOMMUNION. Grant, we humbly beseech Thee, Almighty God, that those whom Thou refreshest with Thy Sacraments may serve Thee worthily by a life well-pleasing to Thee. Through Our Lord Jesus Christ, etc. *Amen.*

THIRD SUNDAY IN LENT

INTROIT. Mine eyes are ever toward the Lord: for He shall pluck my feet out of the snare: look Thou upon me, and have mercy on me, for I am alone and poor.

To Thee, O Lord, have I lifted up my soul: in Thee, O my God, I put my trust: let me not be ashamed.

Glory be to the Father, etc.

COLLECT. We beseech Thee, Almighty God, look upon the desires of Thy humble servants, and stretch forth the right hand of Thy Majesty, to be our defense. Through Our Lord Jesus Christ, etc. *Amen.*

EPISTLE. Eph 5:1–9. Brethren: Be ye followers of God, as beloved children; and walk in love, as Christ also hath loved us, and delivered Himself up for us an Offering and Sacrifice to God, for a sweet-smelling savor. But let not fornication, and all uncleanness, or covetousness, be even named among you, as it becometh saints; or filthiness, or foolish talking, or buffoonery, which is not to the purpose: but rather thanksgiving. For know ye this, understanding that no fornicator, or unclean or covetous man, which is idolatry, hath inheritance in the Kingdom of the Christ, and God. Let no man deceive you with vain words: for because of these things the anger of God cometh on the children of unbelief. Be not therefore partakers with them. For ye were once darkness, but now light in the Lord. Walk as children of light: for the fruit of the light is in all goodness, and justice, and truth.

GRADUAL. Arise, O Lord, let not man prevail: let the Gentiles be judged in Thy sight. When mine enemy shall be turned back, they shall be weakened and perish before Thy face.

GOSPEL. Lk 11:14–28. At that time: Jesus was casting out a devil, and it was dumb; and when he had cast out the devil, the dumb man spake, and the crowds wondered; but some of them said: He casteth out devils through Beelzebub, the prince of devils. But others, tempting, sought of Him a sign from heaven. But seeing their thoughts, He said to them: Every kingdom divided against itself is brought to desolation, and house against house falleth. And if Satan also is divided against himself, how shall his kingdom stand? since ye say, that by Beelzebub I cast out the devils. Now if I cast out the devils by Beelzebub, by whom do your children cast them out? Therefore, they shall be your judges. But if, by the finger of God, I cast out the devils, doubtless the Kingdom of God is come upon you. When the strong one armed guardeth his court, his goods are secure, but if one stronger than he come upon him, and overcome him, he taketh away all his armor wherein he trusted, and distributeth his spoils. He who is not with Me, is against Me: and he who gathereth not with Me, scattereth. When the unclean spirit is gone out of a man, he walketh through places without water, seeking rest; and not finding it, he saith: I will return to my house, whence I came out; and when he cometh, he findeth it swept and adorned. Then he goeth and taketh with him seven other spirits more wicked than himself, and they enter in, and dwell there; and the last state of that man becometh worse than the first. And it came to pass, as He spake these things, that a certain woman from the crowd, lifting up her voice, said to Him: Happy is the womb which bore Thee, and the breasts which Thou hast sucked. But He said: Yea, rather happy are they who hear the Word of God, and keep it.

OFFERTORY. The justices of the Lord are right, rejoicing hearts, and His judgments are sweeter than honey and the honeycomb; for Thy servant keepeth them.

SECRET. May this Victim, O Lord, we beseech Thee, cleanse us from our sins; and sanctify the bodies and minds of Thy servants for the celebration of this sacrifice. Through Our Lord Jesus Christ, etc. *Amen.*

COMMUNION. The sparrow hath found herself a house, and the turtle a nest, where she may lay her young ones: Thine altars, O Lord of hosts, my King, and my God; blessed are they that dwell in Thy house, they shall praise Thee forever and ever.

POSTCOMMUNION. Mercifully absolve us, we beseech Thee, O Lord, from all guilt and danger, since Thou dost admit us to be partakers of this great mystery. Through Our Lord Jesus Christ, etc. *Amen.*

FOURTH SUNDAY IN LENT

INTROIT. Rejoice, O Jerusalem, and come together all ye that love her; rejoice with joy, ye that have been in sorrow: that ye may exult, and be filled from the breasts of your consolation.

I was glad at the things that were said unto me: We will go into the house of the Lord.

Glory be to the Father, etc.

COLLECT. Grant, we beseech Thee, Almighty God, that we who for our deeds are justly punished, by the comfort of Thy grace may mercifully be relieved. Through Our Lord Jesus Christ, etc. *Amen.*

EPISTLE. Gal 4:22–31. Brethren: It is written: Abraham had two sons; one by a bond-maid, and one by a free-woman. But he by the bond-maid was born after the flesh; and he by the free-woman, by promise. Which things are an allegory. For these are two covenants: one indeed on Mount Sinai, which engendereth to bondage, which is Agar; for Sinai is a mount in Arabia, which correspondeth with the present Jerusalem, and is in bondage with her children. But that Jerusalem which is above is free; which is our mother. For it is written: Rejoice, thou barren, who bearest not: break forth and cry, thou who travailest not; for many are the children of the desolate one, rather than of her who hath a husband. But we, brethren, according to Isaac are children of promise. But as then he who was born according to the flesh persecuted him who was according to the spirit, so now also. But what saith the Scripture? Cast forth the bond-maid and her son; for the son of the bond-maid shall not be heir with the son of the free-woman. Therefore, brethren, we are not children of the bond-maid, but of the free-woman: with the liberty wherewith Christ hath made us free.

GRADUAL. I rejoiced at the things that were said to me: We shall go into the house of the Lord. Let peace be in thy strength, and abundance in thy towers.

GOSPEL. Jn 6:1–15. At that time: Jesus went over the lake of Galilee, which is that of Tiberias; and a great crowd followed Him, because they saw the miracles which He performed on those who were infirm. Jesus therefore went up the mountain, and there sat with His disciples. Now the Passover, the festival day of the Jews, was at hand. When Jesus therefore lifted up His eyes, and saw that a great crowd was coming to Him, He said to Philip: Whence shall we buy bread that these may eat? And this He said to try him, for He Himself knew what He would do. Philip answered Him: Loaves to the amount of two hundred shillings are not sufficient for them that every one may take a little. One of His disciples, Andrew, the brother of Simon Peter, saith to Him: There is a boy here who hath five barley loaves, and two fishes: But what are these among so many? Then Jesus said: Make the men sit down. Now there was much grass in the place. The men therefore sat down, in number about five thousand. And Jesus took the loaves; and when He had given thanks, He distributed to those who were seated; in like manner also of the fishes, as much as they would. And when they were filled, He said to His disciples: Gather up the broken meat which remaineth, lest it be lost. They gathered up, therefore, and filled twelve baskets with the broken meat, of the five barley loaves, which remained over and above to those who had eaten. Now those men, when they had seen what a sign Jesus had performed, said: This is, of a truth, the prophet Who is to come into the world. Jesus, therefore, knowing that they would come to take Him by force, and make Him king, fled again into the mountain by Himself.

OFFERTORY. Praise ye the Lord, for He is good: sing ye to His name for He is sweet: whatsoever He pleased He hath done in heaven and in earth.

SECRET. Favorably regard, we beseech Thee, O Lord, these present sacrifices: that they may profit us both unto devotion and salvation. Through Our Lord Jesus Christ, etc. *Amen.*

COMMUNION. Jerusalem, which is built as a city, which is compact together; for thither did the tribes go up, the tribes of the Lord, to praise Thy name, O Lord.

POSTCOMMUNION. Grant, we beseech Thee, O merciful God, that we may sincerely respect and receive with faith Thy holy mysteries, with which Thou daily feedest us. Through Our Lord Jesus Christ, etc. *Amen.*

PASSION SUNDAY

INTROIT. Judge me, O God, and distinguish my cause from the nation that is not holy: deliver me from the unjust and deceitful man, for Thou art my God and my strength.

Send forth Thy light and Thy truth, they have led me, and brought me unto Thy holy hill, and into Thy tabernacles.

COLLECT. We beseech Thee, Almighty God, to look down mercifully upon this Thy family; that by Thy great goodness they be governed in body, and by Thy holy keeping be guarded in mind. Through Our Lord Jesus Christ, etc. *Amen.*

EPISTLE. Heb 9:11–15. Brethren: Christ being come a High Priest of the good things to come, by the greater and better tabernacle not made with hands, that is, not of this building, neither by the blood of goats or calves, but by His own blood, entered once into the sanctuary, having obtained an eternal redemption. For if the blood of goats and bulls, and the ashes of a heifer, being sprinkled, sanctify unto the cleansing of the flesh those who are defiled, how much more shall the blood of Christ, Who, through the Holy Spirit, offered Himself without blemish to God, cleanse our conscience from dead works, to worship the living God? And for this, He is Mediator of a new covenant, that death intervening for the redemption of the transgressions, which were under the former covenant, they who are called may receive the promise of the eternal inheritance, in Christ Jesus Our Lord.

GRADUAL. Deliver me from mine enemies, O Lord: teach me to do Thy will. Thou art my deliverer, O Lord, from the angry nations: Thou wilt lift me up above them that rise up against me: from the unjust man Thou wilt deliver me.

GOSPEL. Jn 8:46–59. At that time: Jesus said to the multitudes of the Jews: Which of you shall convict Me of sin? If I say the truth of you, why do ye not believe Me? He that is of God heareth the words of God. Therefore ye hear them not, because ye are not of God. The Jews therefore answered, and said to Him: Do not we say well, that Thou art a Samaritan and hast a devil? Jesus answered: I have not a devil; but I honor my Father, and ye have dishonored Me. But I seek not Mine own glory; there is One who seeketh and judgeth. Truly, truly, I say to you: if any man keep My word, he shall not see death ever. The Jews therefore said: Now we know that Thou hast a devil. Abraham is dead, and the prophets; and Thou sayest: If any man keep My word, he shall not taste death ever. Art Thou greater than our father Abraham, who is dead? And the prophets are dead. Whom dost Thou make Thyself? Jesus answered: If I glorify Myself, My glory is nothing. It is My Father that glorifieth Me, of Whom ye say that He is your God. And ye know Him not; but I know Him. And if I should say that I know Him not, I shall be like to you, a liar. But I know Him, and keep His word. Abraham your father rejoiced that he might see My day: he saw it, and was glad. The Jews therefore said to Him: Thou art not yet fifty years old, and hast Thou seen Abraham? Jesus said to them: Truly, truly, I say to you: before Abraham was made, I am. They took up stones, therefore, to cast at Him; but Jesus hid Himself, and went out of the temple.

OFFERTORY. I will confess to Thee, O Lord, with my whole heart: render to Thy servant; I shall live and keep Thy words: enliven me according to Thy word, O Lord.

SECRET. May these offerings, we beseech Thee, O Lord, both free us from the bonds of our malice, and procure for us the gifts of Thy mercy. Through Our Lord Jesus Christ, etc. *Amen.*

COMMUNION. This is My Body which shall be delivered for you; this is the chalice of the New Testament in My Blood, saith the Lord; this do as often as you receive it, in commemoration of Me.

POSTCOMMUNION. Be present with us, O Lord our God; and defend with continual support those whom Thou hast refreshed with Thy mysteries. Through Our Lord Jesus Christ, etc. *Amen.*

PALM SUNDAY

INTROIT. O Lord, remove not Thy help far from me; look toward my defense; save me from the lion's mouth, and my lowliness from the horns of the unicorns.

O God, my God, look upon me: Why hast Thou forsaken me? Far from my salvation are the words of my sins.

COLLECT. Almighty and everlasting God, Who hast caused our Savior to take upon Him our flesh, and to suffer death upon the Cross, that all mankind should follow the example of His humility; mercifully grant that we may deserve both to keep in mind the lessons of His patience, and also to be made partakers of His Resurrection. Through the same Our Lord Jesus Christ, etc. *Amen.*

EPISTLE. Phil 2:5–11. Brethren: Have this mind in yourselves, which also was in Christ Jesus; Who, being in the form of God, thought it not robbery to be equal with God; but emptied Himself and took the form of a servant, being made in the likeness of men, and in fashion found as a man. He humbled Himself, and became obedient unto death, even the death of the Cross. Wherefore also God hath highly exalted Him, and given Him the name which is above every name: (*here all kneel*) that at the name of Jesus every knee should bend of those that are in heaven, on earth, and under the earth; and every tongue should confess that the Lord Jesus Christ is in the glory of God the Father.

GRADUAL. Thou hast held me by my right hand, and by Thy will Thou hast conducted me; and with Thy glory Thou hast received me. How good is God to Israel, to those with an upright heart; but my feet were almost moved, my steps had well-nigh slipped; because I was jealous of sinners, seeing the peace of sinners.

TRACT. O God, my God, look upon me: Why hast Thou forsaken me? Far from help are the words of my anguish. O my God, I cry by day, and Thou wilt not hear; and by night, and it shall not be reputed as folly in me. But Thou dwellest in the holy place, the praise of Israel. In Thee have our fathers hoped, they have hoped, and Thou hast delivered them. They cried to Thee, and they were saved, they trusted in Thee, and were not confounded. But I am a worm, and no man, the reproach of men, and the outcast of the people. All they that saw me have laughed me to scorn: they have spoken with the lips, and wagged the head. He hoped in the Lord, let Him deliver him: let Him save him, seeing He delighted in him. And they have looked and stared upon me. They parted my garments amongst them: and upon my vesture they cast lots. Save me from the lion's mouth; and my lowness from the horns of the unicorns. Ye that fear the Lord, praise Him: all ye the seed of Jacob, glorify Him. There shall be declared to the Lord a generation to come: and the heavens shall show forth His justice to a people that shall be born, which the Lord hath made.

The Passion of Our Lord Jesus Christ according to St. Matthew, 26–27.

At that time: Jesus said to His disciples: Ye know that after two days will be the Passover, and the Son of Man will be delivered up to be crucified. Then were gathered together the chief priests and ancients of the people into the court of the high priest, who was called Caiphas: and they consulted together, that they might take Jesus by craft, and put Him to death. But they said: Not on the festival, lest there be a tumult among the people. And when Jesus was in Bethany, in the house of Simon the leper, a woman came to Him having an alabaster box of precious ointment, and poured it on His head, as He reclined at table. And when the disciples saw it, they were displeased, saying: To what purpose is this waste? For this might have been sold for much, and given to the poor. And Jesus, knowing it, said to them: Why trouble ye this woman? for she hath wrought a good work on Me. For the poor ye have always with you: but Me ye have not always. For in pouring this ointment on My body, she hath done it for My burial. Truly I say to you, wherever this gospel shall be preached in the whole world, this also which she hath done shall be told in memory of her. Then one of the Twelve, who was called Judas Iscariot, went to the chief priests, and said to them: What will ye give me, and I will deliver Him to you? And they assigned him thirty pieces of silver. And thenceforth he sought opportunity to betray Him. And on the first day of unleavened bread, the disciples came to Jesus, saying: Where wilt Thou that we prepare for Thee to eat the Passover? But Jesus said: Go into the city to a certain man, and say to him: The Master saith: My time is at hand; with thee I keep the Passover with My disciples. And the disciples did as Jesus ordered them, and prepared the Passover. And when it was evening, He sat down with His twelve disciples. And whilst they were eating, He said: Truly I say to you, that one of you will betray Me. And they, being very much troubled, began every one to say: Is it I, Lord? But He answered and said: He that dippeth his hand with Me in the dish, he will betray Me. The Son of Man indeed goeth, as it is written of Him: but woe to that man by whom the Son of Man is betrayed. It were better for that man if he had not been born. And Judas, who betrayed Him, answered and said: Rabbi, is it I? He saith to him: Thou hast said it. And whilst they were at supper, Jesus took bread, and blessed, and broke, and gave to His disciples, and said: Take and eat: this is My Body. And He took the cup, and gave thanks, and gave to them, saying: Drink ye all of this. For this is My Blood of the New Testament which shall be shed for many, unto remission of sins. And I say to you, I will not drink henceforth of this fruit of the vine until that day when I drink it new with you in the kingdom of My Father. And when they had sung a hymn, they went out unto Mount Olivet. Then Jesus saith to them: All of you will be scandalized in regard to Me this night. For it is written: I will strike the Shepherd, and the sheep of the flock shall be scattered. But after I am risen, I will go before you into Galilee. And Peter answered and said to Him: Although all shall be scandalized in regard to Thee, I will never be scandalized. Jesus said to him: Truly I say to thee, that this night, before a cock crow, thou wilt deny Me thrice. Peter saith to Him: Yea, though I should die with Thee, I will not deny Thee. And in like manner spoke all the disciples. Then Jesus came with them into a country place called Gethsemani, and said to His disciples: Sit ye here while I go yonder, and pray. And taking with him Peter and the two sons of Zebedee, He began to grow sorrowful and to be very sad. Then He saith to them: My soul is sorrowful even unto death: stay ye here, and watch with Me. And He went a little further, and fell upon His face, and prayed, saying: My Father, if it be possible, let this cup pass away from Me. Nevertheless, not as I will, but as Thou. And He cometh to His disciples, and findeth them asleep, and saith to Peter: So, could ye not watch with Me one hour? Watch and pray, that ye enter not into temptation. The spirit indeed is willing, but the flesh is weak. Again, a second time He went away and prayed, saying: My Father, if this cup cannot pass away, except I drink it, Thy will be done. And He cometh again, and findeth them sleeping: for their eyes were heavy. And leaving them, He went away again and prayed the third time, saying the same words! Then He cometh to His disciples, and saith to them: Sleep on now, and take your rest: behold, the hour is at hand, and the Son of Man shall be betrayed into the hands of sinners. Rise, let us go: behold, he that will betray Me is at hand. While He was yet speaking, behold, Judas, one of the Twelve, came, and with him a great crowd with swords and clubs, sent from the chief priests and the ancients of the people. And His betrayer gave them a sign, saying: Whom I shall kiss, that is He; hold Him fast. And forthwith he came to Jesus, and said: Hail, Rabbi: and he kissed Him. And Jesus said to him: Friend, for what art thou come? Then they came up, and laid hands on Jesus, and held Him. And behold one of those with Jesus stretched forth his hand, and drew his sword, and struck the servant of the high priest, and cut off his ear. Then Jesus saith to him: Put up again thy sword into its place, for all they that take the sword shall perish by the sword. Thinkest thou that I cannot ask My Father, and He will give Me presently more than twelve legions of angels? How, then, shall the Scripture be fulfilled, that thus it must be done? In that hour Jesus said to the crowds: Ye are come out, as if to a robber, with swords and clubs to take Me. I sat among you daily teaching in the temple, and ye did not lay hands on Me. Now all this was done, that the Scriptures of the prophets might be fulfilled. Then the disciples all left Him, and fled. But they that held Jesus, led Him to Caiphas, the high priest, where the scribes and the ancients were assembled. And Peter followed Him afar off, even to the court of the high priest. And going in, he sat with the servants, that he might see the end. And the chief priests, and the whole council sought false testimony against Jesus, that they might put Him to death. And they found none, although many false witnesses had come forward. And last of all came two false witnesses and said: This man said, I am able to destroy the temple of God, and to build it in three days. And the high priest arose, and said to Him: Answerest Thou nothing to the things which these testify against Thee? But Jesus was silent. And the high priest said to Him: I adjure Thee by the living God that Thou tell us whether Thou art the Christ, the Son of God. Jesus saith to him: Thou hast said it. But I say to you, hereafter ye shall see the Son of Man sitting at the right hand of the power of God, and coming in the clouds of heaven. Then the high priest rent his garments, saying: He hath blasphemed. What further need have we of witnesses? Behold, now ye have heard the blasphemy. What think ye? They answered and said: He is worthy of death. Then they spat in His face, and buffeted Him; and some struck His face with the palms of their hands, saying: Prophesy to us, O Christ, who is he that struck Thee? But Peter sat without in the court; and there came to him a servant-maid, saying: Thou also wast with Jesus, the Galilean. But he denied it before all, saying: I know not what thou sayest. And as he went out of the gate, another maid saw him, and she saith to those who were there: This man also was with Jesus of Nazareth.

And again he denied it with an oath: I do not know the man. And after a while, they who stood by came and said to Peter: Surely thou also art one of them, for even thy speech doth discover thee. Then he began to invoke curses on himself, and to swear that he knew not the man. And immediately a cock crowed. And Peter remembered the words of Jesus which He had said: Before a cock crow thou wilt deny Me thrice. And he went out and wept bitterly. And when morning was come, all the chief priests and ancients of the people took counsel against Jesus, that they might put Him to death. And having bound Him, they led Him away: and delivered Him to Pontius Pilate, the governor. Then Judas, who betrayed Him, seeing that He was condemned, repented, and brought back the thirty pieces of silver to the chief priests and the ancients, saying: I have sinned by betraying just blood. But they said: What is that to us? Look thou to it. And casting down in the temple the pieces of silver, he departed; and went and hanged himself. But the chief priests took the pieces of silver, and said: It is not lawful to put them into the treasury, because it is the price of blood. And after they had consulted together, they bought with them the potter's field, to be a burying place for strangers. For this cause that field was called Hakeldama, the Field of Blood, even to this day. Then was fulfilled that which was spoken by Jeremiah the prophet, who saith: And they took the thirty pieces of silver, the price of Him Who was prized, Whom they of the children of Israel did prize. And they gave them for the potter's field, as the Lord appointed me. And Jesus stood before the governor, and the governor asked Him, saying: Art Thou the King of the Jews? Jesus saith to him: Thou sayest it. And when He was accused by the chief priests and ancients, He made no answer. Then Pilate saith to Him: Dost Thou not hear how many things they testify against Thee? And He answered not a word, so that the governor wondered exceedingly. Now on the solemn day, the governor was accustomed to release to the people one prisoner, whom they would. And he had then a notorious prisoner, called Barabbas. When therefore they were gathered together, Pilate said: Whom will ye that I release to you, Barabbas, or Jesus, Who is called Christ? For he knew that they had delivered Him up through envy. And as he was sitting on the tribunal, his wife sent to him, saying: Have nothing to do with that just man: for I have suffered much this day in a dream on account of Him. But the chief priests and the ancients persuaded the crowds that they should ask Barabbas, and destroy Jesus. And the governor answered and said to them: Which of the two will ye that I release to you? But they said: Barabbas. Pilate saith to them: What then shall I do with Jesus Who is called Christ? They all say: Let Him be crucified. The governor said to them: Why, what evil hath He done? But they cried out the more, saying: Let Him be crucified. And Pilate seeing that he did no good, but that rather a tumult was made, took water and washed his hands before the crowd, saying: I am innocent of the blood of this just man: look ye to it. And all the people answered and said: His blood be on us, and on our children. Then he released to them Barabbas, and having scourged Jesus, delivered Him to them to be crucified. Then the soldiers of the governor took Jesus into the hall, and gathered together unto Him the whole band, and stripped Him, and put a scarlet cloak about Him. And having platted a crown of thorns, they put it on His head, and a reed in His right hand. And they bowed the knee before Him, and mocked Him, saying: Hail, King of the Jews. And they spat upon Him, and took the reed and struck His head. And after they had mocked Him, they took off the cloak from Him, and put on Him His own garments, and led Him away to crucify Him. And as they went out, they found a man of Cyrene, named Simon: him they forced to take up His Cross. And they came to a place called Golgotha, that is, place of a skull. And they gave Him to drink wine mingled with gall. And when He had tasted, He would not drink. And after they had crucified Him, they divided His garments, casting lots, that what was spoken by the prophet might be fulfilled, who saith: They divided My garments among them: and on My vesture they cast lots. And they sat and watched Him. And they put over His head His charge, written: This is Jesus the King of the Jews. Then were crucified with Him two robbers: one on the right hand, and one on the left. And they that passed by blasphemed Him, wagging their heads, and saying: Vah, Thou Who destroyest the temple of God, and in three days dost rebuild it, save Thyself: if Thou art the Son of God, come down from the Cross. In like manner also the chief priests with the scribes and ancients, mocking, said: He saved others; Himself He cannot save: if He is King of Israel, let Him now come down from the Cross, and we will believe Him. He trusted in God: let Him now deliver Him, if He love Him: for He said: I am the Son of God. And the robbers also, who were crucified with Him, reproached Him in like manner. Now from the sixth hour there was darkness over the whole earth, until the ninth hour. And about the ninth hour, Jesus cried out with a loud voice, saying: Eli, Eli, lamma sabacthani? that is, My God, My God, why hast Thou forsaken Me? And some who stood there and heard, said: This man calleth Elias. And immediately one of them ran and took a sponge, and soaked it in vinegar, and put it on a reed, and gave Him to drink. And the others said: Hold, let us see whether Elias will come to deliver Him. And Jesus again crying with a loud voice, yielded up His Spirit.

[*Here all kneel, and briefly pause awhile.*]

And behold the veil of the temple was rent in twain from the top even to the bottom, and the earth quaked, and the rocks were rent. And the monuments were opened, and many bodies of the saints, who had slept, arose. And they came out of the monuments, after His Resurrection, and went into the holy city, and appeared to many. Now when the centurion, and they who were with him watching Jesus, saw the earthquake, and the things which took place, they were greatly terrified, saying: Indeed this was the Son of God. And many women were there, afar off, who had followed Jesus from Galilee, ministering to Him: among whom was Mary Magdalene, and Mary the mother of James and Joseph, and the mother of the sons of Zebedee. And when it was evening, there came a rich man of Arimathea, named

Joseph, who himself also was a disciple of Jesus. He went to Pilate, and asked the body of Jesus. Then Pilate commanded that the body should be delivered up. And Joseph, taking the body, wrapped it in a clean linen cloth, and laid it in his own new monument, which he had hewn out in the rock. And rolled a great stone to the door of the monument, and went away. And Mary Magdalene was there, and the other Mary, sitting over against the tomb.

[*Here the priest says the* Munda cor meum, *p. 92.*]

And the next day, which followed the day of preparation, the chief priests and the Pharisees came together to Pilate, saying: Sir, we remember that that deceiver said while He was yet alive: After three days I will rise. Command, therefore, the tomb to be made secure until the third day: lest His disciples come, and steal Him away, and say to the people: He is risen from the dead; and the last error will be worse than the first. Pilate said to them: Ye have a guard: Go, make it secure, as ye know how. And they went and made the tomb secure, sealing the stone with the guard.

OFFERTORY. My heart hath expected reproach and misery: and I looked for one that would grieve together with Me, and there was none: I sought for one to comfort Me, and I found none; and they gave Me gall for My food, and in My thirst they gave Me vinegar to drink.

SECRET. Grant, we beseech Thee, O Lord, that the gift we offer in the eyes of Thy Majesty may obtain for us the grace of devotion and the fruit of a blessed eternity. Through Our Lord Jesus Christ, etc. *Amen.*

COMMUNION. Father, if this chalice may not pass away, but I must drink it, Thy will be done.

POSTCOMMUNION. By the operation of this mystery, O Lord, may our vices be purged away, and our just desires fulfilled. Through Our Lord Jesus Christ, etc. *Amen.*[45]

EASTER SUNDAY

INTROIT. I have arisen, and am still with Thee, allelulia: Thou hast laid Thine hand upon me, alleluia: Thy knowledge is become wonderful, alleluia, alleluia.

Lord, Thou hast proved me and known me: Thou hast known my sitting down and my rising up.

Glory be to the Father, etc.

COLLECT. O God, Who through Thine only begotten Son hast on this day overcome death, and opened unto us the gate of everlasting life: as by Thy preventing grace Thou dost prosper our good desires, so do Thou accompany them with Thy continual help. Through the same Our Lord Jesus Christ, etc. *Amen.*

---

[45] For the offices of *Holy Week* see note on p. 190.

EPISTLE. 1 Cor 5:7–8. Brethren: Purge out the old leaven, that ye may be a new paste, as ye are unleavened. For our Passover, Christ, is sacrificed. Therefore let us feast, not with old leaven, nor with the leaven of malice and wickedness, but with unleavened bread of sincerity and truth.

GRADUAL. This is the day which the Lord hath made: let us be glad and rejoice therein. Give praise to the Lord, for He is good: for His mercy endureth forever. Alleluia, alleluia. Christ our Pasch is immolated.

SEQUENCE. *Victimæ Paschali.*

Unto the Paschal Victim bring,
Christians, your thankful offering.
The Lamb redeemed the flock,
So Christ the spotless, without guile,
To God did sinners reconcile.
In wondrous deadly shock
Lo! death and life contend and strive;
The Lord of life, Who died, doth reign and live.
What thou sawest, Mary, say,
As thou wentest on the way.
I saw the grave which could not Christ retain;
I saw His glory as He rose again;
I saw th' angelic witnesses around;
The napkin and the linen clothes I found.
Yea, Christ my hope is risen, and He
Will go before you into Galilee.
We know that Christ indeed has risen from the grave:
Hail, Thou King of victory!
Have mercy, Lord, and save.
Amen. Alleluia.

GOSPEL. Mk 16:1–7. At that time: Mary Magdalen, and Mary the mother of James, and Salome, bought sweet spices, that they might come and anoint Jesus. And very early in the morning, the first day of the week, they come to the monument, the sun being now risen. And they said, one to another: Who shall roll us back the stone from the door of the monument? And looking, they saw the stone rolled back, for it was very great. And entering into the monument, they saw a young man sitting on the right side, clothed with a white robe, and they were affrighted. But he saith to them: Be not affrighted: ye seek Jesus of Nazareth, Who was crucified: He is risen. He is not here; behold the place where they laid Him. But go, tell His disciples and Peter that He goeth before you into Galilee: there ye will see Him, as He told you.

OFFERTORY. The earth trembled and was still, when God arose in judgment, alleluia.

SECRET. Receive, O Lord, we beseech Thee, the prayers and sacrifices of Thy people: and grant that what we have begun at these paschal mysteries may by Thy power avail us as a healing remedy unto everlasting life. Through Our Lord Jesus Christ, etc. *Amen.*

COMMUNION. Christ our Pasch is immolated, alleluia: therefore let us feast with the unleavened bread of sincerity and truth, alleluia, alleluia, alleluia.

POSTCOMMUNION. Pour forth upon us, O Lord, the spirit of Thy love; that by Thy mercy Thou mayest make those of one mind whom Thou hast fed with Thy paschal mysteries. Through Our Lord Jesus Christ, etc. *Amen.*

LOW SUNDAY

INTROIT. As newborn babes, alleluia: desire rational, guileless milk, alleluia, alleluia, alleluia.

Rejoice unto God our helper; sing aloud unto the God of Jacob.

Glory be to the Father, etc.

COLLECT. Grant, we beseech Thee, O Almighty God, that we for whom the feast of the Passover hath now come to an end, may, through Thy merciful bounty, always retain in our life and manners the influence of the same. Through Our Lord Jesus Christ, etc. *Amen.*

EPISTLE. 1 Jn 5:4–10. Dearly beloved: All that is born of God overcometh the world; and this is the victory which overcometh the world, our faith. Who is it that overcometh the world, unless he that believeth that Jesus is the Son of God? This is He Who came by water and blood, Jesus the Christ; not in water alone, but in water and blood. And it is the Spirit Who testifieth that Christ is Truth. For there are Three Who give testimony in heaven: the Father, the Word, and the Holy Spirit; and these Three are One. And there are three who give testimony on earth: the spirit, and water, and blood; and these three are one. If we receive the testimony of men, the testimony of God is greater; for this is the testimony of God, which is greater, because He hath testified of His Son. He who believeth in the Son of God hath the testimony of God in himself.

ALLELUIA. Alleluia, alleluia. On the day of My Resurrection, saith the Lord, I will go before you into Galilee. Alleluia. After eight days, the doors being shut, Jesus stood in the midst of His disciples, and said: Peace be with you. Alleluia.

GOSPEL. Jn 20:19–31. At that time: When it was late that same day, the first of the week, and the doors were shut, where the disciples were gathered together, through fear of the Jews, Jesus came and stood in the midst, and said to them: Peace be to you. And when He had said this, He showed them His hands and side. The disciples, therefore, were glad when they saw the Lord. He said, therefore, to them again: Peace be to you: as the Father hath sent Me, I also send you. When He had said this, He breathed on them; and said to them: Receive ye the Holy Spirit;

whose sins ye shall forgive, they are forgiven them; and whose sins ye shall retain, they are retained. Now Thomas, one of the Twelve, who is called Didymus, was not with them when Jesus came. The other disciples, therefore, said to him: We have seen the Lord. But he said to them: Unless I see in His hands the print of the nails, and put my finger into the place of the nails, and put my hand into His side, I will not believe. And after eight days, His disciples were again within, and Thomas was with them. Jesus cometh, the doors being shut, and stood in the midst, and said: Peace be to you. Then He saith to Thomas: Put thy finger in hither, and see My hands, and bring hither thy hand, and put it into My side; and be not incredulous, but believing. Thomas answered, and said to Him: My Lord, and my God. Jesus saith to him: Because thou hast seen Me, Thomas, thou believest: blessed are they who have not seen, and yet believed. Many other signs also Jesus performed in the sight of His disciples, which are not written in this book. But these are written, that ye may believe that Jesus is the Christ, the Son of God; and that, believing, ye may have life in His name.

OFFERTORY. An angel of the Lord descended from heaven and said to the women: He Whom you seek is risen, as He said, Alleluia.

SECRET. Receive, we beseech Thee, O Lord, the gifts of Thy joyful Church: and grant that she to whom Thou hast given cause for so great joy, may obtain also the fruit of perpetual gladness. Through Our Lord Jesus Christ, etc. *Amen.*

COMMUNION. Put in thy hand, and know the place of the nails, alleluia; and be not incredulous, but believing, alleluia, alleluia.

POSTCOMMUNION. We beseech Thee, O Lord our God, that Thou wouldst make these most holy mysteries, which Thou hast bestowed for the perfection of our renewal, to be to us both a present and future remedy. Through Our Lord Jesus Christ, etc. *Amen.*

SECOND SUNDAY AFTER EASTER

INTROIT. The earth is full of the mercy of the Lord, alleluia: by the Word of the Lord were the heavens established, alleluia, alleluia.

Rejoice in the Lord, O ye just: praise becometh the upright.

Glory be to the Father, etc.

COLLECT. O God, Who in the humility of Thy Son hast raised up a fallen world: grant to Thy faithful people perpetual gladness; and as Thou hast delivered them from the perils of eternal death, make them to rejoice with everlasting joy. Through Our Lord Jesus Christ, etc. *Amen.*

EPISTLE. 1 Pt 2:21–25. Dearly beloved: Christ suffered for us, leaving to you an example, that ye should follow in the steps of Him, Who committed no sin, nor was guile found in His mouth; Who when He was reviled, reviled not; when He suffered, threatened not, but delivered Himself up to him who judged Him unjustly: Who Himself bore our sins in His body on the Tree; that we, being dead to sin, should live to justice: by Whose stripes ye were healed. For ye were as sheep going astray, but are now converted to the Shepherd and Bishop of your souls.

ALLELUIA. Alleluia, alleluia. The disciples knew the Lord Jesus in the breaking of bread. Alleluia. I am the Good Shepherd: and I know My sheep, and Mine know Me. Alleluia.

GOSPEL. Jn 10:11–16. At that time: Jesus said to the Pharisees: I am the Good Shepherd. The good shepherd giveth his life for his sheep. But the hireling, and he that is not the shepherd, whose own the sheep are not, seeth the wolf coming, and leaveth the sheep, and fleeth; and the wolf seizeth, and scattereth the sheep: and the hireling fleeth, because he is a hireling, and hath no care for the sheep. I am the Good Shepherd; and I know Mine, and Mine know Me. As the Father knoweth Me, and I know the Father: and I lay down My life for My sheep. And other sheep I have, which are not of this fold: them also I must bring, and they shall hear My voice, and there shall be one fold and one Shepherd.

OFFERTORY. O God, my God, to Thee do I watch at break of day: And in Thy name I will lift up my hands, alleluia.

SECRET. May this holy sacrifice, O Lord, ever bring to us a blessing unto salvation: that by its power what it represents in mystery it may bring to pass in reality. Through Our Lord Jesus Christ, etc. *Amen.*

COMMUNION. I am the Good Shepherd, alleluia: and I know My sheep, and Mine know Me, alleluia, alleluia.

POSTCOMMUNION. Grant us, we beseech Thee, O Almighty God, that, obtaining the grace of Thy Resurrection, we may ever glory in Thy gift. Through Our Lord Jesus Christ, etc. *Amen.*

THIRD SUNDAY AFTER EASTER

PATRONAGE OF ST. JOSEPH

INTROIT. The Lord is our helper and protector: in Him shall our heart rejoice, and in His holy name we have trusted, alleluia, alleluia.

Give ear, O Thou that rulest Israel: Thou that leadest Joseph like a sheep.

Glory be to the Father, etc.

COLLECT. O God, Who in Thine unspeakable providence didst vouchsafe to choose blessed Joseph to be the husband of Thy most holy Mother: mercifully grant that, as we venerate him for our protector on earth, we may deserve to be aided by his intercession in heaven. Who livest and reignest, etc. *Amen.*

COLLECT OF THE SUNDAY. Almighty God, Who showest to those that are in error the light of Thy truth, that they may return into the way of justice; grant unto all those who are admitted into the fellowship of Christ's religion, that they may avoid those things that are contrary to that name, and follow such things as are agreeable thereto. Through the same Our Lord Jesus Christ, etc. *Amen.*

LESSON. Gn 49:22–26. Joseph is a growing bough, a growing bough and fair to behold: the branches run to and fro upon the wall. But the archers provoked him, and quarreled with him, and envied him. His bow rested upon the strong, and the bands of his arms and his hands were loosed, by the hands of the Mighty One of Jacob: thence he came forth the shepherd, the stone of Israel. The God of thy father will be thy helper, and the Almighty will bless thee with the blessings of heaven above, with the blessings of the deep which lieth beneath, with the blessings of the breasts and of the womb. The blessings of thy father are strengthened with the blessings of his fathers, until the desire of the everlasting hills come: may they be upon the head of Joseph, and upon the crown of the Nazarite among his brethren.

ALLELUIA. Alleluia, alleluia. In whatever tribulation they shall cry to me, I will hear them, and be their protector always. Alleluia. Obtain for us, O Joseph, to lead an innocent life; and may it ever be safe through thy patronage. Alleluia.

GOSPEL. Lk 3:21–23. At that time: It came to pass, when all the people were baptized, that Jesus also being baptized and praying, the heaven was opened; and the Holy Spirit descended in a bodily form, like a dove, upon Him, and a voice came from heaven: Thou art My beloved Son: in Thee I am well pleased. And Jesus Himself was beginning about the age of thirty years; being (as it was supposed) the son of Joseph.

OFFERTORY. Praise the Lord, O Jerusalem, because He hath strengthened the bolts of thy gates: He hath blessed thy children within thee, alleluia, alleluia.

SECRET. Under the patronage of the spouse of Thy most holy Mother, we beseech Thy clemency, O Lord, that Thou wouldst make our hearts despise all earthly things, and love Thee, the true God, with perfect charity: Who livest and reignest, etc. *Amen.*

SECRET OF THE SUNDAY. Grant us, O Lord, through these mysteries, that subduing our earthly desires we may learn to love heavenly things. Through Our Lord Jesus Christ, etc. *Amen.*

COMMUNION. Now Jacob begat Joseph, the husband of Mary, of whom was born Jesus, Who is called Christ, alleluia, alleluia.

POSTCOMMUNION. Refreshed at the fountain of divine blessing, we beseech Thee, O Lord our God, that as Thou makest us rejoice in the protection of blessed Joseph, so by his merits and intercession Thou wouldst make us partakers of celestial glory. Through Our Lord Jesus Christ, etc. *Amen.*

POSTCOMMUNION OF THE SUNDAY. May the Sacrament which we have received, O Lord, both revive us with spiritual nourishment and defend us by bodily succor. Through Our Lord Jesus Christ, etc. *Amen.*

LAST GOSPEL. Jn 16:16–22. At that time: Jesus said to His disciples: A little while, and ye will not see Me; and again a little while, and ye will see Me; because I go to the Father. Then some of His disciples said, one to another: What is this that He saith to us: A little while, and ye will not see Me; and again a little while, and ye will see Me; and, because I go to the Father? They said therefore: What is this that He saith: A little while? We know not what He speaketh. And Jesus knew that they had a mind to ask Him, and He said to them: Of this do ye inquire among yourselves, because I said: A little while, and ye will not see Me; and again a little while, and ye will see Me. Truly, truly, I say to you, that ye shall lament and weep, but the world shall rejoice; and ye shall be made sorrowful, but your sorrow shall be turned into joy. A woman, when she is in labor, hath sorrow, because her hour is come; but when she hath brought forth the child, she remembereth no more the anguish, for joy that a man is born into the world. So also ye now indeed have sorrow, but I will see you again, and your heart will rejoice, and your joy no man shall take from you.

FOURTH SUNDAY AFTER EASTER

INTROIT. Sing unto the Lord a new song, alleluia; for the Lord hath done wonderful things, alleluia. He hath revealed His justice in the sight of the Gentiles, alleluia, alleluia, alleluia.

His right hand and His holy arm: hath wrought salvation for Him.

Glory be to the Father, etc.

COLLECT. O God, Who makest the minds of the faithful to be of one will: grant unto Thy people to love what Thou commandest, and to desire what Thou dost promise; that, amidst the various changes of the world, our hearts may there be fixed where true joys abide. Through Our Lord Jesus Christ, etc. *Amen.*

EPISTLE. Jas 1:17–21. Dearly beloved: Every excellent gift and every perfect gift is from above, coming down from the Father of lights, with Whom is no change, nor shadow of alteration. For of His own will He hath begotten us by the word of truth, that we may be some firstfruits of His creatures. Ye know, my dearly beloved brethren; and let every man be quick to hear, but slow to speak, and slow to anger. For the anger of man worketh not the justice of God. Wherefore, casting away all uncleanness, and abundance of malice, receive with meekness the engrafted word, which can save your souls.

ALLELUIA. Alleluia, alleluia. The right hand of the Lord hath wrought strength: the right hand of the Lord hath exalted me. Alleluia. Christ rising again from the dead dieth now no more; death shall no more have dominion over Him. Alleluia.

GOSPEL. Jn 16:5–14. At that time: Jesus said to His disciples: I go to Him Who sent Me; and none of you asketh Me: Whither art Thou going? But because I have spoken these things to you, sorrow hath filled your heart. But I tell you the truth: it is expedient for you that I go, for if I go not, the Paraclete will not come to you; but if I go, I will send Him to you. And when He is come, He will convict the world of sin, and of justice, and of judgment. Of sin, because they believed not in Me; and of justice, because I go to the Father, and ye will see Me no longer; and of judgment, because the prince of this world is already judged. I have yet many things to say to you, but ye cannot bear them now: but when He, the Spirit of truth shall come, He will teach you all the truth; for He will not speak of Himself; but whatever things He hath heard, He will speak, and the things which are to come, He will show you. He will glorify Me, because He will receive of Mine, and show to you.

OFFERTORY. O God, my God, to Thee do I watch at break of day: And in Thy name I will lift up my hands, alleluia.

SECRET. O God, Who by communion in this venerable sacrifice hast made us partakers of the one supreme Godhead: grant, we beseech Thee, that as we know Thy truth so we may pursue it by a worthy life. Through Our Lord Jesus Christ, etc. *Amen.*

COMMUNION. When the Paraclete shall come, the Spirit of truth, He shall convince the world of sin, and of justice, and of judgment, alleluia, alleluia.

POSTCOMMUNION. Assist us, O Lord our God, that by these mysteries which we faithfully receive, we may be purified from vice and delivered from all dangers. Through Our Lord Jesus Christ, etc. *Amen.*

FIFTH SUNDAY AFTER EASTER

INTROIT. Declare the voice of joy, and let it be heard, alleluia. Declare it even to the ends of the earth; the Lord hath delivered His people, alleluia, alleluia.

O sing joyfully unto God, all the earth: sing ye a psalm unto His name: give glory unto His praise.

Glory be to the Father, etc.

COLLECT. O Lord, from Whom all good things do proceed: grant to us Thy humble servants that by Thy holy inspiration we may think those things that are good, and by Thy guidance may perform the same. Through Our Lord Jesus Christ, etc. *Amen.*

EPISTLE. Jas 1:22–27. Dearly beloved: Be ye doers of the word, and not hearers only, deceiving yourselves. For if any man is a hearer of the word, and not a doer, he is like to a man beholding his natural countenance in a glass. For he beholdeth himself, and goeth away, and presently forgetteth what kind of a man he was. But he who looketh into the perfect law of liberty, and continueth in it, not becoming a forgetful hearer, but a doer of work, this man shall be blessed in his deed. If any man think himself religious, not bridling his tongue, but deceiving his heart, this man's religion is vain. Religion pure and undefiled, with God and the Father is this: to visit orphans and widows in their tribulation, and to keep one's self unspotted from the world.

ALLELUIA. Alleluia, alleluia. Christ is risen, and hath shone upon us, whom He redeemed with His blood. Alleluia. I came forth from the Father, and came into the world: again I leave the world, and go to the Father. Alleluia.

GOSPEL. Jn 16:23–30. At that time: Jesus said to His disciples: Truly, truly, I say to you: if ye ask the Father anything in My name, He will give it you. Hitherto ye have not asked anything in My name: ask, and ye shall receive, that your joy may be full. These things I have spoken to you in proverbs: the hour cometh when I will no more speak to you in proverbs, but I will show you plainly of the Father. On that day, ye will ask in My name; and I say not to you that I will ask the Father for you, for the Father Himself loveth you, because ye have loved Me, and have believed that

I came forth from God. I came forth from the Father, and am come into the world: again I leave the world, and go to the Father. His disciples say to Him: Behold, now Thou speakest plainly, and speakest no proverb. Now we know that Thou knowest all things, and Thou needest not that any man should ask Thee: by this we believe that Thou comest forth from God.

OFFERTORY. O bless the Lord our God, ye Gentiles, and make the voice of His praise to be heard: Who hath set my soul to live, and hath not suffered my feet to be moved: blessed be the Lord, Who hath not turned away my prayer, nor His mercy from me, alleluia.

SECRET. Receive, O Lord, the prayers and sacrifices of Thy faithful people; that through the service of our loving devotion we may attain to heavenly glory. Through Our Lord Jesus Christ, etc. *Amen.*

COMMUNION. Sing ye to the Lord, alleluia; sing ye to the Lord, and bless His name: show forth His salvation from day to day, alleluia, alleluia.

POSTCOMMUNION. Grant us, O Lord, whom Thou hast filled with the virtue of Thy heavenly table, both to desire those things which are right, and to obtain what we desire. Through Our Lord Jesus Christ, etc. *Amen.*

ASCENSION DAY

INTROIT. Ye men of Galilee, why wonder ye, looking into heaven? alleluia: in like manner as ye have seen Him ascending into heaven, so shall He come, alleluia, alleluia, alleluia.

O clap your hands, all ye nations: shout unto God with the voice of joy.

Glory be to the Father, etc.

COLLECT. Grant, we beseech Thee, Almighty God, that as we believe Thine only begotten Son our Redeemer to have this day ascended into the heavens, so we may also in heart and mind dwell amid heavenly things. Through the same Our Lord Jesus Christ, etc. *Amen.*

LESSON. Acts 1:1–11. The former treatise I indeed made, O Theophilus, of all things which Jesus began to do and to teach, until the day on which he was taken up, after He had given commandments through the Holy Spirit to the apostles whom He had chosen. To whom, also, He showed Himself alive after His Passion, by many proofs, for forty days appearing to them, and speaking of the Kingdom of God. And eating with them, He commanded them not to depart from Jerusalem, but to wait for the promise of the Father, which ye have heard (He said) from My mouth. For John indeed baptized with water, but ye shall be baptized with the Holy Spirit not many days hence. They, therefore, who were come together, asked Him, saying: Lord, wilt Thou at this time restore the kingdom to Israel? But He said to them: It is not for you to know the times or moments which the Father hath set by His own power; but ye shall receive power when the Holy Spirit shall come upon you, and ye shall be witnesses to Me in Jerusalem, and in all Judea and Samaria, and to the uttermost parts of the earth. And when He had said these things, whilst they looked on, He was raised up, and a cloud received Him out of their sight. And as they looked steadfastly on Him, as He went up to heaven, behold, two men stood by them in white apparel, who also said: Men of Galilee, why stand ye looking up into heaven? This Jesus, Who hath been taken up from you into heaven, shall so come in like manner as ye have seen Him go into heaven.

ALLELUIA. Alleluia, alleluia. God is ascended with jubilee, and the Lord with the sound of trumpet. Alleluia. The Lord is in Sinai, in the holy place: ascending on high. He hath led captivity captive. Alleluia.

GOSPEL. Mk 16:14–20. At that time: Jesus appeared to the Eleven, as they were at table, and upbraided them with their unbelief and hardness of heart, because they did not believe those who had seen Him after He was risen again. And He said to them: Go ye into the whole world, and preach the gospel to every creature. He that believeth and is baptized shall be saved, but he that believeth not shall be condemned. And these signs shall follow those who believe: in My name they shall cast out devils; they shall speak with new tongues; they shall take up serpents; and if they drink any deadly thing, it shall not hurt them; they shall lay their hands upon the sick, and they shall recover. And the Lord Jesus, after He had spoken to them, was taken up into heaven, and sitteth on the right hand of God. But they, going forth, preached everywhere, the Lord working withal, and confirming the word with the signs which followed.

OFFERTORY. God is ascended in jubilee, and the Lord with the sound of trumpet, alleluia.

SECRET. Accept, O Lord, the gifts we offer for the glorious Ascension of Thy Son: and grant, of Thy mercy, that we may be delivered from present dangers, and attain to eternal life. Through the same Our Lord Jesus Christ, etc. *Amen.*

COMMUNION. Sing ye to the Lord, Who mounteth above the heaven of heavens to the east, alleluia.

POSTCOMMUNION. Grant, we beseech Thee, O Almighty and merciful God, that what we have received in visible mysteries we may obtain in its invisible effect. Through Our Lord Jesus Christ, etc. *Amen.*

SUNDAY WITHIN THE OCTAVE OF THE ASCENSION

INTROIT. Hear, O Lord, my voice with which I have cried unto Thee, alleluia. My heart hath said to Thee, I have sought Thy face, Thy face, O Lord, will I seek: hide not Thy face from me, alleluia, alleluia.

The Lord is my light and my salvation: Whom shall I fear?

Glory be to the Father, etc.

COLLECT. Almighty, everlasting God, grant that we may always have a will devoted to Thee, and a sincere heart to serve Thy Majesty. Through Our Lord Jesus Christ, etc. *Amen.*

EPISTLE. 1 Pt 4:7–11. Dearly beloved: Be ye prudent and watch in prayers. And above all things have constant, mutual love among yourselves; for love covereth a multitude of sins. Be hospitable one to another without murmuring. Everyone, as he hath received grace, ministering the same one to another, as good stewards of the manifold grace of God. If any man speak, let him speak as the oracles of God. If any man minister, let him do it as by the strength which God supplieth; that in all things God may be glorified through Jesus Christ Our Lord.

ALLELUIA. Alleluia, alleluia. The Lord hath reigned over all the nations; God sitteth on His holy throne. Alleluia. I will not leave you orphans; I go and I come to you, and your heart shall rejoice. Alleluia.

GOSPEL. Jn 15:26–16:4. At that time: Jesus said to His disciples: When the Paraclete cometh, Whom I will send to you from the Father, the Spirit of truth, Who proceedeth from the Father, He will give testimony of Me; and ye shall give testimony, because ye are with Me from the beginning. These things have I spoken to you, that ye may not be scandalized. They will cast you out of the synagogues; yea, the hour cometh, that whoever killeth you will think that he offereth homage to God. And these things will they do to you, because they know not the Father nor Me. But these things I have told you, that, when their time shall come, ye may remember that I told you.

OFFERTORY. God is ascended in jubilee, and the Lord with the sound of trumpet, alleluia.

SECRET. May these unspotted sacrifices purify us, O Lord, and impart to our souls the strength of heavenly grace. Through Our Lord Jesus Christ, etc. *Amen.*

COMMUNION. Father, while I was with them, I kept them whom Thou gavest Me, alleluia; but now I come to Thee; I pray not that Thou shouldst take them out of the world, but that Thou shouldst keep them from evil, alleluia, alleluia.

POSTCOMMUNION. Being refreshed, O Lord, with sacred gifts, grant us, we beseech Thee, ever to continue in thanksgiving. Through Our Lord Jesus Christ, etc. *Amen.*

PENTECOST, OR WHITSUNDAY

INTROIT. The Spirit of the Lord hath filled the whole world, alleluia: and that which containeth all things hath knowledge of the voice, alleluia, alleluia, alleluia.

Let God arise, and let His enemies be scattered; and let them that hate Him flee from before His face.

Glory be to the Father, etc.

COLLECT. O God, Who on this day didst teach the hearts of Thy faithful people, by the light of Thy Holy Spirit: grant us by the same Spirit to have a right judgment in all things, and evermore to rejoice in His holy comfort. Through Our Lord Jesus Christ, etc. *Amen.*

LESSON. Acts 2:1–11. When the days of Pentecost were completed, the disciples were all together in one place. And suddenly there came a sound from heaven, as of a rushing mighty wind, and it filled the whole house where they were sitting. And there appeared to them parted tongues as of fire, and it sat upon every one of them;

and they were all filled with the Holy Spirit, and began to speak with other tongues, as the Holy Spirit gave them to speak. Now there were dwelling at Jerusalem, Jews, devout men, out of every nation under heaven. And when this voice was spread, the multitude came together, and were confounded in mind, because every man heard them speak in his own tongue: and they were all amazed, and wondered, saying: Behold, are not all these who speak Galileans? And how hear we every man our own tongue wherein we were born! Parthians, and Medes, and Elamites, and the inhabitants of Mesopotamia, Judea, and Cappadocia, Pontus, and Asia, Phrygia and Pamphylia, Egypt, and the parts of Libya about Cyrene, and strangers of Rome, Jews also, and proselytes, Cretans and Arabians: we hear them speak in our tongues the great works of God.

ALLELUIA. Alleluia, alleluia. Send forth Thy Spirit, and they shall be created: and Thou shalt renew the face of the earth. Alleluia. (*Here all kneel.*) Come, O Holy Spirit, fill the hearts of Thy faithful; and kindle in them the fire of Thy love.

SEQUENCE. *Veni, Sancte Spiritus.*

Come, Thou holy Paraclete,
And from Thy celestial seat
Send Thy light and brilliancy:

Father of the poor, draw near,
Giver of all gifts, be here:
Come, the soul's true Radiancy:

Come, of Comforters the best,
Of the soul the sweetest Guest,
Come in toil refreshingly:

Thou in labor Rest most sweet,
Thou art Shadow from the heat,
Comfort in adversity.

O Thou Light most pure and blest,
Shine within the inmost breast
Of Thy faithful company.

Where Thou art not, man hath naught;
Every holy deed and thought
Comes from Thy divinity.

What is soilèd, make Thou pure;
What is wounded, work its cure;

What is parchèd, fructify;

What is rigid, gently bend;
What is frozen, warmly tend;
Strengthen what goes erringly.

Fill Thy faithful, who confide
In Thy power to guard and guide,
With Thy sevenfold mystery.

Here Thy grace and virtue send;
Grant salvation in the end,
And in heaven felicity.
Amen. Alleluia.

GOSPEL. Jn 14:23–31. At that time: Jesus said to His disciples: If anyone love Me, He will keep My word and My Father will love Him, and We will come to Him and make our abode with Him. He who loveth Me not, keepeth not My words: and the word which ye have heard is not Mine, but the Father's Who sent Me. These things have I spoken to you, abiding with you; but the Paraclete, the Holy Spirit, Whom the Father will send in My name, He will teach you all things and bring all things to your mind, whatever I have said to you. Peace I leave you, my peace I give you; not as the world giveth do I give you. Let not your heart be troubled, nor let it be afraid. Ye have heard that I said to you: I go away and I come to you. If ye loved Me, ye would indeed be glad, because I go to the Father; for the Father is greater than I. And now I have told you before it come to pass, that when it shall come to pass, ye may believe. I will not now speak many things with you; for the prince of this world cometh, and in Me he hath nothing. But that the world may know that I love the Father, and as the Father hath given Me commandment, so do I.

OFFERTORY. Confirm this, O God, which Thou hast wrought in us; from Thy temple, which is in Jerusalem, kings shall offer presents to Thee, alleluia.

SECRET. Hallow, O Lord, we beseech Thee, the gifts we offer; and cleanse our hearts by the light of the Holy Spirit. Through Our Lord Jesus Christ, etc. *Amen.*

COMMUNION. There came suddenly a sound from heaven as of a mighty wind coming, where they were sitting, alleluia; and they were all filled with the Holy Ghost, speaking the wonderful works of God, alleluia, alleluia.

POSTCOMMUNION. May the infusion of the Holy Spirit cleanse our hearts, O Lord, and render them fruitful by the inward watering of His heavenly dew. Through Our Lord Jesus Christ, etc. *Amen.*

TRINITY SUNDAY

INTROIT. Blessed be the Holy Trinity and undivided Unity: we will give glory to Him, because He hath shown His mercy to us.

O Lord, Our Lord, how admirable is Thy name in the whole earth.

Glory be to the Father, etc.

COLLECT. Almighty, everlasting God, Who hast granted to Thy servants, in the confession of the true Faith, to acknowledge the glory of the eternal Trinity, and, in the power of Thy Majesty, to adore the Unity: we beseech Thee that, by steadfastness in the same Faith, we may always be defended from all adversities. Through Our Lord Jesus Christ, etc. *Amen.*

COLLECT OF THE SUNDAY. O God, the strength of those who put their trust in Thee, graciously accept our prayers; and because human infirmity without Thee can do nothing, grant us the help of Thy grace; that, in fulfilling Thy commandments, we may please Thee both in will and deed. Through Our Lord Jesus Christ, etc. *Amen.*

EPISTLE. Rom 11:33–36. O depth of riches of wisdom and knowledge of God! How incomprehensible are His judgments, and unsearchable His ways! For who hath known the mind of the Lord? Or who hath been His counselor? Or who hath first given to Him, and recompense shall be made Him? For of Him, and by Him, and in Him, are all things: to Him be glory forever. Amen.

GRADUAL. Blessed art Thou, O Lord, Who beholdest the depths, and sittest upon the cherubim. Blessed art Thou, O Lord, in the firmament of heaven, and worthy of praise forever. Alleluia, alleluia. Blessed art Thou, O Lord God of our fathers, and worthy of praise forever. Alleluia.

GOSPEL. Mt 28:18–20. At that time: Jesus said to His disciples: All power is given to Me in heaven and on earth. Go ye, therefore, and teach all nations, baptizing them in the name of the Father, and of the Son, and of the Holy Spirit: teaching them to observe all things whatsoever I have commanded you; and behold I am with you all days, unto the end of the world.

OFFERTORY. Blessed be God the Father, and the only begotten Son of God, and also the Holy Spirit; because He hath shown His mercy toward us.

SECRET. Sanctify, we beseech Thee, O Lord our God, by the invocation of Thy holy name, the Victim of this sacrifice: and through its means, make of us too an eternal offering to Thee. Through Our Lord Jesus Christ, etc. *Amen.*

SECRET OF THE SUNDAY. Receive favorably, O Lord, we beseech Thee, the offerings we consecrate to Thee: and grant that they may be our succor forevermore. Through Our Lord Jesus Christ, etc. *Amen.*

COMMUNION. We bless the God of heaven, and before all living we will praise Him: because He has shown His mercy to us.

POSTCOMMUNION. May the reception of this Sacrament, O Lord our God, and the confession of the Holy and eternal Trinity, and Its undivided Unity, profit us to the salvation of body and soul. Through Our Lord Jesus Christ, etc. *Amen.*

POSTCOMMUNION OF THE SUNDAY. Grant, we beseech Thee, O Lord, that, filled with so great gifts, we may receive Thy salutary benefits, and never cease from Thy praise. Through Our Lord Jesus Christ, etc. *Amen.*

LAST GOSPEL. Lk 6:36–42. At that time: Jesus said to His disciples: Be therefore merciful, as your Father also is merciful. Judge not, and ye shall not be judged. Condemn not, and ye shall not be condemned. Forgive, and ye shall be forgiven. Give, and it shall be given to you: good measure and pressed down, and shaken together and running over, shall they give into your bosom. For with the same measure with which ye measure, it shall be measured to you again. And He spake also a similitude to them: Can a blind man lead a blind man? Do not both fall into the pit? The scholar is not above his teacher; but everyone will be perfect, if he be as his teacher. And why seest thou the mote in thy brother's eye, and considerest not the beam that is in thine own eye? Or, how canst thou say to thy brother: Brother, let me draw the mote out of thine eye, when thou thyself perceivest not the beam in thine own eye? Hypocrite, cast first the beam out of thine own eye, and then wilt thou see clearly to draw the mote out of thy brother's eye.

CORPUS CHRISTI

INTROIT. He fed them with the fat of wheat, alleluia, and with honey out of the rock He satisfied them, alleluia, alleluia, alleluia.

Rejoice unto God our helper; sing aloud unto the God of Jacob.

Glory be to the Father, etc.

COLLECT. O God, Who under a wonderful Sacrament hast left us a memorial of Thy Passion: grant us, we beseech Thee, so to venerate the sacred mysteries of Thy Body and Blood that we may ever feel within us the fruit of Thy Redemption. Who livest and reignest, etc. *Amen.*

EPISTLE. 1 Cor 11:23–29. Brethren: I have received of the Lord that which also I delivered to you, that the Lord Jesus, on the night in which He was betrayed, took bread, and giving thanks, broke it, and said: Take and eat; this is My Body, which shall be delivered for you; this do for the commemoration of Me. In like manner also He took the cup, after the supper, saying: This cup is the new covenant in My Blood; this do ye, as often as ye shall drink, for the commemoration of Me. For as often as ye shall eat this Bread, and drink the cup, ye shall show the death of the Lord until He come. Therefore, whoever shall eat this Bread, or drink the cup of the Lord unworthily, shall be guilty of the Body and of the Blood of the Lord. But let a man prove himself; and so let him eat of that Bread, and drink of the cup. For he who eateth and drinketh unworthily, eateth and drinketh judgment to himself, not discerning the Body of the Lord.

GRADUAL. The eyes of all hope in Thee, O Lord, and Thou givest them meat in due season. Thou openest Thy hand, and fillest every living creature with Thy

blessing. Alleluia, alleluia. My Flesh is meat indeed, and My Blood is drink indeed: he that eateth My Flesh and drinketh My Blood, abideth in Me, and I in him.
    SEQUENCE. *Lauda Sion.*

Praise high thy Savior, Sion, praise,
With hymns of joy and holy lays,
Thy Guide and Shepherd true.
Dare all thou canst, yea, take thy fill
Of praise and adoration, still
Thou fail'st to reach His due.

A special theme for thankful hearts,
The Bread that lives, and life imparts,
Today is duly set;
Which, at the solemn festal board,
Was dealt around when, with their Lord,
His chosen Twelve were met.

Full be the praise, and sweetly sounding,
With joy and reverence abounding,
The soul's glad festival.
This is the day of glorious state,
When of that feast we celebrate
The high original.

'Tis here our King makes all things new,
And living rules and offerings true
Absorb each legal rite;
Before the new retreats the old,
And life succeeds to shadows cold,
And day displaces night.

His faithful followers Christ hath bid
To do what at the feast He did,
For sweet remembrance' sake;
And, gifted through His high commands,
Of bread and wine their priestly hands
A saving Victim make.

O Truth to Christian love displayed,
The bread His very Body made,
His very Blood the wine;

Nor eye beholds, nor thought conceives,
But dauntless faith the change believes
Wrought by a power divine.

Beneath two differing species
(Signs only, not their substances)
Lie mysteries deep and rare.
His Flesh the meat, the drink His Blood,
Yet Christ entire, our heavenly Food,
Beneath each kind is there.

And they who of the Lord partake
Nor sever Him, nor rend, nor break:
All gain, and naught is lost;
The boon now one, now thousands claim,
Yet one and all receive the same—
Receive, but ne'er exhaust.

The gift is shared by all, yet tends,
In bad and good, to differing ends
Of blessing or of woe;
What death to some, salvation brings
To others: lo! from common springs
What various issues flow!

Nor be thy faith confounded, though
The Sacrament be broke, for know,
The life which in the whole doth glow
In every part remains;
No force the Substance can divide
Which those meek forms terrestial hide:
The sign is broke; the Signified
Nor change nor loss sustains.

The Bread of angels, lo! is sent
For weary pilgrims' nourishment;
The children's Bread, not to be spent
On worthless dogs profane;
In types significant portrayed,
Young Isaac on the altar laid,
And paschal offerings duly made,
And manna's fruitful rain.

O Thou Good Shepherd, very Bread,
Jesu, on us Thy mercy shed;
Sweetly feed us,
Gently lead us,
Till of Thy fullness us Thou give
Safe in the land of those that live.
Thou Who can'st all, and all dost know,
Thou Who dost feed us here below,
Grant us to share
Thy banquet there,
Coheirs and partners of Thy love
With the blest citizens above.
Amen. Alleluia.

GOSPEL. Jn 6:56–59. At that time: Jesus said to the multitudes of the Jews: My Flesh is true food, and My Blood is true drink. He who eateth My Flesh, and drinketh My Blood, abideth in Me, and I in him. As the Father Who liveth sent Me, and I live by the Father, so he that eateth Me, the same also shall live by Me. This is the Bread which came down from heaven. Not as your fathers ate the manna and died. He who eateth this Bread shall live forever.

OFFERTORY. The priests of the Lord offer incense and loaves to God, and therefore they shall be holy to their God, and shall not defile His name, alleluia.

SECRET. In Thy mercy, O Lord, we beseech Thee, grant to Thy Church the gifts of unity and peace, which are mystically shown forth in the offerings we make to Thee. Through Our Lord Jesus Christ, etc. *Amen.*

COMMUNION. As often as you shall eat this Bread, and drink the chalice, you shall show forth the death of the Lord, until He come: whosoever shall eat this Bread or drink the chalice of the Lord unworthily, shall be guilty of the Body and Blood of the Lord, alleluia.

POSTCOMMUNION. Grant us, we beseech Thee, O Lord, to be filled with the everlasting fruition of Thy divinity, which is prefigured by the temporal reception of Thy precious Body and Blood. Who livest and reignest, etc. *Amen.*

SUNDAY WITHIN THE OCTAVE OF CORPUS CHRISTI

INTROIT. The Lord became my protector, and He brought me forth into a large place: He saved me, because He was well pleased with me.

I will love Thee, O Lord, my strength: the Lord is my rock, my refuge, and my deliverer.

Glory be to the Father, etc.

COLLECT. Make us, O Lord, to have a perpetual fear and love of Thy holy name; for Thou never failest to govern those whom Thou dost solidly establish in Thy love. Through Our Lord Jesus Christ, etc. *Amen.*

EPISTLE. 1 Jn 3:13–18. Dearly beloved: Wonder not if the world hate you. We know that we have passed from death to life, because we love the brethren. He who loveth not, abideth in death. Everyone who hateth his brother is a murderer: and ye know that no murderer hath life everlasting abiding in himself. In this we know the love of God, that He laid down His life for us: and we ought to lay down our lives for the brethren. He who hath the substance of this world, and seeth his brother in need, and shutteth up his bowels against him, how doth the love of God abide in him? My little children, let us love, not in word nor tongue, but in deed and truth.

GRADUAL. In my trouble I cried to the Lord, and He heard me. O Lord, deliver my soul from wicked lips and a deceitful tongue. Alleluia, alleluia. O Lord my God, in Thee have I put my trust: save me from all them that persecute me, and deliver me. Alleluia.

GOSPEL. Lk 14:16–24. At that time: Jesus spoke to the Pharisees this parable: A certain man made a great supper, and invited many. And he sent his servant at suppertime, to say to those who had been invited, that they should come, for now all things are ready. And they all began together to make excuse. The first said to him: I have bought a farm, and I must go out and see it; I pray thee, excuse me. And another said: I have bought five yoke of oxen, and I am going to try them; I pray thee, excuse me. And another said: I have married a wife, and, therefore, I cannot come. And the servant returning, told these things to his lord. Then the master of the house, being angry, said to his servant: Go out quickly into the streets and lanes of the city, and bring in hither the poor and the maimed, and the blind and the lame. And the servant said: Sir, it is done as thou hast commanded, and yet there is room. And the lord said to the servant: Go into the highways and hedges, and compel them to come in, that my house may be filled. But I say to you, that none of these men who have been invited shall taste of my supper.

OFFERTORY. Turn to me, O Lord, and deliver my soul: O save me for Thy mercy's sake.

SECRET. May the oblation we dedicate to Thy name cleanse us, O Lord: and make us daily advance in the practice of a heavenly life. Through Our Lord Jesus Christ, etc. *Amen.*

COMMUNION. I will sing to the Lord, Who giveth me good things, and will make melody to the name of the Lord most High.

POSTCOMMUNION. Having received Thy sacred gifts, we beseech Thee, O Lord, that, by the frequent reception of this mystery, the fruit of our salvation may increase. Through Our Lord Jesus Christ, etc. *Amen.*

FEAST OF THE SACRED HEART OF JESUS

FRIDAY AFTER THE OCTAVE OF CORPUS CHRISTI

INTROIT. He will have mercy according to the multitude of His mercies: for He hath not willingly afflicted nor cast off the children of men: the Lord is good to them that hope in Him, to the soul that seeketh Him, alleluia, alleluia.

The mercies of the Lord I will sing forevermore; from generation to generation. Glory be to the Father, etc.

COLLECT. Grant, we beseech Thee, Almighty God, that we who glory in the most Sacred Heart of Thy beloved Son, and celebrate the singular benefits of His love toward us, may rejoice equally in their operation and their fruit. Through the same Our Lord Jesus Christ, etc. *Amen.*

LESSON. Is 12:1–6. I will give thanks to Thee, O Lord, for Thou wast angry with me: Thy wrath is turned away, and Thou hast comforted me. Behold, God is my Savior, I will deal confidently, and will not fear: because the Lord is my strength, and my praise, and He is become my salvation. Ye shall draw waters with joy out of the fountains of salvation. And ye shall say in that day: Praise ye the Lord: and call on His name: make His works known among the peoples: remember that His name is high. Sing ye to the Lord, for He hath done a great thing: show this forth in all the earth. Rejoice, and praise, O thou habitation of Sion: for great in the midst of thee is the Holy One of Israel.

GRADUAL. O all ye that pass by the way, attend and see if there be any sorrow like to my sorrow. Having loved His own who were in the world, He loved them unto the end. Alleluia, alleluia. Learn of Me, because I am meek and humble of Heart: and you shall find rest to your souls. Alleluia.

GOSPEL. Jn 19.31–37. At that time: The Jews, because it was the eve of the Sabbath, that the bodies might not remain on the cross on the Sabbath (for that was a great Sabbath day), besought Pilate that their legs might be broken, and that they might be taken away. The soldiers therefore came; and broke the legs of the first, and of the other who was crucified with him. But after they came to Jesus, when they saw that He was already dead, they did not break His legs. But one of the soldiers pierced His side with a spear, and immediately there came out blood and water. And he who saw it giveth testimony; and his testimony is true.

OFFERTORY. Bless the Lord, O my soul, and never forget all He hath done for thee, Who satisfieth thy desire with good things. Alleluia.

SECRET. Defend us, O Lord, who offer to Thee Thy holocaust; and that our hearts may be more fervently prepared for it, enkindle within them the flames of Thy divine charity. Who livest and reignest, etc. *Amen.*

COMMUNION. My Heart hath expected reproach and misery; and I looked for one that would grieve together with Me, but there was none: and for one that would comfort Me, and I found none. Alleluia.

POSTCOMMUNION. Being fed with peaceful delights and life-giving Sacraments, we humbly beseech Thee, O Lord our God, that Thou, Who art meek and humble of Heart, wouldst make us clean from the stain of every vice, and more steadfastly to abhor the proud vanities of the world. Who livest and reignest, etc. *Amen.*

FEAST OF THE SACRED HEART
OF JESUS (*Revised Propers*)

‡INTROIT. The thoughts of His Heart to all generations: to deliver their souls from death and feed them in famine. Rejoice in the Lord, O ye just, praise becometh the upright.

Glory be to the Father, etc.

COLLECT. O God Who in the Heart of Thy Son, wounded by our sins, dost deign mercifully to bestow upon us the infinite treasures of Thy love; grant, we pray, that we who now pay Him the devout homage of our piety, may also perform the duty of worthy satisfaction. Through the same Our Lord Jesus Christ, etc. *Amen.*

EPISTLE. Eph 3:8–19. Brethren: To me, the least of all the saints, is given this grace, to preach among the Gentiles the unsearchable riches of Christ: and to enlighten all men, that they may see what is the dispensation of the mystery which hath been hidden from eternity in God Who created all things: that the manifold wisdom of God may be made known to the principalities and powers in heavenly places through the Church, according to the eternal purpose which He made in Christ Jesus Our Lord: in Whom we have boldness and access with confidence by the faith of Him. For this cause I bow my knees to the Father of Our Lord Jesus Christ, of Whom all paternity in heaven and earth is named, that He would grant you, according to the riches of His glory, to be strengthened by His Spirit with might unto the inward man: that Christ may dwell by faith in your hearts; that being rooted and founded in charity, you may be able to comprehend, with all the saints, what is the breadth, and length, and height, and depth, to know also the charity of Christ, which surpasseth all knowledge, that you may be filled unto all the fullness of God.

GRADUAL. The Lord is sweet and righteous: therefore He will give a law to sinners in the way. He will guide the mild in judgment: He will teach the meek His ways. Alleluia, alleluia. Take My yoke upon you and learn of Me, because I am meek, and humble of Heart: and you shall find rest to your souls, alleluia.

GOSPEL. Jn 19:31–37. At that time: The Jews (because it was the Parasceve), that the bodies might not remain upon the cross on the Sabbath day (for that was a great Sabbath day) besought Pilate that their legs might be broken, and that they might be taken away. The soldiers therefore came; and they broke the legs of the first, and of the other that was crucified with him. But after they were come to Jesus, when they saw that He was already dead, they did not break His legs. But one of the soldiers with a spear opened His side, and immediately there came out blood and water. And he that saw it hath given testimony; and his testimony is true. And he knoweth that he saith true, that you also may believe. For these things were done that the Scripture might be fulfilled: You shall not break a bone of Him. And again, another Scripture saith: They shall look on Him Whom they pierced.

OFFERTORY. My Heart hath expected reproach and misery, and I looked for one that would grieve together with Me, but there was none: and for one that would comfort Me, and I found none.

SECRET. Look, we pray, O Lord, on the Heart of Thy beloved Son, Whose charity no words can tell; that the gift which we offer may be pleasing to Thee and an expiation for our offenses. Through the same Our Lord Jesus Christ, etc. *Amen.*

COMMUNION. One of the soldiers with a spear opened His side, from which came blood and water.

POSTCOMMUNION. May Thy holy mysteries, O Lord Jesus, impart to us ivine fervor, so that, tasting the sweetness of Thy most gracious Heart, we may learn to despise earthly things and to love those of heaven. Who liveth and reigneth, etc.

THIRD SUNDAY AFTER PENTECOST

INTROIT. Look Thou upon me, and have mercy on me, O Lord; for I am alone and poor: look upon my lowliness and my labor: and forgive me all my sins, O my God.

To Thee, O Lord, have I lifted up my soul: in Thee, O my God, I put my trust; let me not be ashamed.

Glory be to the Father, etc.

COLLECT. O God, the Protector of all that trust in Thee, without Whom nothing is strong, nothing is holy: increase and multiply upon us Thy mercy: that, Thou being our Ruler and Guide, we may so pass through temporal blessings that we finally lose not those which are eternal. Through Our Lord Jesus Christ, etc. *Amen.*

EPISTLE. 1 Pt 5:6–11. Dearly beloved: Humble yourselves under the powerful hand of God; that He may exalt you in the time of visitation: casting all your care on Him; since He is careful of you. Be sober and vigilant, for your adversary, the devil, as a roaring lion, goeth about, seeking whom he may devour: whom resist strong in faith; knowing that the same sufferings befall your brethren in the world. But the God of all grace, Who hath called you to His eternal glory in Christ Jesus, will perfect, confirm, and establish you, after ye have suffered awhile. To Him be glory and empire forever and ever. Amen.

GRADUAL. Cast thy care upon the Lord, and He will sustain thee. Whilst I cried to the Lord, He heard my voice from them that draw near unto me. Alleluia, alleluia. God is a just Judge, strong and patient; is He angry every day? Alleluia.

GOSPEL. Lk 15:1–10. At that time: The publicans and sinners drew near to Him, to hear Him: and the Pharisees and the scribes murmured, saying: This man receiveth sinners and eateth with them. And He spake to them this parable, saying: What man of you hath a hundred sheep, and loseth one of them, doth not leave the ninety-nine in the desert, and go after that which was lost, until he find it? And when he hath found it, layeth it upon his shoulders, rejoicing; and coming home, he calleth together his friends and neighbors, saying to them: Rejoice with me, because I have found my sheep which was lost? I say to you, that even so there shall be joy in heaven over one sinner that repenteth, more than over ninety-nine just men who need not penance. Or what woman having ten pieces of silver, if she lose one piece, doth not light a lamp, and sweep the house, and seek diligently until she find it? And when she hath found it, she calleth together her friends and neighbors, saying: Rejoice with me, because I have found the piece which I had lost. So I say to you, there is joy before the angels of God over one sinner that repenteth.

OFFERTORY. Let them trust in Thee who know Thy name, O Lord: for Thou hast not forsaken them that seek Thee: sing ye to the Lord, Who dwelleth in Sion: for He hath not forgotten the cry of the poor.

SECRET. Look down, O Lord, upon the offerings of Thy suppliant Church: and grant that they may ever be for the salvation and sanctification of those who believe. Through Our Lord Jesus Christ, etc. *Amen.*

COMMUNION. I say to you: There is joy before the angels of God upon one sinner doing penance.

POSTCOMMUNION. May we be renewed, O Lord, by Thy sacred mysteries which we have received; and may they expiate our sins, and prepare us for Thine eternal mercies. Through Our Lord Jesus Christ, etc. *Amen.*

FOURTH SUNDAY AFTER PENTECOST

INTROIT. The Lord is my light and my salvation; whom shall I fear? The Lord is the protector of my life; of whom shall I be afraid? Mine enemies that trouble me have themselves been weakened and have fallen.

If armies in camp should stand together against me, my heart shall not fear.

Glory be to the Father, etc.

COLLECT. Grant, O Lord, we beseech Thee, both that the course of this world may be peaceably ordered by Thy governance, and that Thy Church may joyfully serve Thee in tranquil devotion. Through Our Lord Jesus Christ, etc. *Amen.*

EPISTLE. Rom 8:18–23. Brethren: I think that the sufferings of this present time are not worthy of the glory, which shall be revealed in us. For the expectation of the creature waiteth for the revelation of the sons of God. For the creature was made subject to vanity, not willingly, but by reason of Him who made it subject in hope: because the creature also itself shall be delivered from the bondage of corruption, into the glorious liberty of the children of God. For we know that the whole creation groaneth, and travaileth in pain, until now. And not only it, but ourselves also having the firstfruits of the Spirit, even we ourselves groan within ourselves, waiting for the adoption of the sons of God, the redemption of our body: in Christ Jesus Our Lord.

GRADUAL. Forgive us our sins, O Lord, lest the Gentiles should at any time say: Where is their God? Help us, O God our Savior, and for the honor of Thy name, O Lord, deliver us. Alleluia, alleluia. O God, Who sittest upon the throne and judgest justice, be Thou the refuge of the poor in tribulation. Alleluia.

GOSPEL. Lk 5:1–11. At that time: When the crowd pressed on Jesus to hear the word of God, He stood by the lake of Genesareth, and He saw two barks standing by the lake; but the fishermen were gone out of them, and were washing their nets. And going up into one of the barks, that was Simon's, He desired Him to put off a little from the land. And sitting down, He taught the crowds out of the bark. Now when He had ceased to speak, He said to Simon: Put off into the deep, and let down your nets for a draught. And Simon, answering, said to Him: Master, we have toiled all the night, and taken nothing, but at Thy word I will let down the net. And when they had done this, they enclosed a great multitude of fishes; and their net was breaking. And they beckoned to their partners who were in the other bark, that they should come and help them. And they came, and filled both the barks, so that they were almost sinking. When Simon Peter saw this, he fell down at the knees of Jesus, saying: Depart from me, for I am a sinful man, O Lord! For amazement had seized him, and all who were with him, at the draught of the fishes which they had taken; and so likewise James and John, the sons of Zebedee, who were partners of Simon. And Jesus said to Simon: Fear not, from henceforth thou wilt catch men. And when they had brought their barks to shore, they left all things and followed Him.

OFFERTORY. Enlighten my eyes, that I never sleep in death: lest at any time my enemy say: I have prevailed against him.

SECRET. Be appeased, O Lord, we beseech Thee, by our offerings which Thou dost receive: and in Thy mercy compel even our rebellious wills to yield to Thee. Through Our Lord Jesus Christ, etc. *Amen.*

COMMUNION. The Lord is my firmament, and my refuge and my deliverer; my God is my helper.

POSTCOMMUNION. May the mysteries which we have received purify us, O Lord, we beseech Thee; and defend us by the gifts which they convey. Through Our Lord Jesus Christ, etc. *Amen.*

FIFTH SUNDAY AFTER PENTECOST

INTROIT. Hear, O Lord, my voice with which I have cried unto Thee; be Thou my helper, forsake me not, neither despise me, O God, my Savior.

The Lord is my light and my salvation: whom shall I fear?

Glory be to the Father, etc.

COLLECT. O God, Who hast prepared for those who love Thee good things beyond the vision of man: pour into our hearts such love toward Thee that we, loving Thee in all things and above all things, may obtain Thy promises, which exceed all that we can desire. Through Our Lord Jesus Christ, etc. *Amen.*

EPISTLE. 1 Pt 3:8–15. Dearly beloved: Be ye all of one mind in prayer, sympathizing, loving the brotherhood, merciful, modest, humble; not rendering evil for evil, nor insult for insult, but, on the contrary, blessing: for to this ye are called, that ye may inherit a blessing. For let him who will love life and see good days refrain his tongue from evil, and his lips that they speak no guile; let him turn away from evil, and do good; let him seek peace and pursue it, for the eyes of the Lord are on the just, and His ears are open to their prayers: but the countenance of the Lord is on those who do evil. And who is there, who can hurt you, if ye be zealous for good? But if also ye suffer something for justice, blessed are ye. And fear not their terror, and be not troubled; but sanctify Christ the Lord in your hearts.

GRADUAL. Behold, O God our protector, and look on Thy servants. O Lord God of hosts, give ear to the prayers of Thy servants. Alleluia, alleluia. In Thy strength, O Lord, the king: shall joy; and in Thy salvation he shall rejoice exceedingly. Alleluia.

GOSPEL. Mt 5:20–24. At that time: Jesus said to His disciples: Unless your justice abound more than that of the scribes and Pharisees, ye shall not enter into the kingdom of heaven. Ye have heard that it was said to those of old: Thou shalt not kill: and whoever shall kill shall be in danger of the judgment. But I say to you, that whoever is angry with his brother shall be in danger of the judgment. And whoever shall say to his brother, Raca, shall be in danger of the council. And whoever shall say, Thou fool, shall be in danger of hellfire. If therefore thou bring thy gift to the altar, and there rememberest that thy brother hath anything against thee, leave there thy gift before the altar, and go first and be reconciled to thy brother; and then come and offer thy gift.

OFFERTORY. I will bless the Lord, Who hath given me understanding: I set God always in my sight; for He is at my right hand, that I be not moved.

SECRET. Be appeased, O Lord, by our humble prayers: and graciously receive the gifts of Thy servants and handmaids; that what each doth offer to the honor of Thy name may avail for the salvation of all. Through Our Lord Jesus Christ, etc. *Amen.*

COMMUNION. One thing I have asked of the Lord, this will I seek after; that I may dwell in the house of the Lord all the days of my life.

POSTCOMMUNION. Grant, we beseech Thee, O Lord, that we whom Thou hast fed with a heavenly gift may be cleansed from our hidden sins, and delivered from the snares of our enemies. Through Our Lord Jesus Christ, etc. *Amen.*

SIXTH SUNDAY AFTER PENTECOST

INTROIT. The Lord is the strength of His people, and the protector of the salvation of His anointed: save, O Lord, Thy people, and bless Thine inheritance, and rule them forever.

Unto Thee will I cry, O Lord: O my God, be not Thou silent to me; lest if Thou be silent to me, I become like them that go down into the pit.

Glory be to the Father, etc.

COLLECT. O God of all power and might, to Whom belongeth everything that is best: implant in our hearts the love of Thy name, and increase within us true religion; that Thou mayest nourish in us those things that are good, and by the zeal of our devotion mayest preserve what Thou hast nourished. Through Our Lord Jesus Christ, etc. *Amen.*

EPISTLE. Rom 6:3–11. Brethren: All ye who are baptized in Christ Jesus, are baptized in His death. For we are buried together with Him by Baptism into death; that as Christ is risen from the dead by the glory of the Father, so we also may walk in newness of life. For, if we have been planted together in the likeness of His death, we shall be also of His Resurrection. Knowing this, that our old man is crucified with Him, that the body of sin may be destroyed, and that we may serve sin no longer. For he who is dead is justified from sin. But if we be dead with Christ, we believe that we shall live also together with Christ: knowing that Christ, rising again from the dead, dieth now no more, death shall no more have dominion over Him. For that He died for sin, He died once: but that He liveth, He liveth to God. So ye also reckon yourselves dead indeed to sin, but alive to God, in Christ Jesus Our Lord.

GRADUAL. Return, O Lord, a little; and be entreated in favor of Thy servants. Lord, Thou hast been our refuge from generation to generation. Alleluia, alleluia. In Thee, O Lord, have I hoped, let me never be confounded: deliver me in Thy justice, and release me; bow down Thine ear to me, make haste to deliver me. Alleluia.

GOSPEL. Mk 8:1–9. At that time: When there was a great crowd with Jesus, and they had nothing to eat, He called His disciples together, and said to them: I have compassion on the crowd, for behold, they have now been with Me three days, and have nothing to eat. And if I send them away fasting to their home, they will faint on the way, for some of them have come from afar. And His disciples answered Him: Whence can anyone satisfy them with bread here in the wilderness? And He asked them: How many loaves have ye? They said: Seven. And He commanded the crowd to lie on the ground. And He took the seven loaves, and gave thanks and broke them, and gave to His disciples to set before them: and they set them before the crowd. And they had a few small fishes: and He blessed them, and commanded them to be set before them. And they ate and were satisfied; and they took up the broken meat which remained, seven baskets full. And they who ate were about four thousand: and He sent them away.

OFFERTORY. Perfect Thou my goings in Thy paths, that my footsteps be not moved: incline Thine ear, and hear my words: show forth Thy wonderful mercies, Thou Who savest them that trust in Thee, O Lord.

SECRET. Be appeased, O Lord by our humble prayers, and graciously receive the offerings of Thy people: and, that no prayer may be in vain and no petition void, grant that we may effectually obtain that for which we faithfully pray. Through Our Lord Jesus Christ, etc. *Amen.*

COMMUNION. I will go round, and offer up in His tabernacle a sacrifice of jubilation: I will sing, and recite a psalm to the Lord.

POSTCOMMUNION. Having been filled, O Lord, with Thy gifts, grant, we beseech Thee, that we may be cleansed by their virtue and defended by their help. Through Our Lord Jesus Christ, etc. *Amen.*

SEVENTH SUNDAY AFTER PENTECOST

INTROIT. O clap your hands, all ye nations; shout unto God with the voice of joy. For the Lord is high, and terrible: a great King over all the earth. Glory be to the Father, etc.

COLLECT. O God, the ordering of Whose providence never erreth: we humbly beseech Thee to put away from us all hurtful things, and to give us all those things which are profitable for us. Through Our Lord Jesus Christ, etc. *Amen.*

EPISTLE. Rom 6:19–23. Brethren: I speak a human thing, because of the infirmity of your flesh; for as ye have yielded your members to serve uncleanness and iniquity unto iniquity, so now yield your members to serve justice unto sanctification. For when ye were servants of sin, ye were free from justice. What fruit, therefore, had ye then in those things, of which ye are now ashamed? For the end of them is death. But now being made free from sin, and having become servants of God, ye have your fruit unto sanctification, but the end everlasting life. For the wages of sin is death. But the grace of God is life everlasting, in Christ Jesus Our Lord.

GRADUAL. Come, children, hearken to Me; I will teach you the fear of the Lord. Come ye to Him and be enlightened; and your faces shall not be confounded. Alleluia, alleluia. O clap your hands all ye nations; shout unto God with the voice of joy. Alleluia.

GOSPEL. Mt 7:15–21. At that time: Jesus said to His disciples: Beware of false prophets, who come to you in the clothing of sheep, but inwardly are ravenous wolves. By their fruits ye shall know them. Do men gather grapes of thorns, or figs of thistles? Even so every good tree bringeth forth good fruit, and the evil tree bringeth forth evil fruit. A good tree cannot bring forth evil fruit, neither can an evil tree bring forth good fruit. Every tree that bringeth not forth good fruit shall be cut down, and cast into the fire. Wherefore by their fruits ye shall know them. Not everyone who saith to Me, Lord, Lord, shall enter into the kingdom of heaven; but he who doeth the will of My Father Who is in heaven, he shall enter the kingdom of heaven.

OFFERTORY. As in holocausts of rams and bullocks, and as in thousands of fat lambs; so let our sacrifice be made in Thy sight this day, that it may please Thee: for there is no confusion to them that trust in Thee, O Lord.

SECRET. O God, Who hast ratified the divers victims of the law by one perfect sacrifice: receive the oblation of Thy devoted servants, and hallow it with a blessing like to that wherewith Thou didst hallow the gifts of Abel; so that what each has offered in honor of Thy Majesty may avail for the salvation of all. Through Our Lord Jesus Christ, etc. *Amen.*

COMMUNION. Bow down Thine ear, make haste to deliver me.

POSTCOMMUNION. May Thy healing operation, O Lord, mercifully free us from our perverse inclinations, and lead us to those things which are right. Through Our Lord Jesus Christ, etc. *Amen.*

EIGHTH SUNDAY AFTER PENTECOST

INTROIT. We have received Thy mercy, O God, in the midst of Thy temple; according to Thy name, O God, so also is Thy praise unto the ends of the earth: Thy right hand is full of justice.

Great is the Lord and greatly to be praised; in the city of our God, even upon His holy mountain.

Glory be to the Father, etc.

COLLECT. Mercifully grant to us, O Lord, we beseech Thee, the spirit to think and do always such things as are right; that we, who cannot exist without Thee, may by Thee be enabled to live according to Thy will. Through Our Lord Jesus Christ, etc. *Amen.*

EPISTLE. Rom 8:12–17. Therefore, brethren, we are debtors, not to the flesh, to live after the flesh; for if ye live after the flesh, ye shall die. But if by the spirit ye mortify the deeds of the flesh, ye shall live; for whoever are led by the Spirit of God, they are sons of God. For ye have not received a spirit of bondage again in fear, but ye have received a spirit of adoption of sons, in which we cry: Abba (Father). For the Spirit Himself beareth testimony to our spirit, that we are children of God; and if children, heirs also; heirs indeed of God, and joint heirs with Christ.

GRADUAL. Be Thou unto me a God, a protector, and a place of refuge, to save me. In Thee, O God, have I hoped: O Lord, let me never be confounded. Alleluia, alleluia. Great is the Lord, and exceedingly to be praised; in the city of our God, in His holy mountain. Alleluia.

GOSPEL. Lk 16:1–9. At that time: Jesus spoke to His disciples this parable: There was a certain rich man who had a steward; and he was accused to him of wasting his goods. And he called him, and said to him: What is this that I hear of thee? Give an account of thy stewardship, for thou canst be steward no longer. And the steward said within himself: What shall I do, since my lord taketh away the stewardship from me? To dig I am not able: to beg I am ashamed. I know what I will do, that when I am removed from the stewardship, they may receive me into their houses. Therefore, calling together every one of the debtors of his lord, he said to the first: How much owest thou to my lord? He said: A hundred measures of oil. And he said to him: Take thy note, and sit down quickly, and write fifty. Then he said to another: And how much owest thou? He said: A hundred measures of wheat. He said to him: Take thy bill, and write eighty. And the lord praised the unjust steward, because he had done prudently; for the children of this world are wiser for their generation than the children of light. And I say to you: Make to yourselves friends of the mammon of iniquity, that when ye shall fail, they may receive you into the everlasting mansions.

OFFERTORY. Thou wilt save the humble people, O Lord, and wilt bring down the eyes of the proud; for who is God, but Thou, O Lord?

SECRET. Receive, O Lord, we beseech Thee, the gifts which of Thine own bounty we offer unto Thee: that, through Thy grace, these most holy mysteries may sanctify the conduct of our present life and bring us to eternal joys. Through Our Lord Jesus Christ, etc. *Amen.*

COMMUNION. Taste and see that the Lord is sweet: blessed is the man that hopeth in Him.

POSTCOMMUNION. May this heavenly mystery be to us, O Lord, a reparation of mind and body; that we may experience the effect of that which we celebrate. Through Our Lord Jesus Christ, etc. *Amen.*

NINTH SUNDAY AFTER PENTECOST

INTROIT. Behold, God is my helper, and the Lord is the protector of my soul: turn back evil upon mine enemies, and destroy Thou them in Thy Truth, O Lord my protector.

Save me, O God, by Thy name, and deliver me in Thy strength.

Glory be to the Father, etc.

COLLECT. Let Thy merciful ears, O Lord, be open to the prayers of Thy suppliant people; and that Thou mayest grant them their desires, make them to ask such things as please Thee. Through Our Lord Jesus Christ, etc. *Amen.*

EPISTLE. 1 Cor 10:6–13. Brethren: We may not be covetous of evil things, as even they coveted. Neither become ye idolaters, as some of them, as it is written: The people sat down to eat and drink, and rose up to play. Neither let us fornicate, as some of them fornicated, and twenty-three thousand fell in one day. Neither let us tempt Christ, as some of them tempted, and were destroyed by the serpents. Neither murmur, as some of them murmured, and perished by the destroyer. Now all these things happened to them in figure, and they are written for a warning to us, on whom the ends of the world have come. Therefore let him who thinketh that he standeth, take heed lest he fall. Let no temptation take hold on you, but such as is human: and God is faithful, Who will not suffer you to be tempted above what ye are able; but will even make with temptation an issue, that ye may be able to bear it.

GRADUAL. O Lord, Our Lord, how admirable is Thy name in the whole earth! For Thy magnificence is elevated above the heavens. Alleluia, alleluia. Deliver me from mine enemies, O my God: and defend me from them that rise up against me. Alleluia.

GOSPEL. Lk 19:41–47. At that time: When Jesus drew near to Jerusalem, seeing the city, He wept over it, saying: If thou also hadst known, and that in this thy day, the things which are for thy peace; but now they are hidden from thine eyes. For the days will come upon thee, and thine enemies will cast a trench round about thee, and compass thee round, and straiten thee on every side, and beat thee to the ground, and thy children who are in thee: and they will not leave in thee one stone upon another, because thou hast not known the time of thy visitation. And entering into the temple, He began to cast out those who sold therein, and those who bought, saying to them: It is written: My house is a house of prayer; but ye have made it a den of robbers. And He was teaching daily in the temple.

OFFERTORY. The justices of the Lord are right, rejoicing hearts, and His judgments are sweeter than honey and the honeycomb; for Thy servant keepeth them.

SECRET. Grant us, O Lord, we beseech Thee, worthily to approach these mysteries: for as often as this memorial-sacrifice is celebrated, the work of our Redemption is wrought. Through Our Lord Jesus Christ, etc. *Amen.*

COMMUNION. He that eateth My Flesh, and drinketh My Blood, abideth in Me and I in him, saith the Lord.

POSTCOMMUNION. We beseech Thee, O Lord, that the communion of Thy Sacrament may bestow upon us both purification and unity. Through Our Lord Jesus Christ, etc. *Amen.*

TENTH SUNDAY AFTER PENTECOST

INTROIT. When I cried to the Lord, He heard my voice, from them that draw near against me; and He humbled them, Who is before all ages, and remains forever: cast thy care upon the Lord, and He shall nourish thee.

Hear my prayer, O God, and despise not my supplication, be attentive unto me, and hear me.

Glory be to the Father, etc.

COLLECT. O God, Who dost manifest Thine Almighty power chiefly in showing pardon and pity: increase and multiply upon us Thy mercy; that we, running the way toward the attainment of Thy promises, may be made partakers of Thy heavenly treasures. Through Our Lord Jesus Christ, etc. *Amen.*

EPISTLE. 1 Cor 12:2–11. Brethren: Ye know, that when ye were heathens, ye went to dumb idols, according as ye were led. Wherefore I make known to you, that no man speaking by the Spirit of God saith anathema to Jesus; and no man can say, Lord Jesus, but in the Holy Spirit. Now there are diversities of gifts, but the same Spirit; and there are diversities of ministrations, but the same Lord; and there are diversities of operations, but the same God, Who worketh all in all. And the manifestation of the Spirit is given to every man unto profit. To one indeed, by the Spirit, is given the word of wisdom; and to another, the word of knowledge, according to the same Spirit; to another, faith in the same Spirit; to another, the grace of cures in the one Spirit; to another, the working of miracles; to another, prophecy; to another, the discerning of spirits; to another, kinds of tongues; to another, interpretation of speeches. But all these things the one and the same Spirit worketh, dividing to every one according as He willeth.

GRADUAL. Keep me, O Lord, as the apple of Thine eye; protect me under the shadow of Thy wings. Let my judgment come forth from Thy countenance: let

Thine eyes behold the things that are equitable. Alleluia, alleluia. A hymn, O God, becometh Thee in Sion: and a vow shall be paid to Thee in Jerusalem. Alleluia.

GOSPEL. Lk 18:9–14. At that time: To some who trusted in themselves as just, and despised others, Jesus spoke this parable: Two men went up into the temple to pray; the one a Pharisee, and the other a publican. The Pharisee, standing, prayed thus with himself: O God, I thank Thee that I am not as the rest of men, extortioners, unjust, adulterers; as even this publican. I fast twice in the week; I give tithes of all I possess. And the publican, standing afar off, would not so much as lift his eyes to heaven, but struck his breast, saying: O God, be merciful to me a sinner. I say to you, this man went down to his house justified rather than the other: for everyone who exalteth himself will be humbled, and he who humbleth himself will be exalted.

OFFERTORY. To Thee, O Lord, have I lifted up my soul: in Thee, O my God, I put my trust, let me not be ashamed: neither let mine enemies laugh at me: for none of them that wait on Thee shall be confounded.

SECRET. Let the appointed sacrifices be offered to Thee, O Lord, which Thou hast granted us so to present for the honor of Thy name, that they may also be for the healing of our ills. Through Our Lord Jesus Christ, etc. *Amen.*

COMMUNION. Thou wilt accept the sacrifice of justice, oblations and holocausts, upon Thine altar, O Lord.

POSTCOMMUNION. We beseech Thee, O Lord our God, that in Thy mercy Thou wouldest not leave destitute of Thine aids those whom Thou ceasest not to refresh with Thy divine Sacraments. Through Our Lord Jesus Christ, etc. *Amen.*

ELEVENTH SUNDAY AFTER PENTECOST

INTROIT. God in His holy place; God Who maketh men of one manner to dwell in a house: He will give power and strength unto His people.

Let God arise, and let His enemies be scattered; and let them that hate Him flee from before His face.

Glory be to the Father, etc.

COLLECT. Almighty, everlasting God, Who, in the abundance of Thy loving kindness, dost exceed both the merits and the desires of those who pray unto Thee: pour down upon us Thy mercy; forgiving us those things of which our conscience is afraid, and granting us those good things which our prayer does not presume to ask. Through Our Lord Jesus Christ, etc. *Amen.*

EPISTLE. 1 Cor 15:1–10. Brethren: I make known to you the gospel which I preached to you, which also ye have received, wherein also ye stand; by which also ye are saved, after what manner I preached to you, if ye hold it fast, unless ye have believed in vain. For I delivered to you first of all, that which I also received, that Christ died for our sins, according to the Scriptures; and that He was buried, and that He arose again the third day, according to the Scriptures; and that He was seen by Kephas, and after that by the Eleven; then was He seen by more than five hundred brethren at once, of whom many remain until this present, and some are fallen asleep; afterward, He was seen by James, then by all the apostles; and last of all, as by one born out of time, He was seen by me also. For I am the least of the apostles, who am not worthy to be called an apostle, because I persecuted the Church of God; but by the grace of God I am what I am, and His grace unto me hath not been void.

GRADUAL. In God hath my heart confided, and I have been helped; and my flesh hath flourished again; and with my will I will give praise to Him. Unto Thee have I cried, O Lord: O my God, be not Thou silent; depart not from me. Alleluia, alleluia. Rejoice to God our helper; sing aloud to the God of Jacob: take a joyful psalm with the harp. Alleluia.

GOSPEL. Mk 7:31–37. At that time: Jesus, going out of the borders of Tyre, came by Sidon to the sea of Galilee, through the midst of the borders of Decapolis. And they bring to Him one deaf and dumb, and besought Him to put His hand upon him. And taking him from the multitude apart, He put His fingers into his ears, and He spat and touched his tongue; and looking up to heaven, He groaned, and said to him: Ephpheta, which is, Be opened. And immediately his ears were opened, and the string of his tongue was loosed, and he spake rightly. And He charged them that they should tell no one; but the more He charged them, so much the more a great deal did they publish it; and so much the more did they wonder, saying: He hath done all things well; He maketh both the deaf to hear and the dumb to speak.

OFFERTORY. I will extol Thee, O Lord, for Thou hast upheld me; and hast not made mine enemies to rejoice over me: O Lord, I have cried to Thee, and Thou hast healed me.

SECRET. Look graciously upon our service, O Lord, we beseech Thee, that the gift we offer may be acceptable to Thee, and be to us the support of our weakness. Through Our Lord Jesus Christ, etc. *Amen.*

COMMUNION. Honor the Lord with thy substance, and with the first of all thy fruits: and thy barns shall be filled with abundance, and thy presses shall run over with wine.

POSTCOMMUNION. We beseech Thee, O Lord, that by the reception of Thy Sacrament we may feel support of mind and body; that, saved in both, we may glory in the fullness of the heavenly remedy. Through Our Lord Jesus Christ, etc. *Amen.*

TWELFTH SUNDAY AFTER PENTECOST

INTROIT. Come unto my help, O God: O Lord, make haste to help me: let my enemies be ashamed and put to confusion who seek after my soul.

Let them be turned backward and blush for shame that wish me evil.

Glory be to the Father, etc.

COLLECT. Almighty and merciful God, of Whose gift it cometh that Thy faithful people do Thee worthy and laudable service: grant, we beseech Thee, that we run without stumbling to the attainment of Thy promises. Through Our Lord Jesus Christ, etc. *Amen.*

EPISTLE. 2 Cor 3:4–9. Brethren: Such confidence we have through Christ to God. Not that we are sufficient to think anything of ourselves, as of ourselves; but our sufficiency is from God: Who also hath made us fit ministers of the new covenant, not in the letter, but in the Spirit: for the letter killeth, but the Spirit giveth life. But if the ministration of death formed with letters on stones was glorious, so that the children of Israel could not behold the face of Moses, for the glory of his countenance, which is made void: how shall not the ministration of the spirit be more glorious? For if the ministry of condemnation is glory, much more the ministry of justice aboundeth in glory.

GRADUAL. I will bless the Lord at all times: His praise shall be ever in my mouth. In the Lord shall my soul be praised; let the meek hear, and rejoice. Alleluia, alleluia. O Lord the God of my salvation, I have cried in the day and in the night before Thee. Alleluia.

GOSPEL. Lk 10:23–37. At that time: Jesus said to His disciples: Happy are the eyes that see the things which ye see. For I say to you, that many prophets and kings desired to see the things which ye see, and saw them not; and to hear the things which ye hear, and heard them not. And behold, a certain lawyer stood up, trying Him, and saying: Teacher, what must I do to possess eternal life? But He said to him: What is written in the law? How readest thou? He answering, said: Thou shalt love the Lord thy God with all thy heart, and with all thy soul, and with all thy strength, and with all thy mind, and thy neighbor as thyself. And He said to him: Thou hast answered rightly: this do, and thou shalt live. But he, willing to justify himself, said to Jesus: And who is my neighbor? And Jesus resumed and said: A certain man was going down from Jerusalem to Jericho, and fell in with robbers, who even stripped him and wounded him, and went away, leaving him half dead. And by chance, a certain priest went down by the same road, and seeing him, passed by. In like manner also a Levite, when he was near the place, and saw him, passed by. But a certain Samaritan, traveling, came near him; and seeing him, was moved with compassion. And going up to him, he bound up his wounds, pouring in oil and wine, and set him on his own beast, brought him to an inn, and took care of him. And the next day, he took out two shillings, and gave to the innkeeper, and said: Take care of him, and whatever thou shalt lay out over and above, I will repay thee at my return. Which of these three appeareth to thee to have been a neighbor to him who fell among the robbers? And he said: He who showed mercy to him. And Jesus said to him: Go, and do thou in like manner.

OFFERTORY. Moses prayed in the sight of the Lord his God, and said: Why, O Lord, is Thine indignation enkindled against Thy people? Let the anger of Thy mind cease; remember Abraham, Isaac, and Jacob, to whom Thou didst swear to give a land flowing with milk and honey: and the Lord was appeased from doing the evil, which He had spoken of doing against His people.

SECRET. Graciously regard, O Lord, we beseech Thee, the sacrifices we present at Thy holy altar: that while they win pardon for us they may also give honor to Thy name. Through Our Lord Jesus Christ, etc. *Amen.*

COMMUNION. The earth shall be filled with the fruit of Thy works, O Lord, that Thou mayest bring bread out of the earth, and that wine may cheer the heart of man; that he may make the face cheerful with oil; and that bread may strengthen man's heart.

POSTCOMMUNION. May the holy participation of this mystery give life to us, O Lord, we beseech Thee; and procure for us both expiation and protection. Through Our Lord Jesus Christ, etc. *Amen.*

THIRTEENTH SUNDAY AFTER PENTECOST

INTROIT. Have regard, O Lord, unto Thy covenant, and forsake not forever the souls of Thy poor: arise, O Lord, and judge Thy cause, and forget not the voices of them that seek Thee.

O God, why hast Thou cast us off forever? why is Thy wrath enkindled against the sheep of Thy pasture?

Glory be to the Father, etc.

COLLECT. Almighty and everlasting God, give unto us an increase of faith, hope, and charity; and, that we may worthily obtain that which Thou dost promise, make us to love that which Thou dost command. Through Our Lord Jesus Christ, etc. *Amen.*

EPISTLE. Gal 3:16–22. Brethren: The promises were made to Abraham and his Seed. He doth not say: and seeds, as if of many; but as of one: and thy Seed, which is Christ. And this I say: the covenant confirmed by God, the Law which was made after four hundred and thirty years, doth not annul, so as to make void the promise. For if the inheritance be by the Law, it is no more by promise. But God gave to Abraham by promise. Why, then, was the Law? It was put because of transgressions, until the Seed should come, to Whom He had promised, it being ordained by angels, in the hand of a mediator. Now a mediator is not of one; but God is one. Is the Law, then, against the promises of God? God forbid. For if a law had been given which could give life, truly justice would have been by the Law. But the Scripture hath shut up all things under sin, that the promise by faith in Jesus Christ might be given to those who believe.

GRADUAL. Have regard, O Lord, to Thy covenant, and forsake not to the end the souls of Thy poor. Arise, O Lord, and judge Thy cause; remember the reproach of Thy servants. Alleluia, alleluia. Lord, Thou hast been our refuge, from generation to generation. Alleluia.

GOSPEL. Lk 17:11–19. At that time: As Jesus was going to Jerusalem, He passed through the midst of Samaria and Galilee. And as He entered into a certain town, there met Him ten lepers, who stood afar off, and lifted up their voice, saying: Jesus, Master, have mercy on us. And when He saw them, He said: Go, show yourselves to the priests. And it came to pass that, as they went, they were cleansed. But one of them, when he saw that he was cleansed, went back, and with a loud voice glorified God. And he fell on his face at His feet, giving thanks: and this was a Samaritan. And Jesus answering, said: Were not the ten cleansed? And where are the nine? There is no one found to return, and give glory to God, but this stranger. And He said to him: Arise, and depart, for thy faith hath healed thee.

OFFERTORY. In Thee, O Lord, have I hoped, I said: Thou art my God, my times are in Thy hands.

SECRET. Look graciously, O Lord, upon Thy people, look graciously upon our gifts: that being appeased by this offering, Thou mayest both grant us pardon and give us what we seek. Through Our Lord Jesus Christ, etc. *Amen.*

COMMUNION. Thou hast given us, O Lord, bread from heaven, having in it all that is delicious, and the sweetness of every taste.

POSTCOMMUNION. Having received Thy heavenly Sacraments, O Lord, we beseech Thee that we may profit to the increase of eternal redemption. Through Our Lord Jesus Christ, etc. *Amen.*

FOURTEENTH SUNDAY AFTER PENTECOST

INTROIT. Behold, O God our protector, and look upon the face of Thy Christ; for one day in Thy courts is better than a thousand.

How lovely are Thy tabernacles, O Lord of hosts: my soul longeth and fainteth for the courts of the Lord.

Glory be to the Father, etc.

COLLECT. Keep, we beseech Thee, O Lord, Thy Church with Thy perpetual favor; and, because the frailty of man without Thee cannot but fall, keep it ever by Thy help from all things hurtful, and lead it to all things profitable to salvation. Through Our Lord Jesus Christ, etc. *Amen.*

EPISTLE. Gal 5:16–24. Brethren: Walk in spirit, and ye will not fulfill the lusts of the flesh: for the flesh lusteth against the Spirit, and the Spirit against the flesh: for these are contrary one to another: so that ye do not whatever things ye will. But if ye are led by the Spirit, ye are not under the law. And the works of the flesh are manifest; which are fornication, uncleanness, lasciviousness, luxury, idolatry, witchcraft, enmities, contentions, rivalries, wrath, quarrels, disputes, sects, envying, murders, drunkenness, revelings, and the like; of which I foretell you, as I have before said, that they who do such things shall not obtain the Kingdom of God. But the fruit of the Spirit is charity, joy, peace, patience, mildness, goodness, long-suffering, meekness, faith, modesty, continence, chastity. Against such there is no law. And they who are of Christ have crucified their flesh with its vices and lusts.

GRADUAL. It is good to confide in the Lord, rather than to have confidence in man. It is good to trust in the Lord, rather than to trust in princes. Alleluia, alleluia. Come, let us praise the Lord with joy; let us joyfully sing to God our Savior. Alleluia.

GOSPEL. Mt 6:24–33. At that time: Jesus said to His disciples: No man can serve two masters; for either he will hate one, and love the other, or he will cling to one, and slight the other. Ye cannot serve God and mammon. Therefore I say to you: Be not anxious for your life, what ye shall eat, nor for your body, what ye shall put on. Is not the life more than the food? and the body more than the raiment? Behold the birds of the air, for they neither sow, nor reap, nor gather into barns, yet your heavenly Father feedeth them. Are not ye of much more value than they? And which of you, by anxious thought, can add to his stature one cubit? And for raiment, why are ye anxious? Consider the lilies of the field, how they grow: they labor not, neither do they spin. Yet I say to you, that not even Solomon in all his glory was arrayed as one of these. Wherefore, if God so clothe the grass of the field, which is today, and tomorrow is cast into the oven, how much more you, O ye of little faith? Be not anxious, therefore, saying: What shall we eat, or what shall we drink, or wherewith shall we be clothed? For after all these things the heathen seek. For your Father knoweth that ye have need of all these things. Seek ye, therefore, first the Kingdom of God, and His justice; and all these things shall be added unto you.

OFFERTORY. The angel of the Lord shall encamp round about them that fear Him, and shall deliver them: O taste and see that the Lord is sweet.

SECRET. Grant us, O Lord, we beseech Thee, that this saving victim may be at once the cleansing of our sins and the appeasing of Thy might. Through Our Lord Jesus Christ, etc. *Amen.*

COMMUNION. Seek first the Kingdom of God and all things shall be added unto you, saith the Lord.

POSTCOMMUNION. May Thy Sacraments, O God, ever purify and defend us; and lead us to the end of eternal salvation. Through Our Lord Jesus Christ, etc. *Amen.*

FIFTEENTH SUNDAY AFTER PENTECOST

INTROIT. Incline Thine ear, O Lord, unto me, and hear me: save Thy servant, O my God, that trusteth in Thee: have mercy upon me, O Lord, for unto Thee have I cried all the day.

Give joy to the soul of Thy servant; for unto Thee, O Lord, have I lifted up my soul.

Glory be to the Father, etc.

COLLECT. O Lord, let Thy continual pity cleanse and defend Thy Church; and, because it cannot continue in safety without Thee, govern it evermore by Thy help. Through Our Lord Jesus Christ, etc. *Amen.*

EPISTLE. Gal 5:25–6:10. Brethren: If we live by the Spirit, let us walk also by the Spirit. Let us not be vainglorious, provoking one another, envying one another. Brethren, if even a man be overtaken in any fault, ye who are spiritual correct him in a spirit of gentleness, considering thyself, lest thou also be tempted. Bear ye one another's burdens, and so ye will fulfill the law of Christ. For if any man think himself to be something, whereas he is nothing, he deceiveth himself. But let every man prove his own work, and so he will have glory in himself only, and not in another. For every one shall bear his own burden. And let him who is instructed in the word communicate to him who instructeth him, in all good things. Be not deceived: God is not mocked. For what a man soweth, that shall he reap also. For he who soweth for his flesh, of the flesh shall also reap corruption; but he who soweth for the Spirit, of the Spirit shall reap everlasting life. And let us not be weary in well doing, for in due time we shall reap if we faint not. Therefore, whilst we have time, let us do good to all, but especially to those of the household of the Faith.

GRADUAL. It is good to give praise to the Lord; and to sing to Thy name, O Most High. To show forth Thy mercy in the morning, and Thy truth in the night. Alleluia, alleluia. For the Lord is a great God, and a great King over all the earth. Alleluia.

GOSPEL. Lk 7:11–16. At that time: Jesus was going into a city called Naim; and there went with Him His disciples, and a great crowd. And when He came nigh to the gate of the city, behold, a dead man was carried out, an only son of his mother, and she was a widow; and a great crowd of the city was with her. And the Lord, seeing her, was moved with pity toward her, and said to her: Weep not. And He came near, and touched the bier. (And they that carried it stood still.) And He said: Young man, I say to thee, arise. And he that was dead sat up, and began to speak. And He gave him to his mother. And fear seized all: and they glorified God, saying: A great Prophet is risen up amongst us, and God hath visited His people.

OFFERTORY. With expectation I have waited for the Lord, and He had regard to me; and He heard my prayer, and He put a new canticle into my mouth, a song to our God.

SECRET. May Thy Sacraments, O Lord, be our safeguard, and ever defend us against the assaults of the devil. Through Our Lord Jesus Christ, etc. *Amen.*

COMMUNION. The bread that I will give is My Flesh for the life of the world.

POSTCOMMUNION. We beseech Thee, O Lord, that the operation of Thy heavenly gift may possess both our minds and bodies; that its effect, and not our own senses, may ever have dominion within us. Through Our Lord Jesus Christ, etc. *Amen.*

SIXTEENTH SUNDAY AFTER PENTECOST

INTROIT. Have mercy upon me, O Lord, for unto Thee have I cried all the day: for Thou, O Lord, art sweet and mild, and plenteous in mercy unto all that call upon Thee.

Incline Thine ear unto me, O Lord, and hear me, for I am needy and poor.

Glory be to the Father, etc.

COLLECT. O Lord, we pray Thee that Thy grace may always precede and follow us, and make us continually to be given to all good works. Through Our Lord Jesus Christ, etc. *Amen.*

EPISTLE. Eph 3:13–21. Brethren: I desire that ye faint not in my tribulations for you, which is your glory. For this cause I bend my knees to the Father of Our Lord Jesus Christ, from Whom every paternity in heaven and on earth is named, that He would grant you, according to the riches of His glory, to be strengthened with power by His Spirit in the inner man, that Christ may dwell by faith in your hearts; ye being rooted and founded in charity, that ye may be able to comprehend, with all the saints, what is the breadth, and length, and height, and depth; to know also the love of Christ, which passeth knowledge; that ye may be filled to the whole fullness of God. Now to Him Who is able to do all things more abundantly than we ask or understand, according to the power which worketh in us: to Him be glory in the Church and in Christ Jesus, for all generations, world without end. Amen.

GRADUAL. The Gentiles shall fear Thy name, O Lord, and all the kings of the earth Thy glory. For the Lord hath built up Sion, and He shall be seen in His majesty. Alleluia, alleluia. Sing ye to the Lord a new canticle, because the Lord hath done wonderful things. Alleluia.

GOSPEL. Lk 14:1–11. At that time: When Jesus went into the house of one of the chief of the Pharisees on the Sabbath to eat bread, they were watching Him. And behold, a certain man who had the dropsy was before Him. And Jesus answering, spake to the lawyers and Pharisees, saying: Is it lawful to heal on the Sabbath day? But they were silent. And taking hold of him, He healed him, and sent him away. And He answered them and said: If the ass or ox of any of you fall into a pit, will he not immediately draw him out on the Sabbath day? And they could not answer Him in regard to these things. And He spake a parable also to those who were invited, marking how they chose the first places at table, saying to them: When thou art invited to a wedding, sit not down in the first place, lest one more honorable than thou be invited by him; and he who invited thee and him come and say to thee: Give place to this man; and then thou begin with shame to take the lowest place. But when thou art invited, go, sit down in the lowest place; that, when he who invited thee cometh, he may say to thee: Friend, go up higher; then shalt thou have glory before those who sit at table with thee. For everyone who exalteth himself will be humbled, and he who humbleth himself will be exalted.

OFFERTORY. Look down, O Lord, to help me; let them be confounded and ashamed that seek after my soul to take it away: look down, O Lord, to help me.

SECRET. Cleanse us, O Lord, we beseech Thee, by the virtue of this sacrifice: and, in Thy mercy, make us worthy to participate therein. Through Our Lord Jesus Christ, etc. *Amen.*

COMMUNION. O Lord, I will be mindful of Thy justice alone: Thou hast taught me, O God, from my youth, and unto old age and grey hairs: O God, forsake me not.

POSTCOMMUNION. Mercifully purify our minds, we beseech Thee, O Lord, and renew them with heavenly Sacraments, that by them we may receive for our bodies both present and future aid. Through Our Lord Jesus Christ, etc. *Amen.*

SEVENTEENTH SUNDAY AFTER PENTECOST

INTROIT. Thou art just, O Lord, and Thy judgment is right; deal with Thy servant according to Thy mercy.

Blessed are the undefiled in the way; who walk in the law of the Lord.

Glory be to the Father, etc.

COLLECT. Grant to Thy people, we beseech Thee, O Lord, to avoid the defilements of the devil; and with a pure mind to follow Thee, the only God. Through Our Lord Jesus Christ, etc. *Amen.*

EPISTLE. Eph 4:1–6. Brethren: I, the prisoner in the Lord, beseech you to walk worthy of the vocation wherewith ye are called, with all humility and meekness, with patience, bearing with one another in charity, careful to keep the unity of the Spirit in the bond of peace. One body and one Spirit, as ye are called in one hope of your calling. One Lord, one Faith, one Baptism. One God and Father of all, Who is above all, and through all, and in us all, Who is blessed forever and ever. Amen.

GRADUAL. Blessed is the nation whose God is the Lord: the people whom He hath chosen for His inheritance. By the Word of the Lord the heavens were established, and all the power of them by the spirit of His mouth. Alleluia, alleluia. O Lord, hear my prayer, and let my cry come unto Thee. Alleluia.

GOSPEL. Mt 22:35–46. At that time: The Pharisees came to Jesus, and one of them, a lawyer, asked Him, tempting Him: Teacher, which is the great commandment in the Law? Jesus said to Him: Thou shalt love the Lord thy God with thy whole heart, and with thy whole soul, and with thy whole mind. This is the greatest and first commandment. And the second is like to it: Thou shalt love thy neighbor as thyself. On these two commandments hangeth the whole law and the prophets. And the Pharisees being gathered together, Jesus asked them, saying: What think ye concerning the Christ: whose Son is He? They say to Him: Of David. He saith to them: How then doth David by the Spirit call Him Lord, saying: The Lord said to my Lord: Sit on My right hand, until I make Thine enemies Thy footstool? If then David calleth Him Lord, how is He his Son? And no man was able to answer Him a word; neither durst anyone from that day forth question Him anymore.

OFFERTORY. I, Daniel, prayed to my God, saying: Hear, O Lord, the prayers of Thy servant; show Thy face upon Thy sanctuary, and favorably look down upon this people upon whom Thy name is invoked, O God.

SECRET. We humbly beseech Thy Majesty, O Lord, that these holy mysteries which we celebrate may deliver us both from past and future sins. Through Our Lord Jesus Christ, etc. *Amen.*

COMMUNION. Vow ye, and pay to the Lord your God, all you that round about Him bring presents: to Him that is terrible, even to Him Who taketh away the spirit of princes; to the terrible with all the kings of the earth.

POSTCOMMUNION. By Thy sacred mysteries, O Almighty God, may our vices be cured, and may we receive everlasting remedies. Through Our Lord Jesus Christ, etc. *Amen.*

EIGHTEENTH SUNDAY AFTER PENTECOST

INTROIT. Give peace, O Lord, unto them that patiently wait for Thee, that Thy prophets may be found faithful: hear the prayers of Thy servant, and of Thy people Israel.

I was glad at the things that were said unto me: we will go into the house of the Lord.

Glory be to the Father, etc.

COLLECT. Direct our hearts, we beseech Thee, O Lord, by the working of Thy mercy; because without Thee we are not able to please Thee. Through Our Lord Jesus Christ, etc. *Amen.*

EPISTLE. 1 Cor 1:4–8. Brethren: I give thanks to my God always for you, for the grace of God which is given you, in Christ Jesus: that in everything ye are made rich in Him, in all utterance, and in all knowledge, as the testimony of Christ was confirmed in you, so that ye come behind in no gift, waiting for the revelation of Our Lord Jesus Christ, Who also will confirm you to the end blameless, in the day of the coming of Our Lord Jesus Christ.

GRADUAL. I rejoiced at the things that were said to me: We shall go into the house of the Lord. Let peace be in thy strength, and abundance in thy towers. Alleluia, alleluia. The Gentiles shall fear Thy name, O Lord: and all the kings of the earth Thy glory. Alleluia.

GOSPEL. Mt 9:1–8. At that time: Jesus entered into a boat, and passed over the water, and came into His own city. And behold, they brought to Him a paralytic lying on a bed. And Jesus, seeing their faith, said to the paralytic: Be of good heart, child; thy sins are forgiven thee. And behold, some of the scribes said within themselves: This one blasphemeth. And Jesus, seeing their thoughts, said: Why think ye evil in your hearts? Which is easier to say: Thy sins are forgiven thee; or to say: Rise and walk? But that ye may know that the Son of Man hath power on earth to forgive sins, then saith He to the paralytic: Arise, take up thy bed, and go into thy house. And he rose, and went into his house. And when the crowd saw it, they feared, and glorified God, who gave such power to men.

OFFERTORY. Moses consecrated an altar to the Lord, offering upon it holocausts, and sacrificing victims: he made an evening sacrifice to the Lord God for a savor of sweetness, in the sight of the children of Israel.

SECRET. O God, Who by Thy venerable intercourse with us in this sacrifice makest us partakers of the one supreme Godhead, grant, we beseech Thee, that as we know Thy truth, so we may follow it up by a worthy life. Through Our Lord Jesus Christ, etc. *Amen.*

COMMUNION. Bring up sacrifices, and come into His courts: adore ye the Lord in His holy court.

POSTCOMMUNION. Nourished by Thy sacred gifts, we render thanks unto Thee, O Lord; humbly imploring Thy mercy, that Thou wouldst render us worthy of thus partaking thereof. Through Our Lord Jesus Christ, etc. *Amen.*

NINETEENTH SUNDAY AFTER PENTECOST

INTROIT. I am the salvation of the people, saith the Lord; in whatever tribulation they shall cry unto Me, I will hear them: and I will be their Lord forever.

Give ear, O My people, unto My law; incline your ears unto the words of My mouth.

Glory be to the Father, etc.

COLLECT. O Almighty and merciful God, graciously keep us from all things that may hurt us; that we, being freed both in mind and body, may with ready hearts accomplish those things which Thou commandest. Through Our Lord Jesus Christ, etc. *Amen.*

EPISTLE. Eph 4:23–28. Brethren: Be ye renewed in the spirit of your mind, and put ye on the new man, who is created according to God in justice and holiness of truth. Wherefore, laying aside lying, speak ye truth everyone with his neighbor, since we are members one of another. Be ye angry, and sin not. Let not the sun go down on your anger. Give not place to the devil. Let him who stole, steal no more; but rather let him labor, working with his hands what is good, that he may have whence to give to him that suffereth want.

GRADUAL. Let my prayer be directed as incense in Thy sight, O Lord. The lifting up of my hands as an evening sacrifice. Alleluia, alleluia. Give glory to the Lord, and call upon His name: declare His deeds among the Gentiles. Alleluia.

GOSPEL. Mt 22:1–14. At that time: Jesus spake to the chief priests and the Pharisees in parables, saying: The kingdom of heaven is like to a king, who made a marriage feast for his son. And sent his servants to call those who were invited to the wedding, and they would not come. Again he sent other servants, saying: Tell those who were invited: Behold, I have prepared my dinner; my beeves and fatlings are killed, and all things are ready; come ye to the wedding. But they gave no heed, and went away, one to his farm and another to his merchandise; and the rest laid hands on his servants, and treated them shamefully, or slew them. But when the king heard of it, he was angry; and sent forth his armies, and destroyed those murderers, and burnt their city. Then he saith to his servants: The wedding indeed is ready, but they who were invited were not worthy. Go ye therefore into the highways, and as many as ye shall find, call to the marriage. And his servants went forth into the ways, and gathered together all whom they found, both bad and good; and the wedding was filled with guests. And the king went in to see the guests; and he saw there a man who had not on a wedding garment; and he saith to him: Friend, how camest thou in hither, not having on a wedding garment? But he was silent. Then the king said to the waiters: Bind him hand and foot, and cast him into the outer darkness: there shall be weeping and gnashing of teeth. For many are called, but few are chosen.

OFFERTORY. If I shall walk in the midst of tribulation, Thou wilt quicken me, O Lord; and Thou wilt stretch forth Thy hand against the wrath of mine enemies: and Thy right hand shall save me.

SECRET. Grant, we beseech Thee, O Lord, that the gifts we offer in the sight of Thy Majesty may profit us unto salvation. Through Our Lord Jesus Christ, etc. *Amen.*

COMMUNION. Thou hast commanded Thy commandments to be kept most diligently: O that my ways may be directed to keep Thy justifications.

POSTCOMMUNION. May Thy healing power, O Lord, mercifully deliver us from all our perversities, and make us ever to be devoted to Thy commandments. Through Our Lord Jesus Christ, etc. *Amen.*

TWENTIETH SUNDAY AFTER PENTECOST

INTROIT. All that Thou hast done unto us, O Lord, Thou hast done in true judgment: because we have sinned against Thee, and we have not obeyed Thy commandments: but give glory to Thy name, and deal with us according to the multitude of Thy mercy.

Blessed are the undefiled in the way: who walk in the law of the Lord.

Glory be to the Father, etc.

COLLECT. Grant, in Thy mercy, we beseech Thee, O Lord, to Thy faithful people pardon and peace, that they may be cleansed from all their offenses, and serve Thee with a quiet mind. Through Our Lord Jesus Christ, etc. *Amen.*

EPISTLE. Eph 5:15–21. Brethren: See how ye walk cautiously, not as foolish, but as wise; redeeming the time, because the days are evil. Therefore, be not unwise, but understanding what is the will of God. And be not drunk with wine, wherein is luxury: but be filled with the Holy Spirit, speaking to yourselves in psalms, and hymns, and spiritual songs, singing and making melody in your hearts to the Lord: giving thanks always for all things, in the name of Our Lord Jesus Christ, to God and the Father, subject to one another in the fear of Christ.

GRADUAL. The eyes of all hope in Thee, O Lord; and Thou givest them meat in due season. Thou openest Thy hand, and fillest every living creature with Thy blessing. Alleluia, alleluia. My heart is ready, O God, my heart is ready: I will sing, and I will give praise to Thee, my glory. Alleluia.

GOSPEL. Jn 4:46–53. At that time: There was a certain ruler whose son was sick at Capharnaum. When he heard that Jesus was come from Judea into Galilee, he went to Him, and prayed Him to come down, and heal his son; for he was at the point of death. Jesus therefore said to him: Unless ye see signs and wonders, ye believe not. The ruler saith to Him: Lord, come down before my son die. Jesus saith to him: Go, thy son liveth. The man believed the word which Jesus said to him, and went away. And as he was going down, his servants met him, and brought word, saying that his son lived. He asked of them therefore the hour wherein he grew better. And they said to him: Yesterday at the seventh hour the fever left him. The father therefore knew that it was at the same hour that Jesus said to him: Thy son liveth; and he believed, himself and his whole house.

OFFERTORY. Upon the rivers of Babylon, there we sat and wept, when we remembered Thee, O Sion.

SECRET. May these mysteries, we beseech Thee, O Lord, be unto us a heavenly remedy, and may they cleanse our hearts from vice. Through Our Lord Jesus Christ, etc. *Amen.*

COMMUNION. Be Thou mindful of Thy word to Thy servant, O Lord, in which Thou hast given me hope: this hath comforted me in my humiliation.

POSTCOMMUNION. That we may be made worthy, O Lord, of Thy sacred gifts, grant us, we beseech Thee, ever to obey Thy commandments. Through Our Lord Jesus Christ, etc. *Amen.*

TWENTY-FIRST SUNDAY AFTER PENTECOST

INTROIT. All things are in Thy will, O Lord: and there is none that can resist Thy will: for Thou hast made all things, heaven and earth, and all things which are under the vault of heaven: Thou art Lord of all.

Blessed are the undefiled in the way: who walk in the law of the Lord.

Glory be to the Father, etc.

COLLECT. Keep, O Lord, we beseech Thee, Thy family by Thy continued goodness; that, through Thy protection, it may be free from all adversities, and devoted in good works to the glory of Thy name. Through Our Lord Jesus Christ, etc. *Amen.*

EPISTLE. Eph 6:10–17. Brethren: Be strengthened in the Lord, and in the might of His power. Put ye on the armor of God, that ye may stand against the wiles of the devil. For our wrestling is not against flesh and blood, but against the princes and the powers, against the world rulers of this darkness, against the spirits of wickedness in the high places. Wherefore, take ye the armor of God, that ye may be able to resist in the evil day, and to stand perfect in all things. Stand, therefore, having your loins girt in truth, and having on the breastplate of justice, and your feet shod with the preparation of the gospel of peace; in all things taking the shield of faith, wherewith ye may be able to extinguish all the fiery darts of the wicked one, and take the helmet of salvation, and the sword of the Spirit, which is the Word of God.

GRADUAL. Lord, Thou hast been our refuge, from generation to generation. Before the mountains were made, or the earth and the world was formed; from eternity and to eternity Thou art God. Alleluia, alleluia. When Israel went out of Egypt, the house of Jacob from a barbarous people. Alleluia.

GOSPEL. Mt 18:23–35. At that time: Jesus spake to His disciples this parable: The kingdom of heaven is likened to a king, who wished to settle accounts with his servants. And when he had begun to take the account, one was brought to him who owed him ten thousand talents. And as he had not wherewith to pay, his lord commanded that he should be sold, and his wife and children, and all that he had, and that payment should be made. But that servant, falling down, besought him, saying: Have patience with me, and I will pay thee all. And the lord of that servant, being moved with pity, let him go, and forgave him the debt. But when that servant was gone out, he found one of his fellow servants who owed him a hundred shillings; and he laid hold of him, and seized him by the throat, saying: Pay what thou owest. And his fellow servant, falling down, besought him, saying: Have patience with me, and I will pay thee all. And he would not; but went and cast him into prison, till he paid the debt. Now when his fellow servants saw what had happened, they were very much grieved, and came and told their lord all that had happened. Then his lord called him, and said to him: Thou wicked servant, I forgave thee all the debt, because thou besoughtest me; shouldst not thou then have had compassion also on thy fellow servant, even as I had compassion on thee? And his lord being angry, delivered him to the torturers, until he paid all the debt. So also will My heavenly Father do to you, if ye do not forgive from your hearts every one his brother.

OFFERTORY. There was a man in the land of Hus, whose name was Job, simple, and upright, and fearing God: whom Satan besought that he might tempt: and power was given him from the Lord over his possessions and his flesh; and he destroyed all his substance and his children; and wounded his flesh also with a grievous ulcer.

SECRET. Receive, O Lord, in Thy mercy these victims, by which Thou wouldst that atonement be made to Thee, and, in the might of Thy loving kindness, salvation be restored to us. Through Our Lord Jesus Christ, etc. *Amen.*

COMMUNION. My soul is in Thy salvation, and in Thy word have I hoped: when wilt Thou execute judgment on them that persecute me? The wicked have persecuted me: help me O Lord my God.

POSTCOMMUNION. Having received the Food of immortality, we beseech Thee, O Lord, that what we have received with our mouth we may follow with a pure mind. Through Our Lord Jesus Christ, etc. *Amen.*

TWENTY-SECOND SUNDAY AFTER PENTECOST

INTROIT. If Thou, O Lord, wilt mark iniquities, Lord, who shall abide it? For with Thee there is merciful forgiveness, O God of Israel.

Out of the depths have I cried unto Thee, O Lord: Lord hear my voice.

Glory be to the Father, etc.

COLLECT. O God, our refuge and strength, Who art the Author of all goodness: hear, we beseech Thee, the devout prayers of Thy Church; and grant that what we faithfully ask we may effectually obtain. Through Our Lord Jesus Christ, etc. *Amen.*

EPISTLE. Phil 1:6–11. Brethren: We are confident in the Lord Jesus, that He Who hath begun in you a good work, will complete it until the day of Christ Jesus: as it is meet for me to think this for all of you: because I have you in my heart, both in my bonds, and in the defense and confirmation of the gospel, ye all being partakers of my joy. For God is my witness, how I long after you all in the bowels of Jesus Christ. And this I pray, that your charity may more and more abound in knowledge, and in all understanding; that ye may approve the better things; that ye may be sincere and without offense, until the day of Christ, filled with the fruit of justice through Jesus Christ, to the glory and praise of God.

GRADUAL. Behold how good and how pleasant it is for brethren to dwell together in unity. It is like the precious ointment on the head, that ran down upon the beard, the beard of Aaron. Alleluia, alleluia. They that fear the Lord, let them hope in Him: He is their helper and protector. Alleluia.

GOSPEL. Mt 22:15–21. At that time: The Pharisees went and consulted among themselves how to ensnare Him in speech. And they sent to Him their disciples with the Herodians, saying: Teacher, we know that Thou art true, and teachest the way of God in truth, neither carest Thou for anyone, for Thou dost not regard the person of men. Tell us, therefore, what thinkest Thou? Is it lawful to pay tribute to Cæsar, or not? But Jesus, knowing their wickedness, said: Why tempt ye Me, hypocrites? Show Me the tribute money. And they offered Him a coin. And Jesus saith to them: Whose is this image, and the inscription? They say to Him: Cæsar's. Then saith He to them: Render therefore to Cæsar the things which are Cæsar's, and to God the things which are God's.

OFFERTORY. Remember me, O Lord, Thou Who rulest above all power; and give a well-ordered speech in my mouth, that my words may be pleasing in the sight of the prince.

SECRET. Grant, O merciful God, that this saving oblation may unceasingly purify us from our own guilt and keep us from all harm. Through Our Lord Jesus Christ, etc. *Amen.*

COMMUNION. I have cried, for Thou, O God, hast heard me; O incline Thine ear unto me, and hear my words.

POSTCOMMUNION. We have received, O Lord, the gifts of Thy sacred mysteries; humbly beseeching Thee that what Thou hast commanded us to do in remembrance of Thee may profit us as a help to our infirmity. Through Our Lord Jesus Christ, etc. *Amen.*

TWENTY-THIRD SUNDAY AFTER PENTECOST

If this should be the last Sunday after Pentecost, the Mass is said of the Twenty-Fourth Sunday, and this Mass is said on the preceding Saturday, if not hindered by a double or semi-double feast; if it is, on some other day previously.

INTROIT. The Lord saith, I think thoughts of peace, and not of affliction; you shall call upon Me, and I will hear you; and I will bring back your captivity from all places.

Thou hast blessed Thy land, O Lord: Thou hast turned away the captivity of Jacob.

Glory be to the Father, etc.

COLLECT. O Lord, we beseech Thee, absolve Thy people from their offenses; that through Thy bountiful goodness we may be delivered from the bonds of those sins which by our frailty we have taken upon ourselves. Through Our Lord Jesus Christ, etc. *Amen.*

EPISTLE. Phil 3:17–4:3. Brethren: Be ye followers of me, and observe those who walk so, as ye have our model. For many walk, of whom I often told you (but now I speak even weeping), the enemies of the Cross of Christ; whose end is destruction, whose God is the belly, and glory is in their shame; who mind earthly things. But our citizenship is in heaven; from whence also we look for a Savior, the Lord Jesus Christ, Who will reform our vile body conformably to His glorious body, according to the working whereby He is able to subject all things to Himself. Therefore, my brethren, beloved and longed for, my joy and crown: stand thus in the Lord, beloved. I beseech Evodia, and I beseech Syntyche, to be of one mind in the Lord. I also ask thee likewise, sincere companion, help these women, who have labored with me in the gospel together with Clement, and mine other fellow laborers, whose names are in the book of life.

GRADUAL. Thou hast delivered us, O Lord, from them that afflict us: and hast put them to shame that hate us. In God we will glory all the day: and in Thy name we will give praise forever. Alleluia, alleluia. From the depths I have cried to Thee, O Lord, Lord hear my prayer. Alleluia.

GOSPEL. Mt 9:18–26. At that time: As Jesus was speaking to the multitudes, behold a certain ruler came up, and worshipped Him, saying: Lord, my daughter hath just now died; but come, lay Thy hand on her, and she will live. And Jesus arose and followed him, as did His disciples. And behold, a woman having an issue of blood twelve years came behind Him, and touched the fringe of His garment. For she said within herself: If I may but touch His garment, I shall be healed. But Jesus, turned about, and seeing her, said: Be of good heart, daughter, thy faith hath healed thee. And the woman was healed from that hour. And when Jesus was come into the house of the ruler, and saw the minstrels, and the crowd in an uproar, He said: Retire, for the maid is not dead, but sleepeth. And they laughed Him to scorn. And when the crowd was put forth, He went in, and took her by the hand: and the maid arose. And the fame hereof went abroad into all that country.

OFFERTORY. From the depths I have cried out to Thee, O Lord; Lord, hear my prayer: from the depths I have cried out to Thee. O Lord.

SECRET. For an increase of our service, O Lord, we offer unto Thee this sacrifice of praise, that in Thy mercy Thou mayest accomplish what Thou hast bestowed on Thine unworthy servants. Through Our Lord Jesus Christ, etc. *Amen.*

COMMUNION. Amen I say to you: Whatsoever you ask when you pray, believe that you shall receive, and it shall be done to you.

POSTCOMMUNION. We beseech Thee, Almighty God, that Thou wouldst not permit us to be subject to human dangers, to whom Thou givest to rejoice in this divine participation. Through Our Lord Jesus Christ, etc. *Amen.*

If there should be more than twenty-four Sundays after Pentecost, the Masses after the Twenty-Third are of those Sundays after Epiphany which were passed over. But the following Mass of the Twenty-Fourth Sunday is always said last.

TWENTY-FOURTH SUNDAY AFTER PENTECOST

INTROIT. The Lord saith, I think thoughts of peace, and not of affliction; you shall call upon Me, and I will hear you; and I will bring back your captivity from all places.

Thou hast blessed Thy land, O Lord: Thou hast turned away the captivity of Jacob.

Glory be to the Father, etc.

COLLECT. Quicken, O Lord, we beseech Thee, the wills of Thy faithful people; that they, more earnestly seeking after the fruit of divine grace, may more abundantly receive the healing gifts of Thy mercy. Through Our Lord Jesus Christ, etc. *Amen.*

EPISTLE. Col 1:9–14. Brethren: We cease not to pray for you, and ask that ye may be filled with the knowledge of His will, in all wisdom and spiritual understanding; that ye may walk worthy of God, pleasing in all things, being fruitful in every good work, and increasing in the knowledge of God; strengthened with all might according to His glorious power, in all patience and long-suffering with joy; giving thanks to God the Father, Who hath made us worthy to share in the lot of the saints in light; Who hath delivered us from the power of darkness, and translated us to the kingdom of His beloved Son; in Whom we have redemption through His blood, the forgiveness of sins.

GRADUAL. Thou hast delivered us, O Lord, from them that afflict us: and hast put them to shame that hate us. In God we will glory all the day: and in Thy name we will give praise forever. Alleluia, alleluia. From the depths I have cried to Thee, O Lord, Lord hear my prayer. Alleluia.

GOSPEL. Mt 24:15–35. At that time: Jesus said to His disciples: When you shall see the abomination of desolation, which was spoken of by Daniel the prophet, standing in the holy place (let him who readeth understand), then let those who are in Judea flee to the mountains; and let not him who is on the housetop come down to take anything out of his house; and let not him who is in the field go back to take his coat. And woe to those who are with child, and to those who give suck in those days. But pray that your flight be not in the winter, or on the Sabbath; for there shall be then great tribulation, such as hath not been from the beginning of the world until now, neither shall be. And unless those days had been shortened, no flesh would be saved; but for the sake of the elect, those days shall be shortened. Then, if any man shall say to you, Lo! Here is the Christ; or there; believe it not. For false christs, and false prophets, will arise, and will show great signs and wonders, so as to deceive (if possible) even the elect. Behold, I have told you before. If, therefore, they shall say to you: Behold, He is in the desert; go ye not out; Behold, in the closets; believe it not. For as the lightning cometh forth from the East, and appeareth even unto the West, so will also the coming of the Son of Man be. Wherever the carcass is, there will the eagles also be gathered together. And immediately after the tribulation of those days, the sun will be darkened, and the moon will not give her light, and the stars will fall from heaven, and the powers of heaven will be shaken. And then will appear the sign of the Son of Man in heaven, and then will all the tribes of the earth mourn; and they will see the Son of Man coming in the clouds of heaven with great power and majesty. And He will send His angels with a trumpet and a great voice, and they will gather together His elect from the four winds, from the farthest part of the heavens to the utmost bounds of them. Now learn the parable from the fig tree: when the branch thereof is already become tender, and the leaves come forth, ye know that summer is nigh. So ye also, when ye shall see all these things, know ye that it is nigh, at the doors. Truly I say to you, that this generation shall not pass till all these things be done. Heaven and earth will pass away, but My words will not pass away.

OFFERTORY. From the depths I have cried out to Thee, O Lord; Lord, hear my prayer: from the depths I have cried out to Thee. O Lord.

SECRET. Be favorable, O Lord, to our supplications, and receiving the prayers and offerings of Thy people, turn the hearts of all to Thee: that, being delivered from the greed of earthly treasures, we may pass on to heavenly desires. Through Our Lord Jesus Christ, etc. *Amen.*

COMMUNION. Amen I say to you: Whatsoever you ask when you pray, believe that you shall receive, and it shall be done to you.

POSTCOMMUNION. Grant, we beseech Thee, Almighty God, that, by this Sacrament which we have received, whatsoever is corrupt in our souls may be restored by its healing power. Through Our Lord Jesus Christ, etc. *Amen.*

PRINCIPAL FEASTS
THROUGHOUT THE YEAR

THE IMMACULATE CONCEPTION (Dec. 8)

INTROIT. I will greatly rejoice in the Lord, and my soul shall be joyful in my God; for He hath clothed me with the garments of salvation, and with the robe of justice hath He covered me, as a bride adorned with her jewels.

I will extol Thee, O Lord; for Thou hast lifted me up: and hast not made my foes to rejoice over me.

Glory be to the Father, etc.

COLLECT. O God, Who, by the Immaculate Conception of the Virgin, didst prepare a worthy habitation for Thy Son; we beseech Thee that, as by the foreseen death of the same Thy Son Thou didst preserve her from all stain of sin, so Thou wouldst enable us, being made pure by her intercession, to come unto Thee. Through the same Our Lord Jesus Christ, etc. *Amen.*

LESSON. Prv 8:22–35. The Lord possessed me in the beginning of His ways, before He made anything from the beginning. I was set up from eternity, and of old, before the earth was made. The depths were not as yet, and I was already conceived; neither had the fountains of waters as yet sprung out; the mountains with their huge bulk had not as yet been established: before the hills I was brought forth. He had not yet made the earth, nor the rivers, nor the poles of the world. When He prepared the heavens, I was present; when with a certain law and compass He enclosed the depths; when He established the sky above, and poised the fountains of waters; when He compassed the sea with its bounds, and set a law to the waters, that they should not pass their limits; when He balanced the foundations of the earth; I was with Him, forming all things, and I was delighted every day, playing before Him at all times, playing in the world: and my delight was to be with the children of men. Now, therefore, ye children, hear me: Blessed are they that keep my ways. Hear instruction, and be wise, and refuse it not. Blessed is the man that heareth me, and that watcheth daily at my gates, and waiteth at the posts of my doors. He that shall find me shall find life, and shall have salvation from the Lord.

GRADUAL. Blessed art thou, O Virgin Mary, by the Lord the most high God, above all women upon the earth. Thou art the glory of Jerusalem, thou art the joy of Israel, thou art the honor of our people. Alleluia, alleluia. Thou art all fair, O Mary, and there is in thee no stain of Original Sin. Alleluia.

GOSPEL. Lk 1:26–28. At that time: The angel Gabriel was sent from God into a city of Galilee, called Nazareth, to a Virgin espoused to a man whose name was Joseph, of the house of David: and the name of the Virgin was Mary. And the angel coming in to her, said: Hail, full of grace, the Lord is with thee: blessed art thou among women.

OFFERTORY. Hail Mary, full of grace: the Lord is with thee: blessed art thou among women, alleluia.

SECRET. Receive, O Lord, the saving victim which we offer to thee on the festival of the Immaculate Conception of the Blessed Virgin Mary: and grant that, even as we confess her to have been preserved by Thy grace from every stain, so may we be delivered by her intercession, from all our sins. Through Our Lord Jesus Christ, etc. *Amen.*

COMMUNION. Glorious things are told of thee, O Mary, for He Who is mighty hath done great things unto thee.

POSTCOMMUNION. May the Sacraments which we have received, O Lord our God, repair in us the wounds of that sin from which Thou didst singularly preserve the Immaculate Conception of Blessed Mary. Through Our Lord Jesus Christ, etc. *Amen.*

EXPECTATION OF THE B. V. M. (Dec. 18)

INTROIT. Drop dew, ye heavens, from above, and let the clouds rain the Just One: let the earth be opened, and bud forth a Savior.

The heavens show forth the glory of God: and the firmament declareth the works of His hands.

Glory be to the Father, etc.

COLLECT. O God, Who wast pleased that Thy Word, at the message of an angel, should take flesh in the womb of the Blessed Virgin Mary: grant unto us Thy humble servants that we who believe her to be truly the Mother of God may be assisted by her intercession with Thee. Through the same Our Lord Jesus Christ, etc. *Amen.*

LESSON. Is 7:10–15. In those days: The Lord spoke to Achaz, saying: Ask thee a sign of the Lord thy God, either unto the depth of hell, or unto the height above. And Achaz said: I will not ask: and I will not tempt the Lord. And he said: Hear ye, therefore, O house of David: Is it a small thing for you to weary men, that ye weary my God also? Therefore the Lord Himself will give you a sign. Behold, the Virgin shall conceive, and bear a Son; and His name shall be called Emmanuel. He shall eat butter and honey, that He may know to refuse the evil, and to choose the good.

GRADUAL. Lift up your gates, O ye princes, and be ye lifted up, O eternal gates: and the King of glory shall enter in. Who shall ascend into the mountain of the Lord, or who shall stand in His holy place? The innocent in hands and clean of heart. Alleluia, alleluia. Behold a Virgin shall conceive, and bring forth a Son, Jesus Christ. Alleluia.

GOSPEL. Lk 1:26–38. At that time: The angel Gabriel was sent from God into a city of Galilee, called Nazareth, to a Virgin espoused to a man whose name was Joseph, of the house of David; and the name of the Virgin was Mary. And the angel coming in to her, said: Hail, full of grace, the Lord is with thee: blessed art thou among women. But when she heard it, she was troubled at his saying, and thought with herself what manner of salutation this should be. And the angel said to her: Fear not, Mary, for thou hast found grace with God. Behold, thou wilt conceive in thy womb, and bring forth a Son; and thou shalt call His name Jesus. He will be great, and will be called Son of the Most High, and the Lord God will give Him the throne of David His father: and He will reign over the house of Jacob forever, and of His kingdom there will be no end. And Mary said to the angel: How shall this be, since I know not man? And the angel, answering, said to her: The Holy Spirit will come on thee, and the power of the Most High will overshadow thee. And therefore also that holy thing which will be born of thee will be called the Son of God. And behold thy kinswoman Elizabeth, she also hath conceived a son in her old age; and this is the sixth month with her who is called barren; for with God nothing is impossible. And Mary said: Behold the handmaid of the Lord: be it to me according to thy word.

OFFERTORY. Hail Mary, full of grace, the Lord is with thee: blessed art thou among women, and blessed is the fruit of thy womb.

SECRET. Strengthen in our minds, we beseech Thee, O Lord, the mysteries of the true Faith: that we who confess Him that was conceived of the Virgin to be true God and man, may, by the power of His saving Resurrection, deserve to arrive at eternal happiness. Through the same Our Lord Jesus Christ, etc. *Amen.*

COMMUNION. Behold a Virgin shall conceive, and bear a Son, and His name shall be called Emmanuel.

POSTCOMMUNION. Pour forth, we beseech Thee, O Lord, Thy grace into our hearts; that as we have known the Incarnation of Christ Thy Son by the message of an angel, so, by His Passion and Cross, we may be brought to the glory of His Resurrection; through the same Christ Our Lord. *Amen.*

ESPOUSALS OF THE B. V. M. (Jan. 23)

INTROIT. Hail, holy parent, who didst bring forth the King Who rules heaven and earth forever.

My heart hath uttered a good word; I speak of my works for the King.

Glory be to the Father, etc.

COLLECT. Vouchsafe, O Lord, we beseech Thee, unto us Thy servants, the gift of Thy heavenly grace; that as in the childbirth of the Blessed Virgin our salvation began, so from the votive solemnity of her Espousals we may obtain an increase of peace. Through Our Lord Jesus Christ, etc. *Amen.*

LESSON. Prv 8:22–35. The Lord possessed me in the beginning of His ways, before He made anything from the beginning. I was set up from eternity, and of old, before the earth was made. The depths were not as yet, and I was already conceived; neither had the fountains of waters as yet sprung out; the mountains with their huge bulk had not as yet been established: before the hills I was brought forth. He had not yet made the earth, nor the rivers, nor the poles of the world. When He prepared the heavens, I was present; when with a certain law and compass He enclosed the depths; when He established the sky above, and poised the fountains of waters; when He compassed the sea with its bounds, and set a law to the waters, that they should not pass their limits; when He balanced the foundations of the earth; I was with Him, forming all things, and I was delighted every day, playing before Him at all times, playing in the world: and my delight was to be with the children of men. Now, therefore, ye children, hear me: Blessed are they that keep my ways. Hear instruction, and be wise, and refuse it not. Blessed is the man that heareth me, and that watcheth daily at my gates, and waiteth at the posts of my doors. He that shall find me shall find life, and shall have salvation from the Lord.

GRADUAL. Thou art blessed and venerable, O Virgin Mary, who without any violation of purity, wert found the Mother of our Savior. O Virgin Mother of God, He Whom the whole world is unable to contain, being made man, enclosed Himself in thy womb. Alleluia, alleluia. Thou art happy, O holy Virgin Mary, and most worthy of all praise, because from thee arose the Sun of Justice, Christ Our Lord. Alleluia.

GOSPEL. Mt 1:18–21. Now the generation of the Christ was thus: His Mother Mary being espoused to Joseph before they came together, she proved to be with Child of the Holy Spirit. And Joseph, her husband, being just, and not willing to expose her, had a mind to put her away privately. But while he thought on these things, behold and angel of the Lord appeared to him in a dream, saying: Joseph, son of David, fear not to take to thee Mary, thy wife, for that which is conceived in her is of the Holy Spirit. And she will bring forth a Son: and thou shalt call His name Jesus; for He will save His people from their sins.

OFFERTORY. Blessed art thou, O Virgin Mary, who didst bear the Creator of all: thou didst bring forth Him Who made thee, and thou remainest a Virgin forever.

SECRET. May the manhood of Thine only begotten Son be our help, O Lord; that He, Who when born of the Virgin, not lessening did consecrate His Mother's virginity, may, on this festival of her Espousals, cleanse us from our sins, and make our offering acceptable in Thy sight, even Jesus Christ Our Lord. Who livest and reignest, etc. *Amen.*

COMMUNION. Blessed is the womb of the Virgin Mary, which bore the Son of the eternal Father.

POSTCOMMUNION. Having received, O Lord, the votive mysteries of this annual solemnity: grant, we beseech Thee, that they may confer upon us remedies both for time and eternity. Through Our Lord Jesus Christ, etc. *Amen.*

PURIFICATION OF THE B. V. M. (Feb. 2)

CANDLEMAS

(*For the* Blessing of the Candles *see p. 179.*)

INTROIT. We have received Thy mercy, O God, in the midst of Thy temple: according to Thy name, O God, so also is Thy praise, unto the ends of the earth: Thy right hand is full of justice.

Great is the Lord, and greatly to be praised: in the city of our God, even upon His holy mountain.

Glory be to the Father, etc.

COLLECT. Almighty, everlasting God, we humbly beseech Thy Majesty that as Thine only begotten Son was this day presented in the temple in the substance of our flesh, so we also may, with purified hearts, be presented unto Thee. Through the same Our Lord Jesus Christ, etc. *Amen.*

LESSON. Mal 3:1–4. Thus saith the Lord God: Behold I send My messenger, and he shall prepare the way before My face. And presently the Lord, Whom ye seek, and the messenger of the covenant, whom ye desire, shall come to His temple. Behold He cometh, saith the Lord of hosts; and who shall be able to think of the day of His coming? and who shall stand to see Him? for He is like a refining fire, and like the fuller's herb; and He shall sit refining and cleansing the silver, and He shall purify the sons of Levi, and shall refine them as gold, and as silver, and they will offer sacrifices to the Lord in justice. And the sacrifice of Juda and of Jerusalem shall please the Lord, as in the days of old, and in the ancient years, saith the Lord Almighty.

GRADUAL. We have received Thy mercy, O God, in the midst of Thy temple: according to Thy name, O God, so also is Thy praise unto the ends of the earth. As we have heard, so have we seen in the city of our God, and in His holy mountain. Alleluia, alleluia. The old man carries the Child: but the Child guided the old man. Alleluia.

GOSPEL. Lk 2:22–32. At that time: After the days of Mary's purification, according to the Law of Moses, were passed, they carried Him to Jerusalem, to present Him to the Lord; as it is written in the Law of the Lord: Every male first-born shall be called holy to the Lord; and to offer sacrifice, according to that which is written in the Law of the Lord, a pair of turtle doves, or two young pigeons. And behold, there was a man in Jerusalem named Simeon, and this man was just and devout, waiting for the consolation of Israel, and the Holy Spirit was in him. And it had been revealed to him by the Holy Spirit, that he should not see death before he had seen the Christ of the Lord. And he came by the Spirit into the temple. And when His parents brought in the Child Jesus to do for Him according to the custom of the Law, then he took Him in his arms, and blessed God, and said: Now, O Lord, lettest Thou Thy servant depart in peace, according to Thy word: for mine eyes have seen Thy salvation, which Thou hast prepared in sight of all nations: light to enlighten the Gentiles, and glory of Thy people Israel.

OFFERTORY. Grace is poured abroad in Thy lips: therefore hath God blessed thee forever, and for ages of ages.

SECRET. Hear our prayers, O Lord: and that the gifts we offer in the presence of Thy Majesty may be worthy of Thee, grant us the aid of Thy loving kindness. Through Our Lord Jesus Christ, etc. *Amen.*

COMMUNION. Simeon received an answer from the Holy Ghost, that he should not see death until he had seen the Christ of the Lord.

POSTCOMMUNION. We beseech Thee, O Lord our God, that Thou wouldst make the most holy mysteries which Thou hast bestowed for the preservation of our new life, by the intercession of Blessed Mary ever Virgin, to be to us both a present and a future remedy. Through Our Lord Jesus Christ, etc. *Amen.*

ST. JOSEPH (March 19)

INTROIT. The just shall flourish like the palm tree; he shall grow up like a cedar of Libanus: planted in the house of the Lord, in the courts of the house of our God.

It is good to give praise unto the Lord; and to sing to Thy name, O Thou most High.

Glory be to the Father, etc.

COLLECT. Vouchsafe, O Lord, we beseech Thee, that we may be helped by the merits of the spouse of Thy most holy Mother; that what of ourselves we cannot obtain may be given to us through his intercession. Who livest and reignest, etc. *Amen.*

LESSON. Ecclus 45:1–6. The beloved of God and men, whose memory is in benediction. He made him like the saints in glory, and magnified him so that his enemies feared him, and by his words he made prodigies cease. He glorified him in the sight of kings, and gave him commandments in the sight of His people, and showed him His glory. He sanctified him in his faith and meekness, and chose him out of all flesh. For He heard him and his voice, and He brought him into a cloud. And He gave him commandments before His face, and a law of life and instruction.

GRADUAL. O Lord, Thou hast prevented him with blessings of sweetness; Thou hast set on his head a crown of precious stones. He asked life of Thee, and Thou hast given him length of days forever and ever. Alleluia, alleluia. The just shall flourish like the palm tree; he shall grow up like the cedar of Libanus. Alleluia.

GOSPEL. Mt 1:18–21. Now the generation of the Christ was thus: His Mother Mary being espoused to Joseph before they came together, she proved to be with Child of the Holy Spirit. And Joseph, her husband, being just, and not willing to expose her, had a mind to put her away privately. But while he thought on these things, behold and angel of the Lord appeared to him in a dream, saying: Joseph, son of David, fear not to take to thee Mary, thy wife, for that which is conceived in her is of the Holy Spirit. And she will bring forth a Son: and thou shalt call His name Jesus; for He will save His people from their sins.

OFFERTORY. My truth and My mercy are with him: and in My name his horn shall be exalted.

SECRET. We render unto Thee our due service, O Lord, humbly entreating Thee to preserve in us Thine own gifts through the intercession of blessed Joseph, spouse of the Mother of Thy Son Jesus Christ Our Lord; on whose holy festival we offer unto Thee this sacrifice of praise. Through the same Our Lord Jesus Christ, etc. *Amen.*

COMMUNION. Joseph, son of David, fear not to take unto thee Mary thy wife: for that which is born in her is of the Holy Ghost.

POSTCOMMUNION. Draw nigh unto us, we beseech Thee, O merciful God; and by the intercession of blessed Joseph, Confessor, mercifully guard thy gifts about us. Through Our Lord Jesus Christ, etc. *Amen.*

ANNUNCIATION OF THE B. V. M. (March 25)

LADY DAY

INTROIT. All the rich among the people shall entreat Thy face: after her shall virgins be brought unto the King; her neighbors shall be brought unto Thee with joy and gladness.

My heart hath uttered a good word: I speak of my works for the King.

Glory be to the Father, etc.

COLLECT. O God, Who wast pleased that Thy Word, at the message of an angel, should take flesh in the womb of the Blessed Virgin Mary: grant unto us Thy humble servants that we who believe her to be truly the Mother of God may be assisted by her intercession with Thee. Through the same Our Lord Jesus Christ, etc. *Amen.*

LESSON. Is 7:10–15. In those days: The Lord spoke to Achaz, saying: Ask thee a sign of the Lord thy God, either unto the depth of hell, or unto the height above. And Achaz said: I will not ask: and I will not tempt the Lord. And he said: Hear ye, therefore, O house of David: Is it a small thing for you to weary men, that ye weary my God also? Therefore the Lord Himself will give you a sign. Behold, the Virgin shall conceive, and bear a Son; and His name shall be called Emmanuel. He shall eat butter and honey, that He may know to refuse the evil, and to choose the good.

GRADUAL. Grace is poured abroad in thy lips: therefore hath God blessed thee forever. Because of truth, and meekness, and justice: and thy right hand shall conduct thee wonderfully.

GOSPEL. Lk 1:26–38. At that time: The angel Gabriel was sent from God into a city of Galilee, called Nazareth, to a Virgin espoused to a man whose name was Joseph, of the house of David; and the name of the Virgin was Mary. And the angel coming in to her, said: Hail, full of grace, the Lord is with thee: blessed art thou among women. But when she heard it, she was troubled at his saying, and thought with herself what manner of salutation this should be. And the angel said to her: Fear not, Mary, for thou hast found grace with God. Behold, thou wilt conceive in thy womb, and bring forth a Son; and thou shalt call His name Jesus. He will be great, and will be called Son of the Most High, and the Lord God will give Him the throne of David His father: and He will reign over the house of Jacob forever, and of His kingdom there will be no end. And Mary said to the angel: How shall this be, since I know not man? And the angel, answering, said to her: The Holy Spirit will come on thee, and the power of the Most High will overshadow thee. And therefore also that holy thing which will be born of thee will be called the Son of God. And behold thy kinswoman Elizabeth, she also hath conceived a son in her old age; and this is the sixth month with her who is called barren; for with God nothing is impossible. And Mary said: Behold the handmaid of the Lord: be it to me according to thy word.

OFFERTORY. Hail Mary, full of grace, the Lord is with thee: blessed art thou among women, and blessed is the fruit of thy womb.

SECRET. Strengthen in our minds, we beseech Thee, O Lord, the mysteries of the true Faith: that we who confess Him that was conceived of the Virgin to be true God and man, may, by the power of His saving Resurrection, deserve to arrive at eternal happiness. Through the same Our Lord Jesus Christ, etc. *Amen.*

COMMUNION. Behold a Virgin shall conceive, and bear a Son, and His name shall be called Emmanuel.

POSTCOMMUNION. Pour forth, we beseech Thee, O Lord, Thy grace into our hearts; that as we have known the Incarnation of Christ Thy Son by the message of an angel, so, by His Passion and Cross, we may be brought to the glory of His Resurrection; through the same Christ Our Lord. *Amen.*

☦NATIVITY OF ST. JOHN THE BAPTIST (June 24)

Devotion to the holy Precursor of Our Lord was very popular in ancient times and throughout the Middle Ages. This is proved by the vigil and octave of this feast, the feast of his martyrdom or Beheading on August 29, and the rejoicings which still mark June 24 in some countries.

INTROIT. The Lord hath called me by my name from the womb of my mother, and He hath made my mouth like a sharp sword; in the shadow of His hand He hath protected me, and hath made me as a chosen arrow.

It is good to give praise to the Lord, and to sing to Thy name, O Most High. Glory be to the Father, etc.

COLLECT. O God, Who hast honored this present day by the birth of blessed John: grant to Thy people the grace of spiritual joys, and guide the souls of all the faithful into the way of eternal salvation. Through Our Lord Jesus Christ, etc. *Amen.*

EPISTLE. Is 49:1–7. Give ear, ye islands, and hearken, ye people from afar. The Lord hath called me from the womb, from the bowels of my mother He hath been mindful of my name. And He hath made my mouth like a sharp sword; in the shadow of His hand He hath protected me, and hath made me as a chosen arrow; in His quiver He hath hidden me. And He said to me: Thou art My servant, Israel, for in thee will I glory. And now saith the Lord that formed me from the womb to be His servant: Behold I have given thee to be the light of the Gentiles, that thou mayest be My salvation even to the farthest part of the earth. Kings shall see, and princes shall rise up, and adore for the Lord's sake, and for the Holy One of Israel, Who hath chosen thee.

GRADUAL. Before I formed Thee in the bowels of thy mother, I knew thee; and before thou camest forth out of the womb, I sanctified thee. The Lord put forth His hand, and touched my mouth: and said to me. Alleluia, alleluia. Thou, child, shalt be called the prophet of the Highest; thou shalt go before the Lord to prepare His ways. Alleluia.

GOSPEL. Lk 1:57–68. Elizabeth's full time of being delivered was come, and she brought forth a son. And her neighbors and kinsfolk heard that the Lord had showed His great mercy toward her, and they congratulated with her. And it came to pass, that on the eighth day they came to circumcise the child, and they called him by his father's name, Zachary. And his mother answering, said: Not so, but he shall be called John. And they said to her: There is none of thy kindred that is called by that name. And they made signs to his father, how he would have him called. And demanding a writing-table, he wrote, saying: John is his name; and they all wondered. And immediately his mouth was opened, and his tongue loosed; and he spoke, blessing God. And fear came upon all their neighbors; and all these things were noised abroad over all the hill country of Judaea; and all they that had heard them laid them up in their heart, saying: What a one, think ye, shall this child be? For the hand of the Lord was with him. And Zachary, his father, was filled with the Holy Ghost; and he prophesied saying: Blessed be the Lord God of Israel; because He hath visited, and wrought the redemption of His people.

OFFERTORY. The just man shall flourish like the palm tree: he shall grow up like the cedar of Libanus.

SECRET. We heap our gifts upon Thine altar, O Lord, giving due honor to the birth of him who both foretold the coming of the Savior of the world and pointed Him out when come, even Our Lord Jesus Christ, Thy Son, Who livest and reignest, etc. *Amen.*

COMMUNION. Thou, child, shalt be called the prophet of the Highest; for thou shalt go before the face of the Lord to prepare His ways.

POSTCOMMUNION. Let Thy Church, O God, be glad at the birth of blessed John the Baptist, through whom she recognized the Author of her new birth, even Our Lord Jesus Christ, Thy Son. Who liveth and reigneth, etc. *Amen.*

STS. PETER AND PAUL (June 29)

INTROIT. Now I know truly that the Lord hath sent His angel, and delivered me out of the hand of Herod, and from all the expectation of the people of the Jews.

Lord, Thou hast proved me, and known me; Thou has known my sitting down, and my rising up.

Glory be to the Father, etc.

COLLECT. O God, Who didst hallow this day by the martyrdom of Thy holy apostles Peter and Paul: grant unto Thy Church that as from them it received the Faith, so in all things it may remain faithful to their teaching. Through Our Lord Jesus Christ, etc. *Amen.*

EPISTLE. Acts 12:1–11. In those days: Herod the king stretched forth his hands to maltreat some of the Church; and he killed James, the brother of John, with the sword; and seeing that it pleased the Jews, he proceeded to seize Peter also. Now it was in the days of the unleavened bread; and when he had seized him, he cast him into prison, delivering him to four files of soldiers to guard, intending to bring him forth to the people after the Passover. And Peter indeed was kept in prison; but prayer was made without ceasing by the Church to God for him. And when Herod would have brought him forth, the same night, Peter was sleeping between two soldiers, bound with two chains; and the sentinels before the door guarded the prison. And behold an angel of the Lord stood by, and a light shone in the room; and he struck Peter on the side, and awaked him, saying: Rise up quickly. And the chains fell off from his hands; and the angel said to him: Gird thyself and tie on thy sandals. And he did so. And he said to him: Wrap thy garment about thee and follow me. And he went out and followed him, and knew not that what was done by the angel was real; but thought he saw a vision. And when they had passed the first and the second ward, they came to the iron gate that leadeth to the city, which of itself opened to them. And they went out, and passed on through one street, and immediately the angel departed from him. And Peter coming to himself said: Now I know truly that the Lord hath sent His angel, and delivered me out of the hand of Herod, and from all the expectation of the people of the Jews.

GRADUAL. Thou shalt make them princes over all the earth: they shall remember Thy name, O Lord. Instead of Thy fathers, sons are born to Thee: therefore shall people praise Thee. Alleluia, alleluia. Thou art Peter, and upon this rock I will build My Church. Alleluia.

GOSPEL. Mt 16:13–19. At that time: Jesus came into the district of Cesarea Philippi, and He asked His disciples, saying: Who do men say that the Son of Man is? But they said: Some, John the Baptist, and others, Elias, and others, Jeremiah, or one of the prophets. Jesus saith to them: But Who say ye that I am? Simon Peter answered, and said: Thou art Christ, the Son of the living God. And Jesus answered and said to him: Blessed art thou, Simon Bar-Jona, because flesh and blood hath not revealed it to thee, but My Father Who is in heaven. And I say to thee, that thou art Peter, and on this rock I will build My Church, and the gates of hell shall not prevail against it. And I will give to thee the keys of the kingdom of heaven; and whatever thou shalt bind on earth, shall be bound also in heaven; and whatever thou shalt loose upon earth shall be loosed also in heaven.

OFFERTORY. Thou shalt make them princes over all the earth: they shall remember Thy name, O Lord, throughout all generations.

SECRET. May the prayers of Thine apostles, O Lord, speed the offerings which we present to be consecrated to Thy name; and grant that they may also avail for our cleansing and our defense. Through Our Lord Jesus Christ, etc. *Amen.*

COMMUNION. Thou art Peter: and upon this rock I will build My Church.

POSTCOMMUNION. Preserve, O Lord, from all adversity, by the intercession of Thine apostles, those whom Thou hast fed with heavenly nourishment. Through Our Lord Jesus Christ, etc. *Amen.*

THE MOST PRECIOUS BLOOD (First Sunday of July)

INTROIT. Thou hast redeemed us, O Lord, by Thy blood, out of every tribe, and tongue, and people, and nation: and Thou hast made us a kingdom to our God.

The mercies of the Lord I will sing forevermore: I will show forth Thy truth with my mouth from generation to generation.

Glory be to the Father, etc.

COLLECT. O Almighty and everlasting God, Who hast appointed Thine only begotten Son to be the Redeemer of the world, and hast been pleased to be reconciled unto us by His blood: grant us, we beseech Thee, so to venerate with solemn worship the price of our Redemption, and to be on earth so defended by its power from the evils of this present life, that we may rejoice in its perpetual fruit in heaven. Through the same Our Lord Jesus Christ, etc. *Amen.*

EPISTLE. Heb 9:11–15. Brethren: Christ being come a High Priest of the good things to come, by the greater and better tabernacle not made with hands, that is, not of this building, neither by the blood of goats or calves, but by His own blood, entered once into the sanctuary, having obtained an eternal redemption. For if the blood of goats and bulls, and the ashes of a heifer, being sprinkled, sanctify unto the cleansing of the flesh those who are defiled, how much more shall the blood of Christ, Who, through the Holy Spirit, offered Himself without blemish to God, cleanse our conscience from dead works, to worship the living God? And for this, He is Mediator of a new covenant, that death intervening for the redemption of the transgressions, which were under the former covenant, they who are called may receive the promise of the eternal inheritance, in Christ Jesus Our Lord.

GRADUAL. This is He that came by water and blood, Jesus Christ: not by water only, but by water and blood. There are three Who give testimony in heaven: the Father, the Word, and the Holy Ghost; and these three are one. And there are three that give testimony on earth: the Spirit, the water, and the blood; and these three are one. Alleluia, alleluia. If we receive the testimony of men, the testimony of God is greater. Alleluia.

GOSPEL. Jn 19:30–35. At that time: Jesus, when had taken the vinegar, said: It is consummated. And bowing His head, He expired. Then the Jews (because it was the eve of the Sabbath), that the bodies might not remain on the cross on the Sabbath (for that was a great Sabbath day), besought Pilate that their legs might be broken, and that they might be taken away. The soldiers, therefore, came, and broke the legs of the first, and of the other who was crucified with him. But after they came to Jesus, when they saw that He was already dead, they did not break His legs. But one of the soldiers pierced His side with a spear, and immediately there came out blood and water. And he who saw it giveth testimony, and his testimony is true.

OFFERTORY. The chalice of benediction which we bless, is it not the communion of the Blood of Christ? And the bread which we break, is it not the partaking of the Body of the Lord?

SECRET. Through these divine mysteries, we beseech Thee, may we draw nigh to Jesus, the Mediator of the New Testament; and upon Thine altars, O Lord of hosts, may we renew the sprinkling of the blood which pleadeth better than that of Abel. Through the same Our Lord Jesus Christ, etc. *Amen.*

COMMUNION. Christ was offered once to exhaust the sins of many; the second time, He shall appear without sin to them that expect Him, unto salvation.

POSTCOMMUNION. Admitted, O Lord, to Thy holy table, we have drawn waters with joy out of the fountains of the Savior: may His Blood be to us, we beseech Thee, a well of water springing up unto life everlasting. Who liveth and reigneth, etc. *Amen.*

VISITATION OF THE B. V. M. (July 2)

INTROIT. Hail, holy parent, who didst bring forth the King Who rules heaven and earth forever.

My heart hath uttered a good word; I speak of my works for the King.

Glory be to the Father, etc.

COLLECT. Vouchsafe, O Lord, we beseech Thee, unto us Thy servants the gift of Thy heavenly grace; that as in the childbirth of the Blessed Virgin our salvation began, so from the votive solemnity of her Visitation we may obtain an increase of peace. Through Our Lord Jesus Christ, etc. *Amen.*

LESSON. Cant 2:8–14. Behold, He cometh, leaping upon the mountains, skipping over the hills. My Beloved is like a roe, or a young hart. Behold, He standeth behind our wall, looking through the windows, looking through the lattices. Behold, my Beloved speaketh to me: Arise, make haste, My love, My dove, My beautiful one, and come. For winter is now past, the rain is over and gone. The flowers have appeared in our land, the time of pruning is come; the voice of the turtledove is heard in our land; the fig tree hath put forth its green figs; the vines in flower yield their sweet smell. Arise, My love, My beautiful one, and come: My dove in the clefts of the rock, in the hollow places of the wall, show Me thy face, let thy voice sound in My ears: for thy voice is sweet, and thy face comely.

GRADUAL. Thou art blessed and venerable, O Virgin Mary, who without any violation of purity, wert found the Mother of our Savior. O Virgin Mother of God, He Whom the whole world is unable to contain, being made man, enclosed Himself in thy womb. Alleluia, alleluia. Thou art happy, O holy Virgin Mary, and most worthy of all praise, because from thee arose the Sun of Justice, Christ Our Lord. Alleluia.

GOSPEL. Lk 1:39–47. At that time: Mary arose and went with haste into the hill country, to a city of Juda. And she entered into the house of Zachariah, and saluted Elizabeth. And it came to pass that when Elizabeth heard the salutation of Mary, the babe leaped in her womb. And Elizabeth was filled with the Holy Spirit: and she cried out with a loud voice, and said: Blessed art thou among women, and blessed is the fruit of thy womb. And whence is this to me, that the Mother of my Lord should come to me? For behold, as soon as the voice of thy salutation sounded in mine ears, the babe in my womb leaped for joy. And happy art thou who hast believed, that those things which were spoken to thee by the Lord will be accomplished. And Mary said: My soul doth magnify the Lord, and my spirit rejoiceth in God my Savior.

OFFERTORY. Blessed art thou, O Virgin Mary, who didst bear the Creator of all: thou didst bring forth Him Who made thee, and thou remainest a Virgin forever.

SECRET. May the manhood of Thine only begotten Son be our help, O Lord; that He, Who when born of the Virgin, not lessening did consecrate His Mother's virginity, may, on this festival of her Visitation, cleanse us from our sins, and make our offering acceptable in Thy sight, even Jesus Christ Our Lord. Who livest and reignest, etc. *Amen.*

COMMUNION. Blessed is the womb of the Virgin Mary, which bore the Son of the eternal Father.

POSTCOMMUNION. Having received, O Lord, the votive mysteries of this annual solemnity: grant, we beseech Thee, that they may confer upon us remedies both for time and eternity. Through Our Lord Jesus Christ, etc. *Amen.*

OUR LADY OF MT. CARMEL (July 16)

INTROIT. Let us all rejoice in the Lord, and celebrate a feast day in honor of the Blessed Virgin Mary: on whose solemn feast the angels rejoice, and give praise to the Son of God.

My heart hath uttered a good word: I speak of my works for the King.

Glory be to the Father, etc.

COLLECT. O God, Who hast honored the Carmelite Order with the peculiar title of the most Blessed Mary, ever Virgin, Thy Mother: mercifully grant that as we this day celebrate her Commemoration with solemn worship, so we may be defended by her protecting power, and be found worthy to attain unto everlasting joys. Who livest and reignest, etc. *Amen.*

LESSON. Ecclus 24:23–31. As the vine I have brought forth a pleasant odor: and my flowers are the fruit of honor and riches. I am the mother of fair love, and of fear, and of knowledge, and of holy hope. In me is all grace of the way and of the truth; in me is all hope of life and of virtue. Come over to me, all ye that desire me, and be filled with my fruits. For my spirit is sweet above honey, and my inheritance above honey and the honeycomb. My memory is unto everlasting generations. They that eat me shall yet hunger: and they that drink me shall yet thirst. He that hearkeneth to me shall not be confounded: and they that work by me shall not sin. They that explain me shall have life everlasting.

GRADUAL. Thou art blessed and venerable, O Virgin Mary, who without any violation of purity, wert found the Mother of our Savior. O Virgin Mother of God, He Whom the whole world is unable to contain, being made man, enclosed Himself in thy womb. Alleluia, alleluia. Mother of God, the life that had been lost was given us through thee, who didst receive thine offspring from heaven, and didst bring forth a Savior unto the world. Alleluia.

GOSPEL. Lk 11:27–28. At that time: As Jesus was speaking to the multitudes, a certain woman from the crowd, lifting up her voice, said to Him: Happy is the womb which bore Thee, and the breasts which Thou hast sucked. But He said: Yea, rather happy are they who hear the Word of God, and keep it.

OFFERTORY. Remember, O Virgin Mother, that thou speak good things for us in the sight of God, that He turn away His wrath from us.

COMMUNION. Most worthy Queen of the world, Mary, ever a Virgin, intercede for our peace and safety, who didst bring forth Christ, Our Lord, the Savior of all.

POSTCOMMUNION. We beseech Thee, O Lord, that the venerable intercession of Thy glorious Mother, the ever Virgin Mary, may assist us; and that it may free us from all dangers, and lovingly unite us in harmony, whom it has loaded with perpetual benefits. Through Our Lord Jesus Christ, etc. *Amen.*

TRANSFIGURATION OF OUR LORD JESUS CHRIST (August 6)

INTROIT. Thy lightnings enlightened the world: the earth shook and trembled.

How lovely are Thy tabernacles, O Lord of hosts: my soul longeth and fainteth for the courts of the Lord.

Glory be to the Father, etc.

COLLECT. O God, Who, in the glorious Transfiguration of Thine only begotten Son, didst attest the mysteries of the Faith by the witness of the fathers, and didst wonderfully signify, by a voice out of a bright cloud, the adoption of sons: mercifully grant unto us to be made coheirs with the very King of glory, and bring us to the enjoyment of the same. Through the same Our Lord Jesus Christ, etc. *Amen.*

EPISTLE. 2 Pt 1:16–19. Dearly beloved: We have not followed cunningly devised fables, when we made known to you the power and presence of Our Lord Jesus Christ, but we were eyewitnesses of His majesty. For He received from God the Father honor and glory, when there came such a voice to Him from the excellent glory: This is My beloved Son, in Whom I am well pleased, hear ye Him. And this voice which came from heaven we heard, when we were with Him on the holy mount. We have also the surer word of prophecy, to which ye do well to attend, as to a light that shineth in a dark place, until the day dawn, and the daystar arise in your hearts.

GRADUAL. Thou art beautiful above the sons of men: grace is poured abroad in Thy lips. My heart hath uttered a good word: I speak my works to the King. Alleluia, alleluia. He is the brightness of eternal light, the unspotted mirror, and the image of His goodness. Alleluia.

Mt 17:1–9. At that time: Jesus taketh with Him Peter and James, and John his brother, and bringeth them up on a high mountain apart; and was transfigured before them. And His face shone as the sun, and His garments became white as snow. And behold, there appeared to them Moses and Elias talking with Him. And Peter answered and said to Jesus: Lord, it is good for us to be here; if Thou wilt, let us make here three tents, one for Thee, and one for Moses, and one for Elias. And while he was yet speaking, behold a bright cloud overshadowed them. And lo! a voice from the cloud, saying: This is My beloved Son, in Whom I am well pleased; hear ye Him. And when the disciples heard it, they fell on their face, and were very much afraid. And Jesus came and touched them, and said to them: Arise, and fear not. And when they lifted up their eyes, they saw no one, but Jesus alone. And as they came down from the mountain, Jesus charged them, saying: Tell the vision to no man, till the Son of Man be risen from the dead.

OFFERTORY. Glory and wealth shall be in His house: and His justice remaineth forever and ever, alleluia.

SECRET. Sanctify, O Lord, we beseech Thee, the gifts we offer, through the glorious Transfiguration of Thine only begotten Son, and by the brightness of His glory in that revelation, cleanse us from the stains of our sins. Through the same Our Lord Jesus Christ, etc. *Amen.*

COMMUNION. Tell the vision you have seen to no man, till the Son of Man be risen from the dead.

POSTCOMMUNION. Grant, we beseech Thee, Almighty God, that we may apprehend, by the intelligence of a purified mind, the most holy mystery of the Transfiguration of Thy Son, which we now celebrate with solemn office. Through Our Lord Jesus Christ, etc. *Amen.*

ASSUMPTION OF THE B. V. M. (August 15)

INTROIT. Let us all rejoice in the Lord, and celebrate a feast day in honor of the Blessed Virgin Mary: on whose Assumption the angels rejoice, and give praise to the Son of God.

My heart hath uttered a good word: I speak of my works for the King.

Glory be to the Father, etc.

COLLECT Pardon, O Lord, we beseech Thee, the transgressions of Thy servants; that we, who by our own deeds are unable to please Thee, may be saved by the intercession of the Mother of Thy Son Our Lord. Through the same Our Lord Jesus Christ, etc. *Amen.*

LESSON. Ecclus 24:11–20. In all these I sought rest, and I shall abide in the inheritance of the Lord. Then the Creator of all things commanded, and said to me: and He that made me rested in my tabernacle. And He said to me: Let thy dwelling be in Jacob, and thy inheritance in Israel, and take root in My elect. From the beginning, and before the world, was I created; and unto the world to come I shall not cease to be: and in the holy dwelling place I have ministered before Him. And so was I established in Sion, and in the holy city likewise I rested: and my power was in Jerusalem. And I took root in an honored people, and in the portion of my God which is His inheritance: and my abode is in the full assembly of saints. I was exalted like a cedar in Libanus, and as a cypress tree on Mt. Sion. I was exalted like a palm tree in Cades, and as a rose plant in Jericho: as a fair olive tree in the plains, and as a plane tree by the water in the meadows was I exalted. I gave a sweet smell like cinnamon, and aromatic balm: I yielded a sweet odor like the best myrrh.

GRADUAL. Because of truth, and meekness, and justice, and thy right hand shall conduct thee wonderfully. Hearken, O daughter, and see, and incline thine ear:

for the King hath greatly desired thy beauty. Alelluia, alleluia. Mary is assumed into heaven; the host of angels rejoiceth. Alleluia.

GOSPEL. Lk 10:38–42. At that time: Jesus entered into a certain town, and a certain woman named Martha received Him into her house. And she had a sister called Mary, who, sitting also at the Lord's feet, heard His word. But Martha was busy about much serving: and she stood and said: Lord, dost Thou not care that my sister hath left me to serve alone? Bid her then help me. And the Lord, answering, said to her: Martha, Martha, thou art anxious, and troubled about many things. But one thing is necessary. Mary hath chosen the best part, which shall not be taken away from her.

OFFERTORY. Mary is assumed into heaven: the angels rejoice, praising together, they bless the Lord. Alleluia.

SECRET. May the prayer of the Mother of God assist Thy people, O Lord, that we may experience her intercession for us in heavenly glory, whom we know to have passed out of this life to satisfy the condition of our mortality. Through Our Lord Jesus Christ, etc.

COMMUNION. Mary hath chosen for herself the best part: which shall not be taken from her forever.

POSTCOMMUNION. Having been made partakers of the heavenly table, we implore Thy mercy, O Lord our God, that we who venerate the Assumption of the Mother of God may by her intercession be delivered from all the evils which threaten us. Through the same Our Lord Jesus Christ, etc. *Amen.*

ASSUMPTION OF THE B. V. M.
(August 15) *Revised Propers*

‡ INTROIT. A great sign appeared in heaven. A woman clothed with the sun, and the moon under her feet, and on her head a crown of twelve stars.

Sing to the Lord a new canticle: because He hath done wonderful things.

Glory be to the Father, etc.

COLLECT. O Almighty and everlasting God, Who has taken up, body and soul, to celestial glory the Immaculate Virgin Mary, Mother of Thy Son, grant, we beseech Thee, that, being always intent on heavenly things, we may merit to share in her glory. Through the same Our Lord Jesus Christ, etc. *Amen.*

LESSON. Jdt 13:22–25 and 15:10. The Lord hath blessed thee by His power, because by thee He has brought our enemies to naught. Blessed art thou, O daughter, by the Lord the most high God, above all women upon the earth. Blessed be the Lord Who made heaven and earth. Who hath directed thee to the cutting off the head of the prince of our enemies; because He hath so magnified thy name this day, that thy praise shall not depart out of the mouth of men who shall be mindful of the power of the Lord forever, for that thou hast not spared thy life, by reason of the distress and tribulation of thy people, but hast prevented our ruin in the presence of our God. Thou art the glory of Jerusalem, thou art the joy of Israel, thou art the honor of our people.

GRADUAL. Hear, O daughter, see and incline thy ear, and the King will greatly desire thy beauty. All beautiful, the King's daughter enters, her garment is of the texture of gold. Alleluia, alleluia. Mary is assumed into heaven; the angel hosts rejoice. Alleluia.

GOSPEL. Lk 1:41–50. At that time: Elizabeth was filled with the Holy Ghost and she cried out with a loud voice, and said: Blessed art thou among women, and blessed is the fruit of thy womb. And whence is this to me, that the Mother of my Lord should come to me? For behold as soon as the voice of thy salutation sounded in my ears, the infant in my womb leaped for joy. And blessed art thou that hast believed, because those things shall be accomplished that were spoken to thee by the Lord. And Mary said: My soul doth magnify the Lord. And my spirit hath rejoiced in God my Savior, because He hath regarded the humility of His handmaid; for behold from henceforth all generations shall call me blessed, because He that is mighty hath done great things to me, and holy is His name. And His mercy is from generation unto generations to them that fear Him.

OFFERTORY. I will put enmities between thee and the Woman, and thy seed and her Seed.

SECRET. May the offering of our devotion ascend to Thee, O Lord, and through the intercession of the most Blessed Virgin Mary, assumed into heaven, may our hearts, consumed with the fire of charity, always aspire to Thee. Through Our Lord Jesus Christ, etc. *Amen.*

COMMUNION. All generations shall call me blessed, because He that is mighty hath done great things to me.

POSTCOMMUNION. Grant we beseech Thee, O Lord, that we who have received the saving Sacraments may, through the merits and intercession of the Blessed Virgin Mary assumed into heaven, be brought to the glory of the resurrection. Through Our Lord Jesus Christ, etc. *Amen.*

NATIVITY OF THE B. V. M. (September 8)

INTROIT. Hail, holy parent, who didst bring forth the King Who rules heaven and earth forever.

My heart hath uttered a good word; I speak of my works for the King.

Glory be to the Father, etc.

COLLECT. Vouchsafe, O Lord, we beseech Thee, unto us Thy servants, the gift of Thy heavenly grace; that as in the childbirth of the Blessed Virgin our salvation began, so from the votive solemnity of her Nativity we may obtain an increase of peace. Through Our Lord.

LESSON. Prv 8:22–35. The Lord possessed me in the beginning of His ways, before He made anything from the beginning. I was set up from eternity, and of old, before the earth was made. The depths were not as yet, and I was already conceived;

neither had the fountains of waters as yet sprung out; the mountains with their huge bulk had not as yet been established: before the hills I was brought forth. He had not yet made the earth, nor the rivers, nor the poles of the world. When He prepared the heavens, I was present; when with a certain law and compass He enclosed the depths; when He established the sky above, and poised the fountains of waters; when He compassed the sea with its bounds, and set a law to the waters, that they should not pass their limits; when He balanced the foundations of the earth; I was with Him, forming all things, and I was delighted every day, playing before Him at all times, playing in the world: and my delight was to be with the children of men. Now, therefore, ye children, hear me: Blessed are they that keep my ways. Hear instruction, and be wise, and refuse it not. Blessed is the man that heareth me, and that watcheth daily at my gates, and waiteth at the posts of my doors. He that shall find me shall find life, and shall have salvation from the Lord.

GRADUAL. Thou art blessed and venerable, O Virgin Mary, who without any violation of purity, wert found the Mother of our Savior. O Virgin Mother of God, He Whom the whole world is unable to contain, being made man, enclosed Himself in thy womb. Alleluia, alleluia. Thou art happy, O holy Virgin Mary, and most worthy of all praise, because from thee arose the Sun of Justice, Christ Our Lord. Alleluia.

GOSPEL. Mt 1:1–16. The book of the generation of Jesus Christ, the son of David, the son of Abraham. Abraham begot Isaac; and Isaac begot Jacob; and Jacob begot Judas, and his brethren; and Judas begot Phares and Zara, of Thamar; and Phares begot Esron; and Esron begot Aram; and Aram begot Aminadab; and Aminadab begot Naason; and Naason begot Salmon; and Salmon begot Booz of Rahab; and Booz begot Obed of Ruth; and Obed begot Jesse; and Jesse begot David the king. And David the king begot Solomon, of her that had been the wife of Urias; and Solomon begot Roboam; and Roboam begot Abia; and Abia begot Asa; and Asa begot Josaphat; and Josaphat begot Joram; and Joram begot Ozias; and Ozias begot Joatham; and Joatham begot Achaz; and Achaz begot Ezechias; and Ezechias begot Manasses; and Manasses begot Amon; and Amon begot Josias; and Josias begot Jechonias and his brethren, in the transmigration of Babylon. And, after the transmigration of Babylon, Jechonias begot Salathiel; and Salathiel begot Zorobabel; and Zorobabel begot Abiud; and Abiud begot Eliacim; and Eliacim begot Azor; and Azor begot Sadoc; and Sadoc begot Achim; and Achim begot Eliud; and Eliud begot Eleazar; and Eleazar begot Mathan; and Mathan begot Jacob; and Jacob begot Joseph, the husband of Mary, of whom was born Jesus, Who is called Christ.

OFFERTORY. Blessed art thou, O Virgin Mary, who didst bear the Creator of all: thou didst bring forth Him Who made thee, and thou remainest a Virgin forever.

SECRET. May the manhood of Thine only begotten Son aid us, O Lord; that He Who, born of a Virgin, took not away, but did hallow, His Mother's inviolate purity, may, on this festival of her Birth deliver us from our sins and make our offering agreeable unto Thee, even Jesus Christ Our Lord. Who liveth and reigneth, etc. *Amen.*

COMMUNION. Blessed is the womb of the Virgin Mary, which bore the Son of the eternal Father.

POSTCOMMUNION. Having received, O Lord, the votive mysteries of this annual solemnity: grant, we beseech Thee, that they may confer upon us remedies both for time and eternity. Through Our Lord Jesus Christ, etc. *Amen.*

THE HOLY NAME OF MARY
(SUNDAY WITHIN THE OCTAVE OF THE ABOVE)

INTROIT. All the rich among the people shall entreat Thy face: after her shall virgins be brought unto the King; her neighbors shall be brought unto Thee with joy and gladness.

My heart hath uttered a good word: I speak of my works for the King.

Glory be to the Father, etc.

COLLECT. Grant, we beseech Thee, O Almighty God, that Thy faithful people who rejoice in the name of the most holy Virgin Mary, and enjoy her protection, may, by her loving intercession, be delivered from all evils here on earth, and be found worthy to attain to everlasting joys in heaven. Through Our Lord Jesus Christ, etc. Amen.

LESSON. Ecclus 24:23–31. As the vine I have brought forth a pleasant odor: and my flowers are the fruit of honor and riches. I am the mother of fair love, and of fear, and of knowledge, and of holy hope. In me is all grace of the way and of the truth; in me is all hope of life and of virtue. Come over to me, all ye that desire me, and be filled with my fruits. For my spirit is sweet above honey, and my inheritance above honey and the honeycomb. My memory is unto everlasting generations. They that eat me shall yet hunger: and they that drink me shall yet thirst. He that hearkeneth to me shall not be confounded: and they that work by me shall not sin. They that explain me shall have life everlasting.

GRADUAL. Thou art blessed and venerable, O Virgin Mary, who without any violation of purity, wert found the Mother of our Savior. O Virgin Mother of God, He Whom the whole world is unable to contain, being made man, enclosed Himself in thy womb. Alleluia, alleluia. After childbirth thou didst still remain an inviolate Virgin: Mother of God, intercede for us. Alleluia.

GOSPEL. Lk 1:26–38. At that time: The angel Gabriel was sent from God into a city of Galilee, called Nazareth, to a Virgin espoused to a man whose name was Joseph, of the house of David; and the name of the Virgin was Mary. And the angel coming in to her, said: Hail, full of grace, the Lord is with thee: blessed art thou among women. But when she heard it, she was troubled at his saying, and thought with herself what manner of salutation this should be. And the angel said to her: Fear not, Mary, for thou hast found grace with God. Behold, thou wilt conceive in thy womb, and bring forth a Son; and thou shalt call His name Jesus. He will be great, and will be called Son of the Most High, and the Lord God will give Him the throne of David His father: and He will reign over the house of Jacob forever, and of His kingdom there will be no end. And Mary said to the angel: How shall this be, since I know not man? And the angel, answering, said to her: The Holy Spirit will come on thee, and the power of the Most High will overshadow thee. And therefore also that holy thing which will be born of thee will be called the Son of God. And behold thy kinswoman Elizabeth, she also hath conceived a son in her old age; and this is the sixth month with her who is called barren; for with God nothing is impossible. And Mary said: Behold the handmaid of the Lord: be it to me according to thy word.

OFFERTORY. Hail Mary, full of grace, the Lord is with thee: blessed art thou among women, and blessed is the fruit of thy womb.

SECRET. By Thy clemency, O Lord, and the intercession of Blessed Mary, ever a Virgin, may this oblation profit us unto eternal and also present well-being and peace. Through Our Lord Jesus Christ, etc. *Amen.*

COMMUNION. Blessed is the womb of the Virgin Mary, which bore the Son of the eternal Father.

POSTCOMMUNION. Having received, O Lord, these helps to our salvation, grant, we beseech Thee, that we may be in all places protected by the patronage of Blessed Mary, ever Virgin; in whose honor we have made these offerings unto Thy Majesty. Through Our Lord Jesus Christ, etc. *Amen.*

EXALTATION OF THE HOLY CROSS (SEPT. 14)

INTROIT. It behooves us to glory in the Cross of Our Lord Jesus Christ: in Whom is our salvation, life, and resurrection: by Whom we are saved and delivered.

God be merciful unto us, and bless us: cause the light of His countenance to shine upon us, and have mercy on us.

Glory be to the Father, etc.

COLLECT. O God, Who dost this day gladden us by the yearly feast of the Exaltation of the Holy Cross: grant, we beseech Thee, that as we have understood the mystery thereof upon earth, so we may worthily enjoy in heaven the fruits of its redemption. Through Our Lord Jesus Christ, etc. *Amen.*

EPISTLE. Phil 2:5–11. Brethren: Have this mind in yourselves, which also was in Christ Jesus; Who, being in the form of God, thought it not robbery to be equal with God; but emptied Himself and took the form of a servant, being made in the likeness of men, and in fashion found as a man. He humbled Himself, and became obedient unto death, even the death of the Cross. Wherefore also God hath highly exalted Him, and given Him the name which is above every name: (*here all kneel*) that at the name of Jesus every knee should bend of those that are in heaven, on earth, and under the earth; and every tongue should confess that the Lord Jesus Christ is in the glory of God the Father.

GRADUAL . Christ became obedient for us unto death: even the death of the Cross. For which cause also God hath exalted Him and hath given Him a name which is above all names. Alleluia, alleluia. Sweet the wood, sweet the nails, sweet the load that hangs thereon: to bear up the King and Lord of heaven naught was worthy save thou, O holy Cross. Alleluia.

GOSPEL. Jn 22:31–36. At that time: Jesus said to the multitudes of the Jews: Now is the judgment of the world; now shall the prince of this world be cast out. And I, if I be lifted up from the earth, will draw all things to Myself. Now this He said, signifying what death He should die. The crowd answered Him: We have heard from the Law that Christ remaineth forever; and how sayest Thou: The Son of Man must be lifted up? Who is the Son of Man? Jesus therefore said to them: Yet a little while, the light is in you. Walk whilst ye have the light, that the darkness may not overtake you: for he who walketh in darkness knoweth not whither he goeth. Whilst ye have the light, believe in the light, that ye may be sons of light.

OFFERTORY. Through the sign of the holy Cross, protect Thy people, O Lord, from the snares of all enemies, that we may pay Thee a pleasing service, and our sacrifice be acceptable, alleluia.

SECRET. Being about to be fed with the Body and Blood of Jesus Christ Our Lord, through Whom the banner of the Cross was sanctified, we beseech Thee, O Lord, our God, that, as we have had the grace to adore it, so we may forever enjoy the effect of its salutary glory. Through the same Our Lord Jesus Christ, etc. *Amen.*

COMMUNION. Through the sign of the Cross deliver us from our enemies, O our God.

POSTCOMMUNION. Draw nigh unto us, O Lord our God, and defend, by the perpetual defense of the holy Cross, those whom Thou makest to rejoice in its honor. Through Our Lord Jesus Christ, etc. *Amen.*

THE SEVEN SORROWS OF THE B. V. M.

THIRD SUNDAY OF SEPTEMBER

INTROIT. There stood by the Cross of Jesus, His Mother, and the sister of His Mother, Mary of Cleophas, and Salome, and Mary Magdalen.

Woman, behold thy son, said Jesus; and to the disciple, Behold thy Mother. Glory be to the Father, etc.

COLLECT. O God, in Whose Passion, according to the prophecy of Simeon, a sword of sorrow did pierce through the sweetest soul of Thy glorious Virgin Mother Mary: mercifully grant that we, who celebrate the memory of her sorrows, may obtain the happy effect of Thy Passion. Who livest and reignest, etc. *Amen.*

LESSON. Jdt 13:22–25. The Lord has blessed thee by His power, because by thee He hath brought our enemies to naught. Blessed art thou, O daughter, by the Lord, the most high God, above all women upon the earth. Blessed be the Lord Who made heaven and earth, because He hath so magnified thy name this day, that thy praise shall not depart out of the mouth of men, who shall be mindful of the power of the Lord forever: for that thou hast not spared thy life, by reason of the distress and tribulation of thy people, but hast prevented our ruin in the presence of our God.

GRADUAL. Sorrowful and tearful art thou, O Virgin Mary, standing by the Cross of the Lord Jesus, thy Son and Redeemer. O Virgin Mother of God, He Whom the whole earth containeth not, the Author of life, made man, beareth this anguish of the Cross. Alleluia, alleluia. Holy Mary, Queen of heaven and mistress of the world, stood by the Cross of Our Lord Jesus Christ, sorrowing.

SEQUENCE. *Stabat Mater.* Alleluia *being added at the end.*

At the Cross her station keeping,
Stood the mournful Mother weeping,
Close to Jesus to the last;
Through her Heart, His sorrow sharing,
All His bitter anguish bearing,
Lo! the piercing sword had passed!

O how sad, and sore distressed,
Now was she, that Mother Blessed
Of the sole begotten One;
Woe-begone, with heart's prostration,
Mother meek, the bitter Passion
Saw she of her glorious Son.

Who could mark, from tears refraining,
Christ's dear Mother uncomplaining,
In so great a sorrow bowed?
Who, unmoved, behold her languish
Underneath His Cross of anguish,
'Mid the fierce, unpitying crowd?

For His people's sins rejected,
She her Jesus, unprotected,
Saw with thorns, with scourges rent;
Saw her Son from judgment taken,
Her beloved in death forsaken,
Till His Spirit forth He sent.

Fount of love and holy sorrow,
Mother! may my spirit borrow
Somewhat of thy woe profound;
Unto Christ, with pure emotion,

Raise my contrite heart's devotion,
Love to read in every wound.

Those five wounds on Jesus smitten,
Mother! in my heart be written,
Deep as in thine own they be:
Thou, my Savior's Cross who bearest,
Thou, thy Son's rebuke who sharest,
Let me share them both with thee!

In the Passion of my Maker
Be my sinful soul partaker,
Weep till death, and weep with thee;
Mine with thee be that sad station,
There to watch the great salvation
Wrought upon the atoning Tree.

Virgin thou of virgins fairest,
May the bitter woe thou sharest
Make on me impression deep:
Thus Christ's dying may I carry,
With Him in His Passion tarry,
And His wounds in memory keep.

May His wounds transfix me wholly,
May His Cross and lifeblood holy
Ebriate my heart and mind;
Thus inflamed with pure affection,
In the Virgin's Son protection
May I at the judgment find.

When in death my limbs are failing,
Let Thy Mother's prayer prevailing
Lift me, Jesus! to Thy throne;
To my parting soul be given
Entrance through the gate of heaven,
There confess me for Thine own.
Amen. Alleluia.

GOSPEL. Jn 19:25–27. At that time: There stood by the Cross of Jesus His Mother, and the sister of His Mother, Mary of Cleophas, and Mary Magdalen. When Jesus, therefore, had seen His Mother and the disciple whom He loved standing, He saith to His Mother: Woman, behold thy son! After that, He saith to the disciple: Behold thy Mother! And from that hour the disciple took her to his home.

OFFERTORY. Remember, O Virgin Mother of God, when thou standest in the presence of the Lord, that thou speak good things for us and turn His wrath from us.

SECRET. We offer unto Thee our prayers and oblations, O Lord Jesus Christ, and humbly beseech Thee that, even as in our prayers we recall the piercing of the most sweet soul of Thy Blessed Mother Mary, so through the merits of Thy death, and the multiplied intercession of Thy Mother and her holy companions at the foot of the Cross, we may share in the reward of the blessed. Who livest and reignest, etc. *Amen.*

COMMUNION. Happy the senses of the Blessed Virgin Mary, which, without death, obtained the palm of martyrdom beside the Cross of Our Lord.

POSTCOMMUNION. O Lord Jesus Christ, may the sacrifice of which we have partaken, in the devout celebration of the transfixion of Thy Virgin Mother, obtain for us of Thy tender mercy the effect of every salutary blessing. Who livest and reignest, etc. *Amen.*

ST. MICHAEL, ARCHANGEL (September 29)

MICHAELMAS

INTROIT. Bless the Lord, all ye His angels: ye that are mighty in strength, and fulfill His commandment, hearkening to the voice of His words.

Bless the Lord, O my soul: and let all that is within me bless His holy name.

Glory be to the Father, etc.

COLLECT. O God, Who dost dispose the services of angels and men in a wonderful order: mercifully grant that as Thy holy angels always minister before Thee in heaven, so by them we may be protected in our life on earth. Through Our Lord Jesus Christ, etc. *Amen.*

LESSON. Apoc 1:1–5. In those days: The things which must shortly come to pass God sent and signified, by His angel to His servant John, who testified the word of God, and the testimony of Jesus Christ, whatever things He saw. Blessed is he who readeth and heareth the words of this prophecy, and keepeth the things which are written in it; for the time is at hand. John to the seven churches which are in Asia: Grace to you and peace from Him Who is, and Who was, and Who is to come; and from the seven spirits who are before His throne; and from Jesus Christ Who is a faithful witness, the firstborn from the dead, and the Prince of the kings of the earth, Who hath loved us, and washed us from our sins in His blood.

GRADUAL. Bless the Lord, all ye His angels: ye that are mighty in strength that do His will. Bless the Lord, O my soul: and all that is within me, bless His holy name. Alleluia, alleluia. Holy Archangel Michael, defend us in the battle: that we may not perish in the tremendous judgment. Alleluia.

GOSPEL. Mt 18:1–10. At that time: The disciples came to Jesus, saying: Who is the greatest in the kingdom of heaven? And Jesus called to Him a little child, and set him in the midst of them, and said: Truly I say to you, unless ye be converted, and become as little children, ye shall not enter into the kingdom of heaven. Whoever, therefore, shall humble himself as this little child, the same is greatest in the kingdom of heaven. And he who shall receive one such little child in My name, receiveth Me. But he who shall scandalize one of these little ones that believe in Me, it were better for him that a millstone were hung about his neck, and he were plunged into the depth of the sea. Woe to the world because of scandals. For it must needs be that scandals come; but nevertheless, woe to that man by whom the scandal cometh. And if thy hand, or thy foot, scandalize thee, cut it off, and cast it from thee; it is better for thee to go into life maimed or lame, than, having two hands or two feet, to be cast into everlasting fire. And if thine eye scandalize thee, pluck it out, and cast it from thee; it is better for thee to enter into life with one eye, than having two eyes to be cast into hellfire. See that ye despise not one of these little ones; for I say to you, that their angels in heaven always behold the face of My Father Who is in heaven.

OFFERTORY. An angel stood near the altar of the temple, having a golden censer in his hand; and there was given to him much incense: and the smoke of the perfumes ascended before God.

SECRET. We offer Thee a sacrifice of praise, O Lord, and humbly beseech Thee that, through the prayers of Thy holy angels, who plead for us, Thou wouldst graciously receive it, and grant that it may avail us unto salvation. Through Our Lord Jesus Christ, etc. *Amen.*

COMMUNION. All ye angels of the Lord, bless the Lord: sing a hymn, and extol Him above all forever.

POSTCOMMUNION. Supported by the intercession of Thy blessed archangel Michael, we humbly beseech Thee, O Lord, that what we honor in word we may also experience in our souls. Through Our Lord Jesus Christ, etc. *Amen.*

SOLEMNITY OF THE HOLY ROSARY

FIRST SUNDAY OF OCTOBER

INTROIT. Let us all rejoice in the Lord, and celebrate a feast day in honor of the Blessed Virgin Mary: on whose solemn feast the angels rejoice, and give praise to the Son of God.

My heart hath uttered a good word: I speak of my works for the King.

Glory be to the Father, etc.

COLLECT. O God, Whose only begotten Son, by His life, death, and resurrection, hath purchased for us the rewards of eternal salvation: grant, we beseech Thee, that, meditating upon these mysteries in the most holy Rosary of the Blessed Virgin Mary, we may both imitate what they contain, and obtain what they promise. Through the same Our Lord Jesus Christ, etc. *Amen.*

LESSON. Prv 8:22–35. The Lord possessed me in the beginning of His ways, before He made anything from the beginning. I was set up from eternity, and of old, before the earth was made. The depths were not as yet, and I was already conceived; neither had the fountains of waters as yet sprung out; the mountains with their huge bulk had not as yet been established: before the hills I was brought forth. He had not yet made the earth, nor the rivers, nor the poles of the world. When He prepared the heavens, I was present; when with a certain law and compass He enclosed the depths; when He established the sky above, and poised the fountains of waters; when He compassed the sea with its bounds, and set a law to the waters, that they should not pass their limits; when He balanced the foundations of the earth; I was with Him, forming all things, and I was delighted every day, playing before Him at all times, playing in the world: and my delight was to be with the children of men. Now, therefore, ye children, hear me: Blessed are they that keep my ways. Hear instruction, and be wise, and refuse it not. Blessed is the man that heareth me, and that watcheth daily at my gates, and waiteth at the posts of my doors. He that shall find me shall find life, and shall have salvation from the Lord.

GRADUAL. Because of truth, and meekness, and justice, and Thy right hand shall conduct Thee wonderfully. Hearken, O daughter, and see, and incline thine ear: for the King hath greatly desired thy beauty. Alleluia, alleluia. This is the solemnity of the glorious Virgin Mary, of the race of Abraham of the tribe of Juda, of the illustrious family of David. Alleluia.

GOSPEL. Lk 1:26–38. At that time: The angel Gabriel was sent from God into a city of Galilee, called Nazareth, to a Virgin espoused to a man whose name was Joseph, of the house of David; and the name of the Virgin was Mary. And the angel coming in to her, said: Hail, full of grace, the Lord is with thee: blessed art thou among women. But when she heard it, she was troubled at his saying, and thought with herself what manner of salutation this should be. And the angel said to her: Fear not, Mary, for thou hast found grace with God. Behold, thou wilt conceive in thy womb, and bring forth a Son; and thou shalt call His name Jesus. He will be great, and will be called Son of the Most High, and the Lord God will give Him the throne of David His father: and He will reign over the house of Jacob forever, and of His kingdom there will be no end. And Mary said to the angel: How shall this be, since I know not man? And the angel, answering, said to her: The Holy Spirit will come on thee, and the power of the Most High will overshadow thee. And therefore also that holy thing which will be born of thee will be called the Son of God. And behold thy kinswoman Elizabeth, she also hath conceived a son in her old age; and this is the sixth month with her who is called barren; for with God nothing is impossible. And Mary said: Behold the handmaid of the Lord: be it to me according to thy word.

OFFERTORY. In me is all grace of the way and of the truth; in me is all hope of life and of virtue. As a rose planted by the water-brooks have I budded forth.

SECRET. Make us meet, O Lord, to offer these gifts to Thee, and by means of the mysteries of the most holy Rosary, make us so to keep in mind the life, Passion, and glory of Thine only begotten Son, that we may be made worthy of His promises. Who liveth and reigneth, etc. *Amen.*

COMMUNION. Send forth flowers as the lily, and yield a perfume: and bring forth leaves in grace, and praise with canticles, and bless the Lord in His works.

POSTCOMMUNION. We beseech Thee, O Lord, that we may be assisted by the prayers of Thy most holy Mother, whose Rosary we celebrate: that we may perceive the virtue of the mysteries which we commemorate, and obtain the effect of the Sacrament which we have received. Who livest and reignest, etc. *Amen.*

MATERNITY OF THE B. V. M.

SECOND SUNDAY OF OCTOBER

INTROIT. Hail, holy parent, who didst bring forth the King Who rules heaven and earth forever.

My heart hath uttered a good word; I speak of my works for the King.

Glory be to the Father, etc.

COLLECT. O God, Who wast pleased that Thy Word, at the message of an angel, should take flesh in the womb of the Blessed Virgin Mary: grant unto us Thy humble servants that we who believe her to be truly the Mother of God may be assisted by her intercession with Thee. Through the same Our Lord Jesus Christ, etc. *Amen.*

LESSON. Ecclus 24:23–31. As the vine I have brought forth a pleasant odor: and my flowers are the fruit of honor and riches. I am the mother of fair love, and of fear, and of knowledge, and of holy hope. In me is all grace of the way and of the truth; in me is all hope of life and of virtue. Come over to me, all ye that desire me, and be filled with my fruits. For my spirit is sweet above honey, and my inheritance above honey and the honeycomb. My memory is unto everlasting generations. They that eat me shall yet hunger: and they that drink me shall yet thirst. He that hearkeneth to me shall not be confounded: and they that work by me shall not sin. They that explain me shall have life everlasting.

GRADUAL. There shall come forth a rod out of the root of Jesse, and a flower shall rise up out of his root. And the spirit of the Lord shall rest upon him. Alleluia, alleluia. Behold a Virgin shall conceive, and bear a Son, and His name shall be called Emmanuel. Alleluia.

GOSPEL. Lk 2:43–51. At that time: As they returned, the Child Jesus remained behind in Jerusalem, and His parents knew it not. And thinking that He was in the company, they came a day's journey, and sought Him among their kindred and acquaintance. And not finding Him, they returned to Jerusalem, seeking Him. And it came to pass that after three days they found Him in the temple, sitting in the midst of the doctors, hearing them and asking them questions. And all who heard Him were astonished at His wisdom, and His answers. And when they saw Him they were amazed. And His Mother said to Him: Child, why hast Thou done so to us? Behold, Thy father and I were seeking Thee sorrowing. And He said to them: Why did ye seek Me? Did ye not know that I must be about My Father's business? And they understood not the word which He spake to them. And He went down with them, and came to Nazareth: and He was subject to them.

OFFERTORY. When His Mother Mary was espoused to Joseph, she was found with Child of the Holy Ghost.

SECRET. By Thy clemency, O Lord, and the intercession of Blessed Mary, ever a Virgin, may this oblation profit us unto eternal and also present well being and peace. Through Our Lord Jesus Christ, etc. *Amen.*

COMMUNION. Blessed is the womb of the Virgin Mary, which bore the Son of the eternal Father.

POSTCOMMUNION. May this Communion, O Lord, purge us from guilt; and through the intercession of Blessed Mary, the Virgin-Mother of God, make us partakers of Thy heavenly remedy. Through the same Our Lord Jesus Christ, etc. *Amen.*

‡FEAST OF THE KINGSHIP OF OUR LORD JESUS CHRIST

LAST SUNDAY OF OCTOBER

INTROIT. The Lamb that was slain is worthy to receive power and divinity and wisdom and strength and honor. To Him be glory and empire forever and ever.

Give to the King Thy judgment, O God; and Thy justice unto the King's Son. Glory be to the Father, etc.

COLLECT. Almighty, everlasting God, Who didst will that all things should be made new in thy beloved Son, the universal King; mercifully grant, that all kindreds of the Gentiles, scattered by the ravages of sin, may be brought under the sweet yoke of His rule. Who livest and reignest, etc. *Amen.*

EPISTLE. Col 1:12–20. Brethren: Giving thanks to God the Father, Who hath made us worthy to be partakers of the lot of the saints in light: Who hath delivered us from the power of darkness, and hath translated us into the kingdom of the Son of His love, in Whom we have redemption through His blood, the remission of sins; Who is the image of the invisible God, the firstborn of every creature: for in Him were all things created in heaven and on earth, visible and invisible, whether thrones, or dominations, or principalities, or powers: all things were created by Him and in Him. And He is before all, and by Him all things consist. And He is the Head of the Body, the Church: Who is the beginning, the firstborn from the dead, that in all things He may hold the primacy; because in Him it hath well pleased the Father that all fullness should dwell; and through Him to reconcile all things unto Himself, making peace through the blood of His Cross, both as to the things that are on earth and the things that are in heaven through Christ Jesus Our Lord.

GRADUAL. He shall rule from sea to sea, and from the river unto the ends of the earth. And all kings of the earth shall adore Him: all nations shall do Him service. Alleluia, alleluia. His power is an everlasting power that shall not be taken away: and His kingdom that shall not be destroyed. Alleluia.

In Paschal time, instead of the Gradual, the following is said:

Alleluia, alleluia. His power is an everlasting power that shall not be taken away; and His kingdom that shall not be destroyed. He hath on His garment and on His thigh written: King of Kings, and Lord of Lords. Alleluia.

GOSPEL. Jn 18:33–37. At that time: Pilate said to Jesus: Art Thou the King of the Jews? Jesus answered: Sayest thou this thing of thyself, or have others told it thee of Me? Pilate answered: Am I a Jew? Thine own nation and the chief priests have delivered Thee up to me: What hast Thou done? Jesus answered: My kingdom is not of this world. If My kingdom were of this world, My servants would certainly strive that I should not be delivered to the Jews; but now My kingdom is not from hence. Pilate therefore said to Him: Art thou a king, then? Jesus answered: Thou sayest that I am a king. For this was I born, and for this came I into the world, that I should give testimony to the truth. Everyone that is of the truth, heareth My voice.

OFFERTORY. Ask of Me, and I will give Thee the Gentiles for Thine inheritance, and the uttermost parts of the earth for Thy possession.

SECRET. We offer Thee, O Lord, the Victim of reconciliation for the human race: grant, we beseech Thee, that on all Gentiles may be bestowed the gifts of unity and peace, by Him Whom we immolate in this sacrifice, even Jesus Christ Thy Son Our Lord. Who livest and reignest, etc. *Amen.*

COMMUNION. The Lord shall sit King forever: the Lord will bless His people with peace.

POSTCOMMUNION. Having received the food of immortality, grant, O Lord, that we, whose glory it is to battle under the standard of Christ our King, may reign with Him forever in heaven: Who livest and reignest, etc. *Amen.*

FEAST OF ALL SAINTS (November 1)

INTROIT. Let us all rejoice in the Lord, celebrating a festal day in honor of all the saints; at whose solemnity the angels rejoice and give praise to the Son of God.

Rejoice in the Lord, O ye just: praise becometh the upright.

Glory be to the Father, etc.

COLLECT. Almighty, everlasting God, Who givest us to venerate in one solemnity the merits of all Thy saints: we beseech Thee that, through the multitude of our intercessors, Thou wouldst bestow upon us the fullness of Thy mercy, which we most humbly desire. Through Our Lord Jesus Christ, etc. *Amen.*

LESSON. Apoc 7:2–12. In those days: Behold, I, John, saw another angel ascending from the rising sun, having the seal of the living God. And he cried with a loud voice to the four angels, to whom it was given to hurt the land and sea, saying: Hurt not the land, and the sea, nor the trees, until we seal the servants of our God on their foreheads. And I heard the number of those who were sealed: a hundred and forty-four thousand were sealed, of every tribe of the children of Israel. Of the tribe of Juda twelve thousand were sealed: of the tribe of Reuben twelve thousand were sealed; of the tribe of Gad twelve thousand were sealed; of the tribe of Aser twelve thousand were sealed; of the tribe of Nephthali twelve thousand were sealed; of the tribe of Manasses twelve thousand were sealed; of the tribe of Simeon twelve thousand were sealed; of the tribe of Levi twelve thousand were sealed; of the tribe of Issachar twelve thousand were sealed; of the tribe of Zabulon twelve thousand were sealed; of the tribe of Joseph twelve thousand were sealed; of the tribe of Benjamin twelve thousand were sealed. After these things I saw a great crowd, which no man could number, of all nations and tribes, and peoples, and tongues, standing before the throne, and in sight of the Lamb, clothed with white robes, and palms in their hands; and they cried with a loud voice, saying: Salvation to our God, Who sitteth upon the throne, and to the Lamb. And all the angels stood around the throne, and the ancients, and the four animals: and they fell down on their faces before the throne and they adored God, saying: Amen. Praise, and glory, and wisdom, and thanksgiving, honor, and power, and strength to our God forever and ever. Amen.

GRADUAL. Fear the Lord, all ye His saints; for there is no want to them that fear Him. But they that seek the Lord shall not be deprived of any good. Alleluia, alleluia. Come to Me, all you that labor and are burdened, and I will refresh you. Alleluia.

GOSPEL. Mt 5:1–12. At that time: Jesus, seeing the crowds, went up on to the mountain; and when He had seated Himself, His disciples came to Him. And He opened His mouth, and taught them, saying: Blessed are the poor in spirit; for theirs is the kingdom of heaven. Blessed are the meek; for they shall possess the land. Blessed are they who mourn; for they shall be comforted. Blessed are they who hunger and thirst after justice; for they shall be filled. Blessed are the merciful; for they shall obtain mercy. Blessed are the clean of heart; for they shall see God. Blessed are the peacemakers; for they shall be called children of God. Blessed are they who suffer persecution for justice' sake; for theirs is the kingdom of heaven. Blessed are ye, when men shall revile you, and persecute you, and speak all that is evil against you, untruly, for My sake: be glad and rejoice, for your reward is great in heaven.

OFFERTORY. The souls of the just are in the hand of God, and the torment of malice shall not touch them: in the sight of the unwise they seemed to die, but they are in peace, alleluia.

SECRET. We offer to Thee, O Lord, the gifts of our bounden service; may they be well-pleasing to Thee as honoring all Thy saints, and, of Thy mercy, let them avail also for our salvation. Through Our Lord Jesus Christ, etc. *Amen.*

COMMUNION. Blessed are the clean of heart, for they shall see God: blessed are the peacemakers, for they shall be called the children of God: blessed are they that suffer persecution for justice' sake, for theirs is the kingdom of heaven.

POSTCOMMUNION. Grant, we beseech Thee, O Lord, to Thy faithful people ever to rejoice in the veneration of all the saints, and to be defended by their continual supplication. Through Our Lord Jesus Christ, etc. *Amen.*

ALL SOULS' DAY (November 2)

INTROIT. Eternal rest grant unto them, O Lord, and let perpetual light shine upon them.

A hymn becometh Thee, O God in Sion; and unto Thee shall the vow be paid in Jerusalem: O hear my prayer; unto Thee shall all flesh come.

Eternal rest, etc.

COLLECT. O God, the Creator and Redeemer of all Thy faithful: grant unto the souls of Thy servants and handmaids remission of all their sins; that through our loving supplications they may obtain that pardon which they have always longed for. Who livest and reignest, etc. *Amen.*

EPISTLE. 1 Cor 15:51–57. Brethren: Behold, I tell you a mystery: we shall all indeed rise again, but we shall not all be changed. In a moment, in the twinkling of an eye, at the last trumpet: for the trumpet shall sound, and the dead shall rise incorruptible, and we shall be changed. For this corruptible must put on incorruption, and this mortal put on immortality. And when this mortal shall have put on immortality, then shall be brought to pass the saying, which is written: Death is swallowed up in victory. Death, where is thy victory? Death, where is thy sting? Now the sting of death is sin: and the strength of sin is the law. But thanks be to God, Who hath given us the victory through Our Lord Jesus Christ.

GRADUAL. Eternal rest give unto them, O Lord; and let perpetual light shine upon them. The just shall be in everlasting remembrance; he shall not fear the evil hearing.

SEQUENCE. *Dies Iræ.*
Day of wrath, O day of mourning,
Lo, the world in ashes burning—
Seer and Sibyl gave the warning.

O what fear man's bosom rendeth,
When from heaven the Judge descendeth,
On Whose sentence all dependeth!

Wondrous sound the trumpet flingeth,
Through earth's sepulchres it ringeth,
All before the throne it bringeth.

Death is struck, and Nature quaking,
All creation is awaking—
To its Judge an answer making.

Lo, the Book, exactly worded,
Wherein all hath been recorded—
Thence shall judgment be awarded.

When the Judge His seat attaineth,
And each hidden deed arraigneth,
Nothing unavenged remaineth.

What shall I, frail man, be pleading?
Who for me be interceding
When the just are mercy needing?

King, of majesty tremendous,
Who dost free salvation send us,
Fount of pity, then befriend us.

Think, kind Jesu, my salvation
Caused Thy wondrous Incarnation—
Leave me not to reprobation.

Faint and weary Thou hast sought me,
On the Cross of suffering bought me;
Shall such grace be vainly brought me?

Righteous Judge of retribution,
Grant Thy gift of absolution
Ere that Reck'ning Day's conclusion.

Guilty, now I pour my moaning,
All my shame with anguish owning:
Spare, O God, Thy suppliant groaning.

Thou the sinful Mary savest,
Thou the dying thief forgavest,
And to me a hope vouchsafest.

Worthless are my prayers and sighing,
Yet, good Lord, in grace complying,
Rescue me from fires undying.

With Thy favored sheep O place me;
Nor among the goats abase me,

But to Thy right hand upraise me.

While the wicked are confounded,
Doomed to flames of woe unbounded,
Call me, with Thy saints surrounded.

Low I kneel, with heart-submission;
See, like ashes, my contrition—
Help me in my last condition.

Ah, that day of tears and mourning,
From the dust of earth returning,
Man for judgment must prepare him—

Spare, O God, in mercy spare him.
Lord, Who didst our souls redeem,
Grant a blessed requiem.
Amen.

GOSPEL. Jn 5:25–29. At that time: Jesus said to the multitudes of the Jews: Truly, truly, I say to you, that the hour cometh, and now is, when the dead shall hear the voice of the Son of God; and they who hear shall live. For as the Father hath life in Himself, so He hath given to the Son also to have life in Himself. And He hath given Him power to execute judgment, because He is the Son of Man. Wonder not at this, for the hour cometh in which all that are in the graves shall hear the voice of the Son of God. And they who have done good shall come forth unto the resurrection of life, but they who have done evil, unto the resurrection of judgment.

OFFERTORY. O Lord Jesus Christ, King of glory, deliver the souls of all the faithful departed from the pains of hell and from the deep pit: deliver them from the mouth of the lion, that hell may not swallow them up, and they may not fall into darkness; but may the holy standard-bearer Michael introduce them to the holy light, which Thou didst promise of old to Abraham and to his seed. We offer to Thee, O Lord, a sacrifice of praise and prayers: do Thou receive them in behalf of those souls whom we commemorate this day: grant them, O Lord, to pass from death to that into which Thou didst promise of old to Abraham and to his seed.

SECRET. Mercifully look down upon this sacrifice which we offer to Thee for the souls of Thy servants and handmaids, we beseech Thee, O Lord; that to those to whom Thou didst grant the merit of Christian faith, Thou mayest also grant its reward. Through Our Lord Jesus Christ, etc. *Amen.*

COMMUNION. May light eternal shine upon them, O Lord: With Thy saints forever, because Thou art merciful. Eternal rest give unto them, O Lord; and let perpetual light shine upon them: With Thy saints forever, because Thou art merciful.

POSTCOMMUNION. We beseech Thee, O Lord, that the prayer of Thy suppliant people may benefit the souls of Thy servants departed: that Thou mayest deliver them from all their sins, and make them partakers of Thy Redemption. Who livest and reignest, etc. *Amen.*

ALL SOULS' DAY (November 2) *Revised Propers*

‡ FIRST MASS

INTROIT *as in the Mass for the Dead (p. 422).*

COLLECT. O God, the Creator and Redeemer of all the faithful: grant to the souls of Thy servants and handmaids departed remission of all their sins; that through pious supplications they may obtain the pardon which they have always desired. Who livest and reignest, etc. *Amen.*

EPISTLE. 1 Cor 15:51–57. Brethren: Behold, I tell you a mystery: we shall all indeed rise again, but we shall not all be changed. In a moment, in the twinkling of an eye, at the last trumpet: for the trumpet shall sound, and the dead shall rise again incorruptible, and we shall be changed. For this corruptible must put on incorruption, and this mortal, put on immortality. And when this mortal hath put on immortality, then shall come to pass the saying that is written: Death is swallowed up in victory. O death, where is thy victory? O death, where is thy sting? Now the sting of death is sin: and the strength of sin is the law. But thanks be to God, Who hath given us the victory through Our Lord Jesus Christ.

GRADUAL. Eternal rest give unto them, O Lord; and let perpetual light shine upon them. The just shall be in everlasting remembrance; he shall not fear the evil hearing.

SEQUENCE. Dies Iræ *(p. 625).*

GOSPEL. Jn 5:25–29. At that time: Jesus said to the multitudes of the Jews: Amen, amen, I say unto you, that the hour cometh, and now is, when the dead shall hear the voice of the Son of God; and they that hear shall live. For as the Father hath life in Himself, so He hath given to the Son also to have life in Himself; and He hath given Him power to do judgment, because He is the Son of Man. Wonder not at this, for the hour cometh wherein all that are in the graves shall hear the voice of the Son of God; and they that have done good things shall come forth unto the resurrection of life, but they that have done evil, unto the resurrection of judgment.

OFFERTORY. O Lord Jesus Christ, King of glory, deliver the souls of all the faithful departed from the pains of hell and from the deep pit: deliver them from the mouth of the lion, that hell may not swallow them up, and they may not fall into darkness; but may the holy standard-bearer Michael introduce them to the holy light, which Thou didst promise of old to Abraham and to his seed. We offer to Thee, O Lord, a sacrifice of praise and prayers: do Thou receive them in behalf of those souls whom we commemorate this day: grant them, O Lord, to pass from death to that into which Thou didst promise of old to Abraham and to his seed.

SECRET. Mercifully look down upon this sacrifice which we offer to Thee for the souls of Thy servants and handmaids, we beseech Thee, O Lord; that to those to whom Thou didst grant the merit of Christian faith, Thou mayest also grant its reward. Through Our Lord Jesus Christ, etc. *Amen.*

COMMUNION. May light eternal shine upon them, O Lord: With Thy saints forever, because Thou art merciful. Eternal rest give unto them, O Lord; and let perpetual light shine upon them: With Thy saints forever, because Thou art merciful.

POSTCOMMUNION. We beseech Thee, O Lord, that the prayer of Thy suppliant people may benefit the souls of Thy servants departed: that Thou mayest deliver them from all their sins, and make them partakers of Thy Redemption. Who livest and reignest, etc. *Amen.*

SECOND MASS
As preceding, except the following:

COLLECT. O God, the Lord of mercies, grant to the souls of Thy servants and handmaids a place of refreshment, rest, and happiness, and the glory of Thy light. Through Our Lord Jesus Christ, etc. *Amen.*

LESSON. 2 Mc 12:43–46. In those days: The most valiant man Judas, making a gathering, sent twelve thousand drachms of silver to Jerusalem for sacrifice to be offered for the sins of the dead, thinking well and religiously concerning the resurrection (for if he had not hoped that they that were slain should rise again, it would have seemed superfluous and vain to pray for the dead); and because he considered that they who had fallen asleep with godliness had great grace laid up for them. It is therefore a holy and wholesome thought to pray for the dead, that they may be loosed from sins.

GOSPEL. Jn 6:37–40. At that time: Jesus said to the multitudes of the Jews: All that the Father giveth to Me shall come to Me; and him that cometh to Me, I will not cast out: because I came down from heaven not to do Mine own will, but the will of Him that sent Me. Now this is the will of the Father Who sent Me: that of all that He hath given Me, I should lose nothing; but should raise it up again in the Last Day. And this is the will of My Father that sent Me: that everyone who seeth the Son, and believeth in Him, may have life everlasting: and I will raise him up in the Last Day.

SECRET. Be favorable, O Lord, to our humble prayers on behalf of the souls of Thy servants and handmaids, for whom we offer to Thee the sacrifice of praise; that Thou mayest vouchsafe to grant them fellowship with Thy saints. Through Our Lord Jesus Christ, etc. Amen.

POSTCOMMUNION. Grant, we beseech Thee, O Lord, that the souls of Thy servants and handmaids, purified by this sacrifice, may obtain pardon and everlasting rest. Through Our Lord Jesus Christ, etc. *Amen.*

THIRD MASS

As on p. 629, except the following:

COLLECT. O God, Who grantest forgiveness and desirest the salvation of mankind; we beseech Thee in Thy mercy to grant that by the intercession of the Blessed Mary ever Virgin and of all Thy saints the souls of Thy servants and handmaids, which have passed out of this life, may partake of everlasting bliss. Through Our Lord Jesus Christ, etc. *Amen.*

EPISTLE. Apoc 14:13. In those days: I heard a voice from heaven, saying to me: Write, blessed are the dead who die in the Lord. From henceforth now, saith the Spirit, that they may rest from their labors, for their works follow them.

GOSPEL. Jn 6:51–55. At that time: Jesus said to the multitudes of the Jews: I am the living Bread, which came down from heaven. If any man eat of this Bread, he shall live forever: and the bread that I will give is My Flesh for the life of the world. The Jews therefore strove among themselves, saying: How can this man give us His Flesh to eat? Then Jesus said to them: Amen, amen, I say unto you: Except you eat the Flesh of the Son of Man, and drink His Blood, you shall not have life in you. He that eateth My Flesh, and drinketh My Blood, hath everlasting life: and I will raise him up in the Last Day.

SECRET. O God, Whose mercy is boundless, favorably receive our humble prayers, and by means of these Sacraments of our salvation, grant to the souls of all the faithful departed, who by Thy grace did confess Thy name, the remission of all their sins. Through Our Lord Jesus Christ, etc. *Amen.*

POSTCOMMUNION. Grant, we beseech Thee, Almighty and merciful God, that the souls of Thy servants and handmaids, for whom we offer to Thy Majesty this sacrifice of praise, may by virtue of this Sacrament be cleansed from all sin and by Thy mercy receive the happiness of eternal light. Through Our Lord Jesus Christ, etc. *Amen.*

PATRONAGE OF THE B. V. M.

SECOND SUNDAY OF NOVEMBER

INTROIT. Hail, holy parent, who didst bring forth the King Who rules heaven and earth forever.

My heart hath uttered a good word; I speak of my works for the King.

Glory be to the Father, etc.

COLLECT. Grant, O Lord God, we beseech Thee, that we Thy servants may rejoice in continual health of mind and body; and through the glorious intercession of Blessed Mary ever Virgin, be freed from present sorrow and enjoy eternal gladness. Through Our Lord Jesus Christ, etc. *Amen.*

LESSON. Ecclus 24:14–16. From the beginning, and before the world, was I created; and unto the world to come I shall not cease to be: and in the holy dwelling place I have ministered before Him. And so was I established in Sion, and in the holy city likewise I rested: and my power was in Jerusalem. And I took root in an honored people, and in the portion of my God which is His inheritance: and my abode is in the full assembly of saints.

GRADUAL. Thou art blessed and venerable, O Virgin Mary, who without any violation of purity, wert found the Mother of our Savior. O Virgin Mother of God, He Whom the whole world is unable to contain, being made man, enclosed Himself in thy womb. Alleluia, alleluia. After childbirth thou didst still remain an inviolate Virgin: Mother of God, intercede for us. Alleluia.

GOSPEL. Lk 11:27–28. At that time: As Jesus was speaking to the multitudes, a certain woman from the crowd, lifting up her voice, said to Him: Happy is the womb which bore Thee, and the breasts which Thou hast sucked. But He said: Yea, rather happy are they who hear the Word of God, and keep it.

OFFERTORY. Hail Mary, full of grace, the Lord is with thee: blessed art thou among women, and blessed is the fruit of thy womb.

SECRET. By Thy clemency, O Lord, and the intercession of Blessed Mary, ever a Virgin, may this oblation profit us unto eternal and also present well-being and peace. Through Our Lord Jesus Christ, etc. *Amen.*

COMMUNION. Blessed is the womb of the Virgin Mary, which bore the Son of the eternal Father.

POSTCOMMUNION. Having received, O Lord, these helps to our salvation, grant, we beseech Thee, that we may be in all places protected by the patronage of Blessed Mary, ever Virgin; in whose honor we have made these offerings unto Thy Majesty. Through Our Lord Jesus Christ, etc. *Amen.*

PRESENTATION OF THE B. M. V. (November 21)

INTROIT. Hail, holy parent, who didst bring forth the King Who rules heaven and earth forever.

My heart hath uttered a good word; I speak of my works for the King.

Glory be to the Father, etc.

COLLECT. O God, Who wast pleased that Blessed Mary ever Virgin, being herself the dwelling place of the Holy Ghost, should on this day be presented in the temple: grant, we beseech Thee, that, through her intercession, we may be found worthy to be presented in the temple of Thy glory. Through Our Lord Jesus Christ, etc. *Amen.*

LESSON. Ecclus 24:14–16. From the beginning, and before the world, was I created; and unto the world to come I shall not cease to be: and in the holy dwelling place I have ministered before Him. And so was I established in Sion, and in the holy city likewise I rested: and my power was in Jerusalem. And I took root in an honored people, and in the portion of my God which is His inheritance: and my abode is in the full assembly of saints.

GRADUAL. Thou art blessed and venerable, O Virgin Mary, who without any violation of purity, wert found the Mother of our Savior. O Virgin Mother of God, He Whom the whole world is unable to contain, being made man, enclosed

Himself in thy womb. Alleluia, alleluia. After childbirth thou didst still remain an inviolate Virgin: Mother of God, intercede for us. Alleluia.

GOSPEL. Lk 11:27–28. At that time: As Jesus was speaking to the multitudes, a certain woman from the crowd, lifting up her voice, said to Him: Happy is the womb which bore Thee, and the breasts which Thou hast sucked. But He said: Yea, rather happy are they who hear the Word of God, and keep it.

OFFERTORY. Hail Mary, full of grace, the Lord is with thee: blessed art thou among women, and blessed is the fruit of thy womb.

SECRET. By Thy clemency, O Lord, and the intercession of Blessed Mary, ever a Virgin, may this oblation profit us unto eternal and also present well-being and peace. Through Our Lord Jesus Christ, etc. *Amen.*

COMMUNION. Blessed is the womb of the Virgin Mary, which bore the Son of the eternal Father.

POSTCOMMUNION. Having received, O Lord, these helps to our salvation, grant, we beseech Thee, that we may be in all places protected by the patronage of Blessed Mary, ever Virgin; in whose honor we have made these offerings unto Thy Majesty. Through Our Lord Jesus Christ, etc. *Amen.*

THE ANNIVERSARY OF THE DEDICATION OF A CHURCH

INTROIT. Terrible is this place: This is the house of God, and the gate of heaven; and shall be called the court of God.

How lovely are Thy tabernacles, O Lord of hosts: my soul longeth and fainteth for the courts of the Lord.

Glory be to the Father, etc.

COLLECT. O God, Who dost every year bring round unto us again the day whereon this Thy holy temple was consecrated, and bringest us again in safety to be present at Thy holy mysteries, graciously hear the prayers of Thy people, and grant that whosoever comes into this house to ask good things at Thy hand may rejoice in the obtaining of all his requests. Through Our Lord Jesus Christ, etc. *Amen.*

LESSON. Apoc 21:2–5. In those days: I saw the holy city, the new Jerusalem, coming down out of heaven, from God, prepared as a bride adorned for her husband. And I heard a great voice from the throne, saying: Behold the tabernacle of God with men, and He will dwell with them. And they shall be His people, and God Himself with them will be their God. And God shall wipe away all tears from their eyes; and death shall be no more, nor mourning, nor wailing, nor sorrow shall be anymore, for the former things are passed away. And He Who sat on the throne said: Behold, I make all things new.

GRADUAL. This place has been made by God; it is a mystery beyond measure, it is free from all stain. O God, before Whom the choir of angels stands, give ear to the prayer of Thy servants. Alleluia, alleluia. I will worship toward Thy holy temple, and I will give glory to Thy name. Alleluia.

GOSPEL. Lk 19:1–10. At that time: Jesus entered and walked through Jericho. And behold, there was a man named Zachæus; who was chief of the publicans, and he was rich: and he sought to see who Jesus was, and he could not on account of the crowd, because he was low of stature. And running before, he climbed up into a sycamore tree, to see Him; for He was about to pass that way. And when Jesus was come to the place, looking up, He saw him, and said to him: Zachæus, make haste and come down: for this day I must remain in thy house. And he made haste and came down, and received Him joyfully. And when all saw it, they murmured, saying that He was gone to be a guest with a man who was a sinner. But Zachæus, standing, said to the Lord: Behold, Lord, I give to the poor the half of my goods; and if I have wronged anyone of anything, I restore fourfold. Jesus said to him: This day is salvation come to this house; because he also is a son of Abraham. For the Son of Man is come to seek and to save that which was lost.

OFFERTORY. O Lord God, in the simplicity of my heart I have joyfully offered all these things; and I have seen with great joy Thy people, which are present: O God of Israel, keep this will, alleluia.

SECRET. Give ear, O Lord, we beseech Thee, unto our prayers (and grant that all we who within the precincts of this temple are keeping the anniversary day of its dedication, may, by full and perfect devotion, be acceptable to Thee both in body and in soul); that we who now lay our votive gifts before Thee, may by Thy help be found worthy to win Thy everlasting rewards. Through Our Lord.

The words in parenthesis are only said in the church of which the dedication is being kept.

COMMUNION. My house shall be called the house of prayer, saith the Lord: everyone that asks therein, receives; and he who seeks finds; and to him who knocks, it shall be opened.

POSTCOMMUNION. O God, Who out of living and elect stones dost prepare for Thy Majesty an eternal abode: help Thy people as they pray unto Thee; that as Thy Church advances by bodily extension, so may it ever grow by spiritual increase. Through Our Lord Jesus Christ, etc. *Amen.*

FOR THE DEAD

ON THE DAY OF DECEASE OR BURIAL (see p. 422).

ON THE ANNIVERSARY

INTROIT. Eternal rest grant unto them, O Lord, and let perpetual light shine upon them.

A hymn becometh Thee, O God in Sion; and unto Thee shall the vow be paid in Jerusalem: O hear my prayer; unto Thee shall all flesh come.

Eternal rest, etc.

COLLECT. O God, the Lord of mercies, grant to the souls of Thy servants and handmaids, whose anniversary we commemorate, a place of refreshment, the happiness of rest, and the clearness of Thy light. Through Our Lord Jesus Christ, etc. *Amen.*

LESSON. 2 Mc 12:43–46. In those days: The most valiant man Judas, making a gathering, sent twelve thousand drachms of silver to Jerusalem for sacrifice to be offered for the sins of the dead, thinking well and religiously concerning the resurrection. (For if he had not hoped that they who were slain should rise again, it would have seemed superfluous and vain to pray for the dead.) And because he considered that they who had fallen asleep with godliness, had great grace laid up for them. It is therefore a holy and wholesome thought to pray for the dead, that they may be loosed from sins.

GRADUAL. Eternal rest give to them, O Lord; and let perpetual light shine upon them. The just shall be in everlasting remembrance; he shall not fear the evil hearing.

TRACT. Absolve, O Lord, the souls of all the faithful departed from every bond of sin. And by the help of thy grace let them be found worthy to escape the sentence of vengeance. And to enjoy the full beatitude of the light eternal.

SEQUENCE. *Dies Iræ.*
Day of wrath, O day of mourning,
Lo, the world in ashes burning—
Seer and Sibyl gave the warning.

O what fear man's bosom rendeth,
When from heaven the Judge descendeth,
On Whose sentence all dependeth!

Wondrous sound the trumpet flingeth,
Through earth's sepulchres it ringeth,
All before the throne it bringeth.

Death is struck, and Nature quaking,
All creation is awaking—
To its Judge an answer making.

Lo, the Book, exactly worded,
Wherein all hath been recorded—
Thence shall judgment be awarded.

When the Judge His seat attaineth,
And each hidden deed arraigneth,
Nothing unavenged remaineth.

What shall I, frail man, be pleading?
Who for me be interceding
When the just are mercy needing?

King, of majesty tremendous,
Who dost free salvation send us,
Fount of pity, then befriend us.

Think, kind Jesu, my salvation
Caused Thy wondrous Incarnation—
Leave me not to reprobation.

Faint and weary Thou hast sought me,
On the Cross of suffering bought me;
Shall such grace be vainly brought me?

Righteous Judge of retribution,
Grant Thy gift of absolution
Ere that Reck'ning Day's conclusion.

Guilty, now I pour my moaning,
All my shame with anguish owning:
Spare, O God, Thy suppliant groaning.

Thou the sinful Mary savest,
Thou the dying thief forgavest,
And to me a hope vouchsafest.

Worthless are my prayers and sighing,

Yet, good Lord, in grace complying,
Rescue me from fires undying.

With Thy favored sheep O place me;
Nor among the goats abase me,
But to Thy right hand upraise me.

While the wicked are confounded,
Doomed to flames of woe unbounded,
Call me, with Thy saints surrounded.

Low I kneel, with heart-submission;
See, like ashes, my contrition—
Help me in my last condition.

Ah, that day of tears and mourning,
From the dust of earth returning,
Man for judgment must prepare him—

Spare, O God, in mercy spare him.
Lord, Who didst our souls redeem,
Grant a blessed requiem.
Amen.

GOSPEL. Jn 6:37–40. At that time: Jesus said to the multitudes of the Jews: All that the Father giveth Me shall come to Me; and him that cometh to Me I will not cast out. Because I have come down from heaven, not to do Mine own will, but the will of Him Who sent Me. Now this is the will of the Father Who sent Me: that of all that He hath given Me, I should lose nothing, but should raise it up again on the Last Day. And this is the will of My Father Who sent Me: that everyone who seeth the Son, and believeth in Him, may have life everlasting; and I will raise him up on the Last Day.

OFFERTORY. O Lord Jesus Christ, the King of glory, deliver the souls of all the faithful departed from the pains of hell and from the deep pit; deliver them from the lion's mouth, that hell engulf them not, that they fall not into the darkness; but let Michael, the holy standard-bearer, bring them into the holy light which Thou didst promise of old to Abraham and his seed. ℣. We offer Thee sacrifices and prayers of praise, O Lord; do Thou accept them for those souls of which we this day make commemoration; cause them, O Lord, to pass from death to the life which of old Thou didst promise to Abraham and his seed.

SECRET. Be propitiated, O Lord, by our supplications for the souls of Thy servants and handmaids, whose anniversary is kept today, for whom we offer Thee the sacrifice of praise, that Thou vouchsafe to join them to the company of Thy saints. Through Our Lord Jesus Christ, etc. *Amen.*

COMMUNION. May eternal light shine upon them, O Lord. With Thy saints forever, because Thou art kind. ℣. Grant them everlasting rest, O Lord, and let perpetual light shine upon them. With Thy saints, etc.

POSTCOMMUNION. Grant, we beseech Thee, O Lord, that the *soul* of Thy *servant*, the anniversary of whose death we now commemorate, being purified by this sacrifice, may obtain both pardon and eternal rest. Through Our Lord Jesus Christ, etc. *Amen.*

THE COMMON MASS FOR THE DEAD[46]

INTROIT. Eternal rest grant unto them, O Lord, and let perpetual light shine upon them.

A hymn becometh Thee, O God in Sion; and unto Thee shall the vow be paid in Jerusalem: O hear my prayer; unto Thee shall all flesh come.

Eternal rest, etc.

COLLECT I. O God, Who didst raise Thy servants to the dignity of bishops or priests in the apostolic priesthood: grant, we beseech Thee, that they may be forever united to the company of the same. Through Our Lord Jesus Christ, etc. *Amen.*

II. O God, the Bestower of forgiveness and the Lover of human salvation: we beseech Thee of Thy tender love to grant that the brethren of our congregation, with their relations and benefactors who have passed out of this life, by the intercession of Blessed Mary ever Virgin, and all Thy saints, may come to the fellowship of eternal bliss.

III. O God, the Creator and Redeemer of all Thy faithful: grant unto the souls of Thy servants and handmaids remission of all their sins; that through our loving supplications they may obtain that pardon which they have always longed for. Who livest and reignest, etc. *Amen.*

LESSON. Apoc 14:13. In those days: I heard a voice from heaven, saying to me: Write: blessed are the dead, who die in the Lord. From henceforth now, saith the Spirit, that they may rest from their labors; for their works follow them.

GRADUAL. Eternal rest give unto them, O Lord; and let perpetual light shine upon them. The just shall be in everlasting remembrance, he shall not fear the evil hearing.

The Sequence Dies Iræ (*p. 625*) *is voluntary in this Mass.*

GOSPEL. Jn 6:51–55. At that time: Jesus said to the multitude of the Jews: I am the living Bread, which came down from heaven. If any man eat of this Bread he shall live forever: and the bread that I will give is My Flesh for the life of the world. The Jews therefore strove among themselves, saying: How can this man give His

---

46   The Epistles and Gospels of any one Mass for the Dead may be said also at any other of the Masses for the Dead.

Flesh to eat? Then Jesus said to them: Amen, amen, I say unto you: Unless you eat the Flesh of the Son of Man, and drink His Blood, you shall not have life in you. He that eateth My Flesh, and drinketh My Blood, hath everlasting life; and I will raise him up on the Last Day.

SECRET I. Receive, we beseech Thee, O Lord, the sacrifices which we offer for the souls of Thy servants, bishops or priests; that Thou mayst command those whom on earth Thou didst invest with the episcopal or sacerdotal dignity to be joined to the fellowship of Thy saints in the heavenly kingdom. Through Our Lord Jesus Christ, etc. *Amen.*

II. O God, Whose mercy is boundless, mercifully receive the prayers of our lowliness, and grant, through these Sacraments of our salvation, to the souls of our brethren, kindred, and benefactors, to whom Thou didst grant the confession of Thy name, the remission of all sins.

III. Look down in Thy mercy, we beseech Thee, O Lord, upon this sacrifice, which we offer up to Thee for the souls of Thy servants and handmaids; that to those to whom Thou didst grant the merit of Christian faith, Thou mayest also grant its reward. Through Our Lord Jesus Christ, etc. *Amen.*

COMMUNION. May the light eternal shine upon them, O Lord. With Thy saints forever, because Thou art merciful. Eternal rest give to them O Lord; and let perpetual light shine upon them. With Thy saints.

POSTCOMMUNION I. Grant, we beseech Thee, O Lord, through Thy loving compassion, which we have implored on behalf of the souls of Thy servants, bishops or priests, that by Thy mercy they may eternally enjoy His presence, in Whom they have hoped and believed. Through Our Lord Jesus Christ, etc. *Amen.*

II. Grant, we beseech Thee, O Almighty and merciful God, that the souls of our brethren, friends, and benefactors, for whom we have offered this sacrifice to Thy Majesty, being, by virtue of these mysteries, purified from all sin, may, through Thy mercy, receive the blessing of perpetual light.

III. Grant, we beseech Thee, O Lord, that our humble prayers in behalf of the souls of Thy servants and handmaids may be profitable for them; so that Thou mayest deliver them from all their sins, and make them partakers of Thy Redemption. Who livest and reignest, etc. *Amen.*

Index

Sophia Institute

Sophia Institute is a nonprofit institution that seeks to nurture the spiritual, moral, and cultural life of souls and to spread the gospel of Christ in conformity with the authentic teachings of the Roman Catholic Church.

Sophia Institute Press fulfills this mission by offering translations, reprints, and new publications that afford readers a rich source of the enduring wisdom of mankind.

Sophia Institute also operates the popular online Catholic resource CatholicExchange.com. *Catholic Exchange* provides world news from a Catholic perspective as well as daily devotionals and articles that will help readers to grow in holiness and live a life consistent with the teachings of the Church.

In 2013, Sophia Institute launched Sophia Institute for Teachers to renew and rebuild Catholic culture through service to Catholic education. With the goal of nurturing the spiritual, moral, and cultural life of souls, and an abiding respect for the role and work of teachers, we strive to provide materials and programs that are at once enlightening to the mind and ennobling to the heart; faithful and complete, as well as useful and practical.

Sophia Institute gratefully recognizes the Solidarity Association for preserving and encouraging the growth of our apostolate over the course of many years. Without their generous and timely support, this book would not be in your hands.

www.SophiaInstitute.com
www.CatholicExchange.com
www.SophiaInstituteforTeachers.org

Sophia Institute Press® is a registered trademark of Sophia Institute.
Sophia Institute is a tax-exempt institution as defined by the
Internal Revenue Code, Section 501(c)(3). Tax I.D. 22-2548708.